Key to 1:250 000 Maps, atlas pages 2-121

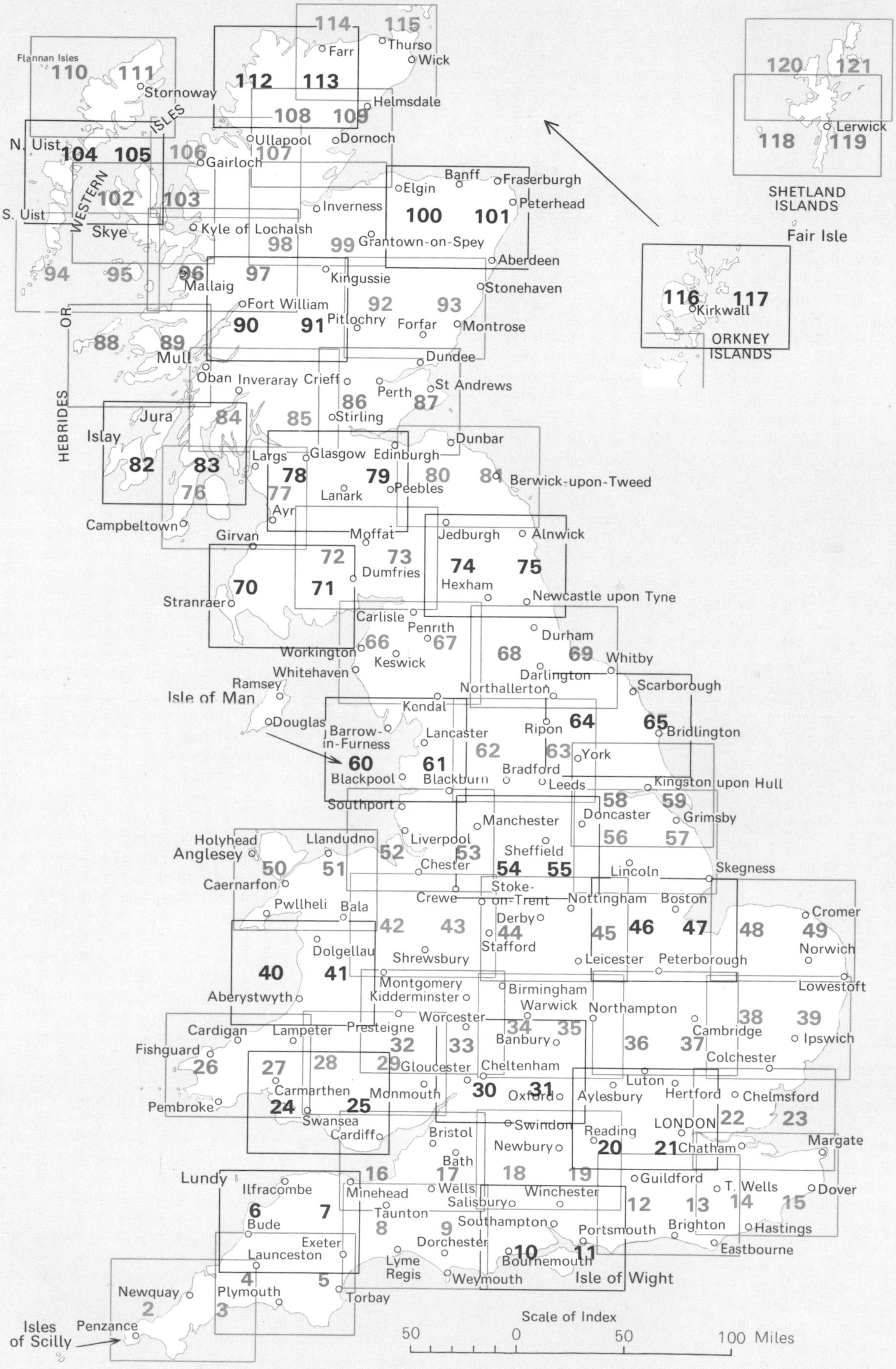

Ordnance Survey

ATLAS

of Great Britain

Ordnance Survey
ATLAS
of Great Britain

Ordnance Survey
Colour Library Books

First published in Great Britain in 1982 by
Ordnance Survey and Country Life Books, a division
of The Hamlyn Publishing Group Ltd

This revised edition published in 1988 by

Ordnance Survey   and   Colour Library Books Ltd
Romsey Road   Godalming Business Centre
Maybush   Catteshall Lane
Southampton SO9 4DH   Godalming
                                Surrey GU7 1XW

1:250 000 maps, key diagrams and text on endpapers and pages
xiv–121, and index on pages 158–188 © Crown Copyright 1982, 1988

Arrangement and all other material © The Hamlyn Publishing Group
Ltd 1982, 1988

ISBN 0-86283-647-6

Printed in Spain

Contents

Page vi   **Introduction**   *M J Wise*
Page viii   Great Britain – Physical
Page ix   Great Britain – Geological
Page xi   Great Britain – Climate

Page xiv   **A Short History of the Ordnance Survey**
Page xv   **Ordnance Survey Products**

Page 1   Legend for Ordnance Survey 1:250 000 Scale Maps

Pages 2–121   **ORDNANCE SURVEY 1:250 000 Maps**

For key see the front and back endpapers of this Atlas

Page 122   **The Historical Geography of Britain**   *R A Butlin*
Page 123   Prehistory to the Romans
Page 125   The Dark Ages
Page 128   Britain to 1350
Page 129   Late Medieval Britain
Page 131   The Agricultural Revolution
Page 133   The Early Industrial Revolution
Page 135   Britain in the Late Nineteenth Century

Page 136   **Modern Britain**   *M J Wise*
Page 137   The Crisis of the 1930s
Page 139   Mineral Resources
Page 140   Industry and Energy
Page 144   The Transport System
Page 146   Agriculture and Fisheries
Page 147   Farming Types
Page 150   Planning for Leisure
Page 151   Planning for Industry
Page 152   Population Patterns
Page 153   Cultural Diversity
Page 156   County Boundaries before 1974
Page 157   County Boundaries since 1974

Page 155   *Acknowledgements and Bibliography*
Page 158   **Index**
Front endpaper The National Grid
                Key to atlas pages 2–121
Back endpaper   Key to atlas pages 2–121
                Key to Ordnance Survey 1:50 000 Scale Maps

Introduction

William Somerville, writing in 1735, described Britain as a 'highly favoured isle'. Today, we may still agree that, while there are many problems of a man-made kind, in most respects Britain is indeed a fortunate country geographically. Its island position near to but separate from Western Europe, its temperate climate, generally plentiful rainfall, great variety of rock types, land forms and soils, its resources of coal and iron, clays and limestones, natural gas and oil, provide a great range of opportunities.

Few areas in the world of similar size offer so great a diversity both of physical and of human characteristics as does Britain. Contrast the remote hamlets of the Scottish Highlands with the thronging streets of Glasgow or London, the open arable lands of East Anglia with the upland grazings of the hills, the industrial landscapes of the Black Country or West Yorkshire with the rural areas that surround them, the New Towns of today with cities, like York, which preserve the fabric of medieval times. The traveller, using this atlas, will be aware, every few miles, of change in the landscape around him. Each observation, each view provokes questions about the evaluations of environment that have been made by people in the past and about the origins of the present use of land. How can we make the best use of the land of Britain today, using it and all its resources fully yet wisely, matching the desire to exploit with the need to conserve?

Diversity of Physical Conditions

Even a swift glance at the relief map shows clear evidence of variety in the contrast between the generally high relief of western and northern Britain and the lower lands of the east and south. Geographers have drawn a broad division between the Highland Zone and the Lowland Zone, separated by an imaginary line drawn across the country from the estuary of the River Tees to that of the Exe. The distinction is not complete for west of the Tees-Exe line there are areas of Lowland, for example in Cheshire and Lancashire and in the Midland Valley of Scotland, while in the Lowland Zone there are uplands and sharp ridges which at points rise to above or near to 305 m (1000 ft). But land over that height dominates in the Highland Zone; there are outstanding mountains such as Ben Nevis (1343 m 4406 ft) and Snowdon (1085 m 3560 ft) and the plains and valleys interrupt or break the generally highland character of the relief.

To a large extent this division reflects geological characteristics. The Highlands are composed mainly of old rocks, primarily of Pre-Cambrian and Palaeozoic ages, which have been folded and fractured in the great Caledonian and Hercynian (Armorican) earth movements and heavily eroded over very long periods of time. The rocks of the Lowland Zone are mainly sedimentary rocks of Mesozoic or Tertiary ages and have been folded into scarplands. The Lowlands have been likened to 'a grained surface' of sawn timber, alternating belts with varied powers to resist denudation – 'grained wood, worn with age'. Even in a nearly continuous outcrop there are many differences in the height and form of the scarps; the local

geological structures vary as do the soils. A full understanding of the land forms in much of Britain must also embrace a knowledge of events subsequent to the deposition and folding of the rocks, especially the effects of the Ice Age, changes in levels of land and sea and erosional processes. Having been the locations of ice caps during the Ice Age, the Highlands bear the clearest signs of glacial erosion: corries or cwms in the mountains, characteristically U-shaped valleys, *roches moutonnées*, hanging valleys. The effects of deposition of materials by ice may also be seen in the Highlands, but these are still more widely exhibited in the Lowlands, by the widespread glacial drifts of the Midlands and East Anglia where deposits of boulder clay smooth the relief and obscure the underlying rocks. The ice sheets and their deposits also altered patterns of drainage and the present courses of rivers such as the Thames, Severn and Warwickshire Avon are, in part, the products of the Ice Age. Even in the areas south of the Thames which were not covered by ice sheets, the effects of near-glacial conditions may be discerned.

The idea of a division into Highland and Lowland Zones is thus a useful way to begin the study of the geography of Britain. Yet there are great differences within the Highland Zone itself, between areas such as Snowdonia or the Scottish Highlands with summits rising to over 1000 m (3300 ft) where sharp relief is a product of geological fracturing and glaciation, and many other extensive areas of the Zone with smoother relief and high-level plateau-like land forms. We may instance the Southern Uplands of Scotland, many parts of the Pennines or the plateau of mid-Wales. For such areas B. W. Sparks has suggested the term Upland Britain, so giving a threefold regional division: Highland, Upland and Lowland.

Regional Contrasts in Climate

Our climate may be a source of both humour and annoyance but, despite occasional extreme events, it is another aspect of the favourability of Britain's physical geography. It is greatly influenced by Britain's maritime situation just off the western edge of the Eurasian land mass. It has been said that, climatically, 'Britain is a battleground', invaded and conquered by one air mass itself soon to be re-conquered by another. The four chief, but not the only, types of air mass are Tropical Maritime, Tropical Continental, Polar Maritime and Polar Continental. Each brings its own type of weather and the battles join along 'fronts', bringing a sequence of sometimes frequent and possibly stormy changes in the weather. There is much variability of weather from day to day and place to place, providing a constant topic of conversation and, according to one's point of view on particular occasions, delight or frustration.

In terms of a world classification of climates the whole island lies within the cool temperate type. Nevertheless notable differences may be discerned within Britain itself. Regional and local differences derive from many factors, including latitude, proximity to the sea, altitude, the relief of the land, aspect, exposure to wind and degree of urban development. Generalising, in winter the west is warmer than the east, while in summer the south is warmer than the north. Precipitation, though, varies from one place to

another more than temperature. The west has more rainfall than the east, with areas of over 1500 mm (60 in) of annual rainfall on the Highland and Upland areas mostly in winter. The east is much drier, with annual totals of less than 750 mm (30 in) over much of the English Lowlands and with the greater proportion falling in the latter six months and, in some areas, in the summer.

Many attempts have been made to divide Britain into climatic regions and to characterise the differences from place to place. One of the simplest attempts superimposes the isotherms for January which run broadly north-south, and for July, which have an east-west trend, to produce four quadrants. The north-west quadrant has cool summers and mild winters, the south-west quadrant has warm summers and mild winters. The north-east quadrant is epitomised by cool summers and cold winters and the south-east, which shows the greatest contrasts in temperature, by warm summers and cold winters. When the general difference in rainfall between west and east is also recalled, a broad regional picture emerges.

A rather more complex pattern of regional climates has been suggested, by S. Gregory. He employs three sets of indicators, the length of the growing season, the magnitude of rainfall and the seasonality of rainfall (*see map page xi*). The growing season of nine or more months of the south-western coasts falls to eight or seven months in Lowland Britain, to six or five months in the Uplands and to four or less in the Grampians and the Western Highlands of Scotland.

Under the heading of rainfall magnitude, Gregory distinguishes those areas that receive at least 1250 mm (50 in) of rain a year with a high probability of its occurrence each year, from those that receive less than 750 mm (30 in) a year with a much lower probability of regularity, with an area of moderate rainfall lying between the two. In terms of rainfall seasonality, he distinguishes the areas of maximum rainfall in the winter half of the year (western Britain and a part of southern England south of the Thames) from the areas of maximum rainfall in the second half of the year. These comprise most of the rest of the country, except for the area between the Thames and the Wash where there is a weakly developed summer maximum.

But yet another distinction should be introduced. About 90% of the population lives in towns and about 11% of the surface area of England and Wales is built upon. Cities, especially large ones, tend to modify the climate. Buildings interrupt air flow and reduce wind speeds; air pollution is higher. The warm air which, particularly by night, covers cities produces what have been termed 'heat islands'. Most towns with high central building densities average 1°-2°C warmer than surrounding countrysides; and on occasions much higher differences are recorded.

It must also be remembered that, even in a temperate climate, departures from the 'norm' and extreme events do occur. A recent example is that of the great drought of 1975-76 which followed a tendency to low rainfall totals in the early 1970s. And, though we do not fully understand the causes, climates do change over time. There have certainly been notable fluctuations in the climatic record of the last 1000 years and it should not be assumed that present climatic conditions will continue unchanged indefinitely.

Climate is one of the factors that influence soil and, broadly speaking, it is possible to draw a distinction between the acidic podsolic soils of the cooler and wetter north and west where high winter rainfall leaches out the soluble salts to leave an impoverished grey soil beneath a black humus layer, and the less leached brown forest soils of the Lowland Zone. But soils also depend upon the parent material, be that solid rock or glacial drift. As we travel from one part of the country to another we notice the rapidity with which changes in the solid rocks occur, very noticeably for example in the scarplands of the Lowland Zone, and soil types reflect such changes. The distribution of glacial drift has been a particularly important factor. We may distinguish between sandy soils, loamy and usually very fertile soils, clay soils often heavy to work, and calcareous soils derived from limestone. A third factor which influences soil type is vegetation, and some soils have a very high content of organic matter. Such soils include the black, fenland soils and peaty and moorland soils. Local elements of geology and relief influence soil type: some areas of hard rock are bare of soil, and the degree of slope may also be important, particularly influencing drainage. It must also be remembered that many of our soils have been tilled, drained and fertilised for centuries, so that they are no longer in a completely natural state.

Atlantic Britain, Highland Britain and Lowland Britain

The concept of Highland and Lowland Zones has also been employed in interpreting the distribution of early settlements. Pioneers in this work were Sir Cyril Fox and Dr L. F. Chitty who in 1932 published a remarkable book, *The Personality of Britain*. They used detailed mapping of archaeological evidence, to examine the distribution of prehistoric settlements in terms both of the physical conditions and what was known of the organisation and technology of each wave of incoming peoples. They recognised two principal sets of embarkation areas for those moving from Europe to Britain. These were the coasts of northwest Europe from Brittany to the Rhine with routes across the narrow seas, and, for those to whom the sea was a highway, the coasts from Spain to Brittany and from the Rhine to the Norwegian fjords.

In Megalithic and early Bronze Age times the Atlantic seaways from Spain were much in use and Britain was in the van of western European progress. But in the middle Bronze Age, land routes across Europe sapped the importance of the Atlantic routes. Britain tended, therefore, to become 'a country on the edge of the known world, the last to receive and absorb cultures moving from east to west'. The Lowland Zone, adjacent to the Continent, was easily invaded and new cultures from the Continent were imposed.

Although later writers have cast doubts upon Fox's ideas, many agree that from about 1000 BC the contrast between Highland and Lowland was very significant. Peoples of the later Bronze and Iron Ages were better equipped than their predecessors to tackle the clearance of the woodlands and to till the heavier soils in the vales. The Romans, it is true, overstepped into the Highland Zone but the boundary

Great Britain – Physical

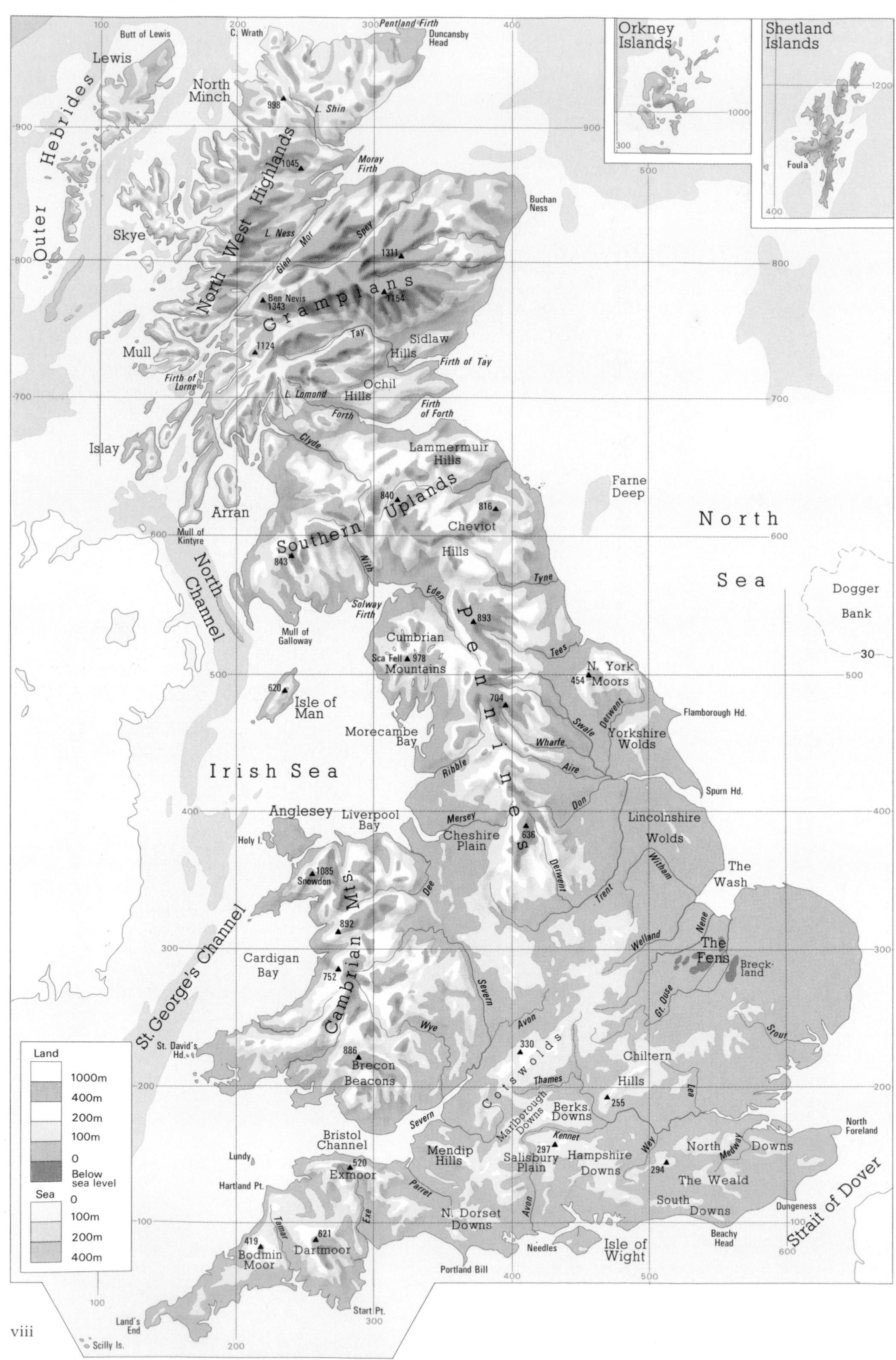

Orkney Islands

Shetland Islands

Butt of Lewis
Lewis
Outer Hebrides
Skye
Mull
Islay
Arran
Mull of Kintyre
North Channel
Mull of Galloway
St. George's Channel
Lundy
Hartland Pt.
Land's End
Scilly Is.
Bodmin Moor
Dartmoor

C. Wrath
Pentland Firth
Duncansby Head
North Minch
L. Shin
North West Highlands
Moray Firth
Ben Nevis 1343
Glen Mor
L. Ness
Spey
Grampians
Tay
Sidlaw Hills
Firth of Tay
Ochil Hills
Firth of Lorne
L. Lomond
Forth
Clyde
Southern Uplands
Lammermuir Hills
Cheviot Hills
Nith
Solway Firth
Eden
Cumbrian Mountains
Sca Fell 978
Pennines
Tyne
Tees
Swale
Wharfe
Aire
Ribble
Don
Derwent
N. York Moors 454
Yorkshire Wolds
Flamborough Hd.
Spurn Hd.
Lincolnshire Wolds
The Wash
Witham
Trent
Nene
The Fens
Breckland
Gt. Ouse
Welland
Stour
Chiltern Hills
Lea
Medway
North Downs
The Weald
South Downs
Beachy Head
Dungeness
Strait of Dover
North Foreland

Buchan Ness
Farne Deep
North Sea
Dogger Bank
30

998
1045
1311
1154
1124
840
816
843
893
704
636
620
1085 Snowdon
892
752
886 Brecon Beacons
620 Isle of Man
Morecambe Bay
Irish Sea
Anglesey
Holy I.
Liverpool Bay
Cheshire Plain
Mersey
Dee
Cambrian Mts.
Cardigan Bay
St. David's Hd.
Wye
Severn
Avon
330
Cotswolds
Thames
Marlborough Downs
Berks. Downs
255
Kennet
297
Salisbury Plain
Hampshire Downs
294
Mendip Hills
Bristol Channel
520 Exmoor
Parret
Exe
N. Dorset Downs
Avon
Wey
Isle of Wight
Needles
Portland Bill
419
621
Tamar
Start Pt.

Land
1000m
400m
200m
100m
0
Below sea level
Sea
0
100m
200m
400m

viii

Great Britain — Geological

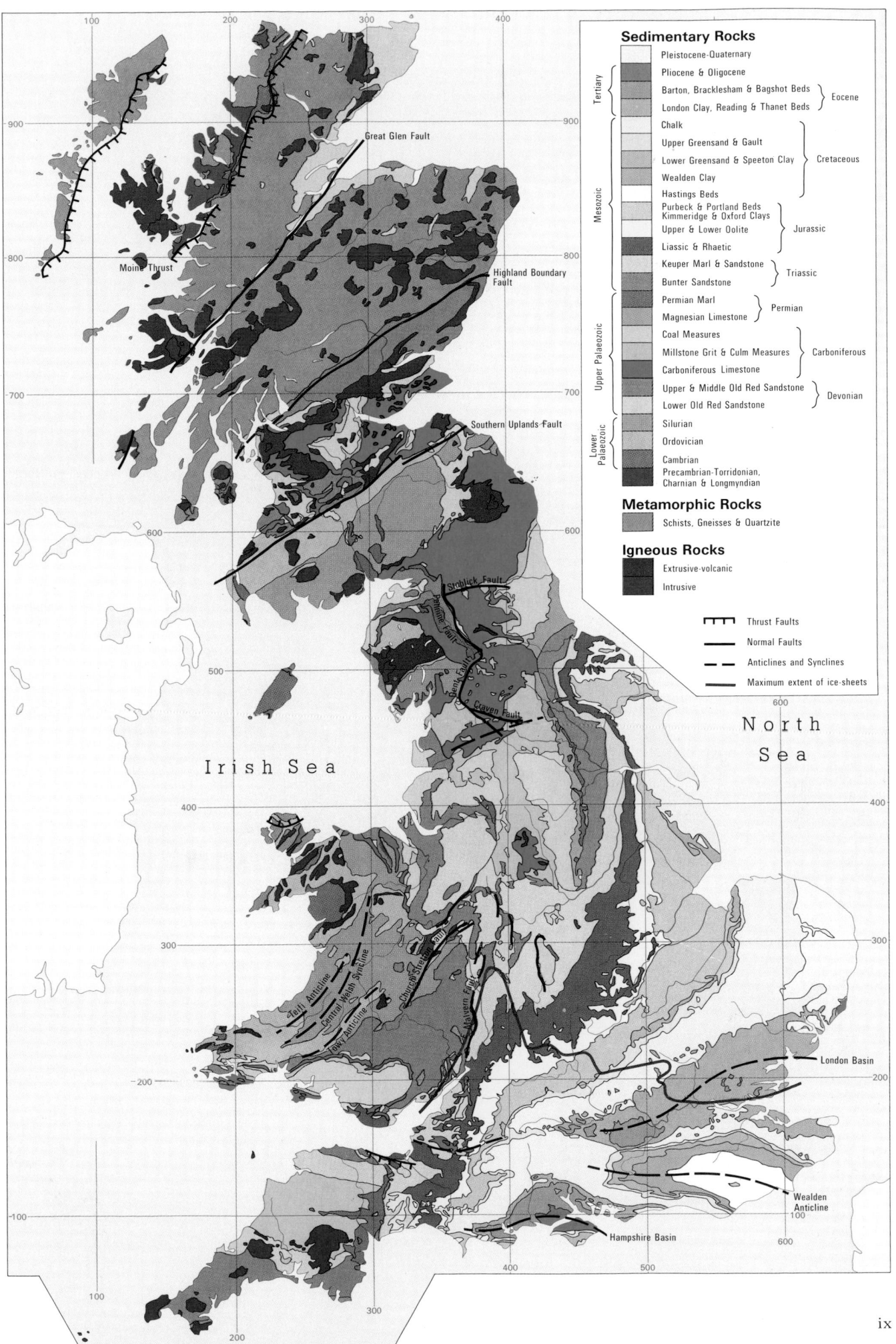

Sedimentary Rocks

Tertiary

- Pleistocene-Quaternary
- Pliocene & Oligocene
- Barton, Bracklesham & Bagshot Beds } Eocene
- London Clay, Reading & Thanet Beds }

Mesozoic

- Chalk
- Upper Greensand & Gault }
- Lower Greensand & Speeton Clay } Cretaceous
- Wealden Clay
- Hastings Beds
- Purbeck & Portland Beds
  Kimmeridge & Oxford Clays
- Upper & Lower Oolite } Jurassic
- Liassic & Rhaetic
- Keuper Marl & Sandstone } Triassic
- Bunter Sandstone }

Upper Palaeozoic

- Permian Marl } Permian
- Magnesian Limestone }
- Coal Measures
- Millstone Grit & Culm Measures } Carboniferous
- Carboniferous Limestone
- Upper & Middle Old Red Sandstone } Devonian
- Lower Old Red Sandstone }

Lower Palaeozoic

- Silurian
- Ordovician
- Cambrian
- Precambrian-Torridonian,
  Charnian & Longmyndian

Metamorphic Rocks

- Schists, Gneisses & Quartzite

Igneous Rocks

- Extrusive-volcanic
- Intrusive

Thrust Faults
Normal Faults
Anticlines and Synclines
Maximum extent of ice-sheets

Great Glen Fault
Moine Thrust
Highland Boundary Fault
Southern Uplands Fault
Stublick Fault
Pennine Fault
Dent Fault
Craven Fault
Teifi Anticline
Central Welsh Syncline
Towy Anticline
Church Stretton Fault
Malvern Fault
London Basin
Wealden Anticline
Hampshire Basin

Irish Sea

North Sea

ix

between the civil and military zones was approximately that between Highland and Lowland Britain (*see map page 123*). Even in Anglo-Saxon times, the western frontier of their influence at the end of the 6th century was aligned along the outcrop of the Palaeozoic rocks (*see map page 125*).

Such observations led Fox to the proposition that historically the Lowland Zone had nourished 'richer cultures' than the Highland. 'Taking Britain as a whole,' he observed, 'the most important centres of any culture or civilisation are likely to be in the south-east of the islands.' Such circumstances, he went on, had led to the 'tragedy' of the early history of Britain. Fresh invasions from the east had, on the one hand, paralysed older cultures by largely destroying them where they were most flourishing and on the other, had tended to cut off the survivals of those cultures in the west from the stimuli of continued contact with Europe.

But the Highland Zone was not simply a barrier to cultural advance nor a region where outliers of former Lowland cultures might precariously survive. There were subtler and more positive influences. Whereas in the Lowland Zone newer cultures were successively imposed on earlier, in Highland Britain they tended to be absorbed by the older cultures. Historically Lowland Britain was characterised by replacement, Highland Britain by fusion and continuity. The power of absorption of the Highland Zone had indeed provided it with a distinctive cultural character of its own. The survival of Celtic languages and traditions was the clearest example.

Later writers have tended to place increased emphasis on one aspect of the geography of the Highland Zone which Fox noted but did not develop, namely the tendency for the shores of the Irish Sea (and its northern and southern approaches) to form a 'culture pool'. R. H. Kinvig (1958), for example, while accepting the value of the idea of a Highland Zone, argued that a better understanding may be gained by subdividing the Highlands into an 'Atlantic Zone' and a 'Moorland Area' lying inland from it.

His Atlantic Zone included the coastal belt of plains and low plateaux along the western and northern coasts and also the islands of Man, the Hebrides, the Shetlands and the Orkneys. He and others distinguished 'Atlantic Britain' on grounds of both physical and historical geography. Historically, the zone had played an active rather than a passive role in that, open southwards to influences *via* sea routes from France, Iberia and the Mediterranean and northwards to influences from Scandinavia, it had been a receiving zone for peoples and cultures. In prehistoric times there was south-north traffic and the builders of the megalithic tombs came by sea. From the 4th century AD onwards contacts between the various parts of Atlantic Britain, and with Gaul and beyond, intensified. Many of the ideas associated with Celtic Christianity came by these routes. By about AD 800 Norse settlers had begun to penetrate and to settle. Eventually the Isle of Man became the capital of an island realm consisting of all the Hebrides. In the 12th century a separate diocese, the Episcopal See of the Isles, was established based on St Patrick's Isle at Peel (*see map page 128*).

E. Estyn Evans (1958) has carried this argument forward into the present day, suggesting a number of aspects of modern social and folk life in the coastlands of western and northwestern Europe which link what he refers to as the 'Atlantic Ends of Europe'. The thesis is that 'these western lands have a cultural heritage which is rich and varied, and signs are not lacking at the present day that some of these areas are once again going to play a more active part than they have done in the immediate past'. Those words remind us of the rise of national pressures and demands for the devolution of government from London, the route centre of the Lowland Zone.

Thus the simple Highland Zone-Lowland Zone concept requires modification. The case for the existence of an Atlantic Britain is strong and the difference between the true Highlands and the Uplands must also be kept in mind. Such broad divisions as have been indicated form a useful starting-point for more detailed studies of the great variety of regional conditions in Britain.

Land and People

The land of Britain, varied in its landscape and in the resources that it offers, is small in area in relation to the demands of its population of 55,060,100 (1985). The total land area of England, Wales and Scotland is about 22,740,000 hectares (56,190,540 acres), allowing only 0.41 HA (1.02 acres) per head of population, and for England and Wales only about 0.3 HA (0.75 acres) per head. The needs are many and include housing, industry, mineral extraction, transport, agriculture, water supply, recreation and defence. Agriculture accounts in England and Wales for about three-quarters of land use, with woodland covering about 7% and urban, industrial and associated development about 11%. There is great variation in the quality of agricultural land: about 13% of the land area is under rough grazing and only 3% is truly of first-class quality (*see maps pages 146 and 147*). In 1900 only about 5% of the land surface was in urban uses, but the proportion has increased more rapidly than has population, and land has been much in demand as cities have spread outwards. In the inter-war years losses of farmland to urban uses amounted at times to over 25,000 HA (60,000 acres) a year. The concern aroused led to the improvement of planning control, and since 1945 about 15,700 HA (38,800 acres) a year or about 0.1% of the total land surface of England and Wales has been transferred from agricultural to urban uses. It is not surprising that land use conflicts have arisen over development proposals, for example for the extension of urban land, motorway construction, the creation of reservoirs, the sinking of new coal mines, the building of new power stations, the enlargement of airports or the improvement for agricultural use of heath or wetlands.

Urban and Industrial Britain

The dominant feature of the human geography of Britain is the existence of a great urban system, the product mainly of the rapid industrial and urban growth of the last 200 years. In 1801 some nine million people lived in England and Wales, and one in three lived in towns. By 1851 the population had grown to 18 million and just over a half were urban dwellers. By the beginning of the 20th century, out of 32.5 million people 78% were urban dwellers. In 1981

Great Britain – Climate

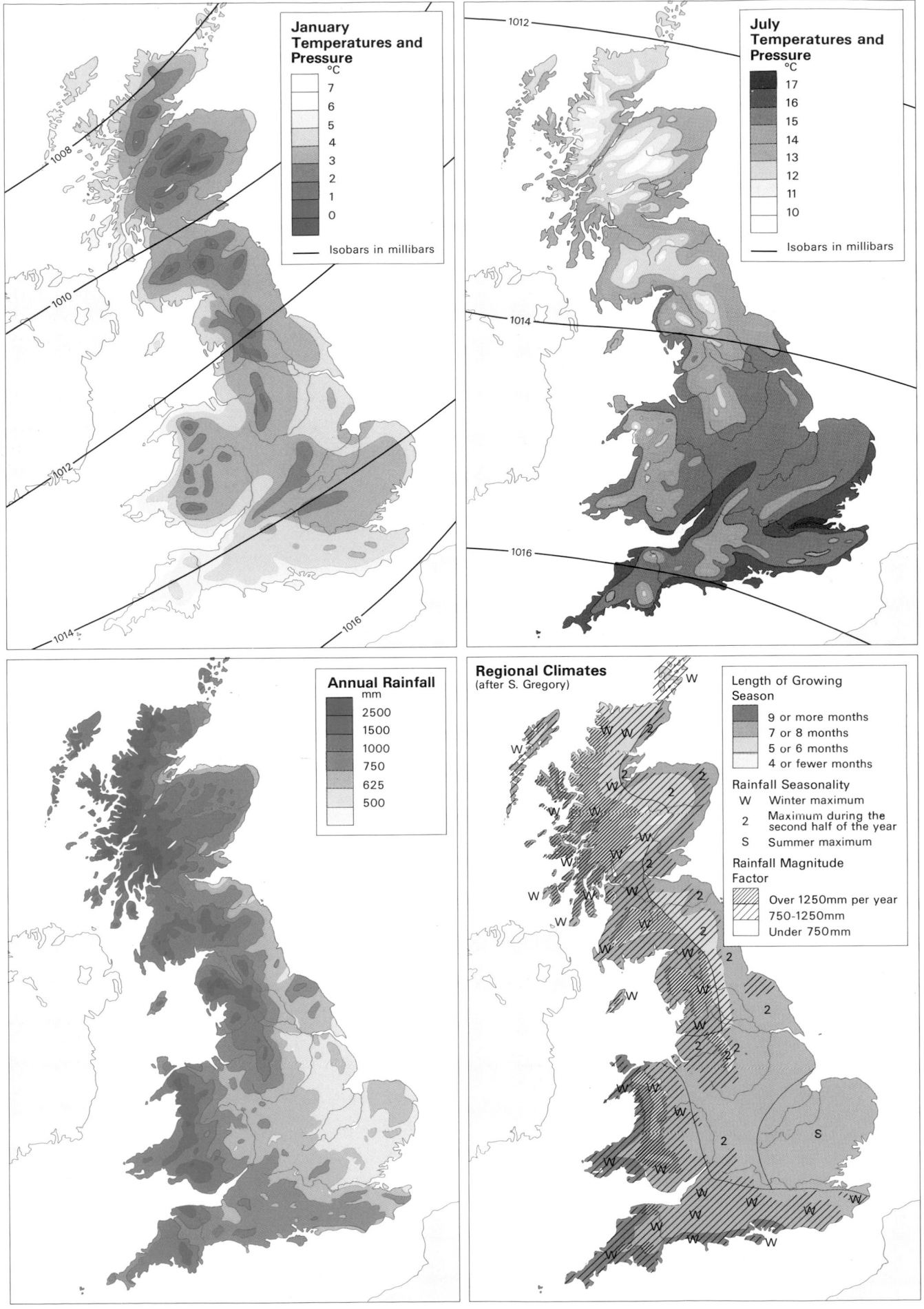

January Temperatures and Pressure

°C
- 7
- 6
- 5
- 4
- 3
- 2
- 1
- 0

— Isobars in millibars

1008
1010
1012
1014
1016

July Temperatures and Pressure

°C
- 17
- 16
- 15
- 14
- 13
- 12
- 11
- 10

— Isobars in millibars

1012
1014
1016

Annual Rainfall

mm
- 2500
- 1500
- 1000
- 750
- 625
- 500

Regional Climates
(after S. Gregory)

Length of Growing Season
- 9 or more months
- 7 or 8 months
- 5 or 6 months
- 4 or fewer months

Rainfall Seasonality
- W Winter maximum
- 2 Maximum during the second half of the year
- S Summer maximum

Rainfall Magnitude Factor
- Over 1250mm per year
- 750-1250mm
- Under 750mm

almost 90% of the population lived in urban areas and the character and shapes of cities have greatly changed due to the general movement of people into urban regions.

Look first at what some call the Central Urban Region, others the British megalopolis (see map page 151). A band of dense population stretches northwestwards from the English Channel across the Thames, through the Midlands, dividing on each side of the Pennines and continuing into Lancashire and Yorkshire. The southern part of this megalopolis is focused around London, the midland and northern parts contain a number of urban groups around, for example, Birmingham, Manchester and Leeds. The urban areas do not actually join together; there are breaks of green land between them. But the whole area is closely bound together by main railway lines and motorways that reflect the strength of the economic links between the cities and their activities in the zone.

Outside this English megalopolis some other important urban and industrial zones occur. Indeed the eye may take another line, starting with the South Wales industrial region and Bristol, continuing to the northeast through the West and East Midlands and terminating on Humberside. Traversing northwards there is the industrial region of northeast England with Newcastle-upon-Tyne as its main centre. The central industrial belt of Scotland with Glasgow and Edinburgh as the principal cities provides homes for about three-quarters of Scotland's population of 5·14 million.

The appearance, character and prosperity of the cities and industrial districts in these strongly urbanised zones vary widely. Some of the cities, Edinburgh, Durham, York, Coventry, above all London, were important in medieval times. But supreme significance must be given to the Industrial Revolution of the 18th and 19th centuries. For this was also a geographical revolution. As new methods for smelting iron using coke were introduced the coalfields became important, and mining and industrial towns began to spring up where none had existed before. Developments in industry, including the introduction of the factory system in the metal-using and textile industries, brought people into rapidly-growing industrial cities such as Birmingham and Manchester. Commercial activities intensified. Canals and, after 1830, railways linked the industrial districts together. External trade prospered and new ports were required: estuaries were deepened, channels constructed, dock systems developed on the Thames, Mersey and Clyde. The Clyde, Tyne, Wear and, for a time, the Thames also built the ships which imported food and commodities for conversion into manufactured products and carried away the finished products and the export coal for the bunkers of the great merchant fleets. London grew as port, manufacturing region, chief centre of commerce, and as the location of government and as the biggest centre of wholesale and retail trade (see maps pages 133 and 135).

These great developments of what has been described as the palaeotechnic phase of industrial development and which underlie present patterns must be seen in terms of Britain's position as the leading industrial power at a time when the world market was expanding. In time it was to be overtaken, but much of the physical fabric constructed at that time remains. Each industrial region developed its own group of specialised activities. The West Midlands was the home of the metal industries, Lancashire of cotton and the West Riding of woollen textiles. South Wales had its iron and steel, coal, tinplate and non-ferrous metal industries. The northeast and Scotland had coal, iron and steel, shipbuilding and marine engineering. Such a system of specialised industrial regions worked well while the market was strong, but in the Great Depression of 1929-31 those areas that had rather narrowly-based industrial structures and were dependent on industries that were declining nationally fared badly. Unemployment soared and poverty struck. South Wales, Clydeside, northeast England, West Cumberland are examples of what for a time were termed Depressed Areas. By contrast, areas such as the West Midlands and Greater London where the industries were more diversified and which possessed strong shares in such industries as electrical engineering and electrical goods, motor vehicles, the food and drink trades and the service industries, which were expanding nationally, remained relatively prosperous.

The contrast in conditions between the regions and the movement of people away from the hard-hit areas to the more prosperous districts raised new questions. To what extent did the nation possess a responsibility towards areas that had contributed greatly to the national wealth but now, for no fault of their own, found themselves in hard straits? If a responsibility existed, how should it be exercised and what methods could be found to rectify the disparities between areas? Preliminary steps to devise remedies were introduced by 1939 but it is since 1945 that 'regional' policies have been developed and more will be said about these in a later section of this atlas.

The 19th-century industrial districts developed their own distinctive landscapes. Mrs Gaskell writing in 1857 described the Yorkshire landscape between Keighley and Haworth: 'what with villas, great worsted factories, with here and there an old fashioned farm-house . . . it can hardly be called "country" any part of the way'. But those who lived there were perhaps more fortunate than those in the slums of inner Manchester or those in the Black Country, 'black by day and red by night' as the flames from the open blast furnaces were reflected from the clouds. The industrial towns threw out branching lines of houses along the roads joining them and by the end of the century a number of great conurbations, areas in which the built-up areas had become contiguous, had been formed. We now find seven major conurbations, each different from the others. London, by far the largest, grew outwards from its central core to engulf land in Middlesex, Hertfordshire, Essex, Kent and Surrey. Its population in 1986 was 6,776,400 (though like all the major conurbations, population has been declining recently. London's population peaked in 1961 at 8 million). The other major conurbations are West Midland, Greater Manchester, Merseyside, Tyneside, West Yorkshire and Clydeside. These conurbations hold about 32% of the population of Great Britain. Outside the conurbations there grew railway towns like Crewe and Swindon, ports such as Southampton, fishing ports such as Grimsby, resort towns like Bournemouth and Blackpool.

Problems of Adaptation and Modernisation

The Great Industrial Age thus contributed vastly to the establishment of the basic pattern of modern urban settlement. Much of its physical structure remains with us; some of it is mean, like the slum houses of the inner areas of the big cities which have been the subject of vigorous clearance, especially since 1945. The street patterns of cities built in the Victorian period were not designed for modern traffic conditions and adapting them to the needs of road transport without damage to the environment poses acute problems. The great railway termini such as St Pancras, Liverpool Street or Waverley remind us of the role of the railway. Some at least of the canals are still at work carrying freight. Although much of the derelict land created by the mines, furnaces and brickworks has been cleared, some still remains: indeed now that the Industrial Age has passed into history a number of industrial museums serve as reminders of the need to create new industries and fresh environments of which we can be proud.

Such changes are symptomatic of the modernisation of the geography of Britain which has been proceeding since the end of the 1939-45 war and especially in the last two decades.

Coal is king no longer. Though still important in the economy, coal production is only about two-fifths of the maximum reached in 1913. For power, we now have a choice of coal, oil, natural gas, or electricity (produced from coal, oil, natural gas, nuclear fuels or, mainly in Scotland, from water power). The period 1965-75 has been described as that of 'a revolution in the UK fuel and power industries unmatched since British coalfields were first developed'. Oil is now more important to the economy than coal and this revolution which began on a basis of imported oil and gas can now draw on the resources of the North Sea. The exploitation of the oil and gas fields has itself produced a revolution in the geography of the North Sea.

The transport system has changed equally radically in the 20th century. The railway system has been reduced in length of rail and transformed technically by electrification and diesel haulage. But except for services such as high speed inter-city trains, commuter traffic and specialised freight, rail has given place to road. Some 2968 km (1855 miles) of motorway have been built in thirty years and the number of motor cars in use has multiplied by six since 1951. There is also the choice of travelling between cities by air and the development of international air traffic has had major consequences for ocean shipping. In freight transport, containerisation in turn has had its effect on 19th-century dock systems, while hovercraft and hydrofoil provide additional types of ferries across the English Channel.

Dramatic changes have also befallen our cities. No longer after 1961 did the population of major conurbations (with one exception) continue to grow. Out-migration exceeded growth by natural increase and in-migration. Decentralisation has provided the key-note. Post-war regional plans, such as that prepared for Greater London by Sir Patrick Abercrombie in 1944, recognised the need to re-create the environment of the inner areas of the industrial conurbations and advocated the delineation of Green Belts to prevent continuing outward sprawl and the creation of New Towns

to house 'overspill' population. Later, other towns beyond the conurbations were designated as 'expanded' towns for the same purpose. To the decentralisation created by planning policies has been added the movement away from the conurbations by families who prefer to live in medium-sized or small towns. Possession of the motorcar has given more freedom of choice in deciding where to live. Thus a new urban form, the 'city region', has been brought into existence. The London city region, for example, has a radius of up to about 65 km (40 miles) comprising a region of towns functionally linked together. It extends to Ashford, Basingstoke, Swindon, Milton Keynes, Bedford and Chelmsford. Many of the industrial enterprises formerly located in the Victorian inner areas have closed or moved out to the towns expanding beyond the conurbation edge, leaving gaps behind in the employment structure of the inner city. Indeed the trend to decentralisation has brought about a degree of polarisation between the more prosperous conditions of life in the outer parts of the city regions and the unemployment, poor social facilities and dreary environments of some parts of the inner cities. In such areas lies one of the great challenges for an age of modernisation and a central problem for the late 1980s and 1990s.

The other lies in the adaptation of industry and the provision of new forms of employment. Economic recession in the last years of the 1970s accelerated the speed at which the older industries have drastically slimmed down their labour forces. Unemployment in 1988 has a different distribution from that of 1931 and is no longer localised only in the coalfield-based industrial areas of the north and Wales.

But while most of the people live in towns and cities, and urban land uses are encroaching on the countryside, agricultural land still makes up about three-quarters of the land use of Britain. The distinction between cities and countryside is less clear than it was. City regions extend their influence and their connecting roads and power lines stamp an artificial pattern on the countryside. City dwellers look to the countryside for recreation. Agriculture too has become more intensive. In the 1960s and early 1970s its production increased at an average rate of 2·5% per year while manpower fell dramatically. It now takes only 2% of the labour force to grow or rear the crops and livestock that supply 80% of the temperate foodstuffs consumed in Britain. City and countryside have become more inter-related. Agriculture supplies milk, meat, cereals, fruit and vegetables for consumption in the cities which, in turn, produce agricultural machinery, farm requisites and fertilisers for the farm. Meanwhile the appearance of the countryside itself changes especially in those areas where hedgerows have been removed in the interests of mechanised farming, where Dutch elm disease has been prevalent, or where farming or forestry takes over hillsides and heathlands. Concern for the countryside and its wildlife has been loudly expressed on such issues. Despite such changes there is a rich and diverse countryside to be studied, valued and cared for. It is hoped that the maps and the chapters on historical geography and modern Britain—sketchy though they inevitably are on such a scale—will add to the awareness of these changes and this diversity.

A Short History of the Ordnance Survey

The formation of the Ordnance Survey owes much to the advocacy of General William Roy, a renowned surveyor engineer and archaeologist of the 18th century. As a young man he was responsible for the production of a military map of Scotland following the 1745 Rebellion. Later he directed the first scientific survey operation carried out in Britain; the precise measurement of a survey base line at Hounslow Heath (now London Airport) and the triangulation connection with France. The establishment of a national organisation to be responsible for survey and mapping of the country was not to take shape, however, until after his death in 1790.

In 1791, Britain found itself under threat of invasion from France. The British Army required accurate mapping of the south coast of England for military purposes at 1 inch to 1 mile scale. The survey was carried out by the Board of Ordnance, a Crown organisation, responsible for army engineering, artillery and other armaments at that time. The name Ordnance Survey stems from this time; their first offices in the Tower of London are commemorated today in the Ordnance Survey coat of arms.

As the threat of invasion receded, civilian applications for the mapping were identified. The industrial revolution was under way, with the associated rapid expansion of towns and road and rail networks, and politicians, administrators, civil engineers and others were quick to recognise the value of accurate maps. The survey was gradually extended to cover other areas of the country and Ordnance Survey was given the task of carrying out the work. Moreover, surveys were undertaken to produce maps at much larger scales to give even more detailed and accurate information. There were scientific applications, too, including the mapping of archaeological sites so that by the mid 19th century, Ordnance Survey had assumed its modern role of providing a national survey for scientific, military, government and public use. The authority for many of its activities is the Ordnance Survey Act of 1841.

As urban and industrial development continued, the demand for more detailed large scale maps increased. The original 1 inch to 1 mile series was retained as a general map but in 1840 the scale of 1:10 560 (6 inches to 1 mile) was authorised for the survey of northern England and Scotland which at that time had not been covered by 1 inch to 1 mile scale mapping. It was found, however, that even this scale was inadequate for all purposes, and there then followed a long controversy surrounding the choice of a suitable base scale for maps of Great Britain. This was resolved in 1863 when it was decided to adopt a scale of 1:2500 (25 inches to 1 mile) for cultivated areas, 1:10 560 (6 inches to 1 mile) for uncultivated areas of mountain and moorland and 1:500 (10 feet to 1 mile) for towns of more than 4000 population. Smaller scale maps including the one-inch map were to be derived from these large-scale surveys.

The first 1:2500 scale survey of cultivated areas was completed in 1893 and by 1914 the first revision had been completed. During the period of the 1:2500 survey there were considerable advances in map production, including the introduction of zincography (a process of etching the map image onto zinc plates for printing; previously the image had been transferred to or hand drawn on special smooth limestone blocks), photography and colour printing. The design and content of the mapping also developed in response to technical advances, advances, user demand and economic pressures to stem the rising cost of the national survey. The latter led in 1893 to the abandonment of the 1:500 series of town plans unless locally funded.

Economies were intensified by World War I, and Ordnance Survey, in line with other govenment organisations, suffered considerable cutbacks in manpower and resources, so much so that only revision of large scale maps covering areas of rapid change could be continued. It was unfortunate that these restrictions coincided with government legislation on land registration (1925), town planning (1925), land drainage (1926), slum clearance (1930) and land valuation (1931), all of which in one way or another required accurate mapping for implementation. By the early 1930s it became clear that Ordnance Survey had been left ill-equipped to supply sufficiently accurate maps. A Departmental Committee under the chairmanship of Sir J C (later Lord) Davidson was set up in 1935 to consider how to restore the effectiveness of the national survey.

Its report, although published in 1938, could not be implemented until after World War II, but it formed the framework on which the present Ordnance Survey was developed. The major recommendations of the Davidson Report included: the introduction of a metric National Grid as a reference system for all large and small scale maps; the recasting of the 1:2500 series on national instead of county lines using a national projection (the method of depicting the earth's surface as a flat plane) rather than separate county projections which had caused problems of fit and accuracy along county borders; the introduction of a system of continuous revision for large scale maps; the testing of a larger 1:1250 (50 inches to 1 mile) scale of survey for densely populated urban areas; the trial of a 1:25 000 ($2\frac{1}{2}$ inches to 1 mile) medium scale map which, if successful, was to be extended to cover the whole country.

After the war, these recommendations were implemented, with large scale surveys, metric conversion and revision proceeding at 1:1250, 1:2500 and 1:10 000 (6 inches to 1 mile) scales. Smaller scale maps of one inch to one mile, 1:25 000 ($2\frac{1}{2}$ inches to 1 mile), 1:250 000 (1 inch to 4 miles) and 1:625 000 (10 miles to 1 inch) were all published as derivations from the large scale surveys. The one-inch national series was converted to 1:50 000 scale in the early 1970s.

Today, Ordnance Survey is a civilian government department with headquarters in Southampton and a network of small local survey offices throughout the country. The resurvey task initiated after World War II in response to the

Davidson Report has been completed and the emphasis now is on the revision of this huge archive of survey information, to keep it up-to-date and meet user demand. New technology has been used to aid the surveyors and draughtsmen in their task. An increasing number of Ordnance Survey 1:1250 and 1:2500 maps are being produced using automated cartographic techniques. Information collected and recorded by the surveyor in graphic form is converted by electronic means into digital form and stored in a computer databank. The graphic information is recorded as a series of numerical co-ordinates which identify the precise location of the feature on the ground. Once the information is stored on the computer it can be recalled to produce an exact scale map copy, or a larger scale or smaller scale copy as required. Furthermore, selected detail can be recalled rather than the whole map.

While the techniques of survey and mapping have developed and improved dramatically since the early years of the Ordnance Survey, and are still developing, the customers for accurate detailed maps remain basically the same. Computer generated maps are very much in demand from local government, coal, gas, electricity, water and construction industries and others concerned with maintenance and development of the infrastructure of Great Britain. Ordnance Survey's objective is to continue to meet this demand as well as satisfying the general public's need for small scale derived mapping for educational, leisure and many other purposes.

Editor's Note
The reference section of this atlas has been compiled with the aim of providing comprehensive and up-to-date information on many aspects of Great Britain in the 1980s, from geology to government, climate to culture. Facts and figures have come from a wide variety of sources and have been interpreted in as objective a manner as possible. The most recent available statistics have been included but since there is often a lapse of some years before figures are published, the year of the latest information will frequently vary from subject to subject and exact comparisons have not always been feasible. The most recent census, for example, was in 1981 so demographic statistics are limited to that date. Metric units have been used throughout for consistency.

Ordnance Survey Products

Ordnance Survey produces and publishes maps in a variety of forms and scales described below, beginning with large-scale maps from which the wide range of small-scale maps are derived.

LARGE SCALE MAPS
Highly detailed maps of Great Britain for people that need accurate large-scale information.

1:1250 scale maps (1 cm to 12.5 metres or 50 inches to 1 mile)
These are the largest scale maps published by the Ordnance Survey and are available for cities and other significant urban areas throughout Britain. There are over 50 000 maps in this series. Each map represents an area of 500 m by 500 m and carries National Grid lines at 100 metre intervals. Every building, road and most other features are shown, even post boxes. Street names, house names or numbers are included as well as administrative and parliamentary boundaries. Height information and some survey control points are also shown.

1:2500 scale maps (1 cm to 25 metres or 25 inches to 1 mile)
These maps cover all parts of the country other than significant urban areas (1:1250) and mountain and moorland areas (1:10 000 scale). Normally each plan covers an area of 2 km east to west by 1 km north to south. National Grid lines are shown at 100 metre intervals. Areas of land parcels are given in acres and hectares as well as features shown on 1:1250 scale maps.

1:10 000 scale maps (1 cm to 100 metres or about 6 inches to 1 mile)
These maps cover the whole country. They are also the largest scale of mapping to cover mountain and moorland and to show contours. Some maps are at 1:10 560 scale with contours at 25 feet intervals, but they are being replaced by 1:10 000 scale maps with contours at 10 metre intervals in mountainous areas and 5 metre intervals elsewhere.

Updated Survey Information
Two services are provided to make the latest 1:1250 and 1:2500 scales survey information available before a new edition map is printed.

SUSI (Supply of Updated Survey Information) provides the most up-to-date large-scale information available. Anyone can call at their local Ordnance Survey office (listed in the Telephone Directory) and order a copy of the surveyor's working document know as Master Survey Drawings (MSD's) on paper or film

SIM (Survey Information on Microfilm) provides copies of MSD's after a fixed amount of survey change has been recorded. These copies at original map scale are available through Ordnance Survey Agents either on paper or film. Copies of current edition 1:1250 and 1:2500 maps are also provided through the SIM service.

DIGITAL MAPPING
A growing number of 1:1250 and 1:2500 scale maps are available on magnetic tape in the form of numerical co-

ordinates suitable for computer manipulation. Data on the tape can be recalled to produce an exact scale map copy or a larger or smaller scale copy as required. Furthermore selected detail can be recalled rather than the whole map.

A digital topographic database from maps at 1:625 000 scale (10 miles to 1 inch) has also been developed by Ordnance Survey and is now available. The structure of the data allows feature selection by location, type or name, the extraction of information for a named area, and the analysis of road or river networks.

SMALL SCALE MAPS

Pathfinder Maps 1:25 000 scale (4 cm to 1 km or $2\frac{1}{2}$ inches to 1 mile)
These coloured maps are ideal for the walker or rambler showing the countryside in great detail with footpaths, right of way in England and Wales and field boundaries. The maps normally cover an area 20 km ($12\frac{1}{2}$ miles) east to west by 10 km ($6\frac{1}{4}$ miles) north to south. Coverage of the country by Pathfinder mapping will be complete by 1990.

Outdoor Leisure Maps 1:25 000 scale (4 cm to 1 km or $2\frac{1}{2}$ inches to 1 mile)
This series covers selected popular leisure and recreation areas of the country. Packed with detail they are invaluable to the serious walker or climber. A wealth of tourist information makes them equally popular with the less dedicated outdoor enthusiast. The area covered by the map varies but is much larger than the Pathfinder.

Landranger Maps 1:50 000 scale (2 cm to 1 km or about $1\frac{1}{4}$ inches to 1 mile)
Landranger maps are suitable for motoring, walking, educational and business purposes. The series covers the whole of the country in 204 sheets. Each map covers an area of 40 km by 40 km (25 miles by 25 miles). All show tourist information, and sheets covering England and Wales in-clude public rights of way. Like other Ordnance Survey maps National Grid squares are provided so that any feature can be given a unique reference number.

Tourist Maps 1:63 360 scale (1 inch to 1 mile) and 1:50 000 scale
These maps cover popular touring and holiday areas and are designed to help visitors explore the countryside in detail. The mapping is enchanced with additional tourist inform-ation and some include a useful guide to the area. Public rights of way are also shown.

Routemaster Maps 1:250 000 scale (1 cm to 2·5 km or 1 inch to 4 miles)
Nine Routemaster maps cover Great Britain. They are designed for the motorist to help find the shortest or most scenic route. The maps are regularly revised and show motorways, trunk main and secondary routes prominently depicted to ease map reading. Colour shading and contours are used to depict relief. Road distances and tourist information are also included.

Great Britain Routeplanner 1:625 000 scale (1 cm to 6·25 km or approximately 1 inch to 10 miles)
This map covers the whole of Great Britain on one sheet. Southern England and Wales appear on one side with Northern England and Scotland on the other. Frequently updated, the map also features inset diagrams of major towns, and National Parks, Forest Parks and areas of outstanding natural beauty. A mileage chart and gazetteer of towns and cities is also included.

OTHER PRODUCTS AND FURTHER INFORMATION
Further information on Ordnance Survey products and services can be obtained from Information and Enquiries, Ordnance Survey, Romsey Road, Maybush, Southampton SO9 4DH.

1

Legend

ROADS ROUTES STRASSEN

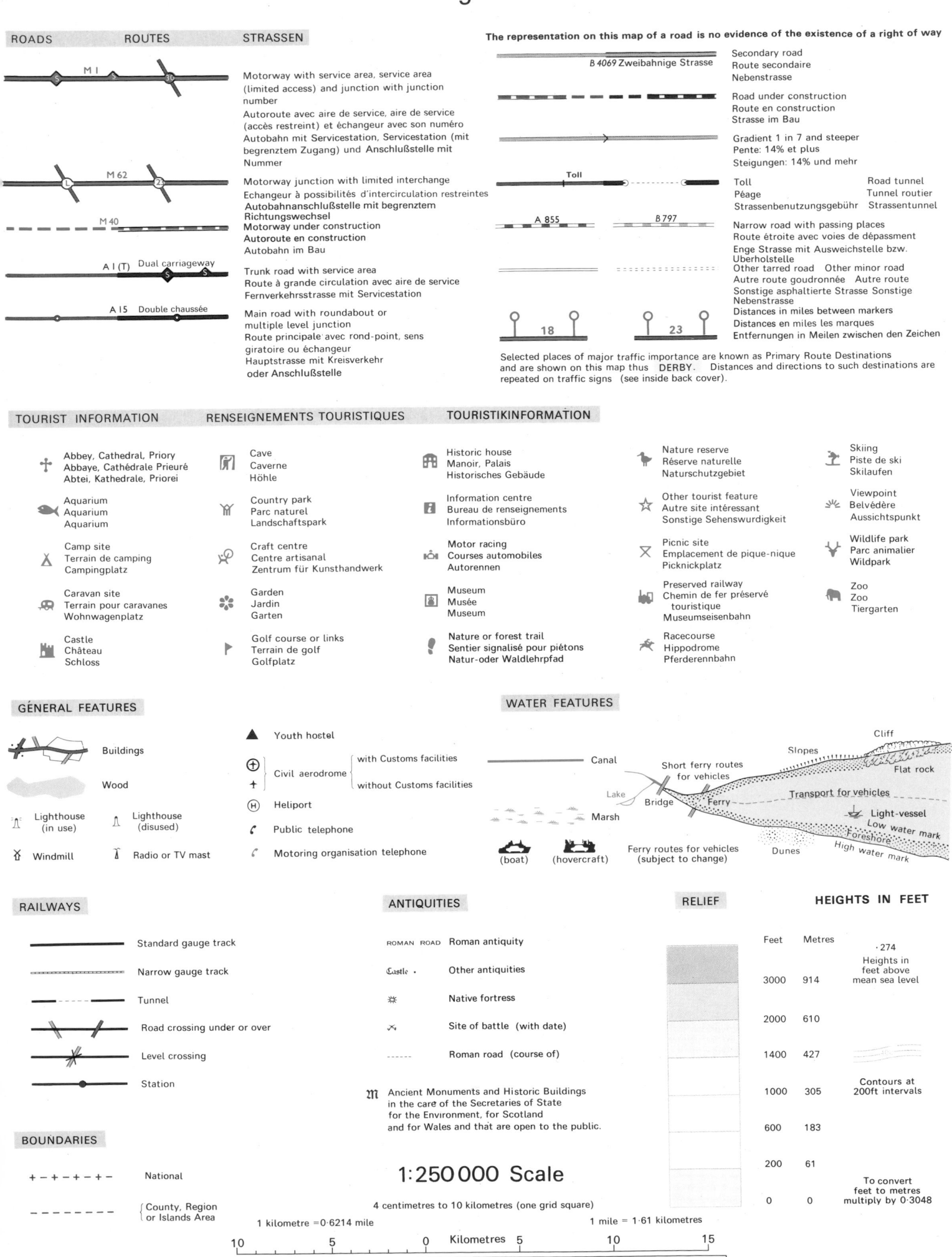

M I — Motorway with service area, service area (limited access) and junction with junction number
Autoroute avec aire de service, aire de service (accès restreint) et échangeur avec son numéro
Autobahn mit Servicestation, Servicestation (mit begrenztem Zugang) und Anschlußstelle mit Nummer

M 62 — Motorway junction with limited interchange
Echangeur à possibilités d'intercirculation restreintes
Autobahnanschlußstelle mit begrenztem Richtungswechsel

M 40 — Motorway under construction
Autoroute en construction
Autobahn im Bau

A I (T) Dual carriageway — Trunk road with service area
Route à grande circulation avec aire de service
Fernverkehrsstrasse mit Servicestation

A I5 Double chaussée — Main road with roundabout or multiple level junction
Route principale avec rond-point, sens giratoire ou échangeur
Hauptstrasse mit Kreisverkehr oder Anschlußstelle

The representation on this map of a road is no evidence of the existence of a right of way

B 4069 Zweibahnige Strasse — Secondary road
Route secondaire
Nebenstrasse

Road under construction
Route en construction
Strasse im Bau

Gradient 1 in 7 and steeper
Pente: 14% et plus
Steigungen: 14% und mehr

Toll — Toll Road tunnel
Péage Tunnel routier
Strassenbenutzungsgebühr Strassentunnel

A 855 B 797 — Narrow road with passing places
Route étroite avec voies de dépassment
Enge Strasse mit Ausweichstelle bzw. Uberholstelle
Other tarred road Other minor road
Autre route goudronnée Autre route
Sonstige asphaltierte Strasse Sonstige Nebenstrasse

18 23 — Distances in miles between markers
Distances en miles les marques
Entfernungen in Meilen zwischen den Zeichen

Selected places of major traffic importance are known as Primary Route Destinations and are shown on this map thus DERBY. Distances and directions to such destinations are repeated on traffic signs (see inside back cover).

TOURIST INFORMATION RENSEIGNEMENTS TOURISTIQUES TOURISTIKINFORMATION

Abbey, Cathedral, Priory
Abbaye, Cathédrale Prieuré
Abtei, Kathedrale, Priorei

Aquarium
Aquarium
Aquarium

Camp site
Terrain de camping
Campingplatz

Caravan site
Terrain pour caravanes
Wohnwagenplatz

Castle
Château
Schloss

Cave
Caverne
Höhle

Country park
Parc naturel
Landschaftspark

Craft centre
Centre artisanal
Zentrum für Kunsthandwerk

Garden
Jardin
Garten

Golf course or links
Terrain de golf
Golfplatz

Historic house
Manoir, Palais
Historisches Gebäude

Information centre
Bureau de renseignements
Informationsbüro

Motor racing
Courses automobiles
Autorennen

Museum
Musée
Museum

Nature or forest trail
Sentier signalisé pour piétons
Natur-oder Waldlehrpfad

Nature reserve
Réserve naturelle
Naturschutzgebiet

Other tourist feature
Autre site intéressant
Sonstige Sehenswurdigkeit

Picnic site
Emplacement de pique-nique
Picknickplatz

Preserved railway
Chemin de fer préservé touristique
Museumseisenbahn

Racecourse
Hippodrome
Pferderennbahn

Skiing
Piste de ski
Skilaufen

Viewpoint
Belvédère
Aussichtspunkt

Wildlife park
Parc animalier
Wildpark

Zoo
Zoo
Tiergarten

GÉNERAL FEATURES

Buildings

Wood

Lighthouse (in use) Lighthouse (disused)

Windmill Radio or TV mast

▲ Youth hostel

⊕ Civil aerodrome with Customs facilities
+ without Customs facilities

Ⓗ Heliport

Public telephone

Motoring organisation telephone

WATER FEATURES

Canal

Lake
Bridge

Marsh

(boat) (hovercraft) Ferry routes for vehicles (subject to change)

Short ferry routes for vehicles
Ferry Transport for vehicles
Cliff
Slopes
Flat rock
Light-vessel
Low water mark
Foreshore
Dunes High water mark

RAILWAYS

Standard gauge track

Narrow gauge track

Tunnel

Road crossing under or over

Level crossing

Station

ANTIQUITIES

ROMAN ROAD Roman antiquity

Castle • Other antiquities

Native fortress

Site of battle (with date)

Roman road (course of)

m Ancient Monuments and Historic Buildings in the care of the Secretaries of State for the Environment, for Scotland and for Wales and that are open to the public.

BOUNDARIES

+ – + – + – + – National

– – – – – – – County, Region or Islands Area

RELIEF HEIGHTS IN FEET

Feet	Metres	
		·274
3000	914	Heights in feet above mean sea level
2000	610	
1400	427	
1000	305	Contours at 200ft intervals
600	183	
200	61	
0	0	To convert feet to metres multiply by 0·3048

1:250 000 Scale

4 centimetres to 10 kilometres (one grid square)

1 kilometre =0·6214 mile   1 mile = 1·61 kilometres

10   5   0   Kilometres   5   10   15

5   0   Miles   5   10

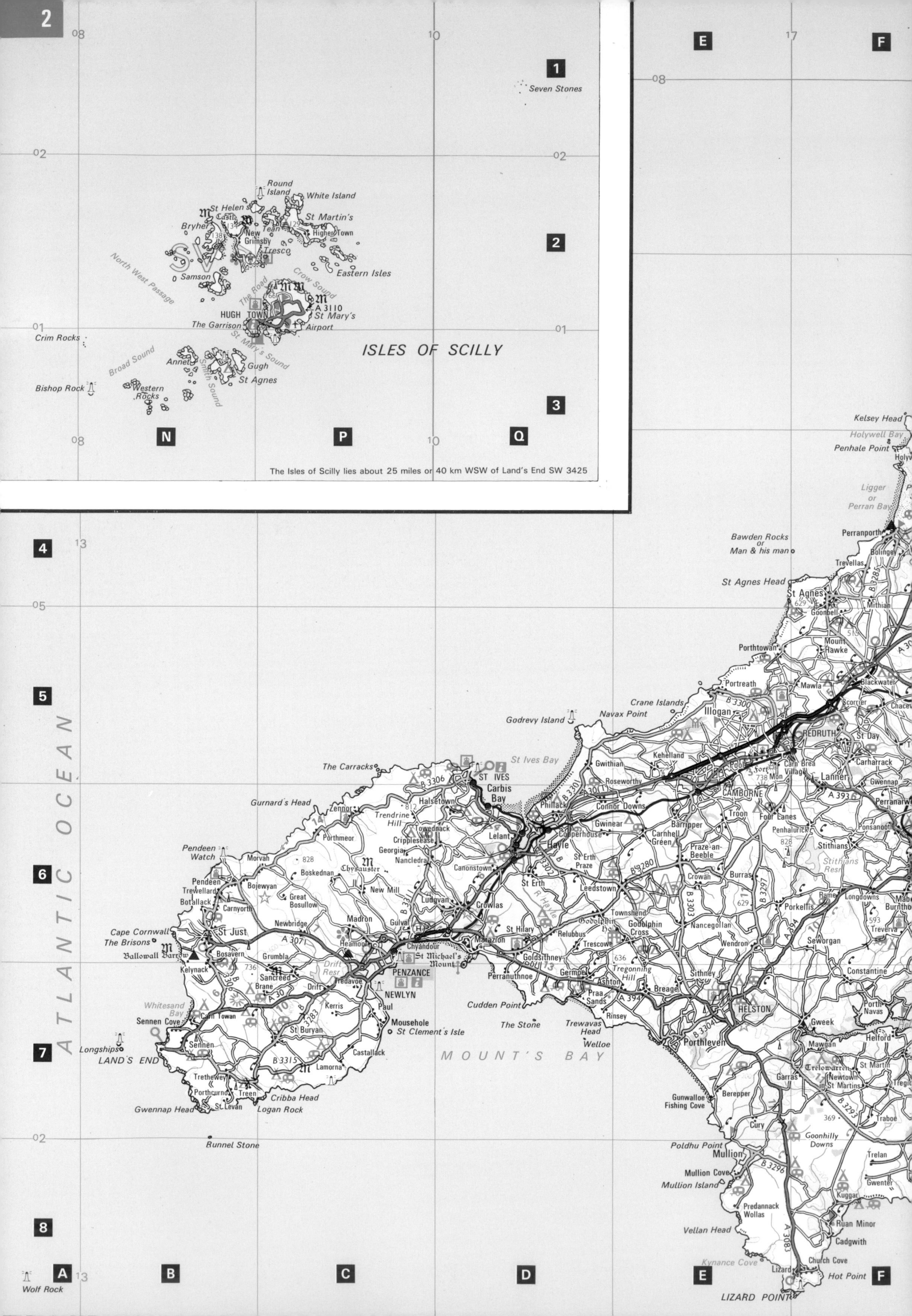

ENGLISH CHANNEL

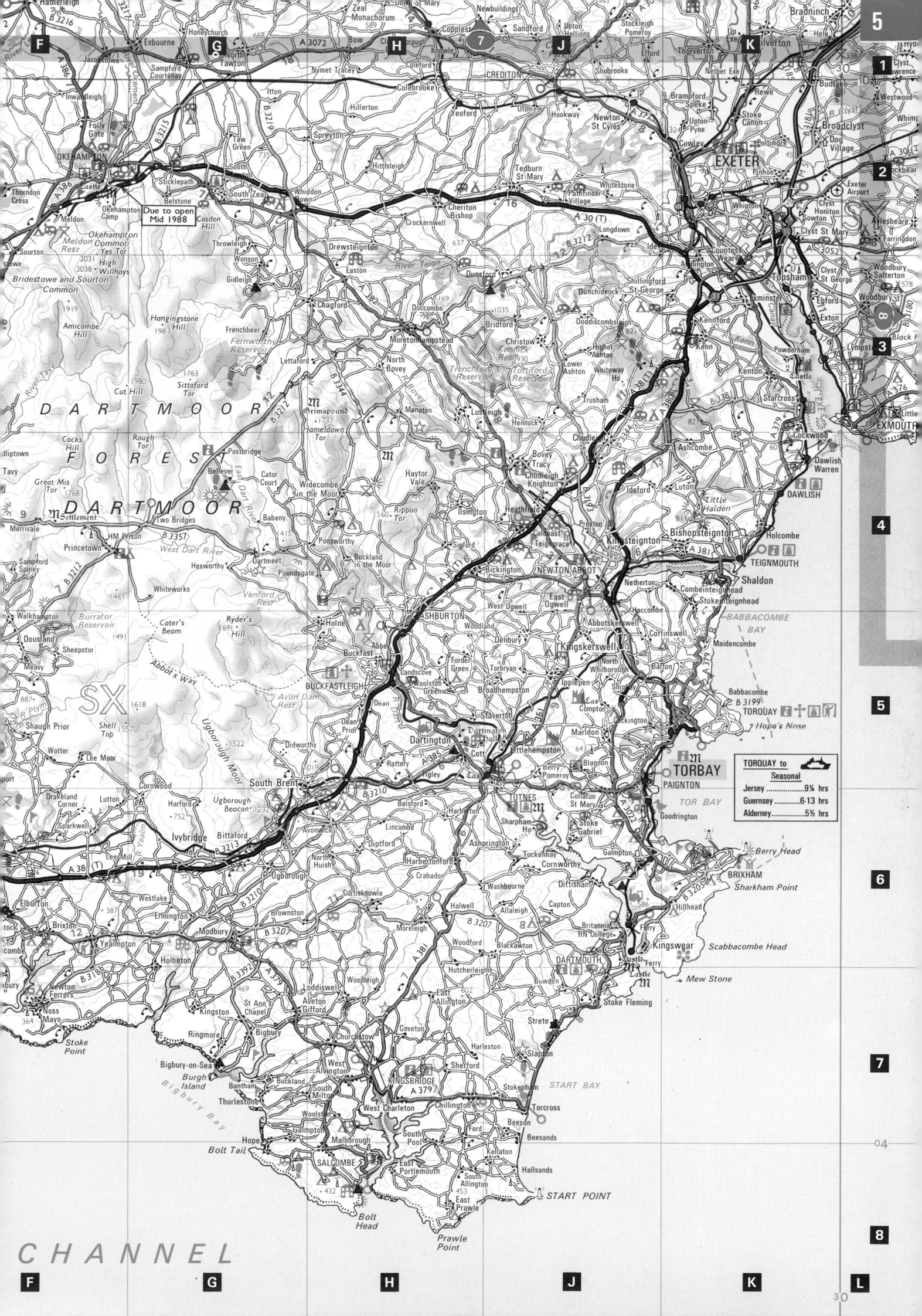

BRISTOL CHANNEL

ILFRACOM

LUNDY

North West Point

South West Point — Rat Island

Bull Point
Rockham Bay
Morte Point
Mortehoe
Woolacombe

Morte Bay

Baggy Point
Pickwell
North Buckland
Georgeham

Croyde Bay
Croyde
Knowle
Saunton

Braunton

Braunton Burrows
Chivenor

Bideford Bar

BARNSTAPLE

OR

BIDEFORD BAY

Appledore
Instow
NORTHAM
Westward Ho!
BIDEFORD
East-the-Water
Woodtown

HARTLAND POINT
Windbury Point
Abbotsham
Alverdisc

Titchberry
Stoke
Hartland
Clovelly
Fairy Cross
Landcross
Littleham
Weare Giffard

Hartland Quay
Dyke
Clovelly Dykes
Buck's Mill
Parkham
Buckland Brewer
Monkleigh

Millford
Philham
Buck's Cross
Woolfardisworthy
Parkham Ash
Frithelstock

Elmscott
Melbury

South Hole
Ashmansworthy
East Putford

Welcombe
Dinworthy
West Putford
Stibb Cross
Langtree

Knaps Longpeak
Gooseham
Eastcott
Youlstone
Bulkworthy
Peters Marland
Winswel

Higher Sharpnose Point
Morwenstow
Shop
Bradworthy
Abbots Bickington
Newton St Petrock

Lower Sharpnose Point
Woodford
Sutcombe
Milton Damerel

Coombe
Kilkhampton
Alfardisworthy
Soldon Cross
Shebbear

Upper Tamar Lake
Lower Tamar Lake
Buckland Filleigh

Stibb
Holsworthy Beacon
Thornbury
Bradford

BUDE
Poughill
Chilsworthy
Sheepwash

Flexbury
Bude Haven
STRATTON
Grimscott
Cookbury
Black Torrington

BUDE
Launcells
Pancrasweek
HOLSWORTHY
Holemoor
Highampton

BAY
Marhamchurch
Pyworthy
Hollacombe
Graddon Moor

Bridgerule
Halwill Junction

Widemouth Bay
Coppathorne
Beaworthy

Dizzard Point
Whitstone
Halwill

Poundstock
Week St Mary
North Tamerton
Clawton

Tregole
Trewint
Tetcott
Lana
Quoditch

Cambeak
St Gennys
Jacobstow
Luffincott
Ashwater

Crackington
Wainhouse Corner
South Wheatley
Clubworthy
West Curry
Northcott
Chapmans Well
Virginstow

Fire Beacon Point
Marshgate
Canworthy Water
Bennacott
Boyton
East Panson

Boscastle
Lesnewth
Otterham
Warbstow
Brazacott
St Giles on the Heath
Broadwoodwidger

Tintagel Head
Trevalga
Bossiney
Halworthy
Tremaine
North Petherwin
Polapit Tamar
Werrington
Cross Green

Tintagel
Treknow
Trewarmett
Trewassa
Davidstow
Tremail
Treneglos
Tresmeer
Tregeare
Yeolmbridge
Egloskerry
Langore
Stowford
Lewdown

Start Point
Treligga
St Clether
Trewen
Red Down
St Stephens
LAUNCESTON
Lifton
Tinhay

Camelford
Laneast
Tregadillett
Lawhitton
Marystow

Port Isaac Bay
Delabole
Helstone
Teath
St Clether
Polyphant
Lewannick
South Petherwin
Kelly
Chillaton

Portgaverne
Pendoggett
Michaelstow
Rough Tor
Altarnun
Lezant
Bradstone
Milton Abbot

Brown Willy
Garrow Tor
Codda
Dunterton

ST GEORGE'S CHANNEL

STRUMBLE HEAD

FISHGUARD to 🚢
Rosslare..............3½ hrs

DINAS HEAD

Carregwastad Point

Fishguard
Bay

Newport
Bay

Cardigan
Island

Cemaes Head

Pwllygranant

St Dogmaels

Abbe

Moylgrove

Monington

Tresinwen
Pen Caer
Pen Brush
Llanwnda
699
GOODWICK
Harbour
625
FISHGUARD

Bryn-
henllan
Dinas
Cross
12
Parrog
Newport

Trwyn y Bwa

645
Glanrhyd

Nevern

Felindre
Farchog
213
330

Eglwyswrw

490

Bridel

592

A 487
(T)

B 4332

Afon Nyfer
Llan
Nant

Manorowen

St Nicholas
Panteg
Granston

Llanychaer
Scleddau

Mynydd Melyn
1007

Mynydd Carningli
1021

1138

Crosswell

Eglwyswen

Penbwchdy

Ynys Deullyn

Abercastle

Trecwn

Pontfaen
1096

931
MYNYDD PRESELI
Foel Eryr
1535

Brynberian

B 4329

Fort

Penclegyr

Porthgain
Trevine

Mathry

Jordanston
Castlemorris

183

Foel
Cwmcerwyn
1759

7
B 4329

Mynachlog-
ddu

Foel-drych

Carreg-gwylan-
fach
Penclegyr

Abereiddy
Berea

Llanrhian
Croes-goch
Square and
Compass
B 4331

SM

Letterston

Little Newcastle

Puncheston
1138

Castlebythe

B 4329
Tufton

Henry's
Moat

Rosebush

Maenclochog

A 478

Llangolman

Penllechwen

Tretio
Treleddyd-
fawr
289

Treglemais
Carnhedryn
292

Treffynnon

Llandeloy

Hayscastle

Hayscastle
Cross
386

Welsh
Hook

Wolf's
Castle

Ambleston

Rinaston

Wallis

412

Llys-y-fran
Resr

645

New Moat

699
B 4313

Efailwen

Llandissilio

Llanycefn

Penffordd

Llanfallteg

ST DAVID'S
HEAD
Whitesand Bay
or Porth-mawr
595
593
Rhosson
Cath
St David's
Solva

Alun
6

Whitchurch
Middle
Mill

Nun
Solva

Penycwm
Newgale

585
Dudwell
Mt
Wolfsdale

Leweston

Treffgarne

Spittal

Scolton

Walton
East

Clarbeston
Clarbeston
Road

387

Wiston

Gelli

Castle

Bethesda
Llawhaden
B 4313

Llanddewi
Velfrey

305

Bishops and Clerks

Ramsey
Island

Ramsey Sound

Green Scar

16
314

Roch

Camrose

Keeston

Pelcom
Cross

A 487

Crundale
209

Robeston
Wathen

4

B 4314

A 478

A 40 (T)

ST BRIDES

BAY

Ricketts
Head

Simpson
Cross
Nolton Haven
Nolton

Druidston

Lambston
Portfield
Gate
385

HAVERFORDWEST

Uzmaston

Conaston
Bridge

NARBERTH

Crinow

Lampeter
Velfrey

B 4314

Skomer
Island
259

Wooltack
Point

Stack
Rocks

Haroldston
West

Broad Haven

Little Haven
Talbenny

B 4341
Walton
West
258

12
268

Merlin's
Bridge

B 4327

Freystrop

Minwear
353

Templeton

A 4115

Ludchurch

BROAD SOUND

Gateholm
Island

Tower Point

St Brides

Hasguard

Walwyn's
Castle

Tiers
Cross

Johnston

Hook

Landshipping

Martletwy

A 4075

287

Reynalton

Loveston

Thomas
Chapel

508

Marloes

183

Oil
Refinery

Robeston
Cross

Steynton

43

A 4076 (T)

Rosemarket

Langwm

Hill
Mountain

Yerbeston

Begelly

Kilgetty

Skokholm
Island

Dale

Gateholm
Island

St Ishmael's

231

Herbrandston

Oil
Refinery

MILFORD
HAVEN
B 4325
Waterston
Oil Refinery
Llanstadwell

477

Houghton

Lawrenny

Cresswell
Quay

Cresselly

Jeffreyston

Saundersfoot
Station

East
Williamston

Saundersfoot

St Ann's
Head

Sheep
Island

Angle

Angle
Bay

Rhoscrowther

Power
Sta

Pwllcrochan

NEYLAND
Toll

Pembroke
Dock

Clanstadwell

PEMBROKE

Palace
Lamphey

Burton

Coshel
Newton

Cosheston

Carew

Milton

Carew
Cheriton
B 4318

Redberth

Carew

Monkstone
Point

New Hedges

Gumfreston

St Florence

TENBY

Freshwater
West

Castlemartin

198

St Twynnells

B 4320
232

Hundleton
293

A 4075

B 4319

Warren

St Petrox

Hodgeston

Freshwater
East

Jameston

Manorbier

A 4139

Lydstep

Penally

Giltar
Point

Caldey Sound

Caldey
Island

SR

Linney
Head

Crow
Rock
Toes

The
Wash

Bosherston

Stackpole

Trewent
Point

Stackpole
Head

Old Castle
Head

Chapel
Point

ST GOVAN'S
HEAD

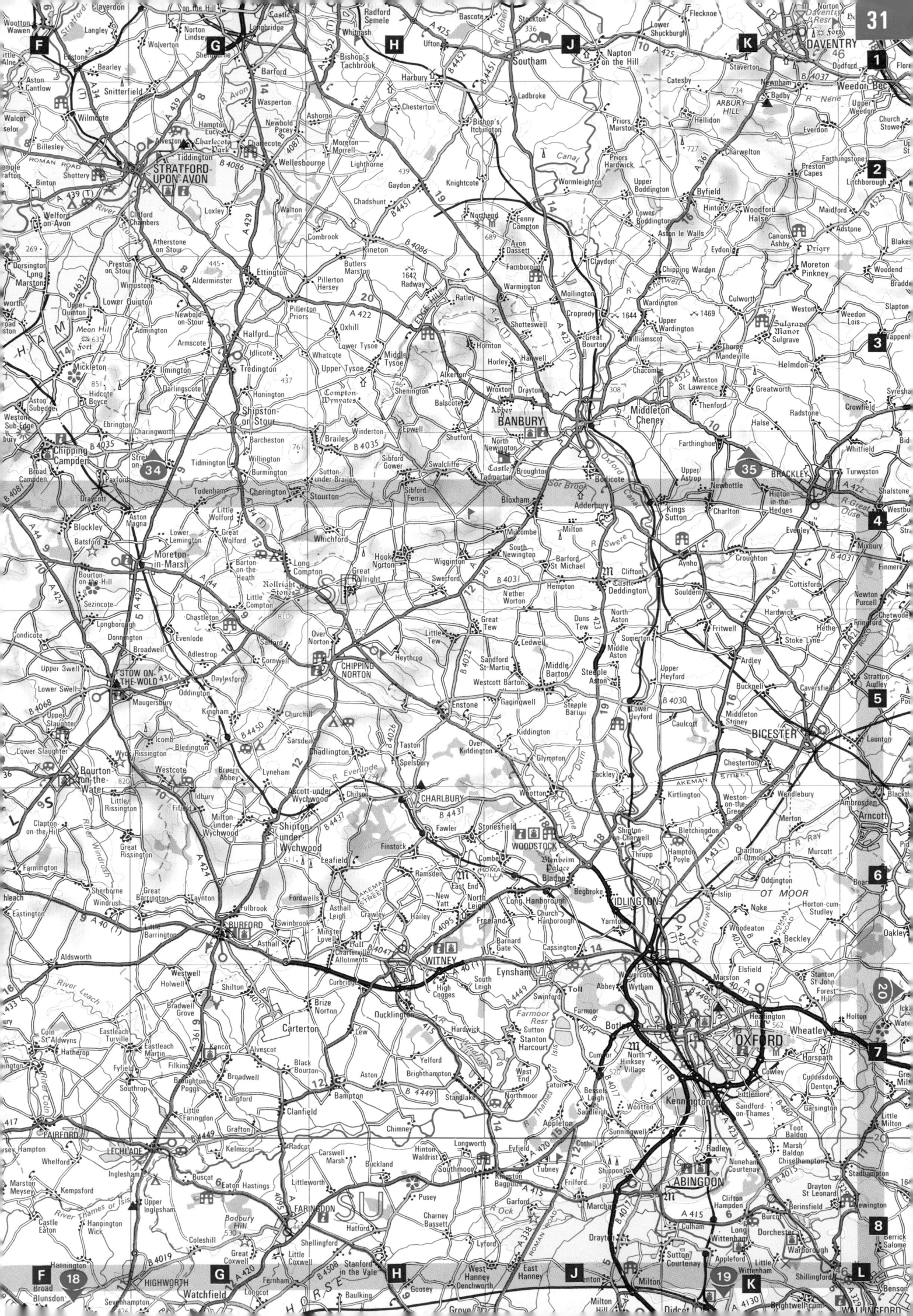

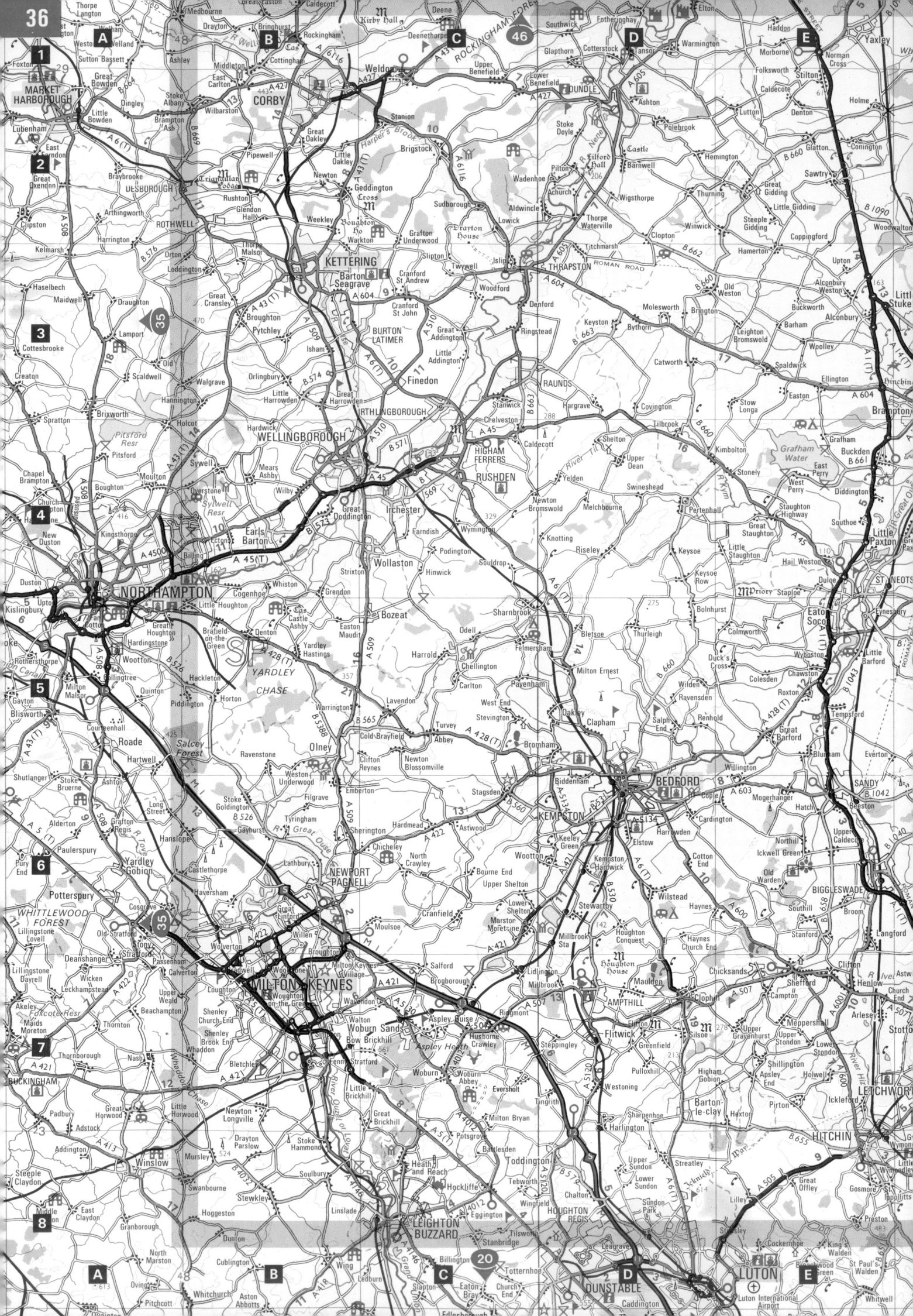

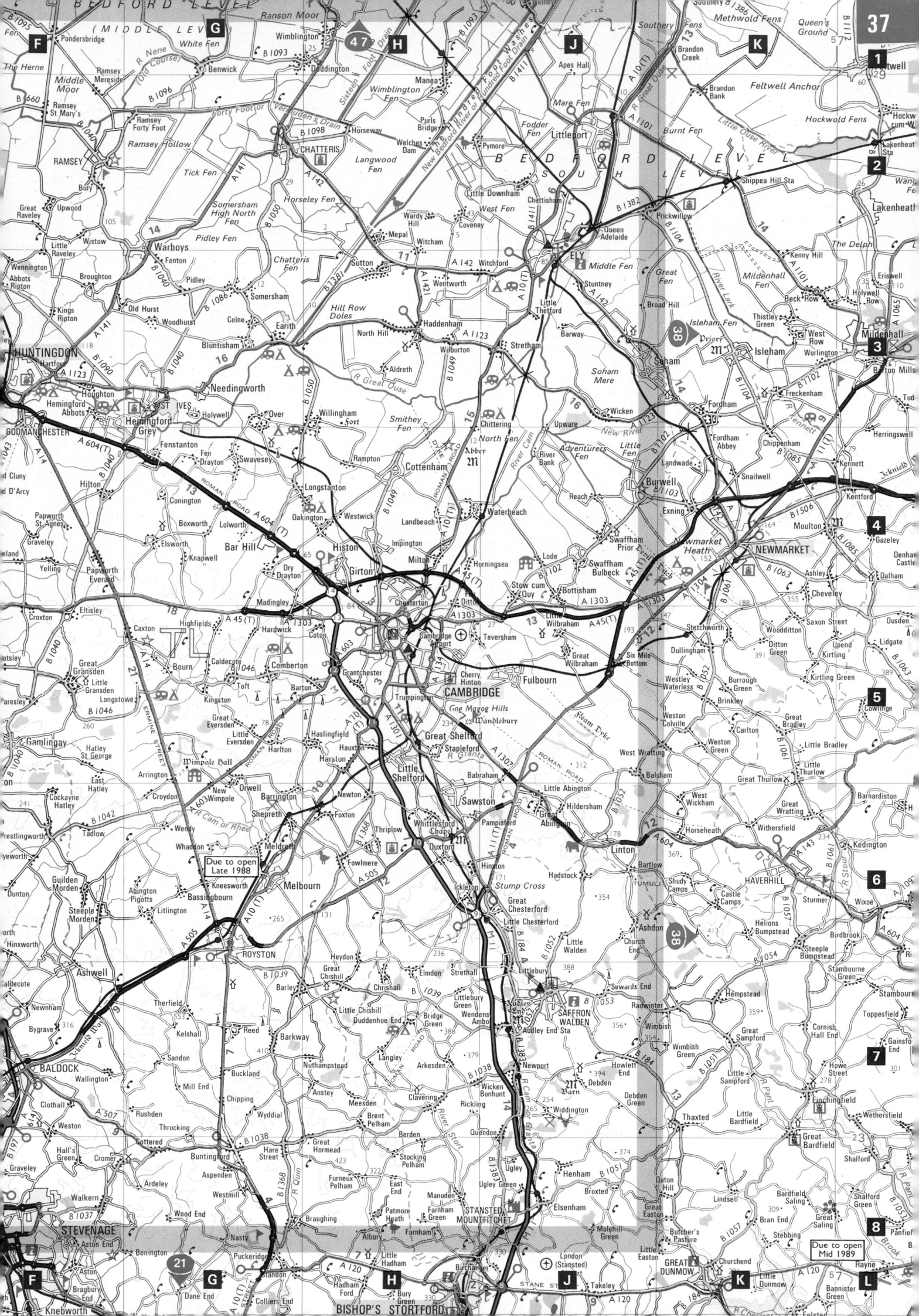

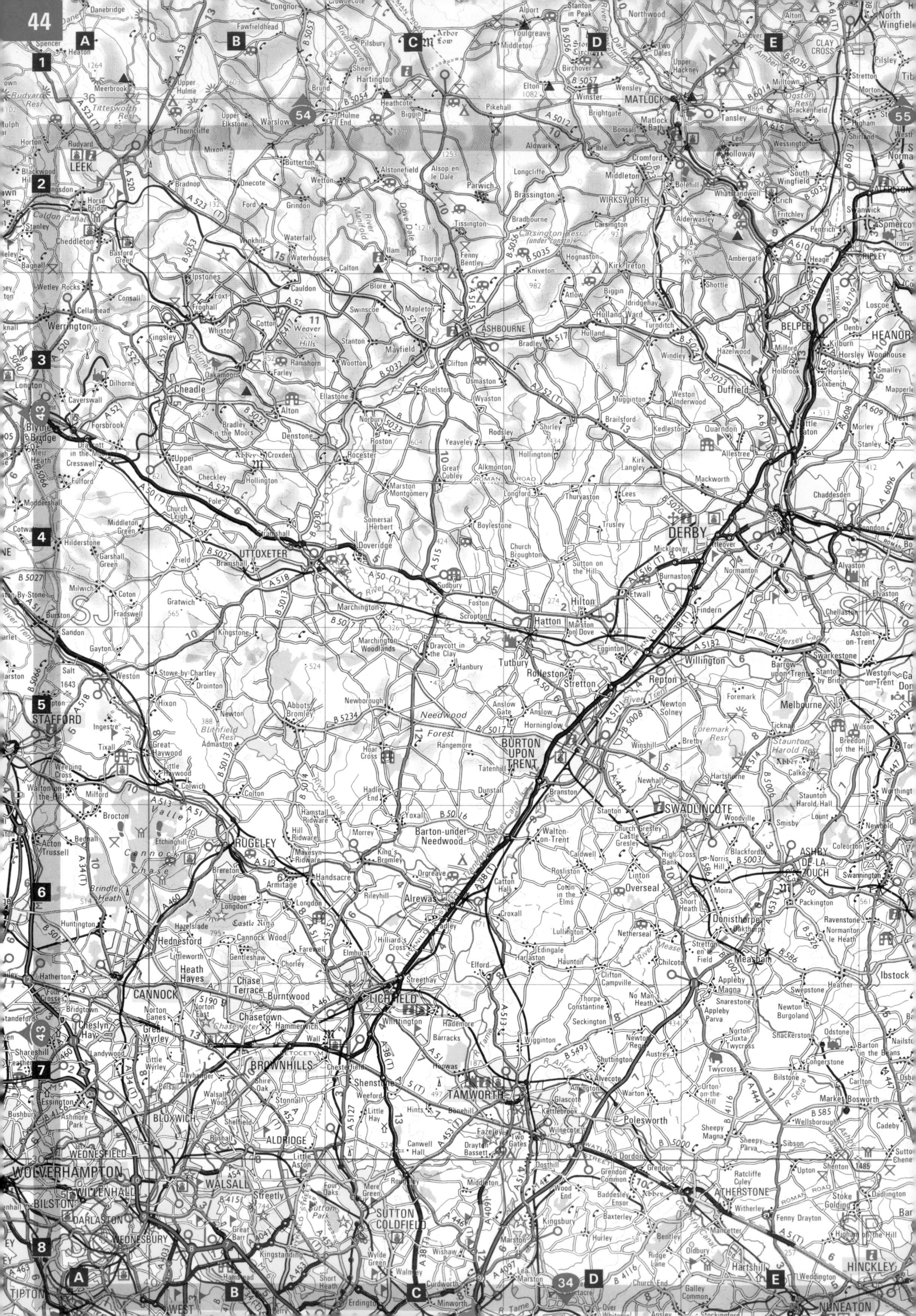

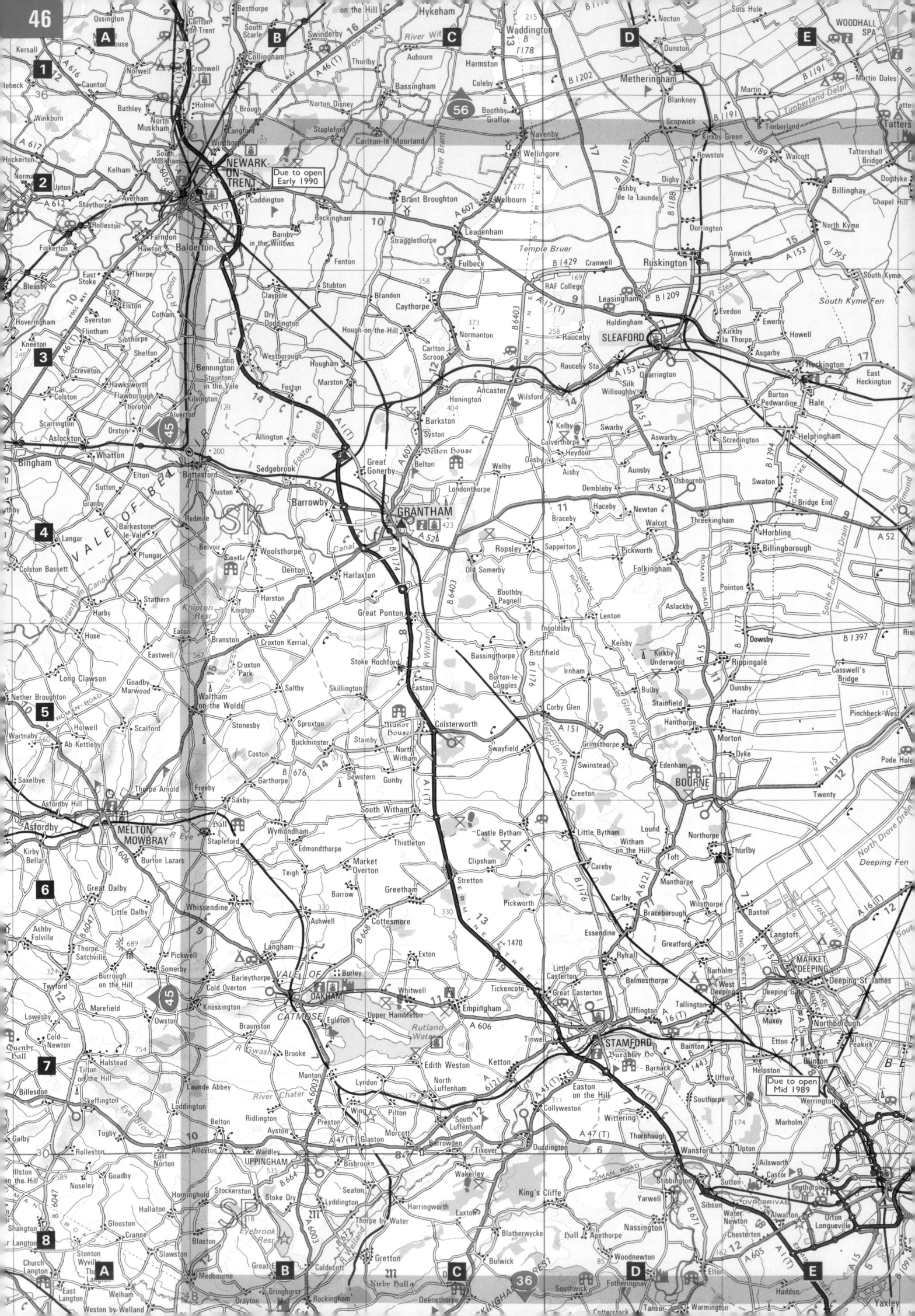

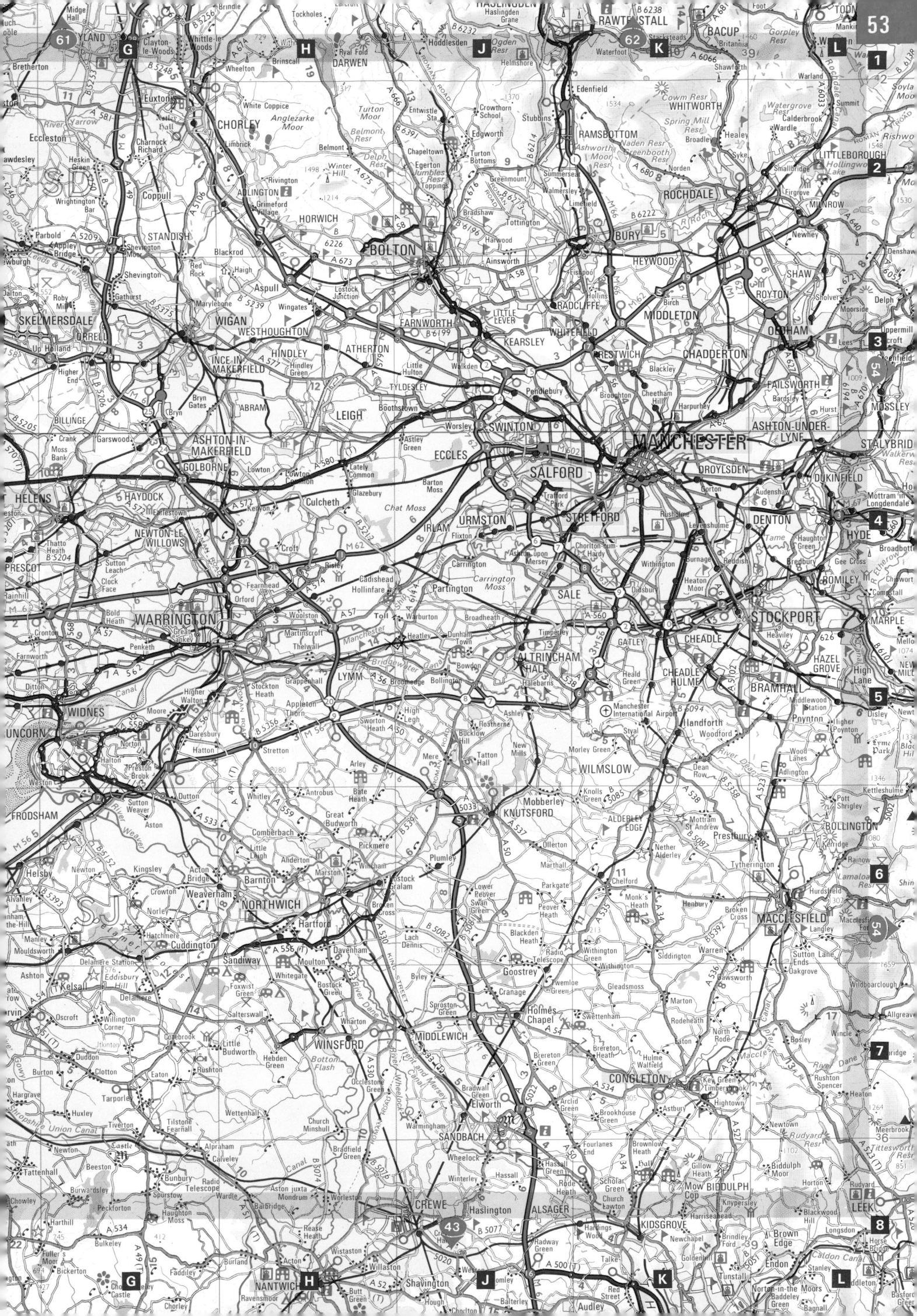

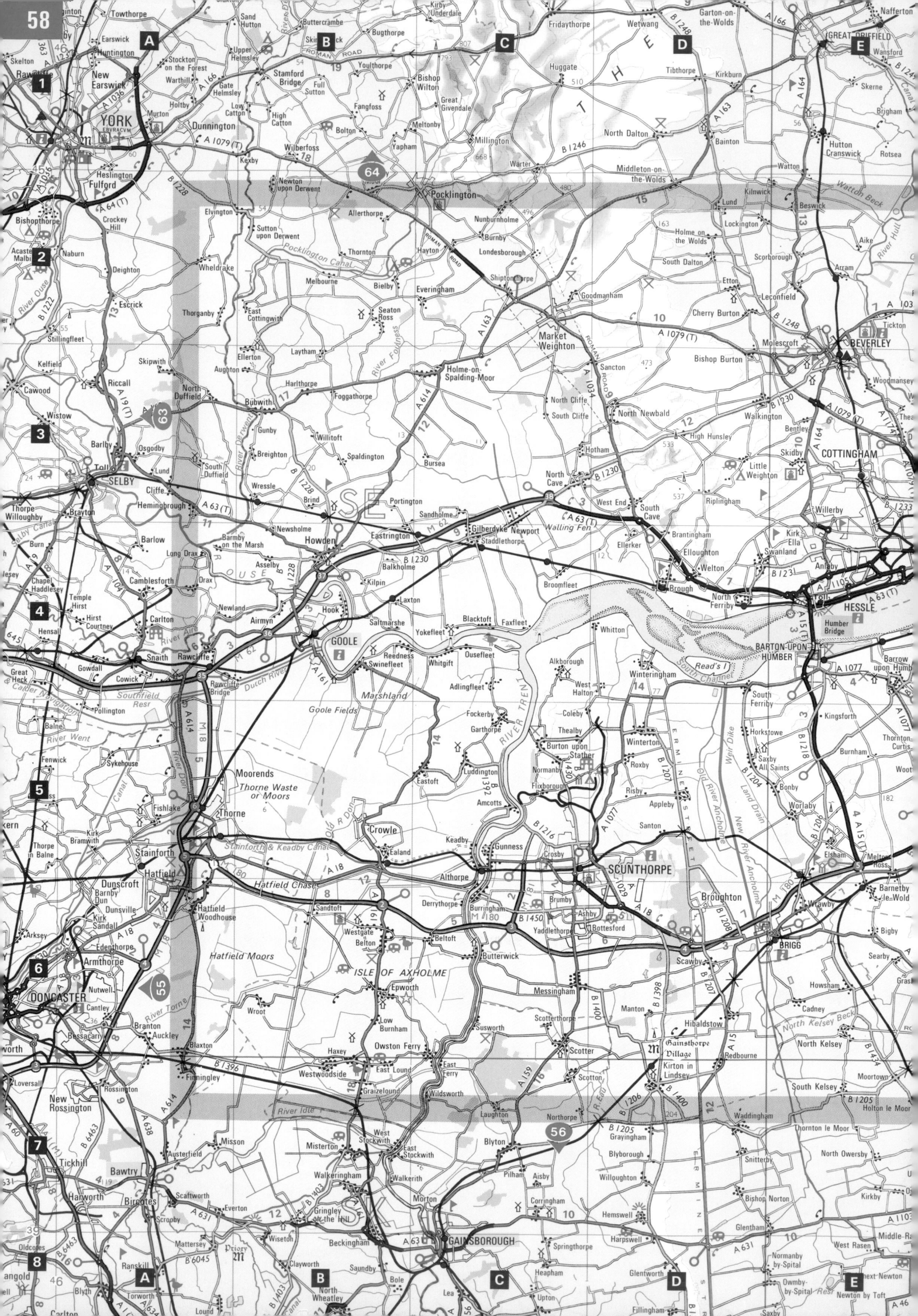

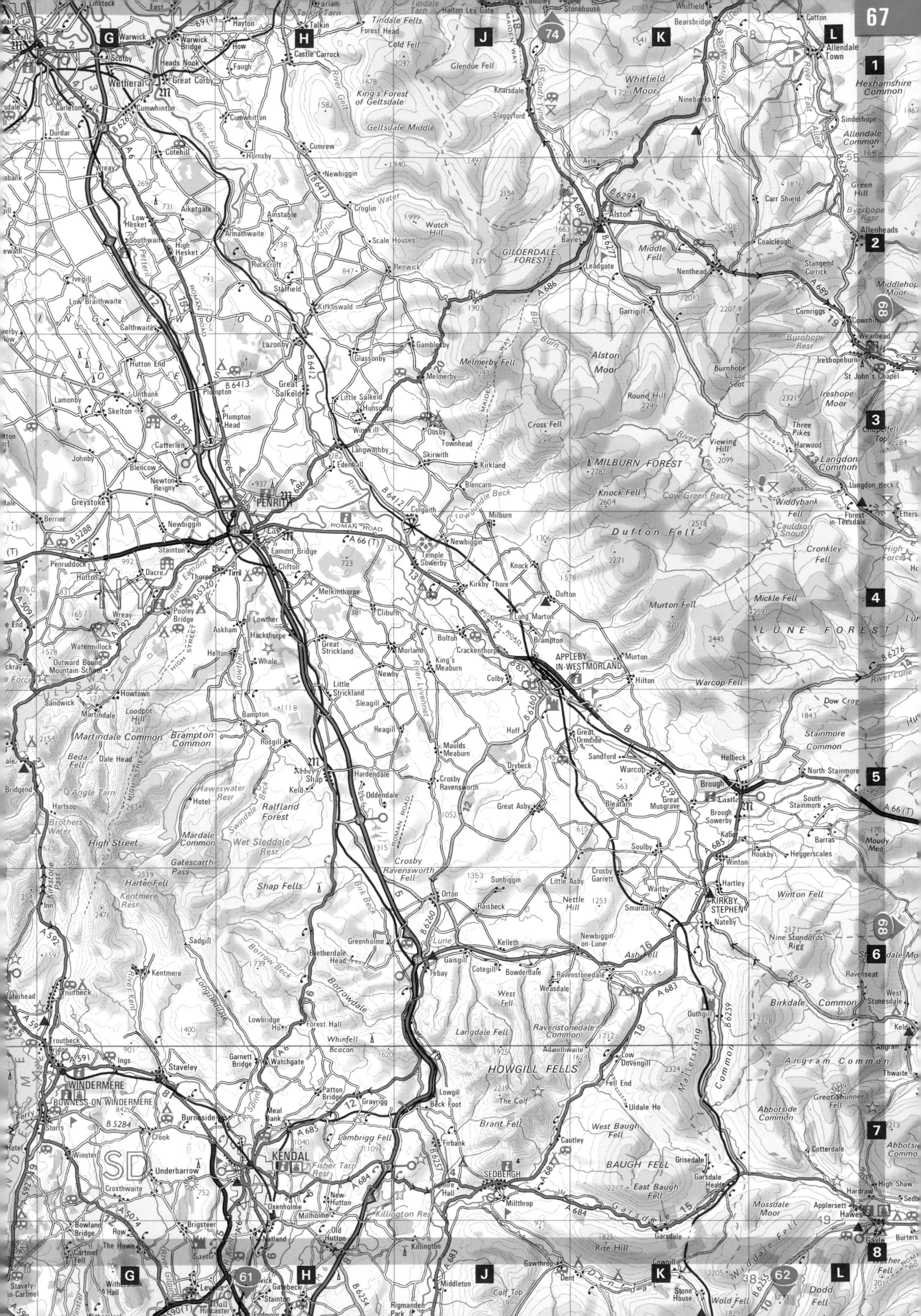

NORTH SEA

SUNDERLAND
Houghton-le-Spring
SEAHAM
PETERLEE
HARTLEPOOL
Hartlepool Bay
Tees Bay
Sedgefield
BILLINGHAM
STOCKTON-ON-TEES
MIDDLESBROUGH
REDCAR
MARSKE-BY-THE-SEA
SALTBURN-BY-THE-SEA
LOFTUS
GUISBOROUGH
Danby
Houlskye
Lealholm
Egton
Egton Bridge
Goathland
NORTHALLERTON
Stokesley
NORTH YORK MOORS
Rosedale Abbey
Hutton-le-Hole

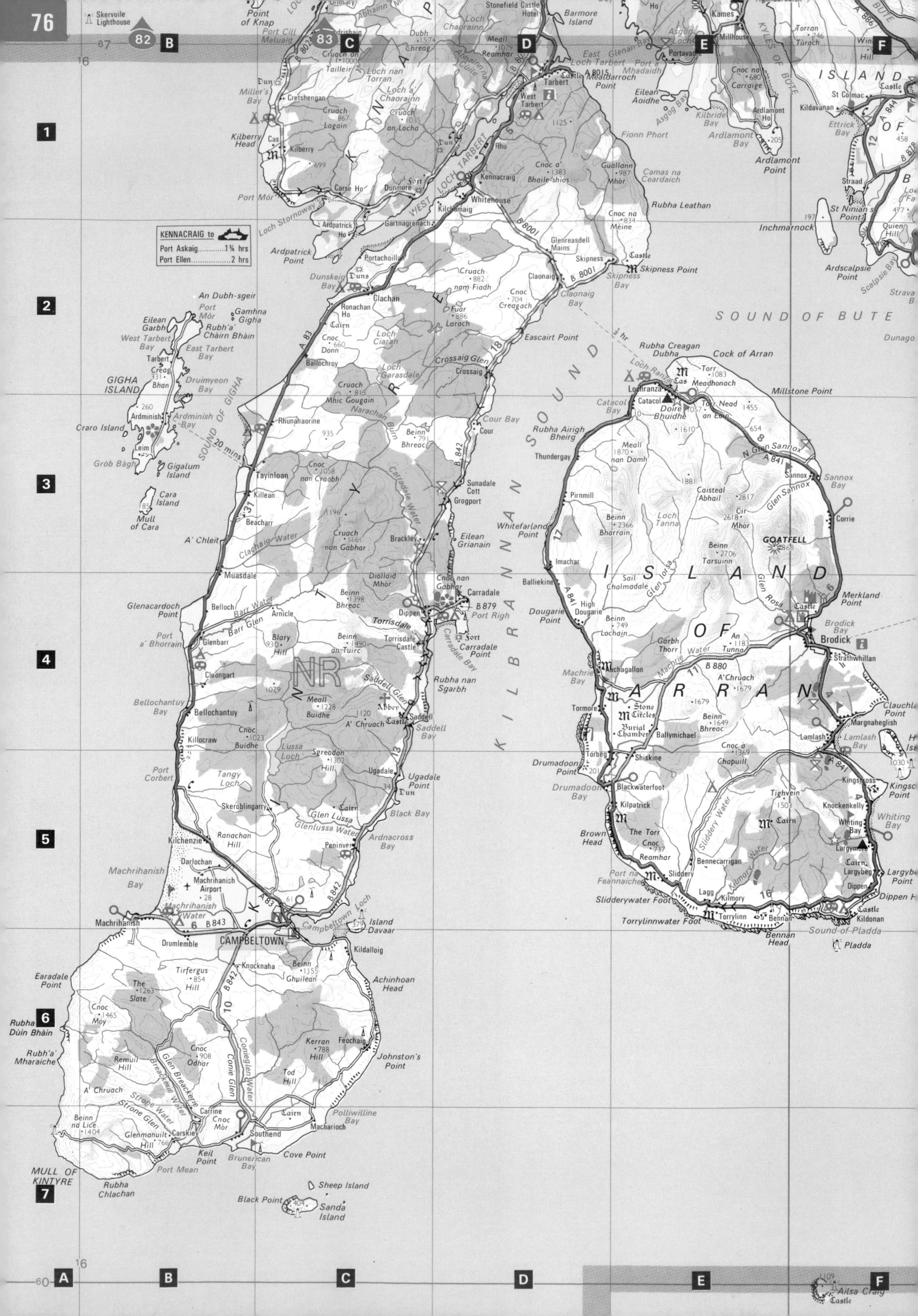

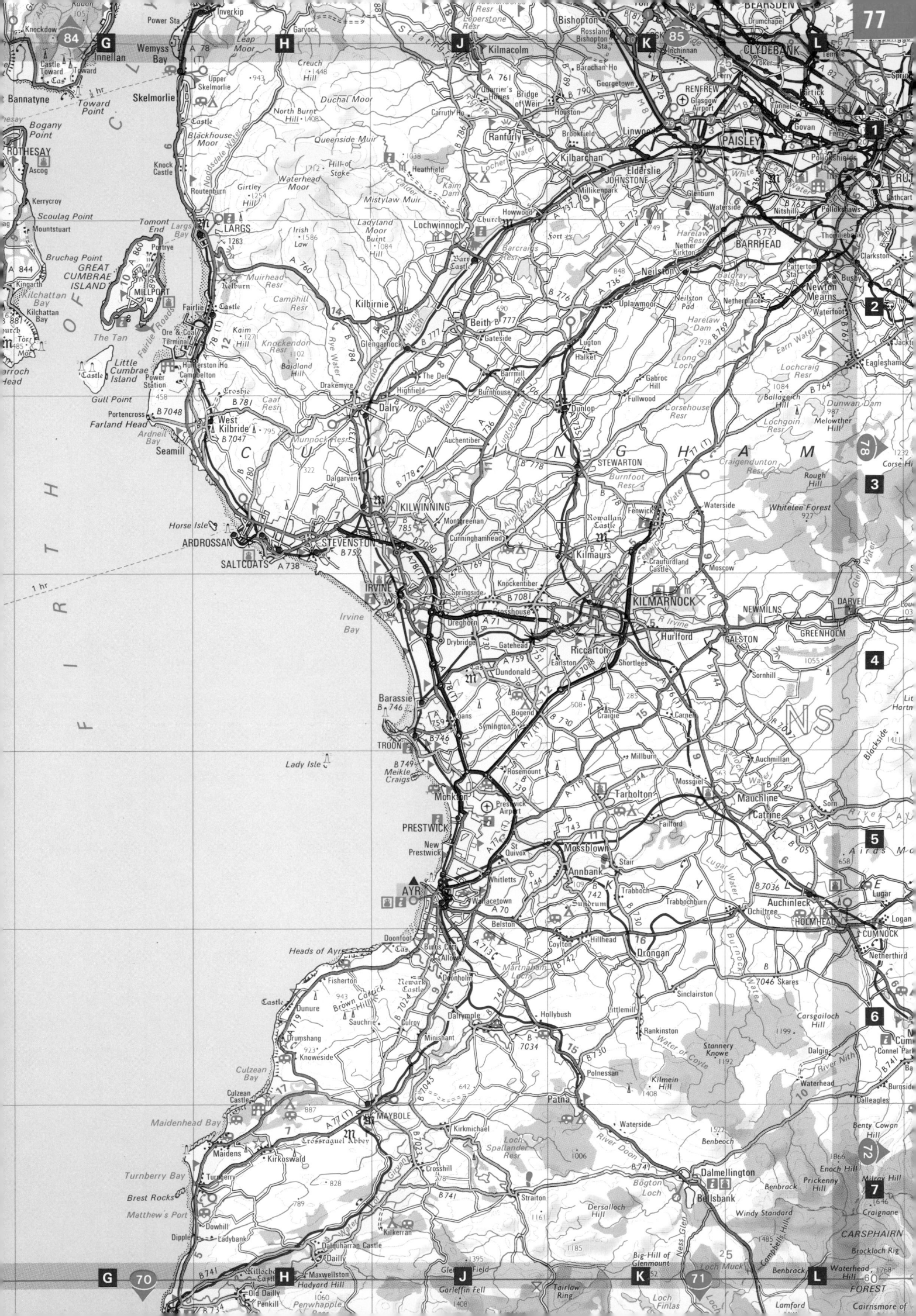

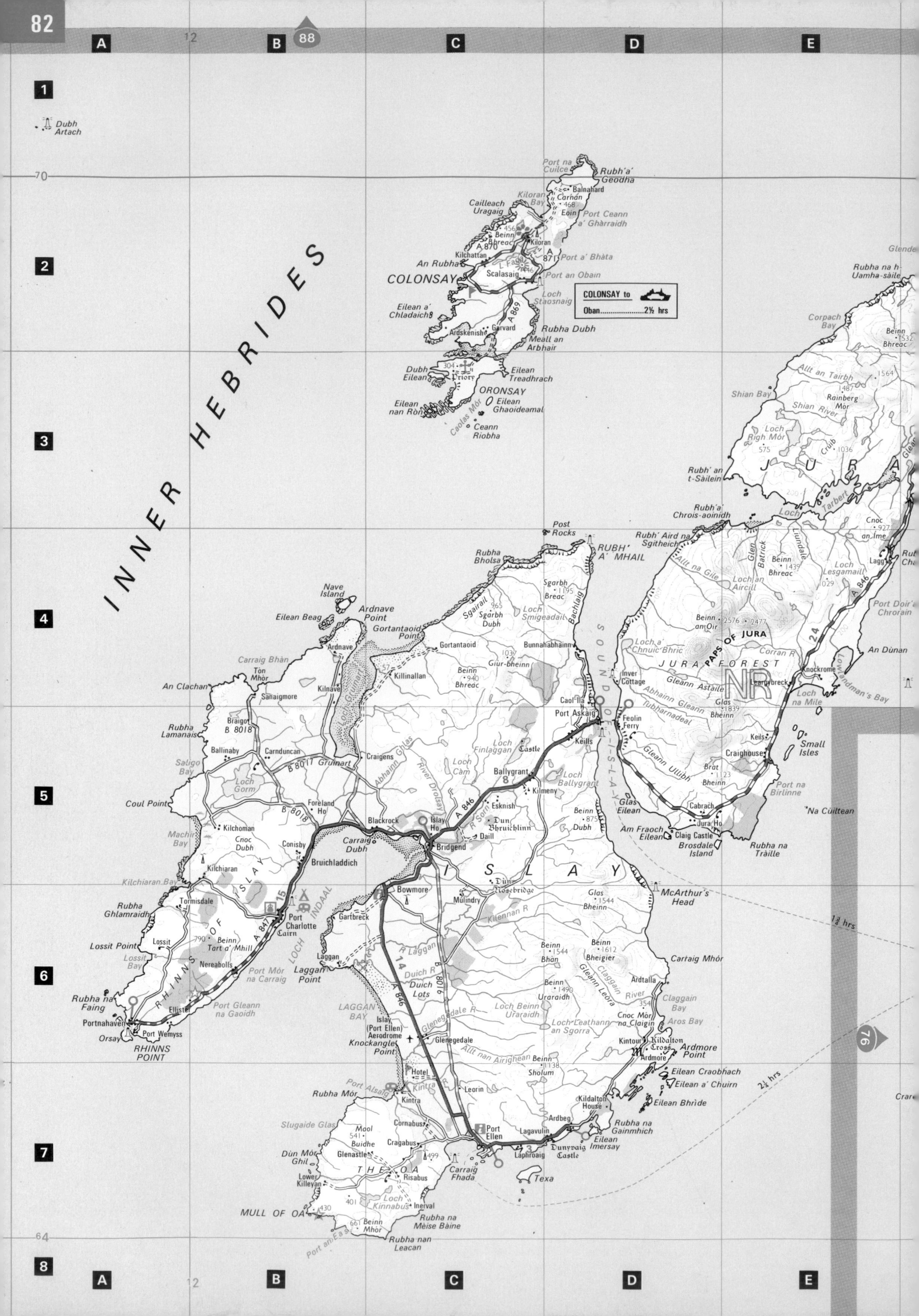

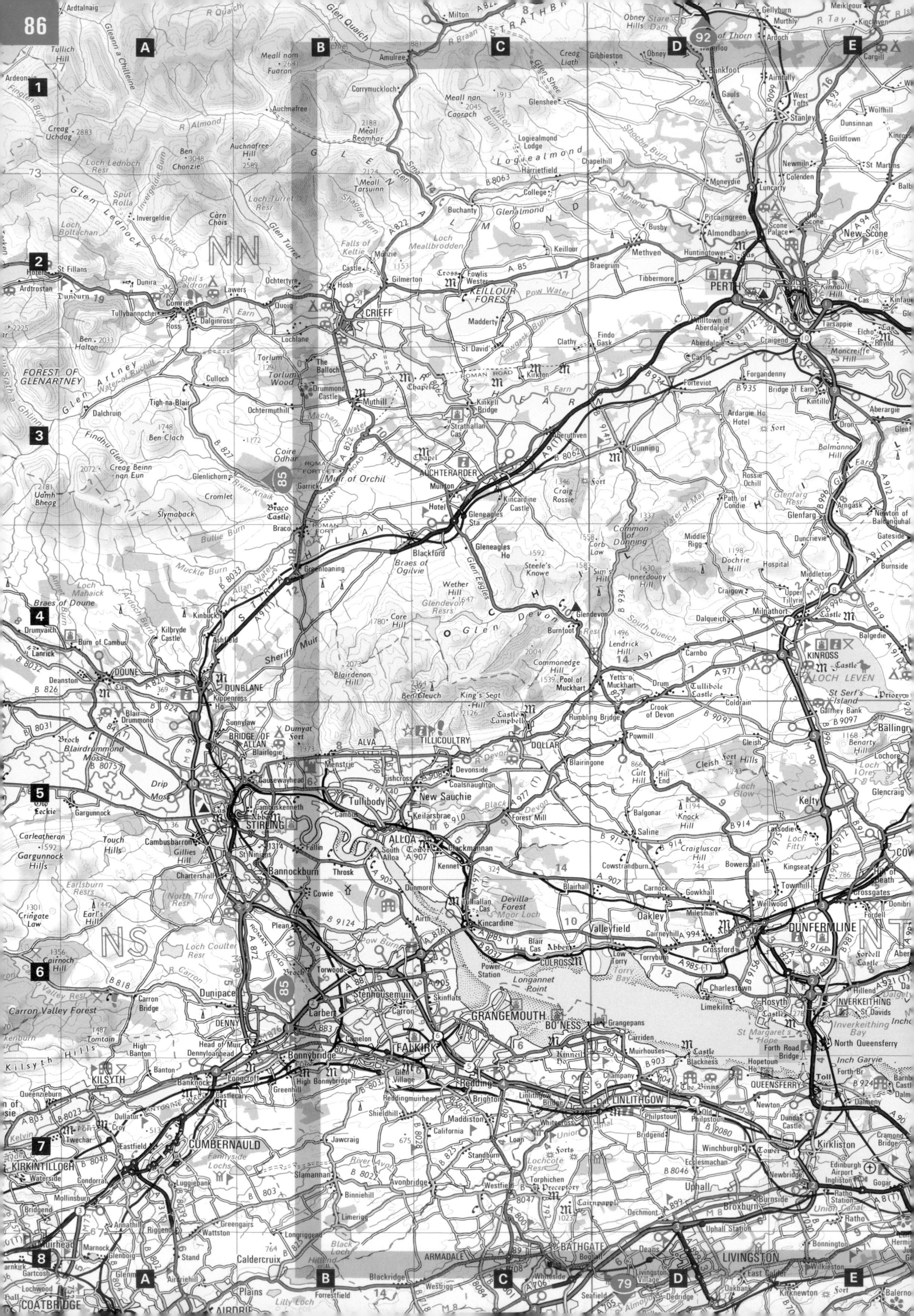

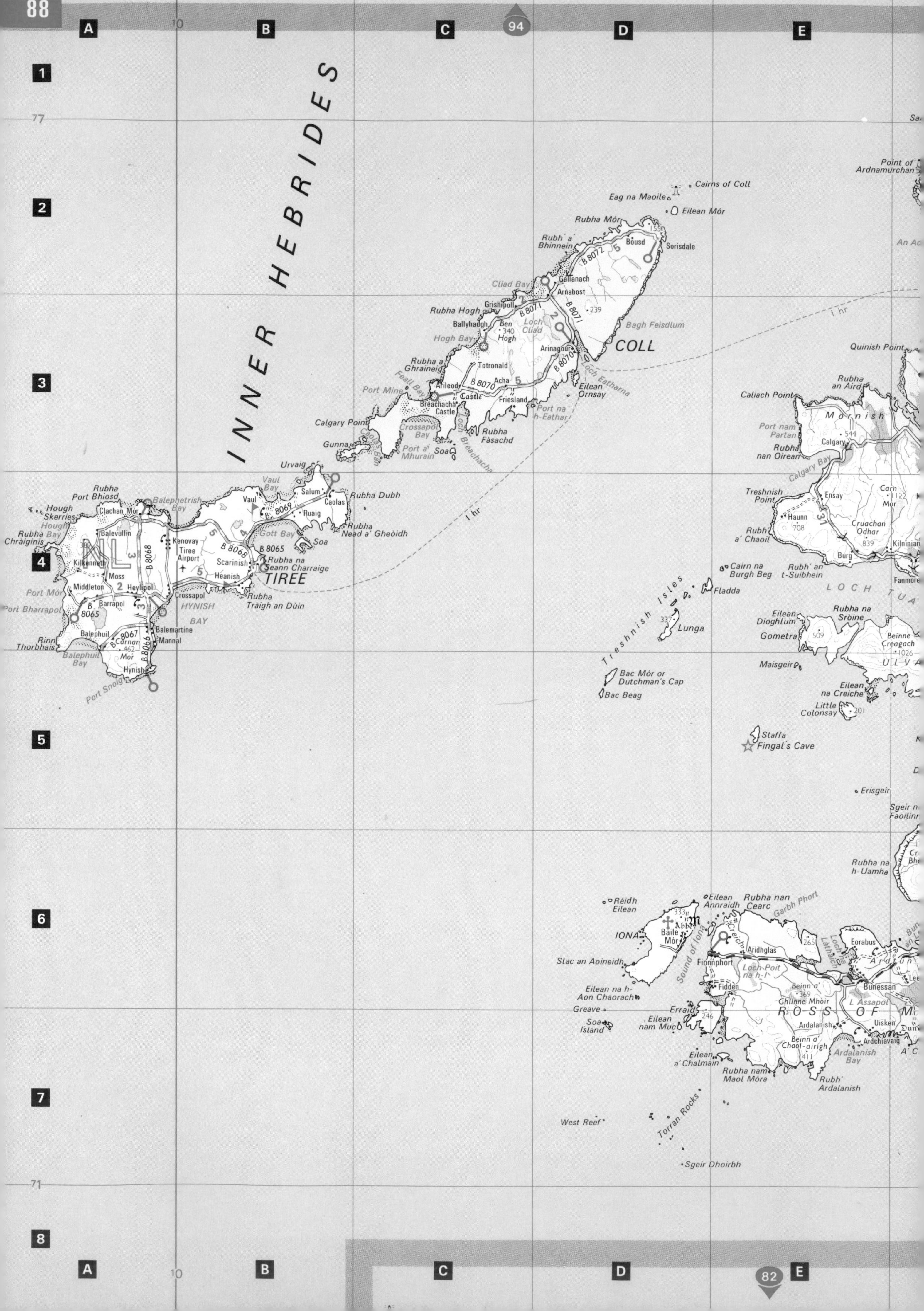

A B C D E

1

77

2

INNER HEBRIDES

Cairns of Coll

Eag na Maoile
Eilean Mór
Rubha Mór
Rubh' a'
Bhinnein
Bousd
Sorisdale
1555
B 8072
Cliad Bay
Gallanach
Arnabost
Rubha Hogh
Grishipoll
B 8071
239
Bagh Feisdlum
Ballyhaugh
Ben
Hogh
340
Loch
Cliad
B 8071
COLL
Hogh Bay
2
1 hr
Rubha a'
Ghraineig
Arinagour
Totronald
B 8070
Acha
Port Mine
Feall Bay
Aileodr
Castle
5
Friesland
B 8070
Loch Eatharna
Eilean
Ornsay
Point of
Ardnamurchan

3

Breachacha
Castle
Port na
h-Eathar
Calgary Point
Rubha
Fàsachd
Quinish Point
Gunna
Crossapol
Bay
Port a'
Soa
Rubha
Rubha
an Aird
Mhurain
Mornish
544
Caliach Point
Port nam
Partan
Rubha
nan Oirean
Calgary
Urvaig
Vaul
Bay
Salum
Rubha Dubh
Calgary Bay
Rubha
Port Bhiosd
Balephetrish
Bay
Vaul
Caolas
Treshnish
Point
Ensay
Carn
Mór
1122
Hough
Skerries
Clachan Mór
B 8069
Ruaig
Rubh'
a' Chaoil
Haunn
708
Cruachan
Odhar
839
Hough
Balevullin
Gott Bay
Rubha
Nead a' Gheòidh
31
Kilninian
Rubha Bay
Chràiginis
NL
B 8068
Kenovay
Tiree
Airport
B 8065
Scarinish
Soa
Rubh' an
t-Suibhein
Burg
Rubha na
Seann Charraige
Kilkenneth
Moss
Heanish
TIREE
Cairn na
Burgh Beg
LOCH TUA
Port Mór
Middleton
Heylipol
Crossapol
Rubha
Tràigh an Dùin
Fladda
Port Bharrapol
Barrapol
B 8065
HYNISH
BAY
Treshnish Isles
Eilean
Dioghlum
Rubha na
Sròine
Balephuil
B 8067
Balemartine
333
Lunga
Gometra
509
Beinne
Creagach
1026
Rinn
Thorbhais
Cörnan
Mór
462
Mannal
Maisgeir
ULVA
Balephuil
Bay
Hynish
Bac Mór or
Dutchman's Cap
Eilean
na Creiche
Port Snoig
Bac Beag
Little
Colonsay
201

5

Staffa
Fingal's Cave

Erisgeir

Sgeir na
Faoilinn

6

Réidh
Eilean
Eilean
Annraidh
Rubha nan
Cearc
Garbh Phort
333
Abbey
Baile
Mór
IONA
Creich
Aridhglas
265
Eorabus
Rubha na
h-Uamha
Stac an Aoineidh
Sound of Iona
Fionnphort
Loch Poit
na h-I
Ardun
Eilean na h-
Aon Chaorach
Fidden
Beinn a'
369
Ghlinne Mhòir
L Assapol
Bunessan
ROSS OF M
Greave
Errard
Soa
Island
Eilean
nam Muc
246
Beinn a'
Chaol-airigh
411
Uisken
Ardchiavaig
Eilean
a' Chalmain
Ardalanish
Bay
Rubha nam
Maol Móra
Ardalanish
Rubh'
Ardalanish

7

71

West Reef
Torran Rocks

Sgeir Dhoirbh

8

A B C D E

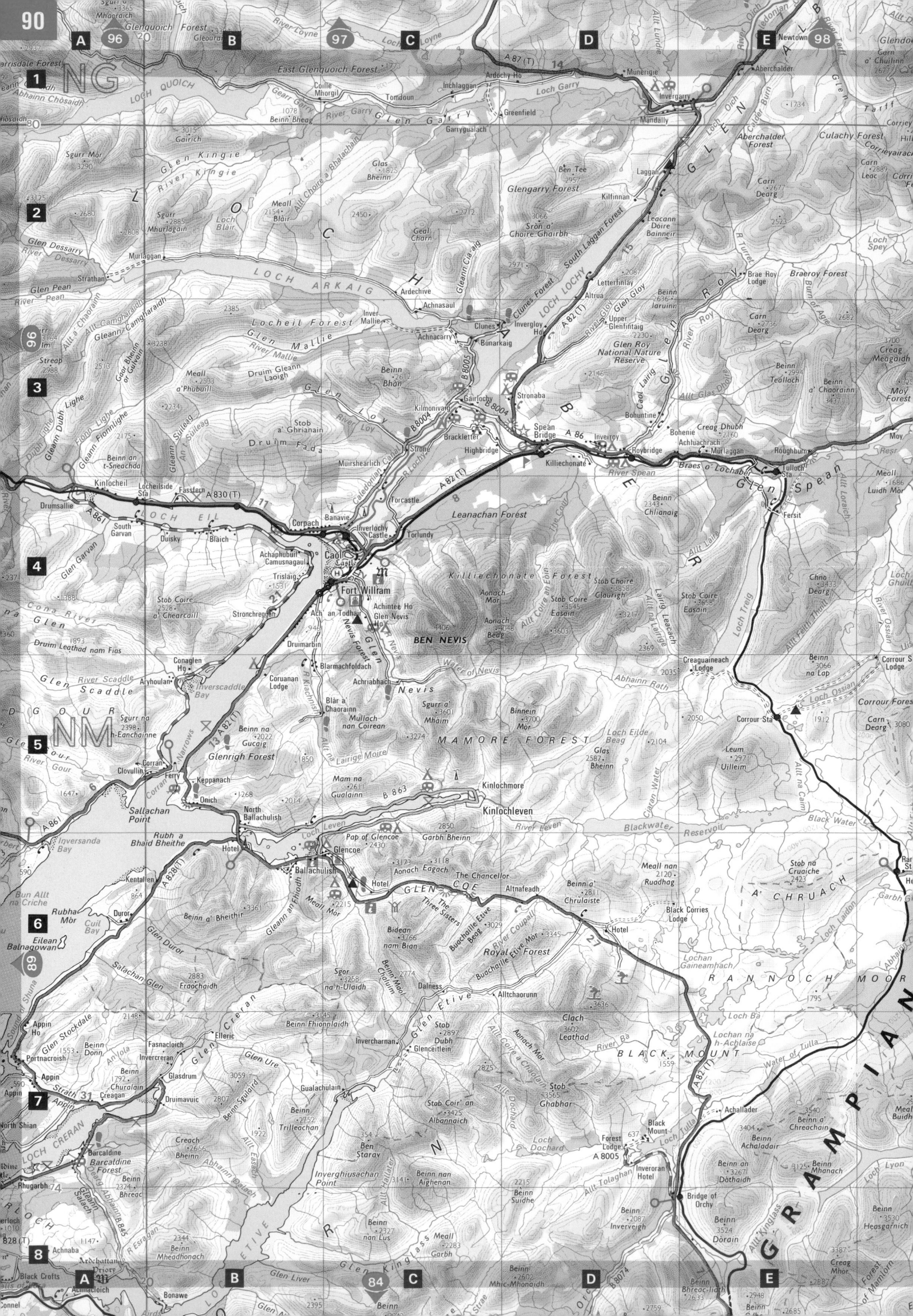

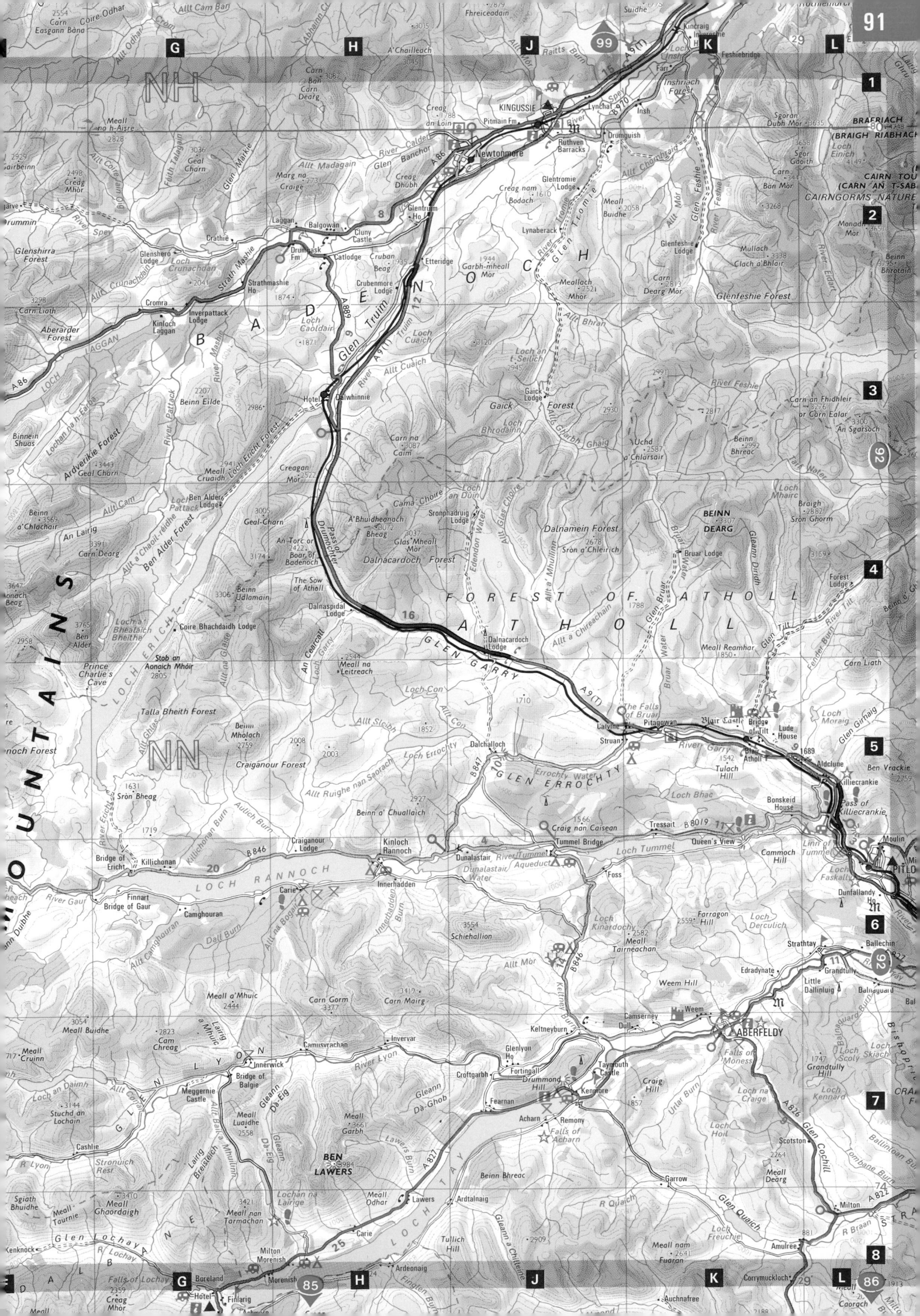

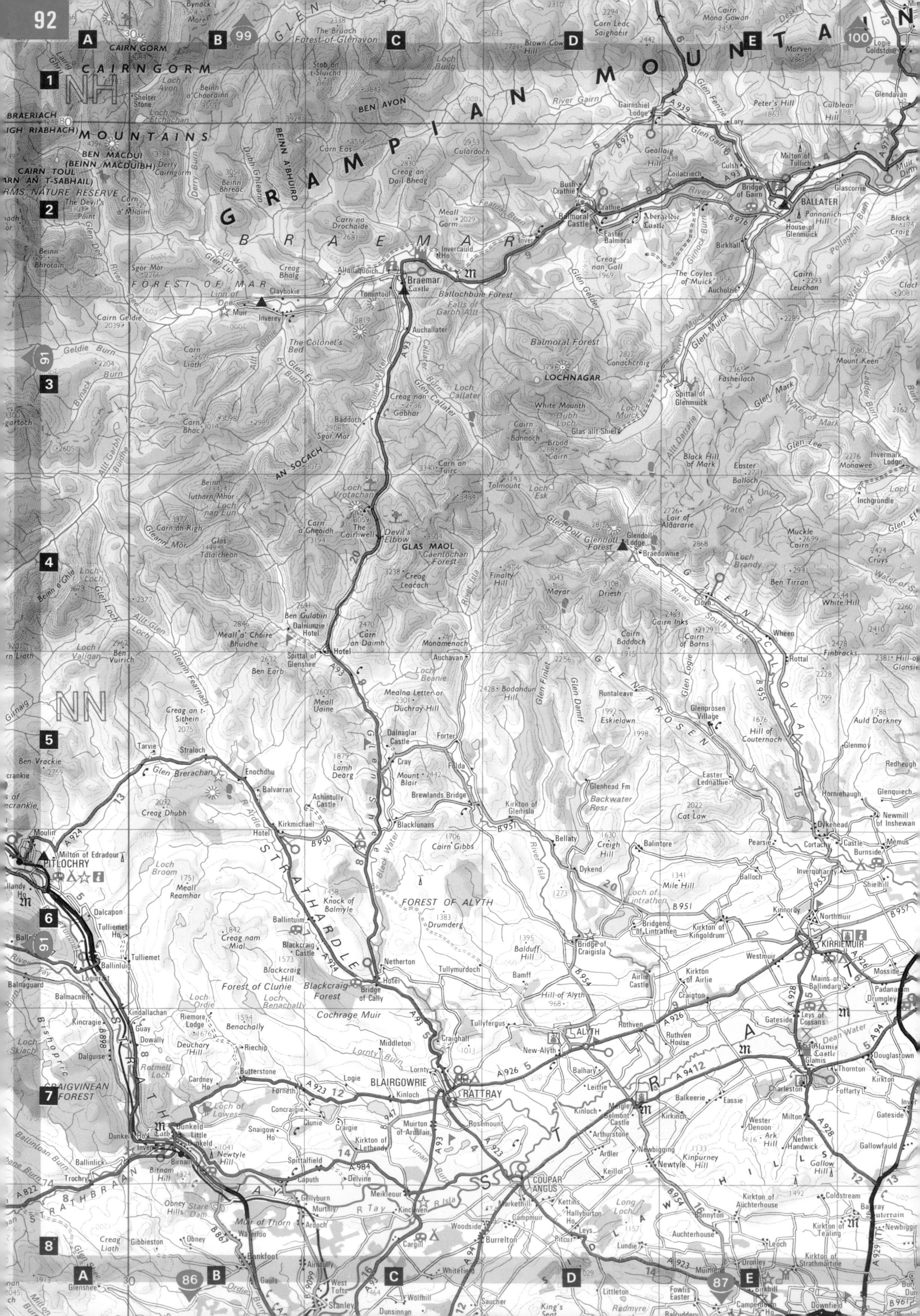

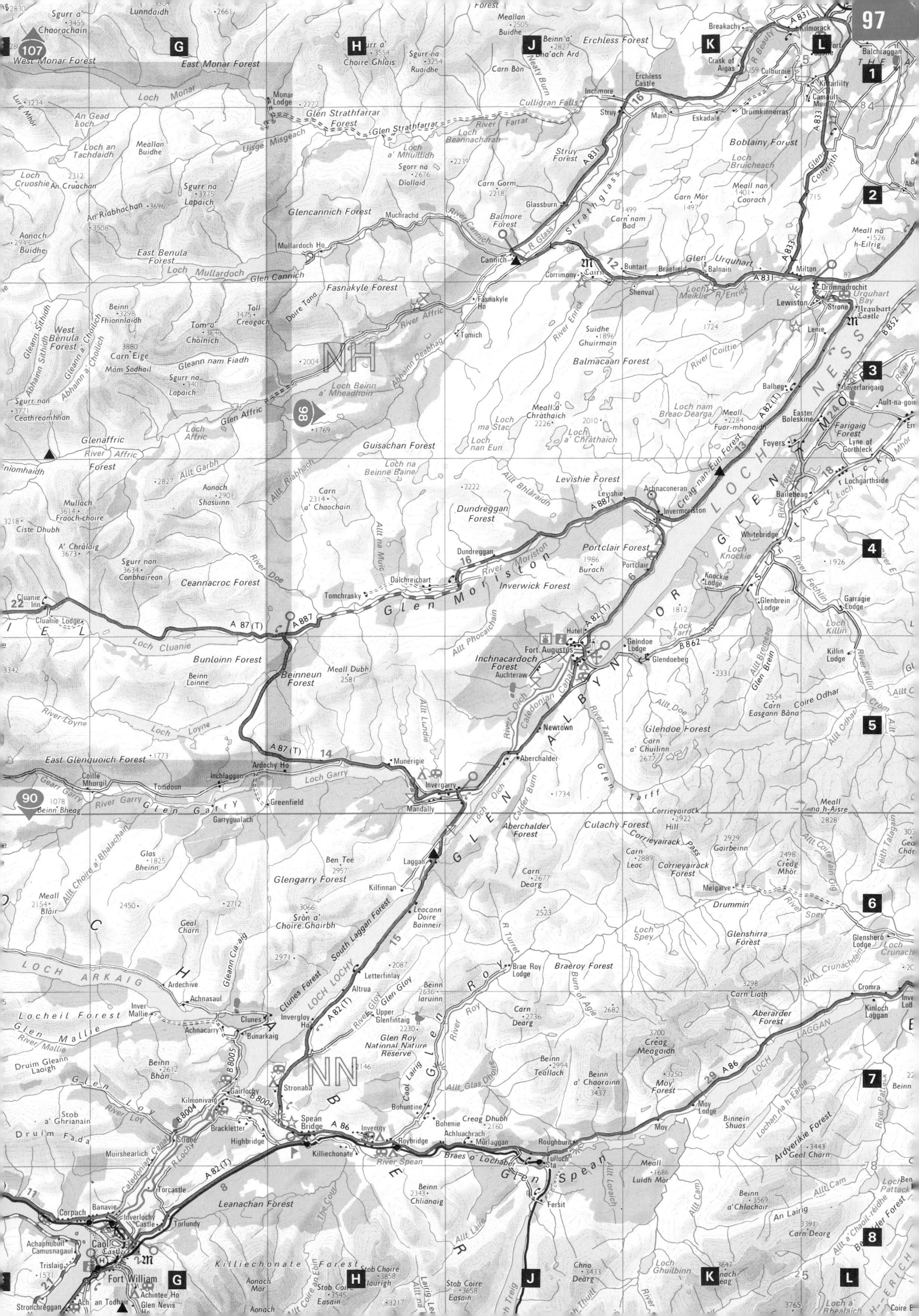

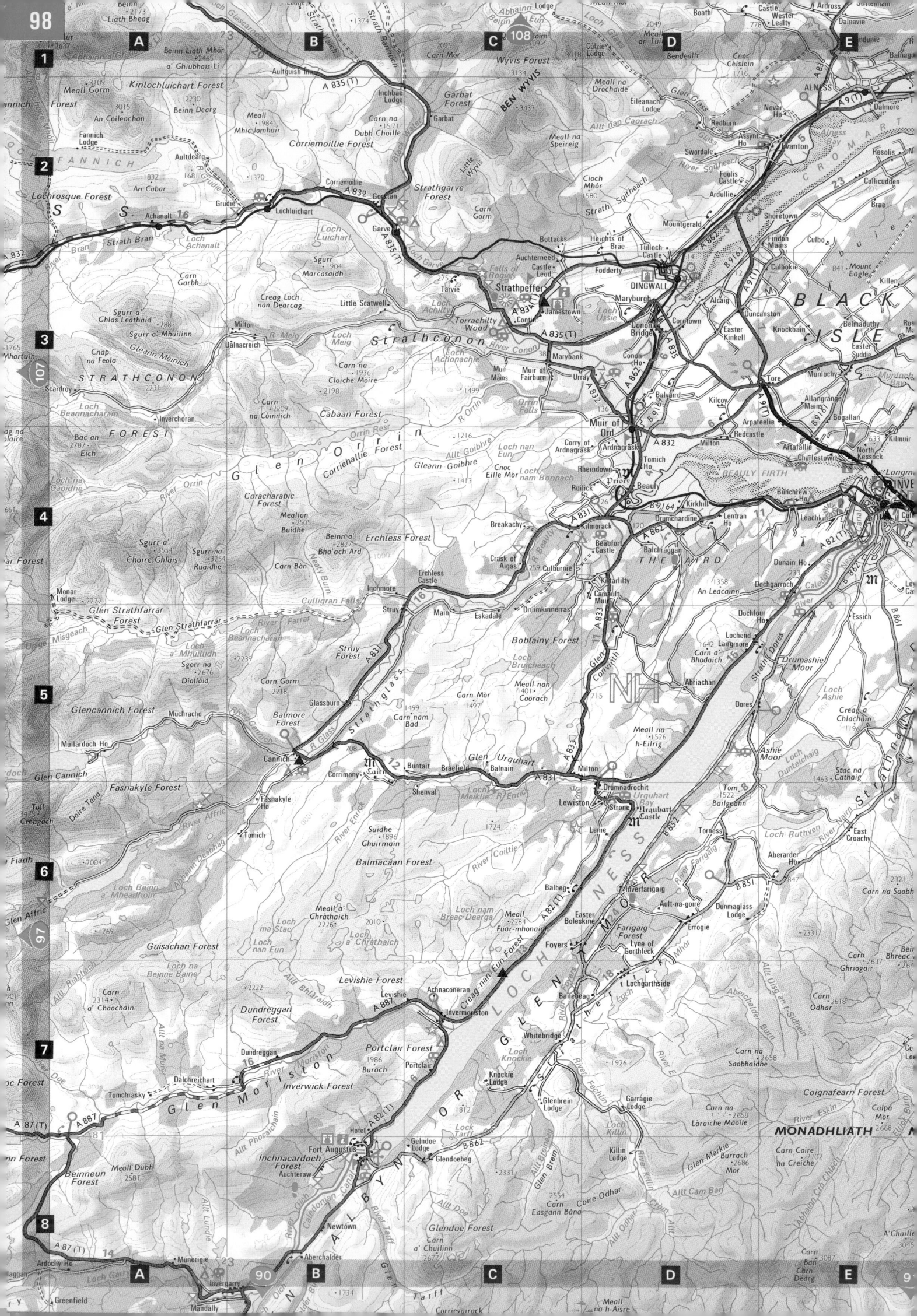

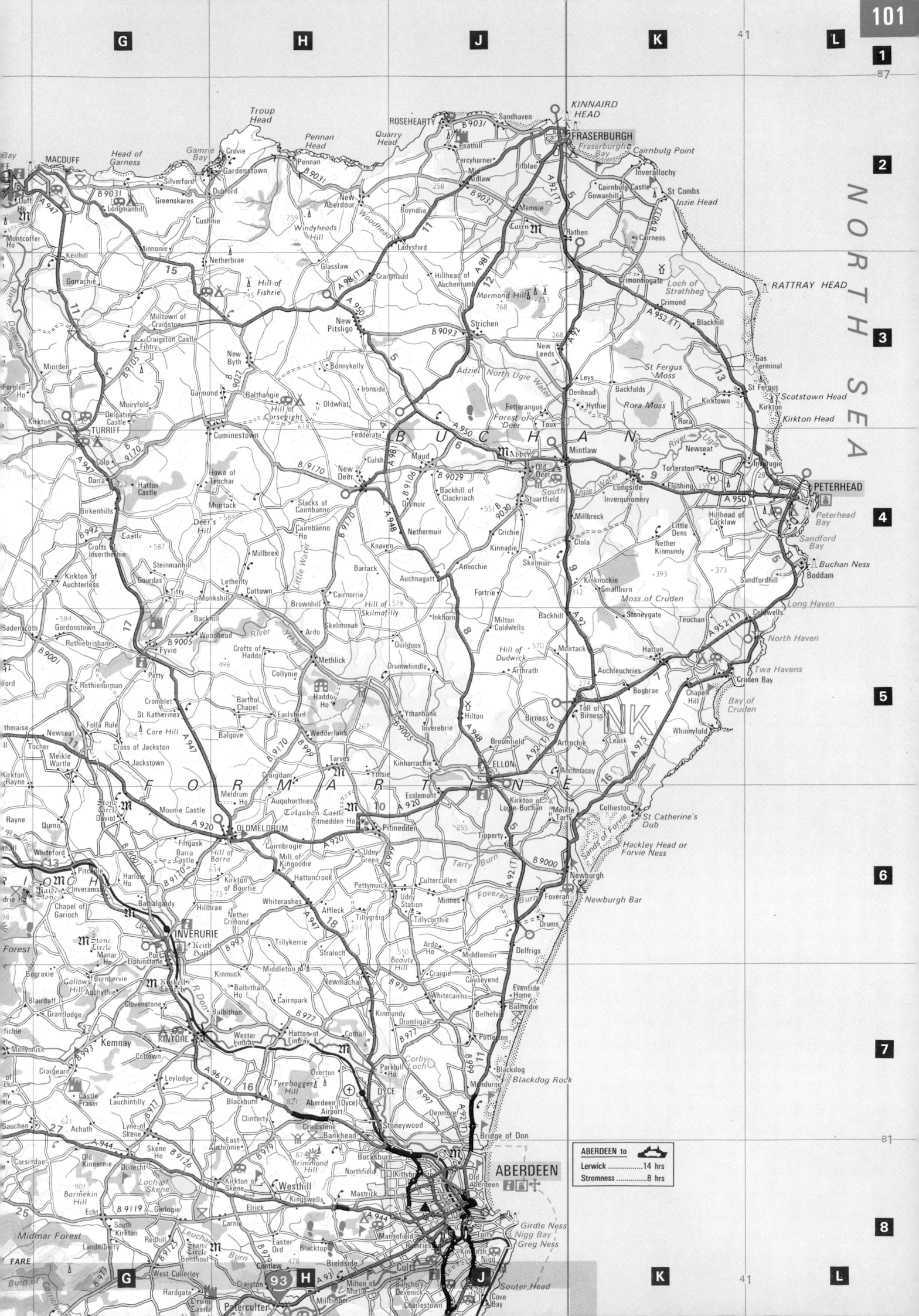

THE HEBRIDES OR WESTERN ISLES

THE LITTLE MINCH

INNER HEBRIDES

OUTER HEBRIDES

THE HEBRIDES

LOCHMADDY to Tarbert .... 2½ hrs

UIG to Tarbert .... 2 hrs

2 hrs

WATERNISH POINT

LOCH SNIZORT

DUNVEGAN HEAD

LOCH DUNVEGAN

LOCH BRACADALE

IDRIGILL POINT

SKYE

ISLAND

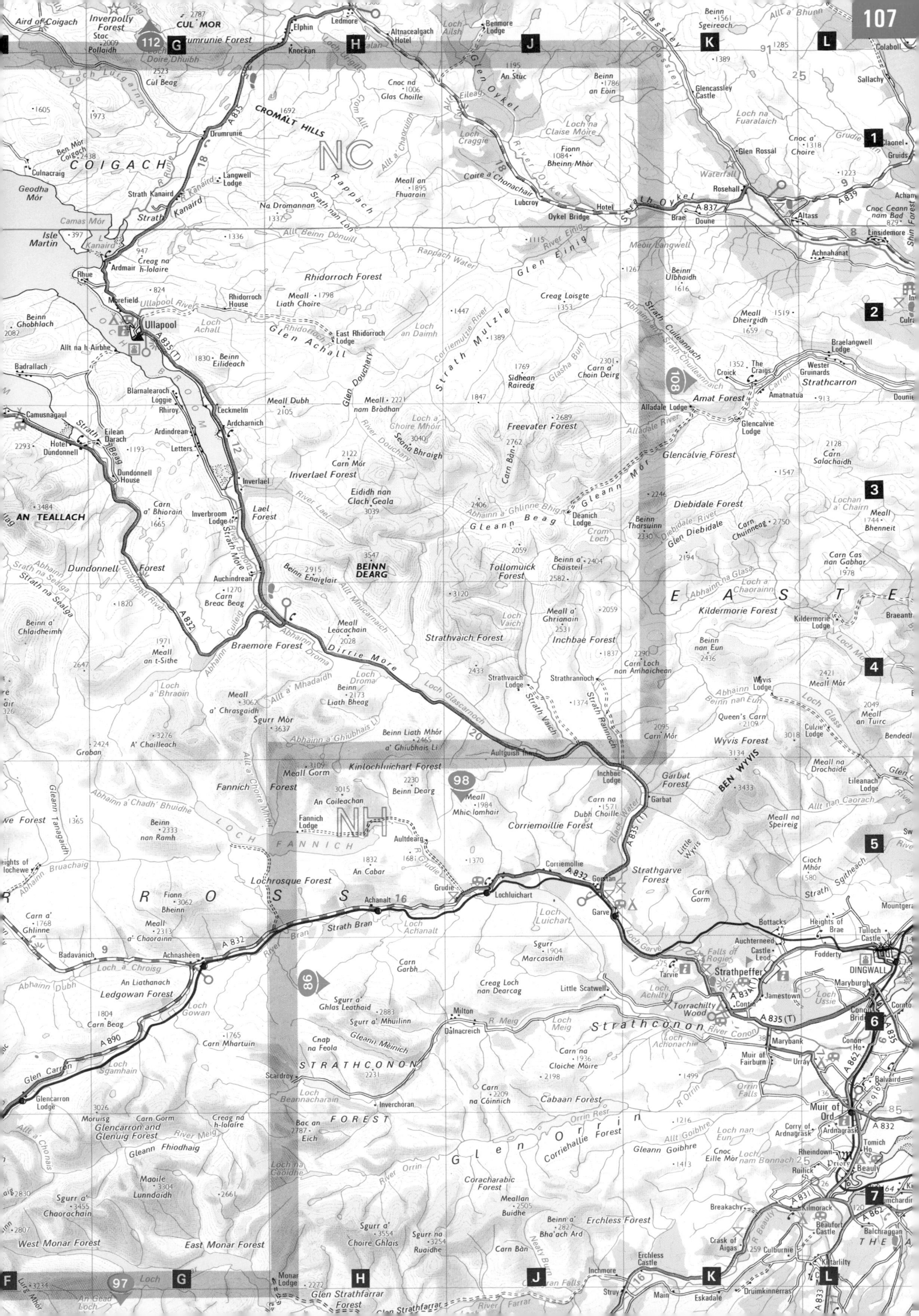

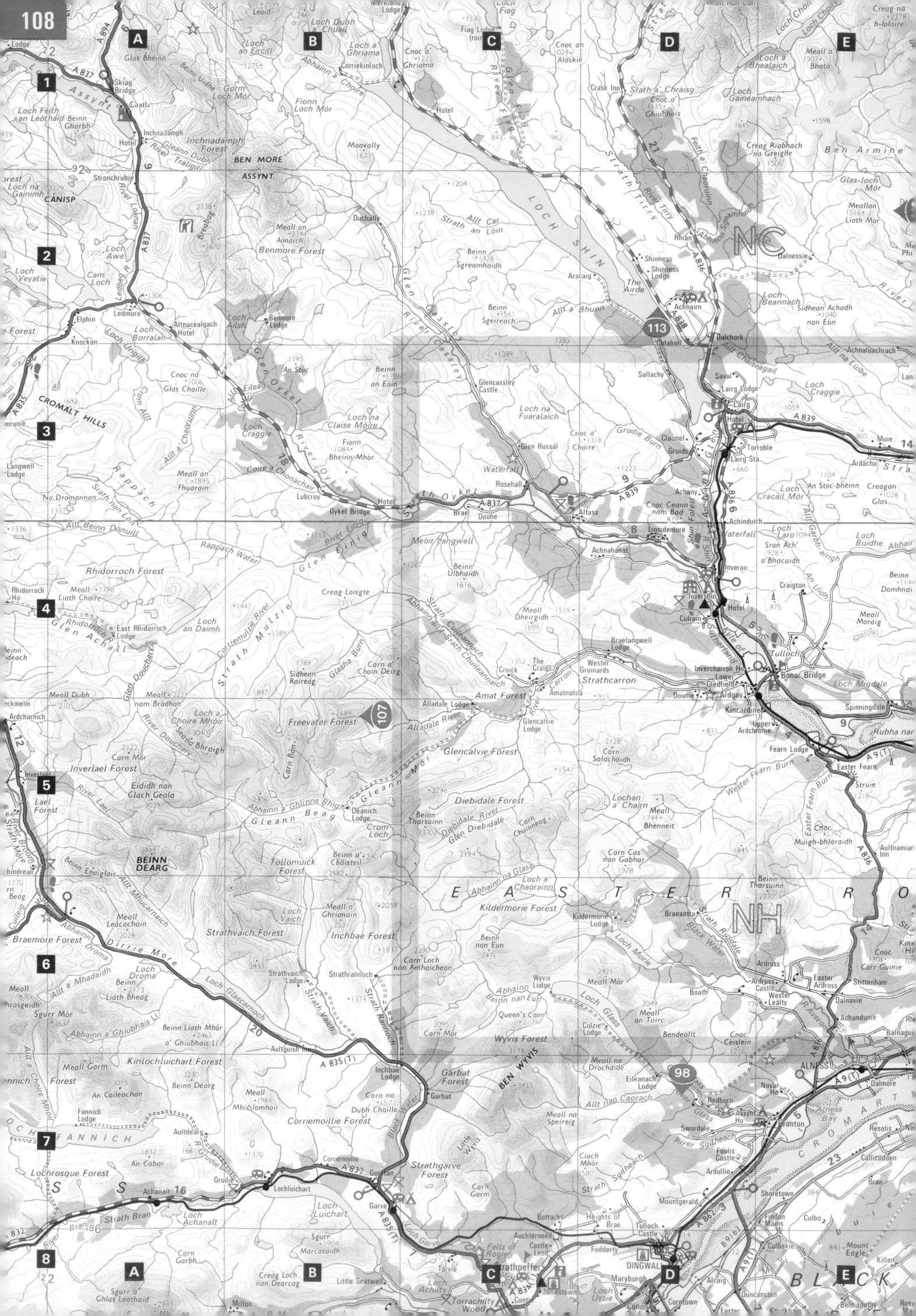

ATLANTIC OCEAN

Flannan
Isles

RONA AND
SULA SGEIR

HW

Lisgear Mhór
Rona
Lòba Sgeir
Gealldruig Mhór

Sula
Sgeir

103

17   18

RONA lies about 44 miles or 70 km NNE of the BUTT OF LEWIS NB 5166

H
E
B
R

Gallan Head
Camas Geodhachan
an Duilisg
Aird
Uig
Geodha Nasavig
670
Forsna
Fiavig Bagh
Sgeir Fiavig Tarris
Crowlista
Ard More
Mangersta   Camas
Uig
Loch
Scaslavat
Ardroil
Mangersta

Aird Fenish
Cleite
Leathann
Staca Leathann   Islivig
Taraίn
Aird Brenish   Mealisval
Brenish
Camas a' Mhoil
1625
Mealista   Laival a
Tuath
Mealasta
Mealasta   Griomaval
Mealasta
Island

R

NA

Kearstay   Gob na h-
Airde Móire
Bràigh Mór
1012
Sron
Romul
SCARP
994
Taran Mór
Manish
Loch a'
Ghlinne
Hushinish   1603
Husival Mór   2227
Tirga
Mór
Hushinish Point
Leosaval
1352
Gasker   Govig   Forest o
105
Horsanish   Amhuinnsuic
Rubha Leacach
104   Taransay Glorigs
Rubha nan Totag   Soay Mór
Sythe Harbour   WEST

NF   TARANSAY   877
Benn
Raah
Aird
Vanish
Paible
324
Rubha   Aird
Sgeirigin   Nisabost
SOUND OF TARANSAY
Rubha Romagi
Rubha Màs   Cleite
a' Chnuic   Nisabost
Toe head   Sgeir

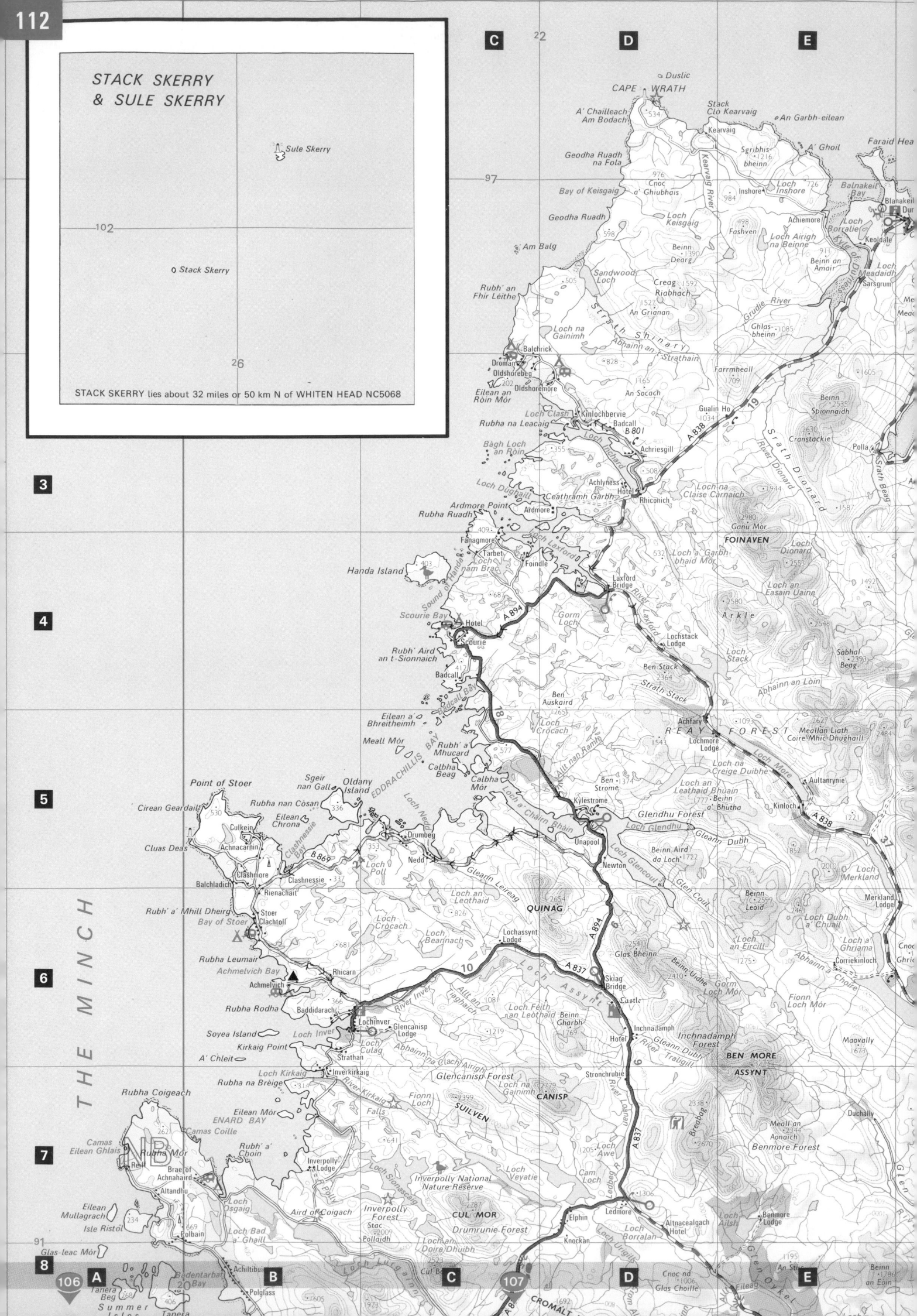

STACK SKERRY
& SULE SKERRY

Sule Skerry

Stack Skerry

STACK SKERRY lies about 32 miles or 50 km N of WHITEN HEAD NC5068

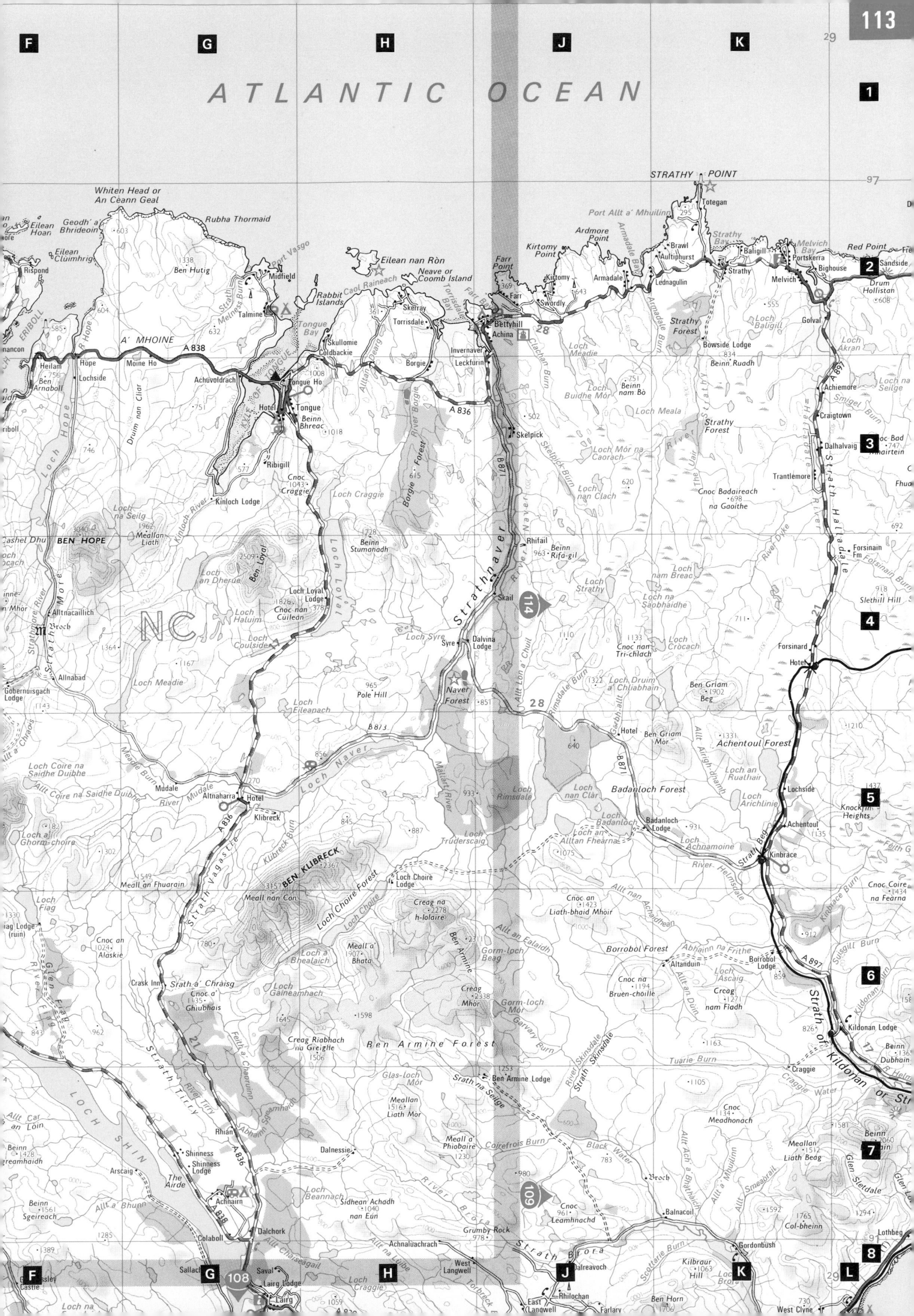

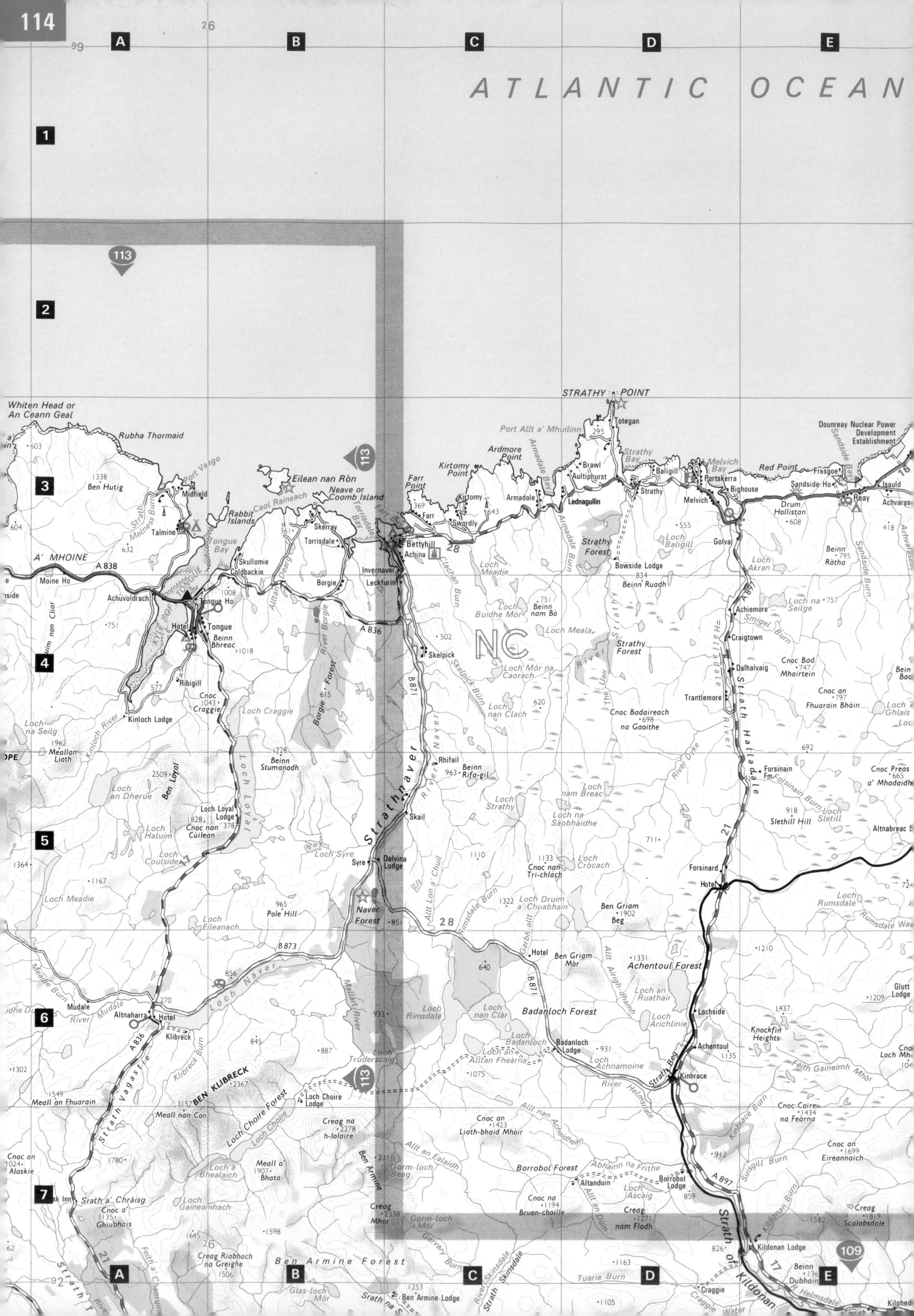

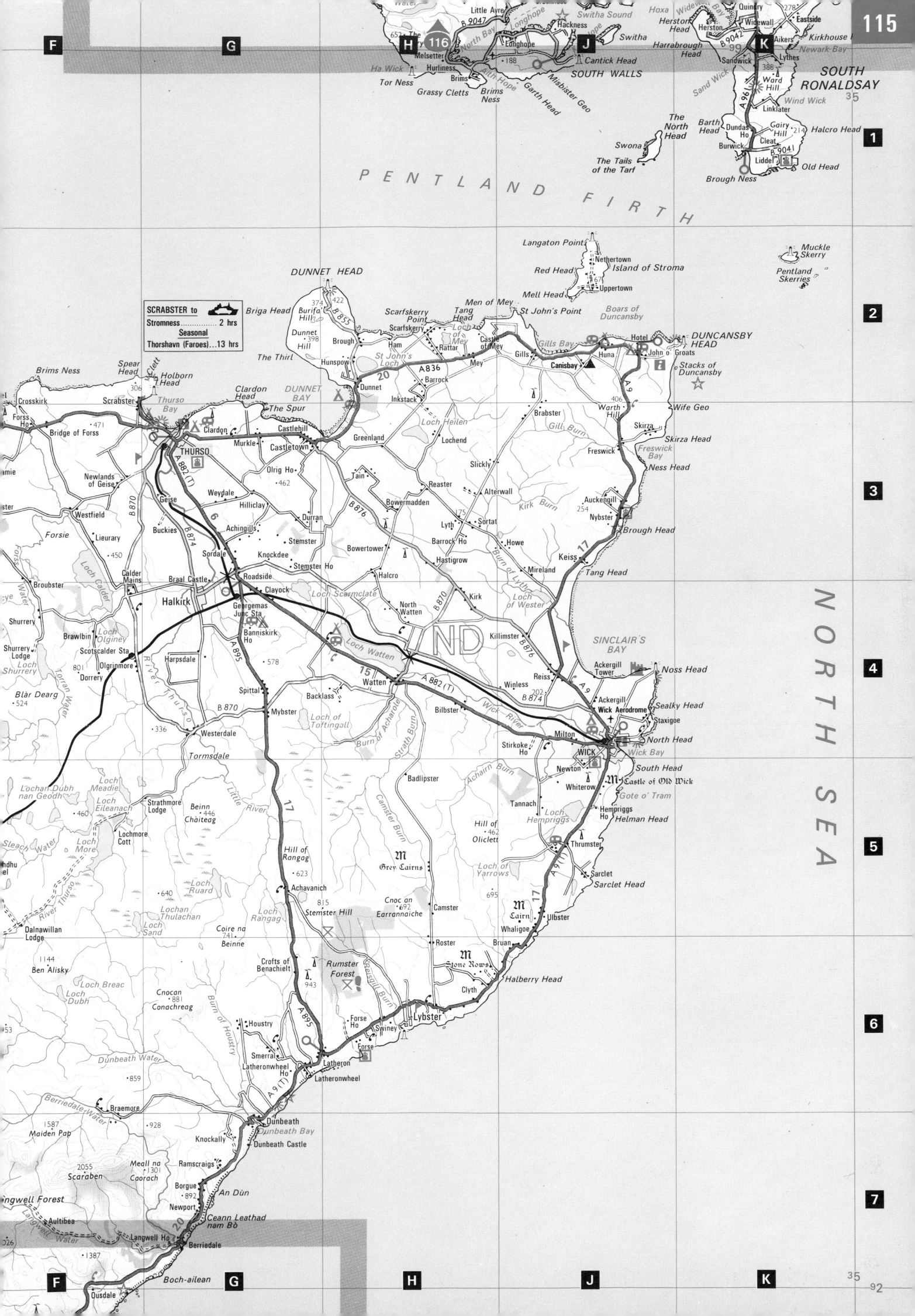

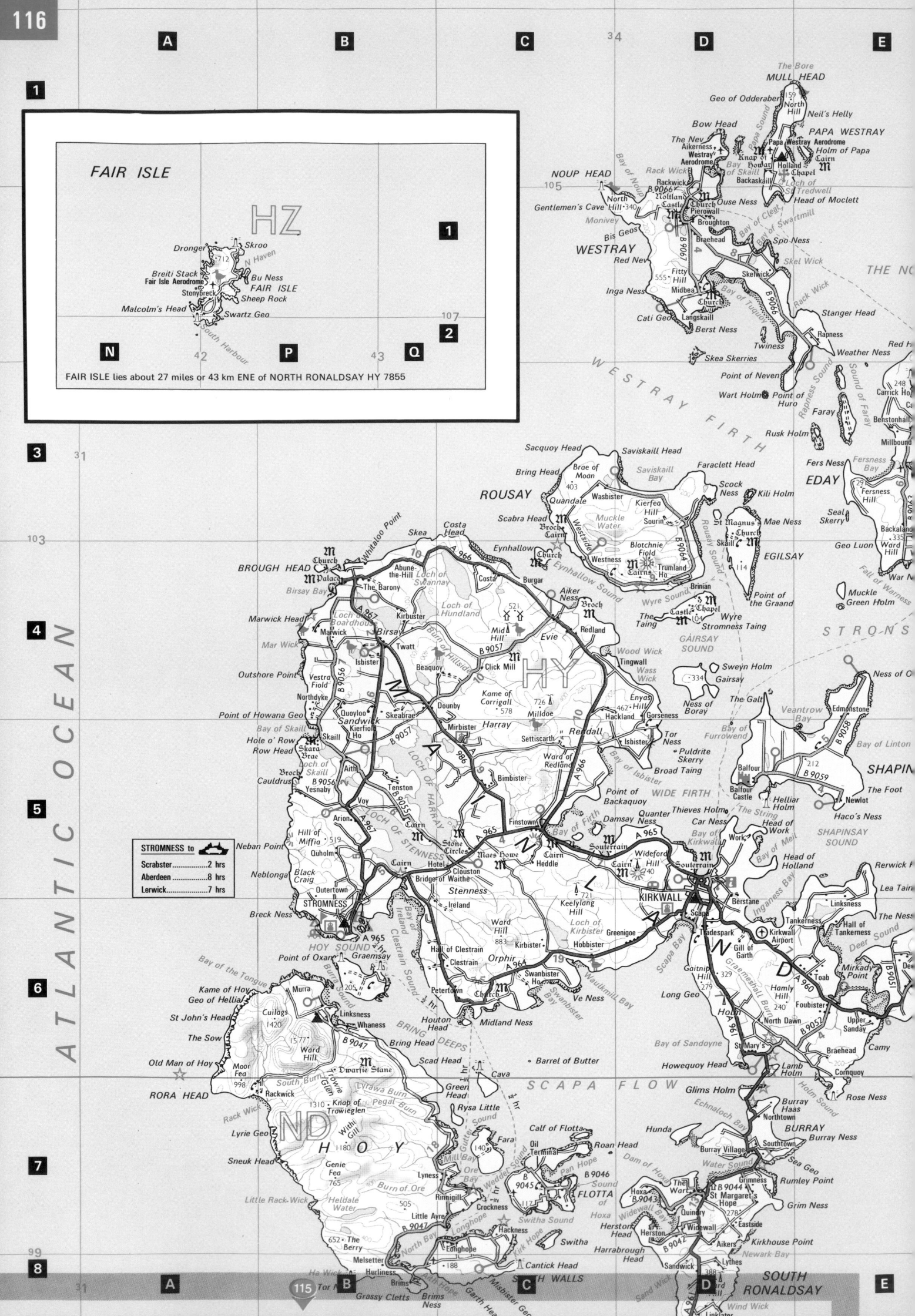

FAIR ISLE

HZ

Dronger
Skroo
N Haven
Breiti Stack
Fair Isle Aerodrome
Bu Ness
Stonybreck
FAIR ISLE
Sheep Rock
Malcolm's Head
Swartz Geo
South Harbour

N   P   Q

FAIR ISLE lies about 27 miles or 43 km ENE of NORTH RONALDSAY HY 7855

STROMNESS to

Scrabster .... 2 hrs
Aberdeen .... 8 hrs
Lerwick .... 7 hrs

ATLANTIC OCEAN

WESTRAY

ROUSAY

EDAY

EGILSAY

SHAPINSAY

HY

MAINLAND

KIRKWALL

STROMNESS

HOY

SCAPA FLOW

FLOTTA

BURRAY

SOUTH RONALDSAY

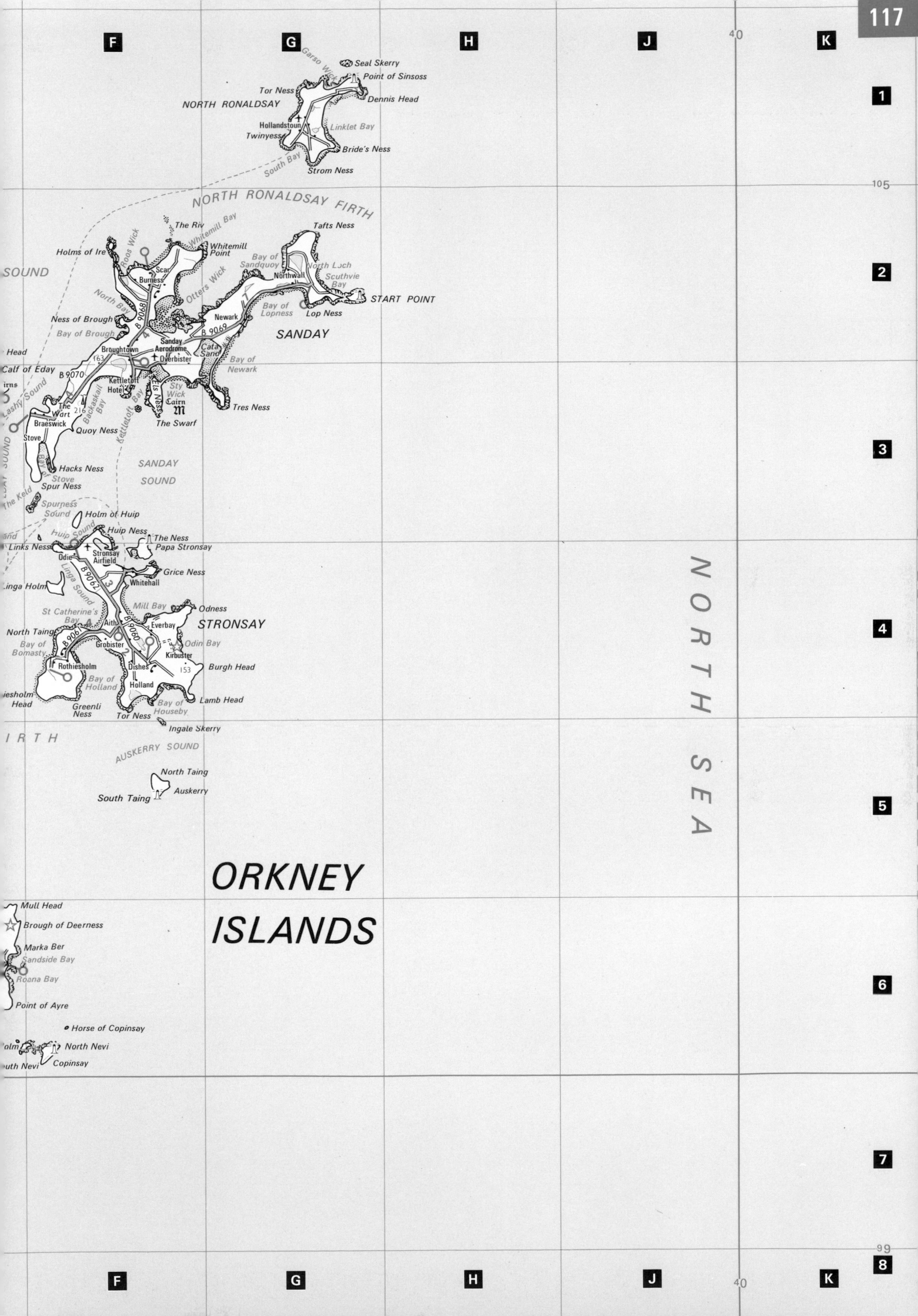

F G H J K

40

105

1

2

3

4

5

6

7

99

8

Seal Skerry
Point of Sinsoss
Tor Ness
Dennis Head
NORTH RONALDSAY
Hollandstoun
Linklet Bay
Twinyess
Bride's Ness
South Bay
Strom Ness

NORTH RONALDSAY FIRTH

The Riv
Roos Wick
Whitemill Bay
Whitemill Point
Tafts Ness
Holms of Ire
SOUND
Scar
Burness
Bay of Sandquoy
North Loch
North Bay
Otters Wick
Northwall
Scuthvie Bay
START POINT
Ness of Brough
Bay of Brough
Newark
Bay of Lopness
Lop Ness
B 9069
SANDAY
Head
Broughtown
Sanday Aerodrome
Cata Sand
Calf of Eday
Overbister
Bay of Newark
irns
B 9070
Kettletoft Hotel
Sty Wick Cairn
The Wart
Backaskaill Bay
Tres Ness
Braeswick
The Swarf
Stove
Quoy Ness
Kettletoft Bay
Ness
SANDAY SOUND
Hacks Ness
Stove
Spur Ness
The Keld
Spurness Sound
Holm of Huip
Huip Ness
Huip Sound
The Ness
Links Ness
Odie
Stronsay Airfield
Papa Stronsay
Grice Ness
Linga Holm
B 9062
Whitehall
Linga Sound
Mill Bay
Odness
St Catherine's Bay
Aith
STRONSAY
North Taing
B 9061
Grobister
B 9060
Everbay
Bay of Bomasty
Dishes
Kirbuster
Odin Bay
Rothiesholm
Bay of Holland
Holland
Burgh Head
iesholm Head
Greenli Ness
Tor Ness
Bay of Houseby
Lamb Head
FIRTH
Ingale Skerry
AUSKERRY SOUND
North Taing
South Taing
Auskerry

NORTH SEA

ORKNEY
ISLANDS

Mull Head
Brough of Deerness
Marka Ber
Sandside Bay
Roona Bay
Point of Ayre
Horse of Copinsay
olm
North Nevi
uth Nevi
Copinsay

ATLANTIC OCEAN

SHETLAND ISLANDS

ST MAGNUS BAY

FOULA

Da Logat
Strem Ness
The Kame
Da Scrodhurdins
Wester Hoevdi
Harrier
The Sneug
373
Ham
Head o'
da Taing
Wick of
Mucklabrek
Hametoun
Hellabrick's Wick
Hesti Geo
South Ness

Ve Skerries

Cribbie
North Ness
Fogla Skerry
285
Virda Field
Biggings
PAPA STOUR
Quilva Taing
Melby Ho
Garth
Sandness
817
Sandness Hill
Pund Head
Bay of Deepdale
Dale
Burn of Dale
Stourbrough Hill
567
Mu Ness
Voe of Dale
246
Mid Walls
Wats Ness
Skarpigarth
Burraland
Walls
Braga Ness
Uskie Geo
Vaila Sound
Vaila Hall
268
Vaila
Ward of Culswick
390
Culswick
Strom Ness
Brock
Housa Water
The Nev
Westerwick
Giltarump
Wester Wick
West Moulie

MUCKLE ROE
Strom Ness
Murbie St
Swarbacks Head
Vementry
Gruna
Isle of West Burrafirth
West Burrafirth
Brindiste
Noonsbr
Unifirth
Sulma Water
Loch on Voxterb
Bridge of Walls
A 971
Browland
Gruting
Gruting Voe
Sell Voe
Sil Wi

Grind of the Navir Ure
Scraada
Scarff
ESHA NESS
Sae Breck
Braehoulland
205
Tangwick
Burnside
The Bruddans
Stenness
Hillswick
Isle of Stenness
Skerry of Eshaness
Dore Holm
Ness of Hillswick
The Drongs
Baa Taing
Isle of Nib
Lang H
Erne
Brae Wo
B 9078

HT

120
117
111
38
38

ATLANTIC OCEAN

Isle of Fet
Garmus Taing
Uyea
Burrier Wick
The Breck
Fugla Ness
South Wick
Hevdadale Head
Lang Clodie Wick
Egga Field
564
Nor Roe
Burn of Sandvoe
Gruna Stack
The Faither
Turls Head
North Roe
Roer
Watir
644
Beorgs of
Skelberry
Muckle Ossa
351 Ketligill
Heillia Head
Stonga
Banks
740
Man
Scord
Housetter
Ockran Head
Burries
Ness
1475
Ronas
Hill
Collafirth
South Head
Gluss
Water
Hamnavoe
Heylors
The
Clifts
Voe
Olla
Whalwick Taing
567
Faan
Hill
Head of Stanshi
Grind of the Navir Ure
Scarff
Scraada
Braehoulland
Sae
Breck
B 9078
Burnside
A 970
Urafirth
Eela
Water
B 9079
ESHA NESS
205 Tangwick
Brae Wick
Hillswick
Ness of
Olnesfirth
Gluss
Barr
The Bruddans
Stenness
Ness of
Hillswick
Isle of Stenness
389
Burraland
Skerry of Eshaness
Dore Holm
The Drongs
Baa Taing
Sullom
Isle of Nibon
Cairn
396
Mangaster
ST MAGNUS
Lang Head
BAY
Egilsay
Islesburgh
Mavis
Grind
Turvalds Head
315
Erne Stack
Busta
Ve Skerries
Strom Ness
Roesound
118
MUCKLE ROE
555
South
Ward
Murbie Stacks
Little-ayre
Linga
Cribbie
North Ness
Swarbacks Head
285
Fogla Skerry
Virda
Field
PAPA STOUR
Vementry
Cairn
Papa
Little
Biggings
298
Gruna
The Rona
Isle of
West Burrafirth
Sound of Papa
Holm of Melby
West
Burrafirth
Brindister
Clousta
Melby Ho
Garth
Noonsbrough

SHETLAND
ISLANDS
Quilva Taing
Sandness
Unifirth
Loch
of
Vaara
Pund Head
817
Sandness
Hill
Burga
Water
Sulma
Water
Aithsting
Bay of Deepdale
Loch of
Voxterby
313
400
Twatt
Mu Ness
Dale
Burn of Dale
567
Stourbrough
Hill
Bixter
Voe of Dale
246
Bridge of Walls
Effirth
Wats Ness
Mid Walls
Walls
Stanydale
Semblister
115
Skarpigarth
Burraland
Gruting
Braga Ness
Vaila
Garderhouse
Uskie Geo
Gruting Voe
Sand

The Historical Geography of Britain

Prehistory

The physical environment in which the early cultures of Britain developed at the end of the Ice Age was very different from our contemporary environment, though the principal structure of this island, the disposition of mountain and lowland, remain much the same. The main changes have occurred in the nature and distribution of vegetation types and the extent of woodland and forest cover, in the reduction of undrained land, and in climate.

The early prehistoric cultures of Britain in the Palaeolithic and Mesolithic periods made very little impact on the landscape, although their cave sites and excavated open sites provide an accurate picture of their essential economic character and artefacts. The basis of the economy was the hunting of wild animals and the collecting of wild plants, but this was eventually replaced during the Neolithic (or New Stone) Age by a food-producing economy. The dating of the beginnings of this new culture is only approximate, but it appears that settlement by farmers in Britain occurred before 4400 BC. The Neolithic period terminated about 2000 years later. The initial phase of cultural development, the 'early' Neolithic, took place in the earlier part of the fourth millennium BC, and is associated with stock-breeding, cereal cultivation, flint- and stone-working industries, and distinctive pottery types. The early Neolithic site at Windmill Hill in Wiltshire has revealed a predominance of bones of 'domesticated' animals rather than wild animals, and of the emmer type of wheat – a cultivated crop. The evidence for early Neolithic settlement is not extensive, but it has been inferred that isolated farmsteads predominated.

Flint was extensively used for axes and other implements, including leaf-shaped arrowheads, and there were important flint mines in Sussex, at Findon, for example. Flint-mining also occurred in Cornwall and in Westmorland, and at a later date the famous mine at Grimes Graves in Norfolk came into operation. Distinctive pottery types included the Grimston type, mainly found in Yorkshire and the North, and the more southern Hembury type. In the later Neolithic, material evidence changes: new forms of pottery appear, with decorations and round bases, such as Peterborough ware and grooved ware, and the use of the older, harder rocks for axes intensifies. The economy seems to have to become more pastoral.

A distinctive and notable feature of the Neolithic is the wide range of burial monuments. The main categories of burial monument are the ubiquitous chambered and unchambered tombs, sometimes covered with earth (such as earthen long barrows), sometimes with stones (cairns). The best-known sites are the 'henge' monuments with large standing stones, the most spectacular of which are sites such as Stonehenge and Avebury in Wiltshire. The dominant relic feature of the Neolithic in Scotland is the chambered tomb and long mound, found extensively in the Clyde region and in the extreme north, and the Orkney and Shetland Islands.

The succeeding culture–the Bronze Age–lasted from 2500 to 900 BC, and whereas there is evidence that the Neolithic culture was strong, spontaneous and regional, the initiation of the Bronze Age apparently occurred through colonisation. The evidence for this occurs in the form of the material culture of a group of people known as the Beaker folk (named for the type of pottery with which they are associated), who began the change from Neolithic to Bronze culture. There was no overall and sharp break between these two phases of British prehistory, for change was rapid in the Lowland Zone of the south and east and slower in the Highland Zone of the north and west. The Bronze Age also brought a change to a warmer and drier climate although a marked deterioration began again about 1100 BC.

The most important innovation of the Bronze Age was the introduction of metal tools–initially in the form of thin copper blades of knives and daggers. The early Bronze Age witnessed a series of stages of copper-working, with main production centres in northwest England, Renfrewshire in Scotland, Wessex, Wales and the Welsh border. Flint exploitation continued in the early Bronze Age, but then declined. Settlements seem to have been small clusters of dwellings; barley became a more important crop than wheat. With the climatic deterioration of the end of the early Bronze Age there was more intensive use of river valleys and watery lowlands–an indication, too, of a changing religious focus. The upper (altitudinal) margins of cultivation declined and new regions of power developed, including north Wales and the Thames valley. The settlements of the middle and later Bronze Age included enclosed farmsteads with associated enclosed fields, and so-called 'Celtic' field systems, and large numbers of stone settlements on the uplands of the southwest. Some hilltop forts and enclosures date from this period, but the most characteristic feature is the round burial barrow or cairn, of which very large numbers survive. Other important features of the Bronze Age are the extensive trade in copper products, the decorative personal bronze ornaments, the continued construction and reconstruction of henge monuments (including work at Stonehenge), and the remarkable settlements at Skara Brae in the Orkneys.

The Iron Age culture was first seen about 900 BC, lasting to the Roman invasion of AD 43, and left its mark extensively in the landscape. Initiated by small groups of continental settlers, the first phase of the Iron Age in Britain continued the traditions of the Bronze Age, using small settlements and the first enclosures of old tribal centres with ramparts. Major innovations began in the 8th century BC, including hillforts, new metallurgy and pottery. The period immediately before the Roman invasion saw strong continental influence from Belgic invaders in the south and east (the north and west undergoing very little change), the emergence of strong regional tribal cultures (such as the Thames region, Arras culture in Yorkshire, Cornwall) and widespread trade with the Roman Empire. The Iron Age invaders were Celtic-speaking; they introduced new crops

Prehistory to the Romans The distribution and types of chambered cairns, chambered tombs and long barrows reflect the diversity of Neolithic Britain, very different from the settlement patterns of Roman Britain.

Prehistory to the Romans

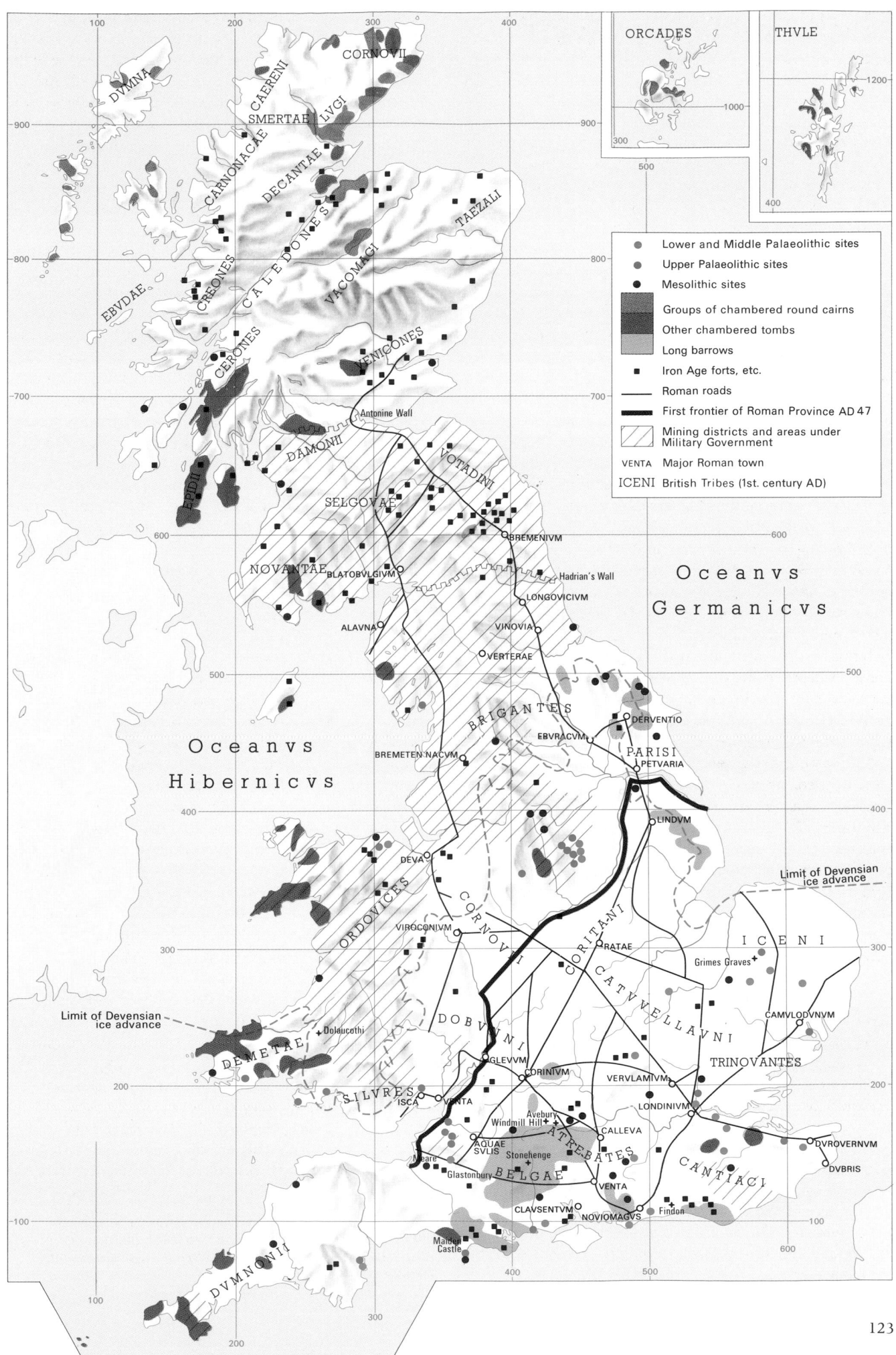

such as rye and oats, and used horse-drawn chariots. The major evidence of the Iron Age in the landscape are the hillfort settlements of England (such as Maiden Castle in Dorset), Wales and Scotland. In addition to the walled hillforts are the lake-villages of the southwest, notably Glastonbury and Meare in Somerset. In the late Iron Age tribal capitals or *oppida* developed, such as St Albans and Colchester, and the heavier soils of the Lowland areas were cultivated by use of the new heavy ploughs. Coinage was introduced, as were new processes for corn-grinding and pottery production.

The Claudian invasion of Britain in AD 43 did not end the Iron Age, nor did it completely 'Romanise' Britain. The Roman cultural influence is mainly to be found in the south and east, partly because of the existence there of indigenous political groups, and was least in the north and west which were primarily zones of military occupation. The whole of Britain was, however, only a frontier province of the Roman Empire and one occupied at a very late stage of that Empire's development; it did not reach the same cultural levels as the more central regions of the continental Empire. Christianity reached Britain in the 4th century, and perhaps helped to accelerate the change away from Celtic Iron Age culture, for Christianity had Roman characteristics. There was therefore both continuity and change between Iron Age and Early Christian-Roman culture. The cultural continuity is best seen at the peasant level in the Highland Zone of the north and west. The cultural provinces of Scotland (Atlantic, Western Isles, Southwest and South) remained much the same, to judge by the distinctive types of settlement, pottery and burial monument. Change was more obvious in the south and east of Britain, but it was rarely total and all-embracing, for 'native' settlements continued to exist, even in the Lowland Zone.

The political map of Roman Britain shortly after the conquest (c. AD 47), indicates a frontier zone which includes most of north England, Wales and Scotland. The construction of Hadrian's Wall in c. AD 123-128 and the Antonine Wall in AD 142 are further testimony to the status of these regions, which remained under military rule.

The major landscape features associated with Roman Britain are towns, roads, mining, and various types of agricultural and rural settlement, notably villas, though there was also continuity of settlement in addition to the more obvious Roman innovations.

Under the Roman system of civic administration, each unit or *civitas* had a capital—in the southeast this was usually a pre-Roman site or *oppidum*, elsewhere a *colonia* or colony town, initially populated by Roman citizens and soldiers. At a lower level in the 'urban' hierarchy were small settlements called *vici*, some of which were walled and built on the site of earlier fortified settlements. The total population of Roman Britain was probably under one million, and there were about 60 towns, which varied considerably in size, though none compared with the larger towns and cities of 20th-century Britain. The dimensions of Roman London, for example, were about 1600 metres by 800 metres (1 mile by $\frac{1}{2}$ mile); this was also about the size of the larger towns such as Verulamium (St Albans), Corinium (Cirencester) and Viriconium (Wroxeter). The other Roman towns were very

much smaller. The larger towns had a planned layout, with the forum at the centre, surrounded by a grid-iron street plan. The public buildings included baths, temples and basilicas, hotels (*mansio*), theatres and amphitheatres. Town defences were constructed in some of the towns at the end of the 2nd century AD.

One of the attractions of Britain to the Romans was its mineral resources—silver, gold and other metals were described as the 'price of victory'. Expectations of gold were high, but the only known Roman mine was at Dolaucothi in Carmarthenshire, where advanced mining techniques were used and an eleven-kilometre (seven-mile) aqueduct channel constructed to convey water to the site. Copper resources were exploited in North Wales and Anglesey, but the most extensively-worked mineral was lead, principally in the Mendips, and also in the Matlock area of Derbyshire, Shropshire, Cheshire, Flintshire, Yorkshire and Cumberland. Lead was a major export. Iron was worked in Sussex and the Forest of Dean.

The network of Roman roads in Britain is impressive and extensive, both in terms of its density and the technological achievement that it represents. Some of the major Roman roads remain as trunk roads to the present day, though others have lost their former status. The Fosse Way and Watling Street are two well-known surviving examples of this network. The best-known farm buildings of Roman Britain are the villas (although this term really refers to a whole rural estate). Villas have been described as 'farms with Romanised buildings'; they were most common in Lowland Britain and parts of South Wales. They were less numerous, however, than non-Roman native settlements in the countryside of Roman Britain. Some were built on the sites of Iron Age farms. The villas themselves changed during the period of the Roman occupation. Most Romanised villas had principal farmsteads constructed to a regular (usually rectangular) plan, but this dates from a rebuilding period of the 2nd century. The largest and most luxurious of the villas are quite late in date, and in a minority.

There were some improvements in agricultural techniques in the Roman period, including corn-drying and threshing and perhaps ploughing, though we know little of the size and shape of fields or of the systems of cultivation.

Britain in the Dark Ages

There was no sharp discontinuity between the Roman and Saxon phases of colonisation of Britain: we know, for example, that Anglo-Saxons were used as mercenaries by the Romans in Britain to assist with town defences at the time of the withdrawal of the Roman administration around AD 400. The period of most intense settlement by the Anglo-Saxons was c.400-800. These people were of Germanic origin and their culture was very different from the Roman; they took control of parts of eastern England in the period 400-450, when it seems that Kent and Sussex may have been settled by these rebellious mercenaries. Other pockets of

The Dark Ages The earliest Saxon settlement is denoted by areas in which pagan burials have been found, followed by places with names ending in *-ingas*. The burhs are of later date. Place-names in *-by* indicate Scandinavian settlements, and 'maerdref' sites named *llys-* are sites of royal courts in Wales.

The Dark Ages

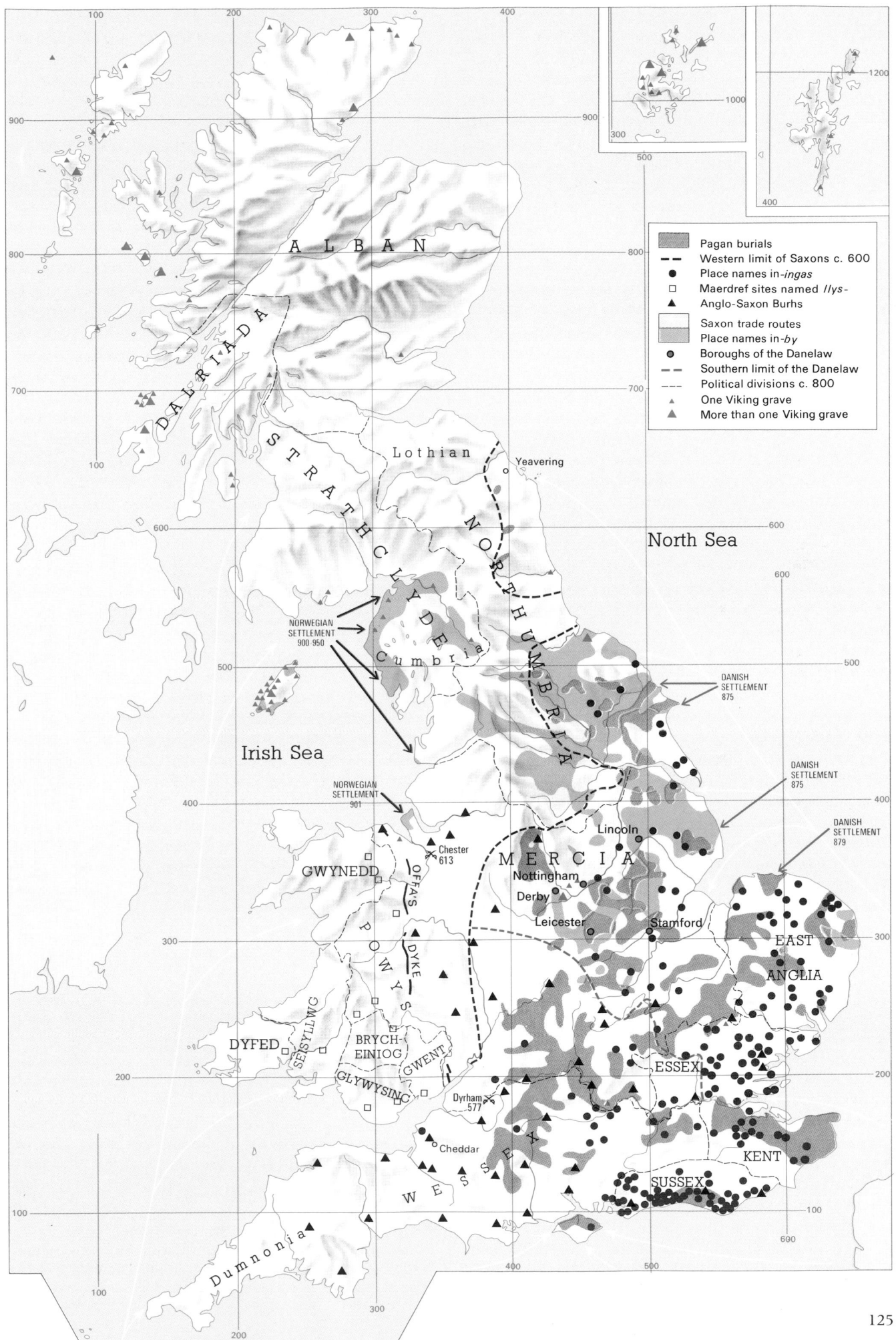

Legend:
- Pagan burials
- Western limit of Saxons c. 600
- Place names in-*ingas*
- Maerdref sites named *llys-*
- Anglo-Saxon Burhs
- Saxon trade routes
- Place names in-*by*
- Boroughs of the Danelaw
- Southern limit of the Danelaw
- Political divisions c. 800
- One Viking grave
- More than one Viking grave

ALBAN

DALRIADA

STRATHCLYDE

Lothian

Yeavering

NORTHUMBRIA

North Sea

Cumbria

NORWEGIAN SETTLEMENT 900-950

DANISH SETTLEMENT 875

Irish Sea

DANISH SETTLEMENT 875

NORWEGIAN SETTLEMENT 901

DANISH SETTLEMENT 879

Chester 613

Lincoln

GWYNEDD

OFFA'S

MERCIA

Nottingham

Derby

DYKE

P O W Y S

Leicester

Stamford

EAST ANGLIA

DYFED

SEISYLLWG

BRYCH-EINIOG

GWENT

GLYWYSINC

ESSEX

Dyrham 577

KENT

Cheddar

SUSSEX

W E S S E X

Dumnonia

settlement were established along the east and south coasts, and, in spite of resistance from the Britons to the Anglo-Saxons, by the mid-6th century the earliest kingdoms had emerged in the south and east. The more powerful kingdoms were those which emerged in the southwest (Wessex), midlands (Mercia) and north (Northumbria). These were involved in struggles not only with each other but also the Britons of the Highland Zone. The early Anglo-Saxon period was one of pagan belief—the distribution of pagan burials is a good indicator of early settlement patterns, as is the distribution of place-names ending in -ingas—but the mission of St Augustine in 597 led to the conversion of the Saxons to Christianity by 670. Evidence of territorial struggle, particularly against the Welsh, survives in the dramatic form of Offa's Dyke, a 192-kilometre (120-mile) earthwork, built in the late 8th century. The general trend of territorial control towards the 10th century involved a reduction in the number and the control of the English kingdoms as Wessex became dominant, the emergence of a major territory—Gwynedd, centred in Snowdonia—in Wales, and the beginnings of a national identity for Scotland.

The effect of the Anglo-Saxon colonisation on the economy and life of Britain, especially Lowland Britain, was profound. A new language was introduced and a new colonisation initiated which changed the intensity of settlement. Much of our evidence for these activities comes from the place-names of the period and from archaeology. The Saxon settlements were not all in virgin territory, for in southern England there was already a fairly dense pattern of Roman-British settlement. There is evidence of Saxon settlement being influenced by pre-existing patterns. The earliest evidence (in the 'mercenary' phase before the Roman withdrawal) is of settlement in Roman towns, villas and forts, but the evidence for later periods also reflects the class structure of society. Two royal palaces have been identified, one at Yeavering in Northumberland, dating from the 7th century, the other at Cheddar in Somerset—a rural palace of the kings of Wessex. At the other end of the scale were the dwellings and farmsteads of yeomen and peasant farmers. It has been suggested that the poorer peasants lived in villages with large numbers of small huts with sunken floors, the best example of which is at Mucking in Essex. The German long-house seems not to have been used widely.

The agricultural mix obviously varied from region to region. Generally the commonest cereals were oats, barley and wheat. Ploughing of the possibly 'open' fields may have been done with a heavy plough pulled by oxen or horses. Animal husbandry was more important in the Highland Zone, and associated with migration to summer pastures.

The early Saxons were not accustomed to town life and it is difficult to assess the degree of continuity of occupation of the Roman towns. Some Roman towns were immediately deserted on the Roman withdrawal, and it is clear that the urban system as a whole declined and decayed. The question of the continued occupation of Roman British town sites is complex, but there is evidence to suggest that life continued in many of these towns, albeit under changed circumstances, and, as Martin Biddle says, 'far from there being a complete break between Roman Britain and Anglo-Saxon England, the new evidence shows that the roots of the English settlements were planted while Britain was still part of the empire and were strengthened for as long as the civitates remained in being' (Archaeology of Anglo-Saxon England, ed D M Wilson). Roman defence lines were followed by the walls of some medieval towns – London, Lincoln, Canterbury and Chichester, for example. In towns such as Colchester and Winchester continuity was initially preserved by the construction of Saxon royal palaces on the Roman sites. From the late 7th century, however, there were signs of a new town growth, and these early Anglo-Saxon towns were mainly trading and industrial centres, frequently coastal or riverine in location, such as Hamwih (Southampton), Dover, Sandwich, Ipswich. The major commercial centres were London and York. By 880 there were about ten English towns, but by the early 10th century there were about 50, with some of the newer towns built for military rather than commercial reasons. By the end of the Anglo-Saxon period it is thought that there were about 100 places that might be described as towns, in which lived about 10% of the population. Much of this later urban growth came in the form of burhs, fortified against the Danish invaders.

During the course of the 9th century a new element entered Britain's social, cultural and political mix in the form of Scandinavian attacks and settlements. The first recorded raid on England took place in 793—on the monastery at Lindisfarne; the raids intensified in the 9th century, and in 851 the Vikings first wintered in England. In midland and eastern England the primary influence was that of the Danes, who had previously attacked the coastal lowlands of northwestern continental Europe, and moved inland along the major rivers. From 860 to 880, notwithstanding the strength of the Wessex army of King Alfred, the Danes took eastern Mercia, East Anglia and most of Northumbria. This Danish-held and settled area became the Danelaw, at the centre of which were a group of five fortified towns in the East Midlands: Lincoln, Stamford, Nottingham, Leicester and Derby. A different wave of attacks and settlement occurred in the northwest of England, where from the early 10th century the Norwegians, mainly from the Dublin kingdom, occupied the region west of the Pennines up to the Solway Firth. Attempts were made to found a Norse kingdom east of the Pennines, at York, but a renewed campaign by the Mercian and Wessex kings reduced the area of the Danelaw. Danish raids on England were renewed early in the 10th century, resulting in the conquest and unification of the whole country except for the southwest, under Canute.

The largest area of Scandinavian settlement in England was the Danelaw, which was formally recognised in 886 by Alfred of Wessex and Guthrum. Its four principal regions were Northumbria, East Anglia, the southeast Midlands and the Five Boroughs. The laws and customs of the Danelaw differed from those of Anglo-Saxon England.

The Scandinavians also exercised powerful influence in Scotland, though Wales was less affected. In the 9th century Norwegians (Vikings) took the Orkneys and Shetlands and moved south from Caithness to the Moray Firth. They settled the Western Islands and founded kingdoms in Ireland and

the Isle of Man. There were frequent attacks by the Vikings from Dublin and the Isle of Man on the Welsh coast, and though no permanent settlements resulted the Scandinavian influence is seen in Norse topographical names of coastal features. The Scandinavian settlement affected both rural and urban life, producing an extension of arable cultivation and a stimulus to urban growth.

Against the background of conquest and war, the conversion of Britain to Christianity proceeded at varying pace and with development of different institutions. At the end of the 10th century a revival of monastic life in England occurred, mainly in the south and east, but the main extension of monasticism occurred after the Norman conquest. In Wales early monastic sites had been established by the 'Celtic' saints in the period from the 5th to the 7th century, and these monasteries were of great importance in Welsh religious life for a long period. There were bishops in Wales, but no division into sees, whereas in England the dioceses dated from the 7th-century Augustinian conversion, even though the territories of the sees changed rapidly during troubled times. In Scotland territorial bishoprics are evident by the 11th century, together with a crude parochial system (*see map page 128*). In England the development of a parochial system was well under way, though not complete by 1066.

Medieval Britain

On 14 October 1066, the Anglo-Saxon kingdom ended with the defeat in battle of Harold Godwinson by William, Duke of Normandy (a Norman duchy which had developed in the 10th century). The Conquest represents, however, less of a dramatic change in life in Britain than is sometimes thought, for many of the innovations with which the Normans are associated, including the feudal and manorial systems, were pre-Norman in origin. The administrative geography of Britain before and after the Norman Conquest was varied and complex. There existed in 1066 a number of earldoms—heritages from the Anglo-Saxon administrative system—including Northumbria, East Anglia and Wessex, which comprised groupings of shires. After the Conquest the existing administrative and judicial system of England was used, and co-operation envisaged with the existing officials such as sheriffs, bishops and abbots. The principal innovations of the new regime were a more rigid social structure and a greater emphasis on military skill and defensive systems. The latter was represented in the construction of a national system of royal and baronial castles, many in the larger towns and others constructed along the Welsh Marches and the Scots border.

From the end of the 10th century there began a period of economic expansion in Britain which had a profound effect on regional economies and on landscapes. This expansion began from a small population, a low-technology and predominantly rural economy, a limited urban and commercial base, and a pyramidal social structure. The population of England at the end of the 11th century was about two million, and by 1347 had reached between six and seven million. Little can be known of the equivalent figures for Wales, although one estimate for 1300 is of a population of less than 250,000. Estimates for Scotland suggest a population of c.250,000 for the late 11th century, reaching c.450,000 by the late 14th century. On the whole, what is postulated is a relatively general rapid increase in population in the 12th and 13th centuries, followed by a period of decline, though the rates of increase obviously varied locally and regionally. The population of 11th-century England had a highly uneven distribution, with the highest densities in the Lowlands, notably East Anglia, and the lowest in the Uplands, waste and forest areas. In the Lincolnshire fenland, for example, there were dramatic increases in the village populations in the 12th and 13th centuries. As there was still much under-used space, an inevitable consequence of the rising population was colonisation on a large scale. The major expansion of settlement in England took place in woodland areas, such as the Forest of Arden. Another indication of the advance of settlement and cultivation can be seen in the attempts at disafforestation of royal forest, that is to release some of the legal restraints on 'assarting' (or clearance) in them. Examples of this occurred in the 12th and 13th centuries in Surrey, Devon, Essex, Hampshire and the Southern Uplands of Scotland. Reclamation of marshland was another important feature of colonisation, with major drainage and settlement activity in the Somerset Levels, the Pevensey levels in Sussex, Holderness, the Romney and Walland marshes in Kent. Inroads were also made into the margins of the high moorland areas, including the Pennines, Dartmoor, Exmoor, and the uplands of Southern Scotland and central and north Wales. Much of the land reclamation of early medieval Britain was carried out by the initiative and under the control of the monastic orders, notably the Cistercians. The pace of colonisation was uneven, and in some areas there was already a shortage of land by the 14th century.

The nature of the rural economy in Britain in the 11th, 12th and 13th centuries is impossible to describe in detail, for local and regional variance was considerable. In those areas where arable cultivation was possible on a relatively large scale, much of the land was arranged and managed in 'open' or sub-divided fields (fields divided into tenurial strips), as in parts of the south and east Midlands, but in other areas, such as southwestern England and west Wales, much land was enclosed and held in severalty rather than in common. In many areas there was a mixture of 'open' and 'enclosed' land. The system of farming the open fields, particularly in heavy soil areas, involved the ploughing-up of substantial cultivation ridges, separated by drainage furrows, and these can still be seen, notably in Midland England, as 'ridge-and-furrow' topography. The most mature form of field-system was the two-and-three-field system, found in a broad belt of territory running from northeast England through the Midlands to south central England and with outliers in South Wales, and involving the

Britain to 1350 The Domesday survey of 1086 produced an unparalleled wealth of information about 11th-century England. Steady inroads were made by 1350 on the areas of unfarmed land covered by forest and marsh.

Late Medieval Britain The indication of farming regions at this date are only tentative, but the enclosures of the 15th and 16th centuries were primarily concentrated in regions of arable farming, converting them to sheep-rearing.

Britain to 1350

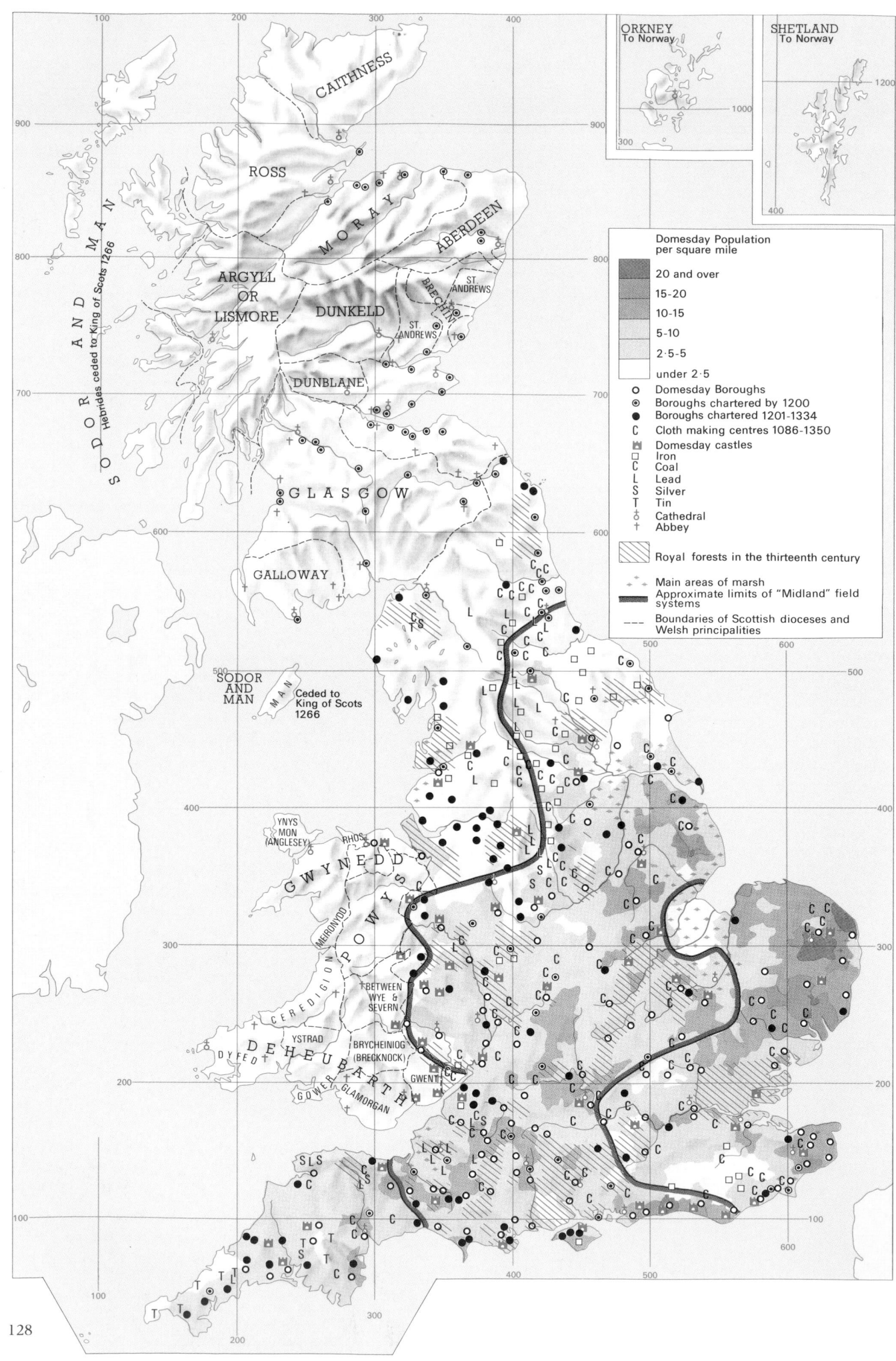

ORKNEY
To Norway

SHETLAND
To Norway

Domesday Population
per square mile

20 and over
15-20
10-15
5-10
2·5-5
under 2·5

○ Domesday Boroughs
◉ Boroughs chartered by 1200
● Boroughs chartered 1201-1334
C Cloth making centres 1086-1350
⌂ Domesday castles
▫ Iron
C Coal
L Lead
S Silver
T Tin
⸸ Cathedral
† Abbey

Royal forests in the thirteenth century

Main areas of marsh
Approximate limits of "Midland" field systems
Boundaries of Scottish dioceses and Welsh principalities

CAITHNESS

ROSS

M O R A Y

ABERDEEN

ARGYLL
OR
LISMORE

DUNKELD

BRECHIN

ST.
ANDREWS

ST.
ANDREWS

DUNBLANE

S O D O R   A N D   M A N
Hebrides ceded to King of Scots 1266

GLASGOW

GALLOWAY

SODOR
AND
MAN
Ceded to
King of Scots
1266

MAN

YNYS
MON
(ANGLESEY)

RHOS

G W Y N E D D

MEIRONYDD

P O W Y S

CEREDIGION

D Y F E D

YSTRAD

DEHEUBARTH

GOWER

GLAMORGAN

BETWEEN
WYE &
SEVERN

BRYCHEINIOG
(BRECKNOCK)

GWENT

128

Late Medieval Britain

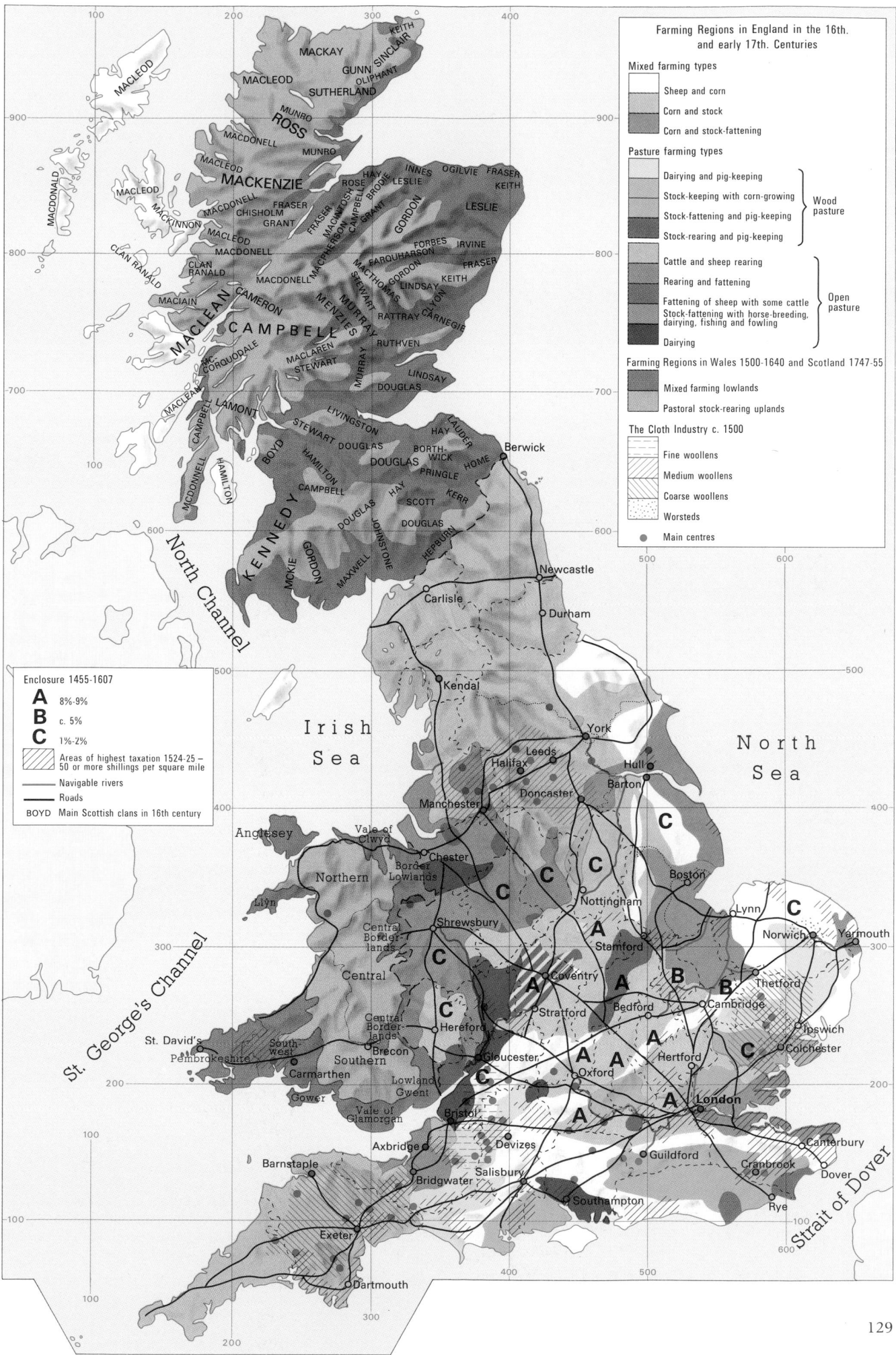

Farming Regions in England in the 16th. and early 17th. Centuries

Mixed farming types
- Sheep and corn
- Corn and stock
- Corn and stock-fattening

Pasture farming types
- Dairying and pig-keeping — Wood pasture
- Stock-keeping with corn-growing
- Stock-fattening and pig-keeping
- Stock-rearing and pig-keeping

- Cattle and sheep rearing — Open pasture
- Rearing and fattening
- Fattening of sheep with some cattle
- Stock-fattening with horse-breeding, dairying, fishing and fowling
- Dairying

Farming Regions in Wales 1500-1640 and Scotland 1747-55
- Mixed farming lowlands
- Pastoral stock-rearing uplands

The Cloth Industry c. 1500
- Fine woollens
- Medium woollens
- Coarse woollens
- Worsteds
- • Main centres

Enclosure 1455-1607

A 8%-9%
B c. 5%
C 1%-2%

Areas of highest taxation 1524-25 – 50 or more shillings per square mile

— Navigable rivers
— Roads
BOYD Main Scottish clans in 16th century

MACLEOD
MACKAY
GUNN SINCLAIR
MACLEOD OLIPHANT
SUTHERLAND
MACDONELL ROSS
MUNRO
MACDONALD MACLEOD MUNRO
MACLEOD INNES OGILVIE FRASER
MACKINNON ROSE HAY KEITH
CHISHOLM MACKINTOSH LESLIE
FRASER MACPHERSON CAMPBELL GORDON LESLIE
MACLEOD GRANT GRANT
MACDONELL FORBES IRVINE
CLAN FARQUHARSON FRASER
RANALD GORDON KEITH
MACDONELL LINDSAY
MACIAIN STEWART MACTHOMAS
CAMERON LYON CARNEGIE
CAMPBELL MENZIES MURRAY RATTRAY CARNEGIE
CAMPBELL MACLAREN RUTHVEN
MC CORQUODALE STEWART LINDSAY
MACLEAN DOUGLAS
CAMPBELL LAMONT
MCDONNELL HAMILTON LIVINGSTON
BOYD STEWART HAY LAUDER
KENNEDY HAMILTON DOUGLAS BORTH-WICK HOME
CAMPBELL PRINGLE KERR
MCKIE DOUGLAS HAY SCOTT
GORDON MAXWELL JOHNSTONE DOUGLAS
HEPBURN

North Channel
Irish Sea
North Sea
St. George's Channel
Strait of Dover

Berwick
Newcastle
Carlisle
Durham
Kendal
York
Leeds
Halifax
Hull
Barton
Manchester
Doncaster
Anglesey
Vale of Clwyd
Chester
Northern
Boston
Llŷn
Nottingham
Lynn
Central Borderlands
Shrewsbury
Norwich
Yarmouth
Stamford
Thetford
Central
Coventry
Cambridge
Ipswich
St. David's
Central Borderlands
Stratford
Bedford
Colchester
Pembrokeshire
Southwest
Hereford
Hertford
Brecon
Gloucester
Oxford
London
Carmarthen
Southern
Lowland Gwent
Bristol
Gower
Vale of Glamorgan
Canterbury
Axbridge
Devizes
Guildford
Cranbrook
Barnstaple
Salisbury
Dover
Bridgwater
Rye
Southampton
Exeter
Dartmouth

129

sub-division of the two or three major arable fields into furlongs, and the division of the arable area usually into three cropping zones, one of which was normally left fallow. Elsewhere, particularly in upland and heavy woodland areas, there were smaller fields and less regular cropping systems. In many of the upland and marshland areas there was no arable cultivation, except perhaps for very isolated pockets, and the rural economy was essentially pastoral, the main activity being the rearing of sheep and cattle. The large sheep flocks of the lowland coastal marshes, of Kent and Essex, for example, were paralleled by the 'vaccaries' of the Pennines and central Wales. Natural habitats, including woods and marshes, provided fodder and habitat for both domesticated animals and for wild game. An important feature of the medieval landscape was the royal forest and its diminutive form, the deer park. The rural settlements of medieval Britain varied widely in size and form from the undoubtedly large villages of parts of Midland England and East Anglia to the more isolated hamlets and farmsteads of many of the uplands and recently-colonised areas of the west and north of Britain.

The increase in monastic orders in Britain after the Conquest was a significant feature of medieval life. It is estimated that in 1066 there were about 280 religious houses in England and Wales, a figure that had increased to over 1,300 by the end of the 12th century (largely by the establishment of houses of monks, regular canons and nuns, military orders and hospitals). By the 14th century the number had increased to over 2,000, mainly with the addition of mendicant orders of friars after 1221, but the total had declined by 1500. The larger monastic houses were very substantial landowners, and are epitomised best by the relics of the spectacular Cistercian abbeys at Fountains, Rievaulx, Tintern and Melrose. In Scotland 'innovative' monasteries came later, beginning in the 12th century and including the founding of houses by the Augustinians and the Cistercians.

The towns of medieval Britain were small in comparison with their modern counterparts. According to the data of the Domesday Book of 1086, there were 111 boroughs in England, some of which were very small indeed. London was the largest, with a population of about 10,000. There was only one borough in Wales at this time—Rhuddlan. The period of economic expansion, however, witnessed a growth in the number of boroughs in England, which numbered 480 by the beginning of the 14th century. There was an increase in the towns in Wales consequent on the Norman Conquest, notably in south Wales and, in the late 13th century, in northwest Wales. In Scotland, urbanisation appears to have begun during the Norman period and notably after 1124 when David I became King of Scots. Prior to this date he had given burgh charters to Roxburgh and Berwick, and between 1124 and 1153 created eleven royal burghs, including Edinburgh, Stirling and Dunfermline. Burghs were also given charters by the Church, and the early ecclesiastical burghs include Glasgow and Aberdeen.

Industrial activity in medieval Britain was generally not highly location-specific, for the major industries were those that supplied the everyday needs of the populace—food, drink, clothing and materials for building—and were relatively ubiquitous. The towns were important centres of a wide variety of industries, though in the 13th century there are signs that some industries, notably textiles, moved away from the towns to the countryside. By the late Middle Ages the major textile regions of England included Wiltshire and Gloucestershire (producing broad cloth), the West Riding of Yorkshire (low-grade cloth), the Norwich worsted region and the cloth regions of Suffolk and Essex (which became progressively more specialised in production), and the cloth regions of Somerset and Devon. These developments reflected a general change from the export of wool to the export of cloth.

The principal areas of iron production were the Weald of Sussex and Kent, the Forest of Dean and the Cleveland Hills. The efficiency of production was increased by the introduction of a form of blast furnace. In the later Middle Ages there was also an increase in the production of coal, encouraged by a growing timber shortage. The main mining areas were the Tyne valley, south Nottinghamshire, west Yorkshire, south Wales and around the Forth and in Fife in Scotland. Lead, together with silver, was produced in Derbyshire, the Pennine valleys of Yorkshire and Durham, in Cumberland, and north and south Wales. Tin production took place in Cornwall, and copper ore was extracted in Devonshire, Cumberland and Wales. The products of the agriculture and industries of medieval Britain were mainly consumed and used within the mainland, but trade was nevertheless an important feature of economic activity. The largest ports were London, Southampton and Bristol. Much of the trade of the western ports, including Southampton, was with the Gascony wine area. Southampton and Bristol imported wine and exported wool and cloth. The east-coast ports mainly traded with the Baltic and the Low Countries, while London had trading connections with most parts of continental Europe.

The dynamic character and the vicissitudes of life in medieval Britain should be stressed, for the economic and human geographies of regions and settlements were continually changing. There was a decline in the population of England from six or seven million in 1348 to about 2·75 million in the early 16th century, with changes of a similar order in Wales and Scotland. This was mainly due to the effects of epidemic and infectious diseases. The best-known epidemic was the Black Death, which affected Britain from 1348 to 1350, though there were many other epidemics including tuberculosis, measles and smallpox. In some respects the decrease of population which began in the late 14th century was related to a weakening of a feudal mode of production, and paved the way for the early advent of rural and urban capitalism, culminating in the Agricultural and Industrial Revolutions. It has been suggested that in 1509, when Henry VIII succeeded to the throne of England, Britain was still medieval in many aspects: by the end of the Tudor dynasty this medievalism was rapidly disappearing, and nearly all traces of it had vanished by 1700.

The Agricultural Revolution Enclosures at this period affected both the commons and the open-fields that had been communally cultivated since medieval times. Agricultural societies formed an important channel for the spreading of new farming ideas and techniques.

The Agricultural Revolution

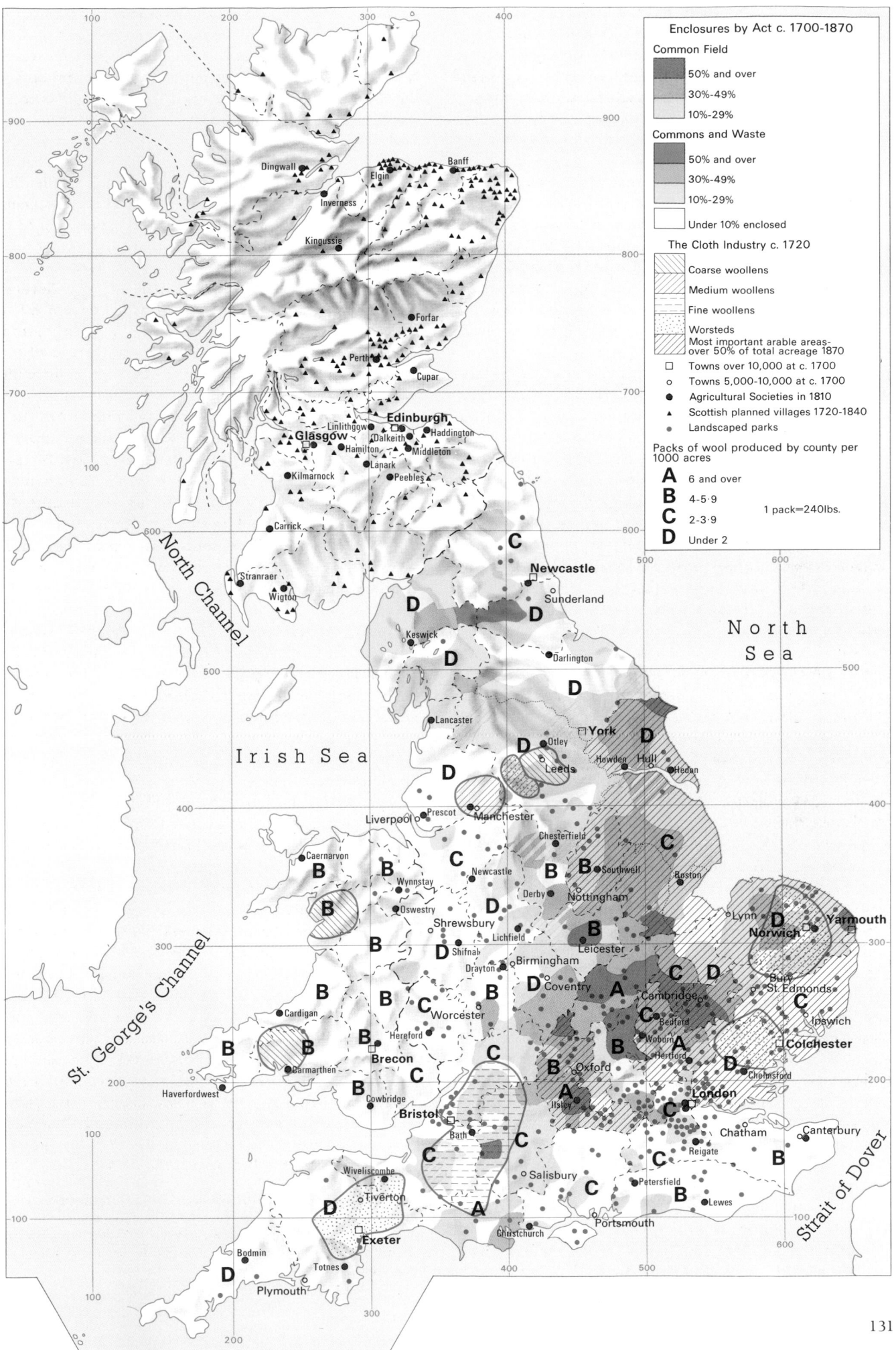

Enclosures by Act c. 1700-1870

Common Field
- 50% and over
- 30%-49%
- 10%-29%

Commons and Waste
- 50% and over
- 30%-49%
- 10%-29%

Under 10% enclosed

The Cloth Industry c. 1720
- Coarse woollens
- Medium woollens
- Fine woollens
- Worsteds
- Most important arable areas- over 50% of total acreage 1870

□ Towns over 10,000 at c. 1700
○ Towns 5,000-10,000 at c. 1700
● Agricultural Societies in 1810
▲ Scottish planned villages 1720-1840
• Landscaped parks

Packs of wool produced by county per 1000 acres

A 6 and over
B 4-5·9
C 2-3·9
D Under 2

1 pack=240lbs.

The Agricultural Revolution

The 16th and 17th centuries witnessed widespread change of an economic and political nature. In England population trends saw a continuing recovery, probably beginning after about 1470; in 1541 the total was about three million, increasing to four million by 1600, to 5·5 million by 1651, followed by a slight decline before further increase in the 18th century. Estimates for Scotland put the population at 550-800,000 for the late 16th century, and at between 800,000 and one million for 1700.

These population increases mirror the beginning of major changes in the sectoral and space-economies of the regions of Britain. Generally labelled the Agricultural and Industrial Revolutions, the phenomena thus classified were extremely complex and extending over quite a long period of time.

In the rural and agricultural sectors the main indices of change are well known, although their local and regional manifestations require further investigation. Enclosure and technical innovations are the best-known features. Enclosure had been a continuous process over a very long period of time, but accelerated in the 16th and 17th centuries prior to the major burst of 'Parliamentary' enclosure in the 18th and 19th centuries. In the late 15th and the 16th century the conversion of arable land to pasture, on account of the relative profitability of sheep farming, led to a 'de-populating' form of enclosure and the desertion of settlements, particularly in the Midlands. The amount of land enclosed in this fashion was quite small, although more 'silent' forms of enclosure also occurred. By 1600 there were regions which had few or no open fields (though these were mainly peripheral to the great central swathe of open fields), and during the 17th century various methods of enclosure, including enclosure 'by agreement', were used to continue the elimination of the open fields. Enclosure by private Act of Parliament was the major mechanism in the 18th and 19th centuries, and quantitatively was the most important method. In this period there were some 5286 Enclosure Acts, of which 3105 effected the enclosure of open-field arable. The total effect was the enclosure in England of nearly 2·8 million HA (seven million acres) or 21% of the total surface area. The counties most affected were Lincolnshire, West Yorkshire, Norfolk, Northamptonshire and East Yorkshire, and those least affected were Middlesex, Essex, Devon, Rutland, Sussex, Hereford, Cheshire, Monmouth, Cornwall and Kent. The degree of enclosure varied in time, but the periods of greatest intensity were 1760-80 and 1793-1815, the latter being the period of the Napoleonic wars. The acreage for Parliamentary enclosure in Wales is estimated to be 167,000 HA (414,000 acres), with the greatest intensity in the period 1793-1815.

The legal system of enclosure in Scotland differed from that of England and Wales, and landowners were not as constrained from enclosing. Acts of the late 16th century facilitated changes in land tenure, and the Act against Lands Lying in Run-rig of 1695 gave power for division of commons. In the Lowlands, arable enclosure was mainly completed by 1770 in Berwickshire and the Lothians, but had only just begun in Ayrshire and Perthshire. In addition, about 200,000 HA (500,000 acres) of common were enclosed in the Lowlands between 1720 and 1850. The pattern of enclosure in the Scottish Highlands was different, particularly after 1745 with the 'clearance' and amalgamation of Highland farms, which were subsequently let to Lowland sheep graziers. This process initially affected the Central Highlands, and later the northwest Highlands and Islands, leading to large-scale emigration.

The landscape effects of enclosure at this time are plain to see—in the form of regular, usually square or rectangular fields, mainly bounded by hedgerows or stone walls. The economic effects of enclosure in the shorter term are more difficult to measure, for in spite of its association with agricultural improvement it is difficult to prove direct causal relationships. The social consequences of enclosures have tended to be neglected, though opinions tend to polarise around the 'improvement' effects and the 'depopulation' effects.

Enclosure was but one of several manifestations of the advent of a capitalist system of production in the rural economy. We associate the Agricultural Revolution with technical improvements in farming, and usually with improvers, such as Thomas Coke of Norfolk, Robert Bakewell of Leicestershire, the Culleys of Northumberland, Jethro Tull and 'Turnip' Townshend. While it is more accurate to describe some of these as popularisers rather than direct innovators, it is certainly the case that many of the technical improvements of this period are associated with large estates, such as Coke's Norfolk estate, and the estates of innovating landlords in East Lothian. The technical innovations included the introduction of short leys with improved grasses (known as convertible husbandry), new crops (clover, turnips, the potato, ryegrass, sainfoin), new rotations (especially the Norfolk system), the application of fertilisers and the new implements such as Tull's seed drill. The area of improved land was increased by major reclamation schemes (notably the Fenland and of areas of moorland and heathland). The regional chronologies of adoption are very complex, and there is no overall pattern or 'national' picture. Incentives for improving and intensifying agricultural production included the rapidly growing population and the increase in the proportion of the population living in towns, particularly London and the towns of the industrial areas. Improvement is also seen in the newer residences, planned estate villages and the land-scaped gardens and parks. What has been described as the flowering or re-building of rural England commenced in the late 16th century, but the architectural expression of the Agricultural Revolution is usually associated with the great buildings of the 18th century and the classical Palladian styles. Landscape gardening also reached its peak in the 18th century, the major practitioners being William Kent, Lancelot Brown and Humphrey Repton.

Agricultural change did not stop in the early 19th century, although progress and advancement were not always universal in rural areas. In the 19th century the legislative context of farming continued to change with

The Early Industrial Revolution The geography of early industrialisation depended on the availability of coal or water for power, and on canals for communications. The concentration of industry into relatively small areas was fed by a dramatic movement of people from rural areas to the towns.

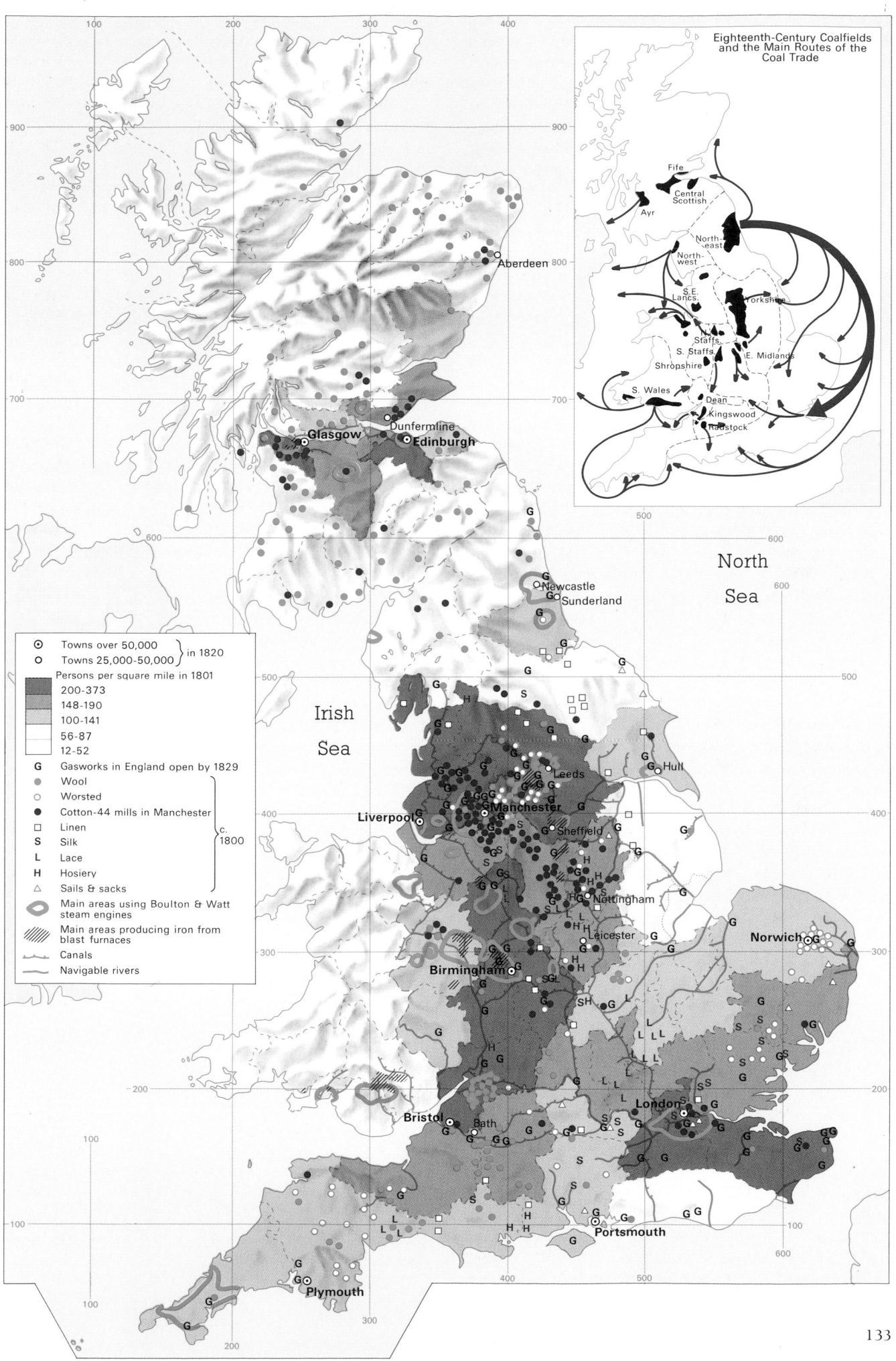

Eighteenth-Century Coalfields
and the Main Routes of the
Coal Trade

Fife

Central
Scottish

Ayr

North-
east

North-
west

S.E.
Lancs.

Yorkshire

Staffs.

S. Staffs.

E. Midlands

Shropshire

S. Wales

Dean

Kingswood

Radstock

North
Sea

Irish
Sea

Aberdeen

Glasgow

Dunfermline

Edinburgh

Newcastle
Sunderland

Hull

Leeds

Liverpool

Manchester

Sheffield

Nottingham

Leicester

Norwich

Birmingham

Bristol

Bath

London

Portsmouth

Plymouth

| | Towns over 50,000 | in 1820 |
| | Towns 25,000–50,000 | |

Persons per square mile in 1801
- 200–373
- 148–190
- 100–141
- 56–87
- 12–52

G   Gasworks in England open by 1829
•   Wool
○   Worsted
●   Cotton–44 mills in Manchester
□   Linen
S   Silk
L   Lace
H   Hosiery
△   Sails & sacks

c. 1800

Main areas using Boulton & Watt
steam engines

Main areas producing iron from
blast furnaces

Canals

Navigable rivers

more Enclosure Acts and the repeal of the Corn Laws (ending the artificial maintenance of prices), the subsidy of land drainage by the Public Money Drainage Act of 1846, and the strengthening of the rights of tenants by the Agricultural Holdings Acts. Farming became a more and more capitally-intensive commercial enterprise, responding to the demands of a rapidly growing population for cheaper food. This process, assisted by new technology (including under-draining, chemical fertilisers and better transport to markets), resulted in improved productivity. It also produced a massive decline in the rural labour force in the course of the 19th century. High investment at the time of high farming could be very profitable, but at other times, particularly the 1880s and 1890s, low prices produced considerable depression and widespread bankruptcy, notably in eastern England.

The Industrial Revolution

The other 'revolution' of the 18th and 19th centuries was 'industrial', a term which has associations not merely with manufacturing and extractional industries but also with rapid urbanisation, rapid population increase and major changes in the transport system. In the mid-18th century the population of Britain was about eleven million, and this figure had risen spectacularly to 45 million by 1911 (of whom less than 10% were engaged in agriculture). The increase was most rapid in mid-century. In the late 18th century, a decline in the death-rate and rise in birth rate because of earlier age at marriage gave a national increase in population of about 40%. The overall figures do, however, mask regional and local variations: in the mid-19th century rural areas of Wales, Scotland and (to a lesser extent) England experienced population decline. Immigration from Ireland was important, though offset by overseas emigration from Britain, giving a net loss of over one million people in the period 1801 to 1911. For the 19th century population growth varied between 11% and 14% a decade, falling, however, to 10% in the first decade of the 20th century. Population growth was highest in the rapidly industrialising and urbanising regions of north and midland England, London, Clydeside and South Wales.

The Industrial Revolution did not start from a totally new base. The textile industries which had developed in the 16th and 17th centuries retained regional distinctiveness. Until the mid-18th century the woollen industry provided about 33% of Britain's industrial output. The wool textile regions changed balance, however, with the decline of the Somerset and Devon and Suffolk producers, and a greater concentration in Gloucestershire, Wiltshire, Norwich and the West Riding (*see map page 131*). The cotton industry experienced a rapid rise in the 18th century, particularly with the increased demand from the home market after 1750, and the technical advances after 1770. The major areas of production were Lancashire, the East Midlands and the Glasgow region. Coal output also increased rapidly in the 18th century: the total for 1700 was about 2·5 million tons, which increased to 10 million by 1800. The turning point for expansion in coal production was about 1770, with the beginning of the canal era providing a cheaper means of distribution. The largest coalfield was that of northeast England, much of whose output was shipped down the east coast to London. Other smaller areas of production included the coalfields of the Midlands, Yorkshire, Lancashire, the Forest of Dean, the Rhondda and the Firth of Forth. Iron production was mainly concentrated in South Wales, Shropshire, Staffordshire, Yorkshire, and the Central valley of Scotland. Other major industries of the 18th century included silk textiles, glassmaking, and shipbuilding.

Changes in the form of power (especially steam) allied to technological changes—the smelting of iron using coal in the early 18th century, the advent of a wide range of machines and of the factory systems—accelerated industrial activity, particularly in the regions on the developing coalfields. By the mid-19th century the Industrial Revolution had reached its peak. Deeper mining and greater demand led to increased production—from 21 million tons in 1826 to 154 million tons in 1880, with the Northumberland and Durham field the major producer, followed by Lancashire, South Wales and Yorkshire. The iron industry was tied to coal production, and of the mid-century total of 2·7 million tons of pig-iron, the largest producers were Staffordshire, Scotland and South Wales. The working of the iron was not so tied, and metal industries were located in Sheffield and the Black Country, with different locations for shipbuilding and locomotive engineering. The textile industries experienced further concentration, with Lancashire dominating cotton production. There was less regional dominance by a single region in the woollen industry, although the major concentration was in West Yorkshire.

The railway age (from 1825 onwards) brought massive change in population distribution, with the increasing concentration in the towns of the coalfield and industrial regions. Over 50% of the English population were urban-dwellers in 1851, and 70% by 1881. Urban development was marked in Yorkshire, Lancashire, the Black Country and Birmingham, Tyneside, Central Scotland, London, South Wales and, later in the century, along the coast of southeast England.

As with agriculture, so there was also depression in industry in late-Victorian Britain, especially in the period 1873-1896, when industrial productivity fell, though new industries developed and partly offset decline elsewhere. These included the chemical and electrical engineering industries, food processing, and steel. On the eve of World War I the main trends of the Industrial Revolution had changed, as some of the older industrial areas began to lose population with a drift of population towards the southeast. These trends have continued to dominate throughout the 20th century.

Britain in the Late Nineteenth Century Between 1835 and 1900 the country was covered by a network of railways, often to the detriment of competing canals and roads. London's role as capital of the Empire helped to attract immigrants sufficient to make it one of the world's largest cities, despite a higher-than-normal mortality rate.

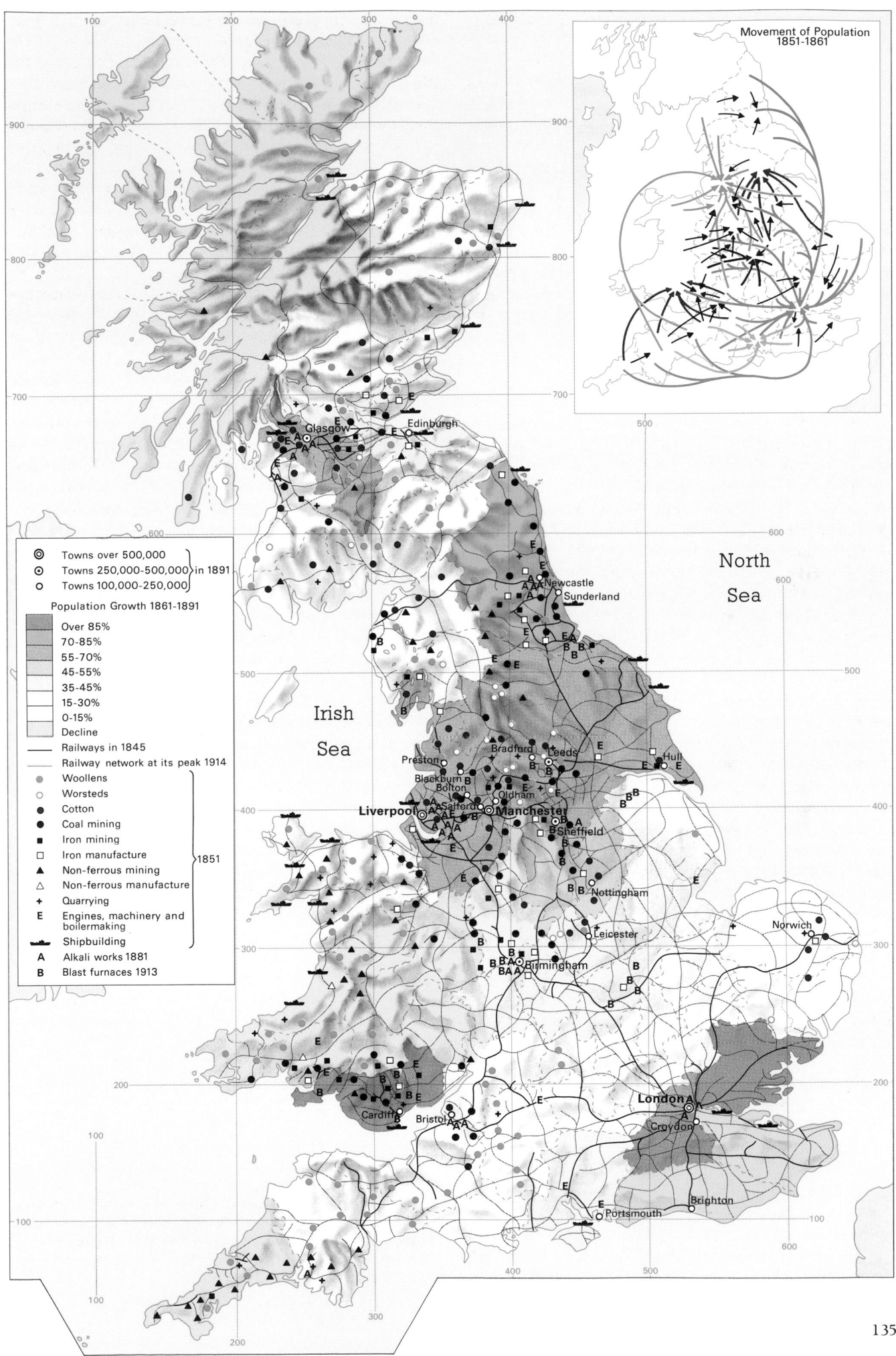

Movement of Population
1851-1861

North
Sea

Irish
Sea

Legend:

⊚ Towns over 500,000
⊙ Towns 250,000-500,000 } in 1891
○ Towns 100,000-250,000

Population Growth 1861-1891

Over 85%
70-85%
55-70%
45-55%
35-45%
15-30%
0-15%
Decline

— Railways in 1845
— Railway network at its peak 1914
● Woollens
○ Worsteds
● Cotton
● Coal mining
■ Iron mining
□ Iron manufacture
▲ Non-ferrous mining
△ Non-ferrous manufacture
+ Quarrying
E Engines, machinery and boilermaking
⛴ Shipbuilding
A Alkali works 1881
B Blast furnaces 1913

} 1851

Place names on map:

Glasgow
Edinburgh
Newcastle
Sunderland
Preston
Bradford
Leeds
Hull
Blackburn
Bolton
Oldham
Liverpool
Salford
Manchester
Sheffield
Nottingham
Leicester
Norwich
Birmingham
Cardiff
Bristol
London
Croydon
Brighton
Portsmouth

Modern Britain

The Legacy of the 1930s

Contrasts between the north and south of Britain are often made in the spirit of rivalry and jest. The Scottish people have their own history and pride. The people of the north of England, it has been remarked, offer 'the backbone of the country' and the superior robustness of the north is contrasted with the agility of intellect, but softer character, of the south. Behind the sometimes provocative jesting about the differences between Yorkshiremen and Londoners, Geordies and Brummies, there lay in the 1930s very great differences in the prosperity and ways of life of the 'two Britains'. Although there were exceptions to the rule, it was in the north that depression was concentrated, in the south that new industries were developing and the cities growing rapidly. Many northerners were moving away seeking the wider opportunities of London and the West Midlands. There was a 'drift' of population to the south of about 1,160,000 between 1923 and 1936. Wales, in this respect, was to be linked with the north rather than the south. Between 1923 and 1937 the insured population of the three southern divisions of the Ministry of Labour increased by 1,396,000 or 41% and the Midlands by 445,000 (27%). The insured population of the rest of Britain increased by only 576,000 or 10%. In terms of actual jobs, the three southern divisions increased by 47%, the Midlands by 32% and the North, Scotland and Wales by only 4%.

This situation was a product of the localisation of industries which had grown before 1914 but were now declining. There were falls in employment in cotton, coal, shipbuilding and some sectors of the iron and steel industries. The industrial districts of the north and Wales were heavily dependent on such industries. To pick out some extremes, unemployment rates in 1932 reached 60·9% in Merthyr Tydfil, 48·9% in Port Talbot, 46·7% in Sunderland, 44·6% in Barnsley, 44% in West Cumberland, 35% in Dundee. The Birmingham rate was 15·3%, Brighton's was 11·4%. Even East Ham in London was no more than 24·1%. And the unemployment rates fell more quickly in the south and the Midlands as economic recovery from the Great Depression began.

For it was in the southern part of Britain that the growing industries were concentrated. Here were the trades manufacturing for the home market and here could be found employment in the service and constructional industries. Motor-car manufacturing was well established in Dagenham, Luton, Oxford, Coventry and Birmingham. Industries linked to the assembly lines, like electrical engineering and the manufacture of components, tyres, car bodies and gear boxes, were in the south. The Birmingham metal trades prospered and the West Midlands, with its closely knit system of 'linkages' between trades, offered jobs to migrants from Wales and the North. Coventry was one of the fastest-growing cities, with an increase of population of 20% between 1931 and 1938 as against 3% for the country as a whole. Jobs were to be found in motor-car and cycle factories, electrical engineering, firms making components, machine-tool industries and in the rayon industry. With about one-fifth of the population of Great Britain, 'Greater London obtained five-sixths of the net increase in the number of factories between 1932 and 1937, two-fifths of all the employment in new factories and one-third of all the factory extensions'. New factories sprang up in the southeast, south, west and north of Greater London, many of them on speculatively built industrial estates along the main roads and railways out of London. Such estates can still be seen in Acton, Perivale, Park Royal and Wembley. Radio and electrical industries, automobile and aircraft engineering, pharmaceuticals, the food and drink trades, paper and printing, scientific instruments, and furniture, all nationally expanding industries, figured prominently.

While such development was in train the Clyde was in the grip of one of the worst concentrations of persistent unemployment lasting for almost all the inter-war period. Conditions on the Tyne were little, if any, better. The demand for action could not be resisted. The Special Areas Act of 1934 was the first of a series of Acts which gave limited powers to Commissioners for the Special Areas to take action to relieve unemployment in South Wales, northeast England, Cumberland and Clydeside. Industrial trading estates were set up, for example at Treforest (near Cardiff), Team Valley (Gateshead) and Hillington (Glasgow). Local authorities began to muster their resources. The Bank of England made available funds for the building of new blast furnaces, steel works and a continuous strip mill at Ebbw Vale: the original plan had been to build the plant on an iron-ore based location in Lincolnshire. Government plants making war materials were sited in the Special Areas. Government contracts, many for naval vessels, helped to bring life to the Clyde, the Tyne and to Barrow. Some of the depressed regions, eastern South Wales for example, profited more than others. Re-armament and the up-swing of trade achieved more than government policy. In 1938 the Royal Commission on the Distribution of the Industrial Population (the 'Barlow Commission') was established and its report was to influence post-war policy for regional development and industrial location.

The circumstances of regional contrast in employment had further consequences in terms of differences in personal incomes, quality of housing, access to medical and social services, opportunities for advancement. The Beveridge Report's recommendation of 1942 of a plan for 'Social Security as part of a general programme of social policy' must be viewed against this background.

The 1930s must not be seen wholly in terms of regional contrast. There was concern for example that the Axial Belt or 'Coffin' stretching from northwest to southeast from Lancashire to London was coming to house too great a share of the country's population (*see map page 151*). It was an age of technical change: the 'talkies' replaced the silent cinema, almost everybody could afford a radio, and the BBC under Sir John Reith's Directorship had a firm policy from which many young people benefited. New secondary schools were

The Crisis of the 1930s A study carried out in the late 1930s revealed the excessive dependence of many towns on a single industry as a structural problem exacerbating the impact of the depression. This map compares the distribution of these industries with the incidence of unemployment.

The Crisis of the 1930's

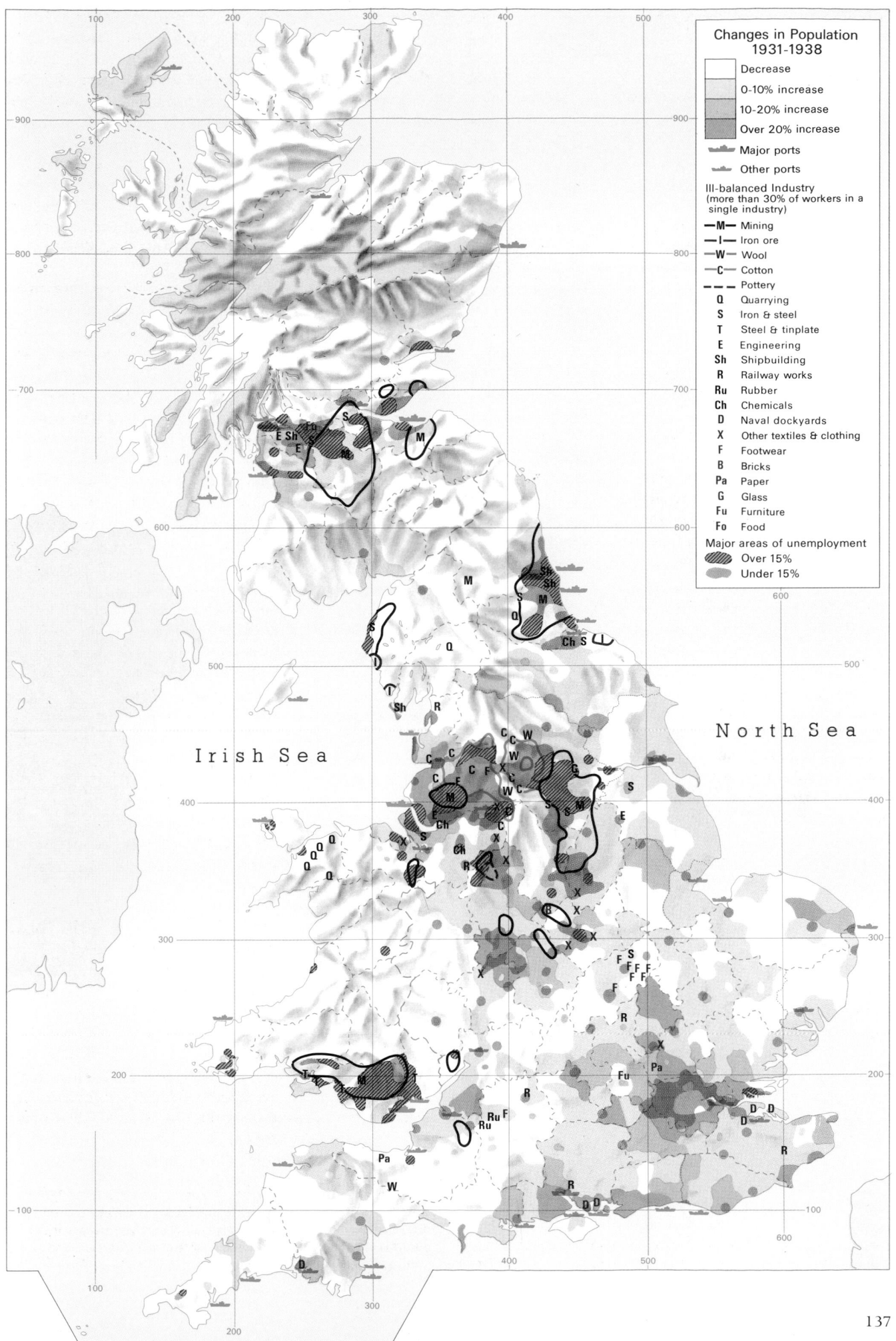

Changes in Population
1931-1938

- Decrease
- 0-10% increase
- 10-20% increase
- Over 20% increase

Major ports
Other ports

Ill-balanced Industry
(more than 30% of workers in a
single industry)

- **M** — Mining
- **I** — Iron ore
- **W** — Wool
- **C** — Cotton
- - - Pottery
- **Q** Quarrying
- **S** Iron & steel
- **T** Steel & tinplate
- **E** Engineering
- **Sh** Shipbuilding
- **R** Railway works
- **Ru** Rubber
- **Ch** Chemicals
- **D** Naval dockyards
- **X** Other textiles & clothing
- **F** Footwear
- **B** Bricks
- **Pa** Paper
- **G** Glass
- **Fu** Furniture
- **Fo** Food

Major areas of unemployment
- Over 15%
- Under 15%

North Sea

Irish Sea

established. Motor-car ownership was extending as the Baby Austin and Morris Minor found ready markets. Some new roads were built, among them the Wolverhampton New Road across the derelict land of the Black Country and the North Circular Road linking the industrial areas of north London.

Competition between the railway companies, especially on the routes from London to Scotland, led to the introduction of new and more efficient steam locomotives and reductions in travel times. Air services to the Continent, notably from Croydon, grew in frequency and a network of internal air services was introduced. British passenger liners registered success in the competition for the Atlantic 'Blue Riband'. An Electricity Grid was built, helping, with the rise of road transport and the growth of light industries, to free industry from coal-based locations.

It was the age of suburbia. More than four million houses were built in Britain between the wars, most of them in the suburbs. The better council housing estates attempted to embody Garden City lines with curving, geometrically designed, tree-lined avenues and nearby playing fields and schools. It was a day for the speculative builder and the semi-detached home, increasingly with garage space or garage. There was some ribbon development but more building of estates with local shops and cinema.

Much of this often-criticised housing remains in the 1980s and commands high prices. As cities expanded outwards, trolley-buses and motor-buses began to supplement and then to supersede the electric tram. In Greater London underground lines were extended and Metroland grew in the northwest, backed by the Metropolitan Railway. Such urban sprawl aroused alarm on many counts. These included concern at the growing size and costs of urban growth, concern at the loss for ever of good agricultural land and, under the shadow of Guernica, forebodings about aerial bombardment. And, as the 1930s drew on, the news from the Continent, the increasing pressure of refugees from Nazi Germany and their stories of persecution led increasingly to the conviction that, at least for a time, domestic problems would have to take second place. But even at the worst times of the war preparation for the future of Britain was in progress and the Barlow Report and the Scott Report, together with the Beveridge Report, laid foundations for the planning of the post-war society.

Fuel and Energy Resources

King Coal provided the heat and energy for Britain's Industrial Revolution of the 18th and 19th centuries. Britain's coals are of Carboniferous age: the formerly-wide extent of the Carboniferous rocks has been broken into a number of separate coalfields by subsequent earth movements and by denudation. Except for the anthracite of the western part of the South Wales Coalfield, the coals in Britain are bituminous in type. Considerable variation in coal types exists, from the steam coals of South Wales (formerly so important in the export trade), to the coking coals such as those of Durham, to the general industrial coals which are widespread but best illustrated in the Yorkshire, Nottinghamshire and Derbyshire coalfields (*see maps pages 139 and 140*).

The Northumberland and Durham coalfields were the first to be developed on a large scale, having the advantages of river and sea transport. As demand increased, mining moved from the shallow pits sunk near the outcrops of the main coal seams to deeper pits working seams at depth and through the overlying later rocks on the 'concealed' coalfields. Coal production increased during the 19th century and reached 230 million tons by 1900 and its maximum of 287 million tons in 1913. Of that total about one-third was exported. South Wales produced 57 million tons, Northumberland and Durham 56 million, Yorkshire 44 million, Scotland 42 million, and Nottinghamshire, Derbyshire and Leicestershire 34 million tons.

Production never again rose to such levels. By 1938 total production had fallen to 227 million tons partly as a result of declining exports. Steamships were replaced by oil-fired vessels; production from South Wales was down to 35 million tons (partly due to the decline in steam-coal production), and from Northumberland and Durham to 33 million, though the East Midlands coalfields held stable.

The industry was nationalised in 1947 and the National Coal Board inherited many problems. Geological problems were increasingly encountered and too little investment in new methods and equipment had taken place. There were complex problems of labour relations, arising in part from the diverse local conditions of mining and the past history of management and of variable demand. Nine hundred and fifty collieries existed of which, according to the *Plan for Coal* of 1950, 250 were to be selected for modernisation and reconstruction to yield about 70% of a planned output of 240 million tons. There was now a high demand for coal, in the phase of economic reconstruction after 1945, and before oil began to invade the general market for industrial, railway and household coal. New mines were sunk, mechanical equipment installed and schemes for improved productivity developed. Open-cast working was introduced. The costs of coal production varied widely, being highest in Kent, South Wales, Lancashire, Durham and Scotland and lowest in the East Midlands and Yorkshire. Despite progress there remained until about 1957 a coal 'gap': the industry could not supply enough to meet the country's needs. Of the 221 million tons produced in that year the main users were power stations (46·5 million), industry (37·5 million), domestic users (35·1 million), coke ovens (30·7 million), gas works (26·4 million), and railways (11·4 million).

The change in the industry's position after this date was dramatic. Competition from other sources of energy and improvements in the efficiency of fuel-burning equipment led to declining demand for coal. By 1967 production had fallen to 174 million tons and by 1977 to 120 million. By 1977 the main users were power stations (77·7 million), coke ovens (19·3 million), domestic (10·4 million), industry (9·1 million); the railways had turned to oil and the gas industry had converted to natural gas. Great changes occurred in the geography of coal production as mines in high-cost coalfields were closed. Now, in 1987, the coalfields of Yorkshire

Mineral Resources The mining of metals is carried on commercially in a number of locations. The widespread availability of sand and gravel is vital to the construction industry, as is chalk and limestone.

Mineral Resources

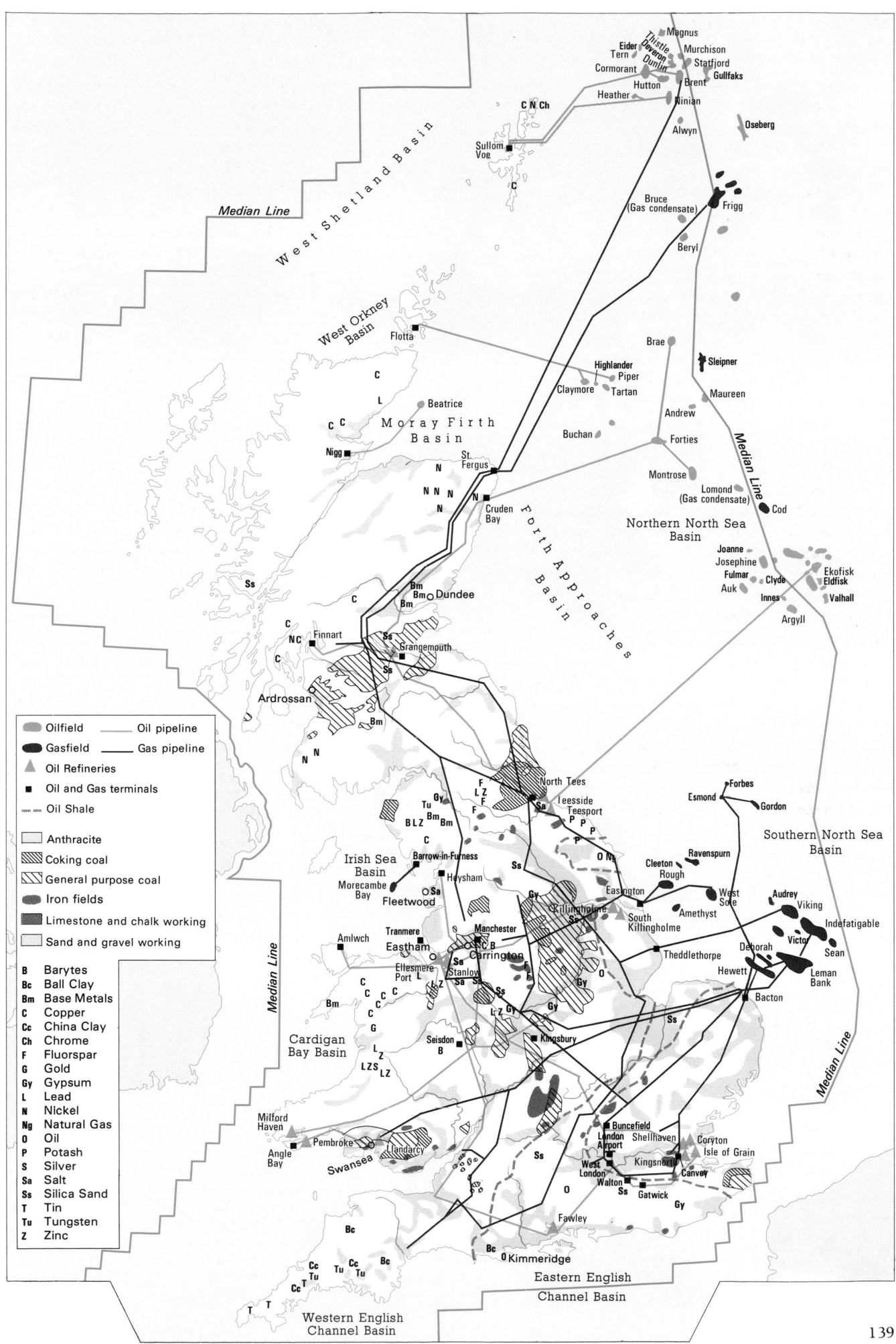

Legend

Oilfield	Oil pipeline		
Gasfield	Gas pipeline		
Oil Refineries			
Oil and Gas terminals			
Oil Shale			
Anthracite			
Coking coal			
General purpose coal			
Iron fields			
Limestone and chalk working			
Sand and gravel working			

B Barytes
Bc Ball Clay
Bm Base Metals
C Copper
Cc China Clay
Ch Chrome
F Fluorspar
G Gold
Gy Gypsum
L Lead
N Nickel
Ng Natural Gas
O Oil
P Potash
S Silver
Sa Salt
Ss Silica Sand
T Tin
Tu Tungsten
Z Zinc

Map labels

West Shetland Basin
Median Line
West Orkney Basin
Flotta
Beatrice
Moray Firth Basin
Nigg
St. Fergus
Cruden Bay
Forth Approaches Basin
Dundee
Finnart
Grangemouth
Ardrossan

Magnus
Eider
Tern
Cormorant
Heather
Hutton
Thistle
Deveron
Dunlin
Brent
Ninian
Alwyn
Murchison
Statfjord
Gullfaks
Oseberg
Bruce (Gas condensate)
Frigg
Beryl
Brae
Sleipner
Highlander
Piper
Claymore
Tartan
Maureen
Andrew
Buchan
Forties
Montrose
Lomond (Gas condensate)
Cod
Northern North Sea Basin
Joanne
Josephine
Fulmar
Auk
Innes
Clyde
Argyll
Ekofisk
Eldfisk
Valhall

Sullom Voe

North Tees
Teesside
Teesport
Esmond
Forbes
Gordon
Ravenspurn
Cleeton
Rough
Southern North Sea Basin
West Sole
Audrey
Viking
Amethyst
Indefatigable
Deborah
Victor
Sean
Hewett
Leman Bank
Bacton
South Killingholme
Easington
Theddlethorpe

Irish Sea Basin
Barrow-in-Furness
Heysham
Morecambe Bay
Fleetwood
Amlwch
Tranmere
Eastham
Ellesmere Port
Stanlow
Manchester
Carrington
Killingholme
Kingsbury
Seisdon
Cardigan Bay Basin

Milford Haven
Pembroke
Angle Bay
Swansea
Llandarcy

Buncefield
London Airport
West London
Walton
Shellhaven
Kingsnorth
Coryton
Isle of Grain
Canvey
Gatwick
Fawley
Kimmeridge
Eastern English Channel Basin
Western English Channel Basin

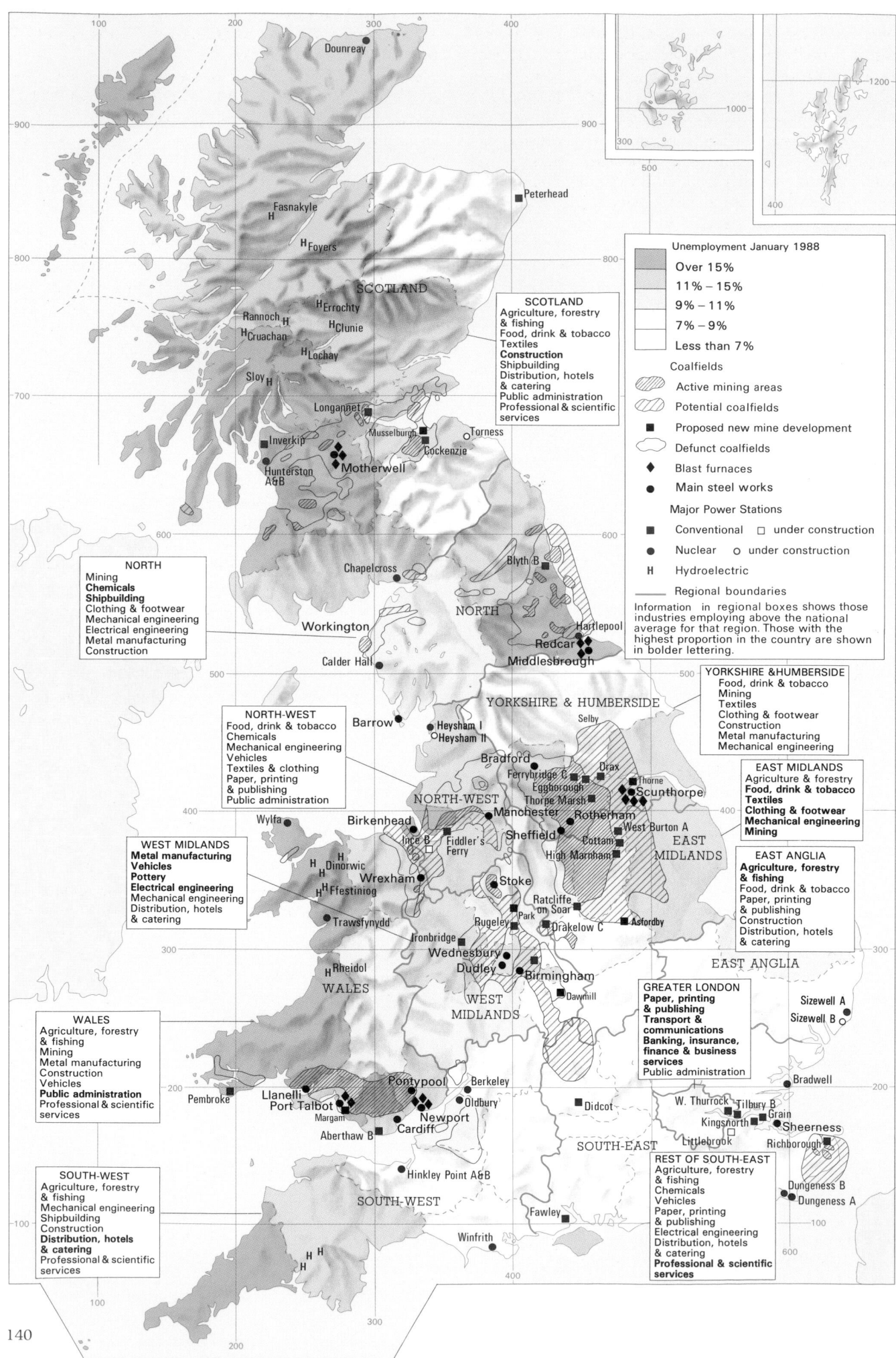

Unemployment January 1988

- Over 15%
- 11% – 15%
- 9% – 11%
- 7% – 9%
- Less than 7%

Coalfields

- Active mining areas
- Potential coalfields
- ■ Proposed new mine development
- Defunct coalfields
- ◆ Blast furnaces
- ● Main steel works

Major Power Stations

- ■ Conventional □ under construction
- ● Nuclear ○ under construction
- H Hydroelectric
- — Regional boundaries

Information in regional boxes shows those industries employing above the national average for that region. Those with the highest proportion in the country are shown in bolder lettering.

SCOTLAND
Agriculture, forestry & fishing
Food, drink & tobacco
Textiles
Construction
Shipbuilding
Distribution, hotels & catering
Public administration
Professional & scientific services

NORTH
Mining
Chemicals
Shipbuilding
Clothing & footwear
Mechanical engineering
Electrical engineering
Metal manufacturing
Construction

NORTH-WEST
Food, drink & tobacco
Chemicals
Mechanical engineering
Vehicles
Textiles & clothing
Paper, printing & publishing
Public administration

YORKSHIRE & HUMBERSIDE
Food, drink & tobacco
Mining
Textiles
Clothing & footwear
Construction
Metal manufacturing
Mechanical engineering

EAST MIDLANDS
Agriculture & forestry
Food, drink & tobacco
Textiles
Clothing & footwear
Mechanical engineering
Mining

WEST MIDLANDS
Metal manufacturing
Vehicles
Pottery
Electrical engineering
Mechanical engineering
Distribution, hotels & catering

EAST ANGLIA
Agriculture, forestry & fishing
Food, drink & tobacco
Paper, printing & publishing
Construction
Distribution, hotels & catering

WALES
Agriculture, forestry & fishing
Mining
Metal manufacturing
Construction
Vehicles
Public administration
Professional & scientific services

GREATER LONDON
Paper, printing & publishing
Transport & communications
Banking, insurance, finance & business services
Public administration

SOUTH-WEST
Agriculture, forestry & fishing
Mechanical engineering
Shipbuilding
Construction
Distribution, hotels & catering
Professional & scientific services

REST OF SOUTH-EAST
Agriculture, forestry & fishing
Chemicals
Vehicles
Paper, printing & publishing
Electrical engineering
Distribution, hotels & catering
Professional & scientific services

Dounreay

Peterhead

Fasnakyle H

H Foyers

SCOTLAND

H Errochty
Rannoch H
H Clunie
H Cruachan
H Lochay

Sloy H

Longannet
Inverkip
Musselburgh
Cockenzie
Torness
Hunterston A&B
Motherwell

Chapelcross

NORTH

Workington
Hartlepool
Redcar
Calder Hall
Middlesbrough

Blyth B

Barrow
Heysham I
Heysham II
Selby

YORKSHIRE & HUMBERSIDE

Bradford
Drax
Ferrybridge C
Thorne
Eggborough
Scunthorpe
NORTH-WEST
Thorpe Marsh
Manchester
Rotherham
Wylfa
Birkenhead
Sheffield
West Burton A
Ince B
Fiddler's Ferry
Cottam
EAST MIDLANDS
High Marnham

H Dinorwic
H
H Ffestiniog
Wrexham
Stoke
Ratcliffe on Soar
Trawsfynydd
Park
Rugeley
Drakelow C
Asfordby
Ironbridge
EAST ANGLIA
Wednesbury
Dudley
Birmingham

H Rheidol
WALES
WEST MIDLANDS
Dawmill

GREATER LONDON
Sizewell A
Sizewell B

Bradwell

WALES
Pontypool
Berkeley
W. Thurrock
Tilbury B
Grain
Pembroke
Llanelli
Port Talbot
Oldbury
Didcot
Kingsnorth
Sheerness
Margam
Newport
Richborough
Aberthaw B
Cardiff
Littlebrook
SOUTH-EAST

SOUTH-WEST
REST OF SOUTH-EAST
Dungeness B
Dungeness A

Hinkley Point A&B

SOUTH-WEST
Fawley

H H
H
Winfrith

and the East Midlands, where costs are lowest and productivity highest produce over 60% of the total. A great local market exists in the thermal electricity generating stations which the Central Electricity Generating Board has erected along the River Trent and the rivers of Yorkshire (*see map page 140*). New reserves have been proved, for example at Selby in Yorkshire, where development is currently in progress, and at Asfordby, in North-East Leicestershire, where plans for development in the Vale of Belvoir aroused controversy on environmental grounds, and elsewhere. However, the problem is not so much one of reserves (for there is enough coal for 400-500 years at present rates of production), but of price and convenience. Output in 1986/7 was 106·9 m. tonnes of which 88·7 was deep mined. 79·5 m. tonnes were used in electricity generation. The 108 collieries now employ about 150,000 workers: productivity has increased to over 2·75 tonnes per manshift.

The ten years after 1965 saw a revolution in the geography of the UK fuel and power industries. The decline of coal was matched by the rise in importance of natural gas, first imported and then extracted from beneath the North Sea, the development of North Sea oil and the emergence of nuclear power.

The West Sole gas field was found in 1964 and offshore gas production began in 1967. By the early 1970s four major fields Leman, Indefatigable, Hewett and Viking were also in production. Since then, Frigg, West Sole, Rough and others have been tapped and natural gas is also produced in association with oil in other fields in the northern North Sea. Four North Sea terminal points, Bacton, Theddlethorpe, Easington and St Fergus are linked to the 5900-km (3700-mile) national high-pressure pipe-line system. North Sea gas meets some 77% of total natural gas supplies: most of the remainder comes from Norway. Further discoveries of natural gas in the North Sea, and the Morecambe field in the Irish Sea, ensure that indigenous production will continue to meet the major part of home needs for the next 20 years at least.

For many years small amounts of oil have been extracted from on-shore fields, notably from Eakring in Nottinghamshire. The discovery of oil in the North Sea in 1969 changed Britain's oil position dramatically, and the first oil flowed ashore in 1975. The scale of investment is indicated by the fact that by the end of 1986, 1109 exploration wells and 246 discoveries had been announced. Over 20 giant and many smaller fields have been proved. The North Sea provides a difficult environment for drilling, with high winds and steep waves, and costs are high. The oil is light and of low sulphur content and production is profitable. Among the largest fields in production and reserve are Forties, Brent, Piper and Ninian. Major investments have been made in 1660 km (1027 miles) of pipeline and in terminal facilities, notably at Sullom Voe in Shetland. Although Britain still needs to import heavy grades of crude oil these have been declining

Industry and Energy The listing of major industries derives from regional employment statistics; as industries such as steel become confined to a very few locations, the provision of a wide range of employment regionally becomes important. The areas of potential coalfields shown on the map are exploratory; by no means all are likely to be exploited.

and exports have increased so that the country has become a net oil exporter. Oil production reached a maximum in 1987 and may now decline slowly.

Our picture of fuel and energy resources must be completed by references to nuclear energy and hydro-electricity (*see map page 140*). Electricity from a nuclear power station (Calder Hall) first entered the Grid in 1956. The commissioning of Berkeley and Bradwell in 1962 marked an important stage in the development of a civil nuclear power programme and 16 stations are now in operation (14 of which are controlled by the electricity authorities). The government views nuclear energy as a major contributor to the future energy needs of the country and the planning of sites for new stations, including Sizewell B, has begun. Controversy exists over the scale of the programme required and the best type of system. Nuclear power stations generate 19% (1986) of Britain's electricity.

The contribution of hydro-electricity is mainly in the more remote areas, especially in Scotland. Hydro-electric power supplies only 2% of electricity requirements overall. Most potential sites for other than very small stations have been employed already. Pumped storage schemes have been developed to increase the scale of power stations.

More will be heard of the search for alternative sources of energy. Studies of the possibilities of tidal energy from the Severn estuary have been made. Experiments with wave energy methods have been begun. Investigations into geo-thermal possibilities are in progress. There are advocates of the greater use of wind power and some experiments. Unfortunately, Britain's climate does not encourage the large-scale development of solar energy even though solar water-heating systems do offer some promise. It will be many years yet before such alternative systems provide other than minor contributions to Britain's needs. Meanwhile there is much to be done in the field of energy conservation.

Industry

Since the end of World War II persistent efforts have been made to influence the location of Britain's industry. The Barlow Commission's Report of 1940 had drawn attention to the problems created by what was regarded as ill-balanced industrial growth in the southeast and the West Midlands, and the narrow industrial structures, declining industries and unemployment in South Wales, Tyneside, Clydeside and the northeast. Measures to remedy the lack of balance and to improve the diversity and the resilience of industries in the Development Areas, as they came to be called, were taken after the war. What has come to be called 'regional policy' developed. There have been, from time to time, changes in the boundaries of the areas delimited as requiring special help; the measures adopted have also varied in kind and in degree. Different governments have given more or less emphasis to regional policy, but the theme has remained a consistent one. Industrial firms seeking to expand their premises or build new plant in the southeast and West Midlands have been, until recently, subject to control through the need to seek Industrial Development Certificates. Those expanding or establishing themselves in Development Areas have been eligible for various forms of financial assistance.

Industrial estates were built in Development Areas and some factories were constructed in advance of need as a further incentive. The original concept of Development Areas was amended over time, and new designations were introduced. These included Special Development Areas where acute problems, such as the rapid decline in coal mining employment, were judged to merit higher levels of assistance, and Intermediate Areas where lesser benefits were made available after 1969 for areas where employment levels or other signs of sluggish economic performance as well as environment problems such as derelict land, a legacy of previous industry, gave rise to concern.

The assisted areas, taken together, came in the 1970s to include about 40% of the country's employed population; too large a share, in the eyes of some, for regional policy to be really effective. Many attempts have been made to evaluate the economic results, especially in terms of employment creation, of a policy which, despite some variations in practice, carried for a long time a strong political consensus. But policy evaluations of this kind are difficult exercises, even employing sophisticated statistical techniques, for it is impossible to know exactly what would have happened in the absence of such policies. Many studies have made favourable assessments of the effects of the measures taken to encourage job creation. One such study estimates that about 241,000 jobs were created in four large development areas (Scotland, Wales, Northern Ireland, Northern England) in the years 1960-76. By contrast, another suggests that we cannot be absolutely certain that regional policy measures have had any serious effect on the national distribution of industrial activity. The balance of view appears to be that without a regional policy matters would have been considerably worse in the assisted areas.

During the later 1970s, years of increasing unemployment, critical voices were raised. The high cost of the financial assistance (projected for 1982-83 in the 1978 White Paper as £609 million at 1979 price levels) was pointed out. In addition, high levels of unemployment were appearing also in certain parts of the so-called growth regions, e.g. in Birmingham and east London. The problem, therefore, was to encourage industrial growth and industrial location wherever it could be located. Industrial growth in the southeast should no longer be restricted for here, where scientific research was strongly located, were possibilities for developing science-based industries. And the southeast was well placed in relation to trade with the EEC.

At the time the Barlow Commission reported in 1940, manufacturing industry was, among the various sectors, the major employer of labour. The location of manufacturing industry was thus seen as the key to the location of employment and hence to the distribution of population. But times have changed and employment in manufacturing industry has declined both relatively and actually. By 1986 only 24·3% of Britain's employed workers were engaged in manufacturing, compared with 67% in the services group. And location policy had had only a limited effect on the distribution of the servicing industries. Between 1978 and 1986 manufacturing industries shed 2,042,000 workers or 28% of their workforce while jobs in the servicing group went up by 1,300,000 (9·8%).

Some writers refer to this change as a process of 'de-industrialisation', others refer to the 'de-skilling' that has arisen from the decline of jobs in the traditional industries located in the assisted areas. The location of manufacturing industry is no longer such an important factor in the general distribution of population as it once was. And, it is argued, the growth of multi-national corporations has placed decisions affecting important British industries in international, rather than national, hands.

A re-interpretation of regional policy in 1979 led to substantial savings in expenditure by 1982-83. The areas eligible for assistance were reduced to include only about 25% of the employed population. Further changes, including the abolition of Special Development Areas, were made in 1984. Early in 1988 it was decided to withdraw the automatic award of regional development grants and to put emphasis on encouraging local enterprise with assistance for small enterprises and innovation. So regional policy in its earlier sense is now less important. However a new development was initiated in 1981 to establish Enterprise Zones, where certain tax and administrative controls are relaxed (see map page 151). Examples may be found in Tyneside, Clydebank, Merseyside, Swansea, Corby and East London.

Since 1981, 7 Urban Development Corporations have also been set up to promote the regeneration of deprived urban areas. Other initiatives to assist Inner City problems have also been taken.

The emphasis so far has been on the effects of regional policy to influence employment location. But there are many other ways in which governments influence industrial location. Some basic industries, like steel, are nationalised: the re-organisation of the steel industry in the late 1970s led to the closure of many plants (eg. Consett, Shelton, Bilston and Corby) and to substantial reductions in the labour force leading to increased efficiency and renewed profitability (see map page 140). Other industries such as cotton textiles and tinplate have been re-organised with help provided under Acts of Parliament. Since 1966 government bodies have assisted rationalisation plans, have promoted new ventures and the introduction of modern technology. The list of industries in which the government has been involved is long. In addition to those already mentioned it includes shipbuilding, the motor-car industry, machine tools, the aerospace industries, not to mention oil, gas and electricity. But government has been withdrawing from direct involvement and pursuing a privatisation programme, e.g. British Gas, British Aerospace, Jaguar, Britoil.

In recent years the trend towards an economy based on 'service industry' has continued. There has also been a strong de-centralisation of employment from most of the major conurbations to the outer parts of the city regions and to medium and small towns and some rural areas. In the period 1971-81, for example, employment in the Greater London Conurbation declined by 8·8% or 378,000 persons and in other major conurbations by 352,000 (12·9%). By contrast, rates of growth in many medium-sized and small cities and towns were of the order of 10 to 15%.

Behind such changes lies the general problem of the decline in the total number of jobs, especially those for men.

Male full-time employment declined by over 1,100,000 in the years 1971-84, and although there has ben a substantial growth in the number of jobs (often part-time) for women, unemployment has become a major issue. In 1965 the general unemployment level was around 1·5%: in 1986 it was 11·7%. By early 1988 there were signs of improvement with the level down to 9·4%. Some writers have given a picture of growing regional economic convergence with a more even distribution of employment than in 1965 (*see map page 140*). 'Big industrial areas such as the South-east, North West and West Midlands,' writes one, 'have declined rapidly relative to small rural or peripheral regions such as East Anglia, the South West, Wales and Northern England.' The appearance of unemployment rates in the West Midlands at levels almost as high as in some development areas has certainly come as an unwelcome shock to an area long renowned for its growth.

So the problems have become more complex than was formerly assumed. To the continuing problem of the development areas created by structural decline of employment in basic and long established industries must be added the changes created by declining employment in other manufacturing industries such as the motor-car and related industries. There have been, too, shifts from big cities to smaller ones, a large-scale decentralisation which has left behind problems of regenerating employment in inner cities. Particular local problems, such as that in East London arising from the closure of the docks, add to the complexity.

Though, in the mid and later 1980s the economy has improved, large-scale unemployment may not disappear quickly. Those industries will benefit that have improved their productivity and international competitiveness. Science- and high-level engineering-based industries, many of which have survived and made progress, should grow further, but they are not mass employers of labour. Those service industries which are often termed 'quaternary industries', demanding high skills and providing international services, have also done well and should strengthen their position. There is great skill and much experience available and the development of imaginative education and re-training schemes could maximise the exploitation of future possibilities for the expansion of the economy.

Transport

'Good roads, canals and navigable rivers by diminishing the expenses of carriage put the remote parts of the country more nearly on a level with those in the neighbourhood of the town. They are upon that account the greatest of all improvements.' So wrote the great economist Adam Smith at the time of the Transport Revolution of the 18th century. However, it may be questioned whether the re-shaping of the British transport system in the past 30 years has had the same effect. It is arguable that recent improvements have emphasised the accessibility of places within the main inter-city network to the relative detriment of the more remote areas, and have worked to the advantage of some, and the disadvantage of other, groups of people.

The British economy depends upon an intensively developed efficient transport network for the rapid movement of people and goods between the principal industrial regions. About 60% of freight traffic is generated by or received in the 'axial belt' extending from Kent to Lancashire. The transport industries are themselves major employers with over 2 million people employed in transport and related industries like the manufacture and repair of motor-cars, railway vehicles and aircraft.

Changes in the use of the different modes of transport and technical changes have, at least over the most densely populated parts of the country, made for speed of transport and communication between cities. In terms of inland transport, road transport is now of the first importance. About 82% of all passenger travel is made by private car: there are some 17·2 million motor-cars in Britain. Over 80% of inland freight, by tonnage (60% of tonne-kilometres), is carried by road. To meet the problems of congestion on roads that are among the most crowded in the world a major improvement programme was initiated in 1955 and the motorway and improved trunk road network is the product of this. About 2968 km (1855 miles) of motorway have been constructed. Many motorways, together with the improved A1(M), focus on London, around which the M25 was completed in 1986. From the M1/M6 junction in the east Midlands motorways extend northwards on both sides of the Pennines. The system extends into south Wales and southwest to Exeter. The midland valley of Scotland has its own network. Except for the extension of the M40 towards Birmingham, few new major motorways are now planned; attention in road improvement will be given to congested strategic roads, e.g. to ports, and to new roads, including bypasses, that will improve the environment of towns and villages. For much of the existing road network originated in the early 18th and early 19th centuries. Towns grew around roads: now we are trying to take traffic around towns. But despite the introduction of traffic management schemes, traffic congestion remains in the main cities, especially London. Birmingham's Inner Ring Road is one successful example of a major new road development within a major city.

About 8% of passenger transport is accounted for by buses and coaches. This is a significant decline since 1960. Much however had been done to improve the organisation of public transport services in the main urban areas. 1987 saw the de-regulation of bus services opening up urban and rural routes to commercial competition.

The railway map exhibits a most dramatic re-shaping. A modernisation scheme of 1955 was overtaken by the Beeching Report of 1963 which brought subsequent closure of lines and stations and withdrawal of stopping train and local services on many other lines. The railway network had been reduced by about one-third to 16,670 km (10,418 miles) by the end of 1986. In 1962 there were 4347 stations open; by 1987 this number had fallen to 2405. The emphasis has been on improving the inter-city services. The main-line permanent way has been re-laid and about 25% of route-mileage is electrified. The Inter-City 125 services, first introduced in 1976, have proved successful; about 1,500 Inter-City expresses run each week-day. Less has been done to improve suburban services although, notably, the Tyne and Wear Metro was opened in 1980 and the London Docklands Light Railway in 1987. Policy for freight has

The Transport System

concentrated on long-distance and bulk traffic. Coal and coke, iron and steel and petroleum products are the most important commodities carried.

Britain's seaports have always played a crucial role in its economic development handling imported materials for manufacture and the exported manufactures. The scale of British seaborne trade, as measured by tonne-kilometes, has declined since 1973, partly because of the economic recession, and partly through the decrease in crude oil imports and the increasing share of European (that is, short-distance) trade. London remains the leading general sea-port though its older docks have now closed and much traffic is handled at Tilbury. Sullom Voe in Shetland is the leading oil port. The handling of North Sea oil has increased the trade of Tees, Forth and Flotta, in Orkney. Tees, Immingham, Port Talbot and Clyde handle imported ores. Recent developments include the growth of container and roll-on traffic which has more than trebled since 1970, especially at Dover, Felixstowe, Tilbury, Southampton and Harwich.

Inland waterways are much less important to the economy than in the days of the Industrial Revolution. Some of the old narrow canals have been closed; others are used by recreational craft. But the wider and deeper canals of Yorkshire and Humberside remain important and development of certain canals, such as that between Doncaster and Rotherham, and their re-equipment with push-tow barge trains are significant developments. The 58-km long (36-mile) Manchester Ship Canal remains in use.

Not the least important of recent changes in the transport network has been the construction of pipelines for the carriage of crude oil, petroleum products and natural gas (*see map page 139*). More than 1660 km (1031 miles) of submarine pipeline link the North Sea oilfields with the refineries and oil ports. Pipeline systems also carry refined products and natural gas to inland markets: one of the longest is the 423 km (263 mile) pipeline from Milford Haven to the Midlands and Manchester.

Of all the developments that illustrate the impact of technical change that of air transport stands out. The present siting of Britain's airports reflects many circumstances, including the needs of the RAF, decisions by government and local authorities and the location of the markets for air traffic. Except for London, there has been little national co-ordination in airport development. Plans for new airports such as the Third London Airport, now to be at Stansted, arouse high controversy especially on environmental grounds. A hierarchy of airports may be discerned ranging from major international (Heathrow) through those operating medium- and short-haul international and domestic services, those operating charter services, to the small airports with limited facilities mainly serving regional needs. Although much discussion of air transport is in terms of passenger movements, its contribution to freight transport should not be overlooked. Less than 1% of Britain's overseas trade measured by weight is carried by air but this amounts to about 20% by value. This is heavily concentrated at London, which in terms of the value of freight handled is now Britain's leading port.

Many tasks remain, for example the Channel Tunnel now under construction, but the modernisation of the transport system has been a remarkable achievement. The Severn, Forth and Humber bridges, the High Speed Train, the virtual completion of the motorway system, the Victoria and Jubilee Lines of London Transport, the North Sea pipelines are symbols of the change. But some argue that the changes which have been designed to link the major industrial areas and to promote resource development and trade have left many rural areas relatively worse off than before, bereft of railway services and with reduced bus services. Also relatively worse off are those like the poor and the elderly who do not own private transport and have been affected by reduced public transport services. But the problem in part reflects the shape of Britain and the concentration of its population. It is theoretically possible to devise a basic route network for a road or railway system of only 1550 km (970 miles) which would reach to within 9 km of half the population and a more extended network of 2800 km (1750 miles) to reach 70%. But to serve the most remote 30% an additional network of over 6000 km (3750 miles) would be required.

Planning for Land

One of the most fruitful aspects of planning since the 1939-45 war has been the care that has been taken over the use of the land of Britain. Although cities and urban life styles have spread outwards, our countryside, though not unchanged, retains its variety and its beauty, even though it provides more and more of the food, water and leisure of the urban population. The Committee on Land Utilisation in Rural Areas (the Scott Committee) in 1942 had expressed concern at the spread of cities over the countryside, and its recommendations provided pathways for fresh thinking and eventual legislation. Another pathway led, after much discussion, to the National Parks and Access to the Countryside Act of 1949, applying to England and Wales (*see map page 150*). The ten National Parks protect some of the most exceptionally beautiful areas of the countryside: they also provide for access and enjoyment by the general public. In so highly developed a country as Britain, it was impossible to draw boundaries around such areas without also including large numbers of towns and villages—and so the National Parks also include the working environments of the communities within them. Out of this situation, many conflicts have developed on such questions as the preservation of scenery and how far development such as new limestone quarries in the Peak District, a new trunk road through the Lake District, minerals exploration in Snowdonia, should be permitted. In Scotland a different scheme was adopted, with the establishment of National Scenic Areas and Forest Parks, and the Forestry Commission there as well as in some English forests has done much to improve the compatibility of tree production and the growing demand for recreation. The problems that exist over the objectives of National Parks should not be allowed to cloud the great benefits which the public have gained from the measures taken both to protect the parks and to display their individually distinctive characteristics.

It is not only in National Parks that special care is taken over new development. there are also 36 Areas of Outstanding Natural Beauty in England and Wales (11% of the area)

Agriculture and Fisheries

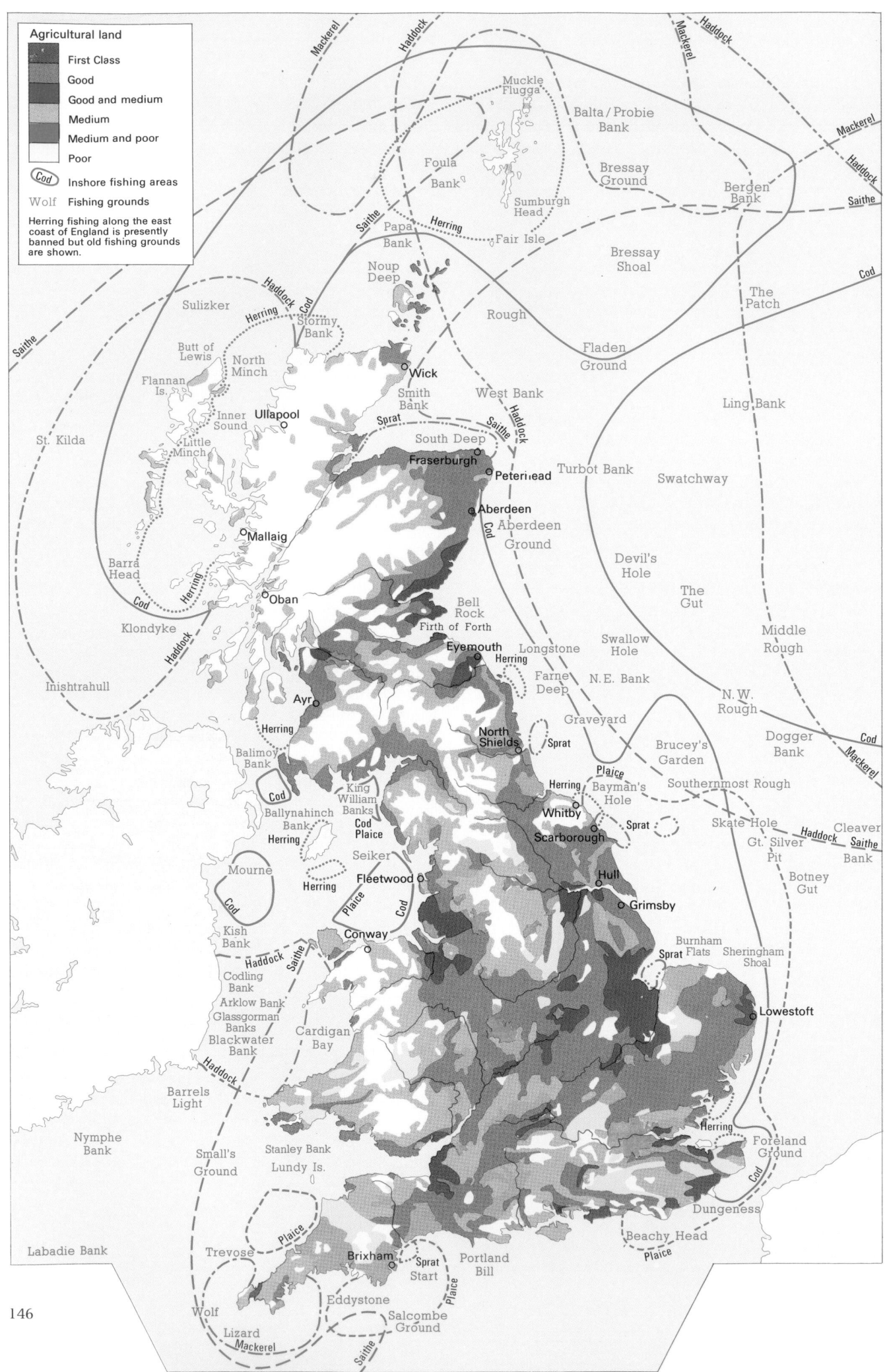

Agricultural land

- First Class
- Good
- Good and medium
- Medium
- Medium and poor
- Poor

(Cod) Inshore fishing areas

Wolf Fishing grounds

Herring fishing along the east coast of England is presently banned but old fishing grounds are shown.

Mackerel   Haddock   Mackerel   Haddock

Muckle Flugga

Balta / Probie Bank

Bressay Ground

Bergen Bank

Mackerel

Haddock

Saithe

Foula Bank

Sumburgh Head

Bressay Shoal

Saithe

Papa Bank

Herring   Fair Isle

Cod

Sulizker

Haddock   Cod

Herring   Stormy Bank

Noup Deep

Rough

Fladen Ground

The Patch

Butt of Lewis

North Minch

Smith Bank

West Bank

Ling Bank

Flannan Is.

Inner Sound

○Wick

Sprat

South Deep

Haddock

Saithe

Turbot Bank

Swatchway

St. Kilda

Ullapool

Little Minch

○Fraserburgh   Peterhead●

Aberdeen

Aberdeen Ground

Devil's Hole

Mallaig

The Gut

Barra Head

Herring

○Oban

Bell Rock

Firth of Forth

Middle Rough

Klondyke

Cod   Haddock

Eyemouth○

Herring

Longstone

Farne Deep

N.E. Bank

Swallow Hole

Inishtrahull

○Ayr

Herring

North Shields●

Sprat

Graveyard

N.W. Rough

Dogger Bank

Cod   Mackerel

Balimoy Bank

Plaice

Brucey's Garden

Southernmost Rough

King William Banks

Cod   Plaice

Herring   Bayman's Hole

Ballynahinch Bank

Whitby●

Skate Hole

Haddock   Cleaver

Saithe   Bank

Herring

Scarborough●

Sprat

Gt. Silver Pit

Seiker

Mourne

Cod

Herring

Fleetwood○   Plaice

Hull●

Botney Gut

Plaice   Cod

○Grimsby

Kish Bank

Conway○

Haddock   Saithe

Burnham Flats   Sheringham Shoal

Codling Bank

Sprat

Arklow Bank

Glassgorman Banks

Cardigan Bay

Blackwater Bank

Haddock

Lowestoft●

Barrels Light

Nymphe Bank

Small's Ground

Stanley Bank

Lundy Is.

Herring

Foreland Ground

Cod

Dungeness

Labadie Bank

Trevose   Plaice   Portland Bill

Beachy Head

Brixham○   Sprat Start   Plaice

Plaice

Wolf   Eddystone   Salcombe Ground

Lizard   Mackerel   Saithe

146

Farming Types

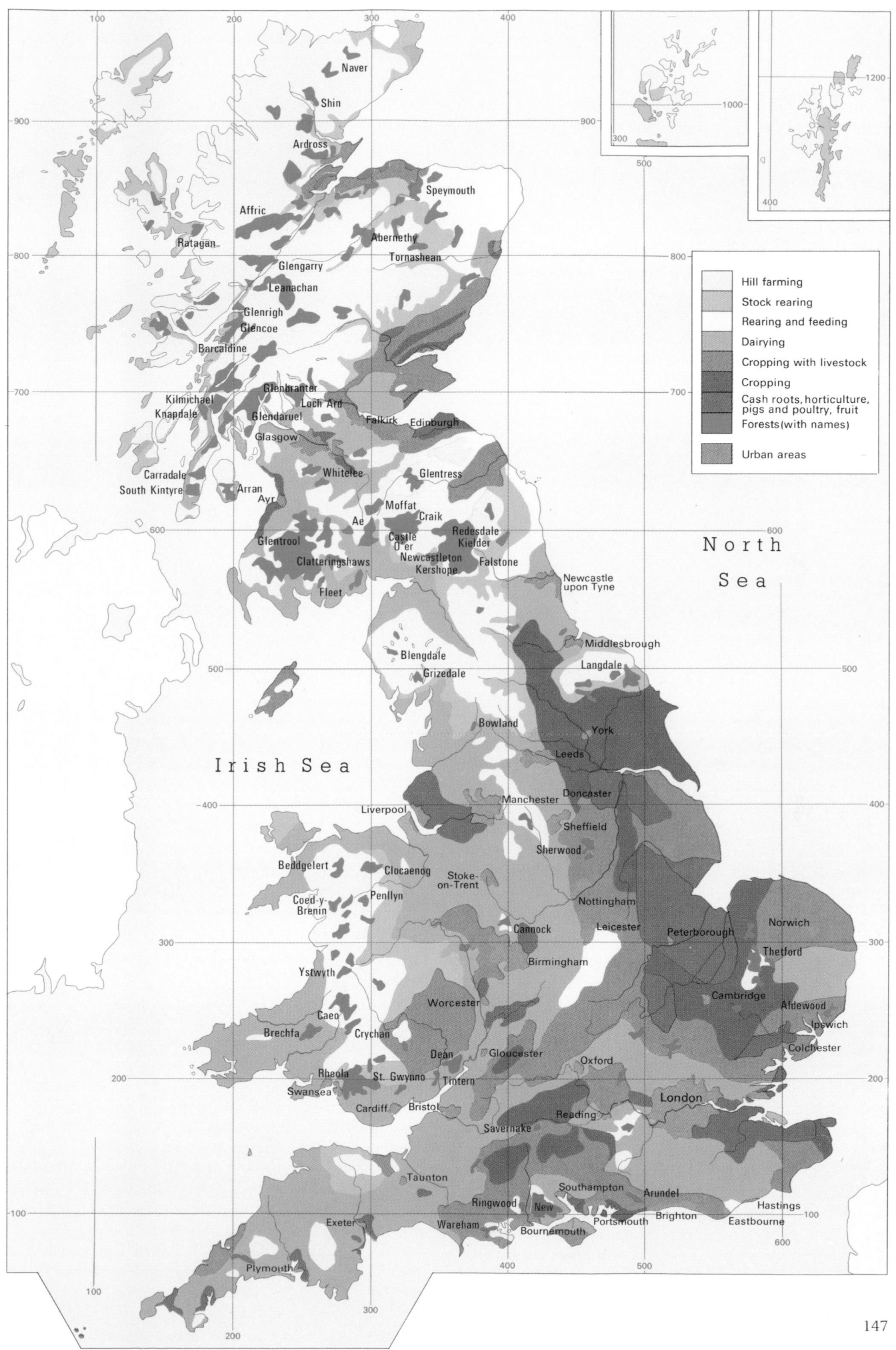

Hill farming
Stock rearing
Rearing and feeding
Dairying
Cropping with livestock
Cropping
Cash roots, horticulture,
pigs and poultry, fruit
Forests (with names)

Urban areas

North
Sea

Irish Sea

Naver
Shin
Ardross
Speymouth
Affric
Abernethy
Ratagan
Tornashean
Glengarry
Leanachan
Glenrigh
Glencoe
Barcaldine
Glenbranter
Kilmichael
Loch Ard
Knapdale
Glendaruel
Falkirk
Edinburgh
Glasgow
Carradale
Whitelee
Glentress
South Kintyre
Arran
Ayr
Moffat
Ae
Craik
Glentrool
Castle
Redesdale
O'er
Kielder
Clatteringshaws
Newcastleton
Falstone
Kershope
Fleet
Newcastle
upon Tyne
Middlesbrough
Blengdale
Langdale
Grizedale
Bowland
York
Leeds
Manchester
Doncaster
Liverpool
Sheffield
Sherwood
Beddgelert
Clocaenog
Nottingham
Coed-y-
Penllyn
Stoke-
on-Trent
Brenin
Cannock
Leicester
Peterborough
Norwich
Birmingham
Thetford
Ystwyth
Cambridge
Caeo
Worcester
Aldewood
Brechfa
Crychan
Ipswich
Dean
Gloucester
Colchester
Rheola
St. Gwynno
Oxford
Swansea
Tintern
London
Cardiff
Bristol
Reading
Savernake
Taunton
Southampton
Arundel
Ringwood
New
Hastings
Exeter
Wareham
Portsmouth
Brighton
Eastbourne
Bournemouth
Plymouth

147

including areas such as the Shropshire hills, the Cotswolds, the Chilterns and the North and South Downs (*see map page 150*). Great progress has also been made in delimiting Heritage Coasts where development is carefully controlled by local authorities. Long-distance footpaths have been signposted and offer splendid opportunities alike for the serious walker and for the gentle stroller.

The need was later seen, and provided for in the Countryside Act of 1968, for recreational access to the smaller but often very lovely areas near to the main cities. By 1986 some 206 Country Parks and 240 Picnic Sites had been established, mainly by local authorities, with the aid of grants from the Countryside Commission for England and Wales. There is a similar, but separate, Commission for Scotland and its plans, based on the distinct landscape characteristics of Scotland and embodying a somewhat different approach from that adopted south of the border, also deserve careful study.

The Scott Committee also argued that good-quality agricultural land should not be used for urban development when land of lesser quality was available. In order to define the extent of the areas of good-, medium- and low-quality farmland a number of land classification schemes have been produced (*see map page 146*). Generally these gradings take account principally of physical conditions such as aspect, height, climate, soil type and drainage conditions but the quality of management is also an important consideration. At present the Ministry of Agriculture recognises five main grades of land and these gradings are used in planning decisions, such as those about urban growth or the lines selected for trunk roads. The amount of truly first-class land is small, about 3% of the total for England and Wales. Grade 2 land, which has minor limitations of soil texture, soil depth or drainage, accounts for about 15%. Including the better areas of Grade 3 (land with moderate limitations) it may be reckoned that about one-third of the agricultural area of England and Wales is of reasonably good quality. Grade 3 land is in fact of diverse qualities ranging from quite good to rather poor and the whole category includes 49% of the total land area. Grades 4 and 5 (poor, but often still useful, land) account for a further one-third of England and Wales.

Taken with what has been written in the Introduction about climatic conditions, it will be seen that farming in Britain has to contend with a very diverse range of conditions. Generally speaking the farming patterns that result (*see map page 147*) represent a sophisticated adjustment to physical conditions, to market demands and to changing agricultural technology. Taken overall Britain is a country of mixed farming: the main arable areas are found mainly in the east and some parts of the Midlands and southern England. By contrast, in the west, where rainfall and relief make arable cropping difficult, grassland for livestock production predominates. The hill areas are very valuable for the production of young livestock.

There are about 260,000 farming units in the United Kingdom. However, many of these are part-time holdings and a recent estimate of the number of *bona fide* farm businesses puts the number at about 130,000, with an average overall size of 106 HA (262 acres). Less than a quarter employ more than four farm workers and the number of regular full-time workers has dropped from about 700,000 in 1946 to about 200,000 today. Of all the countries of Western Europe, Britain has the smallest percentage of its population engaged in agriculture. Output per man is high. About 2% of the country's labour force produces 80% of the country's needs of temperate foodstuffs.

In part this situation is the product of greatly improved technology. The 350,000 horses who worked on farms in 1950 have been replaced by machines. Farming has become capital- and energy-related. About one million tonnes of nitrogen fertilisers are applied to the land each year. Chemical pesticides have played their part. The farming industry has become much more closely related to manufacturing industry and rural-urban interdependence has, in this respect, been intensified.

A second factor behind this position is the support received from the State. After World War II the Government declared its intention to foster a healthy, prosperous and efficient agriculture and under the Agriculture Act of 1948 the Minister of Agriculture supported farmers by deficiency payments on certain commodities, as well as by grants and subsidies of various kinds. The system changed when Britain entered the EEC. Under the Common Agricultural Policy the farmers' prices are maintained by EEC intervention in the marketplace. Argument exists over the Common Agricultural Policy and its effects and it is probably in British interests to obtain changes in its operation. Some reforms were made in 1986: milk production was reduced and beef support prices were lowered.

While many rejoice in the achievements of the industry, others count the cost of change. Many small farms have been amalgamated into larger holdings. In many parts of the country woodlands and hedgerows have been removed, downland and moorland have been ploughed up, and the loss of wild landscape and wildlife is the result. Some complain that too much continuous cropping may eventually affect adversely the quality of the land, others attack factory farming and the over-use of fertilisers. 16 areas of high quality landscape have been designated 'Environmentally Sensitive Areas': farmers in these areas may qualify for payments to continue traditional farming methods and maintain the beauty of the countryside.

The argument may be extended to the fate of villages and rural communities. Some have lost population; churches and shops have closed and public transport services have been reduced or withdrawn. Others, nearer the great cities, have been overwhelmed by the influx of newcomers with urban ways of life, jobs in the city and homes in the countryside. The nature of change varies from area to area. But while the agricultural industry has its critics and while not all that has been done in its name may have been wise, it must be admitted that it has contributed greatly to the maintenance of the British countryside and to the improvement of the British economy.

Planning for the Environment and Regional Change
Several schemes for the future welfare and development of Britain were produced during and immediately after World War II. These included plans for the re-development of cities, many of which had been badly damaged by war-time

bombing and where inherited housing problems existed, plans for the more equitable distribution of industry and employment between the regions, and plans for the rural environment, including conservation of the scenic environment and the future prosperity of agriculture.

The Greater London Plan (1944) by Sir Patrick Abercrombie is a leading example of post-war planning. As was generally thought at the time, it assumed that population would not greatly increase: the problem was the re-distribution of people rather than of growth. It embodied the desire to prevent urban sprawl and to contain the growth of cities and employed the idea of a Green Belt on to which the London conurbation would not expand. The re-building of the bomb-damaged and the poor-quality housing of inner London was a priority. However, to accomplish lower densities and with more open space, it would be necessary to move large numbers of families and jobs out of London and New Towns were to be built for this purpose. The problems of the great city had to be solved on a regional scale. Abercrombie's ideas were applied for Greater London with modifications in detail and the eight New Towns which were begun, Crawley, Bracknell, Hemel Hempstead, Hatfield, Welwyn Garden City, Stevenage, Harlow and Basildon provided exciting opportunities for architects and town planners (see map page 151). Not all the New Towns built then and later have been equally successful and criticisms can be made with hindsight. Nevertheless the post-war New Towns are widely regarded as an achievement for British town planning.

Such ideas of regional-scale planning were not at first adopted so readily in other urban regions, such as in Manchester and Birmingham. However, much was done, especially in Birmingham, to demolish slums and to build a new inner-urban environment with an inner ring road, new housing areas and more green spaces. New Towns were begun also at Corby (Northamptonshire), Newton Aycliffe and Peterlee in the northeast, Cwmbran (south Wales) and East Kilbride, Glenrothes and Cumbernauld in Scotland.

The Town and Country Planning Act (1947) provided powers for local authorities on development control and land-use change. Green Belts were delimited around the conurbations and other cities of special quality.

The 1950s brought a changed situation. Population grew by 5% between 1951 and 1961 and the extra numbers had to be provided for. While, for the time being at least, employment remained concentrated in cities, people began to move their houses to towns and villages beyond the Green Belts. Widespread ownership of motor cars brought more flexibility in movements to work. Supplementary schemes were needed. Around London, 'expanded' towns like Ashford, Thetford and Bletchley were added to the New Towns programme. Cities like Birmingham, constrained by local authority boundaries, had to look outside their boundaries for housing land, and found themselves in conflict with the surrounding county councils. The decentralisation of population from major cities became a still more obvious phenomenon in the 1960s, accompanied now by a relative decentralisation of jobs. The older urban pattern of compact cities was changing into a pattern of 'city regions'. A second wave of New Town construction was embarked upon involving the building of New Towns including Milton Keynes mid-way between London and Birmingham and in the east Midlands (Peterborough, Northampton), the west Midlands (Redditch, Telford), the northwest (Skelmersdale, Runcorn, Warrington, Central Lancashire), the northeast (Washington), Wales (Newtown) and Scotland (Livingston, Irvine). Population grew by a further 5% between 1961 and 1971, and the expectations of a continued growth, the desire to relate plans for town and country with those for transport, the provision of services, and employment, led to a re-thinking for planning on a regional scale in the mid- and later 1960s. Regional Economic Planning Councils (since discontinued) were established for this task and produced a series of reports. Broad 'structure' planning replaced detailed land-use based planning.

Meanwhile the larger cities continued to lose population and jobs, from inner and suburban areas. The tendency for dispersion involving the growth of towns of medium and small sizes produced an extension of urban Britain, confirming the tendency towards 'megalopolis', the functionally-linked zone of city regions and high population densities extending from the Channel coast to Lancashire and Yorkshire. But the 1970s did not bring the expected continued growth in population (an increase of only 0.3% in Great Britain 1971–81), and, as one report put it, 'Britain's main cities are losing population in a big rush to the countryside'. The population of Greater London fell by 10% to 6.77 m (1985), or below the 1901 population of the same area, with the inner London boroughs losing between 12% and 26% of their populations. In 1961 Southwark had 313,000 people; in 1981, 212,000. Manchester (−17%), Liverpool (−16%), Salford (−13%), Newcastle-upon-Tyne (−10%), Nottingham (−10%), Birmingham (−8%) also demonstrate the trend (see map page 152). However in the mid 1980s these rates of population decline began to lessen.

By contrast, population has been increasing in the outer rings around conurbations. There is a crescent of increase in the southeast from Norfolk to the Solent, and smaller but similar areas of increase around the west Midland conurbation, south of Manchester, in the east Midlands and beyond Glasgow and Edinburgh. Northeast Scotland has increased its population, mainly the result of oil and oil-related developments. So has the southwest peninsula to which many retired people have moved. The patterns of decentralisation and dispersion noted for the 1950s and 1960s have intensified and extended in the 1970s and early 1980s.

Not all these changes are the direct results of town planning, though the policies of containing the outward

Planning for Leisure Preservation of the countryside for leisure purposes has involved planning both nationally—with the establishment of the National Parks, areas of outstanding natural beauty and long-distance footpaths—and regionally, by the tourist boards and county councils.

Planning for Industry Post-war planning has attempted to break out of the 'industrial coffin' by the encouragement of Development Areas and New Towns. Green belts and areas of outstanding natural beauty are subject to rigorous development constraints, whereas sites of scientific, landscape and historic interest are given varying degrees of protection.

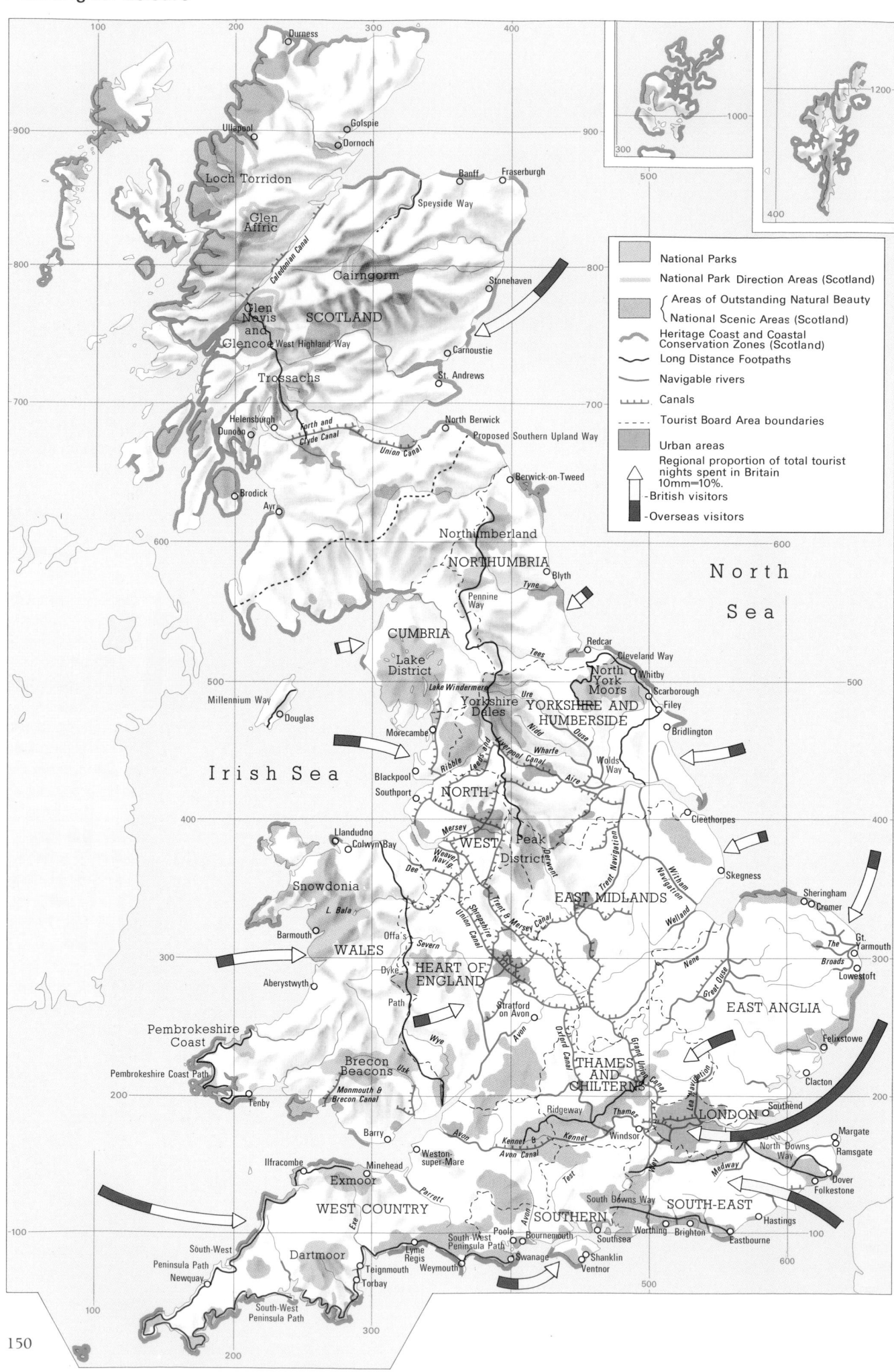

Planning for Industry

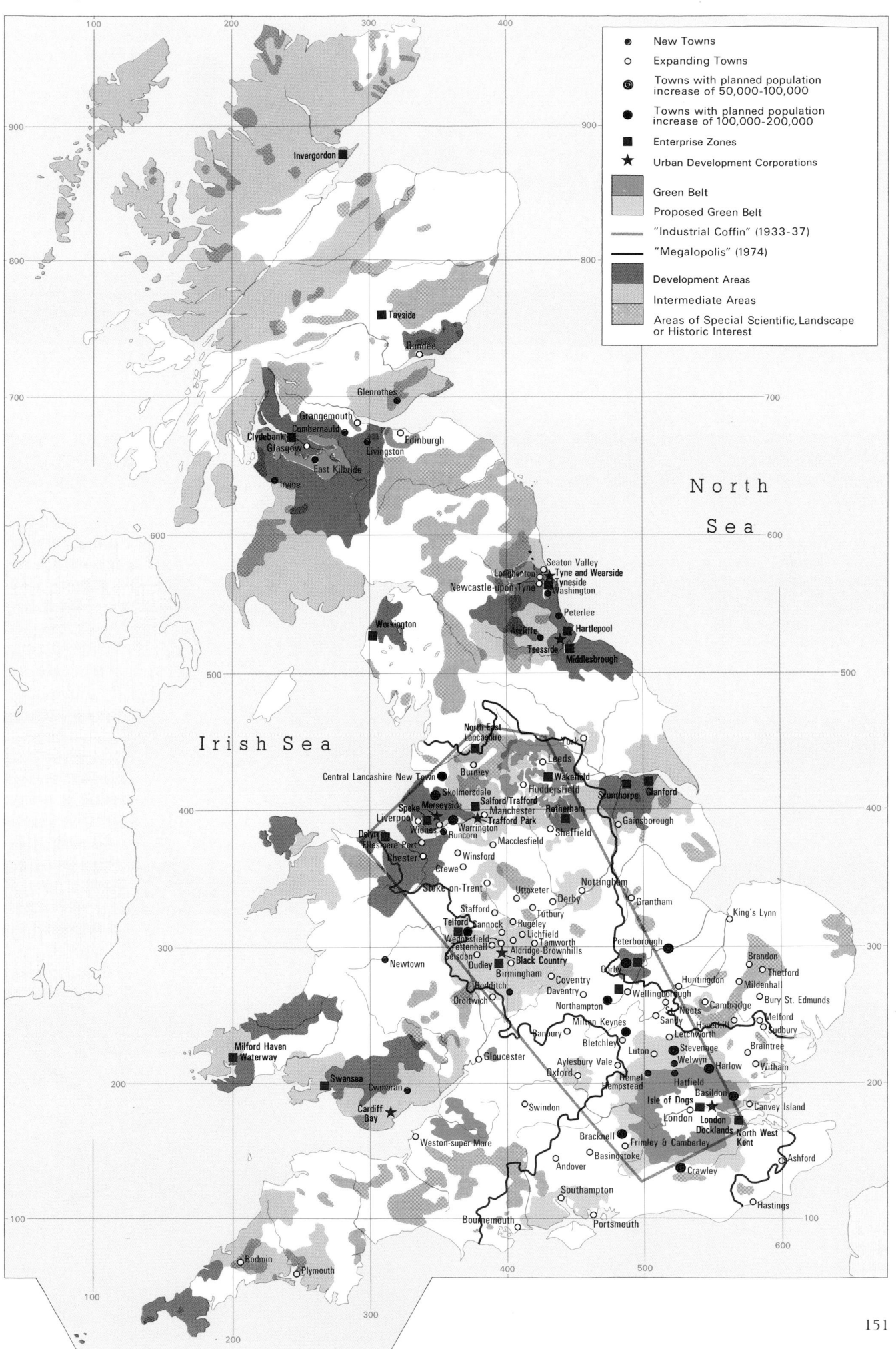

Legend:

- ◉ New Towns
- ○ Expanding Towns
- ◉ Towns with planned population increase of 50,000–100,000
- ● Towns with planned population increase of 100,000–200,000
- ■ Enterprise Zones
- ★ Urban Development Corporations
- Green Belt
- Proposed Green Belt
- "Industrial Coffin" (1933–37)
- "Megalopolis" (1974)
- Development Areas
- Intermediate Areas
- Areas of Special Scientific, Landscape or Historic Interest

North Sea

Irish Sea

Invergordon

Tayside

Dundee

Glenrothes

Grangemouth
Cumbernauld
Clydebank
Glasgow
East Kilbride
Livingston
Edinburgh
Irvine

Seaton Valley
Loughington Tyne and Wearside
Newcastle-upon-Tyne Tyneside
Washington
Peterlee
Workington
Aycliffe Hartlepool
Teesside
Middlesbrough

North East Lancashire
York
Leeds
Burnley
Central Lancashire New Town Wakefield
Skelmersdale Huddersfield
Merseyside Salford/Trafford Scunthorpe Glanford
Speke Manchester Rotherham
Liverpool Trafford Park Gainsborough
Widnes Warrington Sheffield
Delyn Runcorn Macclesfield
Ellesmere Port Winsford
Chester Nottingham
Crewe
Stoke-on-Trent Uttoxeter Derby Grantham
King's Lynn
Stafford Tutbury
Telford Cannock Rugeley Peterborough
Wednesfield Lichfield Brandon
Tettenhall Tamworth Thetford
Seisdon Aldridge-Brownhills Corby Mildenhall
Newtown Dudley Black Country Huntingdon Bury St. Edmunds
Birmingham Cambridge
Redditch Coventry Wellingborough Melford
Droitwich Daventry St. Neots Havehill Sudbury
Northampton Sandy Braintree
Gloucester Milton Keynes Letchworth Witham
Banbury Bletchley Stevenage
Aylesbury Vale Luton Welwyn Harlow
Oxford Hemel Hatfield
Hempstead Isle of Dogs Basildon
Swansea Swindon London Canvey Island
Cwmbran London North West
Cardiff Bay Bracknell Docklands Kent
Weston-super-Mare Frimley & Camberley Ashford
Basingstoke
Andover Crawley
Southampton
Bodmin Hastings
Plymouth Bournemouth Portsmouth

Milford Haven Waterway

151

Population Patterns

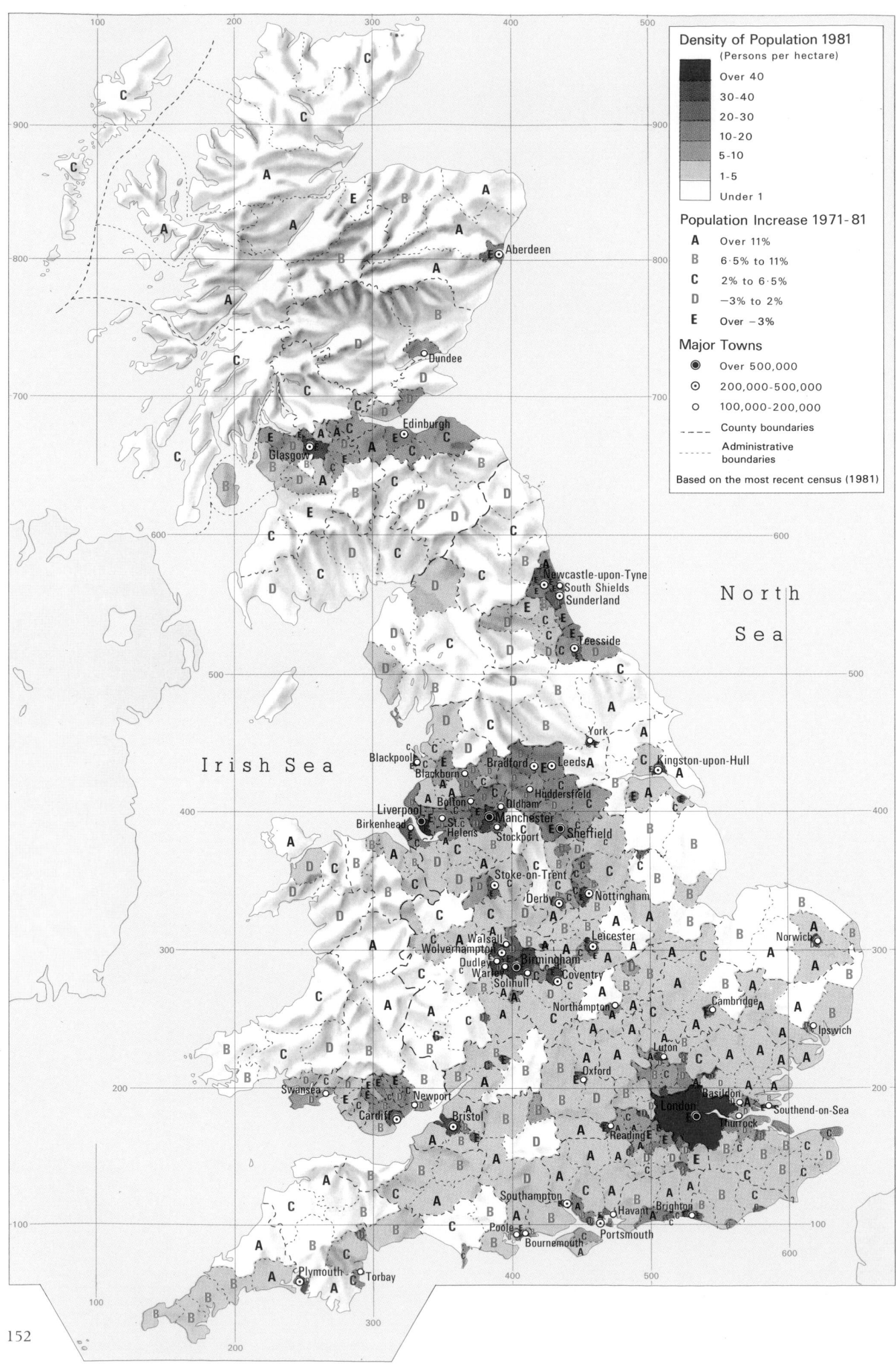

Density of Population 1981
(Persons per hectare)

- Over 40
- 30-40
- 20-30
- 10-20
- 5-10
- 1-5
- Under 1

Population Increase 1971-81

- **A** Over 11%
- **B** 6·5% to 11%
- **C** 2% to 6·5%
- **D** −3% to 2%
- **E** Over −3%

Major Towns

- ◉ Over 500,000
- ⊙ 200,000-500,000
- ○ 100,000-200,000
- - - - County boundaries
- ········· Administrative boundaries

Based on the most recent census (1981)

North Sea

Irish Sea

Aberdeen
Dundee
Edinburgh
Glasgow

Newcastle-upon-Tyne
South Shields
Sunderland
Teesside

York
Kingston-upon-Hull
Blackpool
Blackburn
Bradford
Leeds
Bolton
Oldham
Huddersfield
Liverpool
Manchester
Sheffield
Birkenhead
St. Helens
Stockport
Stoke-on-Trent
Derby
Nottingham
Walsall
Leicester
Norwich
Wolverhampton
Dudley
Birmingham
Warley
Solihull
Coventry
Cambridge
Northampton
Ipswich
Luton
Oxford
Swansea
Basildon
Newport
London
Southend-on-Sea
Cardiff
Bristol
Thurrock
Reading
Southampton
Havant
Brighton
Poole
Portsmouth
Bournemouth
Plymouth
Torbay

Cultural Diversity

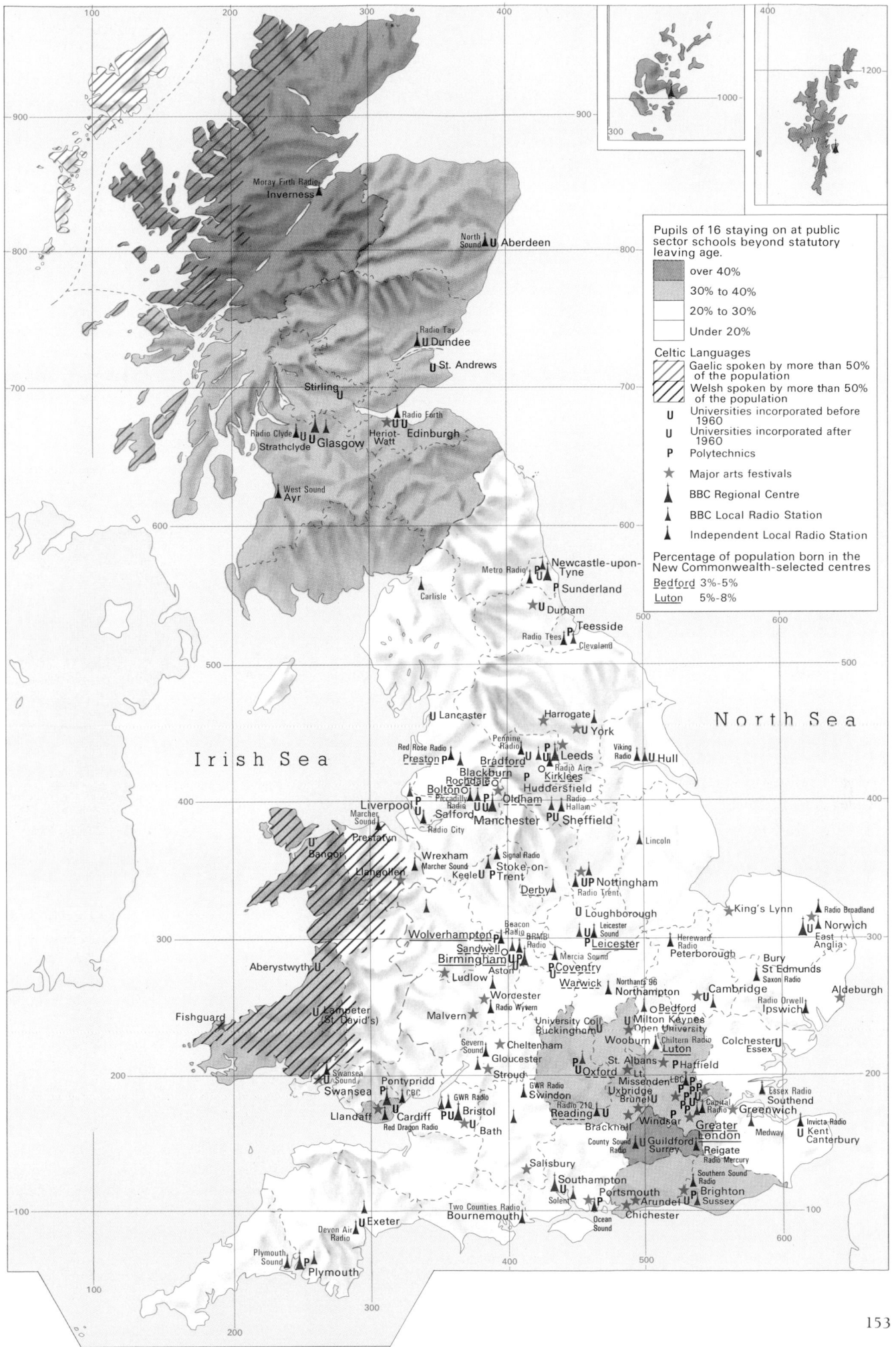

Map legend

Pupils of 16 staying on at public sector schools beyond statutory leaving age.
- over 40%
- 30% to 40%
- 20% to 30%
- Under 20%

Celtic Languages
- Gaelic spoken by more than 50% of the population
- Welsh spoken by more than 50% of the population

- U Universities incorporated before 1960
- U Universities incorporated after 1960
- P Polytechnics
- ★ Major arts festivals
- BBC Regional Centre
- BBC Local Radio Station
- Independent Local Radio Station

Percentage of population born in the New Commonwealth-selected centres
- Bedford 3%-5%
- Luton 5%-8%

Map labels

Irish Sea
North Sea

Moray Firth Radio — Inverness
North Sound — Aberdeen
Radio Tay — U Dundee
St. Andrews
Stirling
Radio Forth — Heriot-Watt Edinburgh
Radio Clyde — Strathclyde Glasgow
West Sound — Ayr

Carlisle
Metro Radio — Newcastle-upon-Tyne
Sunderland
Durham
Radio Tees — Teesside
Cleveland

Lancaster
Harrogate — York
Red Rose Radio — Preston
Pennine Radio — Bradford
Blackburn — Radio Aire
Rochdale — Kirklees
Bolton — Huddersfield
Piccadilly Radio — Oldham
Liverpool — Radio Hallam
Salford — Manchester — Sheffield
Radio City
Viking Radio — Hull

Marcher Sound
Prestatyn
Bangor
Wrexham — Signal Radio
Llangollen — Marcher Sound
Keele — Stoke-on-Trent
Derby
Lincoln
Radio Trent — Nottingham
Loughborough
King's Lynn — Radio Broadland

Aberystwyth
Leicester Sound
Wolverhampton — Beacon Radio
Sandwell — BRMB Radio
Birmingham — Hereward Radio
Aston
Mercia Sound
Ludlow — Coventry
Worcester — Warwick
Radio Wyvern — Northants 96 — Northampton
Malvern — Cambridge
Peterborough
Bury St Edmunds — Saxon Radio
Aldeburgh

Lampeter (St. David's)
University Coll Buckingham
Bedford
Radio Orwell — Ipswich
Fishguard
Severn Sound — Cheltenham
Gloucester
Stroud
Milton Keynes Open University
Wooburn — Chiltern Radio — Luton
Colchester Essex

Swansea Sound
Pontypridd — CBC
GWR Radio — Swindon
GWR Radio
Radio 210
St. Albans — Hatfield
Oxford — Missenden
Brunel — Uxbridge
Capital Radio — Essex Radio
Southend
Greenwich
Llandaff — Cardiff
Red Dragon Radio
Bristol
Bath
Reading — Bracknell
Windsor
Greater London
Guildford Surrey
Reigate — Radio Mercury
Invicta Radio
Medway
Kent Canterbury

Salisbury
County Sound Radio
Southern Sound Radio
Southampton
Solent
Portsmouth
Arundel — Chichester
Brighton Sussex

Two Counties Radio — Bournemouth
Ocean Sound
Devon Air Radio — Exeter
Plymouth Sound — Plymouth

153

spread of the conurbations and decentralisation have set the general pattern. It is the consequences of these changes for the inner city that now cause concern. There is the contrast between the outer parts of the city regions peopled by young, middle-class families and many of the older parts of the inner city with older, poorer and less skilled workers living in pre-1914 houses or more recently-built high-rise blocks and council estates. Industries have moved out or have died. In some areas there are high proportions of ethnic minorities. The inner-city problem has been the most recent major town planning task. But while there is a general problem, each inner-city area presents its own distinctive problems. The London Docklands, now partly re-developed, are very different from Lambeth and Brixton. The tasks of renewal in Inner Birmingham are not the same as in Liverpool or Glasgow. So planning for urban deprivation had taken precedence in the 1970s with many special studies and the emergence of special grants, programmes and partnership schemes between local and central government. The urban riots of 1981 drew further attention to the problem, especially in south London, Manchester and Liverpool. There are signs of progress but the re-creation of the environments of the inner cities continues to be a major task. Funding for the Urban Programme has been greatly increased.

Local Government

The reforms of local government of 1888 and 1894, intended to produce a pattern adapted to the age of the industrial city, also confirmed the existence of units such as the county whose origins lay in early medieval times (*see map page 156*). By the late 1950s and 1960s it had become widely recognised that further major reforms were necessary in the wake of the changes in population distribution, changes in city size, shape and needs and the greater responsibilities, including housing and town planning, which local government had assumed. Royal Commissions on local government in London, England, Wales and Scotland were established. The first result was the establishment in 1963 of the Greater London Council responsible for certain functions for the whole of the London conurbation with a second tier of London Boroughs. The Report of the 'Maud' Royal Commission on Local Government in England in 1969, which included two possible sets of proposals, was hotly argued. The new pattern was set up in 1974 (*see map page 157*). It was based on a smaller number of counties (achieved, for instance, through the amalgamation of Herefordshire and Worcestershire) and county districts, but with metropolitan authorities for major conurbations (such as West Midlands, Merseyside, West Yorkshire, South Yorkshire, and Tyne and Wear). However, the metropolitan government authorities were abolished in 1986.

Population Patterns Although the 1981 census showed overall little growth since 1971, it gave evidence of considerable movement of people, especially from the old cities into the countryside around. Some inner city areas lost more than a quarter of their population.

Cultural Diversity The 1960s and 1970s saw a general growth in cultural activity outside the largest towns, sometimes spontaneous and sometimes deliberately fostered. The revival of Celtic traditions and new ethnic minorities in many towns have brought a new cultural mix to Britain.

Wales now has eight county councils (five with historic Welsh names) and 36 district councils; these replace 13 counties, four county boroughs and 164 district councils.

For Scotland, the 'Wheatley' Royal Commission reported in 1969. Its general principles were accepted with amendments and the pattern established by the Local Government (Scotland) Act 1973, by contrast with that in England, accepted the regional principle. It represents a more logical attempt to establish economic and social entities for cities and countryside. There are nine regions, 53 districts and three all-purpose island councils. Local government responsibilities in Scotland differ in certain respects from those in England.

Meanwhile the wider problems of the devolution of political and administrative responsibilities from Westminster were under study by the Kilbrandon Royal Commission on the Constitution, whose report appeared in 1973. Ever since the Union of Scotland and England in 1707 the arrangements for the government of Scotland have differed in some important respects from those in England. Scotland has its own systems of law and education. In 1885 the office of Secretary of State for Scotland was created, and he discharges functions that for England are exercised by the Home Office, the Departments of the Environment, Education and Science, some aspects of the Department of Health and Social Security, and the Ministry of Agriculture. A separate Welsh Ministry was established in 1951 and strengthened in 1964 but its responsibilities, while wide, are less than those of the Scottish Office.

The re-emergence of national feeling at the political level was channelled in the 1960s and early 1970s into campaigns for devolution. Proposals for devolution were brought forward by the government in 1974 and 1975 based on the preservation of the unity of the UK and rejecting federal solutions. Assemblies were proposed for Scotland and Wales, although that for Scotland was to have much the stronger set of powers. After extensive Parliamentary debates from 1976 the referenda required under the Acts failed to secure the necessary majorities and the issue died away, at least temporarily. But the issue of how to reconcile, in a parliamentary democracy, the need for centralised services with the aspiration of regional feeling, remains for further debate. This central question has a wider application than in Scotland and Wales. Cornishmen claim their own right to political expression, and if, say some, there is devolution to Wales and Cornwall, what of Yorkshire with its own rugged traditions? Too little is still known of the economic aspects of regionalism and discussions could gain strength from the recent trend towards the development of city regions.

Currently the relations between central and local government are under strain. Local govenments see their powers diminishing and more power attaching to the centre: the centre is concerned at the levels of public expenditure incurred by local government. Local governments differ greatly in their ability to generate current income through the rating system. Changes to this system have been made in Scotland and proposals are now before Parliament to replace the system in England by a 'community charge' to be paid by each adult individual. Even though a system of income

equalisation exists through funds made available by central government under the Rate Support Grant, considerable differences exist in the levels of expenditure and of services provided by local governments. What you may get from the social services depends to an extent on where you live. The suggestion is made, for example, that educational attainment is much influenced by the levels of expenditure of Local Education Authorities: some Welsh authorities where education has been highly valued come out well in this respect (*see map page 153*).

Maps which show variations in levels of service provision by local and national authorities tend to show the south and southeast as the best provided regions with a gradation downwards to Wales, to the industrial districts of Northern England and to Scotland. But at a more detailed level the pattern has to be modified to show the contrast between the poorly-provided inner cities and the better-off suburbs.

The issue of how exactly Britain should be governed at national, regional and local levels will not easily be resolved. Differences between central and local government must be seen in the context of a picture in which government has now become a main influence on the geography of life in Britain. Governments at different levels influence the geography of Britain through planning decisions, industrial location policies, decisions on the provision of basic services such as transport, energy, water and housing as well as the social services like health, welfare and education.

Conclusion

The 1980s have seen a change in the economic climate. The economy has become more competitive, more market oriented. The government has withdrawn from some industries in favour of the private sector while exercising close overall controls on national financial policy and public expenditure. There are signs of renewed vigour in manufacturing industry, but unemployment, while somewhat reduced, remains high. The emphasis is on encouraging enterprise. Some social problems, especially in the inner cities, continue to provide concern.

How far do the contrasts between North and South, with which we began, still hold? In some respects they do. The growth of science-based industries (though also in Scotland) has been strongest in the South, around London, Cambridge and in the so-called M4 corridor, for example. It has not been easy to replace the employment loss in the formerly 'heavy' industrial districts of the North. The service industries are stronger in the South. Levels of household expenditure are higher in the South than the North. But, on the other hand, some trends apply to both North and South. High levels of unemployment are not confined to the North. Inner City problems are to be found in all the main cities of the country, and the trend to de-centralisation of population from large cities has been general. Within each region there are contrasts between more and less prosperous areas, between scenes of beauty and those of ugliness. And if we are to contrast North and South, we must also contrast West and East, urban Britain and rural Britain, large cities and small towns. The variety of geographical conditions represented on every map in this Atlas is a great and rewarding challenge to further travel and study.

Acknowledgements and Bibliography

The thematic maps in the Introduction and sections on historical geography and modern Britain were researched by Peter Furtado and made and drawn by Clyde Surveys Ltd., of Maidenhead.

The authors and publishers would like to acknowledge:

Great Britain – Geology: Tectonic Map of Great Britain, the Institute of Geological Sciences 1966; and OUP

Great Britain – Climate: *The Climate of the British Isles,* T J Chandler and S Gregory, Longman 1976.

The Dark Ages: *The Archaeology of Anglo-Saxon England* ed D M Wilson, Methuen 1976.

Britain to 1350: *A New Historical Geography of England* ed H C Darby, Cambridge University Press 1973. *Feudal Britain* G W S Barrow, Edward Arnold 1956.

Late Medieval Britain: *The Agrarian History of England and Wales IV* ed Joan Thirsk, Cambridge University Press 1967.

The Agricultural Revolution: *An Historical Geography of England and Wales* ed R A Dodgshon and R A Butlin, Academic Press 1978. *Man Made the Land* Alan R H Baker and J B Harley, David & Charles 1973.

The Early Industrial Revolution: *The Early Industrial Revolution* E Pawson, Batsford 1979.

Britain in the Late Nineteenth Century: *The Movement of Population* C T Smith, Geographical Journal vol 117, 1951.

Mineral Resources: *The Mineral Resources of Britain* John Blunden, Hutchinson 1975. *A Geography of Energy in the UK* John Fernie, Longman 1981.

Industry and Energy: *Development of the oil & gas resources of the UK* Dept. of Energy, HMSO 1987.

Agriculture and Fisheries: *Fish from the Sea* The White Fish Authority. Fishing grounds – The Watt Committee on Energy, University of Glasgow 1979.

Farming Types: *Types of Farming in Britain* K Buchanan and D J Sinclair, Association of Agriculture 1966.

Planning for Leisure: *Conservation & Recreation in England & Wales* Countryside Commission 1987.

Planning for Industry: *The Containment of Urban England* Peter Hall, George Allen & Unwin 1974. *Britain 1988: an official Handbook* HMSO, 1988.

The Transport System: *Development of the Trunk Road Network* Dept. of Transport 1987.

Further Reading

The Personality of Britain Sir Cyril Fox and L F Chitty, National Museum of Wales 1932.

The UK Space J W House, Weidenfeld & Nicolson 3rd ed, 1981

An Agricultural Atlas of Great Britain J T Coppock, Faber and Faber 1976.

Countryside Conservation Bryn Green, George Allen & Unwin 1981.

National Parks: Conservation or Cosmetics Ann and Malcolm McEwen, George Allen & Unwin 1982.

Britain's Structure and Scenery L D Stamp, Collins 1974.

The Changing Geography of the U.K. R J Johnston and J C Doornkamp, Methuen 1982.

Regional Problems, Problem Regions and Public Policy in the U.K., ed. P Damesick and P Wood, Clarendon Press 1987.

Land Use and Living Space R H Best, Methuen 1981.

A Living History of the British Isles W G V Balchin, Country Life 1981.

A Natural History of the British Isles ed Pat Morris, Country Life 1979.

The Making of the English Landscape W G Hoskins, Penguin 1970.

Wales F V Emery, Longman 1969

The Making of the Scottish Landscape R N Millman, Batsford 1975.

Publications of the Central Statistical Office especially *Regional Trends* and *Social Trends* (annual)

County Boundaries before 1974

ORKNEY

ZETLAND

SCOTLAND

CAITH-NESS

SUTHERLAND

ROSS

AND

CROMARTY

NAIRN

MORAY-SHIRE

BANFFSHIRE

ABERDEEN-SHIRE

Inverness

INVERNESS-SHIRE

Aberdeen

1

ANGUS

PERTH

Dundee

Perth

ARGYLLSHIRE

FIFE

4 5

Stirling Dunfermline

2 3

Edinburgh EAST LOTHIAN

7

6 Glasgow 8

Motherwell

BUTE LANARK-SHIRE

BERWICK-SHIRE

9

Ayr 10

AYRSHIRE

ROXBURGH-SHIRE

DUMFRIES-SHIRE

NORTHUMBERLAND

WIGTOWN-SHIRE KIRKCUD-BRIGHTSHIRE

Newcastle-upon-Tyne

Carlisle Sunderland

CUMBERLAND DURHAM

Darlington Middlesbrough

WESTMOR-LAND

NORTH RIDING

ISLE OF MAN

YORKSHIRE

Lancaster York EAST RIDING

WEST RIDING

IRISH SEA Blackpool Bradford Leeds

Burnley Kingston-upon-Hull

Huddersfield

LANCASHIRE Barnsley Doncaster Grimsby

Wigan Bolton LINDSEY

ANGLESEY Liverpool Manchester Sheffield

ENGLAND

12 CHESHIRE DERBY-SHIRE NOTTINGHAM-SHIRE LINCOLNSHIRE

11 DENBIGH-SHIRE Stoke-on-Trent

13 Derby Nottingham KESTEVEN

MERIONETH-SHIRE STAFFORD-SHIRE HOLLAND

14 Shrewsbury Norwich

WALES LEICESTER-SHIRE 15 Peterborough **NORFOLK**

SHROPSHIRE Leicester 16

RADNOR-SHIRE Birmingham NORTHAMPTON-SHIRE 17 WEST EAST

CARDIGANSHIRE 20 Coventry WARWICK-SHIRE **SUFFOLK**

HEREFORD-SHIRE Worcester Northampton Cambridge Ipswich

BRECKNOCKSHIRE Hereford 18

PEMBROKE-SHIRE OXFORD-SHIRE Luton HERTFORD-SHIRE ESSEX

CARMARTHEN-SHIRE GLOUCESTER-SHIRE BUCKINGHAM-SHIRE

Swansea 19 Oxford GREATER LONDON Southend

GLAMORGAN Bristol Swindon BERK-SHIRE Reading

Cardiff SURREY KENT

WILTSHIRE Dover

HAMPSHIRE SUSSEX

SOMERSET WEST EAST

Southampton Brighton

DEVONSHIRE DORSET

Bournemouth

CORNWALL Plymouth Exeter

NORTH

SEA

1 KINCARDINESHIRE
2 DUNBARTONSHIRE
3 STIRLINGSHIRE
4 CLACKMANNANSHIRE
5 KINROSS-SHIRE
6 RENFREWSHIRE
7 WEST LOTHIAN
8 MIDLOTHIAN
9 PEEBLES-SHIRE
10 SELKIRKSHIRE

11 CAERNARVONSHIRE
12
13 FLINTSHIRE
14 MONTGOMERYSHIRE
15 RUTLAND
16 HUNTINGDON AND PETERBOROUGH
17 CAMBRIDGESHIRE AND ISLE OF ELY
18 BEDFORDSHIRE
19 MONMOUTHSHIRE
20 WORCESTERSHIRE

County Boundaries since 1974

ORKNEY

SHETLAND

WESTERN ISLES

HIGHLAND

Inverness

GRAMPIAN

Aberdeen

SCOTLAND

TAYSIDE

Dundee

Perth

FIFE

CENTRAL

Stirling

Dunfermline

Edinburgh

Glasgow

LOTHIAN

Motherwell

STRATHCLYDE

BORDERS

Ayr

DUMFRIES AND GALLOWAY

NORTHUMBERLAND

Carlisle

Newcastle-upon-Tyne

1

Sunderland

DURHAM

Darlington

2 Middlesbrough

CUMBRIA

NORTH YORKSHIRE

ISLE OF MAN

Lancaster

York

LANCASHIRE

Bradford

Leeds

HUMBERSIDE

Blackpool

Burnley

Kingston-upon-Hull

IRISH SEA

3 Huddersfield

Wigan

Bolton

Doncaster

Grimsby

5

Barnsley

4

Liverpool

Manchester

6

Sheffield

ENGLAND

CHESHIRE

DERBY-SHIRE

NOTTINGHAM-SHIRE

LINCOLNSHIRE

GWYNEDD

CLWYD

Stoke-on-Trent

Derby

Nottingham

STAFFORD-SHIRE

Shrewsbury

LEICESTERSHIRE

NORFOLK

Norwich

SHROPSHIRE

Leicester

Birmingham

7

Peterborough

WALES

Coventry

NORTHAMPTON-SHIRE

CAMBRIDGE-SHIRE

SUFFOLK

POWYS

HEREFORD AND WORCESTER

Worcester

WARWICK-SHIRE

Northampton

Cambridge

Ipswich

Hereford

8

DYFED

GLOUCESTER-SHIRE

OXFORD-SHIRE

Luton

HERTFORD-SHIRE

ESSEX

GWENT

BUCKINGHAM-SHIRE

10

Oxford

GREATER LONDON

Swansea

11

Swindon

9

Southend

12 Cardiff

Bristol

AVON

Reading

Cardiff

WILTSHIRE

SURREY

KENT

SOMERSET

HAMPSHIRE

WEST SUSSEX

EAST SUSSEX

Dover

DEVON

DORSET

Southampton

Brighton

Exeter

Bournemouth

ISLE OF WIGHT

CORNWALL

Plymouth

NORTH SEA

1 TYNE AND WEAR
2 CLEVELAND
3 WEST YORKSHIRE
4 SOUTH YORKSHIRE
5 GREATER MANCHESTER
6 MERSEYSIDE

7 WEST MIDLANDS
8 BEDFORDSHIRE
9 BERKSHIRE
10 WEST GLAMORGAN
11 MID GLAMORGAN
12 SOUTH GLAMORGAN

157

Index to 4 miles: 1 inch Maps

How to use this index

For each entry the Atlas page number is listed and an alpha-numeric map reference is given to the grid square in which the name appears. For example:

Barnstaple............... 7 F2.

Barnstaple will be found on page 7, square F2.

The National Grid

The blue grid lines which appear on the Atlas map pages are from the Ordnance Survey National Grid. The National Grid is a reference system which breaks the country down into squares to enable a unique reference to be given to a place or feature. This reference will always be the same no matter which Ordnance Survey map product is used. The squares which form the basic grid cover an area of 100 kilometres by 100 kilometres and are identified by letters; eg SU, TQ. These squares are subdivided by grid lines each carrying a reference number. The numbering sequence runs East and North from the South West corner of the country.

Grid lines on the Atlas map pages appear at 10 kilometre intervals. The 100 kilometre lines are shown in a darker blue. Those grid lines which fall at the top, bottom and outside edge of each page of Atlas mapping also carry their reference numbers (eg ^{2}4) printed in blue. The larger number is the reference of the actual grid line, the smaller that of the preceding 100 kilometre grid line. The letters which identify each 100 kilometre square appear on the Atlas mapping also printed in blue.

A leaflet on the National Grid referencing system is available from Information and Enquiries, Ordnance Survey, Romsey Road, Maybush, Southampton SO9 4DH.

County Names showing abbreviations used in this Index

England

Avon	Avon
Bedfordshire	Beds
Berkshire	Berks
Buckinghamshire	Bucks
Cambridgeshire	Cambs
Cheshire	Ches
Cleveland	Cleve
Cornwall	Corn
Cumbria	Cumbr
Derbyshire	Derby
Devon	Devon
Dorset	Dorset
Durham	Durham
East Sussex	E. Susx
Essex	Essex
Gloucestershire	Glos
Greater London	G. Lon
Greater Manchester	G. Man
Hampshire	Hants
Hereford & Worcester	H. & W
Hertfordshire	Herts
Humberside	Humbs
Isle of Wight	I. of W
Kent	Kent
Lancashire	Lancs
Leicester	Leic
Lincolnshire	Lincs
Merseyside	Mers
Norfolk	Norf
North Yorkshire	N. Yks
Northamptonshire	Northnts
Northumberland	Northum
Nottinghamshire	Notts
Oxfordshire	Oxon
Shropshire	Shrops
Somerset	Somer
South Yorkshire	S. Yks
Staffordshire	Staffs
Suffolk	Suff

Surrey	Surrey
Tyne and Wear	T. & W
Warwickshire	Warw
West Midlands	W.Mids
West Sussex	W. Susx
West Yorkshire	W. Yks
Wiltshire	Wilts

Other Areas

Isle of Man	I. of M
Isles of Scilly	I. Scilly

Wales

Clwyd	Clwyd
Dyfed	Dyfed
Gwent	Gwent
Gwynedd	Gwyn
Mid Glamorgan	M. Glam
Powys	Powys
South Glamorgan	S. Glam
West Glamorgan	W. Glam

Region & Island Area Names Scotland

Regions

Borders	Border
Central	Central
Dumfries & Galloway	D. & G.
Fife	Fife
Grampian	Grampn
Highland	Highl
Lothian	Lothn
Strathclyde	Strath
Tayside	Tays

Island Areas

Orkney	Orkney
Shetland	Shetld
Western Isles	W. Isles

A

Abbas Combe	9	J2
Abberton, H. & W.	34	A5
Abberton, Essex	23	G2
Abberwick	75	H2
Abbess Roding	21	K2
Abbey	8	C3
Abbeycwmhir	41	K6
Abbey Dore	29	H4
Abbey Hulton	43	L3
Abbey St Bathans	80	F3
Abbeystead	61	J4
Abbeytown	66	D1
Abbots Bickington	6	D4
Abbots Bromley	44	B5
Abbotsbury	9	G6
Abbotsham	6	E3
Abbotskerswell	5	J5
Abbots Langley	20	E3
Abbots Leigh	17	G3
Abbotsley	37	F5
Abbots Morton	34	B5
Abbots Ripton	37	F3
Abbot's Salford	34	B5
Abbotswood	10	E2
Abbotts Ann	18	E6
Abdon	32	E2
Aber	27	J3
Aberaeron	40	D7
Aberaman	25	J4
Aberangell	41	H2
Aberargie	86	E3
Aberarth	40	D7
Aber-banc	27	H3
Aberbargoed	25	K4
Aberbeeg	25	L4
Abercanaid	25	J4
Abercarn	25	L5

Abercastle	26	C4
Abercegir	41	H3
Aberchalder	98	B8
Aberchirder	100	F3
Abercraf	25	G3
Abercych	27	G3
Abercynon	25	J5
Aberdalgie	86	D2
Aberdare	25	J4
Aberdaron	40	A1
Aberdeen	101	J8
Aberdour	87	E6
Aberdulais	25	F5
Aberdyfi	40	F4
Aberedw	28	E3
Abereiddy	26	B4
Abererch	50	C7
Aberfan	25	J4
Aberfeldy	91	K7
Aberffraw	50	C4
Aberffrwd	41	F6
Aberford	63	H6
Aberfoyle	85	H4
Abergavenny	29	H6
Abergele	51	J3
Abergorlech	27	K4
Abergwesyn	28	C2
Abergwili	27	J5
Abergwynant	41	F2
Abergwynfi	25	G5
Abergwyngregyn	51	F3
Abergynolwyn	41	F3
Aberhosan	41	H4
Aberkenfig	25	G6
Aberlady	87	H7
Aberlemno	93	G6
Aberllefenni	41	G3
Abermeurig	27	K2
Abermule	42	C8
Abernant, Dyfed	27	H5

Aber-nant, M. Glam	25	J4
Abernethy	87	E3
Abernyte	87	F1
Aberporth	27	G2
Abersoch	40	C1
Abersychan	29	G7
Abertillery	25	L4
Abertridwr, Powys	41	K2
Abertridwr, M. Glam	25	K6
Abertysswg	25	K4
Aberuthven	86	C3
Aber Village	25	K2
Aberyscir	25	J2
Aberystwyth	40	E5
Abingdon	31	J8
Abinger Common	12	E2
Abington	79	G7
Abington Pigotts	7	G6
Ab Kettleby	45	J5
Ablington	30	F7
Abney	54	E6
Aboyne	93	G2
Abram	53	H3
Abriachan	98	D5
Abridge	21	J4
Abthorpe	35	H6
Abune-the-Hill	116	B4
Aby	57	J6
Acaster Malbis	63	J5
Acaster Selby	63	J5
Accrington	62	A7
Achachork	103	F4
Achahoish	83	G4
Achanalt	98	A2
Achandunie	108	E6
Achany	108	D6
Achaphubuil	90	B4
Acharacle	89	H2
Acharn	91	J7
Achath	101	G7

Achfary	112	D5
Achgarve	106	D2
Achiemore	114	D4
Achiltibuie	106	F1
Achina	113	J2
Achinduich	108	D4
Achingills	115	G3
Achintee	106	E7
Achintraid	96	D2
Achleck	88	F4
Achluachrach	90	E3
Achlyness	112	D3
Achmelvich	112	B6
Achmore, Highld	96	D2
Achmore, W. Isles	111	H5
Achnacarnin	115	F6
Achnacarry	90	C3
Achnacloich	96	A5
Achnaconeran	98	C7
Achnacroish	89	K4
Achnagarron	98	E1
Achnahanat	108	D4
Achnahannet	99	H6
Achnairn	113	G7
Achnamara	83	G3
Achnasaul	90	C3
Achnasheen	107	G6
Achreamie	115	F3
Achriesgill	112	D3
Achurch	36	D2
Ackergill	115	J4
Acklam, N. Yks	64	E6
Acklam, Cleve	69	G5
Ackleton	43	J8
Ackington	75	J3
Acklington	63	H7
Ackworth Moor Top	55	H2
Acle	49	K6
Acock's Green	34	C2
Acol	15	K2

Acomb	74	F7
Aconbury	29	K4
Acre	62	A7
Acrefair	42	D3
Acton, Shrops	32	C2
Acton, Suff	38	D6
Acton, G. Lon	21	G5
Acton, Ches	43	H2
Acton Beauchamp	33	F5
Acton Bridge	53	G6
Acton Burnell	43	G7
Acton Green	33	F5
Acton Pigott	43	G7
Acton Round	43	H8
Acton Scott	32	D2
Acton Trussell	43	L6
Acton Turville	17	K2
Adamthwaite	67	K7
Adbaston	43	J5
Adber	9	G2
Adderbury	31	J4
Adderley	43	H4
Adderstone	81	K6
Addiewell	79	G3
Addingham	62	D5
Addington, Kent	14	C3
Addington, Bucks	35	J8
Addlestone	20	E7
Addlethorpe	57	K7
Adeney	43	J6
Adfa	41	K3
Adforton	32	D3
Adisham	15	J3
Adlestrop	31	G5
Adlingfleet	58	C4
Adlington, Lancs	53	H2
Adlington, Ches	53	L5
Admaston, Staffs	44	B5
Admaston, Shrops	43	H6
Admington	34	D6

Adstock	35	J7
Adstone	35	G5
Advie	99	K5
Adwell	20	A4
Adwick le Street	55	J3
Adwick upon Dearne	55	H3
Ae	72	E5
Affleck	101	H6
Affpuddle	9	K5
Afon-wen	52	C6
Agglethorpe	62	D1
Aignish	111	J4
Aike	58	E2
Aikerness	116	D1
Aikers	116	D7
Aiketgate	67	G2
Aikton	66	E1
Ailey	29	H3
Ailworth	46	E8
Ainderby Quernhow	63	G1
Ainderby Steeple	68	F7
Aingers Green	23	H1
Ainsdale	52	E2
Ainstable	67	H2
Ainsworth	53	J2
Aintree	52	E4
Aird, D. & G.	70	B5
Aird, Strath	83	G1
Aird, W. Isles	111	K4
Aird Dell	111	J1
Aird Mhanais	105	G3
Aird Mheadhonach	105	G2
Aird of Sleat	96	A5
Aird Riabhach	105	H2
Airdrie	78	E3
Airdriehill	78	E3
Aird, The	103	F3
Aird Thunga	111	J4
Aird Uig	110	E4
Airmyn	58	B4

Airntully	86	D1
Airor	96	C5
Airth	86	B6
Airton	62	C4
Aisby, Lincs	56	C4
Aisby, Lincs	46	D4
Aiskew	63	F1
Aislaby, N. Yks	64	E4
Aislaby, N. Yks	64	F2
Aisthorpe	56	D5
Aith, Shetld	119	F3
Aith, Orkney	117	F4
Aithsetter	119	G5
Akeld	81	H7
Akeley	35	J7
Akenham	39	G6
Albaston	4	E4
Alberbury	42	E6
Albourne	12	F5
Albrighton, Shrops	43	F6
Albrighton, Shrops	43	K7
Alburgh	39	H2
Albury, Surrey	12	D2
Albury, Herts	21	J1
Alby Hill	49	G4
Alcaig	98	D3
Alcaston	32	D2
Alcester	34	B5
Alciston	13	J6
Alcombe	7	K1
Alconbury	36	E3
Alconbury Weston	36	E3
Aldborough, Norf	49	G4
Aldborough, N. Yks	63	H3
Aldbourne	18	D3
Aldbrough	5	G3
Aldbrough St John	68	E5
Aldbury	20	D2
Aldclune	91	K5
Aldeburgh	39	K5
Aldeby	49	K8
Aldenham	21	F4
Alderbury	10	C2
Alderford	49	G6
Alderholt	10	C3
Alderley	17	J1
Alderley Edge	53	K6
Aldermaston	19	G4
Alderminster	34	D6
Aldershot	19	K5
Alderton, Glos	30	E4
Alderton, Shrops	43	F5
Alderton, Suff	39	J6
Alderton, Northnts	35	J6
Alderton, Wilts	17	K2
Alderwasley	44	E2
Aldfield	63	F3
Aldford	52	F8
Aldham, Essex	38	E8
Aldham, Suff	38	F6
Aldingbourne	12	C6
Aldingham	61	F2
Aldington, H. & W	34	B6
Aldington, Kent	15	G5
Aldington Frith	15	G5
Aldochlay	84	F5
Aldreth	37	H3
Aldridge	44	B7
Aldringham	39	K4
Aldsworth	31	F6
Aldunie	100	C6
Aldwark, Derby	55	F6
Aldwark, N. Yks	63	H3
Aldwick	12	C7
Aldwincle	36	D2
Aldworth	19	G3
Alexandria	85	F6
Alfardisworthy	6	C4
Alfington	8	C5
Alfold	12	D3
Alford, Grampn	100	E7
Alford, Somer	9	H1
Alford, Lincs	57	J6
Alfreton	44	F2
Alfrick	33	G5
Alfriston	13	J6
Alhampton	9	H1
Alkborough	58	C4
Alkerton	34	E6
Alkham	15	J4
Alkington	43	G4
Alkmonton	44	C4
Allaleigh	5	J6
Allanaquoich	92	C2
Allanton, Strath	79	F4
Allanton, Border	81	G4
Allardice	93	K4
All Cannings	18	C4
Allendale Town	67	L1
Allenheads	67	L2
Allensmore	29	J4
Aller	8	F2
Allerby	66	C3
Allerford	7	K1
Allerston	65	F4
Allerthorpe	58	B2
Allerton	52	F5
Allerton Bywater	63	H7
Allesley	34	D2
Allestree	44	E4
Allexton	46	B7
Allgreave	54	C7
Allhallow-on-Sea	22	E6
Allhallows	14	E1
Alligin Shuas	106	D6
Allimore Green	43	K6
Allington, Lincs	46	B3
Allington, Wilts	18	B4
Allington, Wilts	18	D7
Allithwaite	61	G2
Alloa	86	B5
Allonby	66	C2
Alloway	77	J6
All Saints South Elmham	39	J2
All Stretton	42	F8
Alltforgan	41	J1
Alltmawr	28	E3
Allt_na Airbhe	107	G2
Allt-nan-Sugh	96	E3
Alltwalis	27	J4
Alltwen	24	F4
Almeley	29	H2
Almer	9	L5
Almington	43	J4
Almodbank	86	D2
Almondbury	54	E2
Almondsbury	17	H2
Alne	63	H3
Alness	98	E2
Alnham	75	F2
Alnmouth	75	J2
Alnwick	75	H2
Alphamstone	38	D7
Alpheton	38	D5
Alphington	5	K3
Alport	55	F7
Alpraham	53	G8
Alresford	23	G1
Alrewas	44	C6
Alsager	43	J2
Alsagers Bank	43	K3
Alsop en le Dale	44	C2
Alston	67	L2
Alstone	30	D4
Alstonefield	44	C2
Alswear	7	H3
Altandhu	112	A7
Altarnun	3	L1
Altass	108	D3
Alterwall	115	H3
Altham	62	A6
Althorne	22	F4
Althorpe	58	C6
Altnaharra	113	G5
Altofts	63	G7
Alton, Staffs	44	B3
Alton, Derby	55	G7
Alton, Hants	19	J7
Alton Pancras	9	H4
Alton Priors	18	C4
Altrincham	53	J5
Altrua	90	D2
Alva	86	B5
Alvanley	53	F6
Alvaston	44	E4
Alvechurch	34	B3
Alvecote	44	D7
Alvediston	10	A2
Alveley	33	G2
Alverdiscott	6	F3
Alverstoke	11	H5
Alverstone	11	G6
Alverton	45	J3
Alves	99	K2
Alvescot	31	G7
Alveston, Warw	34	D5
Alveston, Avon	17	H2
Alvie	99	G8
Alvingham	57	H4
Alvington	29	L7
Alwalton	46	E8
Alweston	9	H3
Alwinton	74	F3
Alyth	92	D7
Amatnatua	108	C4
Ambergate	44	E2
Amber Hill	47	F3
Amberley, Glos	30	C7
Amberley, W. Susx	12	D5
Amble-by-the-Sea	75	J3
Amblecote	33	H2
Ambleside	67	F6
Ambleston	26	E5
Ambrosden	31	L6
Amcotts	58	C5
Amersham	20	D4
Amesbury	18	C6
Amhuinnsuidhe	104	F1
Amington	44	D7
Amisfield	72	F5
Amlwch	50	D1
Amlwch Port	50	D1
Ammanford	27	L6
Amotherby	64	E5
Ampfield	10	F2
Ampleforth	63	J2
Ampney Crucis	30	E7
Ampney St Mary	30	E7
Ampney St Peter	30	E7
Amport	18	E6
Ampthill	36	D7
Ampton	38	D3
Amroth	26	F7
Amulree	91	L8
Anaheilt	89	K2
Anancaun	106	F5
An Ard	106	D4
An Caol	106	B6
Ancaster	46	C3
Anchachork	103	F4
Anchor	32	A2
Ancroft	81	J5
Ancrum	80	E7
Ancton	12	C6
Anderby	57	K6
Anderby Creek	57	K6
Anderson	9	K5
Anderton	53	H6
Andover	18	E6
Andover Down	18	E6
Andoversford	30	E6
Andreas	60	R2
Angersleigh	8	C3
Angle	26	C7
Angmering	12	D6
Angram, Lancs	68	A7
Angram, N. Yks	63	J5
Ankerville	109	G6
Anlaby	58	E4
Anmer	48	C5
Annan	73	G7
Annaside	60	D1
Annat, Strath	84	C2
Annat, Highld	106	D6
Annathill	85	K7
Anna Valley	18	E6
Annbank	77	K5
Annesley	45	G2
Annesley Woodhouse	45	F2
Annfield Plain	68	D7
Annochie	101	J4
Annscroft	42	F7
Ansdell	61	G7
Ansford	9	H1
Ansley	34	E1
Anslow	44	D5
Anslow Gate	44	C5
Anstey, Leic	45	G7
Anstey, Herts	37	H7
Anston	55	J5
Anstruther	87	J4
Ansty, Wilts	10	A2
Ansty, Warw	34	E2
Ansty, W. Susx	13	F4
Ansty, Dorset	9	J4
Anthill Common	11	H3
Anthorn	73	G8
Antingham	49	H4
Antony	4	D6
Antrobus	53	H6
Anwick	46	E2
Anwoth	71	G6
Apes Hall	37	J1
Apethorpe	46	D8
Apley	57	F6
Apperknowle	55	G6
Apperley	30	C5
Appersett	67	L7
Appin	90	A7
Appleby	58	D5
Appleby-in-Westmorland	67	J4
Appleby Magna	44	E6
Appleby Parva	44	E7
Applecross	106	C7
Appledore, Devon	8	B3
Appledore, Devon	6	E2
Appledore, Kent	14	F6
Appleford	31	K8
Appleshaw	18	E6
Appleton	31	J7
Appleton-le-Moors	64	E4
Appleton-Le-Street	64	E5
Appleton Roebuck	63	J5
Appleton Thorn	53	H5
Appleton Wiske	69	F6
Appletreehall	74	B2
Appletreewick	62	D3
Appley	8	B2
Appley Bridge	53	G3
Apse Heath	11	G6
Apsley End	36	E7
Apuldram	11	K4
Aquahorthies	101	H6
Aquhythie	101	G7
Arabella	109	G6
Arbirlot	93	H7
Arboll	109	G5
Arborfield	20	B7
Arborfield Cross	20	B7
Arborfield Garrison	20	B7
Arbroath	93	H7
Arbuthnott	93	K4
Archiestown	100	B4
Arclid Green	53	J7
Ardachu	108	E3
Ardalanish	88	E7
Ardanaiseig	84	C2
Ardaneaskan	96	D2
Ardarroch	96	D2
Ardbeg	82	D7
Ardbeg	85	J1
Ardcharnich	107	G3
Ardchiavaig	88	E7
Ardchyle	85	H2
Ardclach	99	H4
Ard-dhubh	96	C1
Arddleen	42	D6
Ardechive	90	C2
Ardeley	37	G8
Ardelve	96	D3
Arden	85	F6
Ardens Grafton	34	C5
Ardentinny	84	D6
Ardeonaig	85	J1
Ardersier	99	F3
Ardessie	107	F3
Ardfern	83	H1
Ardgay	108	D4
Ardgowan	84	F7
Ardhasaig	105	G1
Ardheslaig	106	C6
Ardindrean	107	G3
Ardingly	13	G4
Ardington	18	F2
Ardlair	100	E6
Ardleigh	38	F8
Ardler	92	D7
Ardley	31	K5
Ardlui	84	F3
Ardlussa	83	F3
Ardmair	107	G2
Ardminish	76	B3
Ardmolich	89	J1
Ardnacroish	89	K4
Ardnadam	84	D6
Ardnagrask	98	D4
Ardnarff	96	D2
Ardnastang	89	K2
Ardo	101	H5
Ardoyne	100	F6
Ardrishaig	84	A6
Ardroil	110	E4
Ardross	108	E6
Ardrossan	77	H3
Ardshealach	89	H2
Ardsley	55	G3
Ardsley East	63	G7
Ardtalnaig	91	J8
Ardtoe	89	H1
Ardtornish	89	J4
Ardullie	98	D2
Ardvasar	96	B5
Ardvey, W. Isles	105	F3
Ardvey, W. Isles	105	G2
Ardvourlie	111	F6
Ardwell	70	C7
Areley Kings	33	H3
Aridhglas	88	E6
Arinacrinachd	106	C6
Arinagour	88	D3
Arisaig	96	B7
Arkendale	63	G3
Arkesden	37	H7
Arkholme	61	J2
Arkley	21	G4
Arksey	55	J3
Arkwright Town	55	H6
Arlecdon	66	C5
Arlesey	36	E7
Arleston	43	H6
Arley, Warw	34	D1
Arley, Ches	53	H5
Arlingham	30	B6
Arlington, Glos	30	F7
Arlington, Devon	7	G1
Arlington, E. Susx	13	J6
Armadale, Highld	114	C3
Armadale, Lothn	79	G3
Armathwaite	67	H2
Arminghall	49	H7
Armitage	44	B6
Armscote	34	D6
Armthorpe	55	K3
Arncliffe	62	C2
Arncott	20	A2
Arncroach	87	J4
Arne	10	A6
Arnesby	35	H1
Arnisdale	96	D4
Arnish	106	A7
Arniston Engine	80	B3
Arnol	111	H3
Arnold	45	J3
Arnprior	85	J5
Arrad Foot	61	G1
Arram	58	E2
Arrathorne	68	E7
Arreton	11	G6
Arrington	37	G5
Arrochar	84	E4
Arrow	34	B5
Artafallie	98	E4
Arthington	63	F5
Arthingworth	35	J2
Arthog	41	F2
Arthrath	101	J5
Arundel	12	D6
Asby	66	C4
Ascog	77	G1
Ascot	20	C7
Ascott-under-Wychwood	31	H6
Asenby	63	G2
Asfordby	45	J6
Asfordby Hill	45	J6
Ash, Kent	14	E2
Ash, Somer	9	F2
Ash, Kent	15	J3
Ash, Surrey	19	K5
Ashampstead	19	G3
Ashbocking	39	G5
Ashbourne	44	C3
Ashbrittle	8	C3
Ashburton	5	H5
Ashbury, Oxon	18	D2
Ashbury, Devon	4	F2
Ashby	58	D6
Ashby by Partney	57	J7
Ashby cum Fenby	59	G6
Ashby de la Launde	46	D2
Ashby-de-la-Zouch	44	E6
Ashby Folville	45	J6
Ashby Magna	35	G1
Ashby Parva	35	G2
Ashby St Ledgers	35	G4
Ashby St Mary	49	J7
Ashchurch	30	D4
Ashcombe	5	K4
Ashcott	9	F1
Ashdon	37	J6
Asheldham	23	F3
Ashen	38	C6
Ashendon	20	B2
Ashfield, Suff	39	H4
Ashfield, Central	85	K4
Ashfield Green	39	H3
Ashford, Surrey	20	E6
Ashford, Devon	7	F2
Ashford, Kent	15	G4
Ashford Bowdler	32	E3
Ashford Carbonell	32	E3
Ashford Hill	19	G4
Ashford in the Water	54	E7
Ashgill	78	E5
Ashill, Devon	8	B5
Ashill, Norf	48	D7
Ashill, Somer	8	E3
Ashingdon	22	E4
Ashington, W. Susx	12	E5
Ashington,Northum	75	J5
Ashkirk	80	C7
Ashleworth	30	C5
Ashley, Cambs	38	B4
Ashley, Glos	30	D8
Ashley, Hants	10	E1
Ashley, Devon	7	G4
Ashley, Northnts	35	J3
Ashley, Staffs	43	J4
Ashley, Ches	53	J5
Ashley Green	20	D3
Ashley Heath, Dorset	10	C4
Ashley Heath, Staffs	43	J4
Ash Magna	43	G4
Ashmansworth	18	F5
Ashmansworthy	6	C4
Ashmore	9	L3
Ashmore Park	44	A7
Ashorne	34	E5
Ashover	55	G7
Ashow	34	E3
Asperton	33	F6
Ashprington	5	J6
Ash Priors	8	C2
Ashreigney	7	G4
Ashstead	21	F8
Ash Thomas	7	L4
Ashton, Northnts	36	D2
Ashton, H. & W	32	E4
Ashton, Corn	2	E7
Ashton, Ches	53	G7
Ashton, Northnts	35	J5
Ashton Common	17	K5
Ashton in Makerfield	53	G4
Ashton Keynes	30	E8
Ashton under Hill	34	A7
Ashton-under-Lyne	53	L4
Ashton upon Mersey	53	J4
Ashurst, Hants	10	E3
Ashurst, W. Susx	12	E5
Ashurst, Kent	13	J3
Ashurstwood	13	H3
Ashwater	4	D2
Ashwell, Leic	46	B6
Ashwell, Herts	37	F7
Ashwellthorpe	49	G8
Ashwick	17	H6
Ashwicken	48	C6
Askam in Furness	60	F2
Askern	55	J2
Askerswell	9	G5
Askett	20	C3
Askham, Notts	56	B6
Askham, Cumbr	67	H4
Askham Bryan	63	J5
Askham Richard	63	J5
Asknish	84	B5
Askrigg	68	B7
Askwith	62	E5
Aslackby	46	D4
Aslacton	39	G1
Aslockton	45	J3
Asloun	100	E7
Aspall	39	G4
Aspatria	66	D2
Aspenden	37	G8
Aspley Guise	36	C7
Aspull	53	H3
Asselby	58	B4
Assington	38	E7
Astbury	53	K7
Astcote	35	H5
Asterley	42	E7
Asterton	32	C1
Asthall	31	G6
Asthall Leigh	31	H6
Astley, Warw	34	E2
Astley, H. & W	33	G4
Astley, Shrops	43	G6
Astley Abbots	43	J8
Astley Cross	33	H4
Astley Green	53	J4
Aston, W. Mids	34	B2
Aston, Berks	20	B5
Aston, H. & W	32	D3
Aston, Derby	54	E5
Aston, Herts	21	G1
Aston, Shrops	43	G5
Aston, Ches	53	G6
Aston, Ches	43	H3
Aston, S. Yks	55	H5
Aston, Oxon	31	H7
Aston, Shrops	43	H7
Aston, Staffs	43	J3
Aston Abbotts	20	C1
Aston Botterell	33	F2
Aston-by-Stone	43	L4
Aston Cantlow	34	C4
Aston Clinton	20	C2
Aston Crews	30	A5
Aston End	21	G1
Aston Eyre	43	H8
Aston Fields	34	A4
Aston Flamville	35	F1
Aston Ingham	30	A5
Aston juxta Mondrum	43	H2
Aston le Walls	35	F5
Aston Magna	31	G4
Aston Munslow	32	F2
Aston on Clun	32	C2
Aston-on-Trent	44	F5
Aston Rogers	42	E7
Aston Rowant	20	B4
Aston Sandford	20	B3
Aston Somerville	34	B7
Aston Subedge	19	G2
Aston Tirrold	19	G2
Aston Upthorpe	19	G2
Astwick	36	F7
Astwood	36	C6
Astwood Bank	34	B4
Aswarby	46	D4
Aswardby	57	H6
Atcham	43	G7
Athelington	39	H3
Athelney	8	E2
Athelstaneford	87	J7
Atherington	7	F3
Atherstone	44	E8
Atherstone on Stour	34	D5
Atherton	53	H3
Atlow	44	D3
Attadale	96	E2
Attenborough	45	G4
Attleborough, Warw	34	E1
Attleborough, Norf	48	F8
Attlebridge	49	G6
Attwick	65	J7
Atworth	17	K4
Aubourn	56	D7
Auchagallon	76	D4
Aucharnie	100	F4
Auchattie	93	H2
Auchenblae	93	J4
Auchenbrack	72	C4
Auchencairn	71	J6
Auchencarroch	85	G6
Auchencrow	81	G3
Auchengray	79	G4
Auchenhalrig	100	C2
Auchenheath	79	F5
Auchentiber	77	J3
Auchgourish	99	H7
Auchindrain	84	C4
Auchindrean	107	G3
Auchinleck	100	F4
Auchinleck	77	L5
Auchinloch	85	J7
Auchleuchries	101	K5
Auchleven	100	F6
Auchlochan	79	F6
Auchlossan	93	G1
Auchlyne	85	H2
Auchmillan	77	L5
Auchmithie	93	H7
Auchnacree	93	F5
Auchnagallin	99	J5
Auchnagatt	101	J4
Auchterarder	86	C3
Auchteraw	98	B8
Auchterderran	87	F5
Auchtermuchty	87	F3
Auchterneed	98	C3
Auchtertool	87	F5
Auchtertyre	96	D3
Auchtubh	85	H2
Auckengill	115	J3
Auckley	55	K3
Audenshaw	53	L4
Audlem	43	H3
Audley	43	J2
Auds	100	F2
Aughton, Humbs	58	B3
Aughton, Lancs	52	E3
Aughton, S. Yks	55	H5
Aughton, Lancs	61	J3
Aughton Park	52	F3
Auldearn	99	H3
Aulden	29	J2
Auldhame	87	J6
Auldhouse	78	D4
Ault a' Chruinn	96	E3
Aultbea	106	D3
Aultdearg	98	A2
Aultgrishan	106	C3
Aultiphurst	114	D3
Aultmore	100	D3
Aut-na-goire	98	D6
Aulton	100	F6
Aundorach	99	H7
Aunsby	46	D4
Auquhorthies	101	H6
Aust	17	G2
Austerfield	55	K4
Austrey	44	D7
Austwick	62	A3
Authorpe	57	J5
Authorpe Row	57	K6
Avebury	18	B4
Aveley	21	K5
Avening	30	C8
Averdaron	40	A1
Averffraw	50	C4
Avernish	45	J2
Aveton Gifford	5	G7
Avielochan	99	H7
Aviemore	99	G7
Avington	18	E4
Avoch	99	F3
Avon	10	C5
Avonbridge	86	C7
Avon Dassett	34	F5
Avonmouth	17	G3
Avonwick	5	H6
Awbridge	10	E2
Awkley	17	G2
Awliscombe	8	C4
Awre	30	B7
Awsworth	45	J3
Axbridge	17	F5
Axford, Wilts	18	D3
Axford, Hants	19	H6
Axminster	8	D5
Axmouth	8	D5
Aylburton	29	L7
Ayle	67	K2
Aylesbeare	8	B5
Aylesbury	20	C2
Aylesby	59	G6
Aylesford	14	C7
Aylesham	15	J3
Aylestone	45	G7
Aylmerton	49	G4
Aylsham	49	G5
Aylton	33	F7
Aymestrey	32	D4
Aynho	31	K4
Ayot St Lawrence	21	F2
Ayot St Peter	21	G2
Ayr	77	J5
Aysgarth	62	D1
Ayside	61	G1
Ayston	46	B7
Aythorpe Roding	22	B2
Ayton, N. Yks	65	G4

Ayton, Border......81 H3
Aywick......121 H4
Azerley......63 F2

B

Babbacombe......5 K5
Babbinswood......42 E4
Babcary......9 G2
Babel......25 G1
Babell......52 C6
Babraham......37 J5
Babworth......56 A5
Bac......111 J3
Backaland......116 E3
Backbarrow......61 G1
Backburn, Grampn......100 E5
Backburn, Grampn......93 K2
Backfolds......101 K3
Backford......52 E6
Backhill, Grampn......101 G5
Backhill, Grampn......101 K5
Backhill of Clackriach......101 J4
Backhill of Trustach......93 H2
Backies......109 G3
Backlass......115 H4
Backmuir of New Gilston......87 H4
Back of Keppoch......96 B7
Backwell......17 F4
Backworth......75 K6
Bacon End......22 C2
Baconsthorpe......49 G4
Bacton, Suff......38 F4
Bacton, H. & W......29 H4
Bacton, Norf......49 J4
Bacup......62 B7
Badachro......106 C4
Badbury......18 C2
Badby......35 G5
Badcall, Highld......112 C4
Badcall, Highld......112 D3
Badcaul......106 F2
Baddeley Green......43 L2
Baddesley Ensor......44 D8
Baddidarach......112 B6
Badenscoth......101 G5
Badger......43 J8
Badgers Mount......21 J7
Badgeworth......30 D6
Badgworth......16 E5
Badicaul......96 C3
Badingham......39 J4
Badlesmere......15 G3
Badluarach......106 E2
Badminton......17 K2
Badninish......109 F4
Badrallach......107 F2
Badsey......34 B6
Badsworth......55 H2
Badwell Ash......38 E4
Bagby......63 H1
Bagendon......30 E7
Bage, The......29 G3
Bagillt......52 D6
Baginton......34 E3
Baglan......25 F5
Bagley......42 F5
Bagnall......43 L2
Bagshot, Surrey......20 D7
Bagshot, Wilts......18 E4
Bagthorpe, Norf......48 C4
Bagthorpe, Notts......45 F2
Bagworth......45 F7
Bagwyllydiart......29 J5
Baildon......62 E6
Baile......104 E3
Bailebeag......98 D7
Baile Boidheach......83 G4
Baile Mor......88 D6
Baillieston......78 D3
Bail Uachdraich......104 D5
Bainbridge......68 B7
Bainton, Cambs......46 D7
Bainton, Humbs......65 G7
Bairnkine......74 C2
Bakers End......21 H2
Baker Street......22 C5
Bakewell......54 F7
Bala......51 J7
Balachuirn......96 A1
Balaglas......104 D6
Balallan......111 G5
Balbeg......98 C6
Balbeggie......86 E2
Balbithan......101 G7
Balblair......99 F2
Balcherry......109 G5
Balchladich......112 B5
Balchraggan......98 D4
Balchrick......112 C2
Balcombe......13 G3
Balcurvie......87 G4
Baldersby......63 G2
Balderstone......61 K6
Balderton......46 B2
Baldhu......2 F5
Baldinnie......87 H3
Baldock......37 F7
Baldrine......60 R3
Baldwin......60 O3
Baldwinholme......66 F1
Baldwin's Gate......43 J3
Bale......48 F4
Balemartine......88 A4
Balephuil......88 A4
Balerno......79 J3
Balevullin......88 A4
Balfield......93 G5
Balfour......116 D5
Balfron......85 H6
Balgaveny......100 F4
Balgedie......86 E4
Balgonar......86 D5

Balgove......101 H5
Balgowan......91 H2
Balgown......102 E2
Balgray......92 F8
Balrochan......85 J7
Balgy......106 D6
Balhalgardy......101 G6
Baligill......114 D3
Balintore......109 G6
Balintraid......99 F1
Balivanich......104 C6
Balkholme......58 B4
Balkissock......70 C3
Ball......42 E5
Balla......94 C4
Ballabeg......60 P4
Ballacannell......60 R3
Ballacarnane Beg......60 O3
Ballachulish......90 B6
Ballagyr......60 P3
Ballajora......60 R2
Ballamodha......60 P4
Ballantrae......70 B3
Ballantrushal......111 H2
Ballasalla, I. of M......60 P5
Ballasalla, I. of M......60 Q2
Ballater......92 E2
Ballaugh......60 Q2
Balleigh......109 F5
Ballencrieff......87 H7
Ball Hill......18 F4
Balliasta......121 J2
Balliekine......76 D4
Ballig......60 P3
Ballinaby......82 B5
Ballingham......29 K4
Ballingry......86 E5
Ballinluig......92 A6
Ballintuim......92 C6
Balloch, Highld......99 F4
Balloch, Strath......85 F6
Ballochan......93 G2
Ballygown......89 F4
Ballygrant......82 C5
Ballymichael......76 E4
Balmacara......96 D3
Balmacara Square......96 D3
Balmaclellan......72 B6
Balmae......71 H7
Balmaha......85 G5
Balmartin......104 C4
Balmedie......101 J7
Balmerino......87 G2
Balmer Lawn......10 E4
Balmore......85 J7
Balnaboth......93 G2
Balnabodach......94 C3
Balnacoil......109 G2
Balnacra......106 E7
Balnaguard......91 L6
Balnaguisich......108 E6
Balnahard......89 F5
Balnain......98 C5
Balnakeil......112 E2
Balnaknock......103 F2
Balnapaling......99 F2
Balne......55 J2
Balquhidder......85 H2
Balranald......104 C5
Balsall Common......34 D3
Balscote......34 E6
Balsham......37 J5
Baltasound......121 J2
Balterley......43 J2
Balthangie......101 H3
Baltonsborough......9 G1
Balvaird......98 D3
Balvicar......89 J7
Balvraid......99 G5
Bamber Bridge......61 J7
Bamburgh......81 K6
Bamford......54 F5
Bampton, Cumbr......67 H5
Bampton, Oxon......31 H7
Bampton, Devon......7 K3
Banavie......90 C4
Banbury......35 F6
Banchory......93 J2
Banchory-Devenick......93 L1
Bancyfelin......27 H6
Bancyffordd......27 J4
Banff......101 F2
Bangor......50 E3
Bangor-is-y-coed......42 E3
Banham......38 F2
Bank......10 D4
Bankend, Strath......79 F6
Bankend, D. & G......72 F7
Bankfoot......86 D1
Bankglen......72 A2
Bankhead, Grampn......100 F8
Bankhead, Grampn......101 H7
Bank Newton......62 C4
Banknock......85 K7
Banks, Cumbr......74 B7
Banks, Lancs......52 E1
Bankshill......73 G5
Bank Street......33 F4
Banningham......49 H5
Bannister Green......22 C1
Bannockburn......85 L5
Banstead......21 G8
Bantham......5 G7
Banton......85 K7
Banwell......16 E5
Bapchild......14 F2
Bapton......18 A7
Baramore......89 H1
Barassie......77 J4
Barbaraville......109 F6
Barber Booth......54 E5
Barbon......61 K1
Barbridge......53 H7

Barbrook......7 H1
Barby......35 G3
Barcaldine......90 A7
Barcheston......34 D7
Barcombe......13 H5
Barcombe Cross......13 H5
Barden......68 D7
Bardfield Saling......38 B8
Bardney......57 F7
Bardowie......85 H7
Bardrainney......84 F7
Bardsea......61 G2
Bardsey......63 G5
Bardsley......53 L3
Bardwell......38 E3
Barewood......29 H2
Barford, Warw......34 D4
Barford St Martin......10 B1
Barford, Norf......49 G7
Barford St Michael......31 J4
Barfrestone......15 J3
Bargoed......25 K5
Bargrennan......70 E4
Barham, Cambs......36 E3
Barham, Suff......39 G5
Barham, Kent......15 J3
Barharrow......71 H4
Barholm......46 D6
Barkby......45 H7
Barkestone-le-Vale......45 J4
Barkham......20 B7
Barking, Suff......38 F5
Barking, G. Lon......21 J5
Barkingside......21 J5
Barkisland......54 D2
Barkston, Lincs......46 C3
Barkston, N. Yks......63 H6
Barkway......37 G7
Barkwith......57 F5
Barlaston......43 K4
Barlavington......12 C5
Barlborough......55 H6
Barlby......63 K6
Barlestone......44 F7
Barley, Lancs......62 B5
Barley, Herts......37 G7
Barleythorpe......46 B7
Barling......22 F5
Barlow, Derby......55 G6
Barlow, T. & W......75 H7
Barlow, N. Yks......63 K7
Barmby Moor......64 E8
Barmby on the Marsh......58 A4
Barmer......48 D4
Barmouth......40 F2
Barmpton......68 F5
Barmston......65 J7
Barnacle......34 E2
Barnack......46 D7
Barnard Castle......68 C5
Barnard Gate......31 J4
Barnardiston......38 C6
Barnburgh......55 H3
Barnby......39 K2
Barnby Dun......55 K3
Barnby in the Willows......46 B2
Barnby Moor......55 K5
Barnes......21 G6
Barnet......21 G4
Barnetby le Wold......58 E6
Barney......48 E4
Barnham, W. Susx......12 C6
Barnham, Suff......38 D3
Barnham Broom......49 F7
Barnhead......93 H6
Barnhill......99 K3
Barningham, Durham......68 C5
Barningham, Suff......38 E3
Barnoldby le Beck......59 G6
Barnoldswick......62 B5
Barns Green......12 E4
Barnsley, Glos......30 E7
Barnsley, S. Yks......55 G3
Barnstaple......7 F2
Barnston, Essex......22 C2
Barnston, Mers......52 D5
Barnt Green......34 B3
Barnton......53 H6
Barnwell......36 D2
Barnwood......30 C6
Barony, The......116 B4
Barr......70 D2
Barrachan......70 E7
Barrack......101 H4
Barraglom......111 F4
Barrahormid......83 G3
Barran......84 A2
Barrapol......88 A4
Barras, Grampn......93 K3
Barras, Cumbr......67 L5
Barrasford......74 F6
Barravullin......89 K8
Barregarrow......60 Q3
Barrhead......77 L2
Barrhill......70 D3
Barrington, Somer......8 E3
Barrington, Cambs......37 G6
Barripper......2 E6
Barrmill......77 J2
Barrock......115 H2
Barrow, Leic......46 B6
Barrow, Suff......38 C4
Barrow, Shrops......43 H7
Barrow, Lancs......61 L6
Barroway Drove......47 J7
Barrowby......46 B4
Barrowden......46 C7
Barrowford......62 B6
Barrow Gurney......17 G4
Barrow-in-Furness......60 E3
Barrow Street......9 K1
Barrow upon Humber......58 E4
Barrow upon Soar......45 G6
Barrow upon Trent......44 E5
Barry, Tays......87 J1

Barry, S. Glam......25 K8
Barry Island......25 K8
Barsby......45 H6
Barsham......39 J2
Barston......34 D3
Bartestree......29 K3
Barthol Chapel......101 H5
Bartholomew......43 J2
Bartley......10 E3
Bartlow......37 J6
Barton, Warw......34 C5
Barton, N. Yks......68 E6
Barton, Ches......42 F2
Barton, Glos......30 F5
Barton, Cambs......37 H5
Barton, Lancs......61 J6
Barton, Devon......5 K5
Barton Bendish......48 C7
Barton Hartshorn......35 H7
Barton in Fabis......45 G4
Barton in the Beans......44 E7
Barton-le-Clay......36 D7
Barton-le-Street......64 E5
Barton-le-Willows......64 E6
Barton Mills......38 C3
Barton Moss......53 J4
Barton on Sea......10 D5
Barton-on-the-Heath......31 G4
Barton Seagrave......36 B3
Barton Stacey......18 F6
Baton St David......9 G1
Barton Turf......49 J5
Barton-under-Needwood......44 C6
Barton-upon-Humber......58 E4
Barvas......111 H3
Barway......37 J3
Barwell......45 F8
Barwick......9 G3
Barwick in Elmet......63 H6
Baschurch......42 F5
Bascote......34 F4
Basford Green......44 A2
Bashall Eaves......61 L5
Bashley......10 D5
Basildon......22 D5
Basingstoke......19 H5
Baslow......55 F6
Bason Bridge......16 E6
Bassaleg......16 D2
Bassenthwaite......66 E3
Bassett......10 F3
Bassingbourn......37 G6
Bassingfield......45 H4
Bassingham......56 D8
Bassingthorpe......46 C5
Bastonthorpe......39 G4
Baston......46 E6
Bastwick......49 K6
Batchcott......32 D3
Batcombe, Dorset......9 H4
Batcombe, Somer......17 H7
Bate Heath......53 H6
Bath......17 J4
Bathampton......17 J4
Bathealton......7 J4
Batheaston......17 J4
Bathford......17 J4
Bathgate......79 G3
Bathley......56 B8
Bathpool......4 C4
Bathurst......63 F7
Batley......63 F7
Batsford......31 F4
Battersby......69 H6
Battersea......21 G6
Battisford......38 F5
Battisford Tye......38 F5
Battle, Powys......25 J1
Battle, E. Susx......13 L5
Battlefield......43 G6
Battlesbridge......22 D4
Battlesden......36 C8
Battleton......7 K3
Battramsley......10 E5
Bauds of Cullen......100 D2
Baughton......19 G4
Baulking......18 E1
Baumber......57 G6
Baunton......30 E7
Baverstock......10 B1
Bawburgh......49 G7
Bawdeswell......48 F5
Bawdrip......16 E7
Bawdsey......39 J6
Bawtry......55 K4
Baxenden......62 A7
Baxterley......44 D8
Baycliff......61 F2
Baydon......18 D3
Bayford......21 H3
Bayham Abbey......13 K3
Bayhead......104 C5
Bayles......67 K2
Baylham......39 G5
Bayston Hill......43 F7
Baythorn......33 F3
Beachampton......35 J7
Beachamwell......48 C7
Beachans......99 J4
Beachborough......15 H5
Beachley......17 G1
Beacon......8 C4
Beacon End......22 F1
Beaconsfield......20 D4
Beacravik......105 G2
Beadlam......64 B4
Beadnell......81 L7
Beaford......7 F4
Beal, Northum......81 J5
Beal, N. Yks......63 J7
Bealsmill......4 E4
Beaminster......9 F4
Beamish......68 E1
Beamsley......62 D4
Bean......14 B1

Beanacre......17 L4
Beanley......75 G2
Beaquoy......116 C4
Beare Green......12 E2
Bearley......34 C4
Bearpark......68 E2
earsbridge......67 K1
Bearsden......85 H7
Bearsted......14 D3
Bearwood......10 B5
Beattock......73 F3
Beauchamp Roding......21 K2
Beauchief......55 G5
Beaufort......25 K3
Beaulieu......10 E4
Beauly......98 D4
Beaumaris......50 F3
Beaumont, Essex......39 G8
Beaumont, Cumbr......73 J8
Beausale......34 D3
Beaworthy......4 E2
Beazley End......38 C8
Bebington......52 E5
Bebside......75 J5
Beccles......39 K1
Becconsall......61 H7
Beckbury......43 J7
Beckenham......21 H7
Beckermet......66 C6
Beckermonds......62 B1
Beckfoot, Cumbr......66 C2
Beckfoot, Cumbr......66 D6
Beck Foot, Cumbr......67 J7
Beckford......30 D4
Beckhampton......18 B4
Beck Hole......64 F2
Beckingham, Lincs......46 B2
Beckingham, Notts......56 B4
Beckington......17 K5
Beckley, E. Susx......14 E6
Beckley, Oxon......31 K6
Beck Row......38 B3
Beck Side......60 F1
Beckton......21 J5
Beckwithshaw......63 F4
Becontree......21 J5
Bedale......63 F1
Bedburn......68 D3
Beddau......25 J6
Beddgelert......50 E6
Beddingham......13 H6
Beddington......21 H7
Bedfield......39 H4
Bedford......36 D6
Bedhampton......11 J4
Bedingfield......39 G4
Bedlington......75 J5
Bedlinog......25 J4
Bedmond......20 E3
Bednall......44 A6
Bedrule......74 C2
Bedstone......32 C3
Bedwas......25 K6
Bedworth......34 E2
Beeby......45 H7
Beech, Hants......19 H7
Beech, Staffs......43 K4
Beech Hill......20 A7
Beechingstoke......18 B5
Beedon......19 F3
Beeford......65 J6
Beeley......55 F6
Beelsby......59 G6
Beenham......19 G4
Beer......8 D5
Beer Crocombe......8 E2
Beer Hackett......9 G3
Beesands......5 J7
Beesby......57 J5
Beeson......5 J7
Beeston, Beds......36 E6
Beeston, Norf......48 E6
Beeston, W. Yks......63 F6
Beeston, Notts......45 G4
Beeston, Ches......53 G8
Beeston Regis......49 G3
Beeswing......72 D7
Beetham......61 H2
Beetley......48 E6
Begbroke......31 J6
Begdale......26 F7
Beguildy......32 A3
Beighton, S. Yks......55 H5
Beighton, Norf......49 J7
Beith......77 J2
Bekesbourne......15 J3
Belaugh......49 H6
Belbroughton......33 G2
Belchamp Otten......38 D6
Belchamp St Paul......38 C6
Belchamp Walter......38 D6
Belchford......57 G6
Belford......81 K6
Belhelvie......101 J7
Belhinnie......100 E5
Bellabeg......100 C7
Bellanoch......83 G2
Bell Busk......62 C4
Belleau......57 J6
Belleheiglash......100 A5
Bellerby......68 D7
Bellever......5 G4
Bellingdon......20 D3
Bellingham......74 E5
Belloch......76 B4
Bellochantuy......76 B4
Bellsbank......77 K7
Bellshill, Strath......78 E4
Bellshill, Northum......81 K6
Bellsmyre......85 G7
Bellspool......79 J8
Bellsquarry......79 H3
Bells Yew Green......13 K3
Belmaduthy......98 E4
Belmesthorpe......46 D6
Belmont......53 H2
Belnacraig......100 C7

Belowda......3 H3
Belper......44 E3
Belsay......75 H6
Belses......80 D7
Belsford......5 H6
Belstead......39 G6
Belston......77 J5
Belstone......5 G2
Belthorn......61 L7
Beltinge......15 J2
Beltoft......58 C6
Belton, Humbs......58 B6
Belton, Leic......46 B7
Belton, Lincs......46 C4
Belton, Leic......45 F5
Belton, Norf......49 K7
Belvedere......21 J6
Belvoir......46 B4
Bembridge......11 H6
Bemersyde......80 D6
Bempton......65 J5
Benacre......39 L2
Benbuie......72 C4
Ben Casgro......111 J5
Benderloch......89 L5
Benenden......14 E5
Bengate......49 J5
Benholm......93 K5
Beningbrough......63 J4
Benington, Lincs......47 G3
Benington, Herts......21 H1
Benllech......50 E2
Benmore, Strath......84 D6
Benmore, Central......85 G2
Bennacott......4 C2
Bennan......76 E5
Bennecarrigan......76 E5
Benniworth......57 G5
Benover......13 L2
Benson......20 A4
Benthall......43 H7
Bentham......30 D6
Benthoul......101 H8
Bentley, H. & W......34 A4
Bentley, Warw......44 D8
Bentley, Humbs......58 E3
Bentley, S. Yks......55 J3
Bentley, Hants......19 J6
Bentley Heath......34 C3
Bentpath......73 J4
Bentworth......19 H6
Benwick......37 G2
Beoley......34 B4
Beoraidbeg......96 B6
Bepton......11 K3
Berden......37 H8
Berea......26 B5
Bere Alston......4 E5
Bere Ferrers......4 E5
Berepper......2 E7
Bere Regis......9 K5
Bergh Apton......49 J7
Berinsfield......31 K8
Berkeley......30 A8
Berkhamsted......20 D3
Berkley......17 K6
Berkswell......34 D3
Bermondsey......21 H6
Bernera......96 D3
Bernisdale......103 F3
Berrick Salome......20 A4
Berriedale......109 K1
Berrier......67 G4
Berriew......42 C7
Berrington, Shrops......43 G7
Berrington, Northum......81 J5
Berrow......16 D5
Berrow Geen......33 G5
Berry Hill......29 K6
Berryhillock......100 E2
Berrynarbor......7 F1
Berry Pomeroy......5 J5
Bersham......42 E3
Bersted......12 C6
Berwick......13 J6
Berwick Bassett......18 C3
Berwick Hill......75 H6
Berwick St James......18 B7
Berwick St John......10 A2
Berwick St Leonard......9 L1
Berwick-upon-Tweed......81 H4
Berwyn......42 C3
Besford......33 J6
Bessacarr......55 K3
Bessels Leigh......31 J7
Bessingham......49 G4
Besthorpe, Notts......56 C7
Besthorpe, Norf......48 F8
Beswick......65 H8
Betchworth......12 F1
Bethania, Dyfed......40 E7
Bethania, Gwyn......51 F5
Bethel......50 E4
Bethersden......14 F4
Bethesda, Dyfed......26 E6
Bethesda, Gwyn......51 F4
Bethlehem......24 E2
Bethnal Green......21 H5
Betley......43 J3
Betsham......14 C1
Betteshanger......15 K3
Bettiscombe......8 E5
Bettisfield......42 F4
Betton, Shrops......42 F3
Betton, Shrops......43 H4
Bettws, Gwent......16 D1
Bettws, Gwent......29 G6
Bettws Cedewain......42 C8
Bettws Gwerfil Goch......51 K6
Bettws Newydd......29 H7
Bettyhill......113 J2
Betws, M. Glam......25 H6
Betws, Dyfed......27 K2
Betws Bledrws......27 K2
Betws Garmon......50 E5

Betws Ifan 27 H3
Betws-y-Coed 51 G5
Betws-yn-Rhos 51 J3
Beulah, Powys 28 D2
Beulah, Dyfed 27 G3
Bevendean 13 G6
Bevercotes 56 A6
Beveley 58 E3
Beverston 30 C8
Bevington 30 A8
Bewaldeth 66 E3
Bewcastle 74 B6
Bewdley 33 G3
Bewerley 62 E3
Bewholme 65 J7
Bexhill 13 L6
Bexley 21 J6
Bexwell 48 B7
Beyton 38 E4
Bibury 30 F7
Bicester 31 K5
Bickenhall 8 D3
Bickenhill 34 C2
Bicker 47 F4
Bickerstaffe 52 F3
Bickerton, Ches 43 G2
Bickerton, N. Yks 63 H4
Bickington, Devon 7 F2
Bickington, Devon 5 H4
Bickleigh, Devon 5 F5
Bickleigh, Devon 7 K5
Bickleton 6 F2
Bickley 21 J7
Bickley Moss 43 G3
Bicknacre 22 D3
Bicknoller 16 C7
Bicknor 14 E3
Bickton 10 C3
Bicton, Shrops 32 B2
Bicton, Shrops 42 F6
Bidborough 13 J2
Biddenden 14 E5
Biddenham 36 D5
Biddestone 17 K3
Biddisham 16 E5
Biddlesden 35 H6
Biddlestone 74 F3
Biddulph 53 K8
Biddulph Moor 53 L8
Bideford 6 E3
Bidford-on-Avon 34 C5
Bielby 58 B2
Bieldside 93 K1
Bierley 11 G7
Bierton 20 C2
Bigbury 5 G7
Bigbury-on-Sea 5 G7
Bigby 58 E6
Biggar, Cumbr 60 E3
Biggar, Strath 79 H6
Biggin, Derby 44 D3
Biggin, Derby 54 E8
Biggin, N. Yks 63 J6
Biggings 118 D2
Biggin Hill 21 J8
Biggins 61 K2
Biggleswade 36 E6
Bighton 11 H1
Bignor 12 C5
Big Sand 106 C4
Bigton 119 F6
Bilberry 3 J3
Bilborough 45 G3
Bilbrook 43 K7
Bilbrough 63 J5
Bilbster 115 H4
Bildeston 38 E6
Billericay 22 C4
Billesdon 45 J7
Billesley 34 C5
Billing 35 K4
Billingborough 46 E4
Billinge 53 G3
Billingford, Norf 48 F5
Billingford, Suff 39 G3
Billingham 69 G4
Billinghay 46 E2
Billingley 55 H3
Billingshurst 12 D4
Billingsley 33 G2
Billington, Beds 20 D1
Billington, Lancs 61 L6
Billockby 49 K6
Billy Row 68 D3
Bilsborrow 61 J5
Bilsby 57 J6
Bilsington 15 G5
Bilsthorpe 55 K7
Bilston, W. Mids 44 A8
Bilston, Loth 79 K3
Bilstone 44 E7
Bilting 15 G4
Bilton, Warw 35 F3
Bilton, Humbs 59 F3
Bilton, N. Yks 63 H4
Bilton, Northum 75 J2
Bimbister 116 C5
Binbrook 57 G4
Bincombe 9 H6
Binegar 17 H6
Binfield 20 C6
Binfield Heath 20 B6
Bingfield 75 F6
Bingham 45 J4
Bingley 62 E6
Binham 48 E4
Binley, W. Mids 34 E3
Binley, Hants 18 F5
Binley Woods 34 E3
Binniehill 86 B7
Binstead 11 G5
Binsted 19 J6
Binton 34 C5
Bintree 48 F5
Binweston 42 E7

Birch, Essex 22 F2
Birch, G. Man 53 K3
Bircham Newton 48 C4
Bircham Tofts 48 C4
Birchanger 21 K1
Bircher 32 D4
Birch Green 22 F2
Birchgrove 24 F5
Birchington 15 J2
Birchover 55 F7
Birch Vale 54 D5
Bircotes 55 K4
Birdbrook 38 C6
Birdham 11 K4
Birdingbury 34 F4
Birdlip 30 D6
Birdsall 64 F6
Birds Green 33 G2
Birdston 85 J7
Birdwell 55 G3
Birdwood 30 B6
Birgham 81 F6
Birkdale 52 E2
Birkenhead 52 E5
Birkenhills 101 G4
Birkenshaw, Strath 78 D3
Birkenshaw, W. Yks 62 F7
Birkhall 92 E2
Birkhill 87 G1
Birkin 63 J7
Birley 29 J2
Birling, Kent 14 C2
Birling, Northum 75 J3
Birlingham 33 J6
Birmingham 34 B2
Birnam 92 B7
Birness 101 J5
Birse 93 G2
Birsemore 93 G2
Birstall 45 G7
Birstall Smithies 63 F7
Birstwith 63 F4
Birtley, H. & W 32 C4
Birtley, T. & W 68 E1
Birtley, Northum 74 E6
Birts Street 33 G7
Bisbrooke 46 B8
Bishampton 34 A5
Bishop Auckland 68 E4
Bishopbriggs 85 J7
Bishop Burton 58 D3
Bishop Middleham 68 F3
Bishop Monkton 63 G3
Bishop Norton 56 D4
Bishopsbourne 15 H3
Bishops Cannings 18 B4
Bishop's Castle 32 C2
Bishop's Caundle 9 G3
Bishop's Cleeve 30 D5
Bishop's Frome 33 F6
Bishop's Itchington 34 E5
Bishops Lydeard 8 C2
Bishop's Nympton 7 H3
Bishop's Offley 43 J5
Bishop's Stortford 21 J1
Bishop's Sutton 11 H1
Bishop's Tachbrook 34 E4
Bishop's Tawton 7 F2
Bishopsteignton 5 K4
Bishopstoke 11 F3
Bishopston 24 D6
Bishopstone, Wilts 10 B2
Bishopstone, Bucks 20 C2
Bishopstone, Wilts 18 D2
Bishopstone, E. Susx 13 H6
Bishopstone, H. & W 29 J3
Bishop Sutton 17 G5
Bishop's Waltham 11 G3
Bishopswood, Somer 8 D3
Bishop's Wood, Staffs 43 K7
Bishopsworth 17 G4
Bishop Thornton 63 F3
Bishopthorpe 63 J5
Bishopton, Durham 69 F4
Bishopton, Strath 85 G7
Bishop Wilton 64 E7
Bishton 16 E2
Bisley, Glos 30 D7
Bisley, Surrey 20 D8
Bispham 61 G5
Bissoe 2 F5
Bisterne Close 10 D4
Bitchfield 46 C5
Bittadon 7 F1
Bittaford 5 G6
Bittering 48 E6
Bitterley 32 E3
Bitterne 11 F3
Bitteswell 35 G2
Bitton 17 H4
Bix 20 B5
Bixter 119 F3
Blaby 45 G8
Blackacre 73 F4
Blackadder 81 G4
Blackawton 5 J6
Blackborough 8 B4
Blackborough End 48 B6
Black Bourton 31 G7
Blackboys 13 J4
Blackbrook 43 J4
Blackburn, Loth 79 G3
Blackburn, Grampn 101 H7
Blackburn, Lancs 61 K7
Black Callerton 75 H7
Black Clauchrie 70 D3
Blackden Heath 53 J4
Black Dog, Devon 7 J5
Blackdog, Grampn 101 J7
Blackfield 11 F4
Blackford, Tays 86 B4
Blackford, Somer 16 F6
Blackford, Somer 9 H2

Blackford, Cumbr 73 J7
Blackfordby 44 E6
Blackgang 11 F7
Blackhall 93 H2
Blackhall Rocks 69 G3
Blackham 13 J3
Blackhaugh 80 C6
Blackheath, W. Mids 34 A2
Blackheath, Essex 23 G1
Blackhill 101 K3
Blackland 18 B4
Blackley 53 K3
Blacklunans 92 C5
Black Marsh 42 E8
Blackmill 25 H6
Blackmoor 11 J1
Blackmore 22 C3
Blackmore End 38 C7
Black Mount 90 D7
Blackness 86 D7
Black Notley 22 D1
Blacko 62 B5
Black Pill 24 E5
Blackpool 61 G6
Blackpool Gate 74 B6
Blackridge 79 F3
Blackrock, Strath 82 C5
Blackrock, Gwent 25 L3
Black Rocks 65 H4
Blackrod 53 H2
Blackshaw 73 F7
Blackstone 12 F5
Blackthorn 20 A2
Blackthorpe 38 E4
Blacktoft 58 C4
Blacktop 101 H8
Black Torrington 6 E5
Blackwater, Hants 20 C7
Blackwater, Corn 2 F5
Blackwater, I. of W 11 G6
Blackwaterfoot 76 D5
Blackwell, H. & W 34 A3
Blackwell, Derby 54 E6
Blackwood, Strath 78 E5
Blackwood, Gwent 25 K5
Blackwood Hill 43 L2
Blacon 52 E7
Bladerstone 61 K6
Bladnoch 71 F6
Bladon 31 J6
Blaenannerch 27 G3
Blaenau Ffestiniog 51 G6
Blaenavon 29 G7
Blaendyryn 28 D4
Blaenffos 27 F4
Blaengarw 25 H5
Blaengwrach 25 G4
Blaengwynfi 25 G5
Blaenpennal 41 F7
Blaenplwyf 40 E6
Blaenporth 27 G3
Blaenrhondda 25 H5
Blaenwaun 27 G5
Blagdon, Avon 17 G5
Blagdon, Devon 5 J5
Blagdon Hill 8 D3
Blaich 90 B4
Blaina 25 L4
Blair Atholl 91 K5
Blairdaff 101 F7
Blairgowrie 92 C7
Blairhall 86 D6
Blairingone 86 C5
Blairlogie 85 L5
Blairmore 84 D6
Blaisdon 30 B6
Blakebrook 33 H3
Blakedown 33 H3
Blakelaw 80 F6
Blakemere 29 H3
Blakeney, Glos 30 A7
Blakeney, Norf 48 F3
Blakenhall, Ches 43 J3
Blakenhall, W. Mids 43 L8
Blakeshall 33 H2
Blakesley 35 H5
Blanchland 68 B1
Blandford Camp 9 L4
Blandford Forum 9 K4
Blandford St Mary 9 K4
Bland Hill 62 F4
Blanefield 85 H7
Blankney 56 E7
Blarmachfoldach 90 B5
Blarnalearoch 107 G2
Blashford 10 C4
Blaston 45 K8
Blatherwycke 46 C8
Blawith 61 F1
Blaxhall 39 J5
Blaxton 55 K3
Blaydon 75 H7
Bleadon 16 E5
Blean 15 H2
Bleasby 45 J3
Bleatarn 67 K5
Blebocraigs 87 H3
Bleddfa 32 B4
Bledington 31 G5
Bledlow 20 B3
Bledlow Ridge 20 B4
Blegbie 80 C3
Blencarn 67 J3
Blencogo 66 D2
Blencow 67 G3
Blendworth 11 J3
Blennerhasset 66 D2
Bletchingdon 31 K6
Bletchingley 13 G1
Bletchley, Bucks 36 B7
Bletchley, Shrops 43 H4
Bletherston 26 E5
Bletsoe 36 D5

Blewbury 19 G2
Blickling 49 G5
Blidworth 45 G2
Blindcrake 66 D3
Blindley Heath 13 G2
Blisland 3 K2
Blissford 10 C3
Bliss Gate 33 G3
Blisworth 35 J5
Blockley 31 F4
Blofield 49 J7
Blo' Norton 38 F3
Blore 44 C3
Bloxham 31 J4
Bloxwich 44 B7
Bloxworth 9 K5
Blubberhouses 62 E4
Blue Anchor 16 B6
Blue Bell Hill 14 D2
Blundellsands 52 E4
Blundeston 49 L8
Blunham 36 E5
Blunsdon St Andrew 18 C2
Bluntisham 37 G3
Blyborough 56 D4
Blyford 39 K3
Blymhill 43 K6
Blyth, Northum 75 K5
Blyth, Notts 55 K5
Blyth Bridge 79 J5
Blythburgh 39 K3
Blythe 80 D5
Blythe Bridge 44 A3
Blyton 56 C4
Boarhills 87 J3
Boarhunt 11 H4
Boarshead 13 J3
Boarstall 20 A2
Boasley Cross 4 F2
Boath 108 D6
Boat of Garten 99 H7
Bobbing 14 E2
Bobbington 33 H1
Bocaddon 3 K4
Bockhampton 9 J5
Bocking 22 D1
Bocking Churchstreet 22 D1
Boddam, Shetld 119 F7
Boddam, Grampn 101 L4
Bodedern 50 C2
Bodelwyddan 51 K3
Bodenham, Wilts 10 C2
Bodenham, H. & W 29 K2
Bodewryd 50 D1
Bodfari 51 K3
Bodffordd 50 D3
Bodham 49 G3
Bodiam 14 D6
Bodicote 35 F7
Bodieve 3 H2
Bodinnick 3 K4
Bodle Street Green 13 K5
Bodmin 3 J3
Bodney 48 D8
Boduan 50 C7
Bogallan 98 E3
Bogbrae 101 K5
Bogend 77 J4
Boghall 79 G3
Bogmoor 100 C2
Bogniebrae 100 E4
Bognor Regis 12 C7
Bograxie 101 G7
Bog, The 42 E8
Bogton 100 F3
Bohenie 90 D3
Bohortha 3 G6
Bohuntine 90 D3
Boisdale 94 C4
Bojewyan 2 B6
Bolam 68 D4
Bold Heath 53 G5
Boldon 75 K7
Boldre 10 E5
Boldron 68 C5
Bole 56 C5
Bolehill 44 D2
Boleside 80 C6
Bolham 7 K4
Bolham Water 8 C3
Bolingey 2 F4
Bollington, Ches 53 J5
Bollington, Ches 53 L6
Bolney 12 F4
Bolnhurst 36 D5
Bolsover 55 H6
Bolsterstone 55 F4
Bolstone 29 K4
Boltby 63 H1
Bolton, Humbs 64 E7
Bolton, Northum 75 H2
Bolton, G. Man 53 J3
Bolton, Cumbr 67 J4
Bolton, Loth 87 J7
Bolton Abbey 62 D4
Bolton-by-Bowland 62 A5
Boltonfellend 73 K7
Boltongate 66 E2
Bolton-le-Sands 61 H3
Bolton-on-Swale 63 F1
Bolton Percy 63 J5
Bolton upon Dearne 55 H3
Bolventor 3 K2
Bomere Heath 43 F6
Bonar Bridge 108 E4
Bonawe 84 C1
Bonby 58 E5
Boncath 27 G4
Bonchester Bridge 74 B2
Bondleigh 7 G5
Bonehill 44 C7
Bo'Ness 86 C6
Bonhill 85 F7
Boningale 43 K7
Bonjedward 80 E7

Bonkle 79 F4
Bonnington, Northnts 86 E8
Bonnington, Kent 15 G5
Bonnybridge 85 L6
Bonnykelly 101 H3
Bonnyrigg and Lasswade 80 B3
Bonnyton 93 H6
Bonsall 55 F8
Bont 29 H6
Bontddu 41 F2
Bont Dolgadfan 41 H3
Bont-goch or Elerch 41 F5
Bontnewydd, Gwyn 50 D4
Bont-newydd, Clwyd 51 K3
Bontuchel 51 K5
Bonvilston 25 J7
Booker 20 C4
Booley 43 G5
Boosbeck 69 J5
Boot 66 D6
Boothby Graffoe 56 D8
Boothby Pagnell 46 C4
Boothstown 53 J3
Booth Wood Reservoir 60 E1
Bootle, Cumbr 60 E1
Bootle, Mers 52 E4
Boraston 33 F3
Borcheston 45 F7
Borden 14 E2
Bordley 62 C3
Bordon Camp 11 J1
Boreham, Essex 22 D3
Boreham, Wilts 17 K6
Boreham Street 13 K5
Borehamwood 21 F4
Boreland 73 G4
Borgie 113 H3
Borgue, Highld 115 G7
Borgue, D. & G 71 H7
Borley 38 D6
Borness 71 H7
Bornesketaig 102 E1
Boroughbridge 63 G3
Borough Green 13 K1
Borras Head 42 E2
Borreraig 102 C3
Borrowby 69 G8
Borrowwash 44 F4
Borth 40 F4
Borthwickbrae 73 K2
Borthwickshiels 73 K2
Borth-y-Gest 50 E7
Borve, W. Isles 94 B5
Borve, W. Isles 104 E3
Borve, W. Isles 104 F2
Borve, Highld 103 F4
Borwick 61 J2
Bosavern 2 B6
Bosbury 33 F6
Boscastle 4 A2
Boscombe, Dorset 10 C5
Boscombe, Wilts 18 D7
Bosham 11 K4
Bosherston 26 D8
Boskednan 2 C6
Bosley 53 L7
Bossall 64 E6
Bossiney 3 A3
Bossingham 15 H4
Bossington 7 J1
Bosta 111 F3
Bostock Green 53 H7
Boston 47 G3
Boston Spa 63 H5
Boswinger 3 H5
Botallack 2 B6
Boany Bay 21 G4
Botesdale 38 F3
Bothal 75 J5
Bothamsall 55 K6
Bothel 66 D3
Bothenhampton 9 F5
Bothwell 78 E4
Botley, Bucks 20 D3
Botley, Hants 11 G3
Botley, Oxon 31 J7
Botolphs 12 E6
Bottacks 98 C2
Bottesford, Humbs 58 C6
Bottesford, Leic 45 K4
Bottisham 37 J4
Bottomcraig 87 G2
Botusfleming 4 E5
Botwnnog 50 B7
Boughrood 28 F4
Boughspring 29 K8
Boughton, Norf 48 B7
Boughton, Northnts 35 J4
Boughton, Notts 55 K7
Boughton Aluph 15 G4
Boughton Lees 15 G4
Boughton Malherbe 14 E4
Boughton Monchelsea 13 L1
Boughton Street 15 G3
Boulby 69 K5
Bouldon 32 E2
Boulmer 75 J2
Boulston 26 D6
Boultham 56 D7
Bourn 37 G5
Bourne 46 D5
Bourne End, Bucks 20 C5
Bourne End, Beds 36 C6
Bourne End, Herts 20 E3
Bournemouth 10 B5
Bournes Green 30 D7
Bourneville 34 B2
Bournheath 34 A3
Bournmoor 68 F1
Bourton, Oxon 18 D2
Bourton, Avon 16 E4
Bourton, Shrops 43 G8
Bourton, Dorset 9 J1
Bourton on Dunsmore 34 F3
Bourton-on-the-Hill 31 F4
Bourton-on-the-Water 31 F5

Boveney 20 D6
Boverton 25 H8
Bovey Tracey 5 J4
Bovingdon 20 E3
Bovingdon Camp 9 K6
Bow, G. Lon 21 H5
Bow, Devon 7 H5
Bowbank 68 B4
Bow Brickhill 36 C7
Bowburn 68 F3
Bowcombe 11 F6
Bowd 8 C5
Bowden, Border 80 D6
Bowden, Devon 5 J7
Bowden Hill 18 A4
Bowderdale 67 J6
Bowdon 53 J5
Bowenchalke 10 B2
Bowermadden 115 H3
Bowers Gifford 22 D5
Bowershall 86 D5
Bowertower 115 H3
Bowes 68 B5
Bowhill 80 C7
Bowland 80 C5
Bowland Bridge 67 G8
Bowley 29 K2
Bowlhead Green 12 C3
Bowling 85 G7
Bowling Bank 42 E3
Bowling Green 33 H6
Bowmanstead 66 F7
Bowmore 82 C6
Bowness-on-Solway 73 H7
Bowness-on-Windermere 67 G7
Bowsden 81 H5
Bow Street 41 F5
Bowthorpe 49 G7
Box, Glos 30 C7
Box, Wilts 17 K4
Boxbush 30 B6
Boxford, Suff 38 E6
Boxford, Berks 18 F3
Boxgrove 11 L4
Boxley 14 D3
Boxted, Suff 38 D5
Boxted, Essex 38 E7
Boxworth 37 G4
Boylestone 44 C4
Boyndie 100 F2
Boyndlie 101 J2
Boynton 65 J6
Boyton, Wilts 18 A7
Boyton, Corn 4 D2
Boyton, Suff 39 J4
Bozeat 36 C5
Braaid 60 Q4
Brabling Green 39 H4
Brabourne 15 H4
Brabourne Lees 15 G4
Brabster 115 J3
Bracadale 102 E3
Braceborough 46 D6
Bracebridge Heath 56 D7
Braceby 46 D4
Bracewell 62 B5
Brackenfield 55 G8
Brackletter 90 C3
Brackley, Strath 76 D3
Brackley, Northnts 35 G7
Bracknell 20 C7
Braco 85 L4
Bracobrae 100 E3
Bracon Ash 49 G8
Bracora 96 CG
Bracorina 96 C5
Bradbourne 44 D2
Bradbury 68 F4
Bradda 60 N4
Bradden 35 H6
Braddock 3 K3
Bradenham, Bucks 20 C4
Bradenham, Norf 48 E7
Bradenstoke 18 B3
Bradfield, Essex 39 G7
Bradfield, Berks 19 H3
Bradfield, Norf 49 H4
Bradfield Combust 38 D5
Bradfield Green 53 H8
Bradfield St Clare 38 E5
Bradfield St George 38 E4
Bradford, Devon 6 E5
Bradford, W. Yks 62 E6
Bradford, Northum 81 K6
Bradford Abbas 9 G3
Bradford Leigh 17 K4
Bradford-on-Avon 17 K4
Bradford-on-Tone 8 C2
Bradford Peverell 9 H5
Brading 11 K6
Bradley, Derby 44 D3
Bradley, Humbs 59 F6
Bradley, Hants 19 H6
Bradley, Staffs 43 K6
Bradley Green 34 A4
Bradley in the Moors 44 B3
Bradmore 45 G4
Bradninch 7 K5
Bradnop 44 B2
Bradpole 9 F5
Bradshaw 53 J2
Bradstone 4 D3
Bradwall Green 53 J2
Bradwell, Bucks 36 B7
Bradwell, Essex 22 E1
Bradwell, Derby 54 E5
Bradwell, Norf 49 L7
Bradwell Grove 31 G7
Bradwell-on-Sea 23 G3
Bradwell Waterside 23 F3
Bradworthy 6 D4
Brae, Highld 106 D3
Brae, Highld 98 E2
Brae, Shetld 120 F6
Braeantra 108 D6

Braefield 98 C5
Braehead, Orkney 116 D2
Braehead, Strath 79 F6
Braehead, D. & G. 71 F6
Braehead, Strath 79 G4
Braehead, Tays 93 H6
Braehoulland 120 E5
Braemar 92 C2
Braemore 115 F6
Brae of Achnahaird 112 B7
Brae Roy Lodge 90 E2
Braeside 84 E7
Braes, The 103 G5
Braeswick 117 F3
Brafferton, Durham 68 E4
Brafferton, N. Yks 63 H2
Brafield-on-the-Green 36 B5
Bragar 111 G3
Bragbury End 21 G1
Braides 61 H4
Braidley 62 D1
Braidwood 79 F5
Brailes 34 E7
Brailsford 44 D3
Braintree 22 D1
Braiseworth 39 G3
Braishfield 10 E2
Braithwaite 66 C4
Braithwell 55 J4
Bramber 12 E5
Bramcote 45 G4
Bramdean 11 H2
Bramerton 49 H7
Bramfield, Herts 21 G2
Bramfield, Suff. 39 K3
Bramford 36 E6
Bramhall 53 K5
Bramham 63 H5
Bramhope 63 F5
Bramley, Hants 20 A8
Bramley, Surrey 12 D2
Bramley, S. Yks 55 H4
Brampford Speke 5 K2
Brampton, Cumbr 74 B7
Brampton, Lincs 56 C6
Brampton, Cambs 36 F3
Brampton, S. Yks 55 H3
Brampton, Norf 49 H5
Brampton, Cumbr 67 J4
Brampton, Suff 39 K2
Brampton Abbots 29 L5
Brampton Ash 35 J2
Brampton Bryan 32 C3
Bramshall 44 B4
Bramshaw 10 D3
Bramshott 11 K1
Brancaster 48 C3
Brancepeth 68 E3
Branchill 99 J3
Branderburgh 100 B1
Brandesburton 59 F2
Brandeston 39 H4
Brandiston 49 G5
Brandon, Suff 38 C2
Brandon, Lincs 46 C3
Brandon, Durham 68 E3
Brandon, Warw 34 F3
Brandon, Northum 75 G2
Brandon Bank 38 B2
Brandon Creek 38 B1
Brandon Parva 48 F7
Brandsby 63 J2
Brane 2 C7
Bran End 38 B8
Branksome 10 B5
Branksome Park 10 B5
Branscombe 8 C6
Bransford 33 G5
Bransgore 10 C5
Branston, Leic 46 B5
Branston, taffs 44 D3
Branston, Lincs 56 E7
Branstone 11 H6
Brant Broughton 46 C2
Brantham 36 E7
Branthwaite 66 E3
Brantingham 58 D4
Branton, Northum 75 G2
Branton, S. Yks 55 K3
Branxholme 73 K2
Branxholm Park 73 K2
Branxton 81 G6
Brassington 44 D2
Brasted 13 H1
Brasted Chart 13 H1
Brathens 93 H2
Bratoft 57 J7
Brattleby 56 D5
Bratton 17 L5
Bratton Clovelly 4 E2
Bratton Fleming 7 G2
Bratton Seymour 9 H2
Braughing 37 G8
Braunston, Leic 46 B5
Braunston, Northnts 35 G4
Braunstone 45 G7
Braunton 6 E2
Brawby 64 E5
Brawl 114 D3
Brawlbin 115 F4
Bray 20 D6
Braybrooke 35 J2
Brayford 7 G2
Bray Shop 4 D4
Braystones 66 C6
Brayton 63 K6
Brazacott 4 C2
Breachwood Green 21 F1
Breaclete 111 F4
Breadstone 30 B7
Breage 2 E7
Breakachy 98 C4
Breakish 96 B3
Bream 29 L7
Breamore 10 C3

Brean 16 D5
Brearton 63 G3
Breasclete 111 G4
Breaston 45 F4
Brechfa 27 K4
Brechin 93 G5
Breckles 48 E8
Breckrey 103 G2
Brecon 25 J2
Bredbury 53 L4
Brede 14 E7
Bredenbury 29 L2
Bredfield 39 H5
Bredgar 14 E2
Bredhurst 14 D2
Bredon 33 J7
Bredon's Norton 33 J7
Bredwardine 29 H3
Breedon on the Hill 44 F5
Breich 79 G3
Breighton 58 B3
Bremhill 18 A3
Brenchley 13 K2
Brendon 7 H1
Brenish 110 D5
Brent Eleigh 38 E6
Brentford 21 F6
Brent Knoll 16 E5
Brent Pelham 37 H7
Brentwood 22 B4
Brenzett 15 G6
Brereton 44 B6
Brereton Green 53 J7
Brereton Heath 53 K7
Bressingham 39 F2
Bretby 44 D5
Bretford 34 F3
Bretforton 34 B6
Bretherdale Head 67 H6
Bretherton 53 F1
Brettabister 119 G3
Brettenham, Norf 38 E2
Brettenham, Suff 38 E5
Bretton 52 E7
Brevig 94 B6
Brewham 9 J1
Brewlands Bridge 92 C5
Brewood 43 K7
Briantspuddle 9 K5
Brickendon 21 H3
Bricket Wood 21 F3
Bricklehampton 34 A6
Bride 60 R1
Bridekirk 66 D3
Bridell 26 F3
Bridestowe 4 F3
Brideswell 100 E5
Bridford 5 J3
Bridge 15 H3
Bridge End 46 E4
Bridgefoot 66 C4
Bridge Green 37 H7
Bridgemary 11 G4
Bridgend, Strath 84 A5
Bridgend, Strath 82 C5
Bridgend, Grampn 100 C5
Bridgend, Loth 86 D7
Bridgend, Grampn 100 C5
Bridgend, Cumbr 67 F5
Bridgend, Fife 87 G3
Bridgend, Tays 93 G5
Bridgend, M. Glam 25 H6
Bridgend, Strath 85 J7
Bridgend of Lintrathen 92 D6
Bridge of Alford 100 E7
Bridge of Allan 85 K5
Bridge of Avon 100 A5
Bridge of Brown 99 K6
Bridge of Cally 92 C6
Bridge of Canny 93 H2
Bridge of Dee 72 C7
Bridge of Don 101 J7
Bridge of Dun 93 H6
Bridge of Dye 93 H3
Bridge of Earn 86 E3
Bridge of Feugh 93 J2
Bridge of Forss 115 F3
Bridge of Gairn 92 E2
Bridge of Muchalls 93 K2
Bridge of Orchy 90 D8
Bridge of Walls 118 E3
Bridge of Weir 77 J1
Bridgerule 6 C5
Bridges 42 E8
Bridge Sollers 29 J3
Bridge Street 38 D6
Bridgetown 7 K2
Bridge Trafford 52 F6
Bridge Yate 17 H3
Bridgham 38 E2
Bridgnorth 43 J8
Bridgtown 44 A7
Bridgwater 8 E1
Bridlington 65 J6
Bridport 9 F5
Bridstow 29 K5
Brierfield 62 B6
Brierley, S. Yks 55 H7
Brierley, H. & W 29 J2
Brierley, Glos 29 L6
Brierley Hill 33 J2
Brigg 58 E6
Brigham, Cumbr 66 C3
Brigham, Humbs 65 H7
Brighouse 62 E7
Brighstone 10 F6
Brightgate 55 F8
Brighthampton 31 H7
Brightling 13 K4
Brightlingsea 23 G2
Brighton, E. Susx 13 G6
Brighton, Corn 3 H4
Brightons 86 C7
Brightwalton 18 F3
Brightwell 39 H6

Brightwell Baldwin 20 A4
Brightwell-cum-Sotwell 19 G1
Brignall 68 C5
Brig o' Turk 85 H4
Brigsley 59 G6
Brigsteer 67 G8
Brigstock 36 C2
Brill 20 A2
Brilley 29 G3
Brimfield 32 E4
Brimington 55 H6
Brimpsfield 30 D6
Brimpton 19 G4
Brims 115 H1
Brimscombe 30 C5
Brimstage 52 F5
Brinacory 96 C6
Brind 58 B3
Brindister, Shetld 118 E3
Brindister, Shetld 119 G5
Brindle 61 J7
Brindley Ford 43 K2
Brineton 43 K6
Bringhurst 36 B1
Brington 36 D3
Brinian 116 D4
Briningham 48 F4
Brinkhill 57 H6
Brinkley 38 B5
Brinklow 34 F3
Brinkworth 18 B2
Brinscall 61 K7
Brinsley 45 F3
Brinsop 29 J3
Brinsworth 55 H4
Brisley 48 E5
Brislington 17 H3
Bristol 17 G3
Briston 48 F4
Britannia 62 B7
Britford 10 C2
Brithdir 41 G2
Briton Ferry 25 F5
Britwell Salome 20 A4
Brixham 5 K6
Brixton, Devon 5 F6
Brixton, G. Lon 21 H6
Brixton Deverill 17 K7
Brixworth 35 J3
Brize Norton 31 H7
Broad Blunsdon 18 C1
Broadbottom 54 C4
Broadbridge 11 K4
Broadbridge Heath 12 E3
Broad Campden 34 C7
Broad Chalke 10 B2
Broadclyst 5 K2
Broadford 96 B3
Broad Green 33 G5
Broad Haven 26 C6
Broad Heath, H. & W 33 F4
Broadheath, H. & W 33 H5
Broadheath, G. Man 53 J5
Broadhembury 8 C4
Broadhempston 5 J5
Broad Hill 38 A3
Broad Hinton 18 C3
Broad Laying 18 F4
Broadley, Grampn 100 C2
Broadley, Lancs 53 K2
Broadley Common 21 J3
Broad Marston 34 C6
Broadmayne 9 J6
Broadmeadows 80 C6
Broadmere 19 H6
Broad Oak, E. Susx 14 E6
Broadoak, Dorset 9 F5
Broad Oak, Kent 15 H2
Broad Oak, Dorset 9 J3
Broad Oak, H. & W 29 J5
Broad Oak, E. Susx 13 K4
Broadrashes 100 D3
Broadstairs 15 K2
Broadstone, Dorset 10 B5
Broadstone, Shrops 32 E2
Broad Street 14 E3
Broad Town 18 B3
Broadwas 33 G5
Broadwater 12 E6
Broadway, H. & W 34 C7
Broadway, Somer 8 E3
Broadwell, Warw 35 F4
Broadwell, Glos 31 G5
Broadwell, Oxon 31 G7
Broadwell, Glos 29 K6
Broadwey 9 H6
Broadwindsor 9 F4
Broadwoodkelly 7 G5
Broadwoodwidger 4 E3
Brobury 29 H3
Brochel 106 A7
Brockbridge 11 H3
Brockdish 39 H3
Brockenhurst 10 D4
Brocketsbrae 79 F6
Brockford Street 39 G4
Brockhall 35 H4
Brockham 12 E2
Brockhampton, Glos 30 E5
Brockhampton, H. & W 29 K4
Brockholes 54 E2
Brocklesby 59 F5
Brockley 17 F4
Brockley Green 38 D5
Brockton, Shrops 32 C2
Brockton, Shrops 42 E7
Brockton, Shrops 42 G8
Brockton, Shrops 43 J7
Brockweir 29 K7
Brockwood Park 11 H2
Brockworth 30 C6
Brocton 44 A6
Brodick 76 F4
Brodsworth 55 J3
Brogborough 36 C7
Brokenborough 17 L2

Broken Cross, Ches 53 H6
Broken Cross, Ches 53 K6
Bromborough 52 E5
Bromcote 34 F2
Brome 39 G3
Brome Street 39 G3
Bromeswell 39 J5
Bromfield, Cumbr 66 D2
Bromfield, Shrops 32 D3
Bromham, Wilts 18 A4
Bromham, Beds 36 D5
Bromley 21 J7
Bromley Green 15 G3
Brompton, Kent 14 D2
Brompton, N. Yks 69 F7
Brompton, N. Yks 65 G4
Brompton-on-Swale 68 E7
Brompton Ralph 8 B1
Brompton Regis 7 K2
Bromsash 30 A5
Bromsgrove 34 A3
Bromyard 33 F5
Bromyard Downs 33 F5
Bronaber 51 G7
Bronington 43 F4
Bronllys 25 K1
Bronnant 41 F7
Bronwydd Arms 27 J5
Brongarth 42 D4
Brook, Surrey 12 C3
Brook, Hants 10 D3
Brook, Hants 10 E2
Brook, I. of W 10 E6
Brook, Kent 15 G4
Brooke, Leic 46 B7
Brooke, Norf 49 H8
Brookfield 77 K1
Brookhouse 61 J3
Brookhouse Green 53 K7
Brookland 15 F6
Brookmans Park 21 G3
Brooks 42 C8
Brook Street 21 K4
Brookthorpe 30 C6
Brookwood 12 C1
Broom, Warw 34 B5
Broom, Beds 36 E6
Broome, Shrops 32 D2
Broome, Norf 39 J1
Broome, H. & W 33 J2
Broomedge 53 J5
Broome Park 75 H2
Broomer's Corner 12 E4
Broomfield, Somer 8 D1
Broomfield, Essex 22 D2
Broomfield, Kent 14 E3
Broomfield, Kent 15 H3
Broomfield, Grampn 101 J5
Broomfleet 58 C4
Broom Hill, Dorset 10 B4
Broomhill, Northum 75 J3
Brora 109 H3
Broseley 43 H7
Brotherton 47 F3
Brotherton 63 H7
Brotton 69 J5
Broubster 115 F3
Brough, Notts 56 C8
Brough, Humbs 58 D4
Brough, Derby 54 E5
Brough, Shetld 121 G5
Brough, Shetld 119 H2
Brough, Highld 115 H2
Brough, Shetld 121 H5
Brough, Cumbr 67 K5
Brough Sowerby 67 K5
Broughall 43 G3
Broughton, Northnts 36 B3
Broughton, Bucks 36 B6
Broughton, Cumbr 66 C3
Broughton, N. Yks 62 C4
Broughton, Orkney 116 D2
Broughton, Humbs 58 D6
Broughton, Hants 10 E1
Broughton, N. Yks 64 E5
Broughton, Clwyd 52 E7
Broughton, Cambs 37 F3
Broughton, Oxon 34 F7
Broughton, M. Glam 25 H7
Broughton, Lancs 61 J6
Broughton, Border 79 J6
Broughton, G. Man 53 K3
Broughton Astley 35 G1
Broughton Beck 61 F1
Broughton Gifford 17 K4
Broughton Hackett 33 J5
Broughton i Furness 60 F1
Broughton Mills 66 E7
Broughton Moor 66 C3
Broughton Poggs 31 G7
Broughtown 117 F2
Broughty Ferry 87 H1
Browland 118 E3
Brown Candover 19 G7
Brown Edge 43 L2
Brownhill, Grampn 101 H4
Brownhill, Lancs 61 K6
Brownhills 44 B7
Brownieside 81 K7
Brownlow Heath 53 K7
Brownston 5 G6
Brow Top 61 J4
Broxbourne 21 H3
Broxburn, Lothn 86 D7
Broxburn, Lothn 80 E2
Broxted 37 J8
Broxwood 29 H2
Bruan 115 J6
Brue 111 H3
Bruera 52 F7
Bruern Abbey 31 G5
Bruernish 94 C5
Bruichladdich 82 B5
Bruisyard 39 J4
Brumby 58 C6

Brund 54 E7
Brundall 49 J7
Brundish 39 H4
Brundish Street 39 H3
Brunton, Fife 87 G2
Brunton, Northum 81 L7
Brushford, Devon 7 G5
Brushford, Somer 7 K3
Bruton 9 H1
Bryanston 9 K4
Brydekirk 73 G6
Brymbo 42 D2
Bryn, Shrops 32 B2
Bryn, G. Man 53 G3
Bryn, W. Glam 25 G5
Brynamman 24 F3
Brynberian 26 F4
Bryncethin 25 H6
Bryncir 50 D6
Bryn-coch 25 F5
Bryncroes 50 B7
Bryncrug 40 F3
Bryneglwys 42 C3
Brynford 52 C6
Bryn Gates 53 G3
Bryngwran 50 C3
Bryngwyn, Powys 29 F3
Bryngwyn, Gwent 29 H7
Bryn-henllan 26 E4
Brynhoffnant 27 H2
Brynithe 25 L4
Brynmawr 25 K3
Brynmenyn 25 H6
Brynna 25 H6
Brynrefail 50 D2
Brynsadler 25 J6
Brynsiencyn 50 D4
Brynteg, Gwyn 50 D2
Brynteg, Clwyd 42 E2
Bryn, The 29 H7
Bryn-y-maen 51 H3
Bualintur 103 F6
Bualnaluib 106 D2
Bubbenhall 34 E3
Bubwith 58 B3
Buccleuch 73 J2
Buchlyvie 85 H5
Buckabank 67 F2
Buckden, N. Yks 62 C2
Buckden, Cambs 36 E4
Buckenham 49 J7
Buckerell 8 C4
Buckfast 5 H5
Buckfastleigh 5 H5
Buckhaven 87 G5
Buckholm 80 C6
Buckhorn Weston 9 J2
Buckhurst Hill 21 J4
Buckie 100 D2
Buckies 115 G3
Buckingham 35 H7
Buckland, Glos 34 B7
Buckland, Bucks 20 C2
Buckland, Surrey 12 F1
Buckland, Herts 37 G7
Buckland, Devon 5 G7
Buckland, Oxon 31 H8
Buckland, Kent 15 K4
Buckland Brewer 6 E3
Buckland Common 20 D3
Buckland Dinham 17 J5
Buckland Filleigh 6 E5
Buckland in the Moor 5 H4
Buckland Monochorum 4 E5
Buckland Newton 9 H4
Buckland St Mary 8 D2
Bucklebury 19 G3
Bucklers Hard 10 F4
Bucklesham 39 H6
Buckley 52 E7
Bucklow Hill 53 J5
Buckminster 46 B6
Bucknall, Lincs 57 F7
Bucknall, Staffs 43 L3
Bucknell, Shrops 32 C3
Bucknell, Oxon 31 K5
Bucksburn 101 H4
Buck's Cross 6 D3
Bucks Green 12 D3
Bucks Hill 20 E3
Bucks Horn Oak 19 K6
Buck's Mills 6 D3
Buckton, H. & W 32 C3
Buckton, Northum 81 J6
Buckworth 36 E3
Budbrooke 34 D4
Budby 55 K6
Bude 6 C5
Budlake 5 K1
Budle 81 K6
Budleigh Salterton 8 B6
Budock Water 3 G4
Buerton 43 H3
Bugbrooke 35 H5
Bugle 3 J4
Bugthorpe 64 E7
Builth Road 28 E2
Builth Wells 28 E2
Bulby 46 D5
Buldoo 114 E3
Bulford 18 C6
Bulford Camp 18 C6
Bulkeley 43 G2
Bulkington, Wilts 18 A5
Bulkington, Warw 34 E2
Bulkworthy 6 D4
Bulley 30 B6
Bullwood 84 C7
Bulmer, Essex 38 D6
Bulmer, N. Yks 64 D6
Bulmer Tye 38 D7
Bulphan 22 C3
Bulverhythe 14 D8
Bulwell 45 G3
Bulwick 46 C8
Bumble's Green 21 J3
Bunacaimb 96 B7
Bunarkaig 90 C2
Bunavoneadar 105 G1
Bunbury 53 G8
Bundalloch 96 D3
Bunessan 88 E6
Bungay 39 J2
Bunnahabhainn 82 D4
Bunny 45 G5
Buntait 98 C5
Buntingford 37 G8
Bunwell 49 G8
Burbage, Wilts 18 D4

Burbage, Derby ...54 D6
Burbage, Leic ...35 F1
Burcombe ...10 B1
Burcot ...31 K8
Burdale ...65 F6
Bures ...38 E7
Burford, Shrops ...32 E4
Burford, Oxon ...31 G6
Burg ...88 E4
Burgess Hill ...13 G5
Burgh ...39 H5
Burgh by Sands ...73 J8
Burgh Castle ...49 K7
Burghclere ...19 F4
Burghead ...99 K2
Burghfield ...20 A7
Burghfield Common ...20 A7
Burghfield Hill ...20 A7
Burgh Heath ...12 F1
Burghill ...29 J3
Burgh le Marsh ...57 K7
Burgh next Aylsham ...49 H5
Burgh on Bain ...57 G5
Burgh St Margaret or Fleg-
gburgh ...49 K6
Burgh St Peter ...49 K8
Burghwallis ...55 J2
Burham ...14 D2
Buriton ...11 J2
Burland ...43 H2
Burlawn ...3 H2
Burlescombe ...8 B3
Burleston ...9 J5
Burley, Leic ...46 B6
Burley, Hants ...10 D4
Burleydam ...43 H3
Burley Gate ...29 K3
Burley in Wharfedale ...62 E5
Burley Street ...10 D4
Burlingjobb ...29 G2
Burlton ...42 F5
Burmarsh ...15 H5
Burmington ...34 D7
Burn ...63 J7
Burnage ...53 K4
Burnaston ...44 D4
Burnby ...58 C2
Burneside ...67 H7
Burness ...117 F2
Burneston ...63 G1
Burnett ...17 H4
Burnfoot, Border ...74 B2
Burnfoot, Border ...73 K2
Burnham, Berks ...20 D5
Burnham, Humbs ...58 E5
Burnham Deepdale ...48 D3
Burnham Green ...21 G2
Burnham Market ...48 D3
Burnham Norton ...48 D3
Burnham-on-Crouch ...22 F4
Burnham-on-Sea ...16 E6
Burnham Overy Staithe ...48 D3
Burnham Overy Town ...48 D3
Burnham Thorpe ...48 D3
Burnhead ...72 D4
Burnhervie ...101 G7
Burnhill Green ...43 J7
Burnhope ...68 D2
Burnhouse ...77 J2
Burniston ...65 H3
Burnley ...62 B6
Burnmouth ...81 H3
Burn of Cambus ...85 K4
Burnopfield ...68 D1
Burnsall ...62 D3
Burnside, Strath ...72 A2
Burnside, Lothn ...86 D7
Burnside, Fife ...86 E4
Burnside, Shetld ...120 E5
Burnside of Duntrune ...87 H1
Burntisland ...87 F6
Burntwood ...44 B7
Burnt Yates ...63 F3
Burpham, Surrey ...12 D1
Burpham, W. Susx ...12 D6
Burradon ...75 J6
Burrafirth ...121 J1
Burras ...2 E6
Burravoe, Shetld ...119 F2
Burravoe, Shetld ...121 H5
Burray Village ...116 D7
Burrelton ...92 D8
Burridge ...11 G3
Burrill ...63 F1
Burringham ...58 C6
Burrington, H. & W ...32 D3
Burrington, Avon ...17 F5
Burrington, Devon ...7 G4
Burrough Green ...38 B5
Burrough on the Hill ...45 J6
Burrow Bridge ...8 E1
Burrowhill ...20 D7
Burry Green ...24 C5
Burry Port ...24 C4
Burscough ...52 F2
Burscough Bridge ...52 F2
Bursea ...58 C3
Burshill ...65 H8
Bursledon ...11 F4
Burslem ...43 K3
Burstall ...39 F6
Burstock ...9 K4
Burston, Norf ...39 G2
Burston, Staffs ...43 L4
Burstow ...13 G2
Burstwick ...59 G4
Burtersett ...68 A8
Burtle ...16 F6
Burton, Dorset ...10 C5
Burton, Somer ...16 C6
Burton, Lincs ...56 D6
Burton, Dyfed ...26 D7
Burton, Ches ...52 E6
Burton, Ches ...53 G7
Burton, Wilts ...17 K3

Burton, Northum ...81 K6
Burton Agnes ...65 J6
Burton Bradstock ...9 F6
Burton Constable ...59 F3
Burton Fleming ...65 H5
Burton Green, Warw ...34 D3
Burton Green, Clwyd ...52 E8
Burton Hastings ...34 F2
Burton-in-Kendal ...61 J2
Burton in Lonsdale ...61 K2
Burton Joyce ...45 H3
Burton Latimer ...36 C3
Burton Lazars ...45 J6
Burton-le-Coggles ...46 C5
Burton Leonard ...63 G3
Burton Overy ...45 H8
Burton Pedwardine ...46 E3
Burton Pidsea ...59 G3
Burton Salmon ...63 H7
Burton upon Stather ...58 C5
Burton upon Trent ...44 D5
Burton Wood ...53 G4
Burwardsley ...43 G2
Burwarton ...33 F2
Burwash ...13 K4
Burwash Common ...13 K4
Burwell, Lincs ...57 H6
Burwell, Cambs ...37 J4
Bury, W. Susx ...12 D5
Bury, Cambs ...37 F2
Bury, G. Man ...53 K2
Bury, Somer ...7 K3
Bury Green ...21 J1
Bury St Edmunds ...38 D4
Burythorpe ...64 E6
Busbridge ...12 C2
Busby ...78 C4
Bushbury ...43 L7
Bush Crathie ...92 D2
Bushey ...21 F4
Bushey Heath ...21 F4
Bush Green ...39 H2
Bushley ...30 C4
Bushton ...18 B3
Busta ...119 F2
Butcher's Pasture ...22 C1
Butcombe ...17 G4
Butleigh ...9 G1
Butleigh Wootton ...9 G1
Butlers Marston ...34 E5
Butley ...39 J5
Butsfield ...68 D2
Buttercrambe ...64 E7
Butterleigh ...7 K5
Butterknowle ...68 D4
Buttermere, Cumbr ...66 D5
Buttermere, Wilts ...18 E4
Buttershaw ...62 E7
Butterstone ...92 B7
Butterton ...44 B2
Butterwick, Humbs ...58 C6
Butterwick, N. Yks ...64 E5
Butterwick, Lincs ...47 G3
Butterwick, N. Yks ...65 G5
Butt Green ...43 H2
Buttington ...42 D7
Buttonoak ...33 G3
Buxhall ...38 F5
Buxted ...13 H4
Buxton, Derby ...54 D6
Buxton, Norf ...49 H5
Bwlch ...25 K2
Bwlch-derwin ...50 D6
Bwlchgwyn ...42 D2
Bwlch-Llan ...27 K2
Bwlchtocyn ...40 C1
Bwlch-y-cibau ...42 C6
Bwlch-y-fadfa ...27 J3
Bwlch-y-ffridd ...41 K4
Bwlchygroes ...27 G4
Bwlch-y-sarnau ...41 K6
Byers Green ...68 E3
Byfield ...35 G5
Byfleet ...20 E7
Byford ...29 H3
Bygrave ...37 F7
Byker ...75 J7
Bylchau ...51 J4
Byley ...53 J7
Byrness, Northum ...74 D3
Byrness, Northum ...67 K6
Bythorn ...36 D3
Byton ...32 C4
Byworth ...12 C4

C

Cabourne ...59 F6
Cabrach ...100 C6
Cadbury ...7 K5
Cadbury Barton ...7 G4
Cadder ...85 J7
Caddington ...20 E2
Caddonfoot ...80 C6
Cadeby, Leic ...44 F7
Cadeby, S. Yks ...55 J3
Cadeleigh ...7 K5
Cade Street ...13 K4
Cadgwith ...2 F8
Cadishead ...53 J4
Cadle ...24 E5
Cadley ...18 D4
Cadmore End ...20 B4
Cadnam ...10 D3
Cadney ...58 E6
Cadole ...52 D7
Caeathro ...50 E4
Caehopkin ...25 G3
Caerau, M. Glam ...25 G5
Caerau, S. Glam ...25 K7
Caerdeon ...41 F2

Caergeiliog ...50 C3
Caergwrle ...52 E8
Caerleon ...16 E1
Caer Llan ...29 J7
Caernarfon ...50 D4
Caerphilly ...25 K6
Caersws ...41 K4
Caerwent ...16 F1
Caerwys ...52 C6
Caethle ...40 F4
Caio ...28 A4
Cairnbaan ...83 H2
Cairnborrow ...100 D4
Cairnbrogie ...101 H6
Cairncross, ays ...93 F4
Cairncross, Border ...81 G3
Cairndow ...84 D3
Cairneyhill ...86 D6
Cairngaan ...70 C8
Cairngarroch ...70 B7
Cairnhill ...100 F5
Cairnie ...100 D4
Cairnorrie ...101 H4
Cairnryan ...70 B5
Caister-on-Sea ...49 L6
Caistor ...59 F6
Caistor St Edmund ...49 H7
Caistron ...75 F3
Calbost ...111 J6
Calbourne ...10 F6
Calcot ...20 A6
Caldbeck ...66 F3
Caldbergh ...62 D1
Caldecote, Cambs ...36 E2
Caldecote, Herts ...37 F7
Caldecote, Cambs ...37 G5
Caldecott, Leic ...46 B8
Caldecott, Northnts ...36 C4
Calderbank ...78 E3
Calder Bridge ...66 C6
Calderbrook ...53 L2
Caldercruix ...79 F3
Calder Mains ...115 F4
Caldermill ...78 D5
Calder Vale ...61 J5
Caldicot ...17 F2
Caldwell, N. Yks ...68 D5
Caldwell, Derby ...44 D6
Caldy ...52 D5
Caledrhydiau ...27 J2
Calfsound ...116 E3
Calgary ...88 E3
Califer ...99 J3
California, Central ...86 C7
California, Norf ...41 L6
Calke ...44 E5
Callaly ...75 G3
Callander ...85 J4
Callanish ...111 G4
Callestick ...2 F4
Calligarry ...96 B5
Callington ...4 D5
Callow ...29 J4
Callow End ...33 H6
Callow Hill, Wilts ...18 B2
Callow Hill, H. & W ...33 G3
Callows Grave ...33 E4
Calmore ...10 E3
Calmsden ...30 E7
Calne ...18 B3
Caln St Dennis ...30 E6
Calow ...55 H6
Calshot ...11 F4
Calstock ...4 E5
Calstone Wellington ...18 B4
Calthorpe ...49 G4
Calthwaite ...67 G2
Caltinish ...104 D7
Calton, Staffs ...44 C2
Calton, N. Yks ...62 C4
Calveley ...53 G8
Calver ...55 F6
Calverhall ...43 H4
Calver Hill ...29 H3
Calverleigh ...7 K2
Calverley ...62 F6
Calvert ...20 A1
Calverton, Notts ...45 H3
Calverton, Bucks ...35 J7
Calvine ...91 K5
Cam ...30 B8
Camas-luinie ...96 E3
Camastianavaig ...103 G5
Camasunary ...103 G7
Camault Muir ...98 D4
Camb ...121 H3
Camber ...14 F7
Camberley ...20 C7
Camberwell ...21 H6
Camblesforth ...63 K7
Cambo ...75 G5
Cambois ...75 K5
Camborne ...2 E5
Cambridge, Glos ...30 B7
Cambridge, Cambs ...37 H5
Cambus ...86 B5
Cambusbarron ...85 K5
Cambuskenneth ...85 L5
Cambuslang ...78 D4
Camden Town ...21 G5
Camelford ...4 B3
Camelon ...86 B6
Camelsdale ...11 K1
Camerory ...99 J5
Camerton, Cumbr ...66 C3
Camerton, Avon ...17 H5
Cammachmore ...93 L2
Cammeringham ...56 D5
Campbelton ...77 G2
Campbeltown ...76 C5
Campsall ...55 J2
Campsey Ash ...39 J5
Camp, The ...30 D7
Campton ...36 E7
Camrose ...26 D5

Camster ...115 H5
Camusnagaul, Highld ...90 B4
Camusnagaul, Highld ...107 F3
Camusrory ...96 D6
Camusteel ...106 C7
Camusterrach ...106 C7
Canada ...10 D3
Canal Foot ...61 G2
Candy Mill ...79 H5
Cane End ...20 A6
Canewdon ...22 E4
Canisbay ...115 J2
Cann ...9 K2
Cann Common ...9 K2
Cannich ...98 B5
Cannington ...16 D7
Cannock ...44 A6
Cannock Wood ...44 B6
Canonbie ...73 J6
Canon Bridge ...29 J3
Canon Frome ...33 F6
Canon Pyon ...29 J3
Canons Ashby ...35 G5
Canonstown ...2 D6
Canterbury ...15 H3
Cantley, Norf ...49 J7
Cantley, S. Yks ...55 K3
Cantlop ...43 G7
Canton ...25 K7
Cantraydoune ...99 F4
Cantraywood ...99 F4
Cantsfield ...61 K2
Canvey Island ...22 D5
Canwick ...56 D7
Canworthy Water ...4 C2
Caol ...90 C4
Caolas ...88 B4
Caol Ila ...82 D5
Caolis ...94 B6
Capel ...12 E2
Capel Bangor ...41 F5
Capel Betws Lleucu ...27 L2
Capel Carmel ...40 A1
Capel Coch ...50 D2
Capel Curig ...51 G5
Capel Cynon ...27 H3
Capel Dewi ...27 J3
Capel Garmon ...51 H5
Capel Gwyn, Gwyn ...50 C3
Capel Gwyn, Dyfed ...27 J5
Capel Gwynfe ...24 F2
Capel Hendre ...27 K6
Capel Isaac ...27 K5
Capel Iwan ...27 G4
Capel-le-Ferne ...15 J5
Capel Llanilltterne ...25 J6
Capel Parc ...50 D2
Capel St Mary ...39 F7
Capel-y-ffin ...29 G4
Capenhurst ...52 E6
Capernwray ...61 J2
Capheaton ...75 G5
Cappercleuch ...79 K7
Capstone ...14 D2
Capton ...5 J6
Caputh ...92 B7
Carbis Bay ...2 D6
Carbost, Highld ...102 E5
Carbost, Highld ...103 F4
Carbrooke ...48 E7
Carburton ...55 K6
Car Colston ...45 J3
Carcroft ...55 J2
Cardenden ...87 F5
Cardeston ...42 E6
Cardiff ...25 K7
Cardigan ...27 F3
Cardington, Beds ...36 D6
Cardington, Shrops ...43 G8
Cardinham ...3 K3
Cardow ...100 A4
Cardrona ...80 B6
Cardross ...84 F7
Cardurnock ...73 G8
Careby ...46 D6
Carew ...26 E7
Carew Cheriton ...26 E7
Carew Newton ...26 E7
Carey ...29 K4
Carfrae ...87 J8
Carfin ...72 E6
Cargen ...72 E6
Cargenbridge ...72 E6
Cargo ...73 J8
Cargreen ...4 E5
Carham ...81 F6
Carhampton ...7 L1
Carharrack ...2 F5
Carisbrooke ...11 F6
Carishader ...111 E4
Cark ...61 G2
Carlby ...46 D6
Carlecotes ...54 E3
Carleton, N. Yks ...62 C5
Carleton, Cumbr ...67 G1
Carleton, Lancs ...61 G5
Carleton Forehoe ...49 F7
Carleton Rode ...39 G1
Carlingcott ...17 H5
Carlisle ...67 G1
Carlops ...79 J4
Carloway ...111 G3
Carlton, Cambs ...38 B5
Carlton, Beds ...36 C5
Carlton, N. Yks ...62 D1
Carlton, Leic ...44 E7
Carlton, Cleve ...69 F4
Carlton, S. Yks ...55 G3
Carlton, W. Yks ...63 G7
Carlton, Notts ...45 H3
Carlton, Suff ...39 J4
Carlton, N. Yks ...63 K1
Carlton, N. Yks ...63 K7
Carlton Colville ...39 L1
Carlton Curlieu ...45 H8

Carlton Husthwaite ...63 H2
Carlton in Cleveland ...69 H6
Carlton in Lindrick ...55 J5
Carlton-le-Moorland ...56 D8
Carlton Miniott ...63 H1
Carlton-on-Trent ...56 B7
Carlton Scroop ...46 C3
Carluke ...79 F4
Carmacoup ...78 E7
Carmarthen ...27 J5
Carmel, Gwyn ...50 C2
Carmel, Clwyd ...52 C6
Carmel, Gwyn ...50 D5
Carmel, Dyfed ...27 K3
Carminish ...104 F3
Carmunnock ...78 C4
Carmyle ...78 D3
Carmyllie ...93 G7
Carnaby ...65 J6
Carnach, Highld ...106 F2
Carnach, Highld ...96 F3
Carnach, W. Isles ...105 H2
Carnbee ...87 J4
Carnbo ...86 D4
Carn Brea Village ...2 E5
Carnell ...77 K4
Carnforth ...61 H2
Carn-gorm ...96 E3
Carnhedryn ...26 C5
Carnhell Green ...2 E6
Carnie ...101 H8
Carnish ...104 D5
Carno ...41 J4
Carnock ...86 D6
Carnon Downs ...3 F5
Carnousie ...100 F3
Carnoustie ...87 J1
Carnwath ...79 G5
Carnyorth ...2 B6
Carperby ...68 C8
Carpley Green ...62 C1
Carradale ...76 D4
Carragreich ...105 G2
Carrbridge ...99 H6
Carreglefn ...50 C2
Carrick Castle ...84 D5
Carriden ...86 E6
Carrington, Lothn ...80 B3
Carrington, Lincs ...47 G2
Carrington, G. Man ...53 J4
Carrog ...42 C3
Carron, Grampn ...100 B4
Carron, Central ...86 B6
Carronbridge ...72 D4
Carr Shield ...67 L2
Carrutherstown ...73 G6
Carr Vale ...55 H7
Carrville ...68 F2
Carsaig ...89 G6
Carsegowan ...71 F6
Carsethorn ...72 E8
Carshalton ...21 G7
Carsington ...44 D2
Carskiey ...76 B7
Carsluith ...71 F6
Carsphairn ...72 A4
Carstairs ...79 G5
Carstairs Junction ...79 G5
Carswell Marsh ...31 H8
Carter's Clay ...10 E2
Carterton ...31 G7
Carterway Heads ...68 C1
Carthew ...3 J4
Carthorpe ...63 G1
Cartington ...75 G3
Cartland ...79 F5
Cartmel ...61 G2
Cartmel Fell ...61 H1
Carway ...27 J7
Cas ...76 C1
Cascob ...32 B4
Cashmoor ...10 A3
Cassington ...31 J6
Cassop ...68 F3
Cassiobury Park ...20 E4
Casswell's Bridge ...46 E5
Castallack ...2 C7
Castellau ...25 J6
Castell Howell ...27 J3
Castell-y-bwch ...16 D1
Casterton ...61 K2
Castle Acre ...48 D6
Castle Ashby ...36 B5
Castlebay ...94 B6
Castle Bolton ...68 C7
Castle Bromwich ...34 C1
Castle Bytham ...46 C6
Castlebythe ...26 E5
Castle Caereinion ...42 C7
Castle Camps ...38 B6
Castle Carrock ...67 H1
Castle Cary, Somer ...9 H1
Castlecary, Strath ...85 K7
Castle Combe ...17 K3
Castlecraig, Highld ...99 G2
Castlecraig, Border ...79 J5
Castle Donington ...45 F5
Castle Douglas ...72 C7
Castle Eaton ...31 F8
Castle Eden ...69 G3
Castleford ...63 H7
Castle Frome ...33 F6
Castle Gresley ...44 D6
Castle Heaton ...81 H5
Castle Hedingham ...38 C7
Castlehill, Strath ...79 F4
Castle Hill, Suff ...39 G6
Castle Kennedy ...70 C6
Castlemartin ...26 D8
Castlemilk ...73 G6
Castlemorris ...26 D4
Castlemorton ...33 G7
Castle O'er ...73 H4
Castle Rising ...48 B5
Castle Side ...68 C2

Castlethorpe ...35 J6
Castleton, Strath ...84 A6
Castleton, Gwent ...16 E2
Castleton, N. Yks ...64 D2
Castleton, Derby ...54 E6
Castletown, Highld ...115 G3
Castletown, T. & W ...75 K8
Castletown, I. of M ...60 P5
Caston ...48 E8
Castor ...46 E8
Catacol ...76 E3
Catbrain ...17 G2
Catcliffe ...55 H5
Catcott ...16 E7
Caterham ...21 G1
Catesby ...35 G5
Catfield ...49 J5
Catfirth ...119 G3
Catford ...21 H6
Catforth ...61 H6
Cath ...26 B5
Cathcart ...78 C3
Cathedine ...25 K2
Catherington ...11 J3
Catherton ...33 F3
Catlodge ...91 H2
Catlowdy ...73 K6
Catmore ...19 F2
Caton ...61 J3
Catrine ...77 L5
Cat's Ash ...16 E1
Catsfield ...13 L5
Catshill ...34 A3
Cattal ...63 H4
Cattawade ...39 G7
Catterall ...61 H5
Catterick ...68 E7
Catterick Bridge ...68 E7
Catterick Garrison ...68 D7
Catterlen ...67 G3
Catterline ...93 K4
Catterton ...63 J5
Catthorpe ...35 G3
Cattistock ...9 G5
Catton, N. Yks ...63 G2
Catton, Norf ...49 H6
Catton, Northum ...67 L1
Catwick ...59 F2
Catworth ...36 D3
Caulcott ...31 K5
Cauldhame ...85 J5
Cauldon ...44 B3
Caulkerbush ...66 B1
Caulside ...73 K5
Caunsall ...33 H2
Caunton ...56 B7
Causewayhead ...85 L5
Causeyend ...101 J7
Causey Park Bridge ...75 H4
Cautley ...67 J7
Cavendish ...38 D6
Cavenham ...38 C4
Caversfield ...31 K5
Caversham ...20 B6
Caversta ...111 H6
Caverswall ...44 A3
Cawdor ...99 G3
Cawood ...63 J6
Cawsand ...4 E6
Cawston ...49 G5
Cawthorne ...55 F3
Cawton ...63 K2
Caxton ...37 G5
Caynham ...32 E3
Caythorpe, Lincs ...46 C3
Caythorpe, Notts ...45 H3
Cayton ...65 H4
Ceann-na-Cleithe ...105 G2
Cefn Berain ...51 J4
Cefn-brith ...51 J5
Cefn Coch ...41 L1
Cefn-coed-y-cymmer ...25 J4
Cefn Cribwr ...25 G6
Cefn Cross ...25 G6
Cefn Einion ...32 B2
Cefneithin ...27 K6
Cefn Hengoed ...25 K5
Cefn-mawr ...42 D3
Cefn-y-bedd ...42 E2
Cefn-y-pant ...27 F5
Ceint ...50 D3
Cellan ...27 L3
Cellarhead ...44 A3
Cemaes ...50 C1
Cemmaes ...41 H3
Cemmaes Road ...41 H3
Cenarth ...27 G3
Cennin ...50 D6
Ceres ...87 H3
Cerne Abbas ...9 H4
Cerney Wick ...30 E8
Cerrigceinwen ...50 D3
Cerrigydrudion ...51 J6
Cessford ...80 F7
Chaceley ...30 C4
Chacewater ...2 F5
Chackmore ...35 H7
Chacombe ...35 F6
Chadderton ...53 L3
Chaddesden ...44 E4
Chaddesley Corbett ...33 H3
Chaddleworth ...18 F3
Chadlington ...31 H5
Chadshunt ...34 E5
Chad Valley ...34 B2
Chadwell St Mary ...22 C6
Chadwick End ...34 D3
Chaffcombe ...8 E3
Chagford ...5 H3
Chailey ...13 G5
Chainhurst ...13 L2
Chalbury ...10 B4
Chalbury Common ...10 B4
Chaldon ...13 G1
Chaldon Herring or
East Chaldon ...9 J6

Chale	11 F7
Chale Green	11 F7
Chalfont Common	20 E4
Chalfont St Giles	20 D4
Chalfont St Peter	20 E4
Chalford	30 C7
Chalgrove	20 A4
Chalk	14 C1
Challacombe	7 G1
Challoch	70 E5
Challock	15 G3
Chalton, Beds	36 D8
Chalton, Hants	11 J3
Chalvington	13 J6
Champany	86 D7
Chandler's Cross	20 E4
Chandler's Ford	10 F2
Channerwick	119 G6
Chantry, Suff	39 G6
Chantry, Somer	17 J6
Chapel	87 F5
Chapel Allerton, Somer	16 F5
Chapel Allerton, W. Yks	63 G6
Chapel Amble	3 H2
Chapel Brampton	35 J4
Chapel Chorlton	43 K4
Chapel-en-le-Frith	54 D5
Chapelgate	47 H5
Chapel Haddlesey	63 J7
Chapelhall	78 E3
Chapelhill, Tays	86 D1
Chapel Hill, Lincs	46 F2
Chapel Hill, Grampn	101 K5
Chapel Hill, Gwent	29 K7
Chapelknowe	73 J6
Chapel Lawn	32 C3
Chapel-le-Dale	61 L2
Chapel of Garioch	101 G6
Chapel Row	19 G4
Chapel Stile	66 F6
Chapel St Leonards	57 K6
Chapelton, Strath	78 D5
Chapelton, Devon	7 F3
Chapelton, Tays	93 H7
Chapeltown, Grampn	100 B6
Chapeltown, S. Yks	55 G4
Chapeltown, Lancs	53 J2
Chapmanslade	17 K6
Chapmans Well	4 D2
Chappel	38 D8
Chard	8 E4
Chardstock	8 E4
Charfield	17 J1
Charing	14 F4
Charing Heath	14 F4
Charingworth	34 D7
Charlbury	31 H6
Charlcombe	17 J4
Charlecote	34 D5
Charles	7 G2
Charleston	92 E7
Charlestown, Highld	106 D4
Charlestown, Fife	86 D6
Charlestown, Highld	98 E4
Charlestown, Dorset	9 H7
Charlestown, Corn	3 J4
Charlestown, Grampn	93 L1
Charlestown of Aberlour	100 B4
Charles Tye	38 F5
Charlesworth	54 D4
Charlton, Wilts	18 A2
Charlton, H. & W	34 B6
Charlton, Wilts	10 C2
Charlton, Wilts	18 C5
Charlton, G. Lon	21 J6
Charlton, W. Susx	11 K3
Charlton, Northnts	31 K4
Charlton, Wilts	9 L2
Charlton Abbots	30 E5
Charlton Adam	9 G2
Charlton Horethorne	9 H2
Charlton Kings	30 D5
Charlton Mackrell	9 G2
Charlton Marshall	9 L4
Charlton Musgrove	9 J1
Charlton-on-Otmoor	31 K6
Charlwood	12 F2
Charlynch	8 D1
Charminster	9 H5
Charmouth	8 E5
Charndon	20 A1
Charney Bassett	31 H8
Charnock Richard	53 G2
Charsfield	39 H5
Charter Alley	19 G5
Charterhouse	17 F5
Chartershall	85 L5
Charterville Allotments	31 H6
Chartham	15 H3
Chartham Hatch	15 H3
Chartridge	20 D3
Chart Sutton	14 D3
Charwelton	35 G5
Chase Terrace	44 B7
Chasetown	44 B7
Chastleton	31 G5
Chatburn	62 A5
Chatcull	43 J4
Chatham	14 D2
Chathill	81 K7
Chattenden	14 D1
Chatteris	37 G2
Chattisham	39 F6
Chatto	74 D2
Chatton	81 J7
Chawleigh	7 H4
Chawston	36 E5
Chawton	11 J1
Cheadle, Staffs	44 B3
Cheadle, G. Man	53 K5
Cheadle Hulme	53 K5
Cheam	21 G7
Chearsley	20 B2
Chebsey	43 K5
Checkendon	20 A5

Checkley, Staffs	44 B4
Checkley, Ches	43 J3
Chedburgh	38 C5
Cheddar	17 F5
Cheddington	20 D2
Cheddleton	44 A2
Cheddon Fitzpaine	8 D2
Chedgrave	49 J8
Chedington	9 F4
Chediston	39 J3
Chedworth	30 E6
Chedzoy	8 E1
Cheeseman's Green	15 G5
Cheetham Hill	53 K3
Cheldon	7 H4
Chelford	53 K6
Chellaston	44 E4
Chellington	36 C5
Chelmarsh	33 G2
Chelmondiston	39 H7
Chelmorton	54 E6
Chelmsford	22 D3
Chelsea	21 G6
Chelsfield	21 J7
Chelsworth	38 E6
Cheltenham	30 D5
Chelveston	36 C4
Chelvey	17 F4
Chelwood	17 H4
Chelwood Gate	13 H4
Cheney Longville	32 D2
Chenies	20 E4
Chepstow	29 K8
Cherhill	18 B3
Cherington, Warw	34 D7
Cherington, Glos	30 D8
Cheriton, Devon	8 C4
Cheriton, W. Glam	24 C5
Cheriton, Hants	11 G2
Cheriton Bishop	5 H2
Cheriton Fitzpaine	7 J5
Cherrington	43 H5
Cherry Burton	58 D2
Cherry Hinton	37 H5
Cherry Willingham	56 E6
Chertsey	20 E7
Cheselbourne	9 J5
Chesham	20 D3
Chesham Bois	20 D4
Cheshunt	21 H3
Cheslyn Hay	44 A7
Chessington	21 F7
Chester	52 F7
Chesterblade	17 H6
Chesterfield, Staffs	44 C7
Chesterfield, Derby	55 G6
Chester-le-Street	68 E1
Chesters, Border	74 C2
Chesters, Border	80 E7
Chesterton, Warw	34 E5
Chesterton, Cambs	46 E8
Chesterton, Cambs	37 H4
Chesterton, Staffs	43 K3
Chesterton, Oxon	31 K5
Chestfield	15 H2
Cheswardine	43 H5
Cheswick	81 J5
Cheswick Green	34 C3
Chetnole	9 H4
Chettiscombe	7 K4
Chettisham	37 J2
Chettle	10 A3
Chetton	33 F1
Chetwode	35 H8
Chetwynd Aston	43 H6
Cheveley	38 B4
Chevening	13 H1
Chevington	38 C5
Chevington Drift	75 J4
Chevithorne	7 K4
Chew Magna	17 G4
Chew Stoke	17 G4
Chewton Mendip	17 G5
Chicheley	36 C6
Chichester	11 K4
Chickerell	9 H6
Chicklade	9 L1
Chicksands	36 E7
Chicksgrove	10 A2
Chidden	11 H3
Chiddingfold	12 C3
Chiddingly	13 J5
Chiddingstone	13 H2
Chideock	8 F5
Chidham	11 J4
Chieveley	19 F3
Chignall Smealy	22 C2
Chignall St James	22 C3
Chigwell	21 J4
Chigwell Row	21 J4
Chilbolton	18 E7
Chilcombe	9 G5
Chilcompton	17 H5
Chilcote	44 D6
Childer Thornton	52 E6
Child Okeford	9 J3
Childrey	18 E2
Child's Ercall	43 H5
Childswickham	34 B7
Childwall	52 F5
Chilfrome	9 G5
Chilgrove	11 K3
Chilham	15 G3
Chillaton	4 E3
Chillenden	15 J3
Chillerton	11 F6
Chillesford	39 J5
Chillingham	81 J7
Chillington, Somer	8 E3
Chillington, Devon	5 H7
Chilmark	10 A1
Chilson	31 H6
Chilsworthy, Devon	6 D5
Chilsworthy, Corn	4 E4
Chilthorne Domer	9 G3

Chilton, Bucks	20 A2
Chilton, Durham	68 E4
Chilton, Oxon	19 F2
Chilton Cantelo	9 G2
Chilton Foliat	18 E3
Chilton Lane	68 F3
Chilton Polden	16 E7
Chilton Street	38 C6
Chilton Trinity	16 D7
Chilworth, Surrey	12 D2
Chilworth, Hants	10 F3
Chimney	31 H7
Chineham	19 H5
Chingford	21 H4
Chinley	54 D5
Chinley Head	54 D5
Chinnor	20 B3
Chipnall	43 J4
Chippenham, Cambs	38 B4
Chippenham, Wilts	17 L3
Chipperfield	20 E3
Chipping, Herts	37 G7
Chipping, Lancs	61 K5
Chipping Campden	34 C7
Chipping Hill	22 E2
Chipping Norton	31 H5
Chipping Ongar	21 K3
Chipping Sodbury	17 J2
Chipping Warden	35 F6
Chipstable	8 B2
Chipstead	12 F1
Chirbury	42 D8
Chirk	42 D4
Chirnside	81 G4
Chirnsidebridge	81 G4
Chirton	18 B5
Chisbury	18 D4
Chiselborough	9 F3
Chiseldon	18 C3
Chiselhampton	31 K8
Chislehurst	21 J6
Chislet	15 J2
Chiswell Green	21 F3
Chiswick	21 G6
Chisworth	54 C4
Chitcomb	11 G2
Chithurst	11 K2
Chittering	37 H3
Chitterne	18 A6
Chittlehamholt	7 G3
Chittlehampton	7 G3
Chittoe	18 A4
Chivelstone	5 H7
Chivenor	6 F2
Chobham	20 D7
Cholderton	18 D6
Cholesbury	20 D3
Chollerton	74 F6
Cholsey	19 G2
Cholstrey	29 J2
Choppington	75 J5
Chopwell	75 H8
Chorley, Staffs	44 B6
Chorley, Shrops	33 F2
Chorley, Lancs	53 G2
Chorley, Ches	43 G2
Chorleywood, Herts	20 E4
Chorleywood, Bucks	20 E4
Chorlton	43 J2
Chorlton-cum-Hardy	53 K4
Chorlton Lane	42 F3
Chowley	43 F2
Chrishall	37 H7
Christchurch, Dorset	10 C5
Christchurch, Cambs	47 H8
Christchurch, Glos	29 K6
Christian Malford	18 A3
Christleton	52 F7
Christmas Common	20 B
Christon	16 E5
Christon Bank	81 L7
Christow	5 J3
Chudleigh	5 J4
Chudleigh Knighton	5 J4
Chulmleigh	7 G4
Chunal	54 D4
Church, N. Yks	69 J7
Church, Lancs	61 L7
Churcham	30 B6
Church Aston	43 J6
Church Brampton	35 J4
Church Broughton	44 D4
Church Cove	2 F8
Church Crookham	19 K5
Churchdown	30 C5
Church Eaton	43 K6
Church End, Wilts	18 B3
Church End, Essex	22 C1
Church End, Beds	20 D1
Church End, Warw	34 D1
Church End, Beds	36 E7
Churchend, Essex	23 G4
Church End, Cambs	47 G7
Church End, Hants	19 H5
Church End, Essex	37 J6
Church Fenton	63 J6
Church Gresley	44 D6
Church Hanborough	31 J6
Church Houses	69 J6
Churchill, Avon	17 F5
Churchill, Oxon	31 G5
Churchill, H. & W	33 H3
Churchinford	8 D3
Church Knowle	10 A6
Church Langton	45 J8
Church Lawford	35 F3
Church Lawton	43 K2
Church Leigh	44 B4
Church Lench	34 B5
Church Minshull	53 H7
Church Norton	11 K5
Churchover	35 G2
Church Preen	43 G8
Church Pulverbatch	42 F7
Churchstanton	8 C3
Church Stoke	42 D8

Churchstow	5 H7
Church Stowe	35 H5
Church Street	14 D1
Church Stretton	42 F8
Churchtown, Mers	52 E2
Churchtown, Lancs	61 H5
Churchtown, I. f M	60 R2
Church Village	25 J6
Church Warsop	55 J7
Churt	19 K7
Churton	42 F2
Churwell	63 F7
Chwilog	50 D7
Chyandour	2 C6
Cilan Uchaf	40 B1
Cilcain	52 C7
Cilcennin	27 K1
Cilfor	51 F7
Cilfrew	25 F4
Cilfynydd	25 J5
Cilgerran	27 F3
Cilgwyn	25 F2
Ciliau-Aeron	27 K2
Cilmaengwyn	25 F4
Cilmery	28 E2
Cilrhedyn	27 G4
Ciltwrch	29 F3
Cilwendeg	27 G4
Cilybebyll	25 F4
Cilycwm	28 B3
Cinderford	30 A6
Cirencester	30 E7
City Dulas	50 D2
City of London	21 H5
City, The	20 B4
Clachaig	84 D6
Clachan, Strath	76 C2
Clachan, ighld	103 G5
Clachan, Strath	89 J7
Clachan, Strath	89 K4
Clachan-a-Luib	104 D5
Clachan of Campsie	85 J7
Clachan of Glendaruel	84 B6
Clachan-Seil	89 J7
Clachbreck	83 G4
Clachtoll	112 B6
Clackmannan	86 C5
Clacton-on-Sea	23 H2
Cladach Kirkibost	104 C5
Claggan	89 H4
Claigan	102 D3
Claines	33 H5
Clandown	17 H5
Clanfield, Oxon	31 G7
Clanfield, Hants	11 H3
Clanville	18 E6
Claonaig	76 D2
Claonel	108 D3
Clapgate	10 B4
Clapham, Beds	36 D5
Clapham, W. Susx	12 D6
Clapham, G. Lon	21 G6
Clapham, N. Yks	61 L3
Clappers	81 H4
Clappersgate	66 F6
Clapton	8 F4
Clapton-in-Gordano	17 F3
Clapton-on-the-Hill	31 F6
Clapworthy	7 G3
Clarbeston	26 E5
Clarbeston Road	26 E5
Clarborough	56 B5
Clardon	115 G3
Clare	38 C6
Clarebrand	72 C7
Clarencefield	73 F7
Clarkston	78 C4
Clashmore, Highld	112 B5
Clashmore, Highld	109 F5
Clashnessie	112 B5
Clashnoir	100 B6
Clatt	100 E6
Clatter	41 J4
Clatworthy	8 B1
Claughton, Lancs	61 J3
Claughton, Lancs	61 J5
Claverdon	34 C4
Claverham	17 F4
Clavering	37 H7
Claverley	43 J8
Claverton	17 J4
Clawdd-newydd	51 K5
Clawton	4 D2
Claxby, Lincs	57 F4
Claxby, Lincs	57 J6
Claxton, N. Yks	64 D6
Claxton, Norf	49 J7
Claybokie	92 B2
Claybrooke Magna	35 F2
Clay Coton	35 G3
Clay Cross	55 G7
Claydon, Oxon	35 F5
Claydon, Suff	39 G5
Claygate	21 F7
Claygate Cross	13 K1
Clayhanger, Devon	8 B2
Clayhanger, W. Mids	44 B7
Clayhidon	8 C3
Clayock	115 G2
Claypole	46 B3
Clayton, W. Yks	62 E6
Clayton, W. Susx	13 G5
Clayton, S. Yks	55 H3
Clayton, Staffs	43 K3
Clayton-le-Moors	61 L6
Clayton-le-Woods	61 J7
Clayton West	55 F2
Clayworth	56 B5
Cleadale	95 K7
Cleadon	75 K7
Clearwell	29 K7
Cleasby	68 E5
Cleat, W. Isles	94 B5
Cleat, Orkney	115 K1

Cleatlam	68 D5
Cleator	66 C5
Cleator Moor	66 C5
Cleckheaton	62 E7
Cleedownton	32 E2
Cleehill	33 E3
Clee St Margaret	32 E2
Cleethorpes	59 H6
Cleeton St Mary	33 F3
Cleeve	17 F4
Cleeve Hill	30 D5
Cleeve Prior	34 B6
Clehonger	29 J4
Cleigh	84 A2
Cleish	86 D5
Cleland	78 E4
Clench Common	18 C4
Clenchwarton	48 A5
Clent	33 J3
Cleobury Mortimer	33 F3
Cleobury North	33 F2
Clephanton	99 G3
Clerklands	80 D7
Clestrain	116 C6
Cleughbrae	73 F6
Clevancy	18 B3
Clevedon	16 F3
Cleveleys	61 G5
Cleverton	18 A2
Clewer	17 F5
Cley next the Sea	48 F3
Cliasmol	105 F1
Cliburn	67 H4
Cliddesden	19 H6
Cliffe, Kent	14 D1
Cliffe, N. Yks	63 K6
Cliff End	14 E7
Cliffe Woods	14 D1
Clifford, H. & W	29 G3
Clifford, W. Yks	63 H5
Clifford Chambers	34 C5
Clifford's Mesne	30 B5
Cliffs End	15 K2
Clifton, Derby	44 C3
Clifton, Beds	36 E7
Clifton, Central	84 F1
Clifton, Avon	17 G3
Clifton, Notts	45 G4
Clifton, Cumbr	67 H4
Clifton, Lancs	61 H6
Clifton, H. & W	33 H6
Clifton, Oxon	31 J4
Clifton, Northum	75 J5
Clifton Campville	44 D6
Clifton Hampden	31 K8
Clifton Reynes	36 C5
Clifton upon Dunsmore	35 G3
Clifton upon Teme	33 G4
Climping	12 C6
Clint	63 F4
Clint Green	48 F6
Clintmains	80 E6
Clippesby	49 K6
Clipsham	46 C6
Clipston, Notts	45 H4
Clipston, Northnts	35 J2
Clitheroe	61 L5
Clive	43 G5
Clivocast	121 J2
Clocaenog	51 K
Clochan	100 D2
Clock Face	53 G4
Cloddymoss	99 H2
Clodock	29 H5
Clola	101 K4
Clophill	36 D7
Clopton, Northnts	36 D2
Clopton, Suff	39 H5
Clopton Green	38 C5
Closeburn	72 D4
Close Clark	60 P4
Clothall	37 F7
Clotton	53 G7
Clough Foot	62 C7
Cloughton	65 H3
Cloughton Newlands	65 H3
Clousta	119 F3
Clouston	116 C5
Clova	92 E4
Clovelly	6 D3
Clove Lodge	68 B5
Clovenfords	80 C6
Clovenstone	101 G7
Clovullin	90 B5
Clowne	55 H6
Clows Top	33 G3
Cluanie	97 F5
Cluer	105 G2
Clun	32 C2
Clunbury	32 C2
Clunderwen	26 F6
Clunes	90 D3
Clungunford	32 C3
Clunie	100 F3
Clunton	32 C2
Cluny	87 F5
Clutton, Ches	42 F2
Clutton, Avon	17 H5
Clwyt-y-bont	50 E4
Clydach, W. Glam	24 E4
Clydach, Gwent	25 L3
Clydach Vale	25 H5
Clydebank	85 H4
Clydey	27 G4
Clyffe Pypard	18 B3
Clynder	84 E6
Clynelish	109 G3
Clynnog-fawr	50 D6
Clyro	29 G3
Clyst Honiton	5 K2
Clyst Hydon	8 B4
Clyst St George	5 K3
Clyst St Lawrence	8 B4
Clyst St Mary	5 K2
Clyth	115 H6

Cnoc Amhlaigh	111 K4
Cnwch Coch	41 F6
Coad's Green	4 C3
Coal Aston	55 G6
Coalbrookdale	43 H7
Coalburn	79 F6
Coalcleugh	67 L2
Coaley	30 B7
Coalpit Heath	17 H2
Coalport	43 H7
Coalsnaughton	86 C5
Coaltown of Balgonie	87 G5
Coaltown of Wemyss	87 G5
Coalville	44 F6
Coalway	29 K6
Coast	106 C2
Coatbridge	78 E3
Coatdyke	78 E3
Coate	18 B4
Coates, Glos	30 D7
Coates, Cambs	47 G8
Coatham	69 H4
Coatham Mundeville	68 E4
Coatsgate	73 F3
Cobbaton	7 G3
Coberley	30 D6
Cobham, Kent	14 C2
Cobham, Surrey	21 F7
Cobnash	29 J1
Cockayne	69 J7
Cockayne Hatley	37 F6
Cock Bridge	100 B8
Cockburnspath	80 F2
Cock Clarks	22 E3
Cockenzie and Port Seton	87 H7
Cockerham	61 H4
Cockerington	57 H4
Cockermouth	66 D3
Cockernhoe	21 F1
Cockfield, Durham	68 D4
Cockfield, Suff	38 E5
Cockfosters	21 G4
Cocking	11 K3
Cockington	5 K5
Cocklake	17 F6
Cockley Beck	66 F6
Cockley Cley	48 C7
Cockpole Green	20 B5
Cockshutt	42 F5
Cockthorpe	48 E3
Cockwood	5 K3
Cockyard	29 J4
Coddenham	39 G5
Coddington, Notts	46 B2
Coddington, Ches	42 F2
Coddington, H. & W	33 G6
Codford St Mary	18 A7
Codford St Peter	18 A6
Codicote	21 G2
Codnor	44 F3
Codrington	17 J3
Codsall	43 K7
Codsall Wood	43 K7
Coedely	25 J6
Coedkernew	16 D2
Coedpoeth	42 D2
Coed-y-paen	29 H8
Coed Ystumgwern	40 E1
Coelbren	25 G
Coffinswell	5 J5
Cofton Hackett	34 B3
Cogenhoe	36 B4
Coggeshall	22 E1
Coilacriech	92 E2
Coille Mhorgil	90 C1
Coillore	102 E3
Coity	25 H6
Col	111 J3
Colaboll	113 G2
Colan	3 G3
Colaton Raleigh	8 B6
Colbost	102 D4
Colburn	68 D7
Colby, Norf	49 H4
Colby, Cumbr	67 J4
Colby, I. of M	60 P4
Colchester	38 F8
Cold Ash	19 G3
Cold Ashby	35 H3
Cold Ashton	17 J3
Cold Aston	31 F6
Coldbackie	113 H2
Coldblow	21 K6
Cold Brayfield	36 C5
Coldean	13 G6
Coldeast	5 J4
Colden Common	11 F2
Cold Hanworth	56 E5
Coldharbour	12 E2
Cold Hesledon	69 G2
Cold Higham	35 H5
Coldingham	81 H3
Cold Kirby	63 J1
Cold Newton	45 J7
Cold Norton	22 E3
Cold Overton	46 B6
Coldred	15 J4
Coldridge	7 G5
Coldstream	81 F6
Coldwaltham	12 D5
Coldwells	101 L5
Coldwells Croft	100 E6
Cole	9 H1
Colebatch	32 C2
Colebrook	7 L5
Colebrooke	5 H1
Coleburn	68 E7
Coleby, Humbs	58 C5
Coleby, Lincs	56 D7
Coleford, Devon	7 H5
Coleford, Somer	17 H6
Coleford, Glos	29 K6
Colehill	10 B4
Coleman's Hatch	13 H3

Colemere...42 F4
Colenden...86 E2
Coleorton...44 F6
Colerne...17 K3
Colesbourne...30 D6
Colesden...36 E5
Coleshill, Warw...34 D2
Coleshill, Bucks...20 D4
Coleshill, Oxon...31 G8
Colgate...13 G3
Colgrain...84 F6
Colinsburgh...87 H4
Colinton...87 F8
Colintraive...84 C7
Colkirk...48 E5
Collafirth...120 F4
Collafirth St Mary...5 J5
Collessie...87 F3
Collier Row...21 J4
Colliers End...21 H1
Collier Street...13 L2
Collieston...101 K6
Collin...72 F6
Collingbourne Ducis...18 D5
Collingbourne Kingston...18 D5
Collingham, Notts...56 C7
Collingham, W. Yks...63 G5
Collington...33 F4
Collingtree...35 J5
Colliston...93 H7
Collyweston...46 C2
Colmonell...70 C3
Colmworth...36 E5
Colnabaichin...100 B8
Colnbrook...20 E6
Colne, Lancs...62 B5
Colne, Cambs...37 G3
Colne Engaine...38 D7
Colney...49 G7
Colney Heath...21 G3
Colney Street...21 F3
Coln Rogers...30 E7
Coln St Aldwyns...31 F7
Coln St Dennis...30 E6
Colpy...100 F5
Colsterdale...62 E1
Colsterworth...46 C5
Colston Bassett...45 H4
Coltfield...99 K2
Coltishall...49 H5
Colton, Staffs...44 B5
Colton, Cumbr...61 G1
Colton, Norf...49 G7
Colton, N. Yks...63 J5
Col Uarach...111 J4
Colvend...71 K6
Colvister...121 H3
Colwall Green...33 G6
Colwall Stone...33 G6
Colwell...74 F6
Colwich...44 B5
Colwinston...25 H7
Colworth...12 C6
Colwyn Bay...51 H3
Colyford...8 D5
Colyton...8 D5
Combe, H. & W...32 C4
Combe, Berks...18 E4
Combe, Oxon...31 J6
Combe Florey...8 C1
Combe Hay...17 J3
Combeinteignhead...5 K4
Combe Martin...7 F1
Combe Moor...32 C4
Combe Raleigh...8 C4
Comberbach...53 H6
Comberton...37 G5
Combe St Nicholas...8 E3
Combpyne...28 D5
Combrook...34 E5
Combs, Derby...54 D6
Combs, Suff...38 F5
Combs Ford...38 F5
Combwich...16 D6
Comers...100 F8
Commins Coch...41 H3
Commondale...69 J5
Common Moor...3 L3
Common Side...55 G6
Common, The...10 D1
Compstall...54 C4
Compton, Surrey...12 C2
Compton, Wilts...18 C5
Compton, Hants...11 F2
Compton, Berks...19 G3
Compton, W. Susx...11 J3
Compton, Devon...5 J5
Compton Abbas...9 K3
Compton Abdale...30 E6
Compton Bassett...18 B3
Compton Beauchamp...18 D2
Compton Bishop...16 E5
Compton Chamberlayne...10 B2
Compton Dando...17 H4
Compton Dundon...9 F1
Compton Martin...17 G5
Compton Pauncefoot...9 H2
Compton Valence...9 G5
Comrie...85 K2
Conchra...84 C6
Conderton...34 A7
Condicote...31 F5
Condorrat...85 K7
Condover...43 F7
Coneyhurst...12 E4
Coneysthorpe...64 E3
Coney Weston...38 E3
Congerstone...44 E7
Congham...48 C5
Congleton...53 K7
Congresbury...17 F4
Conicavel...99 H3
Coningsby...57 G8

Conington, Cambs...36 E2
Conington, Cambs...37 G4
Conisbrough...55 J4
Conisby...82 B5
Conisholme...57 J4
Coniston, Humbs...59 F3
Coniston, Cumbr...66 F7
Coniston Cold...62 C4
Conistone...62 C3
Connah's Quay...52 D7
Connel...84 B1
Connel Park...72 B2
Connor Downs...2 D6
Conon Bridge...98 D3
Cononley...62 C5
Conordan...103 G5
Consall...44 A3
Consett...68 D1
Constable Burton...68 D7
Constantine...2 F7
Contin...98 C3
Conwy...51 G3
Conyer...14 F2
Cookbury...6 E5
Cookham...20 C5
Cookham Dean...20 C5
Cookham Rise...20 C5
Cookhill...34 B5
Cookley, H. & W...33 H2
Cookley, Suff...39 J3
Cookley Green...20 A4
Cookney...93 K2
Cooksbridge...13 H5
Cooksmill Green...22 C3
Coolham...12 E4
Cooling...14 D1
Coombe, Corn...6 C4
Coombe, Corn...3 H4
Coombe Bissett...10 C2
Coombe Hill...30 C5
Coombe Keynes...9 K6
Coombes...12 E6
Copdock...39 G6
Copford Green...22 F1
Copister...121 G5
Cople...36 E6
Copley...68 C4
Coplow Dale...54 E6
Copmanthorpe...63 J5
Coppathorne...4 C1
Coppenhall...43 L6
Copperhouse...2 D6
Coppingford...36 E2
Copplestone...7 H5
Coppull...53 G2
Copsale...12 E4
Copster Green...61 K6
Copt Heath...34 C3
Copt Hewick...63 G2
Copthorne...13 G3
Copt Oak...45 F6
Copythorne...10 E3
Corbridge...75 F7
Corby...36 B2
Corby Glen...46 C5
Coreley...33 F3
Corfe...8 D3
Corfe Castle...10 A6
Corfe Mullen...10 A5
Corfton...32 D2
Corgarff...100 B8
Corhampton...11 H2
Corlae...72 B4
Corley...34 E2
Corley Ash...34 D2
Corley Moor...34 D2
Cornelly...25 G6
Corney...66 D7
Cornforth...68 C4
Cornhill...100 E3
Cornhill-on-Tweed...81 G6
Cornholme...62 C7
Cornriggs...67 L2
Cornsay...68 D2
Corntown...98 D3
Cornwell...31 G5
Cornwood...5 G6
Cornworthy...5 J6
Corpach...90 B4
Corpusty...49 G4
Corran, Highld...90 B5
Corran, Highld...96 D5
Corrany...60 R3
Corrie...76 F3
Corrie Common...73 H5
Corriemoillie...98 B2
Corrimony...98 B5
Corringham, Lincs...56 C4
Corringham, Essex...22 D5
Corris...41 G3
Corris Uchaf...41 G3
Corry...96 B3
Corry of Ardnagrask...98 D4
Corscombe...9 G4
Corse...100 F4
Corsham...17 3
Corsindae...101 F8
Corsley...17 K6
Corsley Heath...17 K6
Corsock...72 C6
Corston, Avon...17 H4
Corston, Wilts...17 L2
Corstorphine...87 E7
Corton, Wilts...18 A4
Corton, Suff...49 L8
Corton Denham...9 H2
Corwen...51 K6
Coryton, Essex...22 D5
Coryton, Devon...4 E3
Cosby...45 G8
Coseley...43 L8
Cosgrove...35 J6
Cosham...11 H4

Airntully...86 D1
Airor...96 C5
Airth...86 B6
Cossington, Leic...45 H6
Costa...116 C4
Costessey...49 G6
Costock...45 G5
Coston...46 B5
Cotebrook...53 G7
Cotegill...67 J6
Cotehill...67 G1
Cotes, Leic...45 G5
Cotes, Staffs...43 K4
Cotesbach...35 G2
Cotgrave...45 H4
Cothall...101 H7
Cotham...45 J3
Cothelstone...8 C1
Cotherstone...68 C5
Cothill...31 J8
Cotleigh...8 D4
Coton, Staffs...44 A4
Coton, Northnts...35 H3
Coton, Cambs...37 H5
Coton Clanford...43 K5
Coton in the Elms...44 D6
Cott...5 H5
Cottam, Notts...56 C5
Cottam, Lancs...61 J6
Cottartown...99 J5
Cottenham...37 H4
Cotterdale...67 L7
Cottered...37 G8
Cotterstock...36 D1
Cottesbrooke...35 J3
Cottesmore...46 C6
Cottingham, Northnts...36 B1
Cottingham, Humbs...58 E3
Cottisford...31 K4
Cotton, Staffs...44 B3
Cotton, Suff...38 F4
Cotton End...36 D6
Cottown, Grampn...100 E6
Cottown, Grampn...101 G7
Cottown, Grampn...101 H4
Cotwalton...43 L4
Coughton, Warw...34 B4
Coughton, H. & W...29 K5
Coulags...106 E7
Coull...93 G1
Coulport...84 E6
Coulston...18 A5
Coulter...79 H6
Coulton...63 K2
Cound...43 G7
Coundon...68 E4
Coundon Grange...68 E4
Countersett...62 C1
Countess Wear...5 K3
Countesthorpe...45 G8
Countisbury...7 H1
Coupar Angus...92 D7
Coupland...81 H6
Cour...76 D3
Courteachan...96 B6
Courteenhall...35 J5
Court Henry...27 K5
Courtsend...23 G4
Courtway...8 D1
Cousland...80 B3
Cousley Wood...13 K3
Cove, Highld...106 D2
Cove, Strath...84 E6
Cove, Devon...7 K4
Cove, Hants...19 K5
Cove Bay...93 L1
Covehithe...39 L2
Coven...43 L7
Coveney...37 H2
Covenham St Bartholomew...57 H4
Covenham St Mary...57 H4
Coventry...34 E3
Coverack...3 F8
Coverham...62 E1
Covington...36 D3
Cowan Bridge...61 K2
Cowbeech...13 K5
Cowbit...47 F6
Cowbridge...25 H7
Cowden...13 H2
Cowdenbeath...86 E5
Cowes...11 F5
Cowesby...69 G8
Cowfold...12 F4
Cowgill...62 A1
Cowick...63 K7
Cowie...85 L6
Cowley, Glos...30 D6
Cowley, G. Lon...20 E5
Cowley, Devon...5 K2
Cowley, Oxon...31 K7
Cowling, N. Yks...62 C5
Cowling, N. Yks...63 F1
Cowlinge...38 C5
Cowpen Bewley...69 G4
Cowplain...11 H3
Cowshill...67 L2
Cowstrandburn...86 D5
Coxbank...43 H3
Coxbench...44 E3
Cox Common...39 K2
Coxheath...13 L1
Coxhoe...68 F3
Coxley...17 G6
Coxwold...63 J2
Coychurch...25 H7
Coylton...77 H2
Coylumbridge...99 H7
Coynach...100 D8
Crabbs Cross...34 B4
Crabtree...12 F4
Crabtree Green...42 E3
Crackenthorpe...67 J4
Crackington...4 B2

Crackleybank...43 J6
Crackpot...68 B7
Cracoe...62 C3
Cradley...33 G6
Crafthole...4 D6
Craggan...99 J6
Cragg Vale...62 D7
Craghead...68 E1
Crai...25 G2
Craibstone...101 H7
Craichie...93 G7
Craig, D. & G...72 B6
Craig, Highld...106 F7
Craig Castle...100 D6
Craigcefnparc...24 E4
Craigdam...101 H5
Craigearn...101 G7
Craigellachie...100 B4
Craigendoran...84 F6
Craighouse...82 E5
Craigie, Grampn...101 J7
Craigie, Strath...77 K4
Craiglockhart...87 F7
Craigmaud...101 H3
Craigmillar...87 F7
Craignant...42 D4
Craigneuk, Strath...78 E3
Craigneuk, Strath...78 E4
Craignure...89 J5
Craigo...93 H5
Craigrothie...87 G3
Craigton, Tays...92 E6
Craigton, Tays...93 G8
Craigton, Grampn...93 K1
Craigtown...114 D4
Craik...73 J3
Crail...87 K4
Crailing...80 E7
Crailinghall...80 E7
Crakehall...68 E7
Cramalt...79 J7
Crambe...64 D6
Cramlington...75 J6
Cramond...86 E7
Cramond Bridge...86 E7
Cranage...53 J7
Cranberry...43 K4
Cranbone...10 B3
Cranbourne...20 D6
Cranbrook...14 D5
Cranbrook Common...14 D5
Cranfield...36 C6
Cranford St Andrew...36 C3
Cranford St John...36 C3
Cranham, Glos...30 C6
Cranham, G. Lon...21 K5
Crank...53 G4
Cranleigh...12 D3
Cranmore, I. of W...10 E5
Cranmore, Somer...17 H6
Cranna...100 F3
Crannoch...100 D3
Cransford...39 J4
Cranshaws...80 E3
Cranstal...60 R1
Crantock...3 F3
Cranwell...46 D3
Cranwich...48 C8
Cranworth...48 E7
Crapstone...4 F5
Craskins...100 E8
Crask of Aigas...98 C4
Craster...75 J2
Craswall...29 G4
Cratfield...39 J3
Crathes...93 J2
Crathie, Grampn...92 D3
Crathie, Highld...91 G2
Crathorne...69 G2
Craven Arms...32 D2
Crawcrook...75 H7
Crawford...72 E1
Crawfordjohn...79 F7
Crawick...72 C2
Crawleside...68 B2
Crawley, Hants...10 F1
Crawley, W. Susx...12 F3
Crawley, Oxon...31 H6
Crawley Down...13 G3
Crawshawbooth...62 B7
Crawton...93 K4
Cray...62 B2
Crayford...21 K6
Crayke...63 J2
Crays Hill...22 D4
Cray's Pond...20 A5
Creacombe...7 J4
Creagorry...104 C7
Creaton...35 J3
Creca...73 H6
Credenhill...29 J3
Crediton...5 J1
Creech St Michael...8 D2
Creed...3 H5
Creekmouth...21 K5
Creeting St Mary...38 F5
Creeton...46 D5
Creetown...71 F6
Creggans...84 C4
Cregneish...60 N5
Cregrina...28 F2
Creich...87 G2
Creigiau...25 J6
Cressage...43 G7
Cresselly...26 E7
Cressing...22 D1
Cresswell, Staffs...44 A4
Cresswell, Northum...75 J4
Cresswell Quay...26 E7
Creswell...55 J6
Cretingham...39 H4
Cretshengan...76 C1

Crewe, Ches...42 F2
Crewe, Ches...43 J2
Crew Green...42 E6
Crewkerne...9 F4
Crews Hill...21 H4
Crianlarich...85 F2
Cribyn...27 K2
Criccieth...50 E7
Crich...44 E2
Crichie...101 J4
Crichton...80 B3
Crick, Gwent...17 F1
Crick, Northnts...35 G3
Crickadarn...28 E3
Cricket St Thomas...8 E4
Crickheath...42 D5
Crickhowell...25 L3
Cricklade...30 F8
Cridling Stubbs...63 J7
Crieff...86 B2
Criggion...42 D6
Crigglestone...55 G2
Crimond...101 K3
Crimonmogate...101 K3
Crimplesham...48 B7
Crinan...83 G2
Cringleford...49 G7
Crinow...26 F6
Cripplesease...2 D6
Cripp's Corner...14 C2
Crockenhill...21 K7
Crockernwell...5 H2
Crockerton...17 K6
Crocketford or Ninemile Bar...72 D6
Crockey Hill...63 K5
Crockham Hill...13 H1
Crockleford Heath...38 F8
Croeserw...25 G5
Croes-goch...26 C4
Croesor...51 F6
Croesyceiliog...29 H8
Croesyceilog...27 J6
Croes-y-mwyalch...16 E1
Croft, Leic...45 G8
Croft, Ches...53 H4
Croft, Lincs...57 K7
Croftamie...85 G3
Crofton...55 G2
Croft-on-Tees...68 E6
Crofts of Benachielt...115 G6
Crofts of Haddo...101 H5
Crofts of Inverthernie...101 G4
Crofty...24 D5
Croggan...89 J6
Croglin...67 H2
Croir...111 F4
Cromarty...99 F2
Cromblet...101 G5
Cromdale...99 J6
Cromer, Herts...37 F8
Cromer, Norf...49 H3
Cromford...44 D2
Cromhall...17 H1
Cromhall Common...17 H2
Cromore...111 J5
Cromra...91 G2
Cromwell...56 B7
Cronberry...78 D7
Crondall...19 J6
Cronk, The...60 Q2
Cronk-y-Voddy...60 Q3
Cronton...53 F5
Crook, Durham...68 D3
Crook, Cumbr...67 G7
Crookham, Berks...19 G4
Crookham, Northum...81 H6
Crookham Village...19 J5
Crookhouse...80 F7
Crooklands...61 J1
Crook of Devon...86 D4
Cropredy...35 F6
Cropston...45 G6
Cropthorne...34 A6
Cropton...64 E4
Cropwell Bishop...45 H4
Cropwell Butler...45 H4
Crosby, Cumbr...66 C3
Crosby, Humbs...58 C5
Crosby, Mers...52 E4
Crosby, I. of M...60 Q4
Crosby Garrett...67 K6
Crosby-on-Eden...73 K8
Crosby Ravensworth...67 J5
Croscombe...17 G6
Cross, Somer...16 F5
Cross, W. Isles...111 K1
Crossapol...00 A4
Cross Ash...29 J6
Crossbost...111 H5
Crosscanonby...66 C3
Crossdale Street...49 H4
Crossdougal...94 C3
Crossens...52 E2
Crossford, Fife...86 D6
Crossford, Strath...79 F5
Crossgates, Fife...86 E6
Crossgates, Powys...41 K7
Crossgill...61 J3
Cross Green, Devon...4 D3
Cross Green, Suff...38 E5
Crosshands, Dyfed...27 F5
Cross Hands, Dyfed...27 K6
Crosshill, Fife...86 E5
Crosshill, Strath...77 J7
Crosshouse...77 J4
Cross Houses...43 G7
Cross in Hand...13 J4
Crossings...74 B6
Cross Inn, Dyfed...40 E7
Cross Inn, Dyfed...27 H2
Cross Inn, M. Glam...25 J6
Crosskeys...25 L5
Crosskirk...115 F2
Cross Lanes, Clwyd...42 E3
Crosslanes, Shrops...42 E6

Cross Lanes, N. Yks...63 J3
Crosslee...73 J2
Crossmichael...72 C7
Crossmoor...61 H6
Cross of Jackston...101 G5
Crossroads...93 J2
Crossway...29 J6
Crossway Green...33 H4
Crossways...9 J6
Crosswell...26 F4
Crosthwaite...67 G7
Croston...53 F2
Crostwick...49 H6
Crostwight...49 J4
Croughton...31 K4
Crovie...101 H2
Crowan...2 E6
Crowborough...13 J3
Crowcombe...8 C1
Crowdecote...54 E7
Crowfield, Suff...39 G5
Crowfield, Northnts...35 H6
Crow Hill...30 A5
Crowhurst, Surrey...13 G2
Crowhurst, E. Susx...13 L5
Crowland...47 F6
Crowlas...2 D6
Crowle, Humbs...58 B5
Crowle, H. & W...33 J5
Crowlista...110 E4
Crowmarsh Gifford...20 A5
Crownhill...4 F6
Crownthorpe...49 F7
Crowthorne...20 C7
Crowthorn School...53 J2
Crowton...53 G6
Croxall...44 C6
Croxdale...68 E3
Croxden...44 B4
Croxley Green...20 E4
Croxton, Norf...38 D2
Croxton, Humbs...59 E5
Croxton, Cambs...37 F5
Croxton, Staffs...43 J4
Croxton Kerrial...46 B5
Croxton Park...46 B5
Croy, Highld...99 F4
Croy, Strath...85 K7
Croyde...6 E2
Croydon, Cambs...37 G6
Croydon, G. Lon...21 H7
Cruckmeole...42 F7
Cruckton...42 F6
Cruden Bay...101 K5
Crudgington...43 H6
Crudwell...18 A1
Crug...32 A3
Crugmeer...3 F2
Crugybar...27 L4
Cruliyig...111 F4
Crumlin...25 L5
Crundale, Dyfed...26 D6
Crundale, Kent...15 G4
Cruwys Morchard...7 J4
Crux Easton...18 F5
Crwbin...27 J6
Crymych...27 F4
Crynant...25 F4
Cuaig...106 C6
Cubbington...34 E4
Cubert...3 F4
Cublington...20 C1
Cuckfield...13 G4
Cucklington...9 J2
Cuckney...55 J6
Cuddesdon...31 K7
Cuddington, Bucks...20 B2
Cuddington, Ches...53 G6
Cuddington Heath...43 F3
Cuddy Hill...61 H6
Cudham...21 J8
Cudliptown...5 F4
Cudworth, Somer...8 E3
Cudworth, S. Yks...55 G3
Cuffley...21 H3
Culbo...98 E2
Culbokie...98 E3
Culburnie...98 C4
Culcabock...98 E4
Culcharry...99 G3
Culcheth...53 H4
Cul Doirlinn...89 H1
Culdrain...100 E5
Culduie...96 C1
Culford...38 D3
Culgaith...67 J4
Culham...31 K8
Culkein...112 B5
Culkerton...30 D8
Cullachie...99 H6
Cullen...100 E2
Cullercoats...75 K6
Cullicudden...98 E2
Cullingworth...62 D
Cullipool...89 J7
Cullivoe...121 H2
Cullompton...8 B4
Culmington...32 D2
Culmstock...8 B3
Culnacraig...107 F1
Culnaknock...103 G2
Culrain...108 D4
Culross...86 C6
Culroy...77 J6
Culsh...101 H4
Culswick...118 C4
Cultercullen...101 J6
Cults, Grampn...100 E5
Cults, Grampn...101 H8
Culverstone Green...14 C2
Culverthorpe...46 D3
Culworth...35 G6
Cumbernauld...85 K7
Cumberworth...57 K6
Cuminestown...101 h3

Cummersdale Durness

Cummersdale 67 F1
Cummertrees 73 G7
Cummingstown 99 K2
Cumnock 72 A1
Cumnor 31 J7
Cumrew 67 H1
Cumwhinton 67 G1
Cumwhitton 67 H1
Cundall 63 H2
Cunninghamhead 77 J3
Cunnister 121 H3
Cupar 87 G3
Cupar Muir 87 G3
Curbar 55 F6
Curbridge, Hants 11 G3
Curbridge, Oxon 31 H7
Curdridge 11 G3
Curdworth 44 C8
Curland 8 D3
Currie 79 J3
Curry Mallet 8 E2
Curry Rivel 8 E2
Curtisden Green 13 L2
Curtisknowle 5 H6
Cury 2 E7
Cushnie 101 G2
Cushuish 8 C1
Cusop 29 G3
Cutiau 41 F2
Cutnall Green 33 H4
Cutsdean 30 E4
Cutthorpe 55 G6
Cuxham 20 A4
Cuxton 14 D2
Cuxwold 59 F6
Cwm, Clwyd 51 K3
Cwm, Gwent 25 K4
Cwmafan 25 F5
Cwmaman 25 J5
Cwmann 27 K3
Cwmavon 29 G7
Cwmbach, Dyfed 27 G5
Cwmbach, M. Glam 25 J4
Cwmbelan 41 J5
Cwmbran 29 G8
Cwmcarn 25 L5
Cwmcarvan 29 J7
Cwm-Cewydd 41 H2
Cwm-Cou 27 G3
Cwmdare 25 H4
Cwmdu, Powys 25 K2
Cwmdu, Dyfed 27 L4
Cwmduad 27 H4
Cwmfelin Boeth 27 F6
Cwmfelinfach 25 K5
Cwmfelin Mynach 27 G5
Cwmffrwd 27 J6
Cwmgwrach 25 G4
Cwm Irfon 28 C3
Cwmisfael 27 J6
Cwm-Llinau 41 H3
Cwmllynfell 25 F3
Cwmparc 25 H5
Cwmpengraig 27 H4
Cwmsychbant 27 J3
Cwmtillery 25 L4
Cwm-twrch Isaf 25 F3
Cwm-twrch Uchaf 25 F3
Cwm-y-glo 50 E4
Cwmyoy 29 H5
Cwmystwyth 41 G6
Cwrtnewydd 27 J3
Cwrt-y-cadno 28 A3
Cwrt-y-gollen 29 G6
Cyffylliog 51 K5
Cyfronydd 42 C7
Cymmer, W. Glam 25 G5
Cymmer, M. Glam 25 J5
Cynghordy 28 C4
Cynwyd 51 K6
Cynwyl Elfed 27 H5

D

Dacre, N. Yks 62 E3
Dacre, Cumbr 67 G4
Dacre Banks 62 E3
Daddry Shield 68 A3
Dadford 35 H7
Dalington 44 F8
Dafen 24 D4
Dagenham 21 K5
Daglingworth 30 D7
Dagnall 20 D2
Dailly 77 H7
Dairsie or Osnaburgh 87 H3
Dalavich 84 B3
Dalbeattie 72 D7
Dalbeg 111 G3
Dalblair 72 B2
Dalby 60 P4
Dalchalloch 91 J5
Dalchenna 84 C4
Dalchreichart 98 A7
Dalderby 57 G7
Dale, Dyfed 26 C7
Dale, Shetld 118 D3
Dale, Derby 44 F4
Dale Head 67 G5
Dalgarven 77 H3
Dalgety Bay 86 E6
Dalginross 85 K2
Dalhalvaig 114 D4
Dalham 38 C4
Daliburgh 94 C3
Dalkeith 80 B3
Dallas 99 K3
Dalleagles 77 L6
Dallinghoo 39 H5
Dallington 13 K5
Dalmally 84 D2
Dalmary 85 H5
Dalmellington 77 K7
Dalmeny 86 E7
Dalmore, Highld 98 E2
Dalmore, W. Isles 111 G3
Dalnabreck 89 J2
Dalnacreich 98 B3
Dalnavie 108 E6
Dalreavoch 109 F3
Dalry 77 H3
Dalrymple 77 J3
Dalserf 78 E4
Dalston 66 F1
Dalswinton 72 E5
Dalton, N. Yks 68 D6
Dalton, Lancs 53 F3
Dalton, Northum 74 F8
Dalton, D. & G 73 G6
Dalton, N. Yks 63 H2
Dalton, S. Yks 55 H4
Dalton, Northum 75 H6
Dalton-in-Furness 60 F2
Dalton-le-Dale 69 G2
Dalton-on-Tees 68 E6
Dalton Piercy 69 G3
Dalwhinnie 91 H3
Dalwood 8 D4
Damerham 10 C3
Damgate 49 K7
Damnaglaur 70 C8
Danbury 22 D3
Danby 64 E2
Danby Wiske 68 F7
Danderhall 87 G8
Danebridge, Staffs 54 C7
Danebridge, Ches 54 C7
Dane End 21 H1
Danehill 13 H4
Darenth 21 K6
Daresbury 53 G5
Darfield 55 H3
Dargate 15 G2
Darite 3 L3
Darlaston 44 A8
Darlingscote 34 D6
Darlington 68 E5
Darliston 43 G4
Darlton 56 B6
Darowen 41 H3
Darra 101 G4
Darras Hall 75 H6
Darrington 55 H1
Darsham 39 K4
Dartford 21 K6
Dartington 5 H5
Dartmeet 5 G4
Dartmouth 5 J6
Darton 55 G2
Darvel 78 C6
Darwen 61 K7
Datchet 20 D6
Datchworth 21 G2
Daugh of Kinermony 100 B4
Dauntsey 18 A2
Davenham 53 H6
Daventry 35 G4
Davidstow 4 B3
Davington 73 H3
Daviot, Highld 99 F5
Daviot, Grampn 101 G6
Davoch of Grange 100 D3
Dawley 43 H7
Dawlish 5 K4
Dawlish Warren 5 K4
Dawn 51 H3
Daws Heath 22 E5
Dawsmere 47 H4
Daylesford 31 G5
Ddol Cownwy 41 K2
Deal 15 K3
Dean, Cumbr 66 C4
Dean, Hants 11 G3
Dean, Devon 5 H5
Dean, Somer 17 H6
Deanburnhaugh 73 J2
Deane 19 G5
Deanland 10 A3
Dean Prior 5 H5
Dean Row 53 K5
Deans 79 H3
Deanscales 66 C4
Deanshanger 35 J7
Deanston 85 K4
Dearham 66 C3
Dearne 55 H3
Debach 39 H5
Debden 37 J7
Debden Green 37 J7
Debenham 39 G4
Dechmont 86 D7
Deddington 31 J4
Dedham 38 F7
Dedridge 79 H3
Deene 36 C1
Deenethorpe 36 C1
Deepcut 19 L5
Deepdale 61 L1
Deeping Gate 46 E7
Deeping St James 46 E7
Deeping St Nicholas 46 F6
Deerhill 100 D3
Deerhurst 30 C5
Deerness 116 E6
Defford 33 J6
Defynnog 25 H2
Deganwy 51 G3
Deighton, N. Yks 69 F6
Deighton, N. Yks 63 K5
Deiniolen 50 E4
Delabole 4 A3
Delamere 53 G7
Delfrigs 101 J6
Dell 111 J1
Delliefure 99 J5
Delph 54 C3
Dembleby 46 D4
Denbigh 51 K4
Denbury 5 J5
Denby 44 E3
Denby Dale 55 F3
Denchworth 18 E1
Denford 36 C3
Dengie, Essex 23 F3
Dengie, Essex 23 F3
Denham, Suff 38 C4
Denham, Bucks 20 E5
Denham, Suff 39 G3
Denham Green 20 E5
Denham Street 39 G3
Denhead, Fife 87 H3
Denhead, Grampn 101 K3
Denholm 74 B2
Denholme 62 D6
Denmead 11 H3
Denmore 101 J7
Denne Park 12 E4
Dennington 39 H4
Denny 85 L6
Dennyloanhead 85 L6
Denshaw 54 C2
Denside 93 K2
Densole 15 J4
Denston 38 C5
Denstone 44 B3
Dent 61 L1
Den, The 77 J2
Denton, Lincs 46 B4
Denton, Northnts 36 B5
Denton, Cambs 36 E2
Denton, Durham 68 E5
Denton, N. Yks 62 E5
Denton, Norf 39 H2
Denton, E. Susx 13 H6
Denton, Kent 15 J4
Denton, Oxon 31 K7
Denton, G. Man 53 L4
Denver 48 B7
Denwick 75 J2
Deopham 48 F7
Deopham Green 48 F8
Depden Green 38 C5
Deptford, Wilts 10 B1
Deptford, G. Lon 21 H6
Derby 44 E4
Derbyhaven 60 P5
Deri 25 K4
Derrington 43 K5
Derryguaig 89 F5
Derry Hill 18 A3
Derrythorpe 58 C6
Dersingham 48 B4
Dervaig 89 F3
Derwen 51 K5
Desborough 35 K2
Desford 45 F7
Detchant 81 J6
Detling 14 D3
Deuddwr 42 D6
Devauden 29 J8
Devil's Bridge 41 G6
Devizes 18 B4
Devonport 4 E6
Devonside 86 C5
Devoran 3 F6
Dewlish 9 J5
Dewsbury 63 F7
Dhoon 60 R3
Dhoor 60 R2
Dhowin 60 R1
Dial Post 12 E5
Dibden 10 F4
Dibden Purlieu 10 F4
Dickleburgh 39 G2
Didbrook 30 E4
Didcot 19 G2
Diddington 36 E4
Diddlebury 32 E2
Didley 29 J4
Didmarton 17 K2
Didsbury 53 K4
Didworthy 5 G5
Digby 46 D2
Diggle 54 D3
Dihewyd 27 J2
Dilham 49 J5
Dilhorne 44 A3
Dilston 75 F7
Dilton Marsh 17 K6
Dilwyn 29 J2
Dinas, Gwyn 50 B7
Dinas, Dyfed 27 G4
Dinas Cross 26 E4
Dinas Mawddwy 41 H2
Dinas Powys 25 K7
Dinchope 32 D2
Dinder 17 G6
Dinedor 29 K4
Dines Green 33 H5
Dingestow 29 J6
Dingley 35 J2
Dingwall 98 D3
Dinnet 93 F2
Dinnington, Somer 8 F3
Dinnington, S. Yks 55 J5
Dinnington, T. & W 75 J6
Dinorwig 50 E4
Dinton, Wilts 10 B1
Dinton, Bucks 20 B2
Dinwoodie Mains 73 G4
Dinworthy 6 D4
Dippen 76 C4
Dippenhall 19 K6
Dippin 76 F5
Dipple 100 C3
Diptford 5 H6
Dipton 68 D1
Dirleton 87 J6
Discoed 32 B4
Diseworth 45 F5
Dishes 117 F4
Dishforth 63 G2
Disley 54 C5
Diss 39 G3
Disserth 28 E2
Distington 66 C4
Ditcheat 9 H1
Dichingham 39 J1
Ditchling 13 G5
Dittisham 5 J6
Ditton, Ches 53 F5
Ditton, Kent 13 L1
Ditton Green 38 B5
Ditton Priors 33 F2
Dixton, Glos 30 D4
Dixton, Gwent 29 K6
Dlengrasco 103 F4
Dobwalls 3 L3
Doccombe 5 H3
Dochgarroch 98 E4
Docking 48 C4
Docklow 29 K2
Dockray 67 F4
Doddinghurst 22 B4
Doddington, Lincs 56 D6
Doddington, Shrops 33 F3
Doddington, Kent 14 F3
Doddington, Cambs 37 H1
Doddington, Northum 81 H6
Doddiscombsleigh 5 J3
Dodford, Northnts 35 H4
Dodford, H. & W 33 J3
Dodington 17 J2
Dodleston 52 E7
Dodworth 55 G3
Doe Lea 55 H7
Dogmersfield 19 J5
Dog Village 5 K2
Dogyke 46 F2
Dolanog 41 K2
Dolau 32 A4
Dolbenmaen 50 E6
Dolfach 41 J6
Dolfor 41 L5
Dolgarrog 51 G4
Dolgellau 41 G2
Dolgran 27 J4
Doll 109 G3
Dollar 86 C5
Dolley Green 32 B4
Dolphinholme 61 J4
Dolphinton 79 J5
Dolton 7 F4
Dolwen 51 H3
Dolwyddelan 51 G5
Dol-y-cannau 29 G3
Dolyhir 29 G2
Domgay 42 D6
Doncaster 55 J3
Donhead St Andrew 9 L2
Donhead St Mary 9 L2
Donibristle 86 E6
Donington 46 F4
Donington on Bain 57 G5
Donisthorpe 44 E6
Donkey Town 20 D7
Donnington, H. & W 30 B4
Donnington, Berks 19 F4
Donnington, Glos 31 F5
Donnington, Shrops 43 G7
Donnington, Shrops 43 J6
Donnington, W. Susx 11 K4
Donyatt 8 E3
Doonfoot 77 J6
Doonholm 77 J6
Dorchester, Dorset 9 H5
Dorchester, Oxon 31 K8
Dordon 44 D7
Dore 55 G5
Dores 98 D5
Dorking 12 E2
Dormansland 13 H2
Dormanstown 69 H4
Dormington 29 K3
Dorney 20 D6
Dornie 96 D3
Dornoch 109 F5
Dornock 73 H7
Dorridge 34 C3
Dorrington, Lincs 46 D2
Dorrington, Shrops 43 F7
Dorsington 34 C6
Dorstone 29 H3
Dorton 20 A2
Dosthill 44 D7
Doublebois 3 K3
Doughton 17 K1
Douglas, Strath 79 F6
Douglas, I. of M 60 Q4
Douglas and Angus 87 H1
Douglastown 92 F7
Douglas Water 79 F6
Doulting 17 H6
Dounby 116 B4
Doune 85 K4
Douneside 100 D8
Dounie 108 D4
Dousland 5 F5
Dove Holes 54 D6
Dovenby 66 C3
Dover 15 K4
Doverdale 33 H4
Doveridge 44 C4
Dowdeswell 30 E6
Dowland 7 F4
Dowlish Wake 8 E3
Down Ampney 30 F8
Downderry 4 D6
Downe 21 J7
Downend, Berks 19 F3
Downend, I. of W 11 G6
Downfield 87 G1
Downgate 4 D4
Downham, Lancs 62 A5
Downham, Essex 22 D4
Downham, Northum 81 G6
Downham Market 48 B7
Down Hatherley 30 C5
Downhead 17 H6
Downholme 68 D7
Downies 93 L2
Downley 20 C4
Downs 25 K7
Downside Abbey 17 H5
Down St Mary 7 H5
Downton, Wilts 10 C2
Downton, Hants 10 D5
Downton on the Rock 32 D3
Dowsby 46 E5
Dowsdale 47 F6
Dowthwaitehead 67 F4
Doxey 43 L5
Doynton 17 J3
Draethen 25 L6
Draffan 78 E5
Drakeland Corner 5 F6
Drakemyre 77 H2
Drakes Broughton 33 J6
Draughton, N. Yks 62 D4
Draughton, Northnts 35 J3
Drax 63 K7
Draycote 35 F3
Draycott, Glos 31 F4
Draycott, Derby 45 F4
Draycott, Somer 17 F5
Draycott in the Clay 44 C5
Draycott in the Moors 44 A3
Drayton, Leic 36 B1
Drayton, Somer 8 F2
Drayton, Oxon 34 F6
Drayton, Norf 49 G6
Drayton, Hants 11 H4
Drayton, H. & W 33 J3
Drayton, Oxon 31 J8
Drayton Bassett 44 C7
Drayton Camp 18 F6
Drayton Parslow 36 B8
Drayton St Leonard 31 K8
Drefach, Dyfed 27 H4
Dre-fach, Dyfed 27 K3
Drefach, Dyfed 27 K6
Drefelin 27 H4
Dreghorn 77 J4
Drem 87 J7
Drewsteignton 5 H2
Driby 57 H6
Driffield 30 E8
Drift 2 C7
Drigg 66 C7
Drighlington 63 F7
Drimnin 89 G3
Drimpton 8 F4
Drinishader 105 G2
Drinkstone 38 E4
Drinkstone Green 38 E4
Drointon 44 B5
Droitwich 33 H4
Droman 112 C3
Dron 86 E3
Dronfield 55 G6
Dronfield Woodhouse 55 G6
Drongan 77 K6
Droxford 11 H3
Droylsden 53 L4
Druid 51 K6
Druidston 26 C6
Druimarbin 90 B4
Druimdrishaig 83 G4
Druimindarroch 96 B7
Druimkinnerras 98 C5
Drum 86 D4
Drumbeg 112 C5
Drumblade 100 E4
Drumbuie 96 C2
Drumchapel 85 H7
Drumchardine 98 D4
Drumchork 106 D3
Drumclog 78 D6
Drumelzier 79 J6
Drumfearn 96 B4
Drumgley 92 F6
Drumguish 91 J2
Drumin 100 A5
Drumlassie 100 F8
Drumlemble 76 B6
Drumligair 101 J7
Drumlithie 93 J3
Drummore 70 C8
Drumnadrochit 98 D6
Drumnagorrach 100 E3
Drumoak 93 J2
Drums 101 J6
Drumsallie 90 A4
Drumsturdy 87 H1
Drumuie 103 F4
Drumuillie 99 H6
Drumwhindle 101 J5
Drury 52 D7
Drybeck 67 J5
Drybridge, Grampn 100 D2
Drybridge, Strath 77 J4
Drybrook 30 A6
Dry Doddington 46 B3
Dry Drayton 37 G4
Dryhope 79 K7
Drymen 85 G6
Drymuir 101 J4
Drynoch 103 F5
Dubford 101 G2
Dubwath 66 D3
Duckington 43 F2
Ducklington 31 H7
Duck's Cross 36 E5
Duddenhoe End 37 H7
Duddingston 87 F7
Duddington 46 C7
Duddo 81 H5
Duddon 53 G7
Duddon Bridge 60 E1
Dudleston Heath 42 E4
Dudley, W. Mids 33 J1
Dudley, T. & W 75 J6
Duffield 44 E3
Duffryn, Gwent 16 D2
Duffryn, W. Glam 25 G5
Dufftown 100 C4
Duffus 100 A2
Dufton 67 J4
Duggleby 65 F6
Duirinish 96 C2
Duisky 90 B4
Dukestown 25 K3
Dukinfield 53 L4
Dulas 50 D2
Dulcote 17 G6
Dulford 8 B4
Dull 91 K7
Dullingham 38 B5
Dulnain Bridge 99 H6
Duloe, Beds 36 E4
Duloe, Corn 3 L4
Dulsie 99 H4
Dulverton 7 K3
Dulwich 21 H6
Dumbarton 85 F7
Dumbleton 34 B7
Dumcrieff 73 G3
Dumfries 72 E6
Dumgoyne 85 H6
Dummer 19 G6
Dunan 96 A3
Dunball 16 E6
Dunbar 87 K7
Dunbeath 115 G7
Dunbeg 84 A1
Dunblane 85 K4
Dunbog 87 F3
Duncanston 98 D3
Duncanstone 100 E6
Dunchideock 5 J3
Dunchurch 35 F3
Duncote 35 H5
Duncow 72 E5
Duncrievie 86 E4
Duncton 12 C5
Dundee 87 H1
Dundon 9 F1
Dundonald 77 J4
Dundonnell 107 F3
Dundraw 66 E2
Dundreggan 98 B7
Dundrennan 71 J7
Dundry 17 G4
Dunecht 101 G8
Dunfermline 86 D6
Dunford Bridge 54 E3
Dunham-on-the-Hill 53 F6
Dunham on Trent 56 C6
Dunhampton 33 H4
Dunham Town 53 J5
Dunholme 56 E6
Dunino 87 J3
Dunipace 85 L6
Dunkeld 92 B7
Dunkeswell 8 C4
Dunkirk 15 G3
Dunk's Green 13 K1
Dunley 33 G4
Dunlop 77 K3
Dunmore, Central 86 B6
Dunmore, Strath 76 C1
Dunnet 115 H2
Dunnichen 93 G7
Dunning 86 D3
Dunnington, Warw 34 B5
Dunnington, Humbs 65 J7
Dunnington, N. Yks 63 K4
Dunnockshaw 62 B7
Dunollie 84 A1
Dunoon 84 E7
Dunragit 70 C6
Duns 81 F4
Dunsby 46 E5
Dun Scaich 96 A4
Dunscore 72 D5
Dunscroft 55 K3
Dunsden Green 20 B6
Dunsfold 12 D3
Dunsford 5 J3
Dunshelt 87 F3
Dunsley 69 L5
Dunsmore 20 C3
Dunsop Bridge 61 K4
Dunstable 20 E1
Dunstall 44 C5
Dunstall Green 38 C4
Dunstan 75 J2
Dunster 7 K1
Duns Tew 31 J5
Dunston, Lincs 56 E7
Dunston, Norf 49 H7
Dunston, T. & W 75 J7
Dunston, Staffs 43 L6
Dunsville 55 K3
Dunswell 58 E3
Dunterton 4 D4
Duntisbourne Abbots 30 D7
Duntisbourne Leer 30 D7
Duntisbourne Rouse 30 D7
Duntish 9 H4
Duntocher 85 G7
Dunton, Bucks 20 C1
Dunton, Norf 48 D4
Dunton, Beds 37 F6
Dunton Bassett 35 G1
Dunton Green 13 J1
Dunure 77 H6
Dunvant 24 D5
Dunvegan 102 D4
Dunwich 39 K3
Durdar 67 G1
Durham 68 E2
Durisdeer 72 D3
Durleigh 8 D1
Durley, Wilts 18 D4
Durley, Hants 11 G3
Durnamuck 106 F2
Durness 112 F2

Durno ... 101 G6
Durran ... 115 G3
Durrington, Wilts ... 18 C6
Durrington, W. Susx ... 12 K6
Dursley ... 30 B8
Durston ... 8 D2
Durweston ... 9 K4
Dury ... 119 G2
Duston ... 35 J4
Duthil ... 99 H6
Dutlas ... 32 B3
Duton Hill ... 38 B8
Dutton ... 53 G6
Duxford ... 37 H6
Dwygyfylchi ... 51 G3
Dwyran ... 50 D4
Dyce ... 101 H7
Dye House ... 74 F8
Dyffryn, Gwyn ... 50 B3
Dyffryn, M. Glam ... 25 G5
Dyffryn Ardudwy ... 40 E1
Dyffryn Ceidrych ... 24 F2
Dyffryn Cellwen ... 25 G3
Dyke, Devon ... 6 D3
Dyke, Lincs ... 46 E5
Dyke, Grampn ... 99 H3
Dykehead, Tays ... 92 E5
Dykehead, Strath ... 79 F4
Dylife ... 41 H4
Dymchurch ... 15 H6
Dymock ... 30 B4
Dyrham ... 17 J3
Dysart ... 87 G5
Dyserth ... 51 K3

E

Eagland Hill ... 61 H5
Eagle ... 56 C7
Eaglescliffe ... 69 G5
Eaglesfield, Cumbr ... 66 C4
Eaglesfield, D. & G ... 73 H6
Eaglesham ... 78 C4
Eairy ... 60 P4
Eakring ... 55 K7
Ealand ... 58 B5
Ealing ... 21 F5
Eamont Bridge ... 67 H4
Earby ... 62 C5
Earcroft ... 61 K7
Eardington ... 33 G1
Eardisland ... 29 J2
Eardisley ... 29 H3
Eardiston, Shrops ... 42 E5
Eardiston, H. & W ... 33 F4
Earith ... 37 G3
Earle ... 81 H7
Earlestown ... 53 G4
Earlham ... 49 G7
Earlish ... 102 E2
Earls Barton ... 36 B4
Earls Colne ... 38 D8
Earl's Croome ... 33 H6
Earlsdon ... 34 E3
Earlsferry ... 87 H5
Earlsford ... 101 H5
Earl's Green ... 38 F4
Earl Shilton ... 45 F8
Earl Soham ... 39 H4
Earl Sterndale ... 54 D7
Earlston, Border ... 80 D6
Earlston, Strath ... 77 K4
Earl Stonham ... 39 G5
Earlswood, Warw ... 34 C3
Earlswood, Gwent ... 29 J8
Earnley ... 11 K5
Earsary ... 94 C6
Earsdon ... 75 K6
Earsham ... 39 J2
Earswick ... 63 K4
Eartham ... 12 C6
Easby ... 69 H6
Easdale ... 89 J7
Easebourne ... 11 K2
Easenhall ... 35 F3
Easington, Bucks ... 20 A2
Easington, Humbs ... 59 H5
Easington, Cleve ... 69 K5
Easington, Northum ... 81 K6
Easington Lane ... 69 F2
Easingwold ... 63 J3
Easole Street ... 15 J3
Eassie ... 92 E7
East Aberthaw ... 25 J8
East Allington ... 5 H7
East Anstey ... 7 J3
East Ashling ... 11 K4
East Auchronie ... 101 H8
East Barkwith ... 57 F5
East Barming ... 13 L1
East Barnet ... 21 G4
East Barsham ... 48 E4
East Beckham ... 49 G4
East Bedfont ... 20 E6
East Bergholt ... 38 F7
East Bilney ... 48 E6
East Blatchington ... 13 H6
East Boldre ... 10 E4
Eastbourne ... 13 K7
East Brent ... 16 E5
Eastbridge ... 39 K4
East Bridgford ... 45 H3
East Buckland ... 7 G2
East Budleigh ... 8 B6
East Burrafirth ... 119 F3
East Burton ... 9 K6
Eastbury, Berks ... 18 E3
Eastbury, Herts ... 20 E4
East Calder ... 79 H3
East Carleton ... 49 G7
East Carlton ... 36 B2
East Chaldon or
  Chaldon Herring ... 9 J6

East Challow ... 18 E2
East Chiltington ... 13 G5
East Chinnock ... 9 F3
East Chisenbury ... 18 C5
Eastchurch ... 15 F1
East Clandon ... 12 D1
East Claydon ... 35 J8
East Coker ... 9 G3
East Combe, Somer ... 8 C1
Eastcombe, Glos ... 30 C7
East Compton ... 17 H6
Eastcote, W. Mids ... 34 C3
Eastcote, G. Lon ... 21 F5
Eastcott, Wilts ... 18 B5
Eastcott, Corn ... 6 C4
East Cottingwith ... 58 B2
Eastcourt ... 18 A1
East Cowes ... 11 G5
East Cowton ... 68 F6
East Cramlington ... 75 J4
East Creech ... 10 A6
East Croachy ... 98 E6
East Davoch ... 100 D8
East Dean, Hants ... 10 D2
East Dean, E. Susx ... 13 J7
East Dean, W. Susx ... 11 L3
East Dereham ... 48 E6
East Down ... 7 G1
East Drayton ... 56 B6
East End, Dorset ... 10 A5
East End, Hants ... 10 E5
East End, Kent ... 14 E5
East End, Avon ... 17 F3
East End, Hants ... 18 F4
East End, Oxon ... 31 H6
East End, Herts ... 37 H8
Easter Ardross ... 108 E6
Easter Balmoral ... 92 D2
Easter Boleskine ... 98 D6
Easter Compton ... 17 G2
Easter Fearn ... 108 E5
Eastergate ... 12 C6
Easter Kinkell ... 98 D3
Easter Lednathie ... 92 E5
Easter Muckovie ... 99 F4
Eastern Green ... 34 D3
Easter Ord ... 101 H8
Easter Quaff ... 119 G5
Easter Skeld ... 119 F4
Easterton ... 18 B5
Eastertown ... 16 E5
East Farleigh ... 13 L1
East Farndon ... 35 J2
East Ferry ... 58 C7
Eastfield, Strath ... 79 F3
Eastfield, N. Yks ... 65 H4
Eastfield, Strath ... 85 K7
East Garston ... 18 E3
Eastgate, Durham ... 68 B3
Eastgate, Norf ... 49 G5
East Ginge ... 19 F2
East Goscote ... 45 H6
East Grafton ... 18 D4
East Grimstead ... 10 D2
East Grinstead ... 13 G3
East Guldeford ... 14 F6
East Haddon ... 35 H4
East Hagbourne ... 19 G2
East Halton ... 59 F5
Eastham, Mers ... 52 E5
East Ham, G. Lon ... 21 J5
Easthampstead ... 20 C7
East Hanney ... 18 F1
East Hanningfield ... 22 D3
East Hardwick ... 55 H2
East Harling ... 38 E2
East Harlsey ... 69 G7
East Harptree ... 17 G5
East Hartford ... 75 J6
East Harting ... 11 J3
East Hatley ... 37 F5
East Hauxwell ... 68 D7
East Haven ... 93 G8
East Heckington ... 46 E3
East Hedleyhope ... 68 D2
East Hendred ... 19 F2
East Heslerton ... 65 G5
East Hoathly ... 13 J5
Easthope ... 43 G8
Easthorpe ... 22 F1
East Horrington ... 17 G6
East Horsley ... 12 D1
East Hyde ... 21 F2
East Ilsley ... 19 F2
Eastington, Glos ... 30 B7
Eastington, Glos ... 31 F6
Eastington, Devon ... 7 H5
East Kennett ... 18 C4
East Keswick ... 63 G5
East Kilbride ... 78 D4
East Kirkby ... 57 H7
East Knighton ... 9 K6
East Knoyle ... 9 K1
East Lambrook ... 9 F3
East Lamington ... 109 F6
East Langdon ... 15 K4
East Langton ... 35 J1
East Langwell ... 109 F3
East Lavington ... 12 C5
East Layton ... 68 D6
Eastleach Martin ... 31 G7
Eastleach Turville ... 31 F7
East Leake ... 45 G5
East Lexham ... 48 D6
East Lilburn ... 81 J7
Eastling ... 14 F3
East Linton ... 87 J7
East Liss ... 11 J2
East Lound ... 58 B7
East Lulworth ... 9 K6
East Mains ... 93 H2
East Malling ... 13 K1

East Marden ... 11 K3
East Markham ... 56 B6
East Marton ... 62 C4
East Meon ... 11 H2
East Mersea ... 23 G2
East Molesey ... 21 F7
East Morden ... 9 L5
East Morton ... 62 E5
Eastney ... 11 H5
Eastnor ... 33 G7
East Norton ... 45 J7
East Oakley ... 19 G5
Eastoft ... 58 C5
East Ogwell ... 5 J4
Easton, Lincs ... 46 C5
Easton, Cambs ... 36 E3
Easton, Hants ... 11 G1
Easton, Norf ... 49 G6
Easton, Somer ... 17 G6
Easton, Devon ... 5 H3
Easton, Suff ... 39 H5
Easton, Dorset ... 9 H7
Easton, Cumbr ... 73 K6
Easton Grey ... 17 K2
Easton-in-Gordano ... 17 G3
Easton Maudit ... 36 B5
Easton on the Hill ... 46 D7
Easton Royal ... 18 D4
East Ord ... 81 H4
East Panson ... 4 D2
East Peckham ... 13 K2
East Pennard ... 9 G1
East Perry ... 36 E4
East Portlemouth ... 5 H8
East Prawle ... 5 H8
East Preston ... 12 D6
East Putford ... 6 D4
East Quantoxhead ... 16 C6
East Rainton ... 68 F2
East Ravendale ... 59 G7
East Raynham ... 48 D5
Eastrea ... 47 F8
East Retford ... 56 B5
Eastriggs ... 73 H7
Eastrington ... 58 B3
East Rudham ... 48 D5
East Runton ... 49 G3
East Ruston ... 49 J5
Eastry ... 15 K3
East Saltoun ... 80 C3
East Sleekburn ... 75 J5
East Stockwith ... 56 B4
East Stoke, Notts ... 45 J3
East Stoke, Dorset ... 9 K6
East Stour ... 9 J2
East Stourmouth ... 15 J2
East Stratton ... 19 G7
East Studdal ... 15 K4
East Taphouse ... 3 K3
East-the-Water ... 6 E3
East Tilbury ... 22 C6
East Tisted ... 11 J1
East Torrington ... 57 F5
East Tuddenham ... 48 F6
East Tytherley ... 10 D2
East Tytherton ... 18 A3
East Village ... 7 J5
Eastville ... 57 J8
East Wall ... 43 G8
East Walton ... 48 C6
Eastwell ... 45 J5
East Wellow ... 10 E2
Eastwell Park ... 15 G4
East Wemyss ... 87 G5
East Whitburn ... 79 G3
Eastwick ... 21 J2
East Williamston ... 26 E7
East Winch ... 48 B6
East Wittering ... 11 J5
East Witton ... 62 E1
Eastwood, W. Yks ... 62 C7
Eastwood, Essex ... 22 E5
Eastwood, Notts ... 45 F3
East Woodhay ... 18 F4
East Worldham ... 19 J7
Eathorpe ... 34 E4
Eaton, Notts ... 56 B6
Eaton, Shrops ... 32 C2
Eaton, Shrops ... 32 E1
Eaton, Ches ... 53 G7
Eaton, Norf ... 49 H7
Eaton, Leic ... 45 J5
Eaton, Oxon ... 31 J7
Eaton, Ches ... 53 K7
Eaton Bishop ... 29 J4
Eaton Bray ... 20 D1
Eaton Constantine ... 43 G7
Eaton Hastings ... 31 G8
Eaton Socon ... 36 E5
Eaton upon Tern ... 43 H5
Ebberston ... 65 F4
Ebbesbourne Wake ... 10 A2
Ebbw Vale ... 25 K4
Ebchester ... 68 D1
Ebford ... 5 K3
Ebrington ... 34 C6
Ecchinswell ... 19 F5
Ecclaw ... 80 F3
Ecclefechan ... 73 G6
Eccles, Kent ... 14 D2
Eccles, Border ... 80 F5
Eccles, G. Man ... 53 J4
Ecclesall ... 55 G4
Ecclesfield ... 55 H3
Ecclesgreig ... 93 K5
Eccleshall ... 43 K5
Ecclesmachan ... 86 D7
Eccles Road ... 38 F1
Eccleston, Mers ... 53 F4
Eccleston, Ches ... 52 F7
Eccleston, Lancs ... 53 G2
Eccup ... 63 F5
Echt ... 101 G8
Eckford ... 80 F7
Eckington, Derby ... 55 H6

Eckington, H. & W ... 33 J6
Ecton ... 36 B4
Edale ... 54 E5
Edburton ... 12 F5
Eddleston ... 79 K5
Eddlington, Cambs ... 36 E3
Edenbridge ... 13 H2
Edenfield ... 53 K2
Edenhall ... 67 H3
Edenham ... 46 D5
Eden Park ... 21 H7
Edensor ... 55 F6
Edenthorpe ... 55 K3
Edern ... 50 B7
Edgbaston ... 34 B2
Edgcott ... 20 A1
Edgcott ... 42 E7
Edge ... 43 G5
Edgebolton ... 43 G5
Edge End ... 29 K6
Edgefield ... 49 F4
Edgefield Street ... 49 F4
Edgeworth ... 30 D7
Edgmond ... 43 J6
Edgmond Marsh ... 43 J5
Edgton ... 32 C2
Edgware ... 21 G4
Edgworth ... 53 J2
Edinbane ... 102 E3
Edinburgh ... 87 F7
Edingale ... 44 D6
Edingley ... 45 H2
Edingthorpe ... 49 J4
Edington, Somer ... 16 E7
Edington, Wilts ... 17 L5
Edithmead ... 16 E6
Edith Weston ... 46 C7
Edlesborough ... 20 D2
Edlingham ... 75 H3
Edlington ... 57 G6
Edmondsham ... 10 B3
Edmondsley ... 68 E2
Edmondthorpe ... 46 B6
Edmonstone ... 116 E4
Edmonton ... 21 H4
Edmundbyers ... 68 C1
Ednam ... 80 F6
Ednaston ... 44 D3
Edrom ... 81 G4
Edstaston ... 43 G4
Edstone ... 34 C4
Edvin Loach ... 33 F5
Edwalton ... 45 G4
Edwardstone ... 38 E6
Edwinsford ... 27 L4
Edwinstowe ... 55 K7
Edworth ... 37 F6
Edwyn Ralph ... 33 F5
Edzell ... 93 H5
Efail Isaf ... 25 J6
Efailnewydd ... 50 C7
Efailwen ... 26 F5
Efenechtyd ... 42 C2
Effingham ... 12 E1
Effirth ... 119 F3
Efford ... 7 J5
Egdon ... 33 H5
Egerton, Kent ... 14 F4
Egerton, G. Man ... 53 J2
Egerton Forstal ... 14 E4
Eggesford Station ... 7 G4
Eggington ... 36 C0
Egginton ... 44 D5
Egglescliffe ... 69 G5
Eggleston ... 68 B4
Egham ... 20 E6
Egleton ... 46 B7
Eglingham ... 75 H2
Egloshayle ... 3 J2
Egloskerry ... 4 C3
Eglwysbach ... 51 H3
Eglwys-Brewis ... 25 J8
Eglwyswen ... 26 F4
Eglwyswrw ... 26 F4
Egmanton ... 56 B7
Egremont ... 66 C5
Egton ... 64 F2
Egton Bridge ... 64 F2
Eight Ash Green ... 38 E8
Eilanreach ... 96 D4
Eilean Darach ... 107 G3
Eilean Glas ... 105 H2
Eilean Iarmain or Isleornsay ... 96 B4
Eishken ... 111 H6
Eisingrug ... 50 F7
Elan Village ... 41 J7
Elberton ... 17 H2
Elburton ... 5 F6
Elcombe ... 18 C2
Eldersfield ... 30 C4
Elderslie ... 77 K1
Eldroth ... 62 A3
Eldwick ... 62 E5
Elerch or Bont-goch ... 41 F5
Elford, Staffs ... 44 C6
Elford, Northum ... 81 K6
Elgin ... 100 B2
Elgol ... 103 G2
Elham ... 15 H4
Elie ... 87 H4
Elim ... 50 C2
Eling ... 10 E3
Elishader ... 103 G2
Elishaw ... 74 F4
Elkesley ... 56 A6
Elkstone ... 30 D6
Elland ... 62 E7
Ellary ... 83 G4
Ellastone ... 44 C3
Ellemford ... 80 F3
Ellenhall ... 43 K5
Ellen's Green ... 12 D3
Ellerbeck ... 69 G7
Ellerby ... 69 K5
Ellerdine Heath ... 43 H5
Ellerker ... 58 D4
Ellerton, Humbs ... 58 B3
Ellerton, Shrops ... 43 J5

Ellesborough ... 20 C3
Ellesmere ... 42 F4
Ellesmere Port ... 52 E6
Ellingham, Norf ... 39 J1
Ellingham, Northum ... 81 K7
Ellingstring ... 62 E1
Ellington, Cambs ... 36 E3
Ellington, Northum ... 75 J4
Ellisfield ... 19 H6
Ellistown ... 44 F6
Ellon ... 101 J5
Ellough ... 39 J2
Elloughton ... 58 D4
Ellwood ... 29 K7
Elm ... 47 H7
Elmbridge ... 33 J4
Elmdon, W. Mids ... 34 C2
Elmdon, Essex ... 37 H7
Elmdon Heath ... 34 C2
Elmesthorpe ... 45 F8
Elmhurst ... 44 C6
Elmley Castle ... 34 A6
Elmley Lovett ... 33 H4
Elmore ... 30 B6
Elmore Back ... 30 B6
Elm Park ... 21 K5
Elmscott ... 6 C3
Elmsett ... 38 F6
Elmstead Market ... 23 G1
Elmsted ... 15 H4
Elmstone ... 15 J2
Elmstone Hardwicke ... 30 D5
Elmswell ... 38 E4
Elmton ... 55 J6
Elphin ... 112 D7
Elphinstone ... 87 G7
Elrick ... 101 H8
Elrig ... 70 E7
Elsdon ... 74 F4
Elsecar ... 55 G3
Elsenham ... 37 J8
Elsfield ... 31 K6
Elsham ... 58 E5
Elsing ... 48 F6
Elslack ... 62 C5
Elsrickle ... 79 H5
Elstead ... 12 C2
Elsted ... 11 K3
Elston ... 45 J3
Elstone ... 7 G4
Elstow ... 36 D6
Elstree ... 21 F4
Elstronwick ... 59 G3
Elswick ... 61 H6
Elsworth ... 37 G4
Elterwater ... 66 F6
Eltham ... 21 J6
Eltisley ... 37 F5
Elton, Glos ... 30 B6
Elton, H. & W ... 32 D3
Elton, Cambs ... 46 D8
Elton, Ches ... 52 F6
Elton, Derby ... 55 F7
Elton, Cleve ... 69 G5
Elton, Notts ... 45 J4
Elvanfoot ... 72 E2
Elvaston ... 44 F4
Elveden ... 38 D3
Elvingston ... 87 G7
Elvington, N. Yks ... 58 B2
Elvington, Kent ... 15 J3
Elwick, Cleve ... 69 G3
Elwick, Northum ... 81 K6
Elworth ... 53 J7
Elworthy ... 8 B1
Ely, Cambs ... 37 J2
Ely, S. Glam ... 25 K7
Emberton ... 36 B6
Embleton, Cumbr ... 66 D3
Embleton, Northum ... 81 L7
Embo ... 109 G4
Emborough ... 17 H5
Embsay ... 62 D4
Emery Down ... 10 D4
Emley ... 55 F2
Emmer Green ... 20 B6
Emmington ... 20 B3
Emneth ... 47 H7
Emneth Hungate ... 47 J7
Empingham ... 46 C7
Empshott ... 11 J1
Emsworth ... 11 J4
Enaclete ... 111 F5
Enborne ... 18 F4
Enchmarsh ... 43 G8
Enderby ... 45 G8
Endmoor ... 61 J1
Endon ... 43 L2
Enfield ... 21 H4
Enford ... 18 C5
Engine Common ... 17 H2
Englefield ... 20 A6
Englefield Green ... 20 D6
English Bicknor ... 29 K6
English Frankton ... 42 F5
Enham-Alamein ... 18 E6
Enmore ... 8 D1
Ennerdale Bridge ... 66 C5
Enochdhu ... 92 B5
Ensbury ... 10 B5
Ensdon ... 42 F6
Ensis ... 7 F3
Enstone ... 31 H5
Enterkinfoot ... 72 D3
Enville ... 33 H2
Eochar ... 104 C7
Eolaigarry ... 94 C5
Eorabus ... 88 E6
Eoropie ... 111 K1
Epperstone ... 45 H3
Epping ... 21 J3
Epping Green, Herts ... 21 G3
Epping Green, Essex ... 21 J3
Eppleby ... 68 D5

Epsom ... 21 G7
Epwell ... 34 E6
Epworth ... 58 B6
Erbistock ... 42 E3
Erbusaig ... 96 C3
Erdington ... 34 C1
Eredine ... 84 B4
Ericstane ... 73 F2
Eridge Green ... 13 J3
Eriswell ... 38 C3
Erith ... 21 K6
Erlestoke ... 18 A5
Ermington ... 5 G6
Erpingham ... 49 G4
Errogie ... 98 D3
Errol ... 87 F2
Erskine ... 85 G7
Erskine Bridge ... 85 G7
Erwarton ... 39 H7
Erwood ... 28 C3
Eryholme ... 68 F6
Eryrys ... 52 D8
Escomb ... 68 D3
Escrick ... 63 K5
Esgairgeiliog ... 41 G3
Esh ... 68 D2
Esher ... 21 F7
Eshott ... 75 J4
Eshton ... 62 C4
Esh Winning ... 68 D2
Eskadale ... 98 C5
Eskbank ... 80 B3
Eskdale Green ... 66 D6
Eskdalemuir ... 73 H4
Esknish ... 82 C5
Esprick ... 61 H6
Essendine ... 46 D6
Essendon ... 21 G3
Essich ... 98 E5
Essington ... 44 A7
Esslemont ... 101 J6
Eston ... 69 H5
Etal ... 81 H6
Etchilhampton ... 18 B4
Etchingham ... 13 L4
Etchinghill, Staffs ... 44 B6
Etchinghill, Kent ... 15 H5
Etherley ... 68 D4
Eton ... 20 D6
Etteridge ... 91 H2
Ettersgill ... 68 A4
Ettington ... 34 D6
Etton, Humbs ... 58 D2
Etton, Cambs ... 46 E7
Ettrick ... 73 H2
Ettrickbridge ... 80 B7
Etwall ... 44 D4
Euston ... 38 D3
Euxton ... 53 G2
Evanton ... 98 E2
Evedon ... 46 D3
Evelix ... 109 F4
Evenjobb ... 32 B4
Evenley ... 31 K4
Evenlode ... 31 G5
Evenwood ... 68 D4
Everbay ... 117 E4
Evercreech ... 17 H7
Everdon ... 35 G5
Everingham ... 58 C2
Everleigh ... 18 D5
Everley ... 65 F3
Eversholt ... 36 c7
Evershot ... 9 G4
Eversley ... 20 B7
Eversley Cross ... 20 B7
Everton, Notts ... 56 A4
Everton, Hants ... 10 D5
Everton, Beds ... 36 F5
Evertown ... 73 J6
Evesbatch ... 33 F6
Evesham ... 34 B6
Evington ... 45 H7
Ewden Village ... 55 F4
Ewell ... 21 G7
Ewell Minnis ... 15 J4
Ewelme ... 20 A4
Ewen ... 30 E8
Ewenny ... 25 H7
Ewerby ... 46 E3
Ewes ... 73 J4
Ewhurst ... 12 D2
Ewhurst Green ... 14 D6
Ewloe ... 52 E7
Eworthy ... 4 E2
Ewshot ... 19 K6
Ewyas Harold ... 29 H5
Exbourne ... 7 G5
Exbury ... 10 F4
Exebridge ... 7 K3
Exelby ... 63 F1
Exeter ... 5 K2
Exford ... 7 J2
Exhall ... 34 C5
Exminster ... 5 K3
Exmouth ... 5 L3
Exnaboe ... 119 F7
Exning ... 38 B4
Exton, Leic ... 46 C6
Exton, Hants ... 11 H2
Exton, Somer ... 7 K2
Exton, Devon ... 5 K3
Eyam ... 54 F6
Eydon ... 35 G5
Eye, H. & W ... 32 D4
Eye, Cambs ... 47 F7
Eye, Suff ... 39 G3
Eyemouth ... 81 H3
Eyeworth ... 37 F6
Eyhorne Street ... 14 E3
Eyke ... 39 J5
Eynesbury ... 36 E4
Eynort ... 102 E6
Eynsford ... 21 K7
Eynsham ... 31 J7

Eype 9 F5
Eyre 103 F3
Eythorne 15 J4
Eyton, Shrops 32 C2
Eyton, H. & W. 32 D4
Eyton upon the Weald Moors ..43 H6

F

Faccombe 18 E5
Faceby 69 G6
Faddiley 43 G2
Fadmoor 69 J8
Faerdre 24 E4
Faifley 85 H7
Failand 17 G3
Failford 77 K5
Failsworth 53 K3
Fairbourne 40 F2
Fairburn 63 H7
Fairfield 34 A3
Fairford 31 F7
Fairlie 77 H2
Fairlight 14 E7
Fairmile 8 B5
Fairmilehead 79 K3
Fair Oak, Hants 11 F3
Fairoak, Staffs 43 J4
Fairseat 14 C2
Fairstead 22 D2
Fairwarp 13 H4
Fairy Cross 6 E3
Fakenham 48 E4
Fala 80 C3
Fala Dam 80 C3
Falahill 80 B4
Faldingworth 56 E5
Falfield 30 A8
Falkenham 39 H7
Falkirk 86 B6
Falkland 87 F4
Falla 74 D2
Fallin 85 L5
Falmer 13 G6
Falmouth 3 G6
Fanagmore 112 C4
Fangdale Beck 69 H7
Fangfoss 64 C7
Fanmore 88 F4
Fans 80 E5
Farcet 46 F8
Far Cotton 35 J5
Farden 32 E3
Fareham 11 G4
Farewell 44 B6
Far Forest 33 G3
Faringdon 31 G8
Farington 61 J7
Farleigh, Avon 17 F4
Farleigh, Surrey 21 H7
Farleigh Hungerford 17 K5
Farleigh Wallop 19 H6
Farlesthorpe 57 J6
Farleton 61 J1
Farley, Staffs 44 B3
Farley, Wilts 10 D2
Farley, Shrops 42 E7
Farley Green 12 D2
Farley Hill 20 B7
Farleys End 30 B6
Farlington 63 K3
Farlow 33 F2
Farmborough 17 H4
Farmcote 30 E5
Farmington 31 F6
Farmoor 31 J7
Farmtown 100 E3
Farnborough, Warw 34 F6
Farnborough, G. Lon 21 J7
Farnborough, Hants 19 K5
Farncombe 12 C2
Farndish 36 C4
Farndon, Ches 42 F2
Farndon, Notts 45 J2
Farnell 93 H6
Farnham, Dorset 10 A3
Farnham, N. Yks 63 G3
Farnham, Essex 21 J1
Farnham, Suff 39 J4
Farnham, Surrey 19 K6
Farnham Common 20 D5
Farnham Green 37 H8
Farnham Royal 20 D5
Farningham 21 K7
Farnley 62 F5
Farnley Tyas 54 E2
Farnsfield 45 H2
Farnworth, Ches 53 G5
Farnworth, G. Man 53 J3
Farr, Highld 114 C3
Farr, Highld 98 E5
Farrington 8 B5
Farrington Gurney 17 H5
Farsley 62 F6
Farthinghoe 35 G7
Farthingstone 35 H5
Farway 8 C5
Fascadale 89 G1
Fasnacloich 90 B7
Fassfern 90 B4
Fatfield 68 F1
Fattahead 100 F3
Faugh 67 H1
Fauldhouse 79 G3
Faulkbourne 22 D2
Faulkland 17 J5
Fauls 43 G4
Faversham 15 G2
Favillar 100 B5
Fawfieldhead 54 D7
Fawkham Green 21 K7
Fawler 31 H6
Fawley, Bucks 20 B5

Fawley, Berks 18 E2
Fawley, Hants 11 F4
Fawley Chapel 29 K5
Faxfleet 58 C4
Faygate 12 F3
Fazeley 44 D7
Fearby 62 E1
Fearnan 91 J7
Fearnbeg 106 C6
Fearnhead 53 H4
Fearnmore 106 C5
Featherstone, W. Yks 63 H7
Featherstone, Staffs 43 L7
Feckenham 34 B4
Fedderate 101 H4
Feering 22 E1
Feetham 68 B7
Feizor 62 A3
Felbridge 13 G3
Felbrigg 49 H4
Felcourt 13 G2
Felden 20 E3
Felindre, Powys 32 A2
Felindre, W. Glam 24 E4
Felindre, Dyfed 24 F2
Felindre, Dyfed 27 H4
Felindre Farchog 26 F4
Felinfach 25 J1
Felinfoel 24 D4
Felingwmuchaf 27 K5
Felixkirk 63 H1
Felixstowe 39 H7
Fell End 67 K7
Felling 75 J7
Fell Side 66 F3
Felmersham 36 C5
Felmingham 49 H5
Felpham 12 C7
Felsham 38 E5
Felsted 22 C1
Feltham 21 F6
Felthorpe 49 G6
Felton, Avon 17 G4
Felton, Northum 75 H3
Felton, H. & W. 29 K3
Felton Butler 42 E6
Feltwell 38 C1
Fence 62 B6
Fence Houses 68 F1
Fencote 68 E7
Fen Ditton 37 H4
Fen Drayton 37 G4
Fen End 34 D3
Feniscowles 61 K7
Feniton 8 C5
Fenny Bentley 44 C2
Fenny Bridges 8 C5
Fenny Compton 34 F5
Fenny Drayton 44 E8
Fenny Stratford 36 B7
Fen Pitton 37 H4
Fenrother 75 H4
Fenstanton 37 G4
Fenton, Lincs 46 B2
Fenton, Lincs 56 C6
Fenton, Cambs 37 G3
Fenton, Northum 81 H6
Fenton, Staffs 43 K3
Fenwick, Northum 75 G6
Fenwick, S. Yks 55 J2
Fenwick, Northum 81 J5
Fenwick, Strath 77 K3
Feochaig 76 C6
Feock 3 G6
Feolin Ferry 82 D5
Feriniquarrie 102 C3
Fern 93 F5
Ferndale 25 J5
Ferndown 10 B4
Ferness 99 H4
Fernham 18 D1
Fernhill Heath 33 H5
Fernhurst 11 K2
Fernilea 102 E5
Fernilee 54 D6
Ferrensby 63 G3
Ferrindonald 96 B5
Ferring 12 D6
Ferrybridge 63 H7
Ferryden 93 J6
Ferryhill 68 E3
Ferryside 27 H6
Fersfield 38 F2
Fersit 90 E4
Feshiebridge 99 G8
Fetcham 21 E1
Fetterangus 101 J3
Fettercairn 93 H4
Fewston 62 E4
Ffairfach ....27· L5
Ffaldybrenin 27 L3
Ffarmers 27 L3
Ffawyddog 25 L3
Ffestiniog 51 G6
Fforest 27 K7
Fforest-fach 24 E5
Ffostrasol 27 H3
Ffrith 42 D2
Ffynnon-ddrain 27 J5
Ffynnongroyw 52 C5
Fidden 88 E6
Fiddington, Glos 30 D4
Fiddington, Somer 16 D6
Fiddleford 9 K3
Fiddlers Hamlet 21 J3
Field 44 B4
Field Broughton 61 G1
Field Dalling 48 F4
Field Head 45 F7
Fifehead Magdalen 9 J2
Fifehead Neville 9 J3
Fifield, Berks 20 D6
Fifield, Oxon 31 G6
Figheldean 18 C6

Filby 49 K6
Filey 65 K4
Filgrave 36 B6
Filkins 31 G7
Filleigh, Devon 7 G3
Filleigh, Devon 7 H4
Fillingham 56 D5
Fillongley 34 D2
Filton 17 H3
Fimber 65 F6
Fincham 48 B7
Finchdean 11 J3
Finchhampstead 20 B7
Finchingfield 38 B7
Finchley 21 G4
Findern 44 E4
Findhorn 99 J2
Findochty 100 D2
Findon, W. Susx 12 E6
Findon, Grampn 93 L2
Finedon 36 C3
Fingal Street 39 H4
Fingask 101 G6
Fingest 20 B4
Finghall 68 D8
Fingland 72 C2
Fingringhoe 23 G1
Finmere 35 H7
Finningham 38 F4
Finningley 55 K4
Finnygaud 100 F3
Finsbay 105 F3
Finsbury 21 H5
Finsthwaite 61 G1
Finstock 31 H6
Finstown 116 C5
Fintry, Grampn 11 G3
Fintry, Strath 85 J6
Finzean 93 H2
Fionnphort 88 E6
Firbank 67 J7
Firbeck 55 J5
Firgrove 53 L2
Firsby 57 J7
Firth 121 G5
Fir Tree 68 D3
Fishbourne, I. of W 11 G5
Fishbourne, W. Susx 11 K4
Fishburn 69 F3
Fishcross 86 C5
Fisherford 100 F5
Fisher's Pond 11 F2
Fisherstreet 12 C3
Fisherton, Highld 99 F3
Fisherton, Strath 77 H6
Fishguard 26 D4
Fishlake 55 K2
Fishpool 53 K3
Fishtoft 47 G5
Fishtoft Drove 47 G3
Fishtown of Usan 93 J6
Fishwick 81 H4
Fiskavaig 102 E5
Fiskerton, Lincs 56 E6
Fiskerton, Notts 45 J2
Fittleton 18 C6
Fittleworth 12 D5
Fitton End 47 H6
Fitz 42 F6
Fitzhead 8 C2
Fitzwilliam 55 H2
Fiunary 89 H4
Five Ashes 13 J4
Fivehead 8 E2
Five Oak Green 13 K2
Five Oaks 12 D4
Five Penny Borve 111 J2
Five Penny Ness 111 K1
Five Roads 27 J7
Flackwell Heath 20 C5
Fladbury 34 A6
Fladdabister 119 G5
Flagg 54 E7
Flamborough 65 K5
Flamstead 20 E2
Flansham 12 C6
Flasby 62 C4
Flash 54 D7
Flashader 102 E3
Flaunden 20 E3
Flawborough 45 J3
Flawith 63 H3
Flax Bourton 17 G4
Flaxby 63 G4
Flaxfleet 58 C4
Flaxley 30 A6
Flaxpool 8 C1
Flaxton 64 D6
Fleckney 45 H8
Flecknoe 35 G4
Fleet, Lincs 47 G5
Fleet, Hants 19 K5
Fleet Hargate 47 G5
Fleetwood 61 G5
Fleggburgh or
  Burgh St Margaret 49 K6
Flemingston 25 J7
Flemington 78 D4
Flempton 38 D3
Fletching 13 H4
Fleuchary 99 F1
Flexbury 6 C5
Flexford 12 C1
Flicham 48 C5
Flimby 66 C2
Flimwll 13 L3
Flint 52 D6
Flintham 45 J3
Flint Mountain 52 D6
Flinton 59 G3
Flitcham 48 C5
Flitton 36 D7
Flitwick 36 D7
Flixborough 58 C5
Flixton, N. Yks 65 H5
Flixton, Suff 39 J2

Flixton, G. Man 53 J4
Flockton 55 F2
Flodabay 105 F3
Flodden 81 H6
Flookburgh 61 G2
Flordon 49 G8
Flore 35 H4
Flotterton 75 F3
Flowton 39 F6
Flushing, Corn 3 G6
Flushing, Grampn 101 K4
Flyford Flavell 34 A5
Fobbing 22 D5
Fochabers 100 C3
Fochriw 25 K4
Fockerby 58 C5
Fodderty 98 D3
Foel 41 J2
Foggathorpe 58 B3
Fogo 80 F5
Foindle 112 C4
Folda 92 C5
Foleshill 34 E2
Folke 9 H3
Folkestone 15 J5
Folkingham 46 D4
Folkington 13 J6
Folksworth 36 E2
Folkton 65 H5
Folla Rule 101 G5
Follifoot 63 G4
Folly Gate 5 F2
Fonthill Bishop 10 A1
Fonthill Gifford 9 L1
Fontmell Magna 9 K3
Fontwell 12 C6
Foolow 54 E6
Foots Cray 21 J6
Forcett 68 D5
Ford, Strath 84 A4
Ford, Staffs 44 B2
Ford, Bucks 20 B3
Ford, W. Susx 12 D6
Ford, Mers 52 E4
Ford, Glos 30 E5
Ford, Shrops 42 F6
Ford, Northum 81 H6
Ford, Devon 5 H7
Ford, Wilts 17 K3
Fordcombe 13 J2
Fordell 86 E6
Forden 42 D7
Ford End 22 C2
Forder Green 5 H5
Fordham, Cambs 38 B3
Fordham, Norf 48 B8
Fordham, Essex 38 E8
Fordingbridge 10 C3
Fordon 65 H5
Fordoun 93 J4
Ford Street, Somer 8 C3
Fordstreet, Essex 38 E8
Fordwells 31 H6
Fordwich 15 H3
Fordyce 100 E2
Foremark 44 E5
Forestburn Gate 75 G4
Forestfield 79 F3
Forest Gate 21 J5
Forest Green 12 E2
Forest Head 67 H1
Forest Hill 31 K7
Forest-in-Teesdale 68 A4
Forest Mill 86 C5
Forest Row 13 H3
Forestside 11 J3
Forest Town 55 J7
Forfar 92 F6
Forgandenny 86 D3
Forge Side 29 G7
Forgie 100 C3
Forhampton 30 C4
Forncett End 49 G8
Forncett St Mary 49 G8
Forncett St Peter 39 G1
Forneth 92 B7
Fornham All Saints 38 D4
Fornham St Martin 38 D4
Forres 99 J3
Forsbrook 44 A3
Forse 115 H6
Forsinard 114 D5
Forston 9 H5
Fort Augustus 98 B8
Forteviot 86 D3
Fort George 99 F3
Forth 79 G4
Forthampton 30 C4
Forth Road Bridge, Fife 86 E7
Forth Road Bridge, Lothn 86 E7
Fortingall 91 J7
Forton, Somer 8 E4
Forton, Shrops 42 F6
Forton, Lancs 61 H4
Forton, Staffs 43 J5
Fortrie, Grampn 100 F4
Fortrie, Grampn 101 J4
Fortrose 99 F3
Fortuneswell 9 H7
Fort William 90 C4
Forty Hill 21 H4
Forward Green 39 F5
Fosbury 18 E5
Fosdyke 47 G4
Foss 91 J6
Fossebridge 30 E6
Foss-y-ffin 27 J1
Foster Street 21 J3
Foston, Lincs 46 B3
Foston, Derby 44 C4
Foston, N. Yks 64 D6
Foston on the Wolds 65 J7
Fotherby 57 H4
Fotheringhay 46 D8

Foubister 116 E6
Foulden, Norf 48 C8
Foulden, Border 81 H4
Foul Mile 13 K5
Foulridge 62 B5
Foulsham 48 F5
Fountainhall 80 C5
Four Ashes 38 F3
Four Crosses, Staffs 44 A7
Four Crosses, Powys 42 D6
Four Crosses, Powys 41 K3
Four Elms 13 H2
Four Forks 8 D1
Four Gotes 47 H6
Four Lanes 2 E6
Fourlanes End 53 K8
Four Marks 11 H1
Four Mile Bridge 50 B3
Four Oaks, W. Mids 44 C8
Four Oaks, W. Mids 34 D2
Four Oaks, E. Susx 14 E6
Fourpenny 109 G4
Fourstones 74 E7
Four Throws 14 D6
Fovant 10 B2
Foveran 101 J6
Fowey 3 K4
Fowlis 87 G1
Fowlis Wester 86 C2
Fowlmere 37 H6
Fownhope 29 K4
Foxdale 60 P4
Foxearth 38 D6
Foxfield 60 F1
Foxham 18 A3
Foxholes 65 H5
Fox Lane 19 K5
Foxley, Norf 48 F5
Foxley, Wilts 17 K2
Foxt 44 B3
Foxton, Cambs 37 H6
Foxton, Leic 35 J2
Foxup 62 B2
Foxwist Green 53 H7
Foy 29 K5
Foyers 98 C6
Fraddon 3 H4
Fradley 44 C6
Fradswell 44 A4
Fraisthorpe 65 J6
Framfield 13 H4
Framingham Earl 49 H7
Framingham Pigot 49 H7
Framlingham 39 H4
Frampton, Lincs 47 G4
Frampton, Dorset 9 H5
Frampton Cotterell 17 H2
Frampton Mansell 30 D7
Frampton on Severn 30 B7
Frampton West End 47 G3
Framsden 39 G5
Framwellgate Moor 68 E2
Franche 33 H3
Frankby 52 D5
Frankley 34 A2
Frankton 34 F3
Frant 13 J3
Fraserburgh 101 J2
Frating Green 23 G1
Fratton 11 H4
Freathy 4 D6
Freckenham 38 B3
Freckleton 61 H7
Freeby 45 K5
Freeland 31 J6
Freester 119 G3
Freethorpe 49 K7
Freiston 47 G3
Fremington, N. Yks 68 C7
Fremington, Strath 78 D4
Fremington, Devon 6 F2
Frenchbeer 5 G3
Frensham 19 K6
Fresgoe 114 E3
Freshfield 52 D3
Freshford 17 J4
Freshwater 10 E6
Freshwater East 26 E8
Fressingfield 39 H3
Freston 39 G7
Freswick 115 J3
Fretherne 30 B7
Frettenham 49 H6
Freuchie 87 F4
Friar's Gate 13 H3
Friday Bridge 47 H7
Fridaythorpe 65 F7
Friern Barnet 21 G4
Friesthorpe 56 E5
Frieth 20 B4
Frilford 31 J8
Frilsham 19 G3
Frimley 20 C8
Frindsbury 14 D2
Fring 48 C4
Fringford 31 L5
Frinsted 14 E3
Frinton-on-Sea 23 J1
Friockheim 93 G7
Frisby on the Wreake 45 H6
Friskney 47 H2
Friston, E. Susx 13 J7
Friston, Suff 39 K4
Fritchley 44 E2
Fritham 10 D3
Frith Bank 47 G3
Frith Common 33 F4
Frithelstock 6 E4
Frithville 47 G2
Frittenden 14 E4
Fritton, Norf 39 H1
Fritton, Norf 49 K7
Fritwell 31 K5
Frizington 66 C5

Frocester 30 B7
Frodesley 43 G7
Frodsham 53 G6
Froggatt 55 F6
Froghall 44 B3
Frogmore 20 C7
Frolesworth 35 G1
Frome 17 J4
Fromes Hill 33 F6
Fron, Gwyn 50 C7
Fron, Powys 32 D7
Fron, Powys 41 K7
Froncysyllte 42 D3
Frongoch 51 J7
Frostenden 39 K2
Frosterley 68 C3
Froxfield 18 D4
Froxfield Green 11 J2
Fryerning 22 C3
Fryton 64 D5
Fulbeck 46 C2
Fulbourn 37 J5
Fulbrook 31 G6
Fulford, Staffs 44 A4
Fulford, Somer 8 D2
Fulford, N. Yks 21 K5
Fulham 21 G6
Fulletby 57 G6
Fullerton 18 E7
Full Sutton 64 E7
Fullwood 77 K2
Fulmer 20 D5
Fulmodeston 48 E4
Fulnetby 57 E6
Fulstow 57 H4
Fulwell 75 K8
Fulwood, S. Yks 55 G5
Fulwood, Lancs 61 J6
Funtington 11 K4
Funtley 11 G4
Funzie 121 J3
Furnace 84 C4
Furneux Pelham 37 H8
Furzebrook 10 A6
Fyfett 8 D3
Fyfield, Wilts 18 C4
Fyfield, Hants 18 D6
Fyfield, Glos 31 G7
Fyfield, Oxon 31 J8
Fyfield, Essex 21 K3
Fylingthorpe 65 G2
Fyvie 101 G5

G

Gabroc Hill 77 K2
Gaddesby 45 H6
Gadfa 50 D2
Gaer 25 K2
Gaer-fawr 29 J8
Gaerllwyd 29 J8
Gaerwen 50 D3
Gagingwell 31 J5
Gailey 43 L6
Gainford 68 D5
Gainsborough 56 C5
Gainsford End 38 C7
Gairloch 106 D4
Gairlochy 90 C3
Gaisgill 67 J6
Gaitsgill 67 F2
Galashiels 80 C6
Galby 45 H7
Galgate 61 H4
Galhampton 9 H2
Gallatown 87 F5
Galley Common 34 E1
Galleywood 22 D3
Gallowfauld 92 F7
Galltair 96 D3
Galmisdale 95 K7
Galmpton, Devon 5 G7
Galmpton, Devon 5 J6
Galphay 63 F2
Galson 111 J2
Galston 77 L4
Galtrigill 102 C3
Gamblesby 67 J3
Gamlingay 37 F5
Gamston, Notts 55 B6
Gamston, Notts 45 H4
Ganarew 29 K6
Ganllwyd 41 G1
Ganstead 59 F3
Ganthorpe 64 D5
Ganton 65 G5
Garbat 98 C2
Garbhallt 84 C5
Garboldisham 38 F2
Gardenstown 101 H2
Garderhouse 119 F4
Gare Hill 17 J6
Garelochhead 84 E5
Garenin 111 F3
Garford 31 J8
Garforth 63 H6
Gargrave 62 C4
Gargunnock 85 K5
Garlieston 71 F7
Garlogie 93 H1
Garmond 101 H3
Garmouth 100 C2
Garn 28 B7
Garnant 24 E3
Garn Dolbenmaen 50 D6
Garnett Bridge 67 H7
Garnkirk 78 B4
Garn-yr-erw 29 G6
Garrabost 111 K4

Garras 2 F7
Garreg 50 F6
Garreg Bank 42 D6
Garrigill 67 K2
Garros 103 F2
Garrygualach 90 C1
Garrynamonie 94 C4
Garsdale 67 K8
Garsdale Head 67 K7
Garsdon 18 A2
Garshall Green 44 A4
Garsington 31 K7
Garstang 61 H5
Garston 52 F5
Garswood 53 G4
Gartcosh 78 D3
Garth, Clwyd 42 D3
Garth, Powys 28 D3
Garth, M. Glam 25 G5
Garth, I. of M. 60 Q4
Garthbrengy 25 J1
Gartheli 27 K2
Garthmyl 42 C8
Garthorpe, Leic 46 B5
Garthorpe, Humbs 58 C5
Gartly 100 E5
Gartmore 85 H5
Gartocharn 85 G6
Garton 59 G3
Garton-on-the-Wolds 65 G7
Gartymore 109 J2
Garvald 87 J7
Garvard 82 C2
Garve 98 B2
Garvestone 48 F7
Garvock 93 J4
Garway 29 J5
Garynahine 111 G4
Gastard 17 K4
Gasthorpe 38 E2
Gatcombe 11 F6
Gatebeck 61 J1
Gate Burton 56 C5
Gateforth 63 J7
Gatehead 77 J4
Gate Helmsley 64 D7
Gatehouse of Fleet 71 H6
Gatelawbridge 72 E4
Gateley 48 E5
Gatenby 63 G1
Gateshead 75 J7
Gatesheath 53 F7
Gateside, Fife 86 E4
Gateside, Tays 92 F7
Gateside, Strath 77 J2
Gathurst 53 G3
Gatley 53 K5
Gattonside 80 D6
Gaulby 87 G2
Gaunt's Common 10 B4
Gautby 57 F6
Gavinton 80 F4
Gawber 55 G3
Gawcott 35 H7
Gawsworth 53 K7
Gawthrop 61 K2
Gawthwaite 61 F1
Gaydon 34 E5
Gayhrst 36 B6
Gayle 68 A8
Gayles 68 D6
Gay Street 12 D4
Gayton, Staffs 44 A5
Gayton, Norf 48 C6
Gayton, Mers 52 D5
Gayton, Northnts 35 J5
Gayton le Marsh 57 J5
Gayton Thorpe 48 C6
Gaywood 48 B5
Gazeley 38 C4
Geary 102 D2
Gedding 38 E5
Geddington 36 B2
Gedintailor 103 G5
Gedney 47 H5
Gedney Broadgate 47 H5
Gedney Drove End 47 H5
Gedney Dyke 47 H5
Gedney Hill 47 G6
Gedney Marsh 45 F5
Gee Cross 54 C4
Geise 115 G3
Geldeston 39 J1
Gelli 26 E6
Gellifor 52 C7
Gelligaer 25 K5
Gellilydan 51 F7
Gellioedd 51 J6
Gellywen 27 G5
Gelston 72 C8
Gentleshaw 44 B6
Geocrab 105 G2
Georgeham 6 E2
George Nympton 7 H3
Georgetown 77 K1
Georgia 2 C6
Germansweek 4 E2
Germoe 2 D7
Gerrans 3 G6
Gerrards Cross 20 E5
Geshader 111 F4
Gestingthorpe 38 D7
Geuffordd 42 D6
Geufron 41 H5
Gibraltar 57 K8
Gidea Park 21 K4
Gidleigh 5 G3
Gifford 80 D3
Giggleswick 62 B3
Gilberdyke 58 C4
Gilchriston 80 C3
Gilcrux 66 D3
Gildersome 63 F7
Gildingwells 55 J5
Gileston 25 J8

Gilfach Goch 25 H6
Gilfachreda 27 J2
Gilgarran 66 C4
Gillamoor 64 D3
Gilling East 63 K2
Gillingham, Kent 14 D2
Gillingham, Norf 39 K1
Gillingham, Dorset 9 K2
Gilling West 68 D6
Gillow Heath 53 K8
Gills 115 J2
Gilmanscleuch 80 B7
Gilmerton, Lothn 80 A3
Gilmerton, Tays 86 B2
Gilmorton 35 G2
Gilsland 74 C7
Gilsland Spa 74 C7
Gilston 80 C4
Gilwern 29 G6
Gimingham 49 H4
Gipping 38 F4
Gipsey Bridge 47 F2
Girlsta 119 G3
Girsby 69 F6
Girthon 71 H6
Girton, Notts 56 C7
Girton, Cambs 37 4
Girvan 70 C2
Gisburn 62 B5
Gisla 111 F5
Gisleham 39 L2
Gislingham 38 F3
Gissing 39 G2
Gittisham 8 C5
Gladestry 29 G2
Gladsmuir 87 H7
Glais 24 F4
Glaisdale 64 E2
Glame 106 A7
Glamis 92 E7
Glanaber Terrace 51 G6
Glananaman 24 E3
Glandford 48 F3
Glandwr, Dyfed 27 F5
Glandwr, Gwent 25 L4
Glangrwyney 29 G6
Glanmule 32 A1
Glanrhyd 26 F3
Glanton 75 G2
Glanton Pike 75 G2
Glanvilles Wootton 9 H4
Glan-y-don 52 C6
Glan-yr-afon 51 K6
Glapthorn 36 D1
Glapwell 55 H7
Glasbury 29 F4
Glascoed, Powys 42 C7
Glascoed, Gwent 29 H7
Glascoed, Clwyd 51 J3
Glascote 44 D7
Glascwm 28 F2
Glasdrum 90 B7
Glasfryn 51 J5
Glasgow 78 C3
Glasinfryn 50 E4
Glasnakille 103 G7
Glaspwll 41 G4
Glassburn 98 B5
Glasserton 71 F8
Glassford 78 E5
Glasshouse Hill 30 B5
Glasshouses 62 E3
Glasslaw 101 H3
Glasson, Lancs 61 H4
Glasson, Cumbr 73 H7
Glassonby 67 H3
Glaston 46 B7
Glastonbury 17 F7
Glatton 36 E2
Glazebury 53 H4
Glazeley 33 G2
Gleadless 55 G5
Gleadsmoss 53 K7
Gleaston 60 F2
Glemsford 38 D6
Glenancross 96 B6
Glenastle 82 C7
Glen Auldyn 60 R2
Glenbarr 76 B4
Glenbeg 89 G2
Glen Bernisdale 103 F4
Glenbervie 93 J3
Glenboig 78 E3
Glenborrodale 89 H2
Glenbreck 79 H7
Glenbuck 78 E7
Glenburn 77 K1
Glencaple 72 E7
Glencarse 87 E2
Glencoe 90 C6
Glencraig 86 E5
Glendevon 86 C4
Glendoebeg 98 C8
Glendon Hall 36 B2
Glenegedale 82 C6
Glenelg 96 D4
Glenfarg 86 E3
Glenfield 45 G7
Glenfinnan 96 E7
Glenfoot 86 E3
Glengarnock 77 J2
Glengrasco 103 F4
Glenkerry 73 H2
Glenkindie 100 D7
Glenlee 72 B5
Glenlivet 100 A6
Glenluce 70 C6
Glenmavis 78 E3
Glenmore 103 F4
Glenmoy 92 F5
Glen Parva 45 G2
Glenprosen Village 92 E5
Glenreasdell Mains 76 D2
Glenridding 67 F5

Glenrothes 87 F4
Glenside 111 H6
Glentham 56 E4
Glenton 100 F6
Glentress 79 K6
Glen Trool Lodge 70 F3
Glentrool Village 70 E4
Glentworth 56 C5
Glenuig 96 B8
Glen Village 86 B7
Glen Vine 60 Q4
Glespin 79 F7
Gletness 119 G3
Glewstone 29 K5
Glinton 46 E7
Glooston 45 J8
Glossop 54 D4
Gloster Hill 75 J3
Gloucester 30 C6
Gloup 121 H2
Glusburn 62 D5
Gluss 120 F5
Glympton 31 J5
Glynarthen 27 H3
Glyn Ceiriog 42 D4
Glyncoch 25 J5
Glyncrrwg 25 G5
Glynde 13 H6
Glyndebourne 13 H5
Glyndyfrdwy 42 C3
Glyn Neath 25 G4
Glynogwr 25 H6
Glyntaff 25 J6
Gnosall 43 K5
Gnosall Heath 43 K5
Goadby 45 J8
Goadby Marwood 45 J8
Goatacre 18 B3
Goathill 9 H3
Goathland 64 F2
Goathurst 8 D1
Gobowen 42 E4
Godalming 12 C2
Godington 35 H8
Godmanchester 37 F3
Godmanstone 9 H5
Godmersham 15 G3
Godney 17 F6
Godolphin Cross 2 E6
Godre'r-graig 25 F4
Godshill, Hants 10 C3
Godshill, I. of W 11 G6
Godstone 13 G1
Goff's Oak 21 H3
Gogar 86 E7
Goginan 41 F5
Golan 50 E6
Golant 4 C4
Golberdon 4 D4
Golborne 53 H4
Goldcliff 16 E2
Golden Cross 13 J5
Golden Green 13 K2
Golden Grove 27 K6
Goldenhill 43 K2
Golden Pot 19 J6
Golden Valley 30 D5
Golders Green 21 G5
Goldhanger 22 F3
Golding 43 G7
Goldsborough, N. Yks 63 G4
Goldsborough, N. Yks 69 L5
Goldsithney 2 D6
Goldthorpe 55 H3
Gollanfield 99 G3
Golspie 109 G3
Gomeldon 10 C1
Gomersal 62 F7
Gomshall 12 D2
Gonalston 45 H3
Gonfirth 119 F2
Good Easter 22 C2
Gooderstone 48 C7
Goodleigh 7 F2
Goodmanham 58 C2
Goodnestone, Kent 15 G2
Goodnestone, Kent 15 J3
Goodrich 29 K6
Goodrington 5 J6
Goodshaw 11 K1
Goodwick 26 D4
Goodworth Clatford 18 E6
Goodyers End 34 E2
Goole 58 B4
Goonbell 2 F5
Goonhavern 3 F4
Goosebam 6 C4
Goosetrey 53 J7
Goosey 18 E1
Goosnargh 61 J6
Goostrey 53 J6
Gordon 80 E5
Gordonbush 109 G3
Gordonstown, Grampn 100 E3
Gordonstown, Grampn 101 E3
Gorebridge 80 B3
Gorefield 47 H6
Goring 19 H2
Goring-by-Sea 12 E6
Gorleston-on-Sea 49 L7
Gorran Haven 3 J5
Gors 41 F6
Gorsedd 52 C6
Gorseinon 24 D5
Gorseness 116 D5
Gorsgoch 27 J2
Gorslas 27 K6
Gorsley 30 A5
Gorstan 98 B2
Gorton 53 K4
Gosbeck 39 G5
Gosberton 47 F4
Gosfield 38 C8
Gosforth, Cumbr 66 C6
Gosforth, T. & W 75 J7

Gosmore 36 E8
Gosport 11 H5
Gossabrough 121 H4
Goswick 81 J5
Gotham 45 G4
Gotherington 30 D5
Goudhurst 13 L3
Goulceby 57 G6
Gourdas 101 G4
Gourdon 93 K4
Gourock 84 E7
Govan 77 L1
Goveton 5 H7
Govig 110 E7
Govilon 29 G6
Gowanhill 101 K2
Gowdall 63 K7
Gowerton 24 D5
Gowkhall 86 D6
Goxhill, Humbs 59 F2
Goxhill, Humbs 59 F4
Goytre 25 C5
Grabhair 111 G6
Graffham 12 C5
Grafham 36 E4
Grafton, H. & W 32 E4
Grafton, Oxon 31 G7
Grafton, N. Yks 63 H3
Grafton, H. & W 29 J4
Grafton Flyford 34 A5
Grafton Regis 35 J6
Grafton Underwood 36 C2
Grafty Green 14 E4
Graianrhyd 42 D2
Graig, Gwyn 51 H3
Graig, Clwyd 51 K3
Graig-fechan 42 C2
Graig Penllyn 25 H7
Grain 14 E1
Grainsby 59 G7
Grainthorpe 57 H4
Graizelound 58 B7
Grampound 3 H5
Grampound Road 3 H4
Gramsdale 104 D6
Granborough 35 J8
Granby 45 J4
Grandborough 35 F4
Grandtully 91 L6
Grange, Mers 52 D5
Grange, Cumbr 66 E5
Grange, N. Yks 69 H7
Grange Crossroads 100 D3
Grange Hill 21 J4
Grange Moor 55 F2
Grangemouth 86 C6
Grange-over-Sands 61 H2
Grangepans 86 D6
Grangetown 69 H4
Grange Villa 68 E1
Granish 99 G7
Gransmoor 65 J7
Granston 26 C4
Grantchester 37 H5
Grantham 46 C4
Grantlodge 101 G7
Grantley 63 F3
Granton 87 F7
Grantown-on-Spey 99 J6
Grantshouse 81 G3
Grappenhall 53 H5
Grasby 58 E6
Grasmere 66 F6
Grasscroft 54 C3
Grassendale 52 E5
Grassholme 68 B4
Grassington 62 D3
Grassmoor 55 H7
Grassthorpe 56 B7
Grateley 18 D6
Gratwich 44 B4
Graveley, Cambs 37 F4
Graveley, Herts 37 F8
Gravelly Hill 34 C1
Gravels 42 E7
Graveney 15 G2
Gravesend 14 C1
Gravir 111 H6
Grayingham 56 D4
Grayrigg 67 H7
Grays 14 C1
Grayshott 11 K1
Grayswood 12 C3
Graythorp 69 H4
Grazeley 20 A7
Greasbrough 55 H4
Greasby 52 D5
Great Abington 37 J6
Great Addington 36 C3
Great Alne 34 C5
Great Altcar 52 E3
Great Amwell 21 H2
Great Asby 67 J5
Great Ashfield 38 F4
Great Ayton 69 H5
Great Baddow 22 D3
Great Bardfield 38 B7
Great Barford 36 E5
Great Barr 44 B8
Great Barrington 31 G6
Great Barrow 53 F7
Great Barton 38 D4
Great Bavington 75 F5
Great Bealings 39 H6
Great Bedwyn 18 D4
Great Bentley 23 H1
Great Bircham 48 C4
Great Blakenham 39 G5
Great Bolas 43 H5
Great Bookham 12 E1
Great Bosullow 2 C6
Great Bourton 35 F6
Great Bowden 35 J2
Great Bradley 38 B5
Great Braxted 22 E2
Great Bricett 38 F5

Great Brickhill 36 C7
Great Bridgeford 43 K5
Great Brington 35 H4
Great Bromley 39 F8
Great Broughton 69 H6
Great Budworth 53 H6
Great Burdon 68 F5
Great Burstead 22 C4
Great Busby 69 H6
Great Canfield 22 B2
Great Carlton 57 J5
Great Casterton 46 D7
Great Chart 15 F4
Great Chatwell 43 J6
Great Chesterford 37 J6
Great Cheverell 18 A5
Great Chishill 37 H7
Great Clacton 23 H2
Great Clifton 66 C4
Great Coates 59 G5
Great Comberton 34 A6
Great Corby 67 G1
Great Cornard 38 D6
Great Coxwell 31 G8
Great Cransley 36 B3
Great Cressingham 48 D7
Great Crosby 52 E4
Great Cubley 44 C4
Great Dalby 45 J6
Great Doddington 36 B4
Great Driffield 65 H7
Great Dunham 48 D6
Great Dunmow 22 C1
Great Durnford 18 C7
Great Easton, Leic 46 B8
Great Easton, Essex 38 B8
Great Eccleston 61 H5
Great Edstone 64 E4
Great Ellingham 48 F8
Great Elm 17 J6
Great Eversden 37 G5
Great Finborough 38 F5
Great Fransham 48 D6
Great Gaddesden 20 E2
Great Gidding 36 E2
Great Givendale 64 F7
Great Glemham 39 J4
Great Glen 45 H8
Great Gonerby 46 B4
Great Gransden 37 F5
Great Green 38 E5
Great Habton 64 E5
Great Hallingbury 21 K2
Great Hampden 20 C3
Great Harrowden 36 B3
Great Harwood 61 L6
Great Haseley 20 A3
Great Hatfield 59 F2
Great Haywood 44 B5
Great Heck 63 J7
Great Henny 38 D7
Great Hinton 17 L5
Great Hockham 38 E1
Great Holland 23 J2
Great Horkesley 38 E8
Great Hormead 37 H7
Great Horwood 35 J7
Great Houghton, S. Yks 55 H3
Great Houghton, Northnts 35 J5
Great Hucklow 54 E6
Great Kelk 65 J7
Great Kingshill 20 C4
Great Langton 68 E7
Great Leighs 22 D2
Great Limber 59 F6
Great Linford 36 B6
Great Livermere 38 D3
Great Longstone 54 F6
Great Lumley 68 E2
Great Lyth 42 F7
Great Malvern 33 G6
Great Maplestead 38 D7
Great Marton 61 G6
Great Massingham 48 C5
Great Milton 20 A3
Great Missenden 20 C3
Great Mitton 61 L6
Great Mongeham 15 K3
Great Moulton 39 G1
Great Musgrave 67 K5
Great Ness 42 E6
Great Oakley, Northnts 36 B2
Great Oakley, Essex 39 G8
Great Offley 36 E8
Great Ormside 67 K5
Great Orton 66 F1
Great Oxendon 35 J2
Great Palgrave 48 D6
Great Parndon 21 J3
Great Paxton 36 F4
Great Plumstead 49 J6
Great Ponton 46 C4
Great Preston 63 H7
Great Raveley 37 F2
Great Rissington 31 F6
Great Rollright 31 H4
Great Ryburgh 48 E5
Great Ryle 75 G2
Great Saling 38 C8
Great Salkeld 67 H3
Great Sampford 38 B7
Great Sankey 53 G5
Great Saxham 38 C4
Great Shefford 18 E3
Great Shelford 37 H5
Great Smeaton 69 F6
Great Snoring 48 E4
Great Somerford 18 A2
Great Stainton 68 F4
Great Stambridge 22 F4
Great Staughton 36 E4
Great Steeping 57 J7

Great Stonar 15 K3
Greatstone-on-Sea 15 G6
Great Strickland 67 H4
Great Stukeley 37 F3
Great Sturton 57 G6
Great Swinburne 74 F6
Great Tew 31 H5
Great Tey 38 D8
Great Thurlow 38 B5
Great Torrington 6 E4
Great Tosson 75 G3
Great Totham, Essex 22 E2
Great Totham, Essex 22 E2
Great Wakering 22 F5
Great Waldingfield 38 E6
Great Walsingham 48 E4
Great Waltham 22 C2
Great Warley 21 K4
Great Washbourne 30 D4
Great Welnetham 38 D5
Great Wenham 38 F7
Great Whittington 75 G6
Great Wigborough 23 F2
Great Wilbraham 37 J5
Great Wishford 10 B1
Great Witcombe 30 D6
Great Witley 33 G4
Great Wolford 31 G4
Greatworth 35 G6
Great Wratting 38 B6
Great Wymondley 36 F8
Great Wyrley 44 A7
Great Wytheford 43 G6
Great Yarmouth 49 L7
Great Yeldham 38 C7
Greenburn 79 G3
Greendykes 81 J7
Greenfield, Oxon 20 B4
Greenfield, G. Man 54 C3
Greenfield, Clwyd 52 C6
Greenfield, Highld 90 D1
Greenfield, Beds 36 D7
Greenford 21 F5
Greengairs 85 K7
Greenham 19 F4
Green Hammerton 63 H4
Greenhaugh 74 D5
Greenhead 74 C7
Green Hill, Wilts 18 B2
Greenhill, G. Lon 21 F5
Greenhill, S. Yks 55 G5
Greenhill, Central 85 L7
Greenhithe 14 B1
Greenholm 77 L4
Greenholme 67 H6
Greenhouse 80 D7
Greenhow Hill 62 E3
Greenigoe 116 D6
Greenland 115 H3
Greenlaw 80 F5
Greenloaning 85 L4
Greenmount 53 J2
Greenmow 119 G6
Greenock 84 E7
Greenodd 61 G1
Green Ore 17 G5
Greenside 75 H7
Greensidehill 75 F2
Greenskares 101 G2
Greens Norton 35 H6
Greenstead Green 38 D8
Greensted 21 K3
Green Street 21 F4
Green Street Green 21 J7
Green, The, Cumbr 60 E1
Green, The, Wilts 9 K1
Greenwich 21 J6
Greet 30 E4
Greete 32 E3
Greetham, Leic 46 C6
Greetham, Lincs 57 H6
Greetland 62 D7
Gregson Lane 61 J7
Greinton 8 F1
Grendon, Northnts 36 B4
Grendon, Warw 44 D8
Grendon Common 44 D8
Grendon Green 29 K2
Grendon Underwood 35 A1
Grenitote 104 D4
Grenoside 55 G4
Gresford 42 E2
Gresham 49 G4
Greshornish 102 E3
Gressenhall 48 E6
Gressingham 61 J3
Greta Bridge 68 C5
Gretna 73 J7
Gretna Green 73 J7
Gretton, Northnts 46 B8
Gretton, Glos 30 E4
Gretton, Shrops 43 G8
Grewelthorpe 63 F2
Greygarth 62 E2
Greysouthen 66 C4
Greystoke 67 G3
Greystone 93 G7
Greywell 19 J5
Griais 111 J3
Grianan 111 J4
Griff 34 E2
Griffithstown 29 G8
Grike 66 C5
Grimeford Village 53 H2
Grimethorpe 55 H3
Griminish 104 C3
Grimister 121 G3
Grimley 33 H4
Grimness 116 D7
Grimoldby 57 H5
Grimsargh 61 J6
Grimsby 59 G6
Grimscote 35 H5
Grimscott 6 C5
Grimshader 111 J5

Grimsthorpe 46 D5
Grimston, Norf 48 C5
Grimston, Leic 45 H5
Grimstone 9 H5
Grindale 65 J5
Grindiscol 119 G5
Grindleford 55 F6
Grindleton 62 A5
Grindley Brook 43 G3
Grindlow 54 E6
Grindon, Staffs 44 B2
Grindon, Northum 81 H5
Gringle 43 J7
Gringley on the Hill 56 B4
Grinsdale 73 J8
Grinshill 43 G5
Grinton 68 C7
Grisedale 67 K7
Gristhorpe 65 H4
Griston 48 E8
Grittenham 18 B2
Grittleton 17 K2
Grizebeck 60 F1
Grizedale 66 F7
Grobister 117 F4
Groby 45 G7
Groes, W. Glam 25 F6
Groes, Clwyd 51 K4
Groes-faen 25 J6
Groeslon 50 D5
Grogport 76 D3
Gromford 39 J5
Gronant 51 K2
Groombridge 13 J3
Grosebay 105 G2
Grosmont, N. Yks 64 F2
Grosmont, Gwent 29 J5
Groton 38 E6
Grove, Notts 56 B6
Grove, Oxon 18 F1
Grove, Dorset 9 H7
Grove, Kent 15 J2
Grove Park 21 J6
Grovesend 24 D4
Grudie 98 B2
Gruids 108 D3
Gruline 89 G4
Grumbla 2 C7
Grunasound 119 F5
Grundisburgh 39 H5
Gruting 118 E4
Guardbridge 87 H3
Guarlford 33 H6
Guestling Green 14 E7
Guestwick 48 F5
Guide Post 75 J5
Guilden Morden 37 F6
Guilden Sutton 52 F7
Guildford 12 C2
Guildtown 86 E1
Guilsborough 35 H3
Guilsfield 42 D6
Guisborough 69 J5
Guiseley 62 E5
Guist 48 E5
Guiting Power 30 E5
Gullane 87 H6
Gulval 2 C6
Gumfreston 26 F7
Gumley 35 H1
Gunby, Humbs 58 B3
Gunby, Lincs 46 C5
Gundleton 11 H1
Gunn 7 G2
Gunnerside 68 B7
Gunnerton 74 F6
Gunness 58 C5
Gunnislake 4 E4
Gunnista 119 H4
Gunthorpe, Norf 48 F4
Gunthorpe, Notts 45 H3
Gunwalloe Fishing Cove 2 E7
Gurnard 11 F5
Gurney Slade 17 H6
Gurnos 25 F4
Gussage All Saints 10 B3
Gussage St Michael 10 A3
Guston 15 K4
Gutcher 121 H3
Guthrie 93 G6
Guyhirn 47 G7
Guy's Head 47 H5
Guy's Marsh 9 K2
Guyzance 75 J3
Gwaelod-y-Garth 25 K6
Gwaenysgor 51 K2
Gwalchmai 50 C3
Gwaun-Cae-Gurwen 24 F3
Gwbert 26 F2
Gweek 2 F7
Gwehelog 29 H7
Gwenddwr 28 E3
Gwennap 2 E7
Gwenter 2 F8
Gwernaffield 52 D7
Gwernesney 29 J7
Gwernogle 27 K4
Gwernymynydd 52 D7
Gwersyllt 52 C5
Gwespyr 52 C5
Gwinear 2 D6
Gwithian 2 D5
Gwyddelwern 51 K6
Gwyddgrug 27 J4
Gwytherin 51 H4

H

Habberley, Shrops 42 E7
Habberley, H. & W 33 H3
Habost, W. Isles 111 H6
Habost, W. Isles 111 K1
Habrough 59 F5

Haccombe 5 J4
Haceby 46 D4
Hacheston 39 J5
Hackford 48 F7
Hackforth 68 E7
Hacklete 111 F4
Hackleton 35 K5
Hackness, Orkney 116 C7
Hackness, N. Yks 65 G3
Hackney 21 H5
Hackthorn 56 D5
Hackthorpe 67 H4
Haconby 46 E5
Hadden 81 F6
Haddenham, Bucks 20 B3
Haddenham, Cambs 37 H3
Haddington 87 J7
Haddiscoe 49 K8
Haddon 36 E1
Hademore 44 C7
Hadfield 54 D4
Hadham Cross 21 J2
Hadham Ford 21 J1
Hadleigh, Essex 22 E5
Hadleigh, Suff 38 F6
Hadley 43 H6
Hadley End 44 C5
Hadlow 13 K1
Hadlow Down 13 J4
Hadnall 43 G5
Hadstock 37 J6
Hadzor 33 J4
Haffenden Quarter 14 E4
Hafod-Dinbych 51 H5
Haggbeck 73 K6
Haggerston 81 J5
Hagworthingham 57 H7
Haigh 53 H3
Haighton Green 61 J6
Haile 66 C6
Hailes 30 E4
Hailey, Herts 21 H2
Hailey, Oxon 31 H6
Hailsham 13 J6
Hail Weston 36 E4
Hainault 21 J4
Hainford 49 H6
Hainton 57 F5
Haisthorpe 65 J6
Halam 45 H2
Halberton 7 L4
Halcro 115 H3
Hale, Hants 10 C3
Hale, Lincs 46 E3
Hale, Ches 52 F5
Hale, G. Man 53 H6
Hale Bank 53 F5
Halebarns 53 J5
Hales, Staffs 43 J4
Hales, Norf 49 J8
Halesowen 34 A2
Hales Place 15 H3
Hale Street 13 K2
Halesworth 39 J3
Halewood 52 F5
Halford, Shrops 32 D2
Halford, Warw 34 D6
Halfpenny Green 33 H1
Halfway, Berks 18 F4
Halfway, Powys 25 G1
Halfway, Dyfed 27 L4
Halfway House 42 E6
Halfway Houses 14 F1
Halifax 62 D7
Halistra 102 D3
Halket 77 K2
Halkirk 115 G4
Halkyn 52 D6
Halland 13 J5
Hallaton 45 J8
Hallatrow 17 H5
Hallbankgate 74 C8
Hall Dunnerdale 66 E7
Hallen 17 G2
Hall Green 34 C2
Halliburton 80 E5
Hallin 102 D3
Halling 14 D2
Hallington 75 F6
Hall of the Forest 32 B2
Halloughton 45 H2
Hallow 33 H5
Hallrule 74 B2
Halls 87 K7
Hallsands 5 J8
Hallthwaites 60 L1
Hallworthy 4 B3
Hallyne 79 J5
Halmer End 43 K3
Halmore 30 A7
Halmyre Mains 79 J5
Halnaker 12 C6
Halsall 52 E2
Halse, Somer 8 C2
Halse, Northnts 35 G6
Halsetown 2 D6
Halsham 59 G4
Halsinger 6 F2
Halstead, Essex 38 D7
Halstead, Leic 45 J7
Halstead, Kent 21 J7
Halstock 9 G4
Halsham 57 G7
Haltham 57 G7
Haltoft End 47 G3
Halton, Bucks 20 C2
Halton, Clwyd 42 F4
Halton, Ches 53 G5
Halton, Lancs 61 J7
Halton East 62 D4
Halton Gill 62 B2
Halton Holegate 57 J7
Halton Lea Gate 74 C8
Halton West 62 B4

Haltwhistle 74 D7
Halvergate 49 K7
Halwell 5 H6
Halwill 4 E2
Halwill Junction 4 E1
Ham, Glos 30 A8
Ham, Shetld 118 B5
Ham, Wilts 18 E4
Ham, G. Lon 21 F6
Hamble 11 F4
Hambleden 20 B5
Hambledon, Surrey 12 C3
Hambledon, Hants 11 H3
Hambleton, Lancs 61 G5
Hambleton, N. Yks 63 J6
Hambridge 8 E2
Hambrook, Avon 17 H3
Hambrook, W. Susx 11 J4
Hameringham 57 H7
Hamerton 36 E3
Hametoun 118 B5
Hamilton 78 E4
Hammer 11 L1
Hammerwich 44 B7
Hammond Street 21 H3
Hammoon 9 K3
Hamnavoe, Shetld 119 F5
Hamnavoe, Shetld 121 G4
Hampden Park 13 K6
Hampnett 30 F6
Hampole 55 J2
Hampreston 10 B5
Hampstead 21 G5
Hampstead Norreys 19 G3
Hampsthwaite 63 F4
Hampton, H. & W 34 B6
Hampton, G. Lon 21 F7
Hampton, Shrops 33 G2
Hampton Bishop 29 K4
Hampton Heath 43 F3
Hampton in Arden 34 D2
Hampton Lovell 33 H4
Hampton Lucy 34 D5
Hampton on the Hill 34 D4
Hampton Poyle 31 K6
Hamsey 13 H5
Hamstall Ridware 44 C6
Hamstead, W. Mids 44 B8
Hamstead, I. of W 10 E5
Hamstead Marshall 18 F4
Hamsterley, Durham 68 D1
Hamsterley, Durham 68 D3
Ham Street, Somer 9 G1
Hamstreet, Kent 15 G5
Hamworthy 10 A5
Hanbury, H. & W 34 A4
Hanbury, Staffs 44 C5
Hanchurch 43 K3
Handbridge 52 F7
Handcross 12 F4
Handforth 53 K5
Handley 52 F8
Handsacre 44 B6
Handsworth, W. Mids 34 B1
Handsworth, S. Yks 55 H5
Hanford 43 K3
Hanging Langford 10 B1
Hanham 17 H3
Hankelow 43 H3
Hankerton 18 A1
Hankham 13 K6
Hanley 43 K3
Hanley Castle 33 H6
Hanley Child 33 F4
Hanley Swan 33 H6
Hanley William 33 F4
Hanlith 62 C3
Hanmer 42 F4
Hannington, Northnts 36 B3
Hannington, Wilts 31 F8
Hannington, Hants 19 G5
Hannington Wick 31 F8
Hanslope 35 K6
Hanthorpe 46 D5
Hanwell 34 F6
Hanwood 42 F7
Hanworth, G. Lon 21 F6
Hanworth, Norf 49 G4
Happendon 79 F6
Happisburgh 49 J4
Happisburgh Common 49 J5
Hapsford 53 F6
Hapton, Lancs 62 A6
Hapton, Norf 49 G8
Harberton 5 H6
Harbertonford 5 H6
Harbledown 1 H3
Harborne 34 B2
Harborough Magna 35 F3
Harbottle 74 F3
Harbury 34 E5
Harby, Notts 56 C6
Harby, Leic 45 J4
Harcombe 8 C5
Harden 62 D6
Hardendale 67 H5
Hardgate 93 J1
Hardham 12 D5
Hardhorn 61 G6
Hardingham 48 F7
Hardingstone 35 J5
Hardings Wood 43 K2
Hardington 17 J5
Hardington Mandeville 9 G3
Hardington Marsh 9 G4
Hardley 10 F4
Hardley Street 49 J7
Hardmead 36 C6
Hardraw 68 A7
Hardstoft 55 H7
Hardway, Hants 11 H4
Hardway, Somer 9 J1

Hardwick, Northnts 36 B4
Hardwick, Bucks 20 C2
Hardwick, Cambs 37 G5
Hardwick, Norf 39 H2
Hardwick, Oxon 31 H7
Hardwick, Oxon 31 K5
Hardwicke, Glos 30 C6
Hardwicke, Glos 30 D5
Hardwicke, H. & W 29 G3
Hareby 57 H7
Hareden 61 K4
Harefield 20 E4
Hare Hatch 20 C6
Harehope 75 G1
Harescombe 30 C6
Haresfield 30 C6
Hare Street 37 G8
Harewood 63 G5
Harford 5 G6
Hargrave, Suff 38 C5
Hargrave, Northnts 36 D3
Hargrave, Ches 53 F7
Harker 73 J7
Harkstead 39 G7
Harlaston 44 D6
Harlaxton 46 B4
Harlech 50 E7
Harlesden 21 G5
Harleston, Suff 38 F4
Harleston, Norf 39 H2
Harleston, Devon 5 H7
Harlestone 35 J4
Harle Syke 62 B6
Harley 43 G7
Harlington 36 D7
Harlosh 102 D4
Harlow 21 J2
Harlow Hill 75 G7
Harlsey 69 G7
Harlthorpe 58 B3
Harlton 37 G5
Harman's Cross 10 A6
Harmby 68 D8
Harmer Green 21 G2
Harmer Hill 43 G5
Harmston 56 D7
Harnham 10 C2
Harnhill 30 E7
Harold Hill 21 K4
Haroldston West 26 C6
Haroldswick 121 J1
Harold Wood 21 K4
Harome 63 K1
Harpenden 21 F2
Harpford 8 B5
Harpham 65 H6
Harpley, Norf 48 C5
Harpley, H. & W 33 F4
Harpole 35 H4
Harpsdale 115 G4
Harpsden 20 B5
Harpswell 56 D5
Harpurhey 53 K3
Harpur Hill 54 D6
Harrapool 96 B3
Harrietfield 86 C2
Harrietsham 14 E3
Harrington, Cumbr 66 B4
Harrington, Lincs 57 H6
Harrington, Northnts 35 J2
Harringworth 46 C8
Harriseahead 43 K2
Harrogate 63 G4
Harrold 36 C5
Harrow 21 F5
Harrowbarrow 4 E4
Harrowden 36 D6
Harrow on the Hill 21 F5
Harston, Leic 46 B4
Harston, Cambs 37 H5
Hart 69 G3
Hartburn 75 G5
Hartest 38 D5
Hartfield 13 H3
Hartford, Cambs 37 F3
Hartford, Ches 53 H6
Hartfordbridge 19 J5
Hartford End 22 C2
Harthill 68 D6
Harthill, Ches 43 G2
Harthill, Strath 79 G3
Harthill, S. Yks 55 H5
Hartington 54 E7
Hartland 6 C3
Hartland Quay 6 C3
Hartlebury 33 H3
Hartlepool 69 H3
Hartley, Kent 14 C2
Hartley, Northum 75 K6
Hartley, Cumbr 67 K6
Hartley, Kent 13 L3
Hartley Wespall 20 A8
Hartley Wintney 19 J5
Hartlip 14 E2
Harton, Shrops 32 D2
Harton, N. Yks 64 E6
Harton, T. & W 75 K7
Hartpury 30 C5
Hartshill 44 E8
Hartshorne 44 E5
Hartsop 67 G5
Hartwell 35 J5
Hartwood 79 F4
Harvel 14 C2
Harvington 34 B6
Harwell 19 F2
Harwich 39 H7
Harwood, G. Man 53 J2
Harwood, Durham 67 L3
Harwood Dale 65 G3
Harworth 55 K4
Hascombe 12 C3
Haselbech 35 J3
Haselbury Plucknett 9 F3
Haseley 34 D4

Haselor 34 C5
Hasfield 30 C5
Hasguard 26 C7
Haskayne 52 E3
Hasketon 39 H5
Hasland 55 G7
Haslemere 11 L1
Haslingden 62 A7
Haslingden Grane 62 A7
Haslingfield 37 H5
Haslington 43 J2
Hassall 53 J8
Hassall Green 53 J8
Hassall Street 15 G4
Hassendean 74 B1
Hassingham 49 J7
Hassocks 13 G5
Hassop 55 F6
Hastigrow 115 H3
Hastingleigh 15 G4
Hastings 14 E8
Hastingwood 21 J3
Hastoe 20 D3
Haswell 69 F2
Hatch, Beds 36 E6
Hatch, Hants 19 H5
Hatch, Wilts 9 L2
Hatch Beauchamp 8 E2
Hatch End 21 F4
Hatching Green 21 F2
Hatchmere 53 G6
Hatcliffe 59 G6
Hatfield, Herts 21 G3
Hatfield, H. & W 29 K2
Hatfield, S. Yks 55 K3
Hatfield Broad Oak 21 K2
Hatfield Heath 21 K2
Hatfield Peverel 22 D2
Hatfield Woodhouse 58 A6
Hatford 31 H8
Hatherden 18 E5
Hatherleigh 7 F5
Hathern 45 G5
Hatherop 31 F7
Hathersage 55 F5
Hatherton, Staffs 44 A6
Hatherton, Ches 43 H3
Hatley St George 37 F5
Hatt 4 D5
Hattingley 11 H1
Hatton, Shrops 32 D1
Hatton, Warw 34 D4
Hatton, Derby 44 D4
Hatton, G. Lon 20 E6
Hatton, Lincs 57 F6
Hatton, Ches 53 G5
Hatton, Grampn 101 K5
Hattoncrook 101 H6
Hatton Heath 52 F7
Hatton of Fintray 101 H7
Haugham 57 H5
Haugh Head 81 J7
Haughley 38 F4
Haughley Green 38 F4
Haugh of Glass 100 D5
Haugh of Urr 72 D7
Haughton, Shrops 42 E5
Haughton, Shrops 43 G6
Haughton, Shrops 43 H8
Haughton, Staffs 43 K5
Haughton, Notts 55 K6
Haughton Green 53 L4
Haughton Moss 43 G2
Haunton 44 D6
Hauxley 75 J3
Hauxton 37 H5
Havant 11 J4
Haven 29 J2
Havenstreet 11 G5
Haverfordwest 26 D6
Haverhill 38 B6
Haverigg 60 E2
Havering-atte-Bower 21 K4
Haversham 36 B6
Haverthwaite 61 G1
Hawarden 52 E7
Hawes 68 A8
Hawford 33 H4
Hawick 74 B2
Hawkchurch 8 E4
Hawkedon 38 C5
Hawkeridge 17 K5
Hawkerland 8 B6
Hawkesbury 17 J2
Hawkesbury Upton 17 J2
Hawkes End 34 D2
Hawkhill 75 J2
Hawkhurst 13 L3
Hawkinge 15 J4
Hawkley 11 J2
Hawkridge 7 J2
Hawkshead 66 F7
Hawksland 79 F6
Hawkswick 62 C2
Hawksworth, W. Yks 62 E5
Hawksworth, Notts 45 J3
Hawkwell 22 E4
Hawley, Hants 20 C8
Hawley, Kent 21 K6
Hawling 30 E5
Hawnby 69 H8
Haworth 62 D6
Hawstead 38 D5
Hawthorn 69 G2
Hawthorn Hill 20 C6
Hawton 45 J2
Haxby 64 K4
Haxey 58 B7
Haydock 53 G4
Haydon 9 H3
Haydon Bridge 74 E7
Haydon Wick 18 C2
Haye 4 D5
Hayes, G. Lon 20 E5

Hayes, G. Lon 21 J7
Hayfield 54 D6
Hayle 2 D6
Haynes 36 D6
Haynes Church End 36 D6
Hay-on-Wye 29 G3
Hayscastle 26 C5
Hayscastle Cross 26 D5
Hayton, Notts 56 B5
Hayton, Humbs 58 C2
Hayton, Cumbr 66 D2
Hayton, Cumbr 67 H1
Hayton's Bent 32 E2
Haytor Vale 5 H4
Haywards Heath 13 G4
Haywood Oaks 45 H2
Hazelbank 79 F5
Hazelbury Bryan 9 J4
Hazeley 20 B8
Hazel Grove 53 L5
Hazelrigg 81 J6
Hazelslade 44 B6
Hazelwood 44 E3
Hazlemere 20 C4
Hazlerigg 75 J6
Hazleton 30 E6
Heacham 48 B4
Headbourne Worthy 11 F1
Headcorn 14 E4
Headingley 63 F6
Headington 31 K7
Headlam 68 D5
Headless Cross 34 B4
Headley, Surrey 12 F1
Headley, Hants 19 G4
Headley, Hants 11 K1
Head of Muir 85 L6
Headon 56 B6
Heads Nook 67 G1
Heage 44 E2
Healaugh, N. Yks 68 C7
Healaugh, N. Yks 63 J5
Heald Green 53 K5
Healey, N. Yks 62 E1
Healey, Northum 75 G8
Healey, Lancs 53 K2
Healeyfield 68 C2
Healing 59 G5
Heamoor 2 C6
Heanish 88 B4
Heanor 44 F3
Heanton Punchardon 6 F2
Heapham 56 C5
Hearthstane 79 J7
Heasley Mill 7 H2
Heast 96 B4
Heath, Derby 55 H7
Heath, S. Glam 25 K7
Heath and Reach 36 C8
Heathcote 54 E7
Heath End, Hants 19 G4
Heath End, Hants 19 K6
Heather 44 E6
Heathfield, Somer 8 C2
Heathfield, Strath 77 J1
Heathfield, Devon 5 J4
Heathfield, E. usx 13 J4
Heath Hayes 44 B6
Heath Hill 43 J6
Heath House 16 F6
Heath, The 49 G5
Heathton 33 H1
Heatley 53 J5
Heaton, Staffs 54 C7
Heaton, Lancs 61 H3
Heaton, T. & W 75 J7
Heaton Moor 53 K4
Heaverham 21 K8
Heaviley 53 L5
Hebburn 75 K7
Hebden 62 D3
Hebden Bridge 62 C7
Hebden Green 53 H7
Hebron 75 H5
Heckfield 20 B7
Heckington 46 E2
Heckmondwike 62 F7
Heddington 18 A4
Heddle 116 C5
Heddon-on-the-Wall 75 H7
Hedenham 49 J8
Hedge End 11 F3
Hedgerley 20 D5
Hedging 8 E2
Hedley on the Hill 75 G8
Hednesford 44 B6
Hedon 59 F4
Hedsor 20 D5
Hegdon Hill 29 K2
Heggerscales 67 L5
Heglibister 119 F3
Heighington, Durham 68 E4
Heighington, Lincs 56 E7
Heights of Brae 98 D2
Heights of Kinlochewe 107 F5
Heiton 80 F6
Hele, Devon 7 F1
Hele, Devon 6 E1
Helensburgh 84 E6
Helford 2 F7
Helhoughton 48 D5
Helions Bumpstead 38 B6
Helland 3 J2
Hellesdon 49 H6
Hellidon 35 G5
Hellifield 62 B4
Hellingly 13 J5
Hellington 49 J7
Hellister 119 F4
Helmdon 35 G6
Helmingham 39 G5
Helmsdale 109 J2
Helmshore 62 A7
Helmsley 63 K1

Helperby ... 63 H3
Helperthorpe ... 65 G5
Helpringham ... 46 E3
Helpston ... 46 E7
Helsby ... 53 F6
Helston ... 2 E7
Helstone ... 3 J1
Helton ... 67 H4
Helwith Bridge ... 62 B3
Hemblington ... 49 J6
Hemel Hempstead ... 20 E3
Hemingbrough ... 63 K6
Hemingby ... 57 G6
Hemingford Abbots ... 37 F3
Hemingford Grey ... 37 F3
Hemingstone ... 39 G5
Hemington, Northnts ... 36 D2
Hemington, Somer ... 17 J5
Hemley ... 39 H6
Hempholme ... 65 H7
Hempnall ... 49 H8
Hempnall Green ... 49 H8
Hempriggs ... 99 K2
Hempstead, Essex ... 38 B7
Hempstead, Norf ... 49 G4
Hempstead, Norf ... 49 K5
Hempsted ... 30 C6
Hempton, Norf ... 48 E5
Hempton, Oxon ... 31 J4
Hemsby ... 49 K6
Hemswell ... 56 D4
Hemsworth ... 55 H2
Hemyock ... 8 C3
Henbury, Avon ... 17 G3
Henbury, Ches ... 53 K6
Hendon, T. & W. ... 69 G1
Hendon, G. Lon ... 21 G5
Hendre ... 52 C7
Hendy ... 27 K7
Heneglwys ... 50 D3
Henfield ... 12 F5
Hengoed, Shrops ... 42 D4
Hengoed, Powys ... 29 G2
Hengoed, M. Glam ... 25 K5
Hengrave ... 38 D4
Henham ... 37 J8
Henley, Shrops ... 32 E3
Henley, Somer ... 9 F1
Henley, Suff ... 39 G5
Henley, W. Susx ... 11 K2
Henley-in-Arden ... 34 C4
Henley-on-Thames ... 20 B5
Henley Park ... 12 C1
Henllan, Dyfed ... 27 H3
Henllan, Clwyd ... 51 K4
Henllan Amgoed ... 27 F5
Henllys ... 29 G8
Henlow ... 36 E7
Hennock ... 5 J3
Henryd ... 51 G3
Henry's Moat ... 26 E5
Hensall ... 63 J7
Henshaw ... 74 D7
Henstead ... 39 K2
Henstridge ... 9 J3
Henstridge Marsh ... 9 J2
Henton, Oxon ... 20 B3
Henton, Somer ... 18 F5
Henwood ... 4 C4
Heogan ... 119 G4
Heol Senni ... 25 H2
Heol-y-Cyw ... 25 H6
Hepburn ... 81 J7
Hepple ... 75 F3
Hepscott ... 75 J5
Heptonstall ... 62 C7
Hepworth, Suff ... 38 E3
Hepworth, W. Yks ... 54 E3
Herbrandston ... 26 C7
Hereford ... 29 K3
Hergest ... 29 G2
Heriot ... 80 B4
Hermitage, Border ... 74 B4
Hermitage, Berks ... 19 G3
Hermitage, Dorset ... 9 H4
Hermitage, W. Susx ... 11 J4
Hermitage, The ... 12 F1
Hermon, Gwyn ... 50 C4
Hermon, Dyfed ... 27 G4
Hermon, Dyfed ... 27 H4
Herne ... 15 H2
Herne Bay ... 15 H2
Herner ... 7 F3
Hernhill ... 15 G2
Herodsfoot ... 3 L3
Herongate ... 22 C4
Heronsgate ... 20 E4
Herriard ... 19 H6
Herringfleet ... 49 K8
Herringswell ... 38 C4
Herrington ... 69 F1
Hersden ... 15 J2
Hersham ... 21 F7
Herstmonceux ... 13 K5
Herston ... 116 D7
Hertford ... 21 H2
Hertford Heath ... 21 H2
Hertingfordbury ... 21 H2
Hesketh Bank ... 61 H7
Hesketh Lane ... 61 K5
Hesket Newmarket ... 66 F3
Heskin Green ... 53 G2
Hesleden ... 69 G3
Heslington ... 63 K4
Hessay ... 63 J4
Hessenford ... 4 D6
Hessett ... 38 E4
Hessle ... 58 E4
Hest Bank ... 61 H3
Heston ... 21 F6
Heswall ... 52 D5
Hethe ... 31 K5
Hethersett ... 49 G7
Hethersgill ... 73 K7
Hethpool ... 81 G7

Hett ... 68 E3
Hetton ... 62 C4
Hetton-le-Hole ... 69 F2
Heugh ... 75 G6
Heugh-head ... 100 C7
Heveningham ... 39 J3
Hever ... 13 H2
Heversham ... 61 H1
Hevingham ... 49 G5
Hewelsfield ... 29 K7
Hewish, Somer ... 9 F4
Hewish, Avon ... 16 F4
Hexham ... 74 F7
Hextable ... 21 K6
Hexton ... 36 E7
Hexworthy ... 5 G4
Heybridge, Essex ... 22 C4
Heybridge, Essex ... 22 E3
Heybridge Basin ... 22 E3
Heybrook Bay ... 4 E7
Heydon, Norf ... 49 G5
Heydon, Cambs ... 37 H6
Heydour ... 46 D4
Heylipol ... 88 A4
Heylor ... 120 E4
Heysham ... 61 H3
Heyshott ... 11 K3
Heytesbury ... 17 L6
Heythrop ... 31 H5
Heywood, G. Man ... 53 K2
Heywood, Wilts ... 17 K5
Hibaldstow ... 58 D6
Hickleton ... 55 H3
Hickling, Notts ... 45 H5
Hickling, Norf ... 49 K5
Hickling Green ... 49 K5
Hickling Heath ... 49 K5
Hidcote Boyce ... 34 C6
High Ackworth ... 55 H2
Higham, Lancs ... 62 B6
Higham, Suff ... 38 C4
Higham, Kent ... 14 D1
Higham, Suff ... 38 F7
Higham, Derby ... 55 G8
Higham Dykes ... 75 H6
Higham Ferrers ... 36 C4
Higham Gobion ... 36 E7
Higham on the Hill ... 44 E8
Highampton ... 6 E5
Higham Wood ... 13 K2
High Beach ... 21 J4
High Bentham ... 61 K3
High Bickington ... 7 G3
High Birkwith ... 62 B2
High Blantyre ... 78 D4
High Bonnybridge ... 85 L7
High Borve ... 111 J2
High Bradfield ... 55 F4
Highbridge, Highld ... 90 C3
Highbridge, Somer ... 16 E6
Highbrook ... 13 G3
Highburton ... 54 E2
Highbury ... 17 H6
High Buston ... 75 J3
High Callerton ... 75 H6
High Catton ... 64 E7
Highclere ... 18 F4
Highcliffe ... 10 D5
High Cogges ... 31 H7
High Coniscliffe ... 68 E5
High Cross, Herts ... 21 H2
High Cross, Hants ... 11 J2
High Cross Bank ... 44 D6
High Dougarie ... 76 D4
High Easter ... 22 C2
High Ellington ... 62 E1
Higher Ashton ... 5 J3
Higher Ballam ... 61 G6
Higher Ercall ... 43 G6
Higher End ... 53 G3
Higher Penwortham ... 61 J7
Higher Poynton ... 53 L5
Higher Tale ... 8 B4
Higher Town ... 2 P2
Higher Walreddon ... 4 E4
Higher Walton, Ches ... 53 G5
Higher Walton, Lancs ... 61 J7
Higher Wych ... 43 F3
Highfield, T. & W. ... 75 H8
Highfield, Strath ... 77 J2
Highfields ... 37 G5
High Garrett ... 38 C8
High Grange ... 68 D3
High Green, S. Yks ... 55 G4
High Green, Norf ... 49 G7
High Green, H. & W. ... 33 H6
High Halden ... 14 E5
High Halstow ... 14 D1
High Ham ... 9 F1
High Hatton ... 43 H5
High Hesket ... 67 G2
High Hoyland ... 55 F2
High Hunsley ... 58 D3
High Hurstwood ... 13 H4
High Lane, G. Man ... 54 C5
High Lane, H. & W. ... 33 F4
High Laver ... 21 K3
Highleadon ... 30 B5
High Legh ... 53 J5
Highleigh ... 11 K5
Highley ... 33 G2
High Littleton ... 17 H5
High Melton ... 55 J3
Highmoor Cross ... 20 B5
Highmoor Hill ... 17 F2
Highnam ... 30 B6
High Newton ... 61 H1
High Newton-by-the-Sea ... 81 L7
High Offley ... 43 J5
High Ongar ... 21 K3
High Onn ... 43 K6
High Roding ... 22 C2
High Salvington ... 12 E6
High Shaw ... 68 A7
High Spen ... 75 H8

Highsted ... 14 F2
High Street, Corn ... 3 H4
High Street, Suff ... 39 K5
High Street Green ... 38 F5
Hightae ... 73 H6
Hightown, Mers ... 52 E3
Hightown, Ches ... 53 K7
High Toynton ... 57 G7
High Trewhill ... 75 G3
Highway, Wilts ... 18 B3
Highway, Corn ... 3 K4
Highworth ... 18 D1
High Wray ... 67 F7
High Wych ... 21 J2
High Wycombe ... 20 C4
Hilborough ... 48 D7
Hilcott ... 18 B6
Hildenborough ... 13 J2
Hildersham ... 37 J6
Hilderstone ... 43 L4
Hilderthorpe ... 65 J6
Hilgay ... 48 B8
Hill ... 30 A8
Hillam ... 63 J7
Hillberry ... 60 Q4
Hillbrae, Grampn ... 100 F4
Hillbrae, Grampn ... 101 G6
Hill Brow ... 11 J2
Hilldyke ... 47 G3
Hill End, Durham ... 68 C3
Hill End, Fife ... 86 D5
Hillend, Fife ... 86 E6
Hillerton ... 5 H2
Hillesden ... 35 H8
Hillesley ... 17 J2
Hillfarrance ... 8 C2
Hill Head, Hants ... 11 G4
Hillhead, Strath ... 77 K6
Hillhead, Devon ... 5 K6
Hillhead of Auchentumb ... 101 J3
Hillhead of Cocklaw ... 101 K4
Hilliard's Cross ... 44 C6
Hillliclay ... 115 G3
Hillingdon ... 20 E5
Hillington ... 48 C5
Hillmorton ... 35 G3
Hillockhead ... 100 C8
Hill of Beath ... 86 E5
Hill of Fearn ... 109 G6
Hill Ridware ... 44 B6
Hillside, Shetld ... 119 G2
Hillside, Tays ... 93 J5
Hillside, Grampn ... 93 L2
Hillswick ... 120 E5
Hill, The ... 60 E1
Hilmarton ... 18 B3
Hilperton ... 17 K5
Hilsea ... 11 H4
Hilton, Durham ... 68 D4
Hilton, Dery ... 44 D4
Hilton, Cambs ... 37 F4
Hilton, Cleve ... 69 G5
Hilton, Dorset ... 9 J4
Hilton, Grampn ... 101 J5
Hilton, Shrops ... 43 J8
Hilton, Cumbr ... 67 K4
Hilton of Cadboll ... 109 G6
Himbleton ... 33 J5
Himley ... 33 H1
Hincaster ... 61 J1
Hinckley ... 44 F8
Hinderclay ... 38 F3
Hinderwell ... 69 K5
Hindford ... 42 E4
Hindhead ... 11 K1
Hindley ... 53 H3
Hindley Green ... 53 H3
Hindlip ... 33 H5
Hindolveston ... 48 F5
Hindon ... 9 L1
Hindringham ... 48 E4
Hingham ... 48 F7
Hinkley Point
    Power Station ... 16 D6
Hinstock ... 43 H5
Hintlesham ... 39 F6
Hinton, Hants ... 10 D5
Hinton, Shrops ... 42 F7
Hinton, Northnts ... 35 G5
Hinton, Avon ... 17 J3
Hinton Ampner ... 11 G2
Hinton Blewett ... 17 G5
Hinton Charterhouse ... 17 J5
Hinton-in-the-Hedges ... 35 G7
Hinton Martell ... 10 B4
Hinton on the Green ... 34 B6
Hinton Parva ... 18 D2
Hinton St George ... 9 F3
Hinton St Mary ... 9 J3
Hinton Waldrist ... 31 H8
Hints, Staffs ... 44 C7
Hints, Shrops ... 33 F3
Hinwick ... 36 C4
Hinxhill ... 15 G4
Hinxton ... 37 H6
Hinxworth ... 37 F6
Hipperholme ... 62 E7
Hirn ... 93 J1
Hirnant ... 41 K1
Hirst ... 75 J5
Hirst Courtney ... 63 K7
Hirwaun ... 25 H4
Hiscott ... 7 F3
Histon ... 37 H4
Hitcham ... 38 E5
Hitchin ... 36 E8
Hither Green ... 21 H6
Hittisleigh ... 5 H2
Hixon ... 44 B5
Hoaden ... 15 J3
Hoaldalbert ... 29 H5
Hoar Cross ... 44 C5
Hoarwithy ... 29 K5
Hoath ... 15 J2
Hobarris ... 32 C3

Hobbister ... 116 C6
Hobkirk ... 74 B2
Hobson ... 68 D1
Hoby ... 45 H6
Hockering ... 48 F6
Hockerton ... 45 J2
Hockley ... 22 E4
Hockley Heath ... 34 C3
Hockliffe ... 36 C8
Hockwold cum Wilton ... 38 C2
Hockworthy ... 8 B3
Hoddesdon ... 21 H3
Hoddlesden ... 61 L7
Hodgeston ... 26 E8
Hodnet ... 43 H5
Hodthorpe ... 55 J6
Hoe ... 48 E6
Hoe Gate ... 11 H3
Hoff ... 67 J5
Hoggeston ... 20 C6
Hoghton ... 61 K7
Hognaston ... 44 D2
Hogsthorpe ... 57 K6
Holbeach ... 47 G5
Holbeach Bank ... 47 G5
Holbeach Drove ... 47 G6
Holbeach Hurn ... 47 G5
Holbeach St Johns ... 47 G6
Holbeach St Marks ... 47 G4
Holbeach St Matthew ... 47 H4
Holbeck ... 55 J6
Holberrow Green ... 34 B5
Holbeton ... 5 G
Holbrook, Derby ... 44 E3
Holbrook, Suff ... 39 G7
Holburn ... 81 J6
Holbury ... 10 F4
Holcombe, Somer ... 17 H6
Holcombe, Devon ... 5 K4
Holcombe Rogus ... 8 B3
Holcot ... 35 J4
Holden ... 62 A5
Holdenby ... 35 H4
Holdgate ... 32 E2
Hole in the Wall ... 29 L5
Holemoor ... 6 E5
Holford ... 16 C6
Holker ... 61 G2
Holkham ... 48 D3
Hollacombe, Devon ... 6 D5
Hollacombe, Devon ... 7 G4
Holland-on-Sea ... 23 J2
Hollandstoun ... 117 G1
Hollesley ... 39 J6
Hollinfare ... 53 H4
Hollingbourne ... 14 E3
Hollington, Staffs ... 44 B4
Hollington, Derby ... 44 D4
Hollington, E. Susx ... 14 D7
Hollingworth ... 54 D4
Hollins ... 53 K3
Hollinsclough ... 54 D7
Hollinwood ... 43 G4
Holloway ... 44 E2
Hollowell ... 35 H3
Holl's Green ... 37 F8
Hollybush, H. & W. ... 33 G7
Hollybush, Strath ... 77 J6
Hollybush, Gwent ... 25 K4
Holly End ... 47 H7
Hollym ... 59 H4
Hollywood ... 34 B3
Holm ... 111 J4
Holmbury St Mary ... 12 E2
Holme, Notts ... 56 C8
Holme, Cambs ... 36 E2
Holme, W. Yks ... 54 E3
Holme, Cumbr ... 61 J2
Holme Chapel ... 62 B7
Holme Hale ... 48 D7
Holme Lacy ... 29 K4
Holme Marsh ... 29 H2
Holme next the Sea ... 48 C3
Holme-on-Spalding-Moor ... 58 C3
Holme on the Wolds ... 58 D2
Holmer ... 29 K3
Holmer Green ... 20 D4
Holmes Chapel ... 53 J7
Holmesfield ... 55 G6
Holmeswood ... 52 F2
Holmewood ... 55 H7
Holmfirth ... 54 E3
Holmhead ... 72 A1
Holmpton ... 59 H4
Holmrook ... 66 C7
Holmsgarth ... 119 G4
Holne ... 5 H5
Holnest ... 9 H4
Holsworthy ... 6 D5
Holsworthy Beacon ... 6 D5
Holt, Dorset ... 10 D4
Holt, Clwyd ... 42 F2
Holt, Norf ... 48 F4
Holt, H. & W. ... 33 H4
Holt, Wilts ... 17 K4
Holtby ... 63 K4
Holt End ... 34 B4
Holt Heath ... 33 H4
Holton, Somer ... 9 H2
Holton, Suff ... 39 K3
Holton, Oxon ... 31 L7
Holton cum Beckering ... 57 F5
Holton le Clay ... 59 G6
Holton le Moor ... 58 E7
Holton St Mary ... 38 F7
Holwell, Herts ... 36 E7
Holwell, Oxon ... 31 G7
Holwell, Dorset ... 9 J3
Holwell, Leic ... 45 J5
Holwick ... 68 B4
Holworth ... 9 J6
Holybourne ... 19 J6
Holy Cross ... 33 J3

Holyhead ... 50 B2
Holy Island ... 81 K5
Holymoorside ... 55 G7
Holyport ... 20 C6
Holystone ... 74 F3
Holytown ... 78 E3
Holywell, Clwyd ... 52 C6
Holywell, Corn ... 2 F4
Holywell, Cambs ... 37 G3
Holywell, Dorset ... 9 G4
Holywell Green ... 54 D2
Holywell Lake ... 8 C2
Holywell Row ... 38 C3
Holywood ... 72 E5
Homer ... 43 H7
Homersfield ... 39 H2
Hom Green ... 29 K5
Homington ... 10 C2
Honeybourne ... 34 C6
Honeychurch ... 7 G5
Honey Hill ... 15 H2
Honiley ... 34 D3
Honing ... 49 J5
Honingham ... 49 G6
Honington, Lincs ... 46 C3
Honington, Warw ... 34 D6
Honington, Suff ... 38 E3
Honiton ... 8 C4
Honley ... 54 E2
Hoo ... 39 H5
Hooe, Devon ... 4 F6
Hooe, E. Susx ... 13 K6
Hook, Wilts ... 18 B2
Hook, Humbs ... 58 B4
Hook, Dyfed ... 26 D6
Hook, G. Lon ... 21 F7
Hook, Hants ... 19 J5
Hooke ... 9 G4
Hookgate ... 43 J4
Hook Norton ... 31 H4
Hookway ... 5 J2
Hookwood ... 12 F2
Hoole ... 52 F7
Hoo St Werburgh ... 14 D1
Hooton Levitt ... 55 J4
Hooton Pagnell ... 55 H3
Hooton Roberts ... 55 H4
Hope, Powys ... 42 D7
Hope, Derby ... 54 E5
Hope, Shrops ... 42 E7
Hope, Clwyd ... 52 E8
Hope, Devon ... 5 G7
Hope Bagot ... 33 E3
Hope Bowdler ... 32 D1
Hopeman ... 99 K2
Hope Mansell ... 29 L6
Hopesay ... 32 C2
Hope under Dinmore ... 29 K2
Hopton, Suff ... 38 E3
Hopton, Staffs ... 43 L5
Hopton, Staffs ... 43 L5
Hopton Cangeford ... 32 E2
Hopton Castle ... 32 C3
Hopton on Sea ... 49 L7
Hopton Wafers ... 33 F3
Hopwas ... 44 C7
Hopwood ... 34 B3
Horam ... 13 J5
Horbling ... 46 E4
Horbury ... 55 F2
Horden ... 69 G2
Horderley ... 32 D2
Hordle ... 10 D5
Hordley ... 42 E4
Horeb, Dyfed ... 27 H3
Horeb, Dyfed ... 27 K5
Horham ... 39 H3
Horkstowe ... 58 D5
Horley, Surrey ... 13 F2
Horley, Oxon ... 34 F6
Hornblotton Green ... 9 G1
Hornby, N. Yks ... 69 F6
Hornby, Lancs ... 61 J3
Horncastle ... 57 G7
Hornchurch ... 21 K5
Horncliffe ... 81 H5
Horndean ... 11 J3
Horndon on the Hill ... 22 C5
Horne ... 13 G2
Horn Hill ... 20 E4
Horning ... 49 J6
Horninghold ... 45 K8
Horninglow ... 44 D5
Horningsea ... 37 H4
Horningsham ... 17 K6
Horningtoft ... 48 E5
Hornish Point ... 104 C7
Hornsby ... 67 H1
Hornsea ... 59 G2
Hornsey ... 21 H5
Hornton ... 34 E6
Horrabridge ... 4 F5
Horringer ... 38 D4
Horse Bridge, Staffs ... 44 A2
Horsebridge, Hants ... 10 E1
Horsebridge, E. Susx ... 13 J5
Horsebrook ... 43 K6
Horsehay ... 43 H7
Horseheath ... 38 B6
Horsehouse ... 62 D1
Horsell ... 20 D8
Horseman's Green ... 42 F3
Horseway ... 37 H2
Horsey ... 49 K5
Horsford ... 49 G6
Horsforth ... 63 F6
Horsham, W. Susx ... 12 E3
Horsham, H. & W. ... 33 G5
Horsham St Faith ... 49 H6
Horsington, Lincs ... 57 F7
Horsington, Somer ... 9 J2
Horsley, Glos ... 30 C8
Horsley, Derby ... 44 E3
Horsley, Northum ... 74 E4
Horsley, Northum ... 75 G7
Horsley Cross ... 39 G8

Horsleycross Street ... 39 G8
Horsleyhill ... 74 B2
Horsley Woodhouse ... 44 E3
Horsmonden ... 13 L2
Horspath ... 31 K7
Horstead ... 49 H6
Horsted Keynes ... 13 G4
Horton, Lancs ... 62 B4
Horton, Dorset ... 10 B4
Horton, Wilts ... 18 B4
Horton, Northnts ... 36 B5
Horton, W. Glam ... 24 C6
Horton, Bucks ... 20 D2
Horton, Somer ... 8 E3
Horton, Berks ... 20 E6
Horton, Avon ... 17 J3
Horton, Northum ... 81 J6
Horton, Staffs ... 53 L8
Horton-cum-Studley ... 31 K6
Horton Green ... 42 F3
Horton Heath ... 11 F3
Horton in Ribblesdale ... 62 B2
Horton Kirby ... 21 K7
Horwich ... 53 H2
Horwood ... 6 F3
Hose ... 45 J5
Hosh ... 86 B2
Hostingfield ... 37 H5
Hoswick ... 119 G6
Hotham ... 58 C3
Hothfield ... 14 F4
Hoton ... 45 G5
Hough ... 43 J2
Hougham ... 46 B3
Hougharry ... 104 C4
Hough Green ... 53 F5
Hough-on-the-Hill ... 46 C3
Houghton, W. Susx ... 12 D5
Houghton, Dyfed ... 26 D7
Houghton, Hants ... 10 E1
Houghton, Cambs ... 37 F3
Houghton, Cumbr ... 73 K8
Houghton Conquest ... 36 D6
Houghton-le-Spring ... 69 F2
Houghton on the Hill ... 45 H7
Houghton Regis ... 20 E1
Houghton St Giles ... 48 E4
Houlsyke ... 64 E2
Hound Green ... 20 B8
Houndslow ... 80 E5
Houndwood ... 81 G3
Hounslow ... 21 F6
Housetter ... 120 F4
Houston ... 77 K1
Houstry ... 115 G6
Hove ... 13 F6
Hoveringham ... 45 H3
Hoveton ... 49 J6
Hovingham ... 63 K2
How ... 67 H1
How Caple ... 29 L4
Howden ... 58 B4
Howden-le-Wear ... 68 D3
Howe, Norf ... 49 H8
Howe, Highld ... 115 J3
Howe Green ... 22 D3
Howell ... 46 E3
Howe of Teuchar ... 101 G4
Howe Street, Essex ... 38 B7
Howe Street, Essex ... 22 C2
Howe, The, Cumbr ... 61 H1
Howe, The, I. of M. ... 60 N5
Howey ... 28 E2
Howgate, Border ... 74 D1
Howgate, Lothn ... 79 K4
Howick ... 75 J2
Howle ... 43 H5
Howlett End ... 38 A7
Howmore ... 94 C2
Hownam ... 74 D2
Howsham, Humbs ... 58 E6
Howsham, N. Yks ... 64 E6
Howton ... 29 J5
Howtown ... 67 G5
Howwood ... 77 J1
Hoxa ... 116 D7
Hoxne ... 39 G3
Hoylake ... 52 D5
Hoyland Nether ... 55 G3
Hoyland Swaine ... 55 F3
Hubberholme ... 62 C2
Hubbert's Bridge ... 47 F3
Huby, N. Yks ... 63 F5
Huby, N. Yks ... 63 J3
Hucclecote ... 30 C6
Hucking ... 14 E3
Hucknall ... 45 G3
Huddersfield ... 54 E2
Huddington ... 33 J5
Hudswell ... 68 D6
Huggate ... 65 F7
Hughenden Valley ... 20 C4
Hughley ... 43 G8
Hugh Town ... 2 P2
Huish, Wilts ... 18 C4
Huish, Devon ... 7 F4
Huish Champflower ... 8 B2
Huish Episcopi ... 9 F2
Hulcott ... 20 C2
Hulland ... 44 D3
Hulland Ward ... 44 D3
Hullavington ... 17 K2
Hullbridge ... 22 E4
Hulme End ... 54 E8
Hulme Walfield ... 53 K7
Hulver Street ... 49 K2
Humber Bridge ... 58 E4
Humber Court ... 29 K2
Humberston ... 59 H6
Humbie ... 80 C3
Humbleton, Humbs ... 59 G3
Humbleton, Northum ... 81 H7
Hume ... 80 F5
Humshaugh ... 74 F6
Huna ... 115 J2

Huncoat........................62 A6
Huncote........................45 G8
Hundalee.......................74 C2
Hunderthwaite..................68 B4
Hundleby.......................57 H7
Hundleton......................26 D7
Hundon.........................38 C6
Hundred Acres..................11 G3
Hundred End....................61 H7
Hundred House..................28 F2
Hundred, The...................32 E4
Hungarton......................45 H7
Hungerford.....................18 E4
Hungerford Newtown.............18 E3
Hunmanby.......................65 H5
Hunningham.....................34 E4
Hunsdon........................21 J2
Hunsingore.....................63 H4
Hunsonby.......................67 H3
Hunspow.......................115 H2
Hunstanton.....................48 B3
Hunstanworth...................68 B2
Hunston, Suff..................38 E4
Hunston, W. Susx...............11 K4
Hunstrete......................17 H4
Hunt End.......................34 B4
Hunter's Quay..................84 D7
Huntingdon.....................37 F3
Huntingfield...................39 J3
Huntington, Staffs.............44 A6
Huntington, H. & W.............29 G2
Huntington, Lothn..............87 H7
Huntington, N. Yks.............63 K4
Huntingtower...................86 D2
Huntley........................30 B6
Huntly........................100 E4
Hunton, N. Yks.................68 D7
Hunton, Kent...................13 L2
Hunt's Cross...................52 F5
Huntsham.......................7 L3
Huntspill......................16 E6
Huntworth......................8 E1
Hunwick........................68 D3
Hunworth.......................48 F4
Hurdsfield.....................53 L6
Hurley, Berks..................20 C5
Hurley, Warw...................44 D8
Hurlford.......................77 K4
Hurliness.....................116 B8
Hurn...........................10 C5
Hursley........................10 F2
Hurst, Berks...................20 B6
Hurst, N. Yks..................68 C6
Hurst, G. Man..................53 L3
Hurstbourne Priors.............18 F6
Hurstbourne Tarrant............18 E5
Hurst Green, Surrey............13 G1
Hurst Green, Lancs.............61 K6
Hurst Green, E. Susx...........13 L4
Hurstpierpoint.................13 F5
Hurworth-on-Tees...............68 F5
Hury...........................68 B5
Husbands Bosworth..............35 H2
Husborne Crawley...............36 C7
Hushinish.....................110 D6
Husthwaite.....................63 J2
Hutcherleigh...................5 H6
Huthwaite......................55 H8
Huttoft........................57 K6
Hutton, Essex..................22 C4
Hutton, Avon...................16 E5
Hutton, N. Yks.................64 E6
Hutton, Cumbr..................67 G4
Hutton, Border.................81 H4
Hutton, Lancs..................61 H7
Hutton Bonville................68 F6
Hutton Buscel..................65 G4
Hutton Conyers.................63 G2
Hutton Cranswick...............65 H7
Hutton End.....................67 G3
Hutton Henry...................69 G3
Hutton-le-Hole.................64 E3
Hutton Magna...................68 D5
Hutton Roof, Cumbr.............67 F3
Hutton Roof, Cumbr.............61 J2
Hutton Rudby...................69 G6
Hutton Sessay..................63 H2
Hutton Wandesley...............63 J4
Huxley.........................53 G7
Huyton-with-Roby...............52 F4
Hycemoor.......................66 C8
Hyde, Hants....................10 C3
Hyde, Glos.....................30 C7
Hyde, G. Man...................53 L4
Hyde Heath.....................20 D3
Hydestile......................12 C2
Hynish.........................88 A5
Hyssington.....................42 E8
Hythe, Hants...................10 F4
Hythe, Knt.....................15 H5
Hythe End......................20 E6
Hythie........................101 K3

I

Ibberton.......................9 J4
Ible...........................55 F8
Ibsley.........................10 C4
Ibstock........................44 F6
Ibstone........................20 B4
Ibthorpe.......................18 E5
Ibworth........................19 G5
Ickburgh.......................48 D8
Ickenham.......................20 E5
Ickford........................20 A3
Ickham.........................15 J3
Ickleford......................36 E7
Icklesham......................14 E7
Ickleton.......................37 H6
Icklingham.....................38 C3
Ickwell Green..................36 E6
Icomb..........................31 G5
Idbury.........................31 G5

Iddesleigh.....................7 F5
Ide............................5 J2
Ideford........................5 J4
Ide Hill.......................13 H1
Iden...........................14 F6
Iden Green.....................14 E5
Idlicote.......................34 D6
Idmiston.......................10 D1
Idridgehay.....................44 D3
Idrigill......................102 E2
Idstone........................18 D2
Ifield.........................12 F3
Ifold..........................12 D3
Iford..........................13 H6
Ifton Heath....................42 E4
Ightfield......................43 G4
Ightham........................13 J1
Iken...........................39 K5
Ilam...........................44 C2
Ilchester......................9 G2
Ilderton.......................81 J7
Ilford.........................21 J5
Ilfracombe.....................6 F1
Ilkeston.......................45 F3
Ilketshall St Andrew...........39 J2
Ilketshall St Lawrence.........39 J2
Ilketshall St Margaret.........39 J2
Ilkley.........................62 E5
Illey..........................34 A2
Illingworth....................62 D7
Illogan........................2 E5
Illston on the Hill............45 J8
Ilmer..........................20 B3
Ilmington......................34 D6
Ilminster......................8 E3
Ilsington......................5 H4
Ilston.........................24 D5
Ilton, N. Yks..................62 E2
Ilton, Somer...................8 E3
Immingham......................59 F5
Impington......................37 H4
Ince...........................52 F6
Ince Blundell..................52 E3
Ince-in-Makerfield.............53 G3
Inchbare.......................93 H5
Inchberry.....................100 C3
Inchina.......................106 F5
Inchina.......................106 E2
Inchinnan......................85 G8
Inchlaggan.....................90 C1
Inchmore.......................98 B4
Inchnadamph...................112 D6
Inchture.......................87 F2
Indian Queens..................3 H4
Ingatestone....................22 C4
Ingbirchworth..................55 F3
Ingestre.......................44 A5
Ingham, Suff...................38 D3
Ingham, Lincs..................56 D5
Ingham, Norf...................49 J5
Ingleby Arncliffe..............69 G6
Ingleby Greenhow...............69 H6
Inglesbatch....................17 J4
Inglesham......................31 G8
Ingleton, Durham...............68 D4
Ingleton, N. Yks...............61 K2
Inglewhite.....................61 J5
Ingliston......................86 E7
Ingoe..........................75 G6
Ingoldisthorpe.................48 B4
Ingoldmells....................57 K7
Ingoldsby......................46 D4
Ingram.........................75 G2
Ingrave........................22 C4
Ings...........................67 G7
Ingst..........................17 G2
Ingworth.......................49 G5
Inkberrow......................34 B5
Inkhorn.......................101 J5
Inkpen.........................18 E4
Inkstack......................115 H2
Innellan.......................84 D7
Innerleithen...................80 B6
Innerleven.....................87 G4
Innermessan....................70 B5
Innerwick, Lothn...............80 F2
Innerwick, Tays................91 G7
Innsworth......................30 C5
Insch.........................100 F6
Insh...........................91 K1
Inskip.........................61 H6
Instow.........................6 E2
Inver, Grampn..................92 D2
Inver, Highld.................109 G5
Inveraillort...................96 C7
Inveralligin..................105 D6
Inverallochy..................101 K2
Inveramsay....................101 G6
Inveran.......................108 D4
Inverarity.....................84 C4
Inverarish.....................96 A2
Inverarity.....................92 F7
Inverarnan.....................84 F3
Inverasdale...................106 D3
Inverbervie....................93 K4
Inverbrough....................99 G5
Invercharnan...................98 A3
Invercreran....................98 B7
Inverdruie.....................99 H7
Inverebrie....................101 J5
Invereri......................101 J5
Inveresk.......................87 G7
Inverey........................92 B3
Inverfarigaig..................98 D6
Invergarry.....................90 E1
Invergordon....................99 F2
Invergowrie....................87 G1
Inverguhomery.................101 K4
Inverguseran...................96 C5
Inverharroch..................100 C5
Inverie........................96 C6
Inverinate.....................96 E3
Inverkeilor....................93 H7
Inverkeithing..................86 E6
Inverkeithny..................100 F4
Inverkip.......................84 E7

Inverkirkaig..................112 B7
Invermoidart...................89 H1
Invermoriston..................98 C7
Invernaver....................113 J2
Inverness......................98 E4
Inverroy.......................90 D3
Invershin.....................108 D4
Inverugie.....................101 L4
Inveruglas.....................84 F4
Inverurie.....................101 G6
Invervar.......................91 H7
Inwardleigh....................5 F2
Inworth........................22 E2
Iping..........................11 K2
Ipplepen.......................5 J5
Ipsden.........................20 A5
Ipstones.......................44 B2
Ipswich........................39 G6
Irby...........................52 D5
Irby in the Marsh..............57 J7
Irby upon Humber...............59 F6
Irchester......................36 C4
Ireby, Cumbr...................66 E3
Ireby, Lancs...................61 K2
Ireland, Orkney...............116 C6
Ireland, Shetld...............119 F6
Ireleth........................60 F2
Ireshopeburn...................68 A3
Irlam..........................53 J4
Irnham.........................46 D5
Iron Acton.....................17 H2
Iron-Bridge....................43 H7
Iron Cross.....................34 B5
Ironacannie....................72 B6
Ironside......................101 H3
Ironville......................44 F2
Irstead........................49 J5
Irthington.....................73 K7
Irthlingborough................36 C3
Irton..........................65 H4
Irvine.........................77 J4
Isauld........................114 E3
Isbister, Orkney..............116 B4
Isbister, Orkney..............116 C5
Isbister, Shetld..............119 H2
Isfield........................13 H5
Isham..........................36 B3
Isle Abbotts...................8 E2
Isle Brewers...................8 E2
Isleham........................38 B3
Isle of Whithorn...............71 F8
Isleornsay or
  Eilean Iarmain...............96 B4
Islesburgh....................120 F6
Isleworth......................21 F6
Isley Watton...................44 F5
Islington......................21 H5
Islip, Northnts................36 C3
Islip, Oxon....................31 K6
Islivig.......................110 D5
Istead Rise....................14 C2
Isycoed........................42 F2
Itchen Abbas...................11 G1
Itchen Stoke...................11 G1
Itchingfield...................12 E4
Itchington.....................17 H2
Itteringham....................49 G4
Itton..........................5 G2
Itton Common...................29 J8
Ivegill........................67 G2
Ivelet.........................68 B7
Iver...........................20 E5
Iver Heath.....................20 E5
Iveston........................68 D1
Ivinghoe.......................20 D2
Ivinghoe Aston.................20 D2
Ivington.......................29 J2
Ivington Green.................29 J2
Ivybridge......................5 G6
Ivychurch......................15 G6
Ivy Hatch......................13 J1
Iwade..........................14 E2
Iwerne Courtney
  or Shroton...................9 K3
Iwerne Minster.................9 K3
Ixworth........................38 E3
Ixworth Thorpe.................38 E3

J

Jack Hill......................62 F4
Jackstown.....................101 G5
Jackton........................78 C4
Jacobstow......................4 B2
Jacobstowe.....................7 F5
Jameston.......................26 E8
Jamestown, Highld..............98 C3
Jamestown, Strath..............85 F6
Jamestown, D. & G..............73 H4
Jarrow.........................75 K7
Jawcraig.......................86 B7
Jayes Park.....................12 E2
Jaywick........................23 H2
Jedburgh.......................74 C1
Jeffreyston....................26 E7
Jemimaville....................99 F2
Jevington......................13 J6
Johnby.........................67 G3
John o' Groats................115 J2
Johnshaven.....................93 J5
Johnston.......................26 D6
Johnstone......................77 K1
Johnstonebridge................73 G4
Jordans........................20 D4
Jordanston.....................26 D4
Jump...........................55 G3
Juniper Green..................79 J3
Jurby East.....................60 Q2
Jurby West.....................60 Q2

K

Kaber..........................67 K5
Kaimes.........................79 K3
Kalnakill.....................106 B6
Kames, Strath..................84 B7
Kames, Strath..................78 D7
Kea............................3 G5
Keadby.........................58 C5
Keal...........................57 H7
Keal Cotes.....................57 H7
Kearsley.......................53 J3
Kearstwick.....................61 K1
Kearton........................68 B7
Keasden........................61 L3
Keddington.....................57 H5
Kedington......................38 C6
Kedleston......................44 E3
Keelby.........................59 F6
Keele..........................43 K3
Keeley Green...................36 D6
Keeston.......................26 D6
Keevil.........................17 L5
Kegworth.......................45 F5
Kehelland......................2 E5
Keig..........................100 F7
Keighley.......................62 D5
Keilarsbrae....................86 B5
Keilhill......................101 G3
Keillmore......................83 F3
Keillor........................87 G7
Keills.........................82 D5
Keills.........................82 E5
Keinton Mandeville.............9 G1
Keir Mill......................72 D4
Keisby.........................46 D5
Keiss.........................115 J3
Keith.........................100 D3
Keithock.......................93 H5
Kelbrook.......................62 C5
Kelby..........................46 D3
Keld, N. Yks...................68 A6
Keld, Cumbr....................67 H5
Keldholme......................64 E4
Kelfield.......................63 J6
Kelham.........................45 J2
Kellan.........................89 G4
Kellas, Grampn................100 A3
Kellas, Tays...................87 H1
Kellaton.......................5 H8
Kelleth........................67 J6
Kelling........................49 F3
Kellington.....................63 J7
Kelloe.........................69 F3
Kelly..........................4 D3
Kelly Bray.....................4 D4
Kelmarsh.......................35 J3
Kelmscot.......................31 G8
Kelsale........................39 J4
Kelsall........................53 G7
Kelshall.......................37 G7
Kelso..........................80 F6
Kelsterton.....................17 J4
Kelstneyburn...................91 J7
Kelton.........................68 B4
Kelton Hill or
  Rhonehouse..................72 C8
Kelty..........................86 E5
Kelvedon.......................22 E2
Kelvedon Hatch.................21 K4
Kelynack.......................2 B7
Kemacott.......................7 G1
Kemback........................87 H3
Kemberton......................43 J7
Kemble.........................30 D8
Kemerton.......................33 J7
Kemeys Commander...............29 H7
Kemnay........................101 G7
Kempley........................30 A5
Kempley Green..................30 A5
Kempsey........................33 H6
Kempsford......................31 F8
Kempston.......................36 D6
Kempston Hardwick..............36 D6
Kempton........................32 C2
Kemp Town......................13 G6
Kemsing........................21 K8
Kemnardington..................15 F5
Kenchester.....................29 J3
Kencot.........................31 G7
Kendal.........................67 H7
Kenfig.........................25 G6
Kenfig Hill....................25 G6
Kenilworth.....................34 D3
Kenley, Shrops.................43 G7
Kenley, G. Lon.................21 H8
Kenmore, Highld...............106 C6
Kenmore, Tays..................91 J7
Kenn, Avon.....................16 F4
Kenn, Devon....................5 K3
Kennerleigh....................7 J5
Kennet.........................86 C5
Kennethmont...................100 E6
Kennett........................38 C4
Kenninghall....................38 F2
Kennington, Kent...............15 G4
Kennington, Oxon...............31 K7
Kennoway.......................87 G4
Kenny Hill.....................38 B3
Kennythorpe....................64 E6
Kenovay........................88 A4
Kensaleyre....................103 F3
Kensington.....................21 G6
Kensworth......................20 E2
Kentallen......................90 D4
Kentchurch.....................29 J5
Kentford.......................38 C4
Kentisbeare....................8 B4
Kentisbury.....................7 G1
Kentmere.......................67 G6
Kenton, G. Lon.................21 F5
Kenton, Suff...................39 G4
Kenton, Devon..................5 K3
Kentra.........................89 H2
Kents Bank.....................61 G2
Kent's Green...................30 B5

Kent's Oak.....................10 E2
Kenwick........................42 F4
Kenwyn.........................3 G5
Kenyon.........................53 H4
Keoldale......................112 E2
Keose.........................111 H5
Keppoch........................96 D3
Kepwick........................69 G7
Keresley.......................34 E2
Kerne Bridge...................29 K6
Kerridge.......................53 L6
Kerris.........................2 C7
Kerry..........................32 A1
Kerrycroy......................77 G1
Kerrysdale....................106 D4
Kersall........................56 B7
Kersey.........................38 F6
Kershader.....................111 H5
Kershopefoot...................73 K5
Kersoe.........................34 A6
Kerswell.......................8 B4
Kerswell Green.................33 H6
Kesgrave.......................39 H6
Kessingland....................39 L2
Kestle Mill....................3 G4
Keston.........................21 J7
Keswick, Cumbr.................66 E4
Keswick, Norf..................49 H7
Keswick, Norf..................49 J4
Kettering......................36 B3
Ketteringham...................49 G7
Kettins........................92 D8
Kettlebaston...................38 E5
Kettlebrook....................44 D7
Kettleburgh....................39 H4
Kettleness.....................69 L5
Kettleshulme...................54 C6
Kettlesing Bottom..............63 F4
Kettlestone....................48 E4
Kettlethorpe...................56 C6
Kettletoft....................117 F3
Kettlewell.....................62 C2
Ketton.........................46 C1
Kew............................21 F6
Kewstoke.......................16 E4
Kexbrough......................55 G3
Kexby, Lincs...................56 C5
Kexby, N. Yks..................64 E7
Key Green......................53 K7
Keyham.........................45 H7
Keyhaven.......................10 E5
Keyingham......................59 G4
Keymer.........................13 G5
Keynsham.......................17 H4
Keysoe.........................36 D4
Keysoe Row.....................36 D4
Keyston........................36 D3
Keyworth.......................45 H4
Kibblesworth...................68 E1
Kibworth Beauchamp............45 H8
Kibworth Harcourt.............45 H8
Kidbrooke......................21 J6
Kiddemore Green................43 K7
Kidderminster..................33 H3
Kiddington.....................31 J5
Kidlington.....................31 J6
Kidmore End....................20 A6
Kidsgrove......................43 K2
Kidstones......................62 C1
Kidwelly.......................27 J7
Kielder........................74 C4
Kiells.........................82 D5
Kilbarchan.....................77 K1
Kilbeg.........................96 B5
Kilberry.......................76 C1
Kilbirnie......................77 J2
Kilbride, Strath...............84 A2
Kilbride, Highld...............96 A3
Kilbride, W. Isles.............94 C4
Kilburn, Derby.................44 E3
Kilburn, N. Yks................63 J2
Kilby..........................45 H8
Kilchattan.....................82 C2
Kilchattan Bay.................77 G2
Kilchenzie.....................76 B5
Kilchiaran.....................82 B5
Kilchoan.......................89 F2
Kilchrenan.....................84 C2
Kilconquhar....................87 H4
Kilcot.........................30 A5
Kilcoy.........................98 D3
Kilcreggan.....................84 E6
Kildale........................69 J6
Kildalloig.....................76 C6
Kildary.......................109 F6
Kildonan.......................76 F5
Kildonnan......................95 K7
Kildrummy.....................100 D7
Kildwick.......................62 D5
Kilfinan.......................84 B7
Kilfinnan......................90 D2
Kilgetty.......................26 F7
Kilgwrrwg Common...............29 J8
Kilham, Northum................81 G6
Kilham, Humbs..................65 H6
Kilkenneth.....................88 A4
Kilkhampton....................6 C4
Killamarsh.....................55 H5
Killay.........................24 E5
Killchianaig...................83 F3
Killean........................76 B3
Killearn.......................85 H6
Killen.........................98 E3
Killerby.......................68 D5
Killichonan....................91 G6
Killiechonate..................90 D3
Killiecrankie..................89 G4
Killiecrankie..................91 L5
Killiemor......................89 F5
Killilan.......................96 E2
Killimster....................115 J4
Killin.........................85 H1
Killinghall....................63 F4

Killingholme...................59 F5
Killington.....................61 K1
Killochyett....................80 C5
Killundine.....................89 G4
Kilmacolm......................77 J1
Kilmahumaig....................83 G2
Kilmaluag.....................103 F1
Kilmany........................87 G2
Kilmarie......................103 G7
Kilmarnock.....................77 K4
Kilmartin......................83 H2
Kilmaurs.......................77 K3
Kilmelford.....................89 K7
Kilmeny........................82 C5
Kilmersdon.....................17 H5
Kilmeston......................11 G2
Kilmichael Glassary............84 A3
Kilmichael of Inverlussa.......83 G3
Kilmington, Devon..............8 D5
Kilmington, Wilts..............9 J1
Kilmonivaig....................90 C3
Kilmorack......................98 C4
Kilmore........................96 B5
Kilmory, Strath................76 E5
Kilmory, Highld................89 G1
Kilmory, Strath................83 G4
Kilmuir, Highld...............102 D4
Kilmuir, Highld...............102 E1
Kilmuir, Highld................98 E4
Kilmuir, Highld...............109 F6
Kilnave........................82 B4
Kilncadzow.....................79 F5
Kilndown.......................13 L3
Kilnhurst......................55 H4
Kilninian......................88 F4
Kilninver......................89 K6
Kiln Pit Hill..................68 C1
Kilnsea........................59 J5
Kilnsey........................62 C3
Kilnwik........................65 G8
Kiloran........................82 C2
Kilpatrick.....................76 E5
Kilpeck........................29 J4
Kilpheder......................94 C4
Kilphedir.....................109 H2
Kilpin.........................58 B4
Kilrenny.......................87 J4
Kilsby.........................35 G3
Kilspindie.....................87 F2
Kilsyth........................85 K7
Kiltarlilty....................98 D4
Kilton.........................16 C6
Kilvaxter.....................102 E2
Kilve..........................16 C6
Kilvington.....................45 K3
Kilwinning.....................77 J3
Kimberley, Norf................48 F7
Kimberley, Notts...............45 G3
Kimble.........................20 C2
Kimblesworth...................68 E2
Kimble Wick....................20 C3
Kimbolton, Cambs...............36 D4
Kimbolton, H. & W..............32 E4
Kimcote........................35 G2
Kimmeridge.....................9 L7
Kimmerston.....................81 H6
Kimpton, Wilts.................18 D6
Kimpton, Herts.................21 F2
Kinbrace......................114 D6
Kinbuck........................85 K4
Kincaple.......................87 H3
Kincardine, Fife...............86 C6
Kincardine, Highld............108 D1
Kincardine O'Neil..............93 G2
Kincorth......................101 J8
Kincraig.......................99 G8
Kineton, Warw..................34 E5
Kineton, Glos..................30 E5
Kinfauns.......................86 E2
Kingarth.......................77 F2
Kingcoed.......................29 J7
Kingforth......................58 E5
Kingham........................31 G5
Kingholm Quay..................72 G6
Kinghorn.......................87 F6
Kinglassie.....................86 E5
Kingoodie......................87 G2
King's Acre....................29 J3
Kingsand.......................4 E6
Kingsbarns.....................87 J3
Kingsbridge, Devon.............5 H7
Kingsbridge, Somer.............7 K2
King's Bromley.................44 C6
Kingsburgh....................103 E3
Kingsbury, Warw................44 D8
Kingsbury, G. Lon..............21 F5
Kingsbury Episcopi.............9 F2
King's Caple...................29 K5
Kingsclere.....................19 G5
King's Cliffe..................46 D8
Kingscote......................17 K1
King's Coughton................34 B5
Kingscross.....................76 F5
Kingsdon.......................9 G2
Kingsdown......................15 K3
Kingseat.......................86 E5
Kingsey........................20 B3
Kingsfold......................12 E3
Kingsford......................33 H2
Kingshall Street...............38 E4
King's Heath...................34 B2
Kingskerswell..................5 J5
Kingskettle....................87 G4
Kingsland......................32 D4
Kings Langley..................20 E3
Kingsley, Staffs...............44 B3
Kingsley, Ches.................53 G6
Kingsley, Hants................11 J7
Kingsley Green.................11 K1
King's Lynn....................48 B6
King's Meaburn.................67 J3
Kingsmuir, Tays................93 F7
Kings Muir, Border.............79 K3
Kingsnorth, Kent...............14 E1

Kingsnorth, Kent 15 G5
Kilmichael Glassary 84 A5
Kilmichael of Inverlussa 83 G3
Kilmington, Devon 8 D5
Kilmington, Wilts 9 J1
Kilmonivaig 90 C3
Kilmorack 98 C4
Kilmore 96 B5
Kilmory, Strath 76 E5
Kilmory, Highld 89 G1
Kilmory, Strath 83 G4
Kilmuir, Highld 102 D4
Kilmuir, Highld 102 E1
Kilmuir, Highld 98 E4
Kilmuir, Highld 109 F6
Kilnave 82 B4
Kilncadzow 79 F5
Kilndown 13 L3
Kilnhurst 55 H4
Kilninian 88 F4
Kilninver 89 K6
Kiln Pit Hill 68 C1
Kilnsea 59 J5
Kilnsey 62 C3
Kilnwick 65 G8
Kiloran 82 C2
Kilpatrick 76 E5
Kilpeck 29 J4
Kilpheder 94 C4
Kilphedir 109 H2
Kilpin 58 B4
Kilrenny 87 J4
Kilsby 35 G3
Kilspindie 87 F2
Kilsyth 85 K7
Kiltarlity 98 D4
Kilton 16 C6
Kilvaxter 102 E2
Kilve 16 C6
Kilvington 45 K3
Kilwinning 77 J3
Kimberley, Norf 48 F7
Kimberley, Notts 45 G3
Kimble 20 C3
Kimblesworth 68 E2
Kimble Wick 20 C3
Kimbolton, Cambs 36 D4
Kimbolton, H. & W 32 E4
Kimcote 35 G2
Kimmeridge 9 L7
Kimmerston 81 H6
Kimpton, Wilts 18 D6
Kimpton, Herts 21 F2
Kinbrace 114 D6
Kinbuck 85 K4
Kincaple 87 H3
Kincardine, Fife 86 C6
Kincardine, Highld 108 E5
Kincardine O'Neil 93 G2
Kincorth 101 J8
Kincraig 99 G8
Kineton, Warw 34 E5
Kineton, Glos 30 E5
Kinfauns 86 E2
Kingarth 77 F2
Kingcoed 29 J7
Kingforth 58 E5
Kingham 31 G5
Kingholm Quay 72 E6
Kinghorn 87 F6
Kinglassie 87 F5
Kingoodie 87 G2
King's Acre 29 J3
Kingsand 4 E6
Kingsbarns 87 J3
Kingsbridge, Devon 5 H7
Kingsbridge, Somer 7 K2
King's Bromley 44 C6
Kingsburgh 103 E3
Kingsbury, Warw 44 D8
Kingsbury, G. Lon 21 F5
Kingsbury Episcopi 9 F2
King's Caple 29 K5
Kingsclere 19 G5
King's Cliffe 46 D8
Kingscote 17 K1
Kingscott 7 F4
King's Coughton 34 B5
Kingscross 76 F5
Kingsdon 9 G2
Kingsdown 15 K4
Kingseat 86 E5
Kingsey 20 B3
Kingsfold 12 E3
Kingsford 33 H2
Kingshall Street 38 E4
King's Heath 34 B2
Kingskerswell 5 J5
Kingskettle 87 G4
Kingsland 32 D4
Kings Langley 20 E3
Kingsley, Staffs 44 B3
Kingsley, Ches. 53 G6
Kingsley, Hants 19 J7
Kingsley Green 11 K1
King's Lynn 48 B6
King's Meaburn 67 J4
Kingsmuir, Tays 93 F7
Kings Muir, Border 79 K6
Kingsnorth, Kent 14 E1
Kingsnorth, Kent 15 G5
King's Norton, W. Mids 34 B3
King's Norton, Leic 45 H7
King's Nympton 7 G4
King's Pyon 29 J2
Kings Ripton 37 F3
King's Somborne 10 E1
King's Stag 9 J3
King's Stanley 30 C7
Kings Sutton 35 F7
Kingstanding 44 B8
Kingsteignton 5 J4
King Sterndale 54 D6
Kingsthorne 29 J4
Kingsthorpe 35 J4

Kingston, Grampn 100 C2
Kingston, Hants 10 C4
Kingston, I. of W 11 F6
Kingston, Cambs 37 G5
Kingston, Devon 5 G7
Kingston, Kent 15 H3
Kingston, Dorset 9 J4
Kingston, Lothn 87 J6
Kingston Bagpuize 31 J8
Kingston Blount 20 B4
Kingston by Sea 12 F6
Kingston Deverill 9 K1
Kingstone, Staffs 44 B5
Kingstone, Somer 8 E3
Kingstone, H. & W 29 J4
Kingston, Dorset 10 a7
Kingston Lisle 18 E2
Kingston near Lewes 1 G6
Kingston on Soar 45 G5
Kingston Seymour 16 F4
Kingston St Mary 8 D2
Kingston upon Hull 59 E4
Kingston upon Thames 21 F7
Kingstown 73 J8
King's Walden 21 F1
Kingswear 5 J6
Kingswells 101 H8
Kingswinford 33 H2
Kingswood, Bucks 20 A2
Kingswood, Warw 34 C3
Kingswood, Powys 42 D7
Kingswood, Kent 14 E3
Kingswood, Surrey 12 F1
Kingswood, H. & W 29 G2
Kingswood, Avon 17 H3
Kingswood, Glos 17 J1
King's Worthy 11 F1
Kington, H. & W 34 A3
Kington, Powys 29 H2
Kington Langley 17 L3
Kington Magna 9 J2
Kington St Michael 17 L3
Kingussie 91 J1
Kingweston 9 G1
Kinharrachie 101 J5
Kinknockie 101 K4
Kinlet 33 G2
Kinloch, Highld 96 B4
Kinloch, Tays 92 C7
Kinloch, Highld 112 E5
Kinloch, Highld 95 K6
Kinlochard 85 G4
Kinlochbervie 112 D3
Kinlocheil 90 A4
Kinlochewe 106 F5
Kinloch Hourn 96 E5
Kinloch Laggan 91 G3
Kinlochleven 90 C5
Kinlochmore 90 C5
Kinloch Rannoch 91 H6
Kinlochspelve 89 H6
Kinloss 99 J2
Kinmel Bay 51 J2
Kinmuck 101 H7
Kinmundy 101 H7
Kinnadie 101 J4
Kinnaird 87 F2
Kinnell 93 H6
Kinnerley 42 E5
Kinnersley, H. & W 29 H3
Kinnersley, H. & W 33 H6
Kinnerton, Powys 32 B4
Kinnerton, Clwyd 52 E7
Kinnesswood 86 E4
Kinninvie 68 C4
Kinoulton 45 H4
Kinross 86 E4
Kinrossie 86 E1
Kinsham 32 C4
Kinsley 55 H2
Kintarvie 111 G6
Kintbury 18 E4
Kintessack 99 J2
Kintillo 86 E3
Kintocher 100 E8
Kintore 101 G7
Kintour 82 D6
Kinuachdrachd 83 G2
Kinveachy 99 H7
Kinver 33 H2
Kippax 63 H6
Kippen 85 J5
Kippford or Scaur 71 K6
Kirbister 116 C6
Kirbuster 116 B4
Kirby Bedon 49 H7
Kirby Bellars 45 J6
Kirby Cane 49 J8
Kirby Cross 23 J1
Kirby Grindalythe 65 G6
Kirby Hill, N. Yks 68 D6
Kirby Hill, N. Yks 63 G3
Kirby Knowle 63 H1
Kirby-le-Soken 23 J1
Kirby Mills 64 E4
Kirby Misperton 64 E5
Kirby Muxloe 45 G7
Kirby Row 39 J1
Kirby Sigston 69 G7
Kirby Underdale 64 F7
Kirby Wiske 63 G1
Kirdford 12 D4
Kirivick 111 H4
Kirk 115 H3
Kirkandrews-on-Eden 73 J8
Kirkbampton 66 F1
Kirkbean 72 E8
Kirk Bramwith 55 K2
Kirkbride 66 E1
Kirkbuddo 93 G7
Kirkburn 65 G2
Kirkburton 54 E2
Kirkby, Lincs 56 E4
Kirkby, Mers 52 F4
Kirkby, N. Yks 69 H6

Kirkby Fleetham 68 E7
Kirkby Green 56 E8
Kirkby in Ashfield 45 G2
Kirkby-in-Furness 60 F1
Kirkby la Thorpe 46 D3
Kirkby Lonsdale 61 K2
Kirkby Malham 62 B3
Kirkby Mallory 45 F7
Kirkby Malzeard 63 F2
Kirkby Mills 64 E4
Kirkbymoorside 64 D4
Kirkby on Bain 57 G7
Kirkby Overblow 63 G5
Kirkby Stephen 67 K6
Kirkby Thore 67 J4
Kirkby Underwood 46 D5
Kirkcaldy 87 F5
Kirkcambeck 74 B7
Kirkcarswell 71 J7
Kirkcolm 70 B5
Kirkconnel 72 C2
Kirkcowan 70 E5
Kirkcudbright 71 H6
Kirk Deighton 63 G4
Kirk Ella 58 E4
Kirkfieldbank 79 F5
Kirkgunzeon 72 D7
Kirkham, N. Yks 64 E6
Kirkham, Lancs 61 H6
Kirkhamgate 63 F7
Kirk Hammerton 63 H4
Kirkharle 75 G5
Kirkheaton, W. Yks 54 E2
Kirkheaton, Northum 75 G6
Kirkhill, Highld 98 D4
Kirkhill, Tays 93 H5
Kirkhope 80 B7
Kirkhouse 80 B6
Kirkibost, Highld 96 A4
Kirkibost, W. Isles 111 F4
Kirkinner 71 F6
Kirkintilloch 85 J7
Kirkireton 44 D2
Kirkland, D. & G 72 C2
Kirkland, Cumbr 66 C5
Kirkland, D. & G 72 D4
Kirkland, Cumbr 67 J3
Kirk Langley 44 D4
Kirkleatham 69 H4
Kirklevington 69 G6
Kirkley 39 L1
Kirklington, N. Yks 63 G1
Kirklington, Notts 55 K8
Kirklinton 73 K7
Kirkliston 86 E7
Kirk Merrington 68 E3
Kirkmichael, Tays 92 B5
Kirkmichael, Strath 77 J7
Kirk Michael, I. of M 60 Q2
Kirkmond le Mire 57 F4
Kirknewton, Northum 81 H6
Kirknewton, Lothn 79 J3
Kirk of Shotts 79 F3
Kirkoswald, Cumbr 67 H2
Kirkoswald, Strath 77 H7
Kirkpatrick Durham 72 C6
Kirkpatrick-Fleming 73 H6
Kirk Sandall 55 K3
Kirksanton 60 E1
Kirk Smeaton 55 J2
Kirkstile 100 E5
Kirkton, Border 74 B2
Kirkton, Highld 96 D3
Kirkton, D. & G 72 E5
Kirkton, Highld 106 E7
Kirkton, Grampn 101 F3
Kirkton, Highld 109 F4
Kirkton, Grampn 100 F6
Kirkton, Tays 92 F7
Kirkton, Fife 87 G2
Kirkton, Strath 79 G7
Kirkton, Grampn 101 L3
Kirkton Manor 79 J5
Kirkton of Auchterhouse 92 E8
Kirkton of Auchterless 101 G4
Kirkton of Barevan 99 G4
Kirkton of Bourtie 101 H6
Kirkto of Collace 87 E1
Kirkton of Craig 93 J6
Kirkton of Culsalmond 100 F5
Kirkton of Durris 93 J2
Kirkton of Glenbuchat 100 C7
Kirkton of Glenisla 92 D5
Kirkton of Kingoldrum 92 E6
Kirkton of Largo 87 H4
Kirkton of Lethendy 92 C7
Kirkton of Logie Buchan 101 J6
Kirkton of Maryculter 93 K2
Kirkton of Menmuir 93 G5
Kirkton of Monikie 93 G8
Kirkton of Rayne 101 F5
Kirkton of Skene 101 H8
Kirkton of Strathmartine 87 G1
Kirkton of Tough 100 F7
Kirktown 101 K3
Kirktown of Alvah 100 F4
Kirktown of Bourtie 101 H6
Kirktown of Deskford 100 E2
Kirktown of Fetteresso 93 K3
Kirkwall 116 D5
Kirkwhelpington 75 F5
Kirk Yetholm 81 G7
Kirmington 59 F5
Kirmond le Mire 57 F4
Kirn 84 D7
Kirriemuir 92 E6
Kirstead Green 49 H8
Kirtlebridge 73 H7
Kirtling 38 B5
Kirtling Green 38 B5
Kirtlington 31 K6
Kirtomy 114 C3
Kirton, Notts 56 A7

Kirton, Lincs 47 G4
Kirton, Suff 39 H7
Kirton End 47 F3
Kirton Holme 47 F3
Kirton in Lindsey 58 D7
Kislingbury 35 H5
Kites Hardwick 35 F4
Kittybrewster 101 J8
Kitwood 11 H1
Kiveton Park 55 H5
Knaith 56 C5
Knaphill 20 D8
Knapp 8 E2
Knapton, N. Yks 65 F5
Knapton, Norf 49 J4
Knapton, N. Yks 63 J4
Knaptoft 37 G4
Knapwell 37 G4
Knaresborough 63 G4
Knarsdale 67 J1
Knaven 101 H4
Knayton 63 H1
Knebworth 21 G1
Kneesall 55 K7
Kneesworth 37 G6
Kneeton 45 J3
Knelston 24 C6
Knenhall 40 A2
Knightacott 7 G2
Knightcote 34 E5
Knighton, Powys 32 B3
Knighton, Devon 5 F7
Knighton, Leic 45 H7
Knighton, Staffs 43 J5
Knighton, Staffs 53 J7
Knightwick 33 G5
Knill 29 G1
Knipton 46 B4
Kniveton 44 D2
Knock, Grampn 100 E3
Knock, Strath 89 G5
Knock, W. Isles 111 J4
Knock, Cumbr 67 J4
Knockally 115 G7
Knockan 112 D7
Knockandhu 100 B6
Knockando 100 A4
Knockbain 98 E3
Knockbrex 71 G7
Knock Castle 77 G1
Knockdee 115 G3
Knockenkelly 76 F5
Knockentiber 77 J4
Knockholt 21 J8
Knockholt Pound 21 J8
Knockin 42 E5
Knocknaha 76 B6
Knockrome 82 E4
Knocksharry 60 P3
Knodishall 39 K4
Knolls Green 53 K6
Knolton 42 E4
Knook 18 A6
Knossington 45 K7
Knott End-on-Sea 61 G5
Knotting 36 D4
Knottingley 63 H7
Knotty Green 20 D4
Knowbury 32 E3
Knowehead 72 B4
Knowesgate 75 F5
Knoweside 77 H6
Knowes of Elrick 100 F3
Knowetownhead 74 B2
Knowle, W. Mids 34 C3
Knowle, Devon 6 E2
Knowle, Shrops 33 E3
Knowle, Avon 17 H3
Knowle, Devon 7 H5
Knowle Green 61 K6
Knowl Hill 20 C6
Knowlton 15 J3
Knowsley 52 F4
Knowsley Hall 52 F4
Knowstone 7 J3
Knucklas 32 B3
Knutsford 53 J6
Knypersley 43 K2
Kuggar 2 F8
Kyleakin 96 C3
Kyle of Lochalsh 96 C3
Kylerhea 96 C3
Kylesmorar 96 D6
Kyles Scalpay 105 H2
Kyles Stockinish 105 G2
Kylestrome 112 D5
Kyloe 81 J5
Kynnersley 43 H6
Kyre Park 33 G4

L

Labost 111 G3
Laceby 59 G6
Lacey Green 20 C3
Lach Dennis 53 J6
Lackie 52 E7
Lackalee 105 G2
Lackford 38 C3
Lacock 17 L4
Ladbroke 34 F5
Ladock 3 G4
Ladybank 87 G4
Ladykirk 81 G5
Ladysford 101 J2
Lagavulin 82 D7
Lagg, Strath 82 E4
Lagg, Strath 76 E5
Laggan, Highld 90 D2
Laggan, Highld 91 H2

Lagganulva 89 F4
Laide 106 E2
Lair 106 F7
Lairg 108 D3
Lairgmore 98 D5
Lake 18 C7
Lakenham 49 H7
Lakenheath 38 C2
Lakesend 47 J8
Lakeside 61 G1
Laleham 20 E7
Laleston 25 G7
Lamarsh 38 D7
Lamas 49 H5
Lambden 80 F5
Lamberhurst 13 K3
Lamberton 81 H4
Lambeth 21 H6
Lambfell Moar 60 P3
Lambley, Northum 74 C8
Lambley, Notts 45 H3
Lambourn 18 E3
Lambourne End 21 J4
Lambs Green 12 F3
Lambston 26 D6
Lamerton 4 E4
Lamesley 75 J8
Lamington, Highld 109 F6
Lamington, Strath 79 G6
Lamlash 76 F4
Lamonby 67 G3
Lamorna 2 C7
Lamorran 3 G5
Lampeter 27 K3
Lampeter Velfry 26 F6
Lamphey 26 E7
Lamplugh 66 C4
Lamport 35 J3
Lamyatt 9 H1
Lana 4 D2
Lanark 79 F5
Lancaster 61 H3
Lanchester 68 D2
Landbeach 37 H4
Landcross 6 E3
Landerberry 101 G8
Landford 10 D3
Landimore 24 C5
Landkey 7 F2
Landore 24 E5
Landrake 4 D5
Landscove 5 H5
Landshipping 26 E6
Landulph 4 E5
Landwade 38 B4
Landywood 44 A7
Laneast 4 C3
Lane End 20 C4
Lane Green 44 A7
Laneham 56 C6
Laneshaw Bridge 62 C5
Langar 45 J4
Langbank 85 F7
Langbar 62 D4
Langcliffe 62 B3
Langdale End 65 G3
Langdon Beck 67 L3
Langdon Hills 22 C5
Langenhoe 23 G2
Langford, Devon 8 B4
Langford, Notts 56 C8
Langford, Essex 22 E3
Langford, Beds 36 E6
Langford, Oxon 31 G7
Langford Budville 8 C2
Langham, Leic 46 B6
Langham, Suff 38 E4
Langham, Norf 48 F3
Langham, Essex 38 F7
Langho 61 L6
Langholm 73 J5
Langleeford 81 H7
Langley, Warw 34 C4
Langley, Kent 14 E3
Langley, Berks 20 E6
Langley, Hants 11 F4
Langley, Herts 21 G1
Langley, Essex 37 H7
Langley, W. Susx 11 K2
Langley, Chs 53 L6
Langley Burrell 18 A3
Langley Marsh 8 B2
Langley Park 68 E2
Langley Street 49 J7
Langney 13 K6
Langold 55 J5
Langore 4 D3
Langport 9 F2
Langrick 47 F3
Langridge 17 J4
Langrigg 66 D2
Langrish 11 J2
Langsett 54 F3
Langshaw 80 D6
Langstone 11 J4
Langthorne 68 E7
Langthorpe 63 G3
Langthwaite 68 C4
Langtoft, Lincs 46 E6
Langtoft, Humbs 65 H6
Langton, Durham 68 D5
Langton, N. Yks 64 E6
Langton, Lincs 57 G7
Langton, Lincs 57 H6
Langton by Wragby 57 F6
Langton Green 13 J3
Langton Herring 9 H6
Langton Matravers 10 B7
Langtree 6 E4
Langwathby 67 H3
Langwith 55 J7
Langwith Junction 55 J7
Langworth 56 E6

Lanlivery 3 J4
Lanner 2 F6
Lanreath 3 K4
Lansallos 3 K4
Lanton, Border 80 E7
Lanton, Northum 81 H6
Lapford 7 H5
Laphroaig 82 C7
Lapley 43 K6
Lapworth 34 C3
Larbert 86 B6
Largie 100 F5
Largoward 87 H4
Largs 77 H2
Largybeg 76 F5
Largymore 76 F5
Larkfield 84 E7
Larkhall 78 E4
Larkhill 18 C6
Larling 38 E2
Larriston 74 B4
Lartington 68 C5
Lary 92 E1
Lasham 19 H6
Laskentyre 105 F2
Lassodie 86 E5
Lastingham 64 E3
Latchingdon 22 E3
Latchley 4 E4
Lately Common 53 H4
Lathbury 36 B6
Latheron 115 H6
Latheronwheel 115 G6
Lathones 87 H4
Latimer 20 E4
Latteridge 17 H2
Lattiford 9 H2
Latton 30 E8
Lauchintilly 101 G7
Lauder 80 D5
Laugharne 27 H6
Laughterton 56 C6
Laughton, Lincs 56 C4
Laughton, Leic 35 G4
Laughton, E. Susx 13 J5
Laughton-en-le-Morthen 55 J5
Launcells 6 C5
Launceston 4 D3
Launde Abbey 45 J7
Launton 31 L5
Laurencekirk 93 J4
Laurieston 72 B7
Lavant 11 K4
Lavendon 36 C5
Lavenham 38 E6
Laverhay 73 G4
Laverstock 10 C1
Laverstoke 19 F6
Laverton, Glos 30 E4
Laverton, N. Yks 63 F2
Laverton, Somer 17 J5
Law 79 F4
Lawers 91 H8
Lawford 39 F7
Lawhitton 4 D3
Lawkland 62 A3
Lawley 43 H7
Lawnhead 43 K5
Lawrenny 26 E7
Lawshall 38 D6
Lawton 29 J2
Laxay 111 H5
Laxdale 111 J4
Laxey 60 R3
Laxfield 39 H3
Laxfirth 119 G4
Laxo 119 G2
Laxobigging 121 G5
Laxton, Humbs 58 B4
Laxton, Notts 56 B7
Laxton, Northnts 46 C8
Laycock 62 D5
Layer Breton 22 F2
Layer de la Haye 23 F1
Layham 38 F6
Laytham 58 B3
Lazenby 69 H5
Lazonby 67 H3
Lea, Wilts 18 A2
Lea, H. & W 30 A5
Lea, Shrops 32 C2
Lea, Lincs 56 C5
Lea, Shrops 42 F7
Lea, Derby 55 G8
Leac Eskadale 105 H2
Leachkin 98 E4
Leadburn 79 K4
Leadenham 46 C2
Leaden Roding 22 B2
Leadgate, Durham 68 D1
Leadgate, Cumbr 67 K2
Leadhills 72 D2
Leafield 31 H6
Leagrave 20 E1
Leake Commonside 47 G2
Leake Hurn's End 47 H3
Lealholm 64 E2
Lealt, Strath 83 F2
Lealt, Highld 103 G2
Lea Marston 44 D8
Leamington Hastings 35 F4
Leamington Spa, Royal 34 E4
Leargybreck 82 E4
Learmouth 81 G6
Leasgill 61 H1
Leask 101 K5
Leatherhead 12 E1
Leathley 63 F5
Leaton 42 F6
Lea Town 61 H6
Leaveland 15 G3
Leavenheath 38 E7
Leavening 64 E6
Leaves Green 21 J7

Lebberston................65 H4
Lechlade................31 G8
Leckford................10 E1
Leckfurin................113 J3
Leckhampstead, Berks.....18 F3
Leckhampstead, Bucks.....35 J7
Leckhampton................30 D6
Leckmelm................107 G2
Leckwith................25 K7
Leconfield................58 E2
Ledaig................89 L5
Ledburn................20 D1
Ledbury................33 G7
Ledgemoor................29 J2
Ledicot................32 D4
Ledmore................112 D7
Lednagullin................114 D3
Ledsham, Ches.............52 E6
Ledsham, W. Yks...........63 H7
Ledston................63 H7
Ledwell................31 J5
Lee, Devon................6 E1
Lee, Hants................10 E3
Lee, Shrops................42 F4
Lee, Strath................88 F6
Lee, Lancs................61 J4
Leebotten................119 G6
Leebotwood................43 F8
Lee Brockhurst............43 G5
Leece................60 F3
Lee Clump................20 D3
Leeds, Kent................14 E3
Leeds, N. Yks.............63 G6
Leedstown................2 E6
Leek................44 A2
Leekhampstead............18 F3
Leek Wootton................34 D4
Lee Mill................5 F6
Leeming................68 E8
Leeming Bar................68 E7
Lee Moor................5 F5
Lee-on-the-Solent.........11 G4
Lees, G. Man................54 C3
Lees, Derby................44 D4
Leeswood................52 D7
Lee, Th.................20 D3
Legbourne................57 H5
Legburthwaite............66 F5
Legerwood................80 D5
Legsby................57 F5
Leicester................45 G7
Leicester Forest East.....45 G7
Leigh, Wilts................18 B1
Leigh, Shrops................42 E7
Leigh, Surrey................12 F2
Leigh, H. & W................33 G5
Leigh, G. Man................53 H3
Leigh, Dorset................9 H4
Leigh, Kent................13 J2
Leigh Beck................22 E5
Leigh Delamere............17 K3
Leigh Green................14 F5
Leigh-on-Sea................22 E5
Leigh Sinton................33 G5
Leighterton................17 K1
Leigh, The................30 C5
Leighton, Powys............42 D7
Leighton, Shrops...........43 H7
Leighton, Somer............17 J6
Leighton Bromswold........36 E3
Leighton Buzzard..........36 C8
Leigh upon Mendip.........17 H6
Leigh Woods................17 G3
Leinthall Earls............32 D4
Leinthall Starkes.........32 D4
Leintwardine................32 D3
Leire................35 G1
Leirinmore................113 F2
Leiston................39 K4
Leith................87 F7
Leitholm................81 F5
Lelant................2 D6
Lelley................59 G3
Lem Hill................33 G3
Lemmington Hall...........75 H2
Lempitlaw................81 F6
Lemreway................111 H6
Lendalfoot................70 C3
Lenham................14 E3
Lenham Heath................14 F4
Lenie................98 D6
Lennel................81 G5
Lennoxtown................85 J7
Lenton................46 D4
Lenwade................49 F6
Lenzie................85 J7
Leochel Cushnie...........100 E7
Leominster................29 J2
Leonard Stanley...........30 C7
Lepe................11 F5
Lephin................102 C4
Lephinmore................84 B5
Leppington................64 E6
Lepton................54 F2
Lerryn................3 K4
Lerwick................119 G4
Lesbury................75 J2
Leslie, Grampn............100 E6
Leslie, Fife................87 F4
Lesmahagow................79 F6
Lesnewth................4 B2
Lessingham................49 J5
Lessonhall................66 E1
Leswalt................70 B5
Letchmore Heath...........21 F4
Letchworth................36 F7
Letcombe Bassett..........18 E2
Letcombe Regis............18 E2
Letham, Fife................87 G3
Letham, Tays................93 G7
Lethenty................101 H4
Letheringham................39 H5
Letheringsett..............48 F4
Lettaford................5 H3
Letterewe................106 E4

Letterfearn................96 D3
Letterfinlay................90 D2
Letters................107 G3
Letterston................26 D5
Lettoch................99 K5
Letton, H. & W..............32 C3
Letton, H. & W..............29 H3
Letty Green................21 G2
Letwell................55 J5
Leuchars................87 H2
Leurbost................111 H5
Levedale................43 L6
Leven, Humbs................59 F2
Leven, Fife................87 G4
Levens................61 H1
Levenshulme................53 K4
Levenwick................119 G6
Leverburgh................104 F3
Leverington................47 H6
Leverton................47 G3
Levington................39 H7
Levisham................64 F3
Levishie................98 C7
Lew................31 H7
Lewannick................4 C3
Lewdown................4 E3
Lewes................13 H5
Leweston................26 D5
Lewisham................21 H6
Lewiston................98 D6
Lewknor................20 B4
Leworthy................7 G2
Lewtrenchard................4 E3
Ley................3 K3
Leybourne................14 C3
Leyburn................68 D7
Leycett................43 J3
Leyland................61 J7
Leylodge................101 G7
Leys................101 K3
Leysdown on Sea...........15 G1
Leysmill................93 H7
Leys of Cossans...........92 E7
Leysters................32 E4
Leyton................21 H5
Lezant................4 D4
Lhanbryde................100 B2
Lhen, The................60 Q1
Libanus................25 H2
Libberton................79 G5
Liberton................87 F7
Lichfield................44 C7
Lickey................34 A3
Lickey End................34 A3
Lickfold................12 C4
Liddington................18 D2
Lidgate................38 C5
Lidlington................36 C7
Lieurary................115 F2
Liff................87 G1
Lifton................4 D3
Lighthorne................34 E5
Lightwater................20 D7
Lightwood................43 L3
Lightwood Green...........42 E3
Likisto................105 G2
Lilbourne................35 G3
Lilburn Tower................81 J7
Lilleshall................43 J6
Lilley................36 E8
Lilliesleaf................80 D7
Lillingstone Dayrell......35 J7
Lillingstone Lovell.......35 J6
Lillington................9 H3
Lilstock................16 C6
Limbrick................53 H2
Limefield................53 K2
Limekilns................86 D6
Limerigg................86 B7
Limerstone................9 G2
Limington................9 G2
Limmerhaugh................78 D7
Limpenhoe................49 J7
Limpley Stoke................17 J4
Limpsfield................13 G1
Linby................45 G2
Linchmere................11 K1
Lincoln................56 D6
Lincomb................33 H4
Lindale................61 H1
Lindal in Furness.........60 F2
Linden................80 C6
Lindfield................13 G4
Lindford................11 K1
Lindores................87 F3
Lindridge................33 F4
Lindsell................38 B8
Lindsey................38 E6
Linford, Hants............10 C4
Linford, Essex............22 C6
Lingague................60 P4
Lingdale................69 J5
Lingen................32 C4
Lingfield................13 G2
Lingwood................49 J7
Liniclate................104 C7
Linicro................102 E2
Linkenholt................18 E5
Linkinhorne................4 C3
Linklater................115 K1
Linksness................116 E5
Linktown................87 F5
Linley................32 C1
Linley Green................33 F5
Linlithgow................86 D7
Linlithgow Bridge.........86 C7
Linshader................111 G4
Linshiels................74 E3
Linsidemore................108 D4
Linslade................36 C8
Linstead Parva............39 J3
Linstock................73 K8
Linthwaite................54 E2
Lintlaw................81 G4
Lintmill................100 E2
Linton, H. & W..............30 A5

Linton, N. Yks.............62 C3
Linton, Derby................44 C6
Linton, Border................80 F7
Linton, Cambs................37 J6
Linton, Kent................13 L2
Linton-on-Ouse.............63 H3
Linwood, Hants............10 C4
Linwood, Lincs.............57 F5
Linwood, Strath............77 K1
Lionel................111 K1
Liphook................11 K1
Liskeard................3 L3
Liss................11 J2
Lissett................65 J7
Lissington................57 F5
Lisvane................25 K6
Litcham................48 D6
Litchborough................35 H5
Litchfield................19 F5
Litherland................52 E4
Litlington, Cambs.........37 G6
Litlington, E. Susx.......13 J6
Little Abington...........37 J6
Little Addington..........36 C3
Little Alne................34 C4
Little Asby................67 J6
Little Aston................44 B7
Little Atherfield.........11 F6
Little Ayre................116 C7
Little Ayton................69 H5
Little Baddow................22 D3
Little Badminton..........17 K2
Little Bardfield..........38 B7
Little Barford............38 E5
Little Barningham.........49 G4
Little Barrington.........31 G6
Little Barugh................64 E5
Little Bealings...........39 H6
Little Bedwyn................18 D4
Little Bentley............39 G8
Little Berkhamsted........21 G3
Little Birch................29 K4
Little Blakenham..........39 G6
Littleborough, Notts......56 C5
Littleborough, G. Man.....53 L2
Littlebourne................15 J3
Little Bowden................35 J2
Little Bradley............38 B5
Little Brampton...........32 C2
Little Brechin............93 G5
Littlebredy................9 G6
Little Brickhill..........36 C7
Little Brington...........35 H4
Little Bromley............39 F8
Little Budworth...........53 G7
Little Burstead...........22 C4
Littlebury................37 J7
Littlebury Green..........37 H7
Little Bytham................46 D6
Little Carlton............57 J5
Little Casterton..........46 D7
Little Cawthorpe..........57 H5
Little Chalfont...........20 D4
Little Chart................14 F4
Little Chesterford........37 J6
Little Cheverell..........18 A5
Little Chishill...........37 H7
Little Clacton................23 H2
Little Comberton..........34 A6
Little Common................13 L6
Little Compton................31 G4
Little Cowarne................29 L2
Little Coxwell............31 G8
Little Cressingham........48 D7
Little Dalby................45 J6
Littledean................30 A6
Little Dens................101 K4
Little Dewchurch..........29 K4
Little Downham............37 J2
Little Dunham................48 D6
Little Dunkeld............92 B7
Little Dunmow................22 C1
Little Easton................22 C1
Little Eaton................44 E3
Little Ellingham..........48 F8
Little End................21 K3
Little Eversden...........37 G5
Little Fakenham...........38 D3
Little Faringdon..........31 G7
Little Fenton................63 J6
Littleferry................109 G4
Little Fransham...........48 E6
Little Gaddesden..........20 D2
Little Gidding............36 E2
Little Glemham............39 J5
Little Gransden...........37 F5
Little Gruinard...........106 E3
Little Habton................64 E5
Little Hadham................21 J1
Little Hallingbury........21 K2
Littleham, Devon..........8 B6
Littleham, Devon..........6 E3
Little Hampden................20 C3
Littlehampton................12 D6
Little Harrowden..........36 B3
Little Haseley................20 3
Little Hautbois...........49 H5
Little Haven................26 C6
Little Hay................44 C7
Little Haywood............44 B5
Littlehempston................5 J5
Little Hereford...........32 E4
Little Horkesley..........38 E7
Little Horsted................13 H5
Little Horwood................35 J7
Littlehoughton, Northum...75 J2
Little Houghton, Northnts.35 K5
Little Hucklow............54 E6
Little Hulton................53 J3
Little Kingshill..........20 C4
Little Langdale...........66 F6
Little Langford...........10 B1
Little Laver................21 K3
Little Leigh................53 H6

Little Leighs................22 D2
Little Lever................53 J3
Little London, Hants......20 A8
Little London, Hants......18 A6
Little London, Lincs......47 F5
Little London, Lincs......47 G6
Little London, E. Susx....13 J5
Little Longstone..........54 E6
Little Malvern................33 G6
Little Maplestead.........38 D7
Little Marcle................33 F7
Little Marlow................20 C5
Little Massingham.........48 C5
Little Melton................49 G7
Littlemill, Highld........99 H3
Littlemill, Gwent.........29 H7
Littlemill, Strath........77 K6
Little Milton................20 A3
Little Missenden..........20 D4
Littlemore................31 K7
Little Ness................42 F6
Little Newcastle..........26 D5
Little Newsham............68 D5
Little Oakley, Northnts...36 B2
Little Oakley, Essex......39 H8
Little Orton................66 F1
Littleover................44 E4
Little Paxton................36 E4
Little Petherick.........3 H2
Little Plumstead..........49 J6
Littleport................37 J2
Little Raveley............37 F2
Little Ribston............63 G4
Little Rissington.........31 F6
Little Ryburgh............48 E5
Little Ryle................75 G2
Little Salkeld............67 H3
Little Sampford...........38 B7
Little Saxham................38 C4
Little Scatwell...........98 B3
Little Shelford...........37 H5
Little Singleton.........32 A4
Little Smeaton............55 J2
Little Snoring............48 E4
Little Somerford.........18 A2
Little Stainton...........69 F4
Little Stanney............52 F6
Little Staughton.........36 E4
Little Steeping...........57 J7
Littlestone-on-Sea........15 G6
Little Stonham................39 G4
Little Stretton, Shrops...32 D1
Little Stretton, Leic.....45 H7
Little Strickland.........67 H5
Little Stukeley...........36 F3
Little Tew................31 H5
Little Thetford...........37 J3
Littlethorpe................63 G3
Little Thurlow............38 B5
Little Thurrock...........22 C6
Little Torrington.........6 E4
Little Totham................22 E2
Little Town, Cumbr........66 E5
Littletown, Durham........69 F2
Little Wakering...........22 F5
Little Walden................37 J6
Little Waldingfield.......38 E6
Little Walsingham.........48 E4
Little Waltham................22 D2
Little Warley................22 C4
Little Weighton...........58 D3
Little Welnetham..........38 D4
Little Wenlock............43 H7
Little Whittingham Green..39 H3
Littlewick Green..........20 C5
Little Wilbraham..........37 J5
Little Witley................33 G4
Little Wittenham..........31 K8
Little Wolford............31 G4
Littleworth, Staffs.......44 B6
Littleworth, H. & W.......33 H5
Littleworth, Oxon.........31 H8
Little Wymondley..........36 F8
Little Wyrley................44 B7
Little Yeldham................38 C7
Litton, N. Yks.............62 C2
Litton, Derby................54 E6
Litton, Somer................17 G5
Litton Cheney................9 G5
Liverpool................52 E4
Liversedge................62 F7
Liverton................69 K5
Livingston................79 H3
Livingston Village........79 H3
Lixwm................52 C6
Lizard................2 F8
Llaber................40 F2
Llanaber................40 F2
Llanaelhaearn................50 C6
Llanafan................41 F6
Llanafan-fawr................28 D2
Llanallgo................50 E2
Llanarmon................50 D7
Llanarmon Dyffryn
  Ceiriog................42 C4
Llanarmon-yn-Ial..........42 C2
Llanarth, Gwent............29 H6
Llanarth, Dyfed............27 J2
Llanarthney................27 K5
Llanasa................51 L2
Llanbabo................50 C2
Llanbadarn Fawr...........40 F5
Llanbadarn Fynydd.........41 L6
Llanbadarn-y-garreg.......28 F3
Llanbadrig................50 C1
Llanbeder................16 E1
Llanbedr, Gwyn............40 E1
Llanbedr, Powys............28 E3
Llanbedr, Powys............29 G5
Llanbedr-Dyffryn-Clwyd....50 C8
Llanbedrgoch................50 E2

Llanbedrog................50 C7
Llanbedr-y-cennin.........51 G4
Llanberis................50 E4
Llanbethian................25 H6
Llanboidy................27 G5
Llanbradach................25 K5
Llanbrynmair................41 J3
Llancarfan................25 J7
Llancayo................29 H7
Llancynfelyn................41 F4
Llandaff................25 K7
Llandanwg................40 E1
Llandawke................27 G6
Llanddaniel Fab...........50 D3
Llanddarog................27 K6
Llanddeiniol................40 E6
Llanddeiniolen............50 E4
Llandderfel................51 J7
Llanddeusant, Gwyn........50 C2
Llanddeusant, Dyfed.......25 F2
Llanddew................25 J1
Llanddewi................24 C6
Llanddewi Brefi...........27 L2
Llanddewi'r Cwm...........28 E3
Llanddewi Rhydderch.......29 H6
Llanddewi Velfrey.........26 F6
Llanddewi Ystradenni......32 A4
Llanddoged................51 H4
Llanddona................50 E3
Llanddowror................27 G6
Llanddulas................51 J3
Llandefaelog, Powys.......25 J1
Llandefaelog, Dyfed.......27 J6
Llandefaelog tre'r-graig..25 K1
Llandefalle................25 K1
Llandegai................50 E3
Llandegfan................50 E3
Llandegla................42 C2
Llandegley................32 A4
Llandegveth................29 H8
Llandeilo................27 L5
Llandeilo Graban..........28 E3
Llandeilo'r-Fan...........25 G1
Llandeloy................26 C5
Llandenny................29 J7
Llandevenny................16 F2
Llandinabo................29 K5
Llandinam................41 K5
Llandissilio................26 F5
Llandogo................29 K7
Llandough, S. Glam........25 H7
Llandough, S. Glam........25 K7
Llandovery................25 L1
Llandow................25 H7
Llandre, Dyfed............28 A3
Llandre, Dyfed............41 F5
Llandrillo................51 K7
Llandrillo-yn-Rhos........51 H2
Llandrindod Wells.........41 K7
Llandrinio................42 D6
Llandudno................51 G2
Llandudno Junction........51 H3
Llandudwen................50 B7
Llandwrog................50 D5
Llandybie................27 L6
Llandyfriog................27 H3
Llandyfrydog................50 D2
Llandygwydd................27 G3
Llandynog................51 L4
Llandyssil................42 C8
Llandysul................27 J3
Llanegryn................40 F3
Llanegwad................27 K5
Llaneilian-yn-Rhos........51 H3
Llanelidan................51 L5
Llanelieu................25 K1
Llanellen................29 H6
Llanelli................24 D4
Llanelltyd................41 G2
Llanelly................29 G6
Llanelly Hill................25 L3
Llanelwedd................28 E2
Llanelwy or St Asaph......51 K3
Llanenddwyn................40 E1
Llanengan................40 B1
Llanerchymedd................50 D2
Llanerfyl................41 K3
Llanfachraeth................50 C2
Llanfachreth................41 G1
Llanfaelog................50 C3
Llanfaelrhys................50 C3
Llanfaenor................50 C2
Llanfaes................50 E3
Llanfaethlu................50 C2
Llanfaglan................50 D4
Llanfair................50 E8
Llanfair Caereinion.......41 L3
Llanfair Clydogau.........27 L2
Llanfair Dyffryn Clwyd....42 C2
Llanfairfechan............51 F3
Llanfair Kilgeddin........29 H7
Llanfair-Nant-Gwyn........26 F4
Llanfairpwllgwyngyll......50 E3
Llanfair Talhaiarn........51 J3
Llanfair Waterdine........32 B3
Llanfairyneubwll..........50 C3
Llanfairynghornwy.........50 C1
Llanfallteg................26 F6
Llanfaredd................28 E2
Llanfarian................40 E6
Llanfechain................42 C5
Llanfechan................28 D2
Llanfechell................50 C1
Llanfendigaid................48 E3
Llanferres................52 C7
Llanfflewyn................50 C2
Llanfihangel-ar-arth......27 J4
Llanfihangel Crucorney....29 H5
Llanfihangel Gln Myfyr....51 J6
Llanfihangel Nant Bran....25 H1
Llanfihangel-nant-Melan...29 F4
Llanfihangel Rhydithon....32 A4
Llanfihangel Rogiet.......17 F2
Llanfihangel Tal-y-llyn...25 K2
Llanfihangel-uwch-Gwili...27 J5

Llanfihangel-y-Creuddyn...41 F6
Llanfihangel-yng-Ngwynfa..41 K2
Llanfihangel yn Nhowyn....50 C3
Llanfihangel-y-pennant,
  Gwyn.................50 E6
Llanfihangel-y-pennant,
  Gwyn.................41 F3
Llanfihangel
  Ystum Llwern..........29 J6
Llanfihangel-y-traethau...50 E7
Llanfilo................25 K1
Llanfoist................29 G6
Llanfor................51 J7
Llanfrechfa................29 H8
Llanfrothen................51 F6
Llanfrynach................25 J2
Llanfwrog, Gwyn...........50 C2
Llanfwrog, Clwyd..........52 C8
Llanfyllin................42 C6
Llanfynydd, Clwyd.........42 D2
Llanfynydd, Dyfed.........27 K5
Llanfyrnach................27 G4
Llangadfan................41 K2
Llangadog................24 F2
Llangadwaladr, Gwyn.......50 C4
Llangadwaladr, Clwyd......42 C4
Llangaffo................50 D4
Llangain................27 H6
Llangammarch Wells........28 D3
Llangan................25 H7
Llangarron................29 K5
Llangasty-Talyllin........25 K2
Llangathen................27 K5
Llangattock................29 L3
Llangattock Lingoed.......29 H5
Llangattock-Vibon-Avel....29 J6
Llangedwyn................42 C5
Llangefni................50 D3
Llangeinor................25 H6
Llangeitho................27 L2
Llangeler................27 H4
Llangelynnin................40 E3
Llangendeirne................27 J6
Llangennech................24 D4
Llangennith................24 C5
Llangenny................29 G6
Llangernyw................51 H4
Llangian................40 B8
Llangiwg................24 F4
Llanglydwen................27 F5
Llangoed................50 F3
Llangoedmor................27 G3
Llangollen................42 D3
Llangolman................26 F5
Llangorse................25 K2
Llangorwen................40 F5
Llangovan................29 J7
Llangower................51 J7
Llangranog................27 H2
Llangristiolus................50 D3
Llangrove................29 K6
Llangua................29 H5
Llangunllo................32 B3
Llangunnor................27 J5
Llangurig................41 J5
Llangwm, Dyfed............26 D7
Llangwm, Clwyd............51 J6
Llangwm, Gwent............29 J7
Llangwnnadl................50 B7
Llangwyfan................52 C7
Llangwyllog................50 D3
Llangwyryfon................40 F6
Llangybi, Gwyn............50 D6
Llangybi, Gwent............29 H8
Llangybi, Dyfed............27 L2
Llangyfelach................24 E5
Llangynhafal................52 C7
Llangynidr................25 K2
Llangynin................27 G6
Llangynog, Dyfed..........27 H6
Llangynog, Powys..........41 K1
Llangynwyd................25 G6
Llanhamlach................25 J2
Llanharan................25 J6
Llanharry................25 J6
Llanhennock................16 E1
Llanhilleth................25 L4
Llanidloes................41 J5
Llaniestyn................50 B7
Llanigon................28 F3
Llanilar................41 F6
Llanilid................25 H6
Llanishen, Gwent..........29 J7
Llanishen, S. Glam........25 K6
Llanllechid................51 F4
Llanlleonfel................28 D3
Llanllowell................29 H8
Llanllugan................41 K3
Llanllwchaiarn............32 A1
Llanllwni................27 J3
Llanllyfni................50 D5
Llanmadoc................24 C5
Llanmaes................25 H8
Llanmartin................16 E2
Llanmerewig................42 C8
Llanmihangel................25 H7
Llanmiloe................27 G7
Llanmorlais................24 D5
Llannefydd................51 J3
Llannon................27 K7
Llannor................50 C7
Llanover................29 H7
Llanpumsaint................27 J5
Llanrhaeadr................51 K4
Llanrhaeadr-ym-Mochnant...42 C5
Llanrhian................26 C4
Llanrhidian................24 C5
Llanrhos................50 C2
Llanrhyddlad................50 C2
Llanrhystud................40 E7
Llanrothal................29 K6
Llanrug................50 E4
Llanrwst................51 H4

Llansadurnen ...27 G6
Llansadwrn, Dyfed ...24 E1
Llansadwrn, Gwyn ...50 E3
Llansaint ...27 H7
Llansamlet ...24 E5
Llansannan ...51 J4
Llansannor ...25 H7
Llansantffraed, Dyfed ...40 E7
Llansantffraed, Powys ...25 K2
Llansantffraed-Cwmdeuddwr ...41 J7
Llansantffraed-in-Elwel ...28 E2
Llansantffraid Glan Conwy ...51 H3
Llansantffraid-ym-Mechain ...42 D5
Llansawel ...27 L4
Llansilin ...42 D5
Llansoy ...29 J7
Llanspyddid ...25 J2
Llanstadwell ...26 D7
Llanstephan, Powys ...28 F3
Llanstephan, Dyfed ...27 H6
Llanthony ...29 G5
Llantilio Crossenny ...29 H6
Llantilio Pertholey ...29 H6
Llantrisant, Gwyn ...50 C2
Llantrisant, Gwent ...29 H8
Llantrisant, M. Glam ...25 J6
Llantrithyd ...25 J7
Llantwit Fardre ...25 J6
Llantwit Major ...25 H8
Llanuwchllyn ...51 H7
Llanvaches ...17 F1
Llanvair Discoed ...17 F1
Llanvapley ...29 H6
Llanvetherine ...29 H6
Llanveynoe ...29 H4
Llanvihangel Crucorney ...29 H5
Llanvihangel Gobion ...29 H7
Llanvihangel-Ystern-Llewern ...29 J6
Llanwarne ...29 K5
Llanwddyn ...41 K2
Llanwenog ...27 J3
Llanwern ...16 E2
Llanwinio ...27 G5
Llanwnda, Dyfed ...26 D4
Llanwnda, Gwyn ...50 D5
Llanwnnen ...27 K3
Llanwnog ...41 K4
Llanwrda ...24 F1
Llanwrin ...41 G3
Llanwrthwl ...41 J7
Llanwrtyd ...28 C3
Llanwrtyd-Wells ...28 C3
Llanwyddelan ...41 K3
Llanyblodwel ...42 D5
Llanybri ...27 H6
Llanybydder ...27 K3
Llanycefn ...26 E5
Llanychaer ...26 D4
Llancrwys ...27 L3
Llanymawddwy ...41 J2
Llanymynech, Shrops ...42 D5
Llanymynech, Powys ...42 D5
Llanynghenedl ...50 C2
Llanynys ...51 L4
Llan-y-pwll ...42 E2
Llanyre ...41 K7
Llanystumdwy ...50 D7
Llanywern ...25 K2
Llawhaden ...26 E6
Llawnt ...42 D4
Llawr Dref ...40 B1
Llawryglyn ...41 J4
Llay ...42 E2
Llechcynfarwy ...50 C2
Llechfaen ...25 J2
Llechryd, Dyfed ...27 G3
Llechryd, M. Glam ...25 K4
Lledrod ...41 F6
Llidiad-Nenog ...27 K4
Llithfaen ...50 C6
Llong ...52 D7
Llowes ...29 F3
Llwchmynydd ...40 A1
Llwn-y-groes ...27 K2
Llwydcoed ...25 H4
Llwyn ...32 B2
Llwyncelyn ...27 J2
Llwyndafydd ...27 H2
Llwynderw ...42 D7
Llwyndyrys ...50 C6
Llwyngwril ...40 E3
Llwynhendy ...24 D5
Llwynmawr ...42 D4
Llwynypia ...25 H5
Llynclys ...42 D5
Llynfaes ...50 D3
Llysfaen ...51 H3
Llyswen ...28 F4
Llysworney ...25 H7
Llys-y-fran ...26 E5
Llywel ...25 G1
Loanend ...81 H4
Loanhead ...79 K3
Loans ...77 J4
Lochaber ...90 C2
Lochailort ...96 C7
Lochaline ...89 H4
Lochans ...70 B6
Locharbriggs ...72 E5
Lochawe ...84 D2
Lochboisdale ...94 C4
Lochbuie ...89 H6
Lochcarron ...104 D2
Lochcarron ...96 D2
Lochdon ...89 J5
Lochearnhead ...85 H2
Lochee ...87 G1
Lochend, Highld ...98 D5
Lochend, Highld ...115 H3
Locheport ...104 D5
Locherben ...72 E4
Lochfoot ...72 D6
Lochgair ...84 B3
Lochganvich ...111 G5

Lochgarthside ...98 D7
Lochgelly ...86 E5
Lochgilphead ...84 A6
Lochgoilhead ...84 D4
Lochhill ...100 B2
Lochinver ...112 B6
Lochlane ...85 L2
Lochluichart ...98 B2
Lochmaben ...73 F5
Lochmaddy ...104 E5
Lochore ...86 E5
Lochranza ...76 E2
Lochside ...93 J5
Lochskipport ...94 D2
Lochslin ...109 G5
Lochton ...93 J2
Lochwinnoch ...77 J2
Lochwood ...78 D3
Lockengate ...3 J3
Lockerbie ...73 G5
Lockeridge ...18 C4
Lockerley ...10 E2
Locking ...16 E5
Lockington, Humbs ...58 D2
Lockington, Leic ...45 F5
Lockleywood ...43 H5
Locks Heath ...11 G4
Lockton ...64 F4
Loddington, Northnts ...36 B3
Loddington, Leic ...45 J7
Loddiswell ...5 H7
Loddon ...49 J8
Lode ...37 J4
Loders ...9 F5
Lodsworth ...12 C4
Lofthouse ...62 E2
Lofthouse Gate ...63 G7
Loftus ...69 K5
Logan ...72 A1
Loggerheads ...43 J4
Loggie ...107 G2
Logie, Fife ...87 H2
Logie, Tays ...93 H5
Logie Coldstone ...100 D8
Logie Hill ...109 F6
Logie Newton ...100 F6
Logie Pert ...93 H5
Lgierait ...92 A6
Login ...26 F5
Lolworth ...37 G4
Lonbain ...106 B6
Londesborough ...58 C2
London ...21 H6
London (Gatwick) Airport ...12 F2
London (Heathrow) Airport ...20 E6
London Colney ...21 F3
Londonderry ...63 G1
Londonthorpe ...46 C4
Londubh ...106 D3
Lonemore, Highld ...106 C4
Lonemore, Highld ...109 F5
Long Ashton ...17 G3
Long Bennington ...46 B3
Longbenton ...75 J7
Longborough ...31 F5
Long Bredy ...9 G5
Longbridge, W. Mids ...34 B3
Longbridge, Warw ...34 D4
Longbridge Deverill ...17 K6
Long Buckby ...35 H4
Longburton ...9 H3
Long Clawson ...45 J5
Longcliffe ...44 D2
Long Common ...11 G3
Long Compton, Warw ...31 G4
Long Compton, Staffs ...43 K5
Longcot ...18 D1
Long Crendon ...20 A3
Long Crichel ...10 A3
Longcroft ...85 K7
Longden ...42 F7
Long Ditton ...21 F7
Longdon, Staffs ...44 B6
Longdon, H. & W ...33 H7
Longdon on Tern ...43 H6
Longdown ...5 J2
Longdowns ...2 F6
Long Drax ...58 A4
Long Duckmanton ...55 H6
Long Eaton ...45 F4
Longfield ...14 C2
Longford, Glos ...30 C5
Longford, Derby ...44 D4
Longford, W. Mids ...34 E2
Longford, G. Lon ...20 E6
Longford, Shrops ...43 H4
Longford, Shrops ...43 J6
Longforgan ...87 G1
Longformacus ...80 E4
Longframlington ...75 H3
Long Gill ...62 A4
Longham, Dorset ...10 B5
Longham, Norf ...48 B6
Long Hanborough ...31 J6
Long Hermiston ...86 E7
Longhirst ...75 J5
Longhope, Glos ...30 A6
Longhope, Orkney ...116 C7
Longhorsley ...75 H4
Longhoughton ...75 J2
Long Itchington ...34 F4
Long Lawford ...35 F3
Longley Green ...33 G5
Long Load ...9 F2
Longmanhill ...101 G2
Long Marston, Herts ...20 C2
Long Marston, Warw ...34 C6
Long Marston, N. Yks ...63 J4
Long Marton ...67 J4
Long Melford ...38 D6
Longmoor Camp ...11 J1
Longmorn ...100 B3
Long Newnton ...17 L1
Longnewton, Border ...80 D7
Longnewton, Cleve ...69 F5

Longney ...30 B6
Longniddry ...87 H7
Longnor, Staffs ...54 D7
Longnor, Shrops ...43 F7
Longparish ...18 F6
Long Preston ...62 B4
Longridge, Lothn ...79 G3
Longridge, Lancs ...61 K6
Longriggend ...85 L7
Long Riston ...59 F2
Longsdon ...44 A2
Longside ...101 K4
Longslow ...43 H4
Longstanton ...37 G4
Longstock ...10 E1
Longstowe ...37 G5
Long Stratton ...39 G1
Long Street ...35 J6
Long Sutton, Somer ...9 F2
Long Sutton, Lincs ...47 H5
Long Sutton, Hants ...19 J6
Longthorpe ...46 E8
Longton, Lancs ...61 H7
Longton, Staffs ...43 L3
Longtown, H. & W ...29 H5
Longtown, Cumbr ...73 J7
Longville in the Dale ...43 G8
Long Whatton ...45 F5
Longwick ...20 B3
Long Wittenham ...31 K8
Longwitton ...75 G5
Longworth ...31 H8
Longyester ...80 D3
Lonmore ...102 D4
Looe ...3 L4
Loose ...13 L1
Loosley Row ...20 C3
Lopcombe Corner ...10 D1
Lopen ...9 F3
Loppington ...43 F5
Lopwell ...4 E5
Lorbottle ...75 G3
Lorton ...66 D4
Loscoe ...44 F3
Lossiemouth ...100 B1
Lostock Gralam ...53 H6
Lostock Junction ...53 H3
Lostwithiel ...3 K4
Lothbeg ...109 H2
Lothersdale ...62 C5
Lothmore ...109 H2
Loudwater ...20 D4
Loughborough ...45 G6
Loughor ...24 D5
Loughton, Bucks ...36 B7
Loughton, Shrops ...33 F2
Loughton, Essex ...21 J4
Lound, Notts ...56 5
Lound, Lincs ...46 D6
Lound, Suff ...49 L8
Lount ...44 E6
Louth ...57 H5
Love Clough ...62 B7
Lover ...10 D2
Loversall ...55 J4
Loves Green ...22 C3
Loveston ...26 E7
Lovington ...9 G1
Low Bentham ...61 K3
Low Bradfield ...55 F4
Low Bradley ...62 D5
Low Braithwaite ...67 G2
Low Brunton ...74 F6
Low Burnham ...58 B6
Lowca ...66 B4
Low Catton ...64 E7
Low Coniscliffe ...68 E5
Low Crosby ...73 K8
Lowdham ...45 H3
Low Dinsdale ...69 F5
Low Dovengill ...67 K7
Low Eggborough ...63 J7
Low Ellington ...62 F1
Lower Aisholt ...8 D1
Lower Ashton ...5 J3
Lower Assendon ...20 B5
Lower Basildon ...20 A6
Lower Beeding ...12 F4
Lower Benefield ...36 C2
Lower Boddington ...35 F5
Lower Breinton ...29 J4
Lower Bullingham ...29 K4
Lower Cam ...30 B7
Lower Chapel ...25 J1
Lower Chute ...18 E5
Lower Darwen ...61 K7
Lower Diabaig ...106 C5
Lower Down ...32 C2
Lower Dunsforth ...63 H3
Lower Farringdon ...11 J1
Lower Frankton ...42 E4
Lower Froyle ...19 J6
Lower Gledfield ...108 D4
Lower Green ...48 E4
Lower Halstow ...14 E2
Lower Hardres ...15 H3
Lower Heyford ...31 J5
Lower Higham ...14 D1
Lower Hordley ...42 E5
Lower Killeyan ...82 B7
Lower Langford ...17 F4
Lower Largo ...87 H4
Lower Lemington ...31 G4
Lower Lye ...32 D4
Lower Machen ...25 L6
Lower Maes-coed ...29 H4
Lower Moor ...34 A6
Lower Nazeing ...21 H3
Lower Penarth ...25 K7
Lower Penn ...43 K8
Lower Pennington ...10 E5
Lower Peover ...53 J6
Lower Quinton ...34 C6
Lower Shelton ...36 C6
Lower Shiplake ...20 B6

Lower Shuckburgh ...35 F4
Lower Slaughter ...31 F5
Lower Stanton St Quintin ...17 L2
Lower Stoke ...14 E1
Lower Stondo ...36 E7
Lower Sundon ...36 D8
Lower Swanwick ...11 G4
Lower Swell ...31 F5
Lower Thurlton ...49 K8
Lower Tysoe ...34 E6
Lower Upham ...11 G3
Lower Vexford ...8 C1
Lower Weare ...16 F5
Lower Welson ...29 G3
Lower Wield ...19 H6
Lower Winchendon or Nether Winchendon ...20 B2
Lower Woodend ...20 C5
Lower Woodford ...10 C1
Lowesby ...45 J7
Lowestoft ...49 L8
Loweswater ...66 D4
Lowford ...39 F7
Low Gate ...74 F7
Lowgill, Cumbr ...67 J7
Lowgill, Lancs ...61 K3
Low Ham ...9 F2
Low Hesket ...67 G2
Low Hesleyhurst ...75 G4
Lowick, Northnts ...36 C2
Lowick, Cumbr ...61 F1
Lowick, Northum ...81 J6
Low Leighton ...54 D5
Low Mill ...69 J7
Low Moor ...61 L5
Lownie Moor ...93 F7
Lowood ...80 D6
Low Row, Cumbr ...74 B7
Low Row, N. Yks ...68 B7
Lowsonford ...34 C4
Lowther ...67 H4
Lowthorpe ...65 H6
Lowton ...53 H4
Lowton Common ...53 H4
Low Torry ...86 D6
Low Waters ...78 E4
Low Worsall ...69 F6
Loxbeare ...7 K4
Loxhill ...12 D3
Loxhore ...7 G2
Loxley ...34 D5
Loxton ...16 E5
Loxwood ...12 D3
Lubenham ...35 J2
Luccombe ...7 K1
Luccombe Village ...11 G7
Lucker ...81 K6
Luckett ...4 D4
Luckington ...17 K2
Lucklawhill ...87 H2
Luckwell Bridge ...7 K2
Lucton ...32 D4
Ludag ...94 C4
Ludborough ...57 G4
Ludchurch ...26 F6
Luddenden ...62 D7
Luddesdown ...14 C2
Luddington ...58 C5
Luddington ...57 F5
Ludford ...57 F5
Ludgershall, Bucks ...20 A2
Ludgershall, Wilts ...18 D5
Ludgvan ...2 D6
Ludham ...49 J6
Ludlow ...32 E3
Ludwell ...9 L2
Ludworth ...69 F2
Luffincott ...4 D2
Lugar ...78 C7
Luggate Burn ...87 K7
Luggiebank ...85 K7
Lugton ...77 K2
Lugwardine ...29 K3
Luib ...96 A3
Lullington, Derby ...44 D6
Lullington, Somer ...17 J5
Lulsgate Bottom ...17 G4
Lulsley ...33 G5
Lulworth Camp ...9 K6
Lumb ...62 D7
Lumby ...63 H6
Lumphanan ...100 E8
Lumphinnans ...86 E5
Lumsdaine ...81 G3
Lumsden ...100 D6
Lunan ...93 H6
Lunanhead ...93 F6
Luncarty ...86 D2
Lund, Humbs ...65 G8
Lund, N. Yks ...63 K6
Lundie ...92 D8
Lundin Links ...87 H4
Lunna ...119 H2
Lunning ...119 H2
Lunsford's Cross ...13 L5
Lunt ...52 E3
Luntley ...29 H2
Luppitt ...8 C4
Lupton ...61 J1
Lurgashall ...12 C4
Lusby ...57 H7
Luskentyre ...105 F2
Luss ...84 F5
Lusta ...102 D3
Lustleigh ...5 H3
Luston ...32 D4
Luthermuir ...93 H5
Luthrie ...87 G3
Luton, Kent ...14 D2
Luton, Beds ...20 E1
Luton, Devon ...5 K4
Lutterworth ...35 G2
Lutton, Northnts ...36 E2
Lutton, Devon ...5 F6
Lutton, Lincs ...47 H5

Lutworthy ...7 H4
Luxborough ...7 K2
Luxulyan ...3 J4
Lybster ...115 H6
Lydbury North ...32 C2
Lydd ...15 G6
Lydden ...15 J4
Lyddington ...46 B8
Lydd-on-Sea ...15 G6
Lydeard St Lawrence ...8 C1
Lydford, Devon ...4 F3
Lydford, Somer ...9 G1
Lydgate ...62 C7
Lydham ...32 C1
Lydiard Millicent ...18 B2
Lydiate ...52 E3
Lydlinch ...9 J3
Lydney ...29 L7
Lydstep ...26 E8
Lye ...33 J2
Lye Green ...20 D3
Lyford ...31 H8
Lymbridge Green ...15 H4
Lyme Regis ...8 E7
Lyminge ...15 H4
Lymington ...10 E5
Lyminster ...12 D6
Lymm ...53 H5
Lymore ...10 D5
Lympne ...15 H5
Lympsham ...16 E5
Lympstone ...5 K3
Lynchat ...91 J1
Lyndhurst ...10 E4
Lyndon ...46 C7
Lyne ...20 E7
Lyneal ...42 F4
Lyneham, Wilts ...18 B3
Lyneham, Oxon ...31 G5
Lynemouth ...75 J4
Lyne of Gorthleck ...98 D6
Lyne of Skene ...101 G7
Lyness ...116 C7
Lyng, Somer ...8 E2
Lyng, Norf ...48 F6
Lynmouth ...7 H1
Lynsted ...14 F2
Lynton ...7 H1
Lyon's Gate ...9 H4
Lyonshall ...29 H2
Lytchett Matravers ...10 A5
Lytchett Minster ...10 A5
Lyth ...115 H3
Lytham ...61 G7
Lytham St Anne's ...61 G7
Lythe ...69 L5
Lythes ...116 D8

M

Maaruig ...105 H1
Mabe Burnthouse ...2 F6
Mabie ...72 E6
Mablethorpe ...57 K5
Macclesfield ...53 L6
Macclesfield Forest ...54 C6
Macduff ...101 G2
Machariock ...76 C7
Machen ...25 L6
Machrihanish ...76 B5
Machynlleth ...41 G3
Mackworth ...44 E4
Macmerry ...87 H7
Madderty ...86 C2
Maddiston ...86 C7
Madehurst ...12 C5
Madeley ...43 J3
Madeley Heath ...43 J3
Madingley ...37 G4
Madley ...29 J4
Madresfield ...33 H6
Madron ...2 C6
Maenaddwyn ...50 D2
Maenclochog ...26 E5
Maendy ...25 J7
Maentwrog ...51 F6
Maer ...43 J4
Maerdy, M. Glam ...25 H5
Maerdy, Clwyd ...51 K6
Maesbrook ...42 E5
Maesbury Marsh ...42 E5
Maes-glas ...16 E2
Maeshafn ...52 D7
Maesllyn ...27 H3
Maesmynis ...28 E3
Maesteg ...25 G5
Maesybont ...27 K6
Maesycrugiau ...27 J3
Maesycwmmer ...25 K5
Magdalen Laver ...21 K3
Maggieknockater ...100 C4
Magham Down ...13 K5
Maghull ...52 E3
Magor ...17 F2
Maiden Bradley ...17 K7
Maidencombe ...5 K5
Maidenhead ...20 C5
Maiden Law ...68 D2
Maiden Newton ...9 G5
Maidens ...77 H7
Maidenwell ...3 K2
Maidford ...35 H5
Maids Moreton ...35 J7
Maidstone ...13 L1
Maidwell ...35 J3
Mail ...119 G6
Main ...98 C5
Mains of Clunas ...99 G4
Mains of Drum ...93 K2
Mains of Loch ...100 C2
Mainstone ...32 B2
Maisemore ...30 C5
Makerstoun ...80 E6

Malash ...15 G3
Malborough ...5 H8
Maldon ...22 E3
Malham ...62 C3
Mallaig ...96 B6
Malltraeth ...50 D4
Mallwyd ...41 H2
Malmesbury ...18 A2
Malpas, Gwent ...16 E1
Malpas, Ches ...43 F3
Malpas, Corn ...3 G5
Maltby, Cleve ...69 G5
Maltby, S. Yks ...55 J4
Maltby le Marsh ...57 J5
Maltman's Hill ...14 F4
Malton ...64 E5
Malvern Link ...33 G6
Malvern Wells ...33 G6
Mamble ...33 F3
Manaccan ...2 F7
Manafon ...42 C7
Manaton ...5 H3
Manby ...57 H5
Mancetter ...44 E8
Manchester ...53 K4
Mancot ...52 E7
Mandally ...90 D1
Manea ...37 H2
Manfield ...68 E5
Mangersta ...110 E4
Mangotsfield ...17 H3
Manish ...105 G3
Mankinholes ...62 C7
Manley ...53 G6
Manmoel ...25 K4
Mannal ...88 A4
Manningford Bohune ...18 C5
Manningford Bruce ...18 C5
Mannings Heath ...12 F4
Mannington ...10 B4
Manningtree ...39 G7
Mannofield ...101 J8
Manorbier ...26 E8
Manordeilo ...24 E2
Manorowen ...26 D4
Mansell Gamage ...29 H3
Mansell Lacy ...29 J3
Mansfield, Strath ...72 B2
Mansfield, Notts ...55 J7
Mansfield Woodhouse ...55 J7
Manston ...9 K3
Manswood ...10 A4
Manthorpe ...46 D6
Manton, Leic ...46 B7
Manton, Wilts ...18 C4
Manton, Humbs ...58 D6
Manuden ...37 H8
Maplebeck ...56 B7
Maple Cross ...20 E4
Mapledurham ...20 A6
Mapledurwell ...19 H5
Maplehurst ...12 E4
Mapleton ...44 C3
Mapperley ...44 F3
Mapperton ...9 G5
Mappleborough Green ...34 B4
Mappleton ...59 G2
Mappowder ...9 J4
Marazion ...2 D6
Marbury ...43 G3
March ...47 H8
Marcham ...31 J8
Marchamley ...43 G5
Marchington ...44 C4
Marchington Woodlands ...44 C5
Marchwiel ...42 E3
Marchwood ...10 E3
Marcross ...25 H8
Marden, Wilts ...18 B5
Marden, H. & W ...29 K3
Marden, Kent ...13 L2
Mardy ...29 H6
Marefield ...45 J7
Mareham le Fen ...57 G7
Mareham on the Hill ...57 G7
Maresfield ...13 H4
Marfleet ...59 F4
Margam ...25 F6
Margaret Marsh ...9 K3
Margaret Roding ...22 B2
Margaretting ...22 C3
Margate ...15 K1
Margnaheglish ...76 F4
Marham ...48 C7
Marhamchurch ...4 C5
Marholm ...46 E7
Marian-glas ...50 E2
Mariansleigh ...7 H3
Marishader ...103 F2
Mark ...16 E6
Markbeech ...13 H2
Markby ...57 J6
Mark Causeway ...16 E6
Mark Cross ...13 J3
Market Bosworth ...44 F7
Market Deeping ...46 E6
Market Drayton ...43 H4
Market Harborough ...35 J2
Markethill ...92 D8
Market Lavington ...18 B5
Market Overton ...46 B6
Market Rasen ...57 F5
Market Stainton ...57 G6
Market Weighton ...58 C2
Market Weston ...38 E3
Markfield ...45 F6
Markham ...25 K4
Markinch ...87 F4
Markington ...63 F3
Marksbury ...17 H4
Marks Tey ...22 F1
Markyate ...20 E2
Marlborough ...18 C4
Marlcliff ...34 B5
Marldon ...5 J5

Marlesford....39 J5
Marley Green....43 G3
Marlingford....49 G7
Marloes....26 B7
Marlow....20 C5
Marlpit Hill....13 H2
Marnhull....9 J3
Marnoch....100 E3
Marnock....78 E3
Marple....54 C5
Marr....55 J3
Marrick....68 C7
Marros....27 G7
Marsden....54 D2
Marsett....62 C1
Marsh....8 D3
Marshalls Heath....21 F2
Marsham....49 G5
Marshaw....61 J4
Marsh Baldon....31 K8
Marshborough....15 K3
Marshbrook....32 D2
Marshchapel....59 H7
Marshfield, Gwent....16 D2
Marshfield, Avon....17 J3
Marshgate....4 B2
Marsh Gibbon....20 A1
Marsh Green, Devon....8 B5
Marsh Green, Kent....13 H2
Marsh Green, Shrops....43 H6
Marshland St James....47 J7
Marshside, Mers....52 E2
Marshside, Kent....15 J2
Marsh, The....42 E8
Marshwood....8 E5
Marske....68 D6
Marske-by-the-Sea....69 J4
Marston, Wilts....18 A5
Marston, Lincs....46 B3
Marston, Warw....44 D8
Marston, H. & W.....29 H2
Marston, Ches....53 H6
Marston, Staffs....43 K6
Marston, Oxon....31 K7
Marston, Staffs....43 L5
Marston Green....34 C2
Marston Magna....9 G2
Marston Meysey....31 F8
Marston Montgomery....44 C4
Marston Moretaine....36 C6
Marston on Dove....44 D5
Marston Stannett....29 K2
Marston St Lawrence....35 G6
Marston Trussell....35 H2
Marstow....29 K6
Marsworth....20 D2
Marten....18 D4
Marthall....53 K6
Martham....49 K6
Martin, Hants....10 B3
Martin, Lincs....57 F8
Martindale....67 G5
Martin Dales....57 F7
Martin Drove End....10 B2
Martinhoe....7 G1
Martin Hussingtree....33 H4
Martinscroft....53 H5
Martinstown....9 H6
Martlesham....39 H6
Martlesham Heath....39 H6
Martletwy....26 E6
Martley....33 G4
Martock....9 F3
Marton, Lincs....56 C5
Marton, Shrops....42 D7
Marton, N. Yks....64 E4
Marton, Warw....34 F4
Marton, N. Yks....63 H3
Marton, Cleve....69 H5
Marton, Ches....53 K7
Marvig....111 J6
Marwick....116 B4
Marwood....7 F2
Marybank....98 C3
Maryburgh....98 D3
Marygold....81 G3
Marykirk....93 H5
Marylebone, G. Man....53 G3
Marylebone, G. Lon....21 G5
Marypark....100 A5
Maryport, Cumbr.....66 C3
Maryport, D. & G.....70 C8
Marystow....4 E3
Mary Tavy....4 F4
Maryton....93 H6
Marywell, Grampn....93 G2
Marywell, Tays....93 H7
Masham....63 F1
Mashbury....22 C2
Masongill....61 K2
Mastrick....101 J8
Matching....21 K2
Matching Green....21 K2
Matching Tye....21 K2
Matfen....75 G6
Matfield....13 K2
Mathern....17 G1
Mathon....33 G6
Mathry....26 C4
Matlaske....49 G4
Matlock....55 G7
Matlock Bath....55 F8
Matson....30 C6
Matterdale End....67 F4
Mattersey....56 A5
Mattingley....19 J5
Mattishall....48 F6
Mattishall Burgh....48 F6
Mauchline....77 K5
Maud....101 J4
Maugersbury....31 G5
Maughold....60 R2
Maulden....36 D7
Maulds Meaburn....67 J5
Maunby....63 G1

Maund Bryan....29 K2
Mautby....49 K6
Mavesyn Ridware....44 B4
Mavis Enderby....57 H7
Mawbray....66 C2
Mawdesley....53 F2
Mawgan....2 F7
Mawla....2 F5
Mawnan....3 F7
Mawnan Smith....2 F7
Maxey....46 E7
Maxstoke....34 D2
Maxton....80 E6
Maxwellheugh....80 F6
Maybole....77 H7
Mayfield, Lothn....80 B3
Mayfield, Staffs....44 C3
Mayfield, Surrey....12 D1
Mayfield, E. Susx....13 J4
Mayford....12 C1
Mayland....22 F3
Maypole....29 J6
Maypole Green....49 K8
Maywick....119 F6
Meadle....20 C3
Meadowtown....42 E7
Meal Bank....67 H7
Mealista....110 D3
Mealsgate....66 E2
Mearbeck....62 B3
Mearbrook....62 B3
Meare....17 F6
Meare Green....8 E2
Mears Ashby....36 B4
Measham....44 E6
Meathop....61 H1
Meaux....59 E3
Meavag....105 G2
Meavaig....105 F1
Meavy....5 F5
Medbourne....45 K8
Medburn....75 H6
Meddon....6 C4
Meden Vale....55 J7
Medmenham....20 C5
Meerbrook....54 C7
Meer End....34 D3
Meesden....37 H7
Meeth....7 F5
Meggethead....79 J7
Meidrim....27 G5
Meifod....42 C6
Meikle Earnock....78 E4
Meikleour....92 C8
Meikle Tarty....101 J6
Meikle Wartle....101 G5
Meinciau....27 J6
Meir....43 L3
Meir Heath....43 L3
Melbost....111 J4
Melbost Borve....111 J2
Melbourn....37 G6
Melbourne, Humbs....58 B2
Melbourne, Derby....44 E5
Melbury Abbas....9 K2
Melbury Bubb....9 G4
Melbury Osmond....9 G4
Melby....118 D3
Melchbourne....36 D4
Melcombe Bingham....9 J4
Meldon, Devon....5 F2
Meldon, Northum....75 H5
Meldreth....37 G6
Melfort....89 K7
Melgarve....91 F2
Meliden....51 K2
Melincourt....25 G4
Melin-y-coed....51 H4
Melin-y-ddol....41 K3
Melin-y-grug....41 K3
Melin-y-Wig....51 K6
Melkinthorpe....67 H4
Melkridge....74 D7
Melksham....17 L4
Melldalloch....84 B7
Melling, Mers....52 E3
Melling, Lancs....61 K2
Mellis....39 G3
Mellon Charles....106 D2
Mellon Udrigle....106 D2
Mellor, G. Man....54 C5
Mellor, Lancs....61 K6
Mellor Brook....61 K6
Mells, Somer....17 J6
Mells, Suff....39 K3
Melmerby, N. Yks....62 D1
Melmerby, N. Yks....63 G2
Melmerby, Cumbr....67 J3
Melplash....9 F5
Melrose....80 D6
Melsetter....116 B4
Melsonby....68 D6
Meltham....54 D2
Melton....39 H5
Meltonby....64 E7
Melton Constable....48 F4
Melton Mowbray....45 J6
Melton Ross....58 E5
Melvaig....106 C3
Melverley....42 E6
Melvich....114 D3
Membury....8 D4
Memsie....101 J2
Menabilly....4 C5
Mendham....39 H2
Mendlesham....39 G4
Mendlesham Green....39 F4
Menheniot....4 C5
Mennock....72 D3
Menston....62 E5
Menstrie....85 L5
Mentmore....20 D2
Meoble....83 J1
Meole Brace....43 F6
Meonstoke....11 H3
Meopham....14 C2

Meopham Station....14 C2
Mepal....37 H2
Meppershall....36 E7
Merbach....29 H3
Mere, Ches....53 J5
Mere, Wilts....9 K1
Mere Brow....52 F2
Mereclough....62 B6
Mere Green....44 C8
Mereworth....13 K1
Mergie....93 J3
Meriden....34 D2
Merkadale....102 E5
Merlin's Bridge....26 D6
Merrington....43 F5
Merriott....9 F3
Merrivale....5 F4
Merrymeet....4 C5
Mersham....15 G5
Merstham....13 F1
Merston....11 K4
Merstone....11 G6
Merther....3 G5
Merthyr....27 H5
Merthyr Cynog....28 D4
Merthyr Dyfan....25 K7
Merthyr Mawr....25 G7
Merthyr Tydfil....25 J4
Merthyr Vale....25 J5
Merton, Norf....48 E8
Merton, Devon....7 F4
Merton, G. Lon....21 G7
Merton, Oxon....31 K6
Mervinslaw....74 C2
Meshaw....7 H4
Messing....22 E2
Messingham....58 C6
Metfield....39 H2
Metheringham....56 E7
Methil....87 G5
Methley....63 G7
Methlick....101 H5
Methven....86 D2
Methwold....48 C8
Methwold Hythe....48 C8
Mettingham....39 J2
Mevagissey....3 J5
Mexborough....55 H3
Mey....115 H2
Meysey Hampton....31 F7
Miavaig....111 E4
Michael....60 Q2
Michaelchurch....29 K5
Michaelchurch Escley....29 H4
Michaelchurch-on-Arrow....29 G3
Michaelstone-y-Fedw....16 D2
Michaelston-le-Pit....25 K7
Michaelstow....3 J2
Micheldever....19 G7
Michelmersh....10 E3
Mickfield....39 G4
Mickleby....69 L5
Micklefield....63 H6
Mickleham....12 E1
Mickleover....44 E4
Mickleton, Durham....68 B4
Mickleton, Glos....34 C6
Mickle Trafford....52 F7
Mickley....63 F2
Mickley Square....75 G7
Mid Ardlaw....101 J2
Midbea....116 D2
Mid Beltie....93 H1
Mid Culbeuchly....100 F2
Middle Assendon....20 B5
Middle Aston....31 J5
Middle Barton....31 J5
Middlebie....73 H6
Middle Claydon....35 J8
Middleham....62 E1
Middlehope....32 D2
Middle Littleton....34 B6
Middle Maes-coed....29 H4
Middlemarsh....9 H4
Middle Mill....26 C5
Middle Rasen....56 E5
Middlesmoor....62 D2
Middlesbrough....69 G4
Middleston Moor....68 E3
Middlestown....55 F2
Middleton, Strath....88 A4
Middleton, Northnts....36 B1
Middleton, Lothn....80 B4
Middleton, Norf....48 B6
Middleton, Warw....44 C8
Middleton, Derby....44 D2
Middleton, Essex....38 D7
Middleton, Shrops....42 D8
Middleton, Shrops....32 E3
Middleton, H. & W.....32 E4
Middleton, N. Yks....62 E5
Middleton, Shrops....42 E5
Middleton, N. Yks....62 E5
Middleton, Derby....54 E7
Middleton, Hants....18 F6
Middleton, Northum....75 G5
Middleton, W. Isles....63 G2
Middleton, Lancs....61 H4
Middleton, Northum....81 J7
Middleton, Cumbr....61 K1
Middleton, G. Man....53 K3
Middleton, Suff....39 K4
Middleton, Northum....81 K6
Middleton Cheney....35 F6
Middleton Green....44 A4
Middleton Hall....81 H7
Middleton-in-Teesdale....68 B4
Middleton-on-Sea....12 C7
Middleton on the Hill....32 E4
Middleton-on-the-Wolds....65 G8
Middleton Priors....33 F1
Middleton Scriven....33 F2
Middleton St George....69 F5
Middleton Stoney....31 5
Middleton Tyas....68 E6

Middletown....42 E6
Middle Tysoe....34 E6
Middle Wallop....10 D1
Middle Winterslow....10 D1
Middle Woodford....10 C1
Middlewich....53 J7
Middlewood Green....39 F4
Middlezoy....8 E1
Middridge....68 E4
Midfield....113 G2
Midge Hall....61 J7
Midgeholme....74 C8
Midgham....19 G4
Midgley....62 D7
Midhopestones....55 F4
Midhurst....11 K2
Midlem....80 D7
Midsomer Norton....17 H5
Midtown....106 D3
Midtown of Buchromb....100 C4
Midville....57 H8
Mid Walls....118 E3
Mid Yell....121 H3
Migvie....100 D8
Milborne Port....9 H3
Milborne St Andrew....9 K5
Milborne Wick....9 H2
Milbourne....75 H6
Milbury Heath....17 H1
Milcombe....31 H4
Milden....38 E6
Mildenhall, Suff....38 C3
Mildenhall, Wilts....18 D4
Milebrooke....32 C3
Mile Elm....18 A4
Mile End, Essex....38 E8
Mile End, Glos....29 K6
Mileham....48 D7
Milesmark....86 D6
Milfield....81 H6
Milford, Staffs....44 A5
Milford, Surrey....12 C2
Milford, Devon....6 C3
Milford, Derby....44 E3
Milford Haven....26 D7
Milford on Sea....10 D5
Milkwall....29 K7
Mill Bank....62 D7
Millbounds....116 E3
Millbreck....101 K4
Millbrex....101 H4
Millbridge....19 K6
Millbrook, Beds....36 D7
Millbrook, Hants....10 E3
Millbrook, Corn....4 E6
Millburn....77 K5
Mill Corner....14 E6
Mill End, Bucks....20 B5
Mill End, Herts....37 G7
Millerhill....87 G8
Miller's Dale....54 E6
Mill Green, Essex....22 C3
Mill Green, Shrops....43 H5
Millheugh....78 E4
Mill Hill....21 G4
Millholme....67 H7
Millhouse, Strath....84 B7
Millhouse, Cumbr....66 F3
Millikenpark....77 K1
Millington....64 F7
Mill Lane....19 J5
Millmeece....43 K4
Millom....60 E1
Millport....77 G2
Mill Side....61 H1
Mill Street....48 F6
Millthrop....67 J7
Milltimber....93 K1
Milton of Corsindale....101 F8
Milton of Murtle....93 K1
Milltown, Devon....7 F2
Milltown, Derby....55 G7
Milltown, D. & G....73 J6
Milltown of Aberdalgie....86 D2
Milltown of Auchindoun....100 C4
Milltown of Craigston....101 G3
Milltown of Edinvillie....100 B4
Milltown of Rothiemay....100 E4
Milltown of Towie....100 D7
Milnafua....86 E4
Milnathort....86 E4
Milngavie....85 H7
Milnrow....53 L2
Milnthorpe....61 H1
Milovaig....102 C3
Milson....33 F3
Milstead....14 F3
Milston....18 C6
Milton, Highld....98 B3
Milton, Cumbr....74 B7
Milton, Highld....98 C5
Milton, Highld....98 D4
Milton, D. & G....72 D6
Milton, D. & G....70 D6
Milton, Grampn....100 E2
Milton, Dyfed....26 D7
Milton, Oxon....19 F1
Milton, Highld....109 F6
Milton, Strath....85 G7
Milton, Highld....99 H3
Milton, Cambs....37 H4
Milton, Central....85 H4
Milton, Highld....115 J4
Milton, Oxon....31 J4
Milton, Staffs....43 L2
Milton Abbas....9 K4
Milton Abbot....4 E4
Milton Bridge....79 K3
Milton Bryan....36 C7
Milton Clevedon....9 H1
Milton Coldwells....101 J5
Milton Combe....4 E5
Milton Damerel....6 D4

Miltonduff....100 A2
Milton Ernest....36 D5
Milton Green....52 F8
Milton Hill....19 F1
Milton Keynes....36 B7
Milton Keynes Village....36 B7
Milton Libourne....18 C4
Milton Malsor....35 J5
Milton of Auchinhove....100 E8
Milton of Balgonie....87 G4
Milton of Buchanan....85 G5
Milton of Campfield....93 H1
Milton of Campsie....85 J7
Milton of Corsindae....101 F8
Milton of Cushnie....100 E7
Milton of Lesmore....100 D6
Milton of Murtle....93 K1
Milton of Tullich....92 E2
Milton on Stour....9 K2
Milton Regis....14 F2
Milton-under-Wychwood....31 G6
Milverton....8 C2
Milwich....44 A4
Milwr....52 C6
Minard....84 B5
Minchinhampton....30 C7
Mindrum....81 G6
Minehead....7 K1
Minera....42 D2
Minety....18 B1
Minffordd....50 E7
Mingarry....94 C3
Miningsby....57 H7
Minions....4 C4
Minishant....77 J6
Minllyn....41 H2
Minnes....101 J6
Minnigaff....70 E5
Minshull Vernon....53 H7
Minskip....63 G3
Minstead....10 D3
Minster, Kent....14 F1
Minster, Kent....15 K2
Minsteracres....68 C1
Minsterley....42 E7
Minster Lovell....31 H6
Minsterworth....30 B6
Minterne Magna....9 H4
Minting....57 F6
Mintlaw....101 K4
Minto....74 B1
Minton....32 D1
Minwear....26 E6
Minworth....34 C1
Mirbister....116 C5
Mireland....115 J3
Mirfield....54 F2
Miserden....30 D7
Miskin....25 J6
Misson....56 A4
Misterton, Notts....56 B4
Misterton, Somer....9 F4
Misterton, Leic....3 G2
Mistley....39 G7
Mitcham....21 G7
Mitcheldean....30 A6
Mitchell....3 G4
Mitchel Troy....29 J6
Mitford....75 H5
Mithian....2 F4
Mitton....43 K6
Mixbury....31 L4
Mixon....54 D8
Mobberley....53 J6
Moccas....29 H3
Mochdre, Clwyd....51 H3
Mochdre, Powys....41 K5
Mochrum....70 E7
Mockerkin....66 C4
Modbury....5 G6
Moddershall....43 L4
Moelfre, Clwyd....42 C5
Moelfre, Gwyn....50 E2
Moffat....73 F3
Mogerhanger....36 E6
Moira....44 E6
Mol-chlach....103 F7
Mold....52 D7
Molehill Green....21 K1
Molescroft....58 E2
Molesworth....36 D3
Molland....7 J3
Mollington, Ches....52 E6
Mollington, Oxon....35 F6
Mollinsburn....85 K7
Monachty....40 E7
Monachylemore....85 H4
Mondynes....93 J4
Monewden....39 H5
Moniaive....72 C4
Monifieth....87 H1
Monikie....93 F8
Monimail....87 F3
Monington....26 F3
Monken Hadley....21 G4
Monk Fryston....63 J7
Monkhopton....43 H8
Monkland....29 J2
Monkleigh....6 E3
Monknash....25 H7
Monkokehampton....7 F5
Monks Eleigh....38 E6
Monk's Heath....53 K6
Monk Sherborne....19 H5
Monksilver....8 B1
Monks Kirby....35 F2
Monk Soham....39 H4
Monks Risborough....20 C3
Monkswood....29 H7
Monkton, Devon....8 C4
Monkton, Kent....15 J2
Monkton, Strath....77 J5
Monkton, T. & W.....75 K7
Monkton Combe....17 J4
Monkton Deverill....9 K1
Monkton Farleigh....17 K4

Monkton Heathfield....8 D2
Monkton Up Wimborne....10 B3
Monkwood....11 H1
Monmouth....29 K6
Monnington on Wye....29 H3
Monreith....70 E7
Monreith Mains....70 E7
Montacute....9 F3
Montford....42 F6
Montgarrie....100 E7
Montgomery....42 D8
Montgreenan....77 J3
Montrose....93 J6
Montsale....23 G4
Monxton....18 E6
Monyash....54 E7
Monymusk....101 F7
Monzie....86 B2
Moorby....57 G7
Moorcot....29 H2
Moor Crichel....10 A4
Moordown....10 B5
Moore....53 G5
Moorends....58 A5
Moorhall....55 G6
Moorhampton....29 H3
Moorhouse, Notts....56 B7
Moorhouse, Cumbr....66 F1
Moorland or
  Northmoor Green....8 E1
Moorlinch....8 E1
Moor Monkton....63 J4
Moor of Balvack....100 F7
Moorsholm....69 J5
Moorside....54 C3
Moor, The....13 L4
Moortown, Lincs....58 E7
Moortown, I. of W....10 F6
Morangie....109 F5
Morar....96 B6
Morborne....36 E1
Morchard Bishop....7 H5
Morcombelake....8 F5
Morcott....46 C7
Morda....42 D5
Morden, G. Lon....21 G7
Morden, Dorset....9 L5
Mordiford....29 K4
Mordon....68 F4
More....32 C1
Morebath....7 K3
Morebattle....80 F7
Morecambe....61 H3
Morefield....107 G2
Moreleigh....5 H6
Moresby....66 B4
Moresby Parks....66 B5
Morestead....11 G2
Moreton, Oxon....20 A3
Moreton, Mers....52 D4
Moreton, Staffs....43 J6
Moreton, Essex....21 K3
Moreton, Dorset....9 K6
Moreton Corbet....43 G5
Moretonhampstead....5 H3
Moreton-in-Marsh....31 G4
Moreton Jeffries....29 L3
Moreton Morrell....34 E5
Moreton on Lugg....29 K3
Moreton Pinkney....35 G6
Moreton Say....43 H4
Moreton Valence....30 B7
Morfa Bychan....50 E7
Morfa Glas....25 G4
Morfa Nefyn....50 B6
Morgan's Vale....10 C2
Morland....67 H4
Morley, Durham....68 D4
Morley, Derby....44 E3
Morley, W. Yks....63 F7
Morley Green....53 K5
Morley St Botolph....48 F8
Morningside....87 F7
Morningthorpe....39 H1
Morpeth....75 H5
Morrey....44 C6
Morriston....24 E5
Morston....48 F3
Morthoe....6 E1
Mortimer....20 A7
Mortimer Cross....32 D4
Mortimer West End....20 A7
Mortlake....21 G6
Morton, Lincs....56 C4
Morton, Derby....55 G7
Morton, Shrops....42 D5
Morton, Norf....49 H5
Morton, Avon....17 H1
Morton, Derby....55 H7
Morton Bagot....34 C4
Morton-on-Swale....68 F7
Morvah....2 C6
Morval....4 C6
Morvich, Highld....96 E3
Morvich, Highld....109 F4
Morville....43 H8
Morwenstow....6 C4
Mosborough....55 H5
Moscow....77 K3
Mosedale....66 F3
Moseley, W. Mids....34 B2
Moseley, H. & W.....33 H5
Moss, Strath....88 A4
Moss, Clwyd....52 D7
Moss, S. Yks....55 J2
Mossat....100 D7
Moss Bank, Mers....53 G4
Mossbank, Shetld....121 G5
Mossblown....77 K5
Mossburnford....74 C2
Mossdale....72 B6
Mossend....78 E3
Mossgiel....77 K5
Mossley....54 C3
Moss of Barmuckity....100 B2

Moss Side	61	G6
Mosstodloch	100	C2
Mosterton	9	F4
Mostyn	52	C5
Motcombe	9	K2
Motherwell	78	E4
Mottingham	21	J6
Mottisfont	10	E2
Mottistone	10	F6
Mottram in Longdendale	54	C4
Mottram St Andrew	53	K6
Mouldsworth	53	G6
Moulin	91	L6
Moulsecoomb	13	G6
Moulsford	19	G2
Moulsoe	36	C6
Moulton, Suff	38	B4
Moulton, N. Yks	68	E6
Moulton, Lincs	47	G5
Moulton, Ches	53	H7
Moulton, Northnts	35	J4
Moulton Chapel	47	F6
Moulton Seas End	47	G5
Mount, Corn	3	F4
Mount, Corn	3	K3
Mountain Ash	25	J5
Mountain Cross	79	J5
Mountbenger	80	B7
Mount Bures	38	E7
Mountfield	13	L4
Mountgerald	98	D2
Mount Hawke	2	F5
Mountjoy	3	G3
Mountnessing	22	C4
Mounton	29	K8
Mountsorrel	45	G6
Mousehole	2	C7
Mousen	81	K6
Mouswald	73	F6
Mow Cop, Staffs	53	K8
Mow Cop, Ches	53	K8
Mowhaugh	74	E1
Mowsley	35	H2
Moy	90	F3
Moyles Court	10	C4
Moylgrove	26	F3
Muasdale	76	B3
Muchalls	93	L2
Much Birch	29	K4
Much Cowarne	29	L3
Much Dewchurch	29	J4
Muchelney	9	F2
Much Hadham	21	J1
Much Hoole	61	H7
Muchlarnick	3	L4
Much Marcle	30	A4
Much Wenlock	43	H8
Mucking	22	C5
Mucklestone	43	J4
Muckleton	43	G5
Muckletown	100	E6
Muckton	57	H5
Mudale	113	G5
Muddiford	7	F2
Mudeford	10	C5
Mudford	9	G3
Mudgley	17	F6
Mudgock	85	H7
Mugeary	103	F5
Mugginton	44	D3
Muggleswick	68	C1
Muie	108	E3
Muir	92	B3
Muirden	101	G3
Muirdrum	93	G8
Muirhead, Tays	87	G1
Muirhead, Strath	85	J8
Muirhouses	86	D6
Muirkirk	78	D7
Muir of Fairburn	98	C3
Muir of Fowlis	100	E7
Muir of Lochs	100	C2
Muir of Ord	98	D3
Muirshearlich	90	C3
Muirtack, Grampn	101	H4
Muirtack, Grampn	101	J5
Muirton, Tays	86	C3
Muirton, Highld	99	F2
Muirton of Ardblair	92	C7
Muirton of Ballochy	93	H5
Muker	68	B7
Mulbarton	49	G7
Mulben	100	C3
Mullion	2	E8
Mullion Cove	2	E8
Mumbles, The	24	E6
Mumby	57	K6
Munderfield Row	33	F5
Munderfield Stocks	33	F5
Mundesley	49	J4
Mundford	48	D8
Mundham, Norf	49	J8
Mundham, W. Susx	11	K4
Mundon	22	E3
Munerigie	90	D1
Mungasdale	106	E2
Mungrisdale	66	F3
Munlochy	98	E3
Munsley	33	F6
Munslow	32	E2
Murch	25	K7
Murcott	31	K6
Murkle	115	G3
Murlaggan, Highld	90	B2
Murlaggan, Highld	90	B3
Murrow	47	G7
Mursley	36	B8
Murthly	92	B8
Murton, Durham	69	F2
Murton, Northum	81	H5
Murton, Cumbr	67	K4
Murton, N. Yks	63	K4
Musbury	8	D5
Muscoates	64	D4
Musdale	84	B2

Musselburgh	87	G7
Muston, Leic	46	B4
Muston, N. Yks	65	H5
Mustow Green	33	H3
Mutford	39	K2
Muthill	86	B3
Mutterton	8	B4
Mybster	115	G4
Myddfai	25	F1
Myddle	42	F5
Mydroilyn	27	J2
Mylor Bridge	3	G6
Mynachlog-ddu	26	F4
Myndtown	32	C2
Mynydd-bach	29	J8
Mynydd Isa	52	D7
Mynydd Llandegai	50	F4
Mynydd Mechell	50	C1
Mynytho	50	C7
Myrebird	93	J2
Mytchett	19	K5
Mytholm	62	C7
Mytholmroyd	62	D7
Myton-on-Swale	63	H3

N

Naast	106	D3
Naburn	63	K5
Nackington	15	H3
Nacton	39	H6
Nafferton	65	H7
Nailsea	17	F3
Nailstone	44	F7
Nailsworth	30	C8
Nairn	99	G3
Nancegollan	2	E6
Nancledra	2	C6
Nanhoron	50	B7
Nannerch	52	C7
Nanpantan	45	G6
Nanpean	3	H4
Nanstallon	3	J3
Nant-ddu	25	J3
Nanternis	27	H2
Nantgaredig	27	J3
Nantgarw	25	K6
Nant Glas	41	J7
Nantglyn	51	K4
Nantlle	50	E5
Nantmawr	42	D5
Nantmel	41	K7
Nantmor	50	F6
Nant Peris	50	F5
Nantwich	43	H2
Nant-y-derry	29	H7
Nantyffyllon	25	G5
Nantyglo	25	K3
Nant-y-moel	25	H5
Naphill	20	C4
Nappa	62	B4
Napton on the Hill	35	F4
Narberth	26	F6
Narborough, Norf	48	C6
Narborough, Leic	45	G8
Nasareth	50	D5
Naseby	35	H3
Nash, H. & W	32	C4
Nash, Gwent	16	E2
Nash, Shrops	33	F3
Nash, Bucks	35	J7
Nash Lee	20	C3
Nassington	46	D8
Nasty	21	H1
Nateby, Lancs	61	H5
Nateby, Cumbr	67	K6
Natland	67	H8
Naughton	38	F6
Naunton, Glos	30	F5
Naunton, H. & W	33	H7
Naunton Beauchamp	34	A5
Navenby	56	D8
Navestock Heath	21	K4
Navestock Side	21	K4
Nawton	63	K1
Nayland	38	E7
Nazeing	21	J3
Neacroft	10	C5
Neal's Green	34	C2
Neasham	68	F5
Neath	25	F5
Neatishead	49	J5
Nebo, Gwyn	50	D5
Nebo, Dyfed	40	E7
Nebo, Gwyn	51	H5
Necton	48	D7
Nedd	112	C5
Nedging Tye	38	F6
Needham	39	H2
Needham Market	39	F5
Needingworth	37	G3
Neen Savage	33	F3
Neen Sollars	33	F3
Neenton	33	F2
Nefyn	50	C6
Neilston	77	K2
Nelson, Lancs	62	B6
Nelson, M. Glam	25	K5
Nelson Village	75	J6
Nemphlar	79	F5
Nempnett Thrubwell	17	G4
Nenthall	67	K2
Nenthead	67	K2
Nenthorn	80	E6
Nercwys	52	D7
Nereabolls	82	B6
Nerston	78	D4
Nesbit	81	H6
Ness, N. Yks	64	D3
Ness, Ches	52	E6
Nesscliffe	42	E6
Neston, Ches	52	D6
Neston, Wilts	17	K4
Nether Alderley	53	K6

Netheravon	18	C6
Nether Blainslie	80	D5
Netherbrae	101	G3
Nether Broughton	45	H5
Netherburn	79	F5
Nether Burrow	61	K2
Netherbury	9	F5
Nether Cerne	9	H5
Nether Compton	9	G3
Nether Dallachy	100	C2
Netherend	29	K7
Nether Exe	5	K1
Netherfield	13	L5
Netherhampton	10	C2
Nether Haugh	55	H4
Nether Heyford	35	H5
Nether Howecluch	73	F2
Nether Kellet	61	J3
Nether Kinmundy	101	K4
Nether Kirkton	77	K2
Netherlaw	71	J7
Netherley	93	K2
Nethermill	73	F5
Nether Padley	55	F6
Nether Poppleton	63	J4
Nether Row	66	F3
Netherseal	44	D6
Nether Silton	69	G7
Nether Stowey	16	C7
Netherthird	72	A2
Netherthong	54	E3
Netherton, H. & W	34	A6
Netherton, Mers	52	E3
Netherton, W. Yks	55	F2
Netherton, Northum	75	F3
Netherton, Tays	93	G6
Netherton, Central	85	H7
Netherton, Devon	5	J4
Nethertown, Cumbr	66	B6
Nethertown, Highld	115	J2
Nether Wallop	10	E1
Nether Wasdale	66	D6
Nether Whitacre	44	D8
Nether Winchendon or Lower Winchendon	20	B2
Netherwitton	75	G4
Nether Worton	31	J4
Nethy Bridge	99	J6
Netley	11	F4
Netley Marsh	10	E3
Nettlebed	20	B5
Nettlebridge	17	H6
Nettlecombe	9	G5
Nettleden	20	E2
Nettleham	56	E6
Nettlestead	13	K1
Nettlestead Green	13	K1
Nettlestone	11	H5
Nettleton, Lincs	59	F6
Nettleton, Wilts	17	K3
Neuk, The	93	J2
Nevendon	22	D4
Nevern	26	E3
New Abbey	72	E7
New Aberdour	101	K2
New Addington	21	H7
New Alresford	11	G1
New Alyth	92	D7
Newark, Cambs	46	F7
Newark, Orkney	117	G2
Newark-on-Trent	45	J2
Newarthill	78	E4
New Ash Green	14	C2
New Bewick	75	G1
Newbiggin, Durham	68	B4
Newbiggin, N. Ys	68	B7
Newbiggin, N. Yks	62	C1
Newbiggin, Cumbr	60	F3
Newbiggin, Cumbr	67	G4
Newbiggin, Cumbr	67	H2
Newbiggin, Cumbr	67	J4
Newbiggin-by-the-Sea	75	K5
Newbigging, Tays	92	D7
Newbigging, Tays	92	F8
Newbigging, Tays	93	F8
Newbigging, Strath	79	H5
Newbigging-on-Lune	67	K6
Newbold, Leic	44	F6
Newbold, Derby	55	G6
Newbold on Avon	35	F3
Newbold-on-Stour	34	D6
Newbold Pacey	34	D5
Newbold Verdon	45	F7
New Bolingbroke	57	H8
Newborough, Staffs	44	C5
Newborough, Cambs	46	F7
Newbottle	35	G7
Newbourne	39	H6
New Brancepeth	68	E2
Newbridge, Corn	2	C6
Newbridge, Clwyd	42	D3
Newbridge, Hants	10	D3
Newbridge, Lothn	86	E7
Newbridge, I. of W	11	F6
Newbridge, Gwent	25	L5
Newbridge-on-Usk	29	H8
Newbridge-on-Wye	28	E2
New Brighton	52	E4
New Brinsley	45	F2
Newbrough	74	E7
New Buckenham	39	F1
Newbuildings	5	H2
Newburgh, Lancs	53	F2
Newburgh, Fife	87	F3
Newburgh, Grampn	101	J6
Newburn	75	H7
Newbury	19	F4
Newby, Cumbr	67	H4
Newby, N. Yks	64	D3
Newby, N. Yks	61	L2
Newby Bridge	61	G1
Newby East	73	K8
New Byth	101	H3
Newby West	66	F1

Newby Wiske	63	G1
Newcastle, Shrops	32	B2
Newcastle, Gwent	29	J6
Newcastle Emlyn	27	H3
Newcastleton	73	K5
Newcastle-under-Lyme	43	K3
Newcastle upon Tyne	75	J7
Newchapel, Surrey	13	G2
Newchapel, Dyfed	27	G4
Newchapel, Staffs	43	K2
New Cheriton	11	G2
Newchurch, Powys	29	G2
Newchurch, Kent	15	G5
Newchurch, I. of W	11	G6
Newchurch, Dyfed	27	H5
Newchurch, Gwent	29	J8
Newchurch in Pendle	62	B6
New Clipstone	55	J7
New Costessey	49	G7
Newcott	8	D4
New Cross	41	F6
New Cumnock	72	B2
New Deer	101	H4
Newdigate	12	E2
New Duston	35	J4
New Earswick	63	K4
New Edlington	55	J4
New Ellerby	59	F3
Newell Green	20	C6
New Eltham	21	J6
New End	34	C4
Newenden	14	E6
Newent	30	B5
New Farnley	63	F6
New Ferry	52	E5
Newfield, Durham	68	E3
Newfield, Highld	109	F6
New Fryston	63	H7
Newgale	26	C5
New Galloway	72	B6
Newgate	48	F3
Newgate Street	21	H3
Newhall, Derby	44	D5
Newhall, Ches	43	H3
Newham	81	K7
Newham Hall	81	K7
New Hartley	75	K6
Newhaven	1	H6
New Hedges	26	F7
New Holland	58	E4
Newholm	69	L5
New Horndean	81	G5
New Houghton, Norf	48	C5
New Houghton, Derby	55	H7
Newhouse	78	E3
New Houses	62	B2
New Hutton	67	H7
New Hythe	14	D3
Newick	13	H4
Newington, Kent	14	E2
Newington, Kent	15	H5
Newington, Oxon	31	L8
New Inn, Gwent	29	H8
New Inn, Dyfed	27	J4
New Inn, Gwent	29	J7
New Invention	32	B3
New Kelso	106	E7
New Lanark	79	F5
Newland, N. Yks	58	A4
Newland, H. & W	33	G6
Newlandrig	80	B3
Newlands, Northum	68	C1
Newlands, Grampn	100	C3
Newlands, Highld	99	F4
Newlands of Geise	115	F3
New Lane	52	F2
New Leake	57	J8
New Leeds	101	J3
New Longton	61	J7
New Luce	70	C5
Newlyn	2	C7
Newmachar	101	H7
Newmains	79	F4
New Malden	21	G7
Newmarket, Suff	38	B4
Newmarket, W. Isles	111	J4
New Marske	69	J4
New Marton	42	E4
Newmill, Border	74	B2
New Mill, Corn	2	C6
New Mill, Herts	20	D2
New Mill, W. Yks	54	E3
Newmill of Inshewan	92	F5
New Mills, Derby	54	C5
New Mills, Corn	3	H4
New Mills, Ches	53	J5
New Mills, Powys	41	K3
New Mills, Gwent	29	K7
Newmiln	86	E1
Newmilns	77	L4
New Milton	10	D5
New Moat	26	E5
Newnham, Glos	30	A6
Newnham, Kent	14	F3
Newnham, H. & W	33	F4
Newnham, Herts	37	F7
Newnham, Northnts	35	G5
Newnham, Hants	19	J5
New Ollerton	55	K7
New Pitsligo	101	H3
New Polzeath	3	H2
Newport, Glos	30	B8
Newport, Humbs	58	C3
Newport, Gwent	16	E2
Newport, Dyfed	26	E4
Newport, Devon	7	F2
Newport, I. of W	11	G6
Newport, Highld	115	H7
Newport, Shrops	43	J6
Newport, Essex	37	J7
Newport, Norf	49	L6

Newport-on-Tay	87	H2
Newport Pagnell	36	B6
Newpound Common	12	D4
New Prestwick	77	J5
Newquay, Corn	3	G3
New Quay, Dyfed	27	H2
New Rackheath	49	H6
New Radnor	32	B4
New Romney	15	G6
New Rossington	55	K4
New Row	61	K6
New Sauchie	86	B5
New Scone	86	E2
Newseat	101	G5
Newsham, N. Yks	68	D5
Newsham, Northum	75	K6
Newsholme, Lancs	62	B4
Newsholme, Humbs	58	B4
New Silksworth	69	F1
Newstead, Border	80	D6
Newstead, Notts	45	G2
Newstead, Northum	81	K7
New Stevenston	78	E4
Newthorpe	63	H6
New Tolsta	111	K3
Newton, Gramp	100	A2
Newton, Border	74	B1
Newton, Northnts	36	B2
Newton, Staffs	44	B5
Newton, Strath	84	C5
Newton, Wilts	10	D2
Newton, Strath	78	D3
Newton, S. Glam	16	D3
Newton, W. Isles	104	D4
Newton, Lincs	46	D4
Newton, Norf	48	D6
Newton, Lothn	86	D7
Newton, W. Glam	24	E6
Newton, Suff	38	E6
Newton, Highld	99	F2
Newton, Cumbr	60	F2
Newton, Highld	99	F4
Newton, Warw	35	G3
Newton, Ches	53	G6
Newton, Northum	75	G7
Newton, M. Glam	25	G7
Newton, Ches	53	G8
Newton, H. & W	29	H4
Newton, Lancs	61	H6
Newton, Cambs	37	H6
Newton, Cambs	47	H6
Newton, Lancs	61	J2
Newton, Highld	115	J3
Newton, H. & W	29	K2
Newton, Lancs	61	K4
Newton Abbot	5	J4
Newton Arlosh	66	D1
Newton Aycliffe	68	E4
Newton Bewley	69	G4
Newton Blossomville	36	C5
Newton Bromswold	36	C4
Newton Burgoland	44	E7
Newton by Toft	56	E5
Newton Ferrers	5	F7
Newton Flotman	49	H8
Newtongrange	80	B3
Newton Harcourt	45	H8
Newtonhill	93	L2
Newton Kyme	63	H5
Newton-le-Willows, N. Yks	68	E8
Newton-le-Willows, Mers	53	G4
Newton Longville	36	B7
Newton Mearns	77	L2
Newtonmore	91	J2
Newton of Ardtoe	89	H1
Newton of Balcanquhal	86	E3
Newton-on-Ouse	63	J4
Newton-on-Rawcliffe	64	F3
Newton on the Moor	75	H3
Newton on Trent	56	C6
Newton Poppleford	8	B6
Newton Purcell	35	H7
Newton Regis	44	D7
Newton Reigny	67	G3
Newton Solney	44	D5
Newton St Cyres	5	J2
Newton Stewart	70	F5
Newton St Faith	49	H6
Newton St Loe	17	J4
Newton St Petrock	6	E4
Newton Tony	18	D6
Newton Tracey	7	F3
Newton under Roseberry	69	H5
Newton upon Derwent	64	E8
Newton Valence	11	J1
Newtown, Powys	32	A1
Newtown, Dorset	10	B5
Newtown, Cumbr	74	B7
Newtown, Highld	98	B8
Newtown, Ches	54	C5
Newtown, Derby	54	C5
Newtown, Hants	10	D3
Newtown, Hants	19	F4
Newtown, I. of W	10	F5
Newtown, Northum	75	G3
Newtown, Ches	43	H3
Newtown, Hants	11	H3
Newtown, Northum	81	H6
New Town, Lothn	87	H7
Newtown, Northum	81	J7
Newtown, Grampn	99	K2
Newtown, H. & W	29	L3
Newtown, Staffs	53	L7
Newtown, Hants	19	L3
Newtown, I. of M	60	U4
Newtown-in-St-Martin	2	F7
Newtown Linford	45	G6
Newtown St Boswells	80	D6

New Tredegar	25	K4
Newtyle	92	D7
New Waltham	59	G6
New Wimpole	37	G6
New Winton	87	H7
New Yatt	31	H6
New York, Lincs	47	F2
New York, T. & W	75	K6
Neyland	26	D7
Nibley	17	H2
Nicholashayne	8	C3
Nicholaston	24	D6
Nidd	63	G3
Nigg, Highld	109	G6
Nigg, Grampn	101	J8
Nine Ashes	22	B3
Ninebanks	67	K1
Ninemile Bar or Crocketford	72	D6
Ninfield	13	L5
Ningwood	10	F6
Nisbet	80	E7
Niton	11	G7
Nitshill	77	L1
Niwbwrch	50	D4
Noak Hill	21	K4
Nobottle	35	H4
Nocton	56	E7
Noke	31	K6
Nolton	26	C6
Nolton Haven	26	C6
No Man's Heath, Warw	44	D7
No Man's Heath, Ches	43	G3
Nomansland, Wilts	10	D3
Nomansland, Devon	7	J4
Noneley	43	F5
Nonington	15	J3
Noonsbrough	118	C3
Nor	81	H5
Noranside	93	F5
Norbury, Derby	44	C3
Norbury, Shrops	42	E8
Norbury, Ches	43	G3
Norbury, Staffs	43	J5
Nordelph	47	J7
Norden, Dorset	10	A6
Norden, G. Man	53	K2
Nordley	43	H8
Norham	81	H5
Norley	53	G6
Norleywood	10	E5
Normanby, Humbs	58	C5
Normanby, N. Yks	64	E4
Normanby-by-Spital	56	E5
Normanby le Wold	57	F4
Norman Cross	36	E1
Normandy	12	C1
Norman's Green	8	B4
Normanton, Lincs	46	C3
Normanton, Derby	44	E4
Normanton, W. Yks	63	G7
Normanton, Notts	45	J2
Normanton le Heath	44	E6
Normanton on Soar	45	G5
Normanton-on-the-Wolds	45	H4
Normanton on Trent	56	B7
Normoss	61	G6
Norrington Common	17	K4
Norris Hill	44	E6
Northallerton	69	F7
Northam, Devon	6	E3
Northam, Hants	10	F3
Northampton	35	J4
North Ascot	20	D7
North Aston	31	J5
Northway	21	G3
North Baddesley	10	E3
North Ballachulish	90	B5
North Barrow	9	H2
North Barsham	48	E4
North Benfleet	22	D5
North Berwick	87	J6
North Boarhunt	11	H3
Northborough	46	E7
Northbourne	15	K3
North Bovey	5	H3
North Bradley	17	K5
North Brentor	4	E3
North Buckland	6	E1
North Burlingham	49	J6
North Cadbury	9	H2
North Cairn	70	A4
North Carlton	56	D6
North Cave	58	C3
North Cerney	30	E7
Northchapel	12	C4
North Charford	10	C3
North Charlton	81	K7
North Cheriton	9	H2
Northchurch	20	D3
North Cliffe	58	C3
North Clifton	56	C6
North Cotes	59	H6
Northcott	4	D2
North Cove	39	K2
North Cowton	68	E6
North Crawley	36	C6
North Cray	21	J6
North Creake	48	D4
North Curry	8	E2
North Dalton	65	G7
North Deighton	63	G4
North Duffield	58	A3
Northdyke	116	B4
North Elkington	57	G4
North Elmham	48	E5
Northend, Bucks	20	B4
Northend, Warw	34	E5
North End, W. Susx	12	E6
North End, Hants	18	F4
North End, Avon	16	F4
North End, Hants	11	H4
Northend, Avon	17	J4
North Erradale	106	C3

North Fearns Pendlebury

North Fearns 96 A2
North Ferriby 58 D4
Northfield, W. Mids 34 B3
Northfield, Border 81 H3
Northfield, Grampn 101 J8
Northfleet 14 C1
North Frodingham 65 H7
North Gorley 10 C3
North Green 39 H2
North Greetwell 56 E6
North Grimston 64 F6
North Hayling 11 J4
North Heasley 7 H2
North Heath 12 D4
North Hill, Corn 4 C4
North Hill, Cambs 37 H3
North Hinksey Village 31 J7
North Holmwood 12 E2
North Huish 5 H6
North Hykeham 56 D7
Northiam 14 E6
Northill 36 E6
Northington 11 G1
North Kelsey 58 E6
North Kessock 98 E4
North Kilvington 63 H1
North Kilworth 35 H2
North Kyme 46 E2
North Lancing 12 E6
Northlands 47 G2
Northleach 30 F6
North Lee 20 C3
Northleigh, Devon 8 C5
North Leigh, Oxon 31 H6
North Leverton with Habblesthorpe 56 B5
Northlew 4 F2
North Littleton 34 B6
North Lopham 38 F2
North Luffenham 46 C7
North Marden 11 K3
North Marston 20 B1
North Middleton 80 B4
North Molton 7 H3
Northmoor 31 J7
Northmoor Green or Moorland 8 E1
North Moreton 19 G2
Northmuir 92 E6
North Muskham 56 B8
North Newbold 58 D3
North Newington 34 F7
North Newnton 18 C5
North Newton 8 D1
North Nibley 30 B8
North Oakley 19 G5
North Ockendon 22 B5
Northolt 21 F5
Northop 52 D7
Northop Hall 52 D7
North Ormsby 57 G4
Northorpe, Lincs 56 C4
Northorpe, Lincs 46 D6
North Otterington 69 F8
North Owersby 56 E4
Northowram 62 E7
North Perrott 9 F4
North Petherton 8 D1
North Petherwin 4 C3
North Pickenham 48 D7
North Piddle 34 A5
Northpunds 119 G6
North Queensferry 86 E6
Northrepps 49 H4
North Rigton 63 F5
North Rode 53 K7
North Roe 120 F4
North Runcton 48 B6
North Sandwick 121 H3
North Scale 60 E2
North Scarle 56 C7
North Seaton 75 J5
North Shields 75 K7
North Shoebury 22 F5
North Shore 61 G6
North Side 47 F8
North Somercotes 57 J4
North Stainley 63 F2
North Stainmore 67 L5
North Stifford 22 C5
North Stoke, Oxon 20 A5
North Stoke, W. Susx 12 D5
North Stoke, Avon 17 J4
North Street 11 H1
North Sunderland 81 L6
North Tamerton 4 D2
Noth Tawton 7 G5
North Thoresby 59 G7
North Tidworth 18 D6
North Tolsta 111 K3
Northton 104 E3
Northtown 116 D7
North Tuddenham 48 F6
Northwall 117 G2
North Walsham 49 H4
North Waltham 19 G6
North Warnborough 19 J5
North Water Bridge 93 H5
North Watten 115 H4
Northway 30 D4
North Weald Bassett 21 J3
North Wheatley 56 B5
North Whilborough 5 J5
Northwich 53 H6
Northwick, Avon 17 G2
North Wick, Avon 17 G4
North Widcombe 17 G5
North Willingham 57 F5
North Wingfield 55 H7
North Witham 46 C5
Northwold 48 C8
Northwood, G. Lon 20 E4
Northwood, Shrops 42 F4
Northwood, I. of W 11 F5
Northwood, Derby 55 F7
Northwood Green 30 B6
North Wootton, Norf 48 B5
North Wootton, Somer 17 G6
North Wootton, Dorset 9 H3
North Wraxall 17 K3
Norton, H. & W 34 B6
Norton, Powys 32 C4
Norton, Glos 30 C5
Norton, W. Susx 12 C6
Norton, Shrops 32 D2
Norton, Suff 38 E4
Norton, N. Yks 64 E5
Norton, I. of W 10 E6
Norton, Herts 37 F7
Norton, Cleve 69 G4
Norton, Ches 53 G5
Norton, S. Yks 55 G5
Norton, Shrops 43 G7
Norton, Northnts 35 H4
Norton, H. & W 33 H5
Norton, S. Yks 55 J2
Norton, Notts 55 J6
Norton, Shrops 43 J7
Norton, Wilts 17 K2
Norton Bavant 17 L6
Norton Bridge 43 K4
Norton Canes 44 B7
Norton Canon 29 H3
Norton Disney 56 C8
Norton East 44 B7
Norton Ferris 9 J1
Norton Fitzwarren 8 C2
Norton Green 10 E6
Norton Hawkfield 17 G4
Norton Heath 22 C3
Norton in Hales 43 J4
Norton-in-the-Moors 43 K2
Norton-Juxta-Twycross 44 E7
Norton-le-Clay 63 H2
Norton Lindsey 34 D4
Norton Malreward 17 H4
Norton Mandeville 21 K3
Norton St Philip 17 J5
Norton Subcourse 49 K8
Norton sub Hamdon 9 F3
Norwell 56 B7
Norwell Woodhouse 56 B7
Norwich 49 H7
Norwick 121 J1
Norwood Green 21 F6
Norwood Hill 12 F2
Noseley 45 J8
Noss Mayo 5 F7
Nosterfield 63 F1
Nostie 96 D3
Notgrove 30 F5
Nottage 25 G7
Nottingham 45 G3
Nottington 9 H6
Notton, W. Yks 55 G2
Notton, Wilts 17 L4
Nounsley 22 D2
Noutard's Green 33 G4
Nox 42 F6
Nuffield 20 A5
Nunburnholme 64 F8
Nuneaton 34 E1
Nuneham Courtenay 31 K8
Nun Monkton 63 J4
Nunney 17 J6
Nunnington 63 K2
Nunnykirk 75 G4
Nunthorpe 69 H5
Nunton, Wilts 10 C2
Nunton, W. Isles 104 C6
Nursling 10 E3
Nursted 11 J2
Nutbourne 12 D5
Nutfield 13 G2
Nuthall 45 G3
Nuthampstead 37 H7
Nuthurst 12 E4
Nutley 13 H4
Nutwell 55 K3
Nybster 115 J3
Nyetimber 11 K5
Nyewood 11 K2
Nymet Rowland 7 H5
Nymet Tracey 5 H1
Nympsfield 30 C7
Nynehead 8 C2
Nyton 12 C6

O

Oadby 45 H7
Oad Street 14 E2
Oakamoor 44 B3
Oakbank 79 H3
Oakdale 25 K5
Oake 8 C2
Oaken 43 K7
Oakenclough 61 J5
Oakengates 43 J6
Oakenshaw, Durham 68 E3
Oakenshaw, W. Yks 62 E7
Oakford, Dyfed 27 J2
Oakford, Devon 7 K3
Oakgrove 53 L7
Oakham 46 B7
Oakhanger 11 J1
Oakhill 17 H6
Oakington 37 H4
Oaklands 21 G2
Oakle Street 30 B6
Oakley, Bucks 20 A
Oakley, Beds 36 D5
Oakley, Fife 86 D6
Oakley, Suff 39 G3
Oakley, Hants 19 G5
Oakley Green 20 D6
Oakley Park 41 J5
Oakridge 30 D7
Oaks 42 F7
Oaksey 30 D8
Oakthorpe 44 E6
Oakwoodhill 12 E3
Oakworth 62 D6
Oare, Wilts 18 C4
Oare, Kent 15 G2
Oasby 46 D4
Oathlaw 93 F6
Oban 84 A1
Oborne 9 H3
Occlestone Green 53 H7
Occold 39 G3
Ochiltree 77 L5
Ockbrook 44 F4
Ockham 12 D1
Ockle 89 G1
Ockley 12 E2
Ocle Pychard 29 K3
Odcombe 9 G3
Odd Down 17 J4
Oddendale 67 H5
Oddingley 33 J5
Oddington, Glos 31 G5
Oddington, Oxon 31 K6
Odell 36 C5
Odiham 19 J5
Odstock 10 C2
Odstone 44 E7
Offchurch 34 E4
Offenham 34 B6
Offham, E. Susx 13 H5
Offham, Kent 13 K1
Offord Cluny 37 F4
Offord D'Arcy 37 F4
Offton 38 F6
Offwell 8 C5
Ogbourne Maizey 18 C3
Ogbourne St Andrew 18 C3
Ogbourne St George 18 D3
Ogle 75 H6
Ogmore 25 G7
Ogmoreby-Sea 25 G7
Ogmore Vale 25 H5
Okeford Fitzpaine 9 K3
Okehampton 5 F2
Okehampton Camp 5 F2
Old 35 J3
Old Aberdeen 101 J8
Old Alresford 11 G1
Old Basing 19 H5
Oldberrow 34 C4
Old Bewick 81 J7
Old Bolingbroke 57 H7
Oldborough 7 H5
Old Brampton 55 G6
Old Bridge of Urr 72 C7
Old Buckenham 38 F1
Old Burghclere 19 F5
Oldbury, W. Mids 34 A2
Oldbury, Warw 44 E8
Oldbury, Shrops 33 G1
Oldbury-on-Severn 17 H1
Oldbury on the Hill 17 K2
Old Byland 63 J1
Oldcastle 29 H5
Old Cleeve 16 B6
Old Clipstone 55 K7
Old Colwyn 51 H3
Oldcotes 55 J5
Old Dailly 70 D2
Old Dalby 45 H5
Old Deer 101 J4
Old Denaby 55 H4
Old Ellerby 59 F3
Old Felixstowe 39 J7
Oldfield 33 H4
Oldford 17 J5
Old Hall, The 59 G5
Oldham 53 L3
Oldhamstocks 80 F2
Old Heath 23 G1
Oldhurst 37 G3
Old Hutton 61 J1
Old Kea 3 G5
Old Kilpatrick 85 G7
Old Kinnernie 101 G8
Old Knebworth 21 G1
Oldland 17 H3
Old Leake 47 H2
Old Malton 64 E5
Oldmeldrum 101 H6
Old Milverton 34 E4
Old Monkland 78 E3
Old Newton 38 F4
Old Park 43 H7
Old Philpstoun 86 D7
Old Radnor 29 G2
Old Rayne 100 F6
Old Romney 15 G6
Oldshore Beg 112 C3
Oldshoremore 112 D3
Old Sodbury 17 J2
Old Somerby 46 C4
Oldstead 63 J1
Old Swarland 75 H3
Old Town, Northum 74 E4
Old Town, Cumbr 61 J1
Oldtown of Ord 100 F3
Old Warden 36 E6
Oldways End 7 J3
Old Weston 36 E3
Oldwhat 101 H3
Old Windsor 20 D6
Old Wives Lees 15 G3
Olgrinmore 115 F4
Oliver's Battery 11 F2
Ollaberry 120 F4
Ollach 103 G5
Ollerton, Shrops 43 H5
Ollerton, Ches 53 J6
Ollerton, Notts 55 K7
Olney 36 B5
Olton 34 C2
Olveston 17 H2
Ombersley 33 H4
Ompton 56 A7
Onchan 60 R4
Onecote 44 B2
Ongar Hill 47 J5
Ongar Street 32 C4
Onibury 32 D3
Onich 90 B5
Onllwyn 25 G3
Onneley 43 J3
Onslow Village 12 C2
Opinan, Highld 106 C4
Opinan, Highld 106 D2
Orby 57 J7
Orchard 9 K3
Orchard Portman 8 D2
Orcheston 18 B6
Orcop 29 J5
Orcop Hill 29 J5
Ord 96 B4
Ordhead 100 F7
Ordie 92 F1
Ordiquish 100 C3
Ore 14 E7
Oreton 33 F2
Orford, Ches 53 H4
Orford, Suff 39 K5
Orgreave 44 C6
Orinsay 111 H6
Orleton, H. & W 32 D4
Orleton, H. & W 33 F4
Orlingbury 36 B3
Ormesby 69 H5
Ormesby St Margaret 49 K6
Ormesby St Michael 49 K6
Ormiscaig 106 D2
Ormiston 87 H8
Ormsaigmore 89 F2
Ormskirk 52 F3
Orpington 21 J7
Orrell 53 G3
Orroland 71 J7
Orsett 22 C5
Orslow 4 K6
Orston 45 J3
Orton, Cumbr 67 J6
Orton, Northnts 35 K3
Orton Longueville 46 E8
Orton-on-the-Hill 44 E7
Orwell 37 G5
Osbaldeston 61 K6
Osbaston 44 F7
Osbournby 46 D4
Oscroft 53 G7
Ose 102 E4
Osgathorpe 44 F6
Osgodby, Lincs 56 E4
Osgodby, N. Yks 65 H4
Osgodby, N. Yks 63 K6
Oskaig 103 G5
Oskamull 89 F4
Osmaston 44 D3
Osmington 9 J6
Osmington Mills 9 J6
Osmotherley 69 G7
Osnaburgh or Dairsie 87 H3
Ospisdale 109 F5
Ospringe 15 G2
Ossett 55 F1
Ossington 56 B7
Ostend 22 F4
Oswaldkirk 63 K2
Oswaldtwistle 61 L7
Oswestry 42 D5
Otford 21 K8
Otham 14 D3
Othery 8 E1
Otley, W. Yks 62 F5
Otley, Suff 39 H5
Otterbourne 11 F2
Otterburn, N. Yks 62 B4
Otterburn, Northum 74 E4
Otterburn Camp 74 E4
Otterden Place 14 F3
Otter Ferry 84 B6
Otterham 4 B2
Ottershaw 20 E7
Otterswick 121 H4
Otterton 8 B6
Ottery St Mary 8 C5
Ottringham 59 G4
Oughtershaw 62 B1
Oughtibridge 55 G4
Oulston 63 J2
Oulton, Cumbr 66 E1
Oulton, Norf 49 G5
Oulton, W. Yks 63 G7
Oulton, Staffs 43 L4
Oultn, Suff 49 L8
Oulton Broad 39 L1
Oulton Street 49 G5
Oundle 36 D2
Ousby 67 J3
Ousden 38 C5
Ouseburn 63 H3
Ousefleet 58 C4
Ouston 68 E1
Outertown 116 B5
Outgate 66 F7
Outhgill 67 K6
Outlane 54 D2
Out Newton 59 H4
Out Rawcliffe 61 H5
Outwell, Cambs 47 J7
Outwell, Norf 47 J7
Outwood, Surrey 13 G2
Outwood, W. Yks 63 G7
Ovenden 62 D7
Over, Avon 17 G2
Over, Cambs 37 G3
Overbister 117 F2
Overbury 34 A7
Overcombe 9 H6
Over Haddon 54 F7
Over Kellet 61 J3
Over Kiddington 31 J5
Over Norton 31 H5
Overseal 44 D6
Over Silton 69 G7
Overstone 35 K4
Overstrand 49 H3
Overton, Clwyd 42 E3
Overton, Shrops 32 E3
Overton, D. & G 72 E7
Overton, Hants 19 G6
Overton, Lancs 61 H4
Overton, Grampn 101 H7
Overtown 79 F4
Over Wallop 18 D7
Over Whitacre 34 D1
Oving, Bucks 20 A1
Oving, W. Susx 11 L4
Ovingdean 13 G6
Ovingham 75 G7
Ovington, Essex 38 C6
Ovington, Durham 68 D5
Ovington, Norf 48 E7
Ovington, Hants 11 G1
Ovington, Northum 75 G7
Ower 10 E3
Owermoigne 9 J6
Owlswick 20 B3
Owmby-by-Spital 56 E5
Owslebury 11 G2
Owston 45 J7
Owston Ferry 58 C6
Owstwick 59 G3
Owthorpe 45 H4
Oxborough 48 C7
Oxenholme 67 H8
Oxenhope 62 D6
Oxen Park 61 G1
Oxenton 30 D4
Oxenwood 18 E5
Oxford 31 K7
Oxhill 34 E6
Oxley 43 L7
Oxley's Green 13 K4
Oxnam 74 C2
Oxshott 21 F7
Oxspring 55 F3
Oxted 13 G1
Oxton, Border 80 C4
Oxton, Notts 45 H2
Oxwich 24 C6
Oxwick 48 E5
Oykel Bridge 107 J1
Oyne 100 F6

P

Pabail Iarach 111 K4
Pabail Varach 111 K4
Packington 44 E6
Padanaram 92 F6
Pdbury 35 J7
Paddington 21 G5
Paddlesworth 15 H5
Paddockhaugh 100 B3
Paddock Wood 13 K2
Paddolgreen 43 G4
Padeswood 52 D7
Padiham 62 B6
Padstow 3 H2
Padworth 20 A7
Pagham 11 K5
Paglesham Churchend 22 F4
Paglesham Eastend 22 F4
Paible, W. Isles 104 C5
Paible, W. Isles 104 F2
Paignton 5 J5
Pailton 35 F2
Painscastle 29 F3
Painshawfield 75 G7
Painswick 30 C7
Paisley 77 K1
Pakefield 39 L1
Pakenham 38 E4
Pale 51 J7
Palestine 18 D6
Paley Street 20 C6
Palgrave 39 G3
Palmerstown 25 K8
Palnackie 71 K6
Palnure 71 F5
Palterton 55 7
Pamber End 20 A8
Pamber Green 19 H5
Pamber Heath 20 A7
Pamphill 10 A4
Pampisford 37 H6
Panbride 87 J1
Pancrasweek 6 C5
Pandy, Clwyd 42 C4
Pandy, Gwent 29 H5
Pandy, Powys 41 J3
Pandy Tudur 51 H4
Panfield 38 C8
Pangbourne 20 A6
Pannal 63 G4
Pant 42 D5
Panteg 26 D4
Pant Glas 50 D6
Pantgwyn 27 G3
Pant Mawr 41 H5
Panton 57 F6
Pant-pastynog 51 K4
Pantperthog 41 G3
Pant-y-dwr 41 J6
Pant-y-ffridd 42 C7
Pantyffynnon 27 L6
Panxworth 49 J6
Papcastle 66 D3
Papple 87 J7
Papplewick 45 G2
Papworth Everard 37 F4
Papworth St Agnes 37 F4
Par 3 J4
Parbold 53 F2
Parbrook 9 G1
Parcllyn 27 G2
Parc Seymour 16 F1
Pardshaw 66 C4
Parham 39 J4
Par Corner 20 A5
Park End, Northum 74 E6
Parkend, Glos 29 L7
Parkeston 39 H7
Parkgate, Ches 52 D6
Parkgate, Surrey 12 F2
Parkgate, D. & G 72 F5
Park Gate, Hants 11 G4
Parkgate, Ches 53 J6
Parkham 6 D3
Parkham Ash 6 D3
Parkhouse 29 K7
Parkhurst 11 F5
Parkmill 24 D6
Parkstone 10 B5
Parley Cross 10 B5
Parracombe 7 G1
Parrog 26 E4
Parson Cross 55 G4
Parson Drove 47 G7
Partick 77 L1
Partington 53 J4
Partney 57 J7
Parton, Cumbr 66 B4
Parton, D. & G 72 B6
Partridge Green 12 E5
Parwich 44 C2
Passenham 35 J7
Paston 49 J4
Patcham 13 G6
Patching 12 D6
Patchole 7 G1
Patchway 17 H2
Pateley Bridge 62 E3
Pathfinder Village 5 J2
Pathhead, Strath 72 B2
Pathhead, Lothn 80 B3
Pathhead, Fife 87 F5
Patmore Heath 37 H8
Patna 77 K6
Patney 18 B5
Patrick 60 P3
Patrick Brompton 68 E7
Patrington 59 H4
Patrixbourne 15 J3
Patterdale 67 F5
Pattingham 43 K8
Pattishall 35 H5
Patton Bridge 67 H7
Paul 2 C7
Paulerspury 35 J6
Paull 59 F4
Paulton 17 H5
Pavenham 36 B5
Pawston 81 G6
Paxford 34 C7
Paxton 81 H4
Payhembury 8 B4
Paythorne 62 B4
Pcaston 80 C3
Peacehaven 13 H6
Peak Dale 54 D6
Peak Forest 54 E6
Peakirk 46 E7
Peanmeanach 96 C7
Peasedown St John 17 J5
Peasemore 19 F3
Peasenhall 39 J4
Peaslake 12 D2
Peasmarsh 14 E6
Peaston Bank 80 C3
Peathill 101 J2
Peatling Magna 35 G1
Peatling Parva 35 G2
Peaton 32 E2
Pebmarsh 38 D7
Pebworth 34 C6
Pecket Well 62 C7
Peckforton 43 G2
Peckleton 45 F7
Pedmore 33 J2
Pedwell 9 F1
Peebles 79 K5
Peel 60 P3
Pegswood 75 J5
Peinchorran 103 G5
Peinlich 103 F3
Pelaw 75 J7
Pelcomb Cross 26 D6
Peldon 23 F2
Pelsall 44 B7
Pelon 68 E1
Peluth 66 D2
Pelynt 3 L4
Pembrey 24 C4
Pembridge 29 H2
Pembroke 26 D7
Pembroke Dock 26 D7
Pembury 13 K2
Penallt 29 K7
Penally 26 F8
Penare 3 H5
Penarth 25 K7
Pen-bont Rhydybeddau 41 F5
Penbryn 27 G2
Pencader 27 J4
Pencaitland 80 C3
Pencarreg 27 K3
Pencelli 25 J2
Pen-Clawdd 24 D5
Pencoed 25 H6
Pencombe 29 L2
Pencoyd 29 K5
Pencraig, Powys 41 K1
Pencraig, H. & W 29 K5
Pendeen 2 B6
Penderyn 25 H4
Pendine 27 G7
Pendlebury 53 J3

Pendleton 62 A6
Pendock 30 B4
Pendoggett 3 J2
Pendoylan 25 J7
Penegoes 41 G3
Penffordd 26 E5
Penffridd 50 E5
Penge 21 H6
Pengorffwysfa 50 D1
Penhalurick 2 F6
Penhow 17 F1
Penhurst 13 K5
Penicuik 79 K3
Peniel 51 K4
Penifiler 103 F4
Peninver 76 C5
Penisa'r Waun 50 E4
Peniistone 55 F3
Penketh 53 G5
Penkridge 43 L6
Penley 42 F3
Penllergaer 24 E5
Pen-llyn, Gwyn 50 C2
Penllyn, S. Glam 25 H7
Penmachno 51 G5
Penmaen, W. Glam 24 D6
Penmaen, Gwent 25 K5
Penmaenmawr 51 G3
Penmaenpool 41 F2
Penmark 25 J8
Penmon 51 F2
Penmorfa 50 E6
Penmynydd 50 E3
Penn 20 D4
Pennal 41 G3
Pennan 101 J2
Pennant, Dyfed 40 E7
Pennant, Powys 41 H4
Pennant-Melangell 41 K1
Pennard 24 D6
Pennerley 42 E8
Pennington 60 F2
Pennjerick 2 F6
Penn Street 20 D4
Penny Bridge 61 G1
Pennycross 89 G6
Pennymoor 7 J4
Penparc 27 G3
Penparcau 40 E5
Penperlleni 29 H7
Penpillick 3 J4
Penpol 3 G6
Penpoll 3 K4
Penpont 72 D4
Penrherber 27 G4
Penrhiwceiber 25 J5
Penrhiw-llan 27 H3
Penrhiwpal 27 H3
Penrhos, Gwyn 50 B2
Penrhos, Gwyn 50 C7
Penrhos, Powys 25 G3
Penrhos, Gwent 29 J6
Penrhyn Bay 51 H2
Penrhyn-coch 41 F5
Penrhyndeudraeth 50 F7
Penrhyn-side 51 H2
Penrice 24 C6
Penrith 67 H3
Penrose 3 G2
Penruddock 67 G4
Penryn 3 F6
Pen-sarn, Gwyn 50 D6
Pen-sarn, Gwyn 40 E1
Pensarn, Clwyd 51 J3
Pensax 33 G4
Pensby 52 D5
Penselwood 9 J1
Pensford 17 H4
Penshaw 68 F1
Penshurst 13 J2
Pensilva 4 C5
Pentewan 3 J5
Pentir 50 E4
Pentire 3 F3
Pentney 48 C6
Penton Mewsey 18 E6
Pentraeth 50 E3
Pentre, Clwyd 42 C4
Pentre, Clwyd 42 D3
Pentre, Shrops 42 E6
Pentre, Clwyd 51 K4
Pentre, Powys 41 K5
Pentre-bach, Powys 25 H1
Pentrebach, M. Glam 25 J4
Pentre-bach, Dyfed 27 K3
Pentre Berw 50 D3
Pentre-bont 51 G5
Pentre-celyn 42 C2
Pentre-cwrt 27 H4
Pentre Dolau Honddu 28 D3
Pentredwr, Clwyd 42 C3
Pentre-dwr, W. Glam 24 E5
Pentrefelin, Gwyn 50 E7
Pentrefelin, Gwyn 51 H3
Pentrefoelas 51 H5
Pentregat 27 H2
Pentre-Gwenlais 52 D6
Pentre Halkyn 52 D6
Pentre-llyn-cymmer 51 J5
Pentre'r beirdd 42 C6
Pentre'r-felin 25 H1
Pentre-tafarn-y-fedw 51 H4
Pentre-ty-gwyn 25 G1
Pentrich 44 E2
Pentridge 10 B3
Pentwyn 25 L6
Pentyrch 25 K6
Penuwch 40 E7
Penwithick 3 J4
Penybanc 27 L5
Penybont, Powys 32 A4
Pen-y-bont, Clwyd 42 D5
Pen-y-bont, Dyfed 27 H5
Penybontfawr 41 K1
Pen-y-bryn, Gwyn 41 F2

Penybryn, M. Glam 25 K5
Penycae, Clwyd 42 D3
Pen-y-cae, Powys 25 G3
Pen-y-cae-mawr 29 J8
Pen-y-cefn 52 C6
Pen-y-clawdd 29 J7
Pen-y-coedcae 25 J6
Penycwm 26 C5
Penyffordd 52 E7
Pen-y-garn 27 K4
Pen-y-garnedd, Gwyn 50 E3
Penygarnedd, Powys 41 L1
Penygraig 25 H5
Penygroes, Gwyn 50 D5
Pen-y-groes, Dyfed 27 K6
Penysarn 50 D1
Pen-y-stryt 42 C2
Penywaun 25 H4
Penzance 2 C6
Peopleton 33 J5
Peover Heath 53 J6
Peper Harow 12 C2
Peplow 43 H5
Percie 93 G2
Percyhorner 101 J2
Perivale 21 F5
Perlethorpe 55 K6
Perranarworthal 2 F6
Perranporth 2 F4
Perranuthnoe 2 D7
Perranzabuloe 2 F4
Perry Barr 34 B1
Perry Green 21 J2
Pershore 33 J6
Pert 93 H5
Pertenhall 36 D4
Perth 86 E2
Perthy 42 E4
Perton 43 K8
Peterborough 46 E8
Peterburn 106 C3
Peterchurch 29 H4
Peterculter 93 K1
Peterhead 101 L4
Peterlee 69 G2
Petersfield 11 J2
Peter's Green 21 F2
Peters Marland 6 E4
Peterstone Wentlooge 16 D2
Peterston-super-Ely 25 J7
Peterstow 29 K5
Peter Tavy 4 F4
Petertown 116 C6
Petham 15 H3
Petrockstowe 6 F5
Pett 14 E7
Pettaugh 39 G5
Pettinain 79 G5
Pettistree 39 H5
Petton, Shrops 42 F5
Petton, Devon 7 L3
Petty 101 G5
Pettycur 87 F6
Pettymuick 101 K4
Petworth 12 C4
Pevensey Bay 13 K6
Pewsey 18 C4
Philham 6 C3
Philiphaugh 80 C7
Phillack 2 D6
Philleigh 3 G6
Philpstoun 86 D7
Phoenix Green 19 J5
Pica 66 C4
Piccotts End 20 E3
Pickering 64 E4
Picket Piece 18 E6
Pickhill 63 G1
Picklescott 42 F8
Pickmere 53 H6
Pickwell, Devon 6 E1
Pickwell, Leic 45 J6
Pickworth, Leic 46 C6
Pickworth, Lincs 46 D4
Picton, Ches 52 F6
Picton, N. Yks 69 G6
Piddinghoe 13 H6
Piddington, Oxon 20 A2
Piddington, Northnts 35 K5
Piddlehinton 9 J5
Piddletrenthide 9 J5
Pidley 37 G3
Piercebridge 68 E5
Pierowall 116 D2
Pigdon 75 H5
Pikehall 54 E8
Pilgrims Hatch 21 K4
Pilham 56 C4
Pill 17 G3
Pillaton 4 D5
Pillerton Hersey 34 E6
Pillerton Priors 34 D6
Pilleth 32 B4
Pilley 55 G3
Pilling 61 H5
Pilling Lane 61 G5
Pilning 17 G2
Pilsbury 54 E7
Pilsdon 8 F5
Pilsley, Derby 55 F6
Pilsley, Derby 55 H7
Pilton, Leic 46 C7
Pilton, Northnts 36 D2
Pilton, Somer 17 G6
Pimperne 9 L4
Pinchbeck 47 F5
Pinchbeck West 46 F5
Pinfold 52 E2
Pinhoe 5 K2
Pinmore 70 D2
Pinner 21 F5
Pinvin 34 A6
Pinwherry 70 C3
Pinxton 45 F2
Pipe and Lyde 29 K3

Pipe Gate 53 J7
Piperhill 99 G3
Pipewell 36 B2
Pippacott 7 F2
Pirbright 12 C1
Pirnmill 76 D3
Pirton, Herts 36 E7
Pirton, H. & W 33 H6
Pishill 20 B5
Pistyll 50 C6
Pitblae 101 J2
Pitcairngreen 86 D2
Pitcalnie 109 G6
Pitcaple 101 G6
Pitchcombe 30 C7
Pitchcott 20 B1
Pitchford 43 G7
Pitch Green 20 B3
Pitch Place 12 C1
Pitcombe 9 H1
Pitcox 87 K7
Pitfichie 100 F7
Pitfour Castle 87 E2
Pitgrudy 109 F4
Pitlessie 87 G4
Pitlochry 91 L6
Pitmedden 101 H6
Pitminster 8 D3
Pitmunie 100 F7
Pitney 9 J4
Pitscottie 87 H3
Pitsea 22 D5
Pitsford 35 J4
Pitstone Green 20 D2
Pittendreich 100 A2
Pittentrail 109 F3
Pittenweem 87 J4
Pittington 68 F2
Pitton 10 D1
Pixey Green 39 H3
Place Newton 65 F5
Plains 78 B3
Plaish 43 G8
Plaistow 12 D3
Plaitford 10 D3
Plas 27 J5
Plas Gogerddan 41 F5
Plas Isaf 51 K6
Plas Llwyngwern 41 G3
PlasLlysyn 41 J4
Plastow Green 19 G4
Platt 13 K1
Plawsworth 68 E2
Plaxtol 13 K1
Playden 14 F6
Playford 39 H6
Play Hatch 20 B6
Playing Place 3 G5
Plealey 42 F7
Plean 85 L6
Pleasington 61 K7
Pleasley 55 J7
Plenmeller 74 D7
Pleshey 22 C2
Plockton 96 D2
Plocrapool 105 G2
Plocrapool Point 105 G2
Ploughfield 29 H3
Plowden 32 C2
Ploxgreen 42 E7
Pluckley 14 F4
Plumbland 66 D3
Plumley 53 J6
Plumpton, Cumbr 67 G3
Plumpton, E. Susx 13 G5
Plumpton, Lancs 61 G6
Plumpton Green 13 G5
Plumpton Head 67 H3
Plumstead 49 G4
Plumtree 45 H4
Plungar 45 J4
Plush 9 J4
Plwmp 27 H2
Plymouth 4 E5
Plymstock 4 F6
Plymtree 8 B4
Pockley 63 K1
Pocklington 64 F8
Pode Hole 46 F5
Podimore 9 G2
Podington 36 C4
Podmore 43 J4
Point Clear 23 G2
Pointon 46 E4
Pokesdown 10 C5
Polapit Tamar 4 D3
Polbain 112 A7
Polbathic 4 D6
Polbeth 79 H3
Polebrook 36 D2
Polegate 13 J6
Pole of Itlaw, The 100 F3
Polesworth 44 D7
Polglass 106 F1
Polgooth 3 H4
Poling 12 D6
Polkerris 3 J4
Pollington 55 K2
Polloch 89 J2
Pollokshaws 77 L1
Pollokshields 78 C3
Polmassick 3 H5
Polnessan 77 K6
Polperro 3 L4
Polruan 3 K4
Polsham 17 G6
Polstead 38 E7
Poltalloch 83 H2
Poltimore 5 K2
Polwarth 80 F4
Polyphant 4 C3
Polzeath 3 H2
Ponde 28 E4
Pondersbridge 37 F1
Ponders End 21 H4

Ponsanooth 2 F6
Ponsworthy 5 H4
Pontamman 27 L6
Pontantwn 27 J6
Pontardawe 24 F4
Pontardulais 27 K7
Pontarsais 27 J5
Pont Creuddyn 27 K2
Pont Cyfyng 51 G5
Pontefract 63 H7
Ponteland 75 H6
Ponterwyd 41 G5
Pontesbury 42 F7
Pontfadog 42 D4
Pontfaen, Dyfed 26 E4
Pont-faen, Powys 25 H1
Pont Henri 27 J7
Ponthir 16 E1
Ponthirwaun 27 G3
Pontllanfraith 25 K5
Pontlliw 24 E4
Pont Llogel 41 K2
Pontllyfni 50 D5
Pontlottyn 25 K4
Pontneddfechan 25 H4
Pont Pen-y-benglog 51 F4
Pontrhydfendigaid 41 G7
Pontrhydyfen 25 F5
Pont-rhyd-y-groes 41 G6
Pontrilas 29 H5
Pontrobert 42 C6
Pont-rug 50 E4
Ponts Green 13 K5
Pontshill 30 A5
Pont-Sian 27 J3
Pontsticill 25 J3
Pontyates 27 J7
Pontyberem 27 K6
Pontybodkin 52 D8
Pontyclun 25 J6
Pontycymer 25 H5
Pontymister 16 D1
Pont-y-pant 51 G5
Pontypool 29 G7
Pontypridd 25 J5
Pontywaun 25 L5
Pooksgreen 10 E3
Pool 2 E5
Poole 10 B5
Poole Keynes 30 E8
Poolewe 106 D3
Pooley Bridge 67 G4
Poolhill 30 B5
Pool of Muckhart 86 D4
Pool Quay 42 D6
Poorton 9 G5
Popham 19 G6
Poplar 21 H5
Porchfield 11 F5
Poringland 49 H7
Porkellis 2 E6
Porlock 7 J1
Port-an-eorna 96 C2
Port Ann 84 B6
Port Appin 89 L4
Port Askaig 82 D5
Port Bannatyne 77 F1
Portbury 17 G3
Port Carlisle 73 H7
Port Charlotte 82 B6
Portchester 11 H4
Portclair 98 C7
Port Driseach 84 B7
Port Ellen 82 C7
Port Elphinstone 101 G6
Port Erin 60 N5
Portesham 9 H6
Port e Vullen 60 R2
Port-Eynon 24 C6
Portfield Gate 26 C6
Portgate 4 E3
Portgaverne 3 J1
Port Glasgow 84 F7
Portgordon 100 C2
Portgower 109 J2
Porth 25 J5
Porthallow 3 F7
Porthcawl 25 G7
Porthcurno 2 B7
Port Henderson 106 C4
Porthgain 26 C4
Porthkerry 25 J8
Porthleven 2 E7
Porthllechog 50 D1
Porthmadog 50 E7
Porthmeor 2 C6
Porth Navas 2 F7
Portholland 3 H5
Porthoustock 3 G7
Porthpean 3 J4
Porthtowan 2 E5
Porthyrhyd, Dyfed 28 B4
Porthyrhyd, Dyfed 27 K6
Portincaple 84 E5
Portington 58 B3
Port Isaac 3 H1
Portishead 17 G3
Portknockie 100 D2
Portlethen 93 L2
Portlethen Village 93 L2
Portloe 3 H6
Port Logan 70 B7
Portmahomack 109 H5
Portmeirion 50 E7
Portmellon 3 J5
Port Mholair 111 K4
Port Mor 95 K8
Portmore 10 E5
Port Mulgrave 69 K5
Portnacroish 89 L4
Portnahaven 82 A6
Portnalong 102 E5
Portnaluchaig 96 B7

Portnancon 113 F2
Portobello 87 G7
Port of Menteith 85 H4
Port of Ness 111 K1
Porton 10 C1
Portpatrick 70 B6
Portquin 3 H1
Portreath 2 E5
Portree 103 F4
Portrye 77 G2
Portscatho 3 G6
Portsea 11 H4
Portskerra 114 D3
Portskewett 17 G2
Portslade 12 F6
Portslade-by-Sea 12 F6
Portsmouth 11 H4
Portsoy 100 E2
Port St Mary 60 P5
Port Sunlight 52 E5
Portswood 10 F3
Port Talbot 25 F5
Portway 34 B3
Port Wemyss 82 A6
Port William 70 E7
Portwrinkle 4 D6
Poslingford 38 C6
Postbridge 5 G4
Postcombe 20 B4
Posting 15 H5
Postwick 49 H7
Potarch 93 H2
Potsgrove 36 C8
Potten End 20 E3
Potterhanworth 56 E7
Potter Heigham 49 K6
Potterne 18 A5
Potterne Wick 18 B5
Potters Bar 21 G3
Potter's Cross 33 H2
Potterspury 35 J6
Potter Street 21 J7
Potterton 101 J7
Potto 69 G6
Potton 37 F6
Pott Row 48 C5
Pott Shrigley 53 L6
Poughill, Corn 6 C5
Poughill, Devon 7 J5
Poulshot 18 A5
Poulton 30 F7
Poulton-le-Fylde 61 G6
Pound Bank 33 G3
Pound Hill 13 F3
Poundon 35 H8
Poundsgate 5 H4
Poundstock 4 C2
Powburn 75 G2
Powderham 5 K3
Powerstock 9 G5
Powfoot 73 G7
Powick 33 H5
Powmill 86 D5
Poxwell 9 J6
Poyle 20 E6
Poynings 12 F5
Poyntington 9 H2
Poynton, Ches 53 L5
Poynton Green 43 G6
Poystreet Green 38 E5
Praa Sands 2 D7
Pratt's Bottom 21 J7
Praze-an-Beeble 2 E6
Predannack Wollas 2 E8
Prees 43 G4
Preesall 61 G5
Prees Green 43 G4
Preesgweene 42 D4
Prees Higher Heath 43 G4
Prendwick 75 G2
Pren-gwyn 27 J3
Prenteg 50 E6
Prenton 52 E5
Prescot 53 F4
Prescott 42 F5
Pressen 81 G6
Prestatyn 51 K2
Prestbury, Glos 30 D5
Prestbury, Ches 53 L6
Presteigne 32 C4
Presthope 43 G8
Prestleigh 17 H6
Preston, Glos 30 A4
Preston, Wilts 18 B3
Preston, Leic 46 B7
Preston, Glos 30 E7
Preston, Herts 21 F1
Preston, Humbs 59 F3
Preston, Border 81 F4
Preston, E. Susx 13 G6
Preston, Kent 15 J2
Preston, Devon 5 J4
Preston, Dorset 9 J6
Preston, Lancs 61 J7
Preston, Lothn 87 J7
Preston, Northum 81 K7
Preston Bagot 34 C4
Preston Bissett 35 H8
Preston Brockhurst 43 G5
Preston Brook 53 G5
Preston Candover 19 H6
Preston Capes 35 G5
Preston Gubbals 43 G6
Preston on Stour 34 D5
Preston on Wye 29 H3
Preston upon
   the Weald Moors 43 H6
Preston Wynne 29 K3
Prestwich 53 K3
Prestwick, Northum 75 H6
Prestwick, Strath 77 J5

Prestwood 20 C3
Price Town 25 H5
Prickwillow 38 A2
Priddy 17 G5
Priest Hutton 61 J2
Priest Weston 42 D8
Primethorpe 45 G8
Primrose Green 48 F6
Princes Risborough 20 C3
Princethorpe 34 F3
Princetown 5 F4
Priors Hardwick 35 F5
Priors Marston 35 F5
Priory, The 11 H5
Priory Wood 29 G3
Priston 17 H4
Prittlewell 22 E5
Privett 11 H2
Prixford 7 F2
Probus 3 G5
Proncy 109 F4
Prospect 66 D2
Prudhoe 75 G7
Puckeridge 21 H1
Puckington 8 E3
Pucklechurch 17 J3
Puddington, Ches 52 E6
Puddington, Devon 7 J4
Puddledock 38 F1
Puddletown 9 J5
Pudleston 29 K2
Pudsey 63 F6
Pulborough 12 D5
Puleston 43 J5
Pulford 52 E8
Pulham 9 J4
Pulham Market 39 G2
Pulham St Mary 39 H2
Pulloxhill 36 D7
Pulverbatch 42 F7
Pumsaint 27 L3
Puncheston 26 E5
Puncknowle 9 G6
Punnett's Town 13 K4
Purbrook 11 H4
Purfleet 21 K6
Puriton 16 E6
Purleigh 22 E3
Purley, Berks 20 A6
Purley, G. Lon 21 H7
Purlogue 32 B3
Purls Bridge 37 H2
Purse Caundle 9 H3
Purslow 32 C2
Purston Jaglin 55 H2
Purton, Glos 30 A7
Purton, Glos 30 A7
Purton, Wilts 18 B2
Purton Stoke 18 B1
Pury End 35 J6
Pusey 31 H8
Putley 33 F7
Putney 21 G6
Puttenham, Herts 20 D2
Puttenham, Surrey 12 C2
Puxton 16 F4
Pwll 24 C4
Pwllcrochan 26 D7
Pwllheli 50 C7
Pwllmeyric 17 G1
Pwll-y-glaw 25 F5
Pyecombe 13 F5
Pye Corner 16 E2
Pyle, I. of W 11 F7
Pyle, M. Glam 25 G6
Pylle 17 H7
Pymore 37 H2
Pyrford 20 E8
Pyrton 20 A4
Pytchley 36 B3
Pyworthy 6 D5

Q

Quabbs 32 B2
Quadring 47 F4
Quainton 20 B1
Quarley 18 D6
Quarndon 44 E3
Quarrier's Homes 77 J1
Quarrington 46 D3
Quarrington Hill 68 F3
Quarry Bank 33 J2
Quarry, The 30 B8
Quarrywood 100 A2
Quarter 78 E4
Quatford 33 G1
Quatt 33 G2
Quebec 68 D2
Quedgeley 30 C6
Queen Adelaide 37 H2
Queenborough 14 F1
Queen Camel 9 G2
Queen Charlton 17 H4
Queensbury 14 E6
Queensferry, Clwyd 52 E7
Queensferry, Lothn 86 E7
Queenzieburn 85 J7
Quendale 119 F7
Quendon 37 J7
Queniborough 45 H6
Quenington 30 F7
Quernmore 61 J3
Quethiock 4 D5
Quholm 116 B5
Quidenham 38 E1
Quidhampton, Wilts 10 C1
Quidhampton, Hants 19 G5
Quidinish 105 F3
Quilquox 101 J5
Quindry 116 D7
Quine's Hill 60 Q4
Quinton 35 J5

Quoditch 4 E2
Quorndon or Quorn 45 G6
Quorn or Quorndon 45 G6
Quothquan 79 G6
Quoyloo 116 B4
Quoys 121 J1

R

Raby 52 E5
Rachub 51 F4
Rackenford 7 J4
Rackham 12 D5
Rackheath 49 H6
Racks 73 F6
Rackwick, Orkney 116 B7
Rackwick, Orkney 116 D2
Radcliffe, Northum 75 J3
Radcliffe, G. Man 53 J3
Radcliffe on Trent 45 H4
Radclive 35 H7
Radcot 31 G8
Raddery 99 F3
Radernie 87 H4
Radford Semele 34 E4
Radlett 21 F4
Radley 31 K8
Radnage 20 B4
Radstock 17 H5
Radstone 35 G6
Radway 34 E6
Radway Green 43 J2
Radwell 37 F7
Radwinter 38 B7
Radyr 25 K6
Rafford 99 J3
Ragdale 45 H6
Raglan 29 J7
Ragnall 56 C6
Rainford 53 F3
Rainham, Kent 14 E2
Rainham, G. Lon 21 K5
Rainhill 53 F4
Rainow 54 C6
Rainton 63 G2
Rainworth 55 J8
Raisbeck 67 J6
Rait 87 F2
Raithby, Lincs 57 5
Raithby, Lincs 57 H7
Rake 11 K2
Rame, Corn 4 E7
Rame, Corn 2 F6
Ram Lane 14 F4
Rampisham 9 G4
Rampside 60 F3
Rampton, Notts 56 B6
Rampton, Cambs 37 H4
Ramsbottom 53 J2
Ramsbury 18 D3
Ramscraigs 115 G7
Ramsdean 11 J2
Ramsdell 19 G5
Ramsden 31 H6
Ramsden Bellhouse 22 D4
Ramsden Heath 22 D4
Ramsey, Cambs 37 F2
Ramsey, Essex 39 H7
Ramsey, I. of M 60 R2
Ramseycleuch 73 H2
Ramsey Forty Foot 37 G2
Ramsey Island 22 F3
Ramsey Mereside 37 F2
Ramsey St Mary's 37 F2
Ramsgate 15 K2
Ramsgill 62 E2
Ramshorn 44 B3
Ranby 55 K5
Rand 57 F6
Randwick 30 C7
Ranfurly 84 F8
Rangemore 44 C5
Rangeworthy 17 H2
Ranish 111 J5
Rankinston 77 K6
Ranskill 55 K5
Ranton 43 K5
Ranworth 49 J6
Rapness 116 E2
Rascarrel 71 J7
Raskelf 63 H2
Rassau 25 K3
Rastrick 62 E7
Ratagan 96 E4
Ratby 45 G7
Ratcliffe Culey 44 E8
Ratcliffe on the Wreake ..45 H6
Rathen 101 K2
Rathillet 87 G2
Rathmell 62 B4
Ratho 86 E7
Ratho Station 86 E7
Rathven 100 D2
Ratley 34 E6
Ratlinghope 42 F8
Rattar 115 H2
Ratten Row 61 H5
Rattery 5 H5
Rattlesden 38 E5
Rattray 92 C7
Rauceby 46 D3
Raughton Head 67 F2
Raunds 36 C3
Ravenfield 55 H4
Ravenglass 66 C7
Raveningham 49 J8
Ravenscar 65 G2
Ravensdale 60 Q2
Ravensden 36 D5
Ravenseat 68 A6
Ravenshead 45 G2
Ravensmoor 43 H2
Ravensthorpe, W. Yks 55 F1

Ravensthorpe, Northnts ...35 H3
Ravenstone, Bucks 36 B5
Ravenstone, Leic 44 F6
Ravenstonedale 67 K6
Ravenstown 61 G2
Ravenstruther 79 G5
Ravensworth 68 D6
Raw 65 G2
Rawcliffe, Humbs 58 A4
Rawcliffe, N. Yks 63 J4
Rawcliffe Bridge 58 B4
Rawdon 62 F6
Rawmarsh 55 H4
Rawreth 22 D4
Rawridge 8 D4
Rawtenstall 62 B7
Raydon 38 F7
Raylees 74 F4
Rayleigh 22 E4
Rayne 22 D1
Reach 37 J4
Read 62 A6
Reading 20 B6
Reading Street 14 F5
Reagill 67 J5
Rearquhar 109 F4
Rearsby 45 H6
Reaster 115 H3
Reawick 119 F4
Reay 114 E3
Rechullin 106 D6
Reculver 15 J2
Redberth 26 E7
Redbourn 21 F2
Redbourne 58 D6
Redbrook 29 K6
Redburn 99 H4
Redcar 69 J4
Redcastle 98 D4
Redcliff Bay 17 F3
Red Dial 66 E2
Redding 86 C7
Reddingmuirhead 86 C7
Reddish 53 K4
Redditch 34 B4
Redesdale Camp 74 E4
Redesmouth 74 E5
Redford, Durham 68 C3
Redford, Tays 93 G7
Redfordgreen 73 J2
Redgrave 38 F3
Redhill, Surrey 13 F1
Redhill, Avon 17 F4
Redhill, Grampn 101 F5
Redhill, Grampn 101 G8
Redisham 39 K2
Redland, Orkney 116 C4
Redland, Avon 17 G3
Redlingfield 39 G3
Redlynch, Wilts 10 D2
Redlynch, Somer 9 J1
Redmarley D'Abitot 30 B4
Redmarshall 69 F4
Redmile 45 J4
Redmire 68 C7
Redmoor 3 J3
Rednal 42 E5
Redpath 80 D6
Redpoint 106 C5
Red Rock 53 G3
Red Roses 27 G6
Red Row 75 J4
Redruth 2 F5
Red Street 43 K2
Red Wharf Bay 50 E2
Redwick, Gwent 16 F2
Redwick, Avon 17 G2
Redworth 68 E4
Reed 37 G7
Reedham 49 K7
Reedness 58 B4
Reef 111 F4
Reepham, Lincs 56 E6
Reepham, Norf 49 G5
Reeth 68 C7
Regaby 60 R2
Regoul 99 G3
Reiff 112 A7
Reigate 12 F1
Reighton 65 J5
Reiss 115 J4
Rejerrah 3 G4
Relubbus 2 D6
Relugas 99 H4
Remenham 20 B5
Remenham Hill 20 B5
Rempstone 45 G5
Rendcomb 30 E7
Rendham 39 J4
Rendlesham 39 J5
Renfrew 77 L1
Renhold 36 D5
Renishaw 55 H6
Rennington 75 J2
Renton 85 F7
Renwick 67 H2
Repps 49 K6
Repton 44 E5
Resolis 98 E2
Resolven 25 G4
Reston 81 G3
Retew 3 H4
Rettendon 22 D4
Rettendon Place 22 D4
Revesby 57 G7
Rewe 5 K2
Reydon 39 K3
Reymerston 48 F7
Reynalton 26 E7
Reynoldston 24 C5
Rhadmad 40 E6
Rhandirmwyn 28 B3

Rhayader 41 J7
Rhedyn 50 B7
Rheindown 98 D4
Rhes-y-cae 52 C6
Rhewl, Clwyd 42 C3
Rhewl, Clwyd 51 L4
Rhiconich 112 D3
Rhicullen 108 E6
Rhigos 25 H4
Rhilochan 109 F3
Rhiroy 107 G3
Rhiw 40 B1
Rhiwbryfdir 51 F6
Rhiwderin 16 D2
Rhiwlas, Clwyd 42 C4
Rhiwlas, Gwyn 50 E4
Rhiwlas, Gwyn 51 J7
Rhodesia 55 J5
Rhodes Minnis 15 H4
Rhondda 25 H5
Rhonehouse or
  Kelton Hill 72 C8
Rhoose 25 J8
Rhos, W. Glam 25 F4
Rhos, Dyfed 27 H4
Rhoscefnhir 50 E3
Rhoscolyn 50 B3
Rhoscrowther 26 D7
Rhosesmor 52 D7
Rhos-fawr 50 C7
Rhosgadfan 50 E5
Rhosgoch, Gwyn 50 D2
Rhos-goch, Powys 29 F3
Rhoshirwaun 50 A8
Rhoslan 50 D6
Rhoslefain 40 E3
Rhosllanerchrugog 42 D3
Rhosmeirch 50 D3
Rhosneigr 50 C3
Rhosnesni 42 E2
Rhos-on-Sea 51 H2
Rhossili 24 C6
Rhosson 26 B5
Rhostrehwfa 50 D3
Rhostryfan 50 D5
Rhostyllen 42 E3
Rhosybol 50 D2
Rhos-y-brithdir 42 C5
Rhos-y-gwaliau 51 J7
Rhos-y-llan 50 B7
Rhu 84 E6
Rhuallt 51 K3
Rhuddlan 51 K3
Rhue 107 F2
Rhulen 28 F3
Rhunahaorine 76 C3
Rhyd, Gwyn 50 F6
Rhyd, Powys 41 J3
Rhydargaeau 27 J5
Rhydcymerau 27 K4
Rhydd 33 H6
Rhyd-Ddu 50 E5
Rhydding 25 F5
Rhyd-foel 51 J3
Rhydlewis 27 H3
Rhydlios 50 A7
Rhydlydan 51 H5
Rhydowen 27 J3
Rhyd-Rosser 40 E7
Rhydtalog 42 D2
Rhydwyn 50 C2
Rhyd-y-clafdy 50 C7
Rhydycroesau 42 D4
Rhydyfelin, Dyfed 40 E6
Rhydyfelin, M. Glam 25 J6
Rhyd-y-fro 24 F4
Rhydymain 41 H1
Rhydymwyn 52 D7
Rhyd-yr-onen 40 F3
Rhyl 51 K2
Rhymney 25 K4
Rhynd 86 E2
Rhynie 100 D6
Ribbesford 33 G3
Ribble Head 62 A2
Ribbleton 61 J6
Ribchester 61 K6
Riby 59 F6
Riccall 63 K6
Riccarton 77 K4
Richards Castle 32 D4
Richmond, N. Yks 68 D6
Richmond, G. Lon 21 F6
Rickarton 93 K3
Rickinghall 38 F3
Rickling 37 H7
Rickmansworth 20 E4
Riddell 80 D7
Riddlecombe 7 G4
Riddlesden 62 D5
Ridge, Wilts 10 A1
Ridge, Dorset 10 A6
Ridge, Herts 21 G3
Ridgehill 17 G4
Ridge Lane 44 D8
Ridgeway Cross 33 G6
Ridgewell 38 C6
Ridgewood 13 H5
Ridgmont 36 C7
Riding Mill 75 G7
Ridlington, Leic 46 B7
Ridlington, Norf 49 J4
Ridsdale 74 F5
Rievaulx 63 J1
Rigg 73 H7
Riggend 85 K7
Rigside 79 F6
Rileyhill 44 C6
Rilla Mill 4 C4
Rillington 64 F5
Rimington 62 B5
Rimpton 9 H2
Rimswell 59 H4
Rinaston 26 D5

Ringasta 119 F7
Ringford 71 H6
Ringland 49 G6
Ringmer 13 H5
Ringmore 5 G7
Ringorm 100 B4
Ring's End 47 G7
Ringsfield 39 K2
Ringshall, Herts 20 D2
Ringshall, Suff 38 F5
Ringstead, Norf 48 C3
Ringstead, Northnts 36 C3
Ringwood 10 C4
Ringwould 15 K4
Rinmore 100 D7
Rinnigill 116 C7
Rinsey 2 D7
Ripe 13 J5
Ripley, Hants 10 C5
Ripley, Surrey 12 D1
Ripley, Derby 44 F2
Ripley, N. Yks 63 F3
Riplingham 58 D3
Ripon 63 G2
Rippingale 46 D5
Ripple, H. & W 33 H7
Ripple, Kent 15 K3
Rippondon 54 D2
Rireavach 106 F2
Risabus 82 C7
Risbury 29 K2
Risby, Suff 38 D4
Risby, Humbs 58 D5
Risca 16 D1
Rise 59 F2
Risegate 46 F5
Riseley, Berks 20 B7
Riseley, Beds 36 D4
Rishangles 39 G4
Rishton 61 L6
Rishworth 54 D2
Rising Bridge 62 A7
Risley, Derby 45 F4
Risley, Ches 53 H4
Risplith 63 F3
Rivar 18 E4
Rivenhall End 22 E3
River Bank 37 J4
Riverhead 13 J1
Rivington 53 H2
Roachill 7 J3
Roade 35 J5
Roadmeetings 79 F5
Roadside 115 G3
Roadside of Catterline ...93 K4
Roadside of Kinneff 93 K4
Roadwater 16 B7
Roag 102 D4
Roath 25 K7
Robbingworth 21 K3
Roberton, Strath 79 G7
Roberton, Border 73 K2
Robertsbridge 13 L4
Roberttown 62 E7
Robeston Cross 26 C7
Robeston Wathen 26 E6
Robin Hood's Bay 65 G2
Roborough 7 F4
Roby Mill 53 G3
Rocester 44 C4
Roch 26 C5
Rochdale 53 K2
Rochester, Kent 14 D2
Rochester, Northum 74 E4
Rochford, Essex 22 E4
Rochford, H. & W 33 F4
Rock, H. & W 33 G3
Rock, Corn 3 H2
Rock, Northum 75 J1
Rockbeare 8 B5
Rockbourne 10 C3
Rockcliffe, Cumbr 73 J7
Rockcliffe, D. & G 71 K6
Rock Ferry 52 E5
Rockfield, Highld 109 H5
Rockfield, Gwent 29 J6
Rockhampton 30 A8
Rockingham 36 B1
Rockland All Saints 48 E8
Rockland St Mary 49 J7
Rockland St Peter 48 E8
Rockwell End 20 B5
Rodbourne 18 A2
Rodd 32 C4
Roddam 75 G1
Rodden 9 H6
Rode 17 K5
Rode Heath, Ches 53 K7
Rode Heath, Ches 53 K8
Rodel 104 F3
Roden 43 J8
Rodhuish 16 B7
Rodington 43 J8
Rodley 30 B6
Rodmarton 30 D8
Rodmell 13 H6
Rodmersham 14 F2
Rodney Stoke 17 F5
Rodsley 44 D3
Rodway 63 G3
Roe Green 19 K8
Roecliffe 63 G3
Roehampton 21 G6
Roesound 51 G3
Roewen 51 G3
Roffey 12 E3
Rogart 109 F3
Rogate 11 K2
Rogerstone 16 D2
Rogiet 17 F2
Roke 75 L8
Roker 19 J6
Rollesby 49 K6
Rolleston, Staffs 44 D5
Rolleston, Notts 45 J2

Rolleston, Leic 45 J7
Rolston 59 G2
Rolvenden 14 E5
Rolvenden Layne 14 E5
Romaldkirk 68 B4
Romanby 69 F7
Romannobridge 79 J5
Romansleigh 7 H3
Romford 21 K5
Romiley 53 L4
Romsey 10 E2
Romsley, H. & W 34 A2
Romsley, Shrops 33 G2
Ronague 60 P4
Rookby 67 L5
Rookhope 68 B2
Rookley 11 G6
Rooks Bridge 16 E5
Roos 59 G3
Roosebeck 60 F3
Rootpark 79 G4
Ropley 11 H1
Ropley Deane 11 H1
Ropsley 46 C4
Rora 101 K3
Rorrington 42 E7
Rose 2 F4
Roseacre 61 H6
Rose Ash 7 H3
Rosebank 79 F5
Rosebush 26 E5
Rosedale Abbey 64 E3
Roseden 81 J7
Rosehall 108 C3
Rosehearty 101 J2
Rosehill 43 H4
Roseisle 99 K2
Rosemarket 26 D7
Rosemarkie 99 F3
Rosemary Lane 8 C3
Rosemount, Tays 92 C7
Rosemount, Strath 77 J5
Rosenannon 3 H3
Rosewell 79 K3
Roseworthy 2 E6
Rosgill 67 H5
Roshven 96 C8
Roskhill 102 D4
Rosley 66 F2
Roslin 79 K3
Rosliston 44 D6
Rosneath 84 E6
Ross, D. & G 71 H7
Ross, Northum 81 K6
Rossett 52 E8
Rossington 55 K4
Rossland 85 G7
Ross-on-Wye 29 L5
Roster 115 H6
Rostherne 53 J5
Rosthwaite 66 E5
Roston 44 C3
Rosyth 86 E6
Rothbury 75 G3
Rotherby 45 H6
Rotherfield 13 J4
Rotherfield Greys 20 B5
Rotherfield Peppard 20 B5
Rotherham 55 H4
Rothersthorpe 35 J5
Rotherwick 19 J5
Rothes 100 B4
Rothesay 77 F1
Rothiebrisbane 101 G5
Rothienorman 101 G5
Rothiesholm 117 F4
Rothley 45 G6
Rothmaise 101 F5
Rothwell, Northnts 36 B2
Rothwell, Lincs 59 F7
Rothwell, W. Yks 63 G7
Rotsea 65 H7
Rottal 92 C5
Rottingdean 13 G6
Rottington 66 B5
Roud 11 G6
Rougham 48 D5
Rougham Green 38 E4
Roughburn 90 E3
Rough Close 43 L4
Rough Common 15 H3
Roughlee 62 B5
Roughley 44 C8
Roughsike 74 B6
Roughton, Lincs 57 G7
Roughton, Norf 49 H4
Roughton, Shrops 43 J8
Roundhay 63 G6
Roundstreet Common 12 D4
Roundway 18 B4
Rousdon 8 D5
Rousham 31 G6
Rous Lench 34 B5
Routh 59 F2
Row, Cumbr 67 G8
Row, Corn 3 J2
Rowanburn 73 K6
Rowde 18 A4
Rowfoot 74 C7
Rowhedge 23 G1
Rowhook 12 E3
Rowington 34 D4
Rowland 54 F6
Rowland's Castle 11 J3
Rowlands Gill 75 H8
Rowledge 19 K8
Rowlestone 29 H5
Rowley 42 E7
Rowley Regis 34 A2
Rowly 12 D2
Rowney Green 34 B3
Rowrah 66 C5
Rowsham 20 C2
Rowsley 55 F7
Rowston 46 D2

Rowton, Ches 52 F7
Rowton, Shrops 43 H6
Roxburgh 80 E6
Roxby, Humbs 58 D5
Roxby, N. Yks 69 K5
Roxton 36 D5
Roxwell 22 C3
Royal British Legion
  Village 13 L1
Royal Leamington Spa 34 E4
Royal Tunbridge Wells 13 J3
Roybridge 90 D3
Roydon, Norf 48 C5
Roydon, Norf 39 F2
Roydon, Essex 21 J2
Royston, S. Yks 55 G2
Royston, Herts 37 G6
Royton 53 L3
Ruabon 42 E3
Ruaig 88 B4
Ruan Lanihorne 3 G5
Ruan Minor 2 F8
Ruardean 29 L6
Ruardean Woodside 29 L6
Rubery 34 A3
Rubha Bhocaig 105 G2
Rubha Cam nan Gall 104 D7
Rubha Crago 105 H2
Rubh' Aird-mhicheil 94 C2
Ruckcroft 67 H2
Ruckinge 15 G5
Ruckland 57 H6
Ruckley 43 G7
Ruddington 45 G4
Rudge 17 K5
Rudgeway 17 H2
Rudgwick 12 D3
Rudhall 29 L5
Rudloe 17 K4
Rudry 25 K6
Rudston 65 H6
Rudyard 54 C8
Rufford 52 F2
Rufforth 63 J4
Rugby 35 G3
Rugeley 44 B6
Ruilick 98 D4
Ruisgarry 104 E3
Ruishton 8 D2
Ruislip 20 E5
Ruislip Common 20 E5
Rumbling Bridge 86 D5
Rumburgh 39 J2
Rumford 3 G2
Rumney 25 L7
Runcorn 53 G5
Runcton 11 K4
Runcton Holme 48 B7
Runfold 19 K6
Runhall 48 F7
Runham 49 K6
Runnington 8 C2
Runswick Bay 69 L5
Runwell 22 D4
Ruscombe 20 B6
Rushall, H. & W 30 A4
Rushall, W. Mids 44 B7
Rushall, Wilts 18 C5
Rushall, Norf 39 G2
Rushbrooke 38 D4
Rushbury 32 E1
Rushden, Northnts 36 C4
Rushden, Herts 37 G7
Rushford 38 E2
Rush Green 21 K5
Rushlake Green 13 K5
Rushmere 39 K6
Rushmere St Andrew 39 H6
Rushmoor 19 K6
Rushock 33 H3
Rusholme 53 K4
Rushton, Northnts 36 B2
Rushton, Ches 53 G7
Rushton, Shrops 43 H7
Rushton Spencer 53 L7
Rushwick 33 H5
Rushyford 68 E4
Ruskie 85 J6
Ruskington 46 D2
Rusland 61 G1
Rusper 12 F3
Ruspidge 30 A6
Russel's Water 20 B5
Rustington 12 D6
Ruston Parva 65 H6
Ruswarp 65 F2
Rutherford 80 E6
Rutherglen 78 E3
Ruthernbridge 3 J3
Ruthin 52 C8
Ruthrieston 101 J8
Ruthven, Tays 92 D7
Ruthven, Grampn 100 E4
Ruthven, Highld 99 G5
Ruthvoes 3 H3
Ruthwell 73 G7
Ruyton-X1-Towns 42 E5
Ryal 75 G6
Ryal Fold 61 K7
Ryall 8 F5
Ryarsh 14 C3
Rydal 66 F6
Ryde 11 G5
Rye 14 F6
Rye Foreign 14 F6
Rye Harbour 14 F7
Ryhall 46 D6
Ryhill 55 G2
Ryhope 69 G1
Rylstone 62 C4
Ryme Intrinseca 9 G3
Ryther 63 J6
Ryton, Glos 30 B4
Ryton, N. Yks 64 E5
Ryton, T. & W 75 H7

Ryton, Shrops Shipston-on-Stour

Ryton, Shrops 43 J7
Ryton-on-Dunsmore 34 E3

S

Saasaig 96 B5
Sabden 62 A6
Sacombe 21 H2
Sacriston 68 E2
Sadberge 69 F5
Saddell 76 C4
Saddington 35 H1
Saddle Bow 4 B6
Saddlethorpe 58 C4
Sadgill 67 G6
Saffron Walden 37 J7
Saham Toney 48 E7
Saighton 52 F7
St Abbs 81 H3
St Agnes 2 F4
St Albans 21 F3
St Allen 3 G4
St Andrews 87 J3
St Andrews Major 25 K7
St Annes 61 G7
St Ann's 73 F4
St Ann's Chapel, Corn 4 E4
St Ann's Chapel, Devon 5 G7
St Anthony-in-Meneage 3 F7
St Arvans 29 K8
St Asaph or Llanelwy 51 K3
St Athan 25 J8
St Austell 3 J4
St Bees 66 B5
St Blazey 3 J4
St Boswells 80 D6
St Breock 3 H2
St Breward 3 J2
St Briavels 29 K7
St Brides 26 B6
St Bride's Major 25 G7
St Bride's-super-Ely 25 J7
St Brides Wentlooge 16 D2
St Budeaux 4 E6
Saintbury 34 C7
St Buryan 2 C7
St Catherine 17 J3
St Catherines 84 D4
St Clears 27 G6
St Cleer 3 L3
St Clement 3 G5
St Clether 4 C3
St Colmac 76 F1
St Columb Major 3 H3
St Columb Minor 3 G3
St Columb Road 3 H4
St Combs 101 K2
St Cross South Elmham 39 H2
St Cyrus 93 J5
St David's, Dyfed 26 B5
St David's, Tays 86 C2
St Davids, Fife 86 E6
St Day 2 F5
St Dennis 3 H4
St Dogmaels 26 F3
St Dominick 4 E5
St Donats 25 H8
St Endellion 3 H2
St Enoder 3 G4
St Erme 3 G5
St Erth 2 D6
St Erth Praze 2 D6
St Ervan 3 G2
St Eval 3 G3
St Ewe 3 H5
St Fagans 25 K7
St Fergus 101 K3
St Fillans 85 J2
St Florence 26 E7
St Gennys 4 B2
St George 51 J3
St Georges, Avon 16 E4
St George's, S. Glam 25 K7
St Germans 4 D6
St Giles in the Wood 7 F4
St Giles on the Heath 4 D2
St Harmon 41 J6
St Helen Auckland 68 D4
St Helens, Mers 53 G4
St Helens, I. of W 11 H6
St Hilary, Corn 2 D6
St Hilary, S. Glam 25 J7
Saint Hill 13 G3
St Illtyd 25 L4
St Ippollitts 36 E8
St Ishmael's 26 C7
St Issey 3 H2
St Ive 4 D5
St Ives, Dorset 10 C4
St Ives, Corn 2 D5
St Ives, Cambs 37 G3
St James South Elmham 39 J2
St John 4 E6
St Johns, H. & W 33 H5
St John's, I. of M 60 P3
St John's Chapel 68 A3
St John's Fen End 47 J6
St John's Highway 47 J6
St John's Town of Dalry 72 B5
St Judes 60 Q2
St Just 2 B6
St Just in Roseland 3 G6
St Katherines 101 G5
St Keverne 3 F7
St Kew 3 J2
St Kew Highway 3 J2
St Keyne 3 L3
St Lawrence, Essex 23 F3
St Lawrence, I. of W 11 G7
St Lawrence, Corn 3 J3
St Leonards, Dorset 10 C4
St Leonards, Bucks 20 D3
St Leonards, E. Susx 14 D8
St Leven 2 B7
St Lythans 25 K7
St Mabyn 3 J2
St Margarets 29 H4
St Margaret's at Cliffe 15 K4
St Margaret's Hope 116 D7
St Margaret
South Elmham 39 J2
St Mark's 60 P4
St Martin, Corn 4 C6
St Martin, Corn 2 F7
St Martins, Tays 86 E1
St Martin's, Shrops 42 E4
St Mary Bourne 18 F5
St Mary Church 25 J7
St Mary Cray 21 J7
St Mary Hill 25 H7
St Mary Hoo 14 E1
St Mary in the Marsh 15 G6
St Mary's 116 D6
St Mary's Bay 15 G6
St Mawes 3 G6
St Mawgan 3 G3
St Mellion 4 D5
St Mellons 16 D2
St Merryn 3 G2
St Mewan 3 H4
St Michael Caerhays 3 H5
St Michael Penkevil 3 G5
St Michaels, H. & W 32 E4
St Michaels, Kent 14 E5
St Michael's on Wyre 61 H5
St Michael
South Elmham 39 J2
St Minver 3 H2
St Monance 87 J4
St Neot 3 K3
St Neots 36 E4
St Newlyn East 3 G4
St Nicholas, Dyfed 26 D4
St Nicholas, S. Glam 25 J7
St Nicholas at Wade 15 J2
St Ninians 85 K5
St Osyth 23 H2
St Owen's Cross 29 K5
St Paul's Cray 21 J7
St Paul's Walden 21 F1
St Peter's 15 K2
St Petrox 26 D8
St Pinnock 3 L3
St Quivox 77 J5
St Stephen 3 H4
St Stephens, Corn 4 D3
St Stephens, Corn 4 E6
St Teath 3 J1
St Tudy 3 J2
St Twynnells 26 D8
St Vigeans 93 H7
St Wenn 3 H3
St Weonards 29 J5
St Winnow 3 K4
Salcombe 5 H8
Salcombe Regis 8 C6
Salcott 22 F2
Sale 53 J4
Saleby 57 J6
Sale Green 33 J5
Salehurst 13 L4
Salem, Dyfed 41 F5
Salem, Dyfed 27 L5
Salen, Strath 89 G4
Salen, Highld 89 H2
Salesbury 61 K6
Salford, Beds 36 C7
Salford, Oxon 31 G5
Salford, G. Man 53 K4
Salford Priors 34 B5
Salfords 13 F2
Salhouse 49 H6
Saline 86 D5
Salisbury 10 C2
Sallachy 96 E2
Salle 49 G5
Salmonby 57 H6
Salperton 30 E5
Salph End 36 D5
Salsburgh 79 F3
Salt 44 A5
Saltash 4 E6
Saltburn 99 F2
Saltburn-by-the-Sea 69 J4
Saltby 46 B5
Saltcoats 77 H3
Saltdean 13 G6
Salter 61 K3
Salterforth 62 B5
Salterswall 53 H7
Saltfleet 57 J4
Saltfleetby All Saints 57 J4
Saltfleetby St Clement 57 J4
Saltfleetby St Peter 57 J5
Saltford 17 H4
Salthaugh Grange 59 G4
Salthouse 48 F3
Saltmarshe 58 B4
Salton 64 E4
Saltwood 15 H5
Salum 88 B4
Salwarpe 33 H4
Salwayash 9 F5
Samala 104 C5
Sambourne 34 B4
Sambrook 43 J5
Samlesbury 61 J6
Samlesbury Bottoms 61 K7
Sampford Arundel 8 C3
Sampford Brett 16 B6
Sampford Courtenay 7 G5
Sampford Peverell 8 B3
Sampford Spiney 5 F4
Samuelston 87 H7
Sanachan 96 D1
Sancreed 2 C7
Sand, Highld 106 E2
Sand, Shetld 119 F4
Sandaig 96 C5
Sandbach 53 J7
Sandbank 84 D6
Sandbanks 10 B6
Sandend 100 E2
Sanderstead 21 H7
Sandford, Dorset 10 A6
Sandford, Strath 78 E5
Sandford, Avon 17 F5
Sandford, Devon 7 J5
Sandford, Cumbr 67 K5
Sandfordhill 101 L4
Sandford-on-Thames 31 K7
Sandford Orcas 9 H2
Sandford St Martin 31 J5
Sandgate 15 J5
Sandgreen 71 G6
Sandhaven 101 J2
Sandhead 70 B6
Sandhoe 75 F7
Sandholme, Humbs 58 C3
Sandholme, Lincs 47 G4
Sandhurst, Glos 30 C5
Sandhurst, Berks 20 C7
Sandhurst, Kent 14 D6
Sand Hutton, N. Yks 64 D7
Sandhutton, N. Yks 63 G1
Sandiacre 45 F4
Sandilands 57 K5
Sandiway 53 H6
Sandleheath 10 C3
Sandleigh 31 J7
Sandling 14 D3
Sandness 118 D3
Sandon, Essex 22 D3
Sandon, Herts 37 G7
Sandon, Staffs 43 L5
Sandown 11 G6
Sandplace 3 L4
Sandridge 21 F2
Sandringham 48 B5
Sandsend 69 L5
Sandsound 119 F4
Sandtoft 58 B6
Sandwich 15 K3
Sandwick, W. Isles 104 D7
Sandwick, Cumbr 67 G5
Sandwick, Shetld 119 G6
Sandwick, W. Isles 111 J4
Sandwick, Orkney 115 K1
Sandwith 66 B5
Sandy 36 E6
Sandycroft 52 E7
Sandygate 60 Q2
Sandyhills 66 A1
Sandy Lane 18 A4
Sangobeg 113 F2
Sannox 76 F3
Sanquhar 72 C3
Santon 58 D3
Santon Bridge 66 D6
Santon Downham 38 D2
Sapcote 45 F8
Sapey Common 33 G4
Sapiston 38 E3
Sapperton, Lincs 46 D4
Sapperton, Glos 30 D7
Saracen's Head 47 G5
Sarclet 115 J5
Sarisbury 11 G4
Sarn, Powys 32 B1
Sarn, M. Glam 25 H6
Sarnau, Powys 42 D6
Sarnau, Dyfed 27 H2
Sarnau, Dyfed 27 H6
Sarnau, Gwyn 51 J7
Sarn Bach 40 C1
Sarnesfield 29 H2
Sarn Meyllteyrn 50 B7
Saron, Dyfed 27 H4
Saron, Dyfed 27 L6
Sarratt 20 E4
Sarre 15 J2
Sarsden 31 G5
Satley 68 D2
Satterleigh 7 G3
Satterthwaite 66 F7
Sauchen 101 G7
Saucher 87 E1
Sauchieburn 93 H5
Sauchrie 77 J6
Saughall 52 E6
Saughtree 74 B4
Saul 30 B7
Saundby 56 B5
Saundersfoot 26 F7
Saunderton 20 B3
Saunton 6 E2
Sausthorpe 57 H7
Saval 108 D3
Savon Street 38 B5
Sawbridgeworth 21 J2
Sawdon 65 G4
Sawley, Lancs 62 A5
Sawley, N. Yks 63 F3
Sawley, Derby 45 F4
Sawrey 67 F7
Sawston 37 H6
Sawtry 36 E2
Saxby, Leic 46 B5
Saxby, Lincs 56 E5
Saxby All Saints 58 D5
Saxelbye 45 J5
Saxilby 56 C6
Saxlingham 48 F4
Saxlingham Nethergate 49 H8
Saxmundham 39 J4
Saxondale 45 H4
Saxtead 39 H4
Saxtead Green 39 H4
Saxthorpe 49 G4
Saxton 63 H6
Sayers Common 12 F5
Scackleton 63 K2
Scadabay 105 G2
Scaftworth 55 K4
Scagglethorpe 64 F5
Scalasaig 82 C2
Scalby 65 H3
Scaldwell 35 J3
Scaleby 73 K7
Scaleby Hill 73 K7
Scale Houses 67 H2
Scales, Cumbr 60 F2
Scales, Cumbr 66 F4
Scalford 45 J5
Scaling 69 K5
Scalloway 119 G5
Scamblesby 57 G6
Scampston 64 F5
Scampton 56 D6
Scarastavore 104 F2
Scarborough 65 H4
Scarcliffe 55 H7
Scarcroft 63 G5
Scardroy 98 A3
Scarfskerry 115 H2
Scargill 68 C5
Scarinish 88 B4
Scarisbrick 52 E2
Scarning 48 E6
Scrrington 45 J3
Scarth Hill 52 F3
Scartho 59 G6
Scaur or Kippford 71 K6
Scawby 58 D6
Scawton 63 J1
Scayne's Hill 13 G4
Scethrog 25 K2
Scholar Green 53 K8
Scholes, W. Yks 54 E3
Scholes, W. Yks 63 G6
Scleddau 26 D4
Scole 39 G3
Scolpaig 104 C4
Scolton 26 D5
Sconser 103 G5
Scoor 88 F7
Scopwick 56 E8
Scoraig 106 F2
Scorborough 58 E2
Scorrier 2 F5
Scorton, N. Yks 68 E6
Scorton, Lancs 61 J5
Sco Ruston 49 H5
Scotasay 105 G2
Scotby 67 G1
Scotch Corner 68 E6
Scotforth 61 H4
Scothern 56 E6
Scotland Gate 75 J5
Scotlandwell 86 E4
Scotsburn 109 F6
Scots' Gap 75 G5
Scots Hole 57 F7
Scotstown 89 K2
Scottas 96 C5
Scotter 58 C6
Scotterthorpe 58 C6
Scotton, Lincs 58 C7
Scotton, N. Yks 68 D7
Scotton, N. Yks 63 G4
Scottow 49 H5
Scoughall 87 K6
Scoulton 48 E7
Scourie 112 C4
Scousburgh 119 F7
Scrabster 115 F2
Scrainwood 75 F3
Scrane End 47 G3
Scraptoft 45 H7
Scratby 9 L6
Scrayingham 64 E6
Screapadal 106 A7
Scredington 46 D3
Scremby 57 J7
Scremerston 81 J5
Scriven 63 G4
Scrooby 55 K4
Scropton 44 C4
Scrub Hill 47 F2
Scruton 68 F7
Sculthorpe 48 D4
Scunthorpe 58 C5
Scurlage 24 C6
Seaborough 9 F4
Seacombe 52 E4
Seacroft 57 K7
Seaford 13 H7
Seaforth 52 E4
Seaforth Head 111 G6
Seagrave 45 H6
Seaham 69 G2
Seahouses 81 L6
Seal 13 J1
Sealand 52 E7
Seamer, N. Yks 69 G5
Seamer, N. Yks 65 H4
Seamill 77 H3
Sea Palling 49 K5
Searby 58 E6
Seasalter 15 G2
Seascale 66 C6
Seathorne 57 K7
Seathwaite, Cumbr 66 E5
Seathwaite, Cumbr 66 E7
Seaton, Cumbr 66 C3
Seaton, Leic 46 C8
Seaton, Devon 8 D5
Seaton, Corn 4 D6
Seaton, Humbs 59 F2
Seaton, Durham 69 F2
Seaton, Northum 75 K6
Seaton Burn 75 J6
Seaton Carew 69 H4
Seaton Delaval 75 K6
Seaton Ross 58 B2
Seaton Sluice 75 K6
Seatown 9 F5
Seave Green 69 H6
Seaview 11 H5
Seavington St Mary 8 E3
Seavington St Michael 8 F3
Sebastapol 29 G8
Sebergham 66 F2
Seckington 44 D7
Sedbergh 67 J7
Sedbury 29 K8
Sedbusk 68 A7
Sedgeberrow 34 B7
Sedgebrook 46 B4
Sedgefield 69 F4
Sedgeford 48 C4
Sedgehill 9 K2
Sedgley 43 L8
Sedgwick 61 J1
Sedlescombe 14 D7
Seend 18 A4
Seend Cleeve 18 A4
Seer Green 20 D4
Seething 49 J8
Sefton 52 E3
Seghill 75 J6
Seifton 32 D2
Seighford 43 K5
Seilebost 105 F2
Seisdon 43 K8
Seisiadar 111 K4
Selattyn 42 D4
Selborne 11 J1
Selby 63 K6
Selham 12 C4
Selkirk 80 C7
Sellack 29 K5
Sellafirth 121 H3
Sellindge 15 H5
Selling 15 G3
Sells Green 18 A4
Selly Oak 34 B2
Selmeston 13 J6
Selsdon 21 H7
Selsey 11 K5
Selsfield Common 13 G3
Selside 62 A2
Selston 45 F2
Selworthy 7 K1
Semer 38 F6
Semington 17 K4
Semley 9 K2
Send 12 D1
Senghenydd 25 K5
Sennen 2 B7
Sennen Cove 2 B7
Sennybridge 25 H2
Sereveton 45 J3
Sessay 63 H2
Setchey 48 B6
Setley 10 E4
Setter 121 G4
Settiscarth 116 C5
Settle 62 B3
Settrington 64 F5
Sevenhampton, Wilts 18 D1
Sevenhampton, Glos 30 E5
Seven Kings 21 J5
Sevenoaks 13 J1
Sevenoaks Weald 13 J1
Seven Sisters 25 G4
Severn Beach 17 G2
Severn Stoke 33 H6
Sevington 15 G4
Sewards End 37 J7
Sewerby 65 J6
Seworgan 2 F6
Sewstern 46 B5
Sezincote 31 F4
Shabbington 20 A3
Shackerstone 44 E7
Shackleford 12 C2
Shader 111 H2
Shadforth 69 F2
Shadingfield 39 K2
Shadoxhurst 15 F5
Shaftesbury 9 K2
Shafton 55 G2
Shalbourne 18 E4
Shalcombe 10 E6
Shalden 19 H6
Shaldon 5 K4
Shalfleet 10 F6
Shalford, Essex 38 C8
Shalford, Surrey 12 D2
Shalford Green 38 C8
Shalmsford Street 15 H3
Shalstone 35 H7
Shamley Green 12 D2
Shandon 84 E6
Shandwick 109 G6
Shangton 45 J8
Shanklin 11 G6
Shanquhar 100 E5
Shap 67 H5
Shapwick, Dorset 10 A4
Shapwick, Somer 16 F7
Shardlow 44 F4
Shareshill 43 L7
Sharlston 55 G2
Sharnbrook 36 C5
Sharnford 35 F1
Sharoe Green 61 J6
Sharow 63 G2
Sharpenhoe 36 D7
Sharperton 74 F3
Sharpness 30 A7
Sharpthorne 13 G3
Sharrington 48 F4
Shatterford 33 G2
Shaugh Prior 5 F5
Shavington 43 H2
Shaw, Berks 19 F4
Shaw, Wilts 17 K4
Shaw, G. Man 53 L3
Shawbost 111 G3
Shawbury 43 G5
Shawell 35 G2
Shawford 11 F2
Shawforth 53 K1
Shawhead 72 D6
Shaw Mills 63 F3
Shearsby 35 H1
Shebbear 6 E5
Shebdon 43 J5
Shebster 115 F3
Shedfield 11 G3
Sheen 54 E7
Sheepscombe 30 C6
Sheepstor 5 F5
Sheepwash 6 E5
Sheepy Magna 44 E7
Sheepy Parva 44 E7
Sheering 21 K2
Sheerness 14 F1
Sheet 11 J2
Sheffield 55 G5
Sheffield Bottom 20 A7
Shefford 36 E7
Sheinton 43 H7
Shelderton 32 D3
Sheldon, W. Mids 34 C2
Sheldon, Devon 8 C4
Sheldon, Derby 54 E7
Sheldwich 15 G3
Shelf 62 E7
Shelfanger 39 G2
Shelfield 44 B7
Shelford 45 H3
Shelley 54 F2
Shellingford 31 H8
Shellow Bowells 22 C3
Shelsley Beauchamp 33 G4
Shelsley Walsh 33 G4
Shelton, Northnts 36 D4
Shelton, Norf 39 H1
Shelton, Notts 45 J3
Shelton Green 39 H1
Shelve 42 E8
Shelwick 29 K3
Shenfield 22 C4
Shenington 34 E6
Shenley 21 F3
Shenley Brook End 36 B7
Shenleybury 21 F3
Shenley Church End 36 B7
Shenmore 29 H4
Shenstone, Staffs 44 C7
Shenstone, H. & W 33 H3
Shenton 44 E7
Shenval, Grampn 100 B6
Shenval, Highld 98 C6
Shepherd's Green 20 B5
Shepherdswell or
Sibertswold 15 J4
Shepley 54 E3
Shepperdine 29 L8
Shepperton 20 E7
Shepreth 37 G6
Shepshed 45 F6
Shepton Beauchamp 8 F3
Shepton Mallet 17 H6
Shepton Montague 9 H1
Shepway 14 D3
Sheraton 69 G3
Sherborne, Glos 31 F6
Sherborne, Dorset 9 H3
Sherborne St John 19 H5
Sherbourne 34 D4
Sherburn, Durham 68 F2
Sherburn, N. Yks 65 G5
Sherburn in Elmet 63 H6
Shere 12 D2
Shereford 48 D5
Sherfield English 10 D2
Sherfield on Loddon 20 A8
Sherford 5 H7
Sheriffhales 43 J6
Sheriff Hutton 63 K3
Sheringham 49 G3
Sherington 36 B6
Shernborne 48 C4
Sherrington 18 A7
Sherston 17 K2
Sherwood Green 7 F3
Shettpeston 78 D3
Shevington 53 G3
Shevington Moor 53 G2
Sheviock 4 D6
Shiel Bridge 96 E4
Shieldaig, Highld 106 D4
Shieldaig, Highld 106 D6
Shieldhill 86 B7
Shielfoot 89 H1
Shifnal 43 J7
Shilbottle 75 H3
Shildon 68 E4
Shillingford, Oxon 19 G1
Shillingford, Devon 7 K3
Shillingford St George 5 K3
Shillingstone 9 K3
Shillington 36 E7
Shillmoor 74 E3
Shiltenish 111 G6
Shilton, Warw 34 F2
Shilton, Oxon 31 G7
Shimpling, Suff 38 D5
Shimpling, Norf 39 G2
Shimpling Street 38 D5
Shiney Row 68 F1
Shinfield 20 B7
Shinness 113 G7
Shipbourne 13 J1
Shipdham 48 E7
Shipham 17 F5
Shiphay 5 J5
Shiplake 20 B6
Shipley, W. Susx 12 E4
Shipley, W. Yks 62 E6
Shipley, Shrops 43 K8
Shipmeadow 39 J1
Shippon 31 J8
Shipston-on-Stour 34 D6

Shipton, Shrops....................32 E1
Shipton, Glos.......................30 E6
Shipton, N. Yks...................63 J4
Shipton Bellinger................18 D6
Shipton Gorge......................9 F5
Shipton Green....................11 K5
Shipton Moyne...................17 K2
Shipton-on-Cherwell...........31 J6
Shiptonthorpe....................58 C2
Shipton-under-Wychwood.....31 G6
Shirburn............................20 A4
Shirdley Hill......................52 E2
Shirebrook.........................55 J7
Shirehampton....................17 G3
Shiremoor.........................75 K6
Shirenewton.......................29 J8
Shire Oak..........................44 B7
Shireoaks..........................55 J5
Shirkoak...........................14 F5
Shirland............................55 G8
Shirley, W. Mids................34 C3
Shirley, Derby....................44 D3
Shirley, Hants....................10 F3
Shirl Heath........................29 J2
Shirrell Heath....................11 G3
Shirwell.............................7 F2
Shiskine............................76 E4
Shobdon...........................32 D4
Shobrooke..........................7 J5
Shocklach.........................42 F3
Shoeburyness.....................22 F5
Sholden............................15 K3
Sholing............................11 F3
Sholver............................54 C3
Shop, Corn..........................6 C4
Shop, Corn..........................3 G2
Shoreditch.........................21 H5
Shoreham..........................21 K7
Shoreham-by-Sea...............12 F6
Shoresdean........................81 H5
Shoreswood.......................81 H5
Shoretown.........................98 E2
Shorncote.........................30 E8
Shorne..............................14 C1
Shortgate..........................13 H5
Short Heath, W. Mids..........44 C8
Short Heath, Leic...............44 E6
Shortlanesend.....................3 G5
Shortlees..........................77 K4
Shortley Bridge...................68 C1
Shorwell...........................11 F6
Shoscombe........................17 J5
Shotesham........................49 H8
Shotgate...........................22 D4
Shotley............................39 H7
Shotley Gate......................39 H7
Shottenden........................15 G3
Shottermill........................11 K1
Shottery............................34 C5
Shotteswell.......................34 F6
Shottisham.......................39 J6
Shottle.............................44 E3
Shotton, Clwyd...................52 E7
Shotton, Durham................69 G3
Shotton, Northum...............81 G6
Shotts.............................79 F3
Shotwick...........................52 E6
Shoughlaige-e-Caine...........60 Q3
Shouldham........................48 B7
Shouldham Thorpe..............48 B7
Shoulton...........................33 H5
Shrawardine......................42 F6
Shrawley..........................33 H4
Shrewley..........................34 D4
Shrewsbury.......................43 F6
Shrewton..........................18 B6
Shripney...........................12 C6
Shrivenham......................18 D2
Shropham.........................48 E8
Shroton or
  Iwerne Courtney.................9 K3
Shrub End........................23 F1
Shucknall.........................29 K3
Shudy Camps....................38 B6
Shulishader.....................111 K4
Shurdington......................30 D6
Shurlock Row....................20 C6
Shurrery.........................115 F4
Shurton...........................16 D6
Shustoke.........................34 D1
Shute..............................8 D5
Shutford...........................34 E6
Shuthonger......................30 C4
Shutlanger.......................35 J6
Shuttington.......................44 D7
Shuttlewood......................55 H6
Sibbertoft........................35 H2
Sibdon Carwood................32 D2
Sibertswold or
  Shepherdswell................15 J4
Sibford Ferris....................34 E7
Sibford Gower....................34 E7
Sible Hedingham................38 C7
Sibsey............................47 G2
Sibson, Cambs...................46 D8
Sibson, Leic......................44 E7
Sibthorpe.........................45 J3
Sibton............................39 J4
Sicklesmere......................38 D4
Sicklinghall.......................63 G5
Sidbury, Devon....................8 C5
Sidbury, Shrops..................33 F2
Sidcup............................21 J6
Siddington, Glos.................30 E8
Siddington, Ches................53 K6
Sidestrand........................49 H4
Sidford.............................8 C5
Sidinish..........................104 D3
Sidlesham........................11 K5
Sidley............................13 L6
Sidmouth...........................8 C6
Sigford.............................5 H4
Sigglesthorne....................59 F2
Silchester........................20 A7
Sileby.............................45 H6

Silecroft..........................60 E1
Silian..............................27 K2
Silkstone..........................55 F3
Silkstone Common..............55 F3
Silksworth.........................69 F1
Silk Willoughby..................46 D3
Silloth.............................66 D1
Sillyearn.........................100 E3
Siloh...............................28 B4
Silpho.............................65 G3
Silsden............................62 D5
Silsoe.............................36 D7
Silton...............................9 J2
Silverburn.........................79 K3
Silverdale, Cumbr...............61 H2
Silverdale, Staffs................43 K3
Silver End.........................22 E2
Silverford........................101 G2
Silverley's Green................39 H3
Silverstone........................35 H6
Silverton...........................7 K5
Silwick...........................118 E4
Simonburn........................74 E6
Simonsbath.........................7 H2
Simonstone........................62 A6
Simprim...........................81 G5
Simpson............................36 B7
Simpson Cross....................25 G3
Sinclairston.......................77 K6
Sinderby............................63 G1
Sinderhope........................67 L1
Sindlesham........................20 B7
Singleton, Lancs.................61 G6
Singleton, W. Susx..............11 K3
Singlewell.........................14 C1
Sinnahard........................100 D7
Sinnington.........................64 E4
Sinton Green......................33 H4
Sipson.............................20 E6
Sirhowy............................25 K3
Sissinghurst.......................14 D5
Siston..............................17 H3
Sithney.............................2 E7
Sittingbourne.....................14 F2
Six Ashes.........................33 G2
Sixhills.............................57 F5
Sixpenny Handley...............10 A3
Sizewell...........................39 K4
Skares.............................77 L6
Skateraw...........................80 F2
Skaw..............................119 H2
Skeabost.........................103 F4
Skeabrae.........................116 B4
Skeeby.............................68 D6
Skeffington.......................45 J7
Skeffling...........................59 H5
Skegby.............................55 H7
Skegness..........................57 K7
Skelberry.........................119 F7
Skelbo............................109 F4
Skeldyke...........................47 G4
Skellingthorpe....................56 D6
Skellister........................119 G3
Skellow............................55 J2
Skelmanthorpe...................55 F2
Skelmersdale......................52 F3
Skelmorlie........................77 G1
Skelpick..........................114 C4
Skelton, N. Yks..................68 C6
Skelton, Cumbr...................67 G3
Skelton, N. Yks..................63 G3
Skelton, N. Yks..................63 J4
Skelton, Cleve....................69 J5
Skelwick.........................116 D2
Skelwith Bridge..................66 F6
Skendleby.........................57 J7
Skenfrith..........................29 J5
Skerne.............................65 H7
Skerray...........................113 H2
Sketty.............................24 E5
Skewen............................24 F5
Skewsby............................63 K2
Skeyton............................49 H5
Skidbrooke........................57 J4
Skidby.............................58 E3
Skigersta........................111 K1
Skilgate............................7 K3
Skillington........................46 B5
Skinburness.......................66 D1
Skinflats...........................86 C6
Skinidin..........................102 D4
Skinningrove......................69 K5
Skipness...........................76 E2
Skipsea............................65 J7
Skipton............................62 C4
Skipton-on-Swale................63 G2
Skipwith...........................63 K6
Skirling............................79 H6
Skirmett...........................20 B4
Skirpenbeck.......................64 E7
Skirwith...........................67 J3
Skirza............................115 J3
Skulamus..........................96 B3
Skullomie........................113 H2
Skye of Curr......................99 H6
Slack..............................62 C7
Slackhall...........................54 D5
Slackhead........................100 D2
Slacks of Cairnbanno..........101 H4
Slad................................30 C7
Slade................................6 F1
Slade Green......................21 K6
Slaggyford........................67 J1
Slaidburn.........................61 L4
Slaithwaite........................54 D2
Slaley..............................68 B1
Slamannan.........................86 B7
Slapton, Bucks...................20 D1
Slapton, Northnts...............35 H6
Slapton, Devon....................5 J7
Slaugham..........................12 F4
Slawston..........................45 J8
Sleaford, Lincs...................46 D3
Sleaford, Hants..................19 K7
Sleagill............................67 H5

Sleapford..........................43 H6
Sledge Green.....................30 C4
Sledmere..........................65 G6
Sleightholme......................68 B5
Sleights...........................64 F2
Slepe...............................9 L5
Slickly...........................115 J3
Sliddery...........................76 E5
Slimbridge........................30 B7
Slindon, W. Susx................12 C6
Slindon, Staffs...................43 K4
Slinfold............................12 E3
Slingsby............................64 D5
Slip End...........................20 E2
Slipton.............................36 C3
Slochd..............................99 G6
Slockavullin.......................83 H2
Sloley..............................49 H5
Sloothby............................57 J6
Slough, Powys....................32 C4
Slough, Berks.....................20 D5
Slyne...............................61 H3
Smailholm..........................80 E6
Smallbridge.......................53 L2
Smallburgh........................49 J5
Smallburn, Strath................78 D7
Smallburn, Grampn............101 K4
Small Dole........................12 F5
Smalley............................44 F3
Smallfield.........................13 G2
Small Hythe......................14 E5
Smallridge..........................8 E4
Smardale..........................67 K6
Smarden..........................14 E4
Smeatharpe.........................8 C3
Smeeth............................15 G5
Smeeton Westerby..............35 H1
Smerclate..........................94 C4
Smerral..........................115 G6
Smethwick........................34 B2
Smirisary..........................96 B8
Smisby.............................44 E6
Smithfield.........................73 K7
Smithincott.........................8 B3
Smithton...........................99 F4
Snailbeach.........................42 E7
Snailwell..........................38 B4
Snainton...........................65 G4
Snaith.............................63 K7
Snape, N. Yks....................63 F1
Snape, Suff.......................39 J5
Snarestone.........................44 E7
Snarford...........................56 E5
Snargate...........................15 F6
Snave..............................15 G6
Snead..............................32 C1
Sneaton............................65 F2
Sneatonthorpe....................65 G2
Snelland...........................56 E5
Snelston...........................44 C3
Snettisham........................48 B4
Snishival...........................94 C2
Snitter.............................75 G3
Snitterby..........................56 D4
Snitterfield........................34 D4
Snitton.............................32 E3
Snodhill...........................29 H3
Snodland..........................14 D2
Snowshill..........................30 E4
Soberton...........................11 H3
Soberton Heath..................11 H3
Soham.............................38 A3
Soldon Cross.......................6 D4
Soldridge..........................11 H1
Sole Street, Kent................14 C2
Sole Street, Kent................15 G4
Solihull............................34 C3
Sollas............................104 D4
Sollers Dilwyn....................29 J2
Sollers Hope......................29 L4
Sollom.............................52 F2
Solva..............................26 C5
Somerby...........................45 J6
Somercotes........................44 F2
Somerford Keynes...............30 E8
Somerley..........................11 K5
Somerleyton......................49 K8
Somersal Herbert...............44 C4
Somersby..........................57 H6
Somersham, Suff................39 F6
Somersham, Cambs.............37 G3
Somerton, Somer..................9 F2
Somerton, Oxon..................31 J5
Somerton, Norf...................49 K6
Sompting..........................12 E6
Sonning............................20 B6
Sonning Common.................20 B5
Sopley.............................10 C5
Sopworth...........................17 K2
Sorbie..............................71 F7
Sordale...........................115 G3
Sorisdale...........................88 D2
Sorn................................77 L5
Sortat............................115 H3
Sotby..............................57 G6
Sots Hole..........................57 F7
Sotterley..........................39 K2
Soudley............................43 J5
Soughton or Sychdyn............52 D7
Soulbury............................36 B8
Soulby..............................67 K5
Souldern...........................31 K4
Souldrop...........................36 C4
Sound, Shetld...................119 F3
Sound, Shetld...................119 G4
Soundwell.........................17 H3
Sourhope...........................74 E1
Sourin............................116 D3
Sourton.............................5 F2
Soutergate........................60 F1
South Acre........................48 D6
Southall...........................21 F5
South Allington....................5 H8
South Alloa........................86 B5
Southam, Glos....................30 D5

Southam, Warw...................34 F4
South Ambersham...............12 C4
Southampton......................10 F3
Soth Bank.........................69 H4
South Barrow.......................9 H2
South Benfleet....................22 D5
Southborough......................13 J2
Southbourne, Dorset............10 C5
Southbourne, W. Susx..........11 J4
South Brent........................5 G5
Southburgh........................48 E7
South Burlingham................49 J7
South Cadbury......................9 H2
South Carlton.....................56 D6
South Cave.........................58 D3
South Cerney......................30 E8
South Chard........................8 E4
South Charlton....................75 H1
South Cheriton.....................9 H2
Southchurch.......................22 F5
South Cliffe.......................58 C3
South Clifton......................56 C6
South Cove........................39 K2
South Creake......................48 D4
South Croxton.....................45 H6
South Dalton......................58 D2
South Darenth....................21 K7
South Duffield....................58 A3
Southease.........................13 H6
South Elkington..................57 G5
South Elmsall.....................55 H2
Southend, Strath..................76 B7
South End, Cumbr...............60 F3
Southend, Berks..................19 G3
Southend-on-Sea.................22 E5
Southerndown.....................16 B2
Southerness.......................66 B1
South Erradale..................106 C4
Southery...........................48 B8
South Fambridge.................22 E4
South Fawley......................18 E2
South Ferriby.....................58 D4
Southfleet.........................14 C1
South Garvan......................90 A4
Southgate, Norf...................48 B4
Southgate, W. Glam.............24 D6
Southgate, Norf...................49 G5
Southgate, G. Lon................21 H4
South Godstone..................13 G2
South Gorley......................10 C3
South Green........................22 C4
South Hanningfield...............22 D4
South Harting......................11 J3
South Hayling......................11 J5
South Heath........................20 D3
South Heighton....................13 H6
South Hetton......................69 F2
South Hiendley....................55 G2
South Hill...........................4 D4
South Hole..........................6 C4
South Holmwood..................12 E2
South Hornchurch................21 K5
South Hylton......................69 F1
Southill...........................21 E6
South Kelsey......................56 E7
South Kilvington..................63 H1
South Kilworth....................35 H2
South Kirkby......................55 H2
South Kirkton....................101 G8
South Kyme........................46 E3
South Lancing......................12 E6
Southleigh, Devon..................8 D5
South Leigh, Oxon................31 H7
South Leverton....................56 B5
South Littleton....................34 B6
South Lochboisdale..............94 C4
South Lopham......................38 F2
South Luffenham..................46 C7
South Malling......................13 H5
South Marston.....................18 C2
South Milford......................63 H6
South Milton.......................5 G7
South Mimms......................21 G3
Southminster......................22 F4
South Molton.......................7 H3
South Moor, Durham............68 D1
Southmoor, Oxon.................31 J8
South Moreton....................19 G2
South Mundam.....................11 K4
South Muskham....................56 B8
South Newington..................31 J4
South Newton......................10 B1
South Normanton..................45 F2
South Norwood....................21 H7
South Nutfield....................13 G2
South Ockendon..................22 B5
Southoe............................36 E4
Southolt...........................39 G4
South Ormsby......................57 H6
South Otterington................63 G1
Southowram.......................62 E7
South Oxhey.......................21 F4
South Perrott.......................9 F4
South Petherton....................9 F3
South Petherwin...................4 D3
South Pickenham.................48 D7
South Pool..........................5 H7
Southport..........................52 E2
South Raynham....................48 D5
Southrepps........................49 H4
South Reston......................57 J5
Southrey...........................57 F7
Southrop...........................31 G7
Southrope.........................19 H6
South Runcton....................48 B7
South Scarle......................56 C7
Southsea...........................11 H5
South Shields.....................75 K7
South Shore.......................61 G6
South Skirlaugh...................59 F3
South Somercotes................57 J4
South Stainley....................63 G3
South Stainmore.................67 L5
South Stoke, W. Susx...........12 D5

South Stoke, Oxon...............19 G2
Southstoke, Avon................17 J4
South Street......................13 G5
South Tawton.......................5 G2
South Thoresby....................5 J6
South Tidworth...................18 D6
Southtown, Orkney..............116 D7
South Town, Hants...............11 H1
Southwaite........................67 G2
South Walsham....................49 J6
South Warnborough..............19 J6
Southwater........................12 E4
Southway..........................17 G6
South Weald.......................21 K4
Southwell, Dorset..................9 H7
Southwell, Notts..................45 J2
South Weston......................20 B4
South Wheatley.....................4 C2
South Widcombe...................17 G5
South Wigston.....................45 G8
South Willingham................57 F5
South Wingfield...................44 E2
South Witham......................46 C6
Southwold.........................39 L3
South Wonston....................11 F1
Southwood.........................49 J7
South Woodham Ferrers.........22 E4
South Wootton.....................48 B5
South Zeal...........................5 G2
Soutra Mains......................80 C4
Sowerby, W. Yks.................62 D7
Sowerby, N. Yks..................63 H1
Sowerby Bridge...................62 D7
Sowerby Row......................67 F2
Sowton..............................5 K2
Spa Common.......................49 H4
Spalding...........................47 F5
Spaldington........................58 B3
Spaldwick.........................36 E3
Spalford............................56 C7
Sparham............................48 F6
Spark Bridge......................61 G1
Sparkford...........................9 H2
Sparkwell...........................5 F6
Sparrowpit........................54 D5
Sparsholt, Oxon..................18 E2
Sparsholt, Hants..................10 F1
Spaunton..........................64 E4
Spaxton.............................8 D1
Spean Bridge......................90 D3
Speen, Bucks......................20 C4
Speen, Berks......................19 F4
Speeton............................65 J5
Speke..............................52 F5
Speldhurst.........................13 J2
Spellbrook.........................21 J2
Spelsbury..........................31 H5
Spencers Wood...................20 B7
Spennithorne......................62 E1
Spennymoor......................68 E3
Spetchley.........................33 H5
Spetisbury..........................9 L4
Spexhall...........................39 J2
Spey Bay.........................100 C2
Speybridge........................99 J6
Spilsby............................57 J7
Spindlestone......................81 K6
Spinningdale....................108 E5
Spirthill...........................18 A3
Spithurst..........................13 H5
Spittal, Dyfed....................26 D5
Spittal, Highld..................115 G4
Spittal, Lothn.....................87 H7
Spittal, Northum..................81 J4
Spittalfield........................92 C7
Spittal of Glenmuick............92 E3
Spittal of Glenshee..............92 C4
Spixworth.........................49 H6
Spofforth..........................63 G4
Spondon............................44 F4
Spooner Row......................49 F8
Sporle..............................48 D6
Spott...............................87 K7
Spratton............................35 J3
Spreakley..........................19 K6
Spreyton............................5 G2
Spridlington.......................56 E5
Springburn........................78 D3
Springcorrie......................111 G4
Springfield, W. Mids............34 B2
Springfield, Fife..................87 G3
Springfield, Grampn..............99 J2
Springholm........................72 D7
Springside.........................77 J4
Springthorpe......................56 C5
Sproatley..........................59 H5
Sproston Green....................53 J7
Sprotbrough.......................55 J3
Sproughton........................36 E6
Sprowston.........................49 H6
Sproxton, Leic....................46 B5
Sproxton, N. Yks.................63 K1
Spurstow...........................53 G8
Square and Compass.............26 C4
Stackhouse........................62 B3
Stackpole..........................26 D8
Stacksteads........................62 B7
Staddiscombe......................4 F6
Staddlethorpe.....................58 C4
Stadhampton......................31 L8
Staffield...........................67 H2
Staffin...........................103 F2
Stafford............................43 L5
Stagsden...........................36 C6
Stainacre..........................65 G2
Stainburn..........................63 F5
Stainby.............................46 C5
Staincross.........................55 G2
Staindrop..........................68 D4

Staines............................20 E6
Stainfield, Lincs..................46 D5
Stainfield, Lincs..................57 F6
Stainforth, N. Yks................62 B3
Stainforth, S. Yks................55 K2
Staining............................61 G6
Stainland...........................54 D2
Stainsacre.........................65 G2
Stainton, Durham................68 C5
Stainton, N. Yks..................68 D7
Stainton, Cumbr..................67 G4
Stainton, Cleve....................69 G5
Stainton, Cumbr..................61 J1
Stainton, S. Yks..................55 J4
Stainton by Langworth..........56 E6
Staintondale......................65 G3
Stainton le Vale..................57 F4
Stainton with Adgarley...........60 F2
Stair, Cumbr.......................66 E4
Stair, Strath.......................77 K5
Staithes............................69 K5
Stakeford..........................75 J5
Stake Pool.........................61 H5
Stalbridge..........................9 J3
Stalbridge Weston.................9 J3
Stalham...........................49 J5
Stalham Green.....................49 J5
Stalisfield Green..................14 F3
Stallingborough....................59 G5
Stalling Busk......................62 C1
Stalmine............................61 G5
Stalybridge........................54 C4
Stambourne........................38 C7
Stambourne Green................38 C7
Stamford...........................46 D7
Stamford Bridge...................64 E7
Stamfordham.......................75 G6
Stanborough.......................21 G2
Stanbridge, Dorset................10 B4
Stanbridge, Beds..................20 D1
Stand..............................78 E3
Standburn.........................86 C7
Standeford.........................43 L7
Standen............................14 E4
Standford..........................11 K1
Standish............................53 G2
Standlake..........................31 H7
Standon, Hants....................10 F2
Standon, Herts....................21 H1
Standon, Staffs...................43 K4
Stane..............................79 F4
Stanfield...........................48 E5
Stanford, Beds....................36 E6
Stanford, Kent....................15 H5
Stanford Bishop...................33 F5
Stanford Bridge...................33 G4
Stanford Dingley..................19 G3
Stanford in the Vale..............31 H8
Stanford-le-Hope..................22 C5
Stanford on Avon.................35 G3
Stanford on Soar..................45 G5
Stanford on Teme................33 G4
Stanford Rivers...................21 K3
Stanghow..........................69 J5
Stanhoe............................48 D4
Stanhope, Durham...............68 B3
Stanhope, Border.................79 J7
Stanion.............................36 C2
Stanley, Durham..................68 D1
Stanley, Tays......................86 E1
Stanley, Derby....................44 F3
Stanley, W. Yks...................63 G7
Stanley, Staffs....................43 L2
Stanley Crook......................68 D3
Stanmer............................13 G6
Stanmore, Berks..................19 F3
Stanmore, G. Lon.................21 F4
Stannington, S. Yks..............55 G5
Stannington, Northum...........75 J6
Stansbatch.........................32 C4
Stansfield.........................38 C5
Stanstead.........................38 D6
Stanstead Abbotts...............21 H2
Stansted...........................14 C2
Stansted Mountfitchet...........21 K1
Stanton, Staffs...................44 C3
Stanton, Derby....................44 E5
Stanton, Suff.....................38 E3
Stanton, Glos.....................30 E4
Stanton, Gwent....................29 H5
Stanton by Bridge.................44 E5
Stanton-by-Dale..................45 F4
Stanton Drew......................17 G4
Stanton Fitzwarren...............18 C1
Stanton Harcourt.................31 J7
Stanton Hill.......................55 H7
Stanton in Peak...................55 F7
Stanton Lacy......................32 D3
Stanton Long......................32 E1
Stanton-on-the-Wolds............45 H4
Stanton Prior......................17 H4
Stanton St Bernard...............18 B4
Stanton St John...................31 K7
Stanton St Quintin................17 L2
Stanton Street....................38 E4
Stanton under Bardon...........45 F6
Stanton upon Hine Heath........43 G5
Stanton Wick......................17 H4
Stanwardine in the Fields.......42 F5
Stanway, Glos....................30 E4
Stanway, Essex...................22 F1
Stanwell...........................20 E6
Stanwell Moor....................20 E6
Stanwick..........................36 C3
Stanwick-St-John................68 D5
Stanydale........................118 E3
Stape..............................64 E3
Stapehill..........................10 B4
Stapeley...........................43 H3
Staple............................15 J3
Staplecross.......................14 D6
Stapleield........................12 F4
Staple Fitzpaine...................8 B1
Stapleford, Wilts..................10 B1
Stapleford, Leic..................46 B6

Stapleford, Lincs	56 C8	Stockbriggs	78 E6
Stapleford, Notts	45 H4	Stockbury	14 E2
Stapleford, Herts	21 H2	Stockcross	18 F4
Stapleford, Cambs	37 H5	Stockdalewath	67 F2
Stapleford Abbotts	21 K4	Stockeinteignhead	5 K4
Stapleford Tawney	21 K4	Stockerston	46 B8
Staplegrove	8 D2	Stock Green	34 A5
Staplehay	8 D2	Stockingford	34 E1
Staplehurst	14 D4	Stocking Pelham	37 H8
Staplers	11 G6	Stockland	8 D4
Stapleton, Cumbr	74 B6	Stockland Bristol	16 D6
Stapleton, H. & W	32 C4	Stockleigh English	7 J5
Stapleton, N. Yks	68 E5	Stockleigh Pomeroy	7 J5
Stapleton, Somer	9 F2	Stockley	18 B4
Stapleton, Shrops	43 F7	Stocklinch	8 E3
Stapleton, Leic	44 F8	Stockport	53 K4
Stapleton, Avon	17 H3	Stocksbridge	55 F4
Stapley	8 C3	Stocksfield	75 G7
Staploe	36 E4	Stockton, Wilts	18 A7
Star, Somer	17 F5	Stockton, H. & W	32 E4
Star, Dyfed	27 G4	Stockton, Warw	34 F4
Star, Fife	87 G4	Stockton, Norf	49 J8
Starbotton	62 C2	Stockton, Shrops	43 J8
Starcross	5 K3	Stockton Heath	53 H5
Starkigarth	119 G6	Stockton-on-Tees	69 G5
Starston	39 H2	Stockton on Teme	33 G4
Startforth	68 C5	Stockton on the Forest	63 K4
Startley	18 A2	Stock Wood	34 B5
Stathe	8 E2	Stodmarsh	15 J2
Stathern	45 J4	Stoer	112 B6
Station Town	69 G3	Stoford, Wilts	10 B1
Staughton Highway	36 E4	Stoford, Somer	9 G3
Staunton, Glos	30 B5	Stogumber	8 B1
Staunton, Glos	29 K6	Stogursey	16 D6
Staunton in the Vale	45 K3	Stoke, Devon	6 C3
Staunton on Arrow	29 H1	Stoke, Kent	14 E1
Staunton on Wye	29 H3	Stoke, Hants	18 F5
Staveley, N. Yks	63 G3	Stoke, Hants	11 J4
Staveley, Cumbr	67 G7	Stoke Abbott	9 F4
Staveley, Derby	55 H6	Stoke Albany	35 K2
Staveley-in-Cartmel	61 G1	Stoke Ash	39 G3
Staverton, Glos	30 C5	Stoke Bardolph	45 H3
Staverton, Northnts	35 G4	Stoke Bliss	33 F4
Staverton, Devon	5 H5	Stoke Bruerne	35 J6
Staverton, Wilts	17 K4	Stoke by Clare	38 C6
Stawell	16 E7	Stoke-by-Nayland	38 E7
Staxigoe	115 J4	Stoke Canon	5 K2
Staxton	65 H5	Stoke Charity	19 F7
Staylittle	41 H4	Stoke Climsland	4 D4
Staythorpe	45 J2	Stoke D'Abernon	21 F8
Stean	62 D2	Stoke Doyle	36 D2
Stearsby	63 K2	Stoke Dry	46 B8
Steart	16 D6	Stoke Ferry	48 C7
Stebbing	22 C1	Stoke Fleming	5 J7
Stedham	11 K2	Stokeford	9 K6
Steele Road	74 B4	Stoke Gabriel	5 J6
Steen's Bridge	29 K2	Stoke Gifford	17 H2
Steep	11 J2	Stoke Golding	44 E8
Steeple, Essex	22 F3	Stoke Goldington	36 B6
Steeple, Dorset	9 L6	Stokeham	56 B6
Steeple Ashton	17 L5	Stoke Hammond	36 B8
Steeple Aston	31 J5	Stoke Heath	43 H5
Steeple Barton	31 J5	Stoke Holy Cross	49 H7
Steeple Bumpstead	38 B6	Stoke Lacy	29 L3
Steeple Claydon	35 H8	Stoke Lyne	31 K5
Steeple Gidding	36 E2	Stoke Mandeville	20 C2
Steeple Langford	10 B1	Stokenchurch	20 B4
Steeple Morden	37 F6	Stoke Newington	21 H5
Steeton	62 D5	Stokenham	5 J7
Steinmanhill	101 G4	Stoke on Tern	43 H5
Steisay	104 D7	Stoke-on-Trent	43 K3
Stelling Minnis	15 H4	Stoke Orchard	30 D5
Stemster	115 G3	Stoke Poges	20 D5
Stenalees	3 J4	Stoke Prior, H. & W	33 J4
Stenhousemuir	86 B6	Stoke Prior, H. & W	29 K2
Stenton	87 K7	Stoke Rivers	7 G2
Stepney	21 H5	Stoke Rochford	46 C5
Steppingley	36 D7	Stoke Row	20 A5
Stepps	78 D3	Stokesay	32 D2
Sternfield	39 J4	Stokesby	49 K6
Stert	18 B5	Stokesley	69 H6
Stetchworth	38 B5	Stoke St Gregory	8 E2
Stevenage	21 G1	Stoke St Mary	8 D2
Stevenston	77 H3	Stoke St Michael	17 H6
Steventon, Oxon	19 F1	Stoke St Milborough	32 E2
Steventon, Hants	19 G6	Stoke sub Hamdon	9 F3
Stevington	36 C5	Stoke Talmage	20 A4
Stewartby	36 D6	Stoke Trister	9 J2
Stewarton	77 K3	Stolford	16 D6
Stewkley	36 B8	Stondon Massey	21 K3
Stewton	57 H5	Stone, Glos	30 A8
Steyning	12 E5	Stone, Bucks	20 B2
Steynton	26 D7	Stone, H. & W	33 H3
Stibb	6 C4	Stone, Kent	21 K6
Stibbard	48 E5	Stone, Staffs	43 L4
Stibb Cross	6 E4	Stone Allerton	16 F5
Stibb Green	18 D4	Stone Easton	17 H5
Stibbington	46 D8	Stonebroom	55 H8
Stichill	80 F6	Stone Cross	13 K6
Sticker	3 H4	Stonefield	78 D4
Stickford	57 H8	Stonegate	13 K4
Sticklepath	5 G2	Stonegrave	63 K2
Stickney	47 G2	Stonehaugh	74 D6
Stiffkey	48 E3	Stonehaven	93 K3
Stifford's Bridge	33 G6	Stone House, Cumbr	62 A1
Stilligarry	94 C2	Stonehouse, Glos	30 C7
Stillingfleet	63 J5	Stonehouse, Northum	74 C8
Stillington, Cleve	69 F4	Stonehouse, Strath	78 E5
Stillington, N. Yks	63 J3	Stone in Oxney	14 F6
Stilton	36 E2	Stoneleigh	34 E3
Stinchcombe	30 B8	Stonesby	46 B5
Stinsford	9 J5	Stonesfield	31 H6
Stirchley	43 J7	Stones Green	39 G8
Stirling	85 K5	Stoneybridge	94 C2
Stisted	22 E1	Stoneyburn	79 G3
Stithians	2 F6	Stoney Cross	10 D3
Stittenham	108 E6	Stoneygate, Leic	45 H7
Stivichall	34 E3	Stoneygate, Grampn	101 K5
Stixwould	57 F7	Stoneyhills	22 F4
Stoak	52 F6	Stoneykirk	70 B6
Stobo	79 J6	Stoney Middleton	55 F6
Stoborough	9 L6	Stoney Stanton	45 F8
Stoborough Green	9 L6	Stoney Stratton	17 H7
Stock	22 C4	Stoney Stretton	42 E7
Stockbridge	10 E1		

Stoneywood	101 H7	Stretton under Fosse	35 F2
Stonham Aspal	39 G5	Stretton Westwood	43 G8
Stonnall	44 B7	Strichen	101 J3
Stonor	20 B5	Stringston	16 C6
Stonton Wyville	45 J8	Strixton	36 C4
Stonybreck	116 P1	Stroat	29 K8
Stony Stratford	35 J6	Stromeferry	96 D2
Stoodleigh	7 K4	Stromemore	96 D2
Stopham	12 D5	Stromness	116 B6
Stopsley	21 F1	Stronachlachar	85 G3
Storeton	52 E5	Strond	104 F3
Stornoway	111 J4	Strone, Highld	90 C3
Storridge	33 G6	Strone, Strath	84 D6
Storrington	12 D5	Strone, Highld	98 D6
Storrs	67 G7	Stronenaba	90 D3
Storth	61 H2	Stronmilchan	84 D2
Stotfold	36 F7	Strontian	89 K2
Stottesdon	33 F2	Strood	14 D2
Stoughton, Surrey	12 C1	Stroud, Glos	30 C7
Stoughton, Leic	45 H7	Stroud, Hants	11 J2
Stoughton, W. Susx	11 K3	Struan, Highld	102 E5
Stoul	96 C6	Struan, Tays	91 K5
Stoulton	33 J6	Strubby	57 J5
Stourbridge	33 J2	Strumpshaw	49 J7
Stourpaine	9 K4	Strutherhill	78 E5
Stourport-on-Severn	33 H3	Struy	98 C5
Stour Provost	9 J2	Stuartfield	101 J4
Stour Row	9 K2	Stubbington	11 G4
Stourton, Warw	34 D7	Stubbins	53 J2
Stourton, Staffs	33 H2	Stubhampton	9 L3
Stourton, Wilts	9 J1	Stubton	46 B3
Stourton Caundle	9 J3	Studham	20 E2
Stoven	39 K2	Studland	10 B6
Stow	56 C5	Studley, Wilts	18 A3
Stow Bardolph	48 B7	Studley, Warw	34 B4
Stow Bedon	48 E8	Studley Roger	63 F2
towbridge	48 B7	Stuntney	37 J3
Stow cum Quy	37 J4	Sturbridge	43 K4
Stowe	32 C3	Sturmer	38 B6
Stowe-by-Chartley	44 B5	Sturminster Marshall	10 A5
Stowell	9 H2	Sturminster Newton	9 J3
Stowford	4 E3	Sturry	15 H4
Stowlangtoft	38 E4	Sturton by Stow	56 C5
Stow Longa	36 E3	Sturton le Steeple	56 B5
Stow Maries	22 E4	Stuston	39 G3
Stowmarket	38 F5	Stutton, Suff	39 G7
Stow-on-the-Wold	31 F5	Stutton, N. Yks	63 H5
Stowting	15 H4	Styal	53 K5
Stowupland	36 D4	Suckley	33 G5
Straad	76 F1	Sudborough	36 C2
Strachan	93 H2	Sudbourne	39 K5
Strachur	84 C4	Sudbrook, Lincs	56 E6
Stradbroke	39 H3	Sudbrook, Gwent	17 G2
Stradishall	38 C5	Sudbury, Derby	44 C4
Stradsett	48 B7	Sudbury, Suff	38 D6
Stragglethorpe	46 C2	Sudgrove	30 D7
Straiton, Strath	77 J7	Suffield	49 H4
Straiton, Lothn	79 K3	Sugnall	43 K4
Straloch	92 B5	Sulby	60 Q2
Stramshall	44 B4	Sulgrave	35 G6
Stranraer	70 B5	Sulham	20 A6
Strata Florida	41 G7	Sulhamstead	20 A7
Stratfield Mortimer	20 A7	Sullington	12 D5
Stratfield Saye	20 A7	Sullom	120 F1
Stratfield Turgis	20 A7	Sully	25 K8
Stratford	21 H5	Sumburgh	119 G8
Stratford St Andrew	39 J4	Summerbridge	62 F3
Stratford St Mary	38 F7	Summercourt	3 G4
Stratford Tony	10 B2	Summerleaze	17 F2
Stratford-upon-Avon	34 D5	Summerseat	53 J2
Strath	106 C4	Summit	53 L2
Strathan, Highld	90 A2	Sunbiggin	67 J6
Strathan, Highld	112 B6	Sunbury	20 E7
Strathaven	78 E5	Sunderland, Cumbr	66 D3
Strathblane	85 H7	Sunderland, T. & W	69 F1
Strathdon	100 C7	Sunderland Bridge	68 E3
Strath Kanaird	107 G1	Sundhope	80 B7
Strathkinness	87 H3	Sundon Park	36 D8
Strathmiglo	87 F3	Sundridge	13 H1
Strathpeffer	98 C3	Sunk Island	59 G5
Strathrannoch	107 J4	Sunningdale	20 D7
Strathtay	91 L6	Sunninghill	20 D7
Strathwhillan	76 F4	Sunningwell	31 J7
Strathy	114 D3	Sunniside, Durham	68 D3
Strathyre	85 H3	Sunniside, T. & W	75 J8
Stratton, Corn	6 C5	Sunnylaw	85 K5
Stratton, Glos	30 E7	Sunnyside	13 G3
Stratton, Dorset	9 H5	Surbiton	21 F7
Stratton Audley	31 L5	Surfleet	47 F5
Stratton-on-the-Fosse	17 H5	Surfleet Seas End	47 F5
Stratton St Margaret	18 C2	Surlingham	49 J7
Stratton St Michael	49 H8	Sustead	49 G4
Stratton Strawless	49 H5	Susworth	58 C6
Streat	13 G5	Sutcombe	6 D4
Streatham	21 G6	Suton	49 F8
Streatley, Beds	36 D8	Sutterby	57 H6
Streatley, Berks	19 G2	Sutton, Notts	56 A5
Street, N. Yks	64 E2	Sutton, W. Susx	12 C5
Street, Somer	9 F1	Sutton, Cambs	46 D8
Street, Lancs	61 J4	Sutton, Shrops	32 E2
Street End	11 K5	Sutton, Surrey	12 E2
Streethay	44 B8	Sutton, Beds	37 F6
Streetly	34 C6	Sutton, Shrops	33 G2
Strefford	32 D2	Sutton, G. Lon	21 G7
Strensall	63 K3	Sutton, Cambs	37 H3
Strensham	33 J6	Sutton, Shrops	43 H4
Stretcholt	16 D6	Sutton, Notts	45 J4
Strete	5 J7	Sutton, Staffs	43 J5
Stretford	53 J4	Sutton, Norf	49 J5
Stretford Court	29 J2	Sutton, Oxon	31 J7
Strethall	37 H7	Sutton, Kent	15 K4
Stretham	37 J3	Sutton at Hone	21 K6
Strettington	11 K4	Sutton Bassett	35 J1
Stretton, Leic	46 C6	Sutton Benger	18 A3
Stretton, Staffs	44 D5	Sutton Bridge	47 H5
Stretton, Ches	42 F2	Sutton Cheney	44 F7
Stretton, Derby	55 G7	Sutton Coldfield	44 C6
Stretton, Ches	53 H5	Sutton Courtenay	31 K8
Stretton, Staffs	43 K6	Sutton Crosses	47 H5
Stretton en le Fields	44 E6	Sutton Grange	63 F2
Stretton Grandison	29 L3	Sutton Hill	43 J7
Stretton Heath	42 E6	Sutton Howgrave	63 G2
Stretton-on-Dunsmore	34 F3		
Stretton-on-Fosse	34 D7		
Stretton Sugwas	29 J3		

Sutton in Ashfield	55 H8	Symondsbury	9 F5
Sutton-in-Craven	62 D5	Symonds Yat	29 K6
Sutton Lane Ends	53 L6	Synod Inn	27 J2
Sutton Leach	53 G4	Syre	113 H4
Sutton Maddock	43 J7	Syreford	30 E5
Sutton Mallet	8 E1	Syresham	35 H6
Sutton Mandeville	10 A2	Syston, Lincs	46 C3
Sutton Montis	9 H2	Syston, Leic	45 H6
Sutton-on-Hull	59 F3	Sytchampton	33 H4
Sutton-on-the-Forest	63 J3	Sywell	36 B4
Sutton on the Hill	44 D4		
Sutton on Trent	56 B7	**T**	
Sutton Scotney	19 F7		
Sutton St Edmund	47 G6	Tackley	31 J5
Sutton St James	47 G6	Tacolneston	49 G8
Sutton St Nicholas	29 K3	Tadcaster	63 H5
Sutton-under-Brailes	34 E7	Tadden	10 A4
Sutton-under-		Taddington	54 E8
Whitestonecliffe	63 H1	Tadley	19 H4
Sutton upon Derwent	58 B2	Tadlow	37 F6
Sutton Valence	14 E4	Tadmarton	34 E7
Sutton Veny	17 K6	Tadworth	12 F1
Sutton Waldron	9 K3	Tafarnaubach	25 K3
Sutton Weaver	53 G6	Tafarn-y-Gelyn	52 C7
Swaby	57 H6	Taff's Well	25 K6
Swadlincote	44 E5	Tafolwern	41 H3
Swaffham	48 D7	Tai-bach, Clwyd	42 C5
Swaffham Bulbeck	37 J4	Taibach, W. Glam	25 F6
Swaffham Prior	37 J4	Tain, Highld	109 F5
Swafield	49 H4	Tain, Highld	115 H3
Swainbost	111 K1	Tai'n Lon	50 D5
Swainby	69 G6	Takeley	21 K1
Swainshill	29 J3	Talachddu	25 J1
Swainsthorpe	49 H7	Talacre	52 C5
Swalcliffe	34 E7	Talaton	8 B5
Swalecliffe	15 H2	Talbenny	26 C6
Swallow	59 F6	Talerddig	41 J3
Swallowcliffe	10 A2	Talgarreg	27 J2
Swallowfield	20 B7	Talgarth	25 K1
Swallownest	55 H5	Talisker	102 E5
Swanage	10 B7	Talke	43 K2
Swanbister	116 C6	Talkin	67 H1
Swanbourne	35 K8	Talladale	106 E4
Swan Green	53 J6	Tallarn Green	42 F3
Swanland	58 D4	Tallentire	66 D3
Swanley	21 K7	Talley	27 L4
Swanmore	11 G3	Tallington	46 D7
Swannington, Leic	44 F6	Talmine	113 G2
Swannington, Norf	49 G6	Talog	27 H5
Swanscombe	14 C1	Tal-sarn	27 K2
Swansea	24 E5	Talsarnau	50 F7
Swanton Abbot	49 H5	Talskiddy	3 H3
Swanton Morley	48 F6	Talwrn	50 D3
Swanton Novers	48 F4	Tal-y-bont, Gwyn	40 E1
Swanwick, Derby	44 F2	Tal-y-bont, Dyfed	41 F5
Swanwick, Hants	11 G4	Tal-y-Bont, Gwyn	51 G4
Swarby	46 D3	Talybont-on-Usk	25 K2
Swardeston	49 H7	Tal-y-cafn	51 G3
Swarister	121 H4	Tal-y-llyn, Gwyn	41 G3
Swarkestone	44 E5	Talyllyn, Powys	25 K2
Swarland	75 H3	Talysarn	50 D5
Swaton	46 E4	Tal-y-Wern	41 H3
Swavesey	37 G4	Tamerton Foliot	4 E5
Sway	10 D5	Tamworth	44 D7
Swayfield	46 C5	Tandridge	13 G1
Swaythling	10 F3	Tanfield	68 D1
Sweffling	39 J4	Tangasdale	94 B5
Swepstone	44 E6	Tangley	18 E5
Swerford	31 H4	Tangmere	11 L4
Swettenham	53 K7	Tangwick	120 E5
Swffryd	25 L5	Tankerness	116 E5
Swilland	39 G5	Tankersley	55 G4
Swillington	63 G6	Tannach	115 J6
Swimbridge	7 G3	Tannadice	93 H4
Swinbrook	31 G6	Tannington	39 H4
Swinderby	56 C7	Tansley	55 G8
Swindon, Wilts	18 C2	Tansor	36 D1
Swindon, Glos	30 D5	Tantobie	68 D1
Swindon, Staffs	33 H1	Tanton	69 H5
Swine	59 F3	Tanworth-in-Arden	34 C3
Swinefleet	58 B4	Tan-y-fron	51 J4
Swineshead, Northnts	36 D4	Tanygrisiau	51 F6
Swineshead, Lincs	47 F3	Tan-y-groes	27 G3
Swineshead Bridge	46 F3	Taplow	20 D5
Swiney	115 H6	Tarbert, Strath	76 D1
Swinford, Leic	35 G3	Tarbert, Strath	82 F3
Swinford, Oxon	31 J7	Tarbert, W. Isles	105 G1
Swingfield Minnis	15 J4	Tarbet, Highld	112 C4
Swinhoe	81 L7	Tarbet, Highld	96 C6
Swinhope	57 G6	Tarbet, Strath	84 F4
Swinithwaite	68 C8	Tarbock Green	52 F5
Swinside Hall	74 D2	Tarbolton	77 K5
Swinscoe	44 C3	Tarbrax	79 H4
Swinton, N. Yks	64 E5	Tarfside	93 F4
Swinton, N. Yks	62 F2	Tarland	100 D8
Swinton, Border	81 G5	Tarleton	61 H7
Swinton, S. Yks	55 H4	Tarlogie	109 F5
Swinton, G. Man	53 J3	Tarlscough	52 F2
Swintonmill	81 G5	Tarlton	30 D8
Swithland	45 G6	Tarnbrook	61 J4
Swordale	98 D2	Tarporley	53 G7
Swordland	96 C6	Tarr	8 C1
Swordly	114 C3	Tarrant Crawford	9 L4
Sworton Heath	53 H5	Tarrant Gunville	9 L3
Swyddffynnon	41 F7	Tarrant Hinton	10 A3
Swynnerton	43 K4	Tarrant Keyneston	9 L4
Swyre	9 G6	Tarrant Launceston	10 A4
Sychdyn or Soughton	52 D7	Tarrant Monkton	10 A4
Syde	30 D6	Tarrant Rawston	10 A4
Sydenham, Oxon	20 B3	Tarrant Rushton	10 A4
Sydenham, G. Lon	21 H6	Tarrel	109 G5
Sydenham Damerel	4 E4	Tarring Neville	13 H6
Sydling St Nicholas	9 H5	Tarrington	29 L3
Sydmonton	19 F5	Tarskavaig	96 A5
Syerston	45 J3	Tarves	101 H5
Syke	53 K2	Tarvie	98 C3
Sykehouse	55 K2	Tarvin	53 F7
Sykes	61 K4	Tasburgh	49 H8
Syleham	39 H3	Tasley	43 H8
Sylen	27 K7	Taston	31 H5
Symbister	119 H2	Tatenhill	44 D5
Symington, Strath	79 G6	Tatham	61 K3
Symington, Strath	77 J4	Tathwell	57 H5

Tatsfield 13 H1	Thirlestane 80 D5	Thorverton 7 K5	Tilney High End 47 J6	Toppings 53 J2	Trefeglwys 41 J4
Tattenhall 53 F8	Thirn 62 F1	Thrandeston 39 G3	Tilney St Lawrence 47 J6	Topsham 5 K3	Trefenter 40 F7
Tatterford 48 D5	Thirsk 63 H1	Thrapston 36 C3	Tilshead 18 B6	Torbay 5 J5	Treffgarne 26 D5
Tattersett 48 D5	Thistleton 46 C6	Threapwood 42 F3	Tilstock 43 G4	Torbeg 76 E5	Treffynnon 26 C5
Tattershall 57 G8	Thistley Green 38 B3	Three Bridges 13 F3	Tilston 42 F2	Torbryan 5 J5	Trefil 25 K3
Tattershall Bridge 46 E2	Thixendale 64 F6	Three Cocks 29 F4	Tilstone Fearnall 53 G7	Torcross 5 J7	Trefilan 27 K2
Tattershall Thorpe 57 G8	Tholomas Drove 47 H7	Three Crosses 24 D5	Tilsworth 20 D1	Tore 98 E3	Trefnanney 42 D6
Tattingstone 39 G7	Tholthorpe 63 H3	Three Holes 47 J7	Tilton on the Hill 45 J7	Torksey 56 C6	Trefnant 51 K3
Tatworth 8 E4	Thomas Chapel 26 F7	Threekingham 46 D4	Timberland 57 F8	Torlum 104 C6	Trefonen 42 D5
Taunton 8 D2	Thomastown 100 E5	Three Leg Cross 13 K3	Timbersbrook 53 K7	Torlundy 90 C4	Trefor, Gwyn 50 C2
Taverham 49 G6	Thompson 48 E8	Three Legged Cross 10 B4	Timberscombe 7 K1	Tormarton 17 J3	Trefor, Gwyn 50 C6
Tavernspite 27 F6	Thomshill 100 B3	Three Mile Cross 20 B7	Timble 62 E4	Tormitchell 70 D2	Treforest 25 J6
Tavistock 4 E4	Thong 14 C1	Threemilestone 3 F5	Timperley 53 J5	Tormore 76 D4	Trefriw 51 G4
Taw Green 5 G2	Thoralby 62 D1	Threlkeld 66 F4	Timsbury, Hants 10 E2	Tornagrain 99 F4	Tregadillett 4 C3
Tawstock 7 F3	Thoresway 57 F4	Threshfield 62 C3	Timsbury, Avon 17 H5	Tornahaish 100 B8	Tregaian 50 D3
Taxal 54 D6	Thorganby, N. Yks. 58 A2	Thrigby 49 K6	Timworth Green 38 D4	Tornaveen 100 F8	Tregare 29 H6
Tayinloan 76 B3	Thorganby, Lincs 57 G4	Thringarth 68 B4	Tincleton 9 J5	Torness 98 D6	Tregaron 28 A1
Taynish 83 G3	Thorington 39 K3	Thringstone 44 F6	Tindale 74 C8	Torpenhow 66 E3	Tregarth 51 F4
Taynton, Glos. 30 B5	Thorington Street 38 F7	Thrintoft 68 F7	Tingewick 35 H7	Torphichen 86 C7	Tregeare 4 C3
Taynton, Oxon 31 G6	Thorley 21 J2	Thriplow 37 H6	Tingley 63 F7	Torphins 93 H1	Tregeiriog 42 C4
Taynuilt 84 C1	Thormanby 63 H2	Throcking 37 G7	Tingrith 36 D7	Torpoint 4 E6	Tregele 50 C1
Tayport 87 H2	Thornaby-on-Tees 69 G5	Throckley 75 H7	Tinhay 4 D3	Torquay 5 K5	Tregidden 2 F7
Tay Road Bridge, Fife 87 H2	Thornage 48 F4	Throckmorton 34 A6	Tinshill 63 F6	Torquhan 80 C5	Treglemais 26 C5
Tay Road Bridge, Tays. 87 H2	Thornborough, N. Yks. 63 F2	Throphill 75 H5	Tinsley 55 H4	Torran 106 A7	Tregole 4 B2
Tayvallich 83 G3	Thornborough, Bucks 35 J7	Thropton 75 G3	Tintagel 4 A3	Torrance 85 J7	Tregonetha 3 H3
Tealby 57 F4	Thornbury, Devon 6 E5	Throwleigh 5 G2	Tintern Parva 29 K7	Torridon 106 D6	Tregony 3 H5
Teanamachar 104 C5	Thornbury, Avon 17 H1	Throwley 15 F3	Tintinhull 9 F3	Torrin 96 A3	Tregoyd 29 F4
Teangue 96 B5	Thornbury, H. & W. 29 L2	Throwley Forestal 15 F3	Tintwistle 54 D4	Torrisdale 113 H2	Tre-groes 27 J3
Tebay 67 J6	Thornby 35 H3	Thrumpton 45 G4	Tinwald 72 F5	Torrisholme 61 H3	Tregurrian 3 G3
Tebworth 36 C8	Thorncliffe 54 D8	Thrumster 115 J5	Tinwell 46 D7	Torroble 108 D3	Tregynon 41 K4
Tedburn St Mary 5 J2	Thorncombe 8 E4	Thrunton 75 G2	Tipperty 101 J6	Torry, Grampn 100 D4	Trehafod 25 J5
Teddington, Glos. 30 D4	Thorncombe Street 12 D2	Thrupp, Glos 30 C7	Tipton 34 A1	Torry, Grampn 101 J8	Treharris 25 J5
Teddington, G. Lon 21 F6	Thorndon 39 G4	Thrupp, Oxon 31 J6	Tipton St John 8 B5	Torrylinn 76 E5	Treherbert 25 H5
Tedstone Delamere 33 F5	Thorndon Cross 5 F2	Thrushelton 4 E3	Tiptree 22 E2	Torterston 101 K4	Treknow 4 A3
Tedstone Wafre 33 F5	Thorne 58 A5	Thrushgill 61 K3	Tirabad 28 C3	Torthorwald 73 F6	Trelan 2 F8
Teeton 35 H3	Thorner 63 G5	Thruxton, Hants 18 D6	Tirley 30 C5	Tortington 12 D6	Trelawnyd 51 K3
Teffont Evias 10 A1	Thorne St Margaret 8 B2	Thruxton, H. & W. 29 J4	Tirphil 25 K4	Tortworth 30 B8	Trelech 27 G4
Teffont Magna 10 A1	Thorney, Notts 56 C6	Thrybergh 55 H4	Tirril 67 H4	Torvaig 103 F4	Treleddyd-fawr 26 B5
Tegryn 27 G4	Thorney, Cambs 47 F7	Thundersley 22 D5	Tisbury 10 A2	Torver 66 E7	Trelewis 25 K5
Teigh 46 B6	Thorney Hill 10 D5	Thundridge 21 H2	Tissington 44 C2	Torwood 85 L6	Treligga 4 A3
Teigngrace 5 J4	Thornfalcon 8 D2	Thurcaston 45 G6	Titchberry 6 C3	Torworth 55 K5	Trelights 3 H2
Teignmouth 5 K4	Thornford 9 H3	Thurcroft 55 H5	Titchfield 11 G4	Toscaig 96 C2	Trelill 3 J2
Telford 43 H6	Thorngumbald 59 G4	Thurgarton, Norf 49 G4	Titchmarsh 36 D3	Toseland 37 F4	Trelissick 3 G6
Tellisford 17 K5	Thornham 48 C3	Thurgarton, Notts 45 H3	Titchwell 48 C3	Tosside 62 A4	Trelleck 29 K6
Telscombe 13 H6	Thornham Magna 39 G3	Thurgoland 55 F3	Titley 29 H1	Tostock 38 E4	Trelleck Grange 29 J7
Templand 73 F5	Thornham Parva 39 G3	Thurlaston, Warw 35 F3	Titlington 75 G2	Totaig 102 D3	Trelogan 52 C5
Temple, Lothn 80 B4	Thornhaugh 46 D7	Thurlaston, Leic 45 G8	Tittensor 43 K4	Totarol 111 F4	Tremadog 50 E6
Temple, Strath 85 H8	Thornhill, D. & G. 72 D4	Thurlby, Lincs 46 D6	Tittleshall 48 D5	Tote, Highld 103 F4	Tremail 4 B3
Temple, Corn 3 K2	Thornhill, Derby 54 E5	Thurlby, Lincs 56 D7	Tiverton, Ches 53 G7	Tote, Highld 103 G3	Tremain 27 G3
Temple Bar 27 K2	Thornhill, Hants. 11 F3	Thurleigh 36 D5	Tiverton, Devon 7 K4	Totegan 114 D3	Tremaine 4 C3
Temple Cloud 17 H5	Thornhill, Central 85 J5	Thurlestone 5 G7	Tivetshall St Margaret 39 G2	Totland 10 E6	Tremar 3 L3
Templecombe 9 J2	Thornhill, M. Glam 25 K6	Thurloxton 8 D1	Tivetshall St Mary 39 G2	Totley 55 G6	Trematon 4 D6
Temple Ewell 15 J4	Thornhill Edge 55 F2	Thurlstone 55 F3	Tixall 44 A5	Totnes 5 J5	Tremeirchion 51 K3
Temple Grafton 34 C5	Thornicombe 9 K4	Thurlton 49 K8	Tixover 46 C7	Totscore 102 E2	Trenance 3 G3
Temple Guiting 30 E5	Thornley, Durham 68 D3	Thurmaston 45 H7	Toab, Orkney 116 E6	Tottenham 21 H4	Trearren 3 J5
Temple Hirst 63 K7	Thornley, Durham 69 F3	Thurnham, Kent 14 E3	Toab, Shetld 119 F7	Tottenhill 48 B6	Trench 43 H6
Temple Normanton 55 H7	Thornliebank 77 L2	Thurnham, Lancs 61 H4	Tobermory 89 G3	Totteridge, Bucks 20 C4	Treneglos 4 C3
Temple Sowerby 67 J4	Thorns 38 C5	Thurning, Northnts 36 D2	Toberonochy 89 J8	Totteridge, G. Lon 21 G4	Trenewan 3 K4
Templeton, Dyfed 26 F6	Thornthwaite, Cumbr 66 E4	Thurning, Norf. 49 F5	Tobson 111 F4	Totternhoe 20 D1	Trent 9 G3
Templeton, Devon 7 J4	Thornthwaite, N. Yks 62 E4	Thurnscoe 55 H3	Tocher 101 F5	Tottington 53 J2	Trentham 43 K3
Tempsford 36 E5	Thornton, Humbs. 58 B2	Thursby 66 F1	Tockenham 18 B3	Totton 10 E3	Trentishoe 7 G1
Tenbury Wells 33 E4	Thornton, Mers 52 E3	Thursford 48 E4	Tockenham Wick 18 B2	Touchen-end 20 C5	Treoes 25 H7
Tenby 26 F7	Thornton, Humbs. 58 E5	Thursley 19 L7	Tockholes 61 K7	Toux, Grampn 100 E3	Treorchy 25 H5
Tendring 23 H1	Thornton, W. Yks. 62 E6	Thurso 115 G3	Tockington 17 H2	Toux, Grampn 101 J3	Tre'r-ddol 41 F4
Ten Mile Bank 48 B8	Thornton, Fife 87 F5	Thurstaston 52 D5	Tockwith 63 H4	Tovil 13 L1	Tresaith 27 G2
Tenston 116 B5	Thornton, Lancs 61 G5	Thurston 38 E4	Todber 9 J2	Toward 72 B2	Trescott 43 K8
Tenterden 14 E5	Thornton, Lincs 57 G7	Thurstonfield 66 F1	Toddington, Beds 36 D8	Towcester 35 H6	Trescowe 2 D6
Terling 22 D2	Thornton, Northum 81 H5	Thurstonland 54 E2	Toddington, Glos 30 E4	Towednack 2 C6	Tresham 17 J1
Ternhill 43 H4	Thornton, Bucks 35 J7	Thurton 49 J7	Todenham 34 D7	Towersey 20 B3	Tresillian 3 G5
Terregles 72 E6	Thornton Dale 64 F4	Thurvaston 44 D4	Todhills 73 J7	Towie 100 D7	Tresinwen 26 C3
Terrington 63 K2	Thorntonhall 78 C4	Thuxton 48 F7	Todmorden 62 C7	Towiemore 100 C4	Tremeer 4 C3
Terrington St Clement 47 J5	Thornton Hough 52 E5	Thwaite, N. Yks. 68 A7	Toft, Lincs 46 D6	Tow Law 68 D3	Tressait 91 H3
Terrington St John 47 J6	Thornton-in-Craven 62 C5	Thwaite, Suff. 39 G4	Toft, Cambs 37 G5	Town End 47 H8	Tresta 119 F3
Teston 13 L1	Thornton-le-Beans 69 F7	Thwaite St Mary 49 J8	Toft Hill 68 D4	Townhead, D. & G. 71 H7	Treswell 56 B6
Testwood 10 E3	Thornton-le-Clay 64 D6	Thwing 65 H5	Toft Monks 49 K8	Townhead, Cumbr 67 J3	Tre Taliesin 41 F4
Tetbury 30 C8	Thornton le Moor, Lincs 56 E4	Tibbermore 86 D2	Toft next Newton 56 E5	Townhead of Greenlaw 72 C7	Trethewey 2 B7
Tetbury Upton 30 C8	Thornton-le-Moor, N. Yks. 63 G1	Tibberton, Glos. 30 B5	Toftrees 48 D5	Townhill 86 E6	Trethomas 25 K6
Tetchill 42 E4	Thornton-le-Moors 52 F6	Tibberton, Shrops. 43 H5	Toftwood 48 E6	Townshend 2 D6	Trethurgy 3 J4
Tetcott 4 D2	Thorntonloch 80 F2	Tibberton, H. & W. 33 J5	Togston 75 J3	Town Yetholm 81 G7	Tretio 26 B5
Tetford 57 H6	Thornton Rust 62 C1	Tibshelf 55 H7	Tokavaig 96 B4	Towthorpe 63 K4	Tretire 29 K5
Tetney 59 H6	Thornton Steward 62 E1	Tibthorpe 65 G2	Tokers Green 20 A6	Towton 63 H6	Tretower 25 K2
Tetney Lock 59 H6	Thornton Watlass 63 F1	Ticehurst 13 K3	Tolland 8 C1	Towyn 51 J3	Treuddyn 52 D8
Tetsworth 20 A3	Thornwood Common 21 J3	Tichborne 11 G1	Tollard Royal 10 A3	Toynton All Saints 57 H7	Trevalga 4 A2
Tettenhall 43 K7	Thoroton 45 J3	Tickencote 46 C7	Toll Bar 55 J3	Toynton Fen Side 57 H7	Trevanson 3 H2
Teversal 55 H7	Thorp Arch 63 H5	Tickenham 17 F3	Toller Fratrum 9 G5	Toynton St Peter 57 J7	Trevarren 3 H3
Teversham 37 H5	Thorpe, Derby 44 C2	Tickhill 55 J4	Toller Porcorum 9 G5	Toy's Hill 13 H1	Trevarrick 3 H5
Teviothead 73 K3	Thorpe, N. Yks. 62 D3	Ticklerton 32 D1	Tollerton, Notts. 45 H4	Trabboch 77 K5	Trevellas 2 F4
Tewin 21 G2	Thorpe, Surrey 20 E7	Ticknall 44 E5	Tollerton, N. Yks. 63 J3	Trabbochburn 77 K5	Treverva 3 G6
Tewkesbury 30 C4	Thorpe, Cumber 67 G4	Tickton 58 E2	Tollesbury 22 F2	Traboe 2 F7	Trevethin 29 G7
Teynham 14 F2	Thorpe, Notts 45 J3	Tidcombe 18 D5	Tolleshunt D'Arcy 22 F2	Tradespark, Orkney 116 D6	Trevigro 4 D5
Thainston 93 H4	Thorpe, Lincs 57 J3	Tiddington, Oxon 20 A3	Tolleshunt Major 22 F2	Tradespark, Highld 99 G3	Trevine 26 C4
Thakeham 12 E5	Thorpe, Norf 49 K8	Tiddington, Warw. 34 D5	Tolpuddle 9 J5	Trafford Park 53 J4	Treviscoe 3 H4
Thame 20 B3	Thorpe Abbotts 39 G3	Tidebrook 13 K4	Tolsta Chaolais 111 F4	Trallong 25 H2	Trevone 3 G2
Thames Ditton 21 F7	Thorpe Acre 45 G5	Tideford 4 D6	Tolworth 21 F7	Trallwng or Welshpool 42 D7	Trewarmett 4 A3
Thamesmead 21 J5	Thorpe Arnold 45 J5	Tidenham 29 K8	Tomatin 99 G6	Tranent 87 H7	Trewarthenick 3 H5
Thaneston 93 H4	Thorpe Audlin 55 H2	Tideswell 54 E6	Tombreck 98 E5	Trantlemore 114 D4	Trewassa 3 B3
Thanington 15 H3	Thorpe Bassett 64 F5	Tidmarsh 20 A6	Tomchrasky 98 A7	Tranwell 75 H5	Trewellard 2 B6
Thankerton 79 G6	Thorpe Bay 22 F5	Tidmington 34 D7	Tomdoun 90 C1	Trapp 27 L6	Trewen 4 C3
Tharston 49 G8	Thorpe by Water 46 B8	Tidpit 10 B3	Tomich, Highld 98 B6	Traprain 87 J7	Trewidland 3 L4
Thatcham 19 G4	Thorpe Constantine 44 D7	Tiers Cross 26 D6	Tomich, Highld 109 F6	Traquair 80 B6	Trewint 4 B2
Thatto Heath 53 G4	Thorpe End 49 H6	Tiffield 35 H5	Tomintoul, Grampn 100 A7	Trawden 62 C6	Trewithian 3 G6
Thaxted 38 B7	Thorpe Fendykes 57 J7	Tifty 101 G4	Tomintoul, Grampn 92 C2	Trawsfynydd 51 G7	Trewoon 3 H4
Theakston 63 G1	Thorpe Green 38 E5	Tigerton 93 G5	Tomnavoulin 100 B6	Trealaw 25 J5	Treyarnon 3 G2
Thelby 58 C5	Thorpe Hesley 55 G4	Tighnabruaich 84 B7	Tonbridge 13 J2	Treales 61 H6	Treyford 11 K3
Theale, Berks 20 A6	Thorpe in Balne 55 J2	Tighnafiline 106 D3	Tondu 25 G6	Trearddur 50 B3	Trickett's Cross 10 A4
Theale, Somer 17 F6	Thorpe Langton 35 J1	Tigley 5 H5	Tong 43 J7	Treaslane 103 E3	Timdon 69 F3
Thearne 58 E3	Thorpe Larches 69 F4	Tilbrook 36 D4	Tonge 44 F5	Trebartha 4 C4	Timdon Grange 69 F3
Theberton 39 K4	Thorpe le Fallows 56 D5	Tilbury 14 C1	Tongham 19 K6	Trebetherick 3 H2	Trimingham 49 H4
Thedden Grange 19 H7	Thorpe-le-Soken 23 H1	Tile Cross 34 C2	Tongland 71 H6	Treborough 8 B1	Trimley St Martin 39 H7
Theddingworth 35 H2	Thorpe Malsor 36 B3	Tile Hill 34 D3	Tongue 113 G3	Trebudannon 3 G2	Trimley St Mary 39 H7
Theddlethorpe All Saints 57 J5	Thorpe Mandeville 35 G6	Tilehurst 20 A6	Tongwynlais 25 K6	Trebullett 4 D4	Trimpley 33 G3
Theddlethorpe St Helen 57 J5	Thorpe Market 49 H4	Tilford 19 K6	Tonmawr 25 G5	Trebyr 25 G2	Trimsaran 27 J7
Thelbridge Barton 7 H4	Thorpe Morieux 38 E5	Tillathrowie 100 D3	Tonna 25 F5	Trecastle 25 G2	Trimstone 6 F1
Thelnetham 38 F3	Thorpeness 39 K5	Tillicoultry 86 C5	Ton-teg 25 J6	Trecwn 26 D4	Trinant 25 L2
Thelwall 53 H5	Thorpe on the Hill 56 D7	Tillingham 23 F3	Tonwell 21 H2	Trecynon 25 H4	Tring 20 D2
Themelthorpe 48 F5	Thorpe Salvin 55 J5	Tillington, W. Susx. 12 C4	Tonypandy 25 H5	Tredavoe 2 C7	Trinity 93 H5
Thenford 35 G6	Thorpe Satchville 45 J6	Tillington, H. & W. 29 J3	Tonyrefail 25 J6	Tredegar 25 K4	Trislaig 90 B4
Therfield 37 G3	Thorpe St Andrew 49 H7	Tillington Common 29 J3	Toot Baldon 31 K7	Tredington, Glos 34 D6	Trispen 3 G4
Thetford 38 D2	Thorpe Thewles 69 G4	Tillyarie 101 J6	Toothill, Hants 10 E3	Tredington, Warw. 34 D6	Tritlington 75 J4
Theydon Bois 21 J4	Thorpe Underwood 63 H4	Tillycorthie 101 J3	Toot Hill, Essex 21 K3	Tredinnick 3 H2	Trochry 92 A7
Thickwood 17 K3	Thorpe Waterville 36 D2	Tillydrine 93 H2	Topcroft 39 H1	Tredizzick 3 H2	Troedyraur 27 H3
Thimbleby, Lincs 57 G7	Thorpe Willoughby 63 J6	Tillyfourie 100 F7	Topcroft Street 39 H1	Tredomen 25 K1	Troedyrhiw 25 J4
Thimbleby, N. Yks. 69 G7	Thorp St Peter 57 J7	Tillygreig 101 J3	Toppesfield 38 C7	Tredunnock 29 H8	Trofarth 51 H3
Thirkleby 63 H2	Thorrington 23 G1	Tilmanstone 15 K3		Tredustan 25 K1	Trondavoe 121 F5
Thirlby 63 H1		Tilney All Saints 47 J6		Treen 2 B7	Troon, Corn 2 E6

Troon, Strath 77 J4	Tyneham 9 K6	Upper Bucklebury 19 G4	Urlay Nook 69 G5
Troston 38 D3	Tynehead 80 B4	Upper Caldecote 36 E6	Urmston 53 J4
Trottiscliffe 14 C2	Tynemouth 75 K7	Upper Chapel 28 E3	Urquhart 100 B2
Trotton 11 K2	Tynewydd 25 H5	Upper Chute 18 D5	Urra 69 H6
Troutbeck 67 G6	Tyninghame 87 K7	Upper Clatford 19 F6	Urray 98 D3
Troutbeck Bridge 67 G6	Tynron 72 D4	Upper Dallachy 100 C2	Urswick 60 F2
Trowbridge 17 K5	Tyn-y-ffridd 42 C4	Upper Dean 36 D4	Ushaw Moor 68 E2
Trow Green 29 K7	Tyn-y-graig, Powys 28 E2	Upper Denby 55 F3	Usk 29 H7
Trowle Common 17 K5	Tynygraig, Dyfed 41 F7	Upper Derraid 99 J5	Usselby 57 E4
Trows 80 E6	Tyn-y-groes 51 G3	Upper Dicker 13 J5	Uton 5 J2
Trowse Newton 49 H7	Ty Rhiw 25 K6	Upper Dunsforth 63 H3	Utkinton 53 G7
Trudoxhill 17 J6	Tyringham 36 B6	Upper Elkstone 54 D6	Utley 62 D5
Trull 8 D2	Tythby 45 H4	Upper End 54 D6	Utterby 57 H4
Trumisgarry 104 D4	Tythegston 25 G7	Upper Ethie 99 F2	Uttoxeter 44 B4
Trumpan 102 D2	Tytherington, Avon 17 H2	Upper Farringdon 11 J1	Uwchmynydd 40 A1
Trumpet 33 F7	Tytherington, Somer 17 J6	Upper Framilode 30 B6	Uxbridge 20 E5
Trumpington 37 H5	Tytherington, Ches 53 L6	Upper Froyle 19 J6	Uyeasound 121 H2
Trunch 49 H4	Tytherington, Wilts 17 L6	Upper Gravenhurst 36 E7	Uzmaston 26 D6
Truro 3 G5	Tytherleigh 8 E4	Upper Green 18 E4	
Trusham 5 J3	Tywardreath 3 H4	Upper Hackney 55 F7	
Trusley 44 D4	Tywyn, Gwyn 40 E3	Upper Hale 19 K6	**V**
Trusthorpe 57 K5	Tywyn, Gwyn 51 G3	Upper Hambleton 46 C7	
Trysull 43 K8		Upper Hardres Court 15 H3	Valleyfield 86 D6
Tubney 31 J8		Upper Hartfield 13 H3	Valsgarth 121 J1
Tuckenhay 5 J6	**U**	Upper Heath 32 E2	Valtos, W. Isles 111 E4
Tuckhill 33 G2		Upper Helmsley 64 D7	Valtos, Highld 103 G2
Tuddenham, Suff 38 C3	Uachdar 104 D6	Upper Heyford, Northnts 35 H5	Vange 22 D5
Tuddenham, Suff 39 G6	Uags 96 C2	Upper Heyford, Oxon 31 J5	Varteg 29 G7
Tudeley 13 K2	Ubbeston Green 39 J3	Upper Hill 29 J2	Vatersay 94 B6
Tudhoe 68 E3	Ubley 17 G5	Upper Hopton 54 E2	Vatten 102 D4
Tudweiliog 50 B7	Uckerby 68 E6	Upper Hulme 54 D7	Vaul 78 B3
Tuffley 30 C6	Uckfield 13 H4	Upper Inglesham 31 G8	Vaynor 25 J3
Tufton 26 E5	Uckington 30 D5	Upper Killay 24 D5	Vaynor Park 42 C7
Tugby 45 J7	Uddingston 78 D3	Upper Knockando 100 A4	Veensgarth 119 G4
Tugford 32 E2	Uddington 79 F6	Upper Lambourne 18 E2	Velindre 29 F4
Tullibody 86 B5	Udimore 14 E7	Upper Lochton 93 H2	Veness 116 E4
Tullich 84 C3	Udny Green 101 H6	Upper Longdon 44 B6	Vennington 42 E7
Tullich Muir 109 F6	Udny Station 101 J6	Upper Longwood 43 H7	Venn Ottery 8 B5
Tulloch 93 J4	Uffcott 18 C3	Upper Lydbrook 29 L6	Ventnor 11 G7
Tullynessle 100 E7	Uffculme 8 B3	Upper Maes-coed 29 H4	Vernham Dean 18 E5
Tumble 27 K6	Uffington, Lincs 46 D7	Uppermill 54 C3	Vernham Street 18 E5
Tumby Woodside 57 G8	Uffington, Oxon 18 E2	Upper Minety 18 B1	Vernolds Common 32 D2
Tummel Bridge 91 J6	Uffington, Shrops 43 G6	Upper North Dean 20 C4	Verran Island 94 C2
Tunbridge Wells, Royal 13 J3	Ufford, Cambs 46 D7	Upper Poppleton 63 J4	Verwig 27 F3
Tunga 111 J4	Ufford, Suff 39 H5	Upper Quinton 34 C6	Verwood 10 B4
Tunstall, Kent 14 E2	Ufton 34 E4	Upper Sanday 116 E6	Veryan 3 H6
Tunstall, N. Yks 68 E7	Ufton Nervet 20 A7	Upper Sapey 33 F4	Vicarage 8 D6
Tunstall, Humbs 59 H3	Ugadale 76 C5	Upper Seagry 18 A2	Vickerstown 60 E3
Tunstall, Suff 39 J5	Ugborough 5 G6	Upper Shelton 36 C6	Victoria 3 H3
Tunstall, Lancs 61 K2	Uggeshall 39 K2	Upper Sheringham 49 G3	Vidlin 119 G2
Tunstall, Staffs 43 K2	Ugglebarnby 65 F2	Upper Skelmorlie 77 G1	Viewpark 78 E3
Tunstall, Norf 49 K7	Ugley 37 J8	Upper Slaughter 31 F5	Village Abberley, The 33 G4
Tunstead 49 H5	Ugley Green 37 J8	Upper Soudley 30 A6	Village, The 33 H2
Tunworth 19 H6	Ugthorpe 69 K5	Upper Stondon 36 E7	Vinehall Street 13 L4
Tupsley 29 K3	Uig, Highld 102 C3	Upper Stowe 35 H5	Vines Cross 13 J5
Tupton 55 G7	Uig, Highld 103 E2	Upper Street, Hants 10 C3	Virginia Water 20 D7
Turgis Green 20 A8	Uigshader 103 F4	Upper Street, Norf 49 J6	Virginstow 4 D2
Turkdean 30 F6	Uisken 88 E7	Upper Sundon 36 D8	Vobster 17 J6
Tur Langton 45 J8	Ulbster 115 J5	Upper Swainswick 17 J4	Voe 119 G2
Turnastone 29 H4	Ulceby, Humbs 59 F5	Upper Swell 31 F5	Vowchurch 29 H4
Turnberry 77 H7	Ulceby, Lincs 57 J6	Upper Tean 44 B4	
Turnditch 44 D3	Ulcombe 14 E4	Upperthong 54 E3	
Turners Hill 13 G3	Uldale 66 E3	Upper Tillyrie 86 E4	**W**
Turners Puddle 9 K5	Uley 30 B8	Upperton 12 C4	
Turnworth 9 K4	Ulgham 75 J4	Upper Tooting 21 G6	Waberthwaite 66 D7
Turriff 101 G3	Ullapool 107 G2	Uppertown 115 J2	Wackerfield 68 D4
Turton Bottoms 53 J2	Ullenhall 34 C4	Upper Tysoe 34 E6	Wacton 39 G1
Turves 47 G8	Ullenwood 30 D6	Upper Upham 18 D3	Wadborough 33 J6
Turvey 36 C5	Ulleskelf 63 J5	Upper Wardington 35 F6	Waddesdon 20 B2
Turville 20 B4	Ullesthorpe 35 G2	Upper Weald 36 B7	Waddingham 56 D4
Turville Heath 20 B4	Ulley 55 H5	Upper Weedon 35 H5	Waddington, Lincs 56 D7
Turweston 35 H7	Ullingswick 29 K2	Upper Wield 19 H7	Waddington, Lancs 61 L5
Tutbury 44 D5	Ullinish 102 E5	Upper Winchendon 20 B2	Wadebridge 3 H2
Tutnall 34 A3	Ullock 66 C4	Upper Woodford 10 C1	Wadeford 8 E3
Tutshill 29 K8	Ulpha 66 D7	Uppingham 46 B8	Wadenhoe 36 D2
Tuttington 49 H5	Ulsta 121 G4	Uppington 43 G7	Wadesmill 21 H2
Tuxford 56 B6	Ultrome 65 J7	Upsall 63 H1	Wadhurst 13 K3
Twatt, Orkney 116 B4	Ulverston 61 F2	Upshire 21 J3	Wadshelf 55 G6
Twatt, Shetld 119 F3	Ulzieside 72 C3	Up Somborne 10 E1	Wadworth 55 J4
Twechar 85 K7	Umberleigh 7 G3	Upstreet 15 J2	Waen-fach 42 D6
Tweedmouth 81 H4	Unapool 112 D5	Up Sydling 9 H4	Wainfleet All Saints 57 J8
Tweedsmuir 79 J7	Underbarrow 67 G7	Upton, Dorset 10 A5	Wainfleet Bank 57 J8
Twelveheads 2 F5	Underriver 13 J1	Upton, Bucks 20 B2	Wainhouse Corner 4 B2
Twemloe Green 53 J7	Underwood, Gwent 16 E2	Upton, Notts 56 B6	Wainscott 14 D1
Twenty 46 E5	Underwood, Notts 45 F2	Upton, Lincs 56 C5	Wainstalls 62 D7
Twerton 17 J4	Undy 17 F2	Upton, Mers 52 D5	Waitby 67 K6
Twickenham 21 F6	Unifirth 118 D3	Upton, Berks 20 D6	Wakefield 55 G1
Twigworth 30 C5	Union Mills 60 Q4	Upton, Cambs 36 E3	Wakerley 46 C8
Twineham 12 F5	Unstone 55 G6	Upton, Hants 10 E3	Wakes Colne 38 D8
Twinhoe 17 J5	Unthank 67 G3	Upton, Hants 18 E5	Walberswick 39 K3
Twinstead 38 D7	Upavon 18 C5	Upton, Cambs 46 E7	Walberton 12 C6
Twitchen, Shrops 32 C3	Up Cerne 9 H4	Upton, Leic 44 E8	Walcot, Shrops 32 C2
Twitchen, Devon 7 H2	Upchurch 14 E2	Upton, Ches 52 F7	Walcot, Warw 34 C5
Two Bridges 5 G4	Upcott 29 H2	Upton, Oxon 19 G2	Walcot, Lincs 46 D4
Two Dales 55 F7	Upend 38 C5	Upton, W. Yks 55 H2	Walcot, Shrops 43 G6
Two Gates 44 D7	Up Exe 7 K5	Upton, Notts 45 J2	Walcote 35 G2
Twycross 44 E7	Uphall 86 D7	Upton, Northnts 35 J4	Walcott, Lincs 46 E2
Twyford, Berks 20 B6	Uphall Station 86 D7	Upton, Norf 49 J6	Walcott, Norf 49 J4
Twyford, Hants 11 F2	Upham, Hants 11 G2	Upton, Somer 7 K3	Walden 62 D1
Twyford, Norf 48 F5	Upham, Devon 7 J5	Upton Bishop 30 A5	Walden Head 62 C1
Twyford, Bucks 35 H8	Up Hatherley 30 D5	Upton Cheyney 17 H4	Walden Stubbs 55 J2
Twyford, Leic 45 J6	Uphill 16 E5	Upton Cressett 33 F1	Walderslade 14 D2
Twyford Common 29 K4	Up Holland 53 G3	Upton Cross 4 C4	Walderton 11 J3
Twynholm 71 H6	Uplawmoor 77 K2	Upton Grey 19 H6	Walditch 9 F5
Twyning 33 J7	Upleadon 30 B5	Upton Hellions 7 J5	Waldridge 68 E1
Twyning Green 33 J7	Upleatham 69 G5	Upton Lovell 18 A6	Waldringfield 39 H6
Twynllanan 25 F2	Uploders 9 G5	Upton Magna 43 G6	Waldron 13 J5
Twyn-y-Sheriff 29 J7	Uplowman 8 B3	Upton Noble 17 J7	Wales, Notts 55 H5
Twywell 36 C3	Uplyme 8 E5	Upton Pyne 5 K2	Walesby, Notts 56 A6
Tyberton 29 H4	Upminster 21 K5	Upton Scudamore 17 K6	Walesby, Lincs 57 F4
Tyburn 34 C1	Up Nately 19 H5	Upton Snodsbury 33 J5	Walford, H. & W. 32 C3
Tycroes 27 L6	Upnor 14 D1	Upton St Leonards 30 C6	Walford, Shrops 42 F5
Tycrwyn 41 L2	Upottery 8 D4	Upton upon Severn 33 H6	Walford, H. & W. 29 K5
Tydd Gote 47 H6	Upper Affcot 32 D2	Up Wrren 33 J4	Walgherton 43 H3
Tydd St Giles 47 H6	Upper Ardchronie 108 E5	Upwaltham 12 C5	Walgrave 35 K3
Tydd St Mary 47 H6	Upper Arley 33 G2	Upware 37 J3	Walkden 53 J3
Ty-hen 50 A7	Upper Astrop 35 G7	Upwell, Cambs 47 J7	Walker 75 J7
Tyldesley 53 J3	Upper Basildon 19 G3	Upwell, Norf 47 J7	Walkerburn 80 B6
Tyler Hill 15 H2	Upper Beeding 12 F5	Upwey 9 H6	Walker Fold 61 K5
Tylers Green 20 D4	Upper Benefield 36 C2	Upwood 37 F2	Walkeringham 56 B4
Tylorstown 25 J5	Upper Boddington 35 F5	Urafirth 120 F5	Walkerith 56 B4
Tylwch 41 J5	Upper Borth 40 F5	Urchfont 18 B5	Walkern 37 F8
Ty-nant, Gwyn 41 J1	Upper Breinton 29 J3	Urdimarsh 29 K3	Walker's Green 29 K3
Ty-nant, Clwyd 51 J6	Upper Broughton 45 H5	Urgha 105 G2	
Tyndrum 84 F1		Urishay Common 29 H4	

Walkhampton 5 F5	Warnham 12 E3
Walkington 58 D3	Warninglid 12 F4
Walk Mill 62 B6	Warren, Dyfed 26 D8
Wall, Staffs 44 C7	Warren, Ches 53 K6
Wall, Northum 74 F7	Warren Row 20 C5
Wallacetown 77 J5	Warren Street 14 F3
Wallasey 52 D4	Warrington, Bucks 36 B5
Wallingford 19 H2	Warrington, Ches 53 H5
Wallington, Herts 37 F7	Warsash 11 F4
Wallington, Hants 11 G4	Warslow 54 D8
Wallington, G. Lon 21 G7	Warsop 55 J7
Wallis 26 E5	Warter 65 F7
Walliswood 12 E3	Warthill 63 K4
Walls 118 E4	Wartling 13 K6
Wallsend 75 J7	Wartnaby 45 J5
Wall under Heywood 32 E1	Warton, Warw 44 D7
Wallyford 87 G7	Warton, Northum 75 G3
Walmer 15 K3	Warton, Lancs 61 H7
Walmer Bridge 61 H7	Warton, Lancs 61 J2
Walmersley 53 K2	Warwick, Warw 34 D4
Walmley 44 C8	Warwick, Cumbr 67 G1
Walpole 39 J3	Warwick Bridge 67 G1
Walpole Highway 47 J6	Wasbister 116 C3
Walpole St Andrew 47 J6	Wasdale Head 66 D6
Walpole St Peter 47 J6	Washaway 3 J3
Walsall 44 B8	Washbourne 5 H6
Walsall Wood 44 B7	Washfield 7 K4
Walsden 62 C7	Washford 16 B6
Walsgrave on Sowe 34 E2	Washford Pyne 7 J4
Walsham le Willows 38 F3	Washingborough 56 E6
Walsoken 47 H6	Washington, W. Susx 12 E5
Walston 79 H5	Washington, T. & W. 68 F1
Walter's Ash 20 C4	Wasing 19 G4
Walterstone 29 H5	Waskerley 68 C2
Waltham, Humbs 59 F4	Wasperton 34 D5
Waltham, Kent 15 H4	Wass 63 J2
Waltham Abbey 21 H3	Watchet 16 B6
Waltham Chase 11 G3	Watchfield, Oxon 18 D1
Waltham Cross 21 H3	Watchfield, Somer 16 E6
Waltham on the Wolds 45 K5	Watchgate 67 H7
Waltham St Lawrence 20 C6	Watendlath 66 E5
Walthamstow 21 H5	Water 62 B7
Walton, Bucks 36 B7	Waterbeach 37 H4
Walton, Cumbr 74 B7	Waterbeck 73 H6
Walton, Warw 34 D5	Waterden 48 D4
Walton, Somer 9 F1	Water End, Herts 20 E2
Walton, Leic 35 G2	Water End, Herts 21 G3
Walton, W. Yks 55 G2	Waterfall 44 B2
Walton, Powys 29 G2	Waterfoot, Lancs 62 B7
Walton, Shrops 43 G6	Waterfoot, Strath 78 C4
Walton, Derby 55 G7	Waterford 21 H2
Walton, W. Yks 63 H5	Waterhead, Cumbr 67 F6
Walton, Suff 39 H7	Waterhead, Strath 77 L6
Walton Cardiff 30 D4	Waterhouses, Staffs 44 B2
Walton East 26 E5	Waterhouses, Durham 68 D2
Walton Highway 47 H6	Wateringbury 13 K1
Walton-in-Gordano 17 F3	Waterlip 17 H6
Walton-le-Dale 61 J7	Waterloo, Dorset 10 B5
Walton-on-Thames 21 F7	Waterloo, Tays 92 B8
Walton-on-the-Hill, Staffs 44 A5	Waterloo, Mers 52 E4
Walton on the Hill, Surrey 12 F1	Waterloo, Strath 79 F4
Walton-on-the-Naze 23 J1	Waterloo, Norf 49 H6
Walton-on-Trent 44 D6	Waterlooville 11 H4
Walton West 26 C6	Watermeetings 72 E2
Walworth 68 E5	Watermillock 67 G4
Walwyn's Castle 26 C6	Water Newton 46 E8
Wambrook 8 D4	Water Orton 34 C1
Wanborough 18 D2	Waterperry 20 A3
Wandsworth 21 G6	Waterrow 8 B2
Wangford 39 K3	Watersfield 12 D5
Wanlip 45 G6	Waterside, Strath 85 J7
Wanlockhead 72 D2	Waterside, Strath 77 K3
Wansford, Cambs 46 D8	Waterside, Strath 77 K7
Wansford, Humbs 65 H7	Waterside, Strath 77 L1
Wanstead 21 J5	Waterstock 20 A3
Wanstrow 17 J6	Waterston 26 D7
Wanswell 30 A7	Water Stratford 35 H7
Wantage 18 E2	Waters Upton 43 H6
Wapley 17 J3	Waterthorpe 55 H5
Wappenbury 34 E4	Water Yeat 66 E8
Wappenham 35 H6	Watford, Herts 21 F4
Warbleton 13 K5	Watford, Northnts 35 H4
Warborough 31 K8	Wath, N. Yks 62 E3
Warboys 37 G2	Wath, N. Yks 63 G2
Warbstow 4 C2	Wath upon Dearne 55 H3
Warburton 53 J5	Watlington, Oxon 20 A4
Warcop 67 K5	Watlington, Norf 48 B6
Warden 15 G1	Watnall 45 G2
Ward Green 38 F4	Watten 115 H4
Wardington 35 F6	Watterow 8 B2
Wardle, Ches 5 H8	Wattisfield 38 F3
Wardle, G. Man 53 L2	Wattisham 38 F5
Wardley 46 B7	Watton, Norf 48 E7
Wardlow 54 E6	Watton, Humbs 65 H7
Wardy Hill 37 H2	Watton at Stone 21 H2
Ware 21 H2	Wattston 85 K8
Wareham 9 L6	Wattstown 25 J5
Warehorne 15 F5	Wattsville 25 L5
Warenford 81 K7	Waunarlwydd 24 E5
Waren Mill 81 K6	Waunfawr 50 E5
Wareside 21 H2	Wavendon 36 C7
Waresley 37 F5	Waverton, Cumbr 66 E2
Warfield 20 C6	Waverton, Ches 52 F7
Wargrave 20 B6	Wawne 59 E3
Warham 48 E3	Waxham 49 K5
Wark, Northum 74 E6	Waxholme 59 H4
Wark, Northum 81 G6	Wayford 8 F4
Warkleigh 7 G3	Way Village 7 J4
Warkton 36 B3	Weachyburn 100 F7
Warkworth 75 J3	Wealdstone 21 F5
Warlaby 69 F7	Weare 16 F5
Warland 53 L1	Weare Giffard 6 E3
Warleggan 3 J3	Wearhead 67 L3
Warlingham 21 H8	Weasdale 67 J6
Warmfield 55 G1	Weasenham All Saints 48 D5
Warmingham 53 J7	Weasenham St Peter 48 D5
Warmington, Northnts 36 D1	Weaverham 53 H6
Warmington, Warw 34 F6	Weaverthorpe 65 G5
Warminster 17 K6	Webheath 34 B4
Warmsworth 55 J3	Wedderlairs 101 H6
Warmwell 9 J6	Weddington 44 E8
Warndon 33 H5	Wedhampton 18 B5
Warnford 11 H2	Wedmore 17 F6
	Wednesbury 44 A8
	Wednesfield 44 A7

Wedon 20 C2	West Bradley 9 G1	West Horrington 17 G6	West Stoke 11 K4	Whinnyfold 101 K5	Whitton, Suff 39 G6
Weedon Bec 35 H5	West Bretton 55 F2	West Horsley 12 D1	West Stonesdale 68 A6	Whippingham 11 G5	Whittonditch 18 D3
Weedon Lois 35 H6	West Bridgford 45 G4	West Hougham 15 J4	West Stoughton 16 F6	Whipsnade 20 E2	Whittonstall 68 C1
Weeford 44 C7	West Bromwich 34 B1	Westhoughton 53 H3	West Stour 9 J2	Whipton 5 K2	Whitwell, Leic 46 C7
Week 7 H4	West Buckland, Somer 8 C2	Westhouse 61 K2	West Stourmouth 15 J2	Whissendine 46 B6	Whitwell, N. Yks 68 E7
Weekley 36 B2	West Buckland, Devon 7 G2	Westhouses 55 H8	West Stow 38 D3	Whissonsett 48 E5	Whitwell, Herts 21 F1
Week St Mary 4 C2	West Burrafirth 118 E3	Westhumble 12 E1	West Stowell 18 C4	Whistley Green 20 B6	Whitwell, I. of W 11 G7
Weeley 23 H1	West Burton, Lancs 62 C3	West Hyde 20 E4	West Street 14 F3	Whiston, Staffs 44 B3	Whitwell, Derby 55 J6
Weeley Heath 23 H1	West Burton, W. Susx 12 C5	West Ilsley 19 F2	West Tanfield 63 F2	Whiston, Avon 17 H4	Whitwell-on-the-Hill 64 E6
Weem 91 K7	West Burton, N. Yks 62 D1	Westing 121 H2	West Tarbert 76 D1	Whiston, Northnts 36 B4	Whitwick 44 F6
Weeping Cross 43 L5	Westbury, Shrops 42 E7	West Itchenor 11 J4	West Thorney 11 J4	Whiston, Mers 53 F4	Whitwood 63 H7
Weeting 38 C2	Westbury, Bucks 35 H7	West Kennett 18 C4	West Thurrock 21 K6	Whiston, S. Yks 55 H4	Whitworth 53 K2
Weeton, N. Yks 63 F5	Westbury, Wilts 17 K5	West Kilbride 77 H3	West Tilbury 14 C1	Whiston, Staffs 43 K6	Whixall 43 G4
Weeton, Lancs 61 G6	Westbury Leigh 17 K5	West Kingsdown 21 K7	West Tisted 11 H2	Whitbeck 60 E1	Whixley 63 H4
Weir 62 B7	Westbury-on-Severn 30 B6	West Kington 17 K3	West Tofts 86 E1	Whitbourne 33 G5	Whorlton, Durham 68 D5
Welbeck Abbey 55 J6	Westbury-sub-Mendip 17 G6	West Kirby 52 D5	West Torrington 57 F5	Whitbrook 29 K7	Whorlton, N. Yks 69 G6
Welborne 48 F7	Westby 61 G6	West Knighton 9 J6	West Town 17 F4	Whitburn, Lothn 79 G3	Whyle 32 E4
Welbourn 46 C2	West Caister 49 L6	West Knoyle 9 K1	West Tytherley 10 D2	Whitburn, T. & W 75 L7	Whyteleafe 21 H8
Welburn 64 E6	West Calder 79 H3	Westlake 5 G6	West Tytherton 18 A3	Whitby, Ches 52 E6	Wibdon 29 K8
Welbury 69 F6	West Camel 9 G2	West Langdon 15 K4	West Walton 47 H6	Whitby, N. Yks 65 F1	Wibtoft 35 F2
Welby 46 C4	West Challow 18 E2	West Langwell 113 H8	Westward 66 E2	Whitchurch, Oxon 20 A6	Wichenford 33 G4
Welches Dam 37 H2	West Charleton 5 H7	West Lavington, Wilts 18 B5	Westward o! 6 E3	Whitchurch, Bucks 20 C1	Wichling 14 F3
Welcombe 6 C4	West Chelborough 9 G4	West Lavington, W. Susx 11 K2	Westwell, Kent 15 F4	Whitchurch, Dyfed 26 C5	Wick, H. & W 34 A6
Weldon 36 C2	West Chevington 75 J4	West Layton 68 D6	Westwell, Oxon 31 G6	Whitchurch, Devon 4 E4	Wick, Wilts 10 C2
Weldrake 58 A2	West Chiltington 12 D5	West Leake 45 G5	Westwell Leacon 14 F4	Whitchurch, Hants 19 F6	Wick, Dorset 10 C5
Welford, Berks 18 F3	West Chinnock 9 F3	Westleigh, Devon 8 B3	West Wellow 10 D3	Whitchurch, Shrops 43 G3	Wick, W. Susx 12 D6
Welford, Northnts 35 H2	West Clandon 12 D1	Westleigh, Devon 6 E3	West Wemyss 87 G5	Whitchurch, Avon 17 H4	Wick, M. Glam 25 H7
Welford-on-Avon 34 C5	West Cliffe 15 K4	Westleton 39 K4	West Wick, Avon 16 E4	Whitchurch, S. Glam 25 K6	Wick, Avon 17 J3
Welham 35 J1	Westcliff-on-Sea 22 E5	West Lexham 48 D6	Westwick, Cambs 37 H4	Whitchurch, H. & W 29 K6	Wick, Highld 115 J4
Welham Green 21 G3	West Clyne 109 G3	Westley, Suff 38 D4	Westwick, Norf 49 H5	Whitchurch Canonicorum 8 E5	Wickam Street 38 C5
Well, N. Yks 63 F1	West Coker 9 G2	Westley, Shrops 42 E7	West Wickham, Cambs 38 B6	Whitchurch Hill 20 A6	Wicken, Cambs 37 J3
Well, Lincs 57 J6	Westcombe 17 H7	Westley Waterless 38 B5	West Wickham, G. Lon 21 H7	Whitcott Keysett 32 B2	Wicken, Northnts 35 J7
Well, Hants 19 J6	West Compton, Dorset 9 G5	West Lilling 63 K3	West Winch 48 B6	Whitebridge 98 C7	Wicken Bonhunt 37 J7
Welland 33 G6	West Compton, Somer 17 G6	Westlington 20 B2	West Winterslow 10 D1	Whitebrook 29 K7	Wickenby 56 F5
Wellbank 93 F8	Westcote 31 G5	West Linton, Border 79 J4	West Wittering 11 J5	Whitecairns 101 J7	Wickersley 55 H4
Wellesbourne 34 D5	Westcott, Bucks 20 B2	Westlinton, Cumbr 73 J7	West Witton 62 D1	Whitechapel 61 J5	Wickford 22 D4
Well Hill 21 J7	Westcott, Devon 8 B4	West Littleton 17 J3	Westwood, Devon 8 B5	White Coppice 53 H2	Wickham, Berks 18 E3
Wellingborough 36 B4	Westcott, Surrey 12 E2	West Lulworth 9 K6	Westwood, Wilts 17 K5	Whitecraig 87 G7	Wickham, Hants 11 G3
Wellingham 48 D5	Westcott Barton 31 J5	West Lutton 65 G6	West Woodhay 18 E4	Whitecroft 29 L7	Wickham Bishops 22 E2
Wellngore 46 C2	West Cross 24 E6	West Malling 13 K1	West Woodlands 17 J6	Whiteface 109 F5	Wickhambreaux 15 J3
Wellington, Somer 8 C2	West Cullerley 101 G8	West Malvern 33 G6	Westwoodside 58 B7	Whitefield 53 K3	Wickhambrook 38 C5
Wellington, Shrops 43 H6	West Curthwaite 66 F2	West Marden 11 J3	West Worldham 11 J1	Whiteford 101 G6	Wickhamford 34 B6
Wellington, H. & W 29 J3	West Dean, Hants 10 D2	West Markham 56 B6	West Wratting 38 B5	Whitegate 53 H7	Wickham Market 39 J5
Wellington Heath 33 G6	Westdean, E. Susx 13 J7	Westmarsh 15 J2	West Wycombe 20 C4	Whitehall 117 F4	Wickhampton 49 K7
Wellow, I. of W 10 E6	West Dean, W. Susx 11 K3	West Marton 62 B4	West Yell 121 G4	Whitehaven 66 B5	Wickham Skeith 39 F4
Wellow, Avon 17 J5	West Deeping 46 E7	West Meon 11 H2	Wetheral 67 G1	Whitehill 11 J1	Wickham St Paul 38 D7
Wellow, Notts 55 K7	West Derby 52 E4	West Mersea 23 G2	Wetherby 63 H5	Whitehills 100 F2	Wickham Street 39 F4
Wells 17 G6	West Dereham 48 B7	Westmeston 13 G5	Wetherden 38 F4	Whitehouse, Strath 76 D1	Wicklewood 48 F7
Wellsborough 44 E7	West Ditchburn 75 H1	Westmill 37 G8	Wetheringsett 39 G4	Whitehouse, Grampn 100 F7	Wickmere 49 G4
Wells-next-the-Sea 48 E3	West Down 6 F1	West Milton 9 G5	Wethersfield 38 C7	Whitekirk 87 J6	Wick St Lawrence 16 E4
Wellwood 86 D6	West Drayton, Notts 56 B6	Westminster 21 G6	Wethersta 119 F2	White Kirkley 68 C3	Wickwar 17 J2
Welney 47 J8	West Drayton, G. Lon 20 E6	West Monkton 8 D2	Wetherup Street 39 G4	White Ladies Aston 33 J5	Widdington 37 J7
Welshampton 42 F4	West End, Beds 36 C5	West Moors 10 B4	Wetley Rocks 44 A3	Whiteley Village 20 E7	Widdrington 75 J4
Welsh Bicknor 29 K6	West End, Humbs 58 D3	Westmuir, Tays 92 E6	Wettenhall 53 H7	Whitemans Green 13 G4	Widecombe in the Moor 5 H4
Welsh End 43 G4	West End, Surrey 20 D7	West Muir, Tays 93 G5	Wetton 44 C2	Whitemire 99 H3	Widegates 4 C6
Welsh Frankton 42 E4	West End, N. Yks 62 E4	West Newton, Norf 48 B5	Wetwang 65 G7	Whitemoor 3 H4	Widemouth Bay 6 C5
Welsh Hook 26 D5	West End, Hants 11 F3	Westnewton, Cumbr 66 D2	Wetwood 43 J4	White Notley 22 D2	Wide Open 75 J6
Welsh Newton 29 K6	West End, Avon 17 F4	West Newton, Humbs 59 F3	Wexcombe 18 D5	Whiteparish 10 D2	Widewall 116 D7
Welshpool or Trallwng 42 D7	West End, Oxon 31 J7	West Norwood 21 H6	Weybourne 49 G3	Whiterashes 101 H6	Widford, Essex 22 C3
Welsh St Donats 25 J7	West End, Norf 49 K6	West Ogwell 5 J4	Weybread 39 H2	White Rocks 29 J5	Widford, Herts 21 J2
Welton, Humbs 58 D4	West End Green 20 A7	Weston, Staffs 44 A5	Weybridge 20 E7	White Roding or	Widmerpool 45 H5
Welton, Lincs 56 E6	Westerdale, Highld 115 G4	Weston, Notts 56 B7	Weydale 115 G3	White Roothing 21 K2	Widnes 53 G5
Welton, Cumbr 66 F2	Westerdale, N. Yks 69 J6	Weston, N. Yks 62 E5	Weyhill 18 E6	White Roothing or	Wigan 53 G3
Welton, Northnts 35 G4	Westerfield, Shetld 119 F3	Weston, N. Yks 64 E6	Weymouth 9 H7	White Roding 21 K2	Wiggaton 8 C5
Welton le Marsh 57 J7	Westerfield, Suff 39 G6	Weston, Brks 18 F3	Whaddon, Wilts 10 C2	Whiterow 115 J5	Wiggenhall St Germans 48 A6
Welton le Wold 57 G5	Wester Fintray 101 H7	Weston, Lincs 47 F5	Whaddon, Glos 30 C6	Whiteshill 30 C7	Wiggenhall St Mary
Welwick 59 H4	Westergate 12 C6	Weston, Herts 37 F7	Whaddon, Cambs 37 G6	Whiteside 79 G3	Magdalen 48 A6
Welwyn 21 G2	Wester Gruinards 108 D4	Weston, Ches 53 G5	Whaddon, Bucks 35 K7	Whitesmith 13 J5	Wiggenhall St Mary
Welwyn Garden City 21 G2	Westerham 13 H1	Weston, Shrops 43 G5	Whale 67 H4	Whitestaunton 8 D3	the Virgin 47 J6
Wem 43 G5	Westerleigh 17 J3	Weston, Northnts 35 G6	Whaley 55 J6	Whitestone 5 J2	Wiggington 63 J4
Wembdon 8 D1	Wester Quarff 119 G5	Weston, Shrops 43 G8	Whaley Bridge 54 D5	White Waltham 20 C6	Wigginton, Herts 20 D2
Wembley 21 F5	Wester Skeld 118 E4	Weston, Dorset 9 H7	Whaley Thorns 55 J6	Whiteway 30 D6	Wigginton, Staffs 44 D7
Wembury 4 F7	Westerton 93 H6	Weston, Ches 43 J2	Whalley 61 L6	Whitewell 61 K5	Wigginton, Oxon 31 H4
Wembworthy 7 G5	Westerwick 118 E4	Weston, Hants 11 J2	Whalton 75 H5	Whitewreath 100 B3	Wigglesworth 62 B4
Wemyss Bay 84 D8	West Farleigh 13 L1	Weston, Avon 17 J4	Wham 62 A3	Whitfield, Northum 74 D8	Wiggonby 66 F1
Wendens Ambo 37 J7	West Felton 42 E5	Weston Bampfylde 9 H2	Whaness 116 B6	Whitfield, Avon 17 H1	Wighill 63 H5
Wendlebury 31 K6	Westfield, Lothn 86 C7	Weston Beggard 29 K3	Whaplode 47 G5	Whitfield, Bucks 35 H7	Wighton 48 E4
Wendling 48 E6	Westfield, Norf 48 E7	Westonbirt 17 K2	Whaplode Drove 47 G6	Whitfield, Kent 15 K4	Wigmore, H. & W 32 D4
Wendover 20 C3	Westfield, E. Susx 14 E7	Weston by Welland 35 J1	Wharfe 62 A3	Whitford, Clwyd 52 C6	Wigmore, Kent 14 E2
Wendron 2 E6	Westfield, Highld 115 F3	Weston Colville 38 B5	Wharncliffe Side 55 F4	Whitford, Devon 8 D5	Wigsley 56 C6
Wendy 37 G6	West Firle 13 H6	Weston Green 38 B5	Wharram le Street 64 F6	Whitgift 58 C4	Wigsthorpe 36 D2
Wenhaston 39 K3	West Fleetham 81 K7	Weston Heath 43 J6	Wharton, Ches 53 H7	Whitgreave 43 K5	Wigston 45 H8
Wennington, Cambs 37 F3	Westgate, Durham 68 B3	Weston Hills 47 F5	Wharton, H. & W 29 K2	Whithorn 71 F7	Wigtoft 47 F4
Wennington, Lancs 61 K2	Westgate, Humbs 58 B6	Westoning 36 D7	Whashton 68 D6	Whiting Bay 76 F5	Wigton 66 E2
Wennington, G. Lon 21 K5	Westgate, Norf 48 E3	Weston-in-Gordano 17 F3	Whatcombe 9 K4	Whitland 27 G6	Wigtown 71 F6
Wensley, N. Yks 68 C8	Westgate on Sea 15 K1	Weston Jones 43 J5	Whatcote 34 E6	Whitletts 77 J5	Wilbarston 36 B2
Wensley, Derby 55 F7	West Gerinish 104 C7	Weston Longville 49 G6	Whatfield 38 F6	Whitley, Berks 20 B6	Wilberfoss 64 E7
Wentbridge 55 H2	West Ginge 19 F2	Weston Lullingfields 42 F5	Whatley 17 J6	Whitley, Ches 53 H6	Wilburton 37 H3
Wentnor 32 C1	West Grafton 18 D4	Weston-on-the-Green 31 K6	Whatlington 13 L5	Whitley, N. Yks 63 J7	Wilby, Northnts 36 B4
Wentworth, S. Yks 55 G4	West Green 19 J5	Weston-on-Trent 44 F5	Whatstandwell 44 E2	Whitley, Wilts 17 K4	Wilby, Norf 38 F2
Wentworth, Cambs 37 H3	West Grimstead 10 D2	Weston Patrick 19 H6	Whatton 45 J4	Whitley Bay 75 K6	Wilby, Suff 39 H3
Wenvoe 25 K7	West Grinstead 12 E4	Weston Rhyn 42 D4	Whauphill 70 F7	Whitley Chapel 68 B1	Wilcot 18 C4
Weobley 29 J2	West Haddlesey 63 J7	Weston-sub-Edge 34 C6	Wheatacre 49 K8	Whitley Row 13 H1	Wildboarclough 54 C7
Weobley Marsh 29 J2	West Haddon 35 H3	Weston-super-Mare 16 E4	Wheathampstead 21 F2	Whitlock's End 34 C3	Wilden, Beds 36 D5
Wereham 48 B7	West Hagbourne 19 G2	Weston Turville 20 C2	Wheathill 33 F2	Whitminster 30 B7	Wilden, H. & W 33 H3
Wergs 43 K7	West Hall, Cumbr 74 B7	Weston-under-Lizard 43 K6	Wheatley, Hants 19 J6	Whitmore 43 K3	Wildhern 18 E5
Wernrheolydd 29 H6	Westhall, Suff 39 K2	Weston under Penyard 29 L5	Wheatley, Oxon 31 K7	Whitnage 8 B3	Wildsworth 56 C4
Werrington, Corn 4 D3	West Hallam 44 F3	Weston under Wetherley 34 E4	Wheatley Hill 69 F3	Whitnash 34 E4	Wilford 45 G4
Werrington, Cambs 46 E7	West Halton 58 D4	Weston Underwood, Bucks 36 B5	Wheatley Lane 62 B6	Whitney-on-Wye, H. & W 29 H3	Wilkesley 43 H3
Werrington, Staffs 43 L3	Westham, Somer 16 F6	Weston Underwood,	Wheaton Aston 43 K6	Whitney-on-Wye, H. & W 29 G3	Wilkhaven 109 H5
Wervin 52 F6	West Ham, G. Lon 21 J5	Derby 44 D3	Wheddon Cross 7 K2	Whitrigg 66 E3	Wilkieston 79 J3
Wesham 61 H6	Westham, E. Susx 13 K6	Westonzoyland 8 D1	Wheedlemont 100 D6	Whitsbury 10 C3	Willand 8 B3
Wessington 55 G8	Westhampnett 11 K4	West Overton 18 C4	Wheelerstreet 12 C2	Whitsome 81 G4	Willaston, Ches 52 E6
West Acre 48 C6	West Handley 55 G6	West Parley 10 B5	Wheelock 53 J8	Whitson 16 E2	Willaston, Ches 43 H2
West Allerdean 81 H5	West Hanney 18 F1	West Peckham 13 K1	Wheelton 61 K7	Whitstable 15 H2	Willen 36 B6
West Alvington 5 H7	West Hanningfield 22 D4	West Pennard 17 G7	Whelford 31 F8	Whitstone 4 C2	Willenhall, W. Mids 44 A8
West Anstey 7 J3	West Hardwick 55 H2	West Pentire 2 F3	Whelpley Hill 20 D3	Whittingham 75 G2	Willenhall, W. Mids 34 E3
West Ashby 57 G6	West Harptree 17 G5	West Perry 36 E4	Whenby 63 K3	Whittingslow 32 D2	Willerby, Humbs 58 E3
West Ashling 11 K4	Westhay 17 F6	Westport 8 E2	Whepstead 38 D5	Whittington, Staffs 44 C7	Willerby, N. Yks 65 H5
West Ashton 17 K5	Westhead 52 F3	West Putford 6 D4	Wherstead 39 G6	Whittington, Norf 48 C8	Willersey 34 C7
West Aukland 68 D4	West Heath 19 K5	West Quantoxhead 16 C6	Wherwell 18 E6	Whittington, Shrops 42 E4	Willersley 29 H3
West Bagborough 8 C1	West Helmsdale 109 J2	West Rainton 68 F2	Wheston 54 E6	Whittington, Glos 30 E5	Willesborough Lees 15 G4
West Barns 87 K7	West Hendred 19 F2	West Rasen 56 E5	Whetsted 13 K2	Whittington, Derby 55 G6	Willesden 21 G5
West Barsham 48 E4	West Heslerton 65 G5	West Raynham 48 D5	Whetstone 45 G8	Whittington, Staffs 33 H2	Willett 8 C1
West Bay 9 F5	Westhide 29 K3	Westrigg 79 G3	Whicham 60 E1	Whittington, H. & W 33 H5	Willey, Warw 35 F2
West Beckham 49 G4	West Hill, Devon 8 B5	West Row 38 B3	Whichford 31 H4	Whittington, Lancs 61 K2	Willey, Shrops 43 H8
West Bere 15 H2	Westhill, Grampn 101 H8	West Rudham 48 D5	Whickham 75 J7	Whittlebury 35 H6	Williamscot 35 F6
West Bergholt 38 E8	West Hoathly 13 G3	West Runton 49 G3	Whiddon Down 5 G2	Whittle-le-Woods 61 J7	Willian 37 F7
West Bexington 9 G6	West Holme 9 K6	Westruther 80 E4	Whigstreet 93 F7	Whittlesey 47 F8	Willingale 22 B3
West Bilney 48 C6	Westhope, Shrops 32 D2	Westry 47 G8	Whilton 35 H4	Whittlesford 37 H6	Willingdon 13 J6
West Blatchington 13 F6	Westhope, H. & W 29 J2	West Saltoun 80 C3	Whimble 8 B5	Whitton, Powys 32 B4	Willingham 37 H3
Westborough 46 B3	West Horndon 22 C5	West Sandwick 121 G4	Whimpwell Green 49 J5	Whitton, Humbs 58 D4	Willingham by Stow 56 C5
Westbourne, Dorset 10 B5	Westhorpe, Suff 38 F4	West Scrafton 62 D1	Whinburgh 48 F7	Whitton, Shrops 32 E3	Willington, Durham 68 D3
Westbourne, W. Susx 11 J4	Westhorpe, Lincs 46 F4	West Stafford 9 J6		Whitton, Cleve 69 F4	Willington, Derby 44 D5
West Bradford 61 L5		West Stockwith 56 B4		Whitton, Border 80 F7	Willington, Warw 34 D7
				Whitton, Northum 75 G3	

Willington, Beds 36 E6
Willington, T. & W. 75 K7
Willington Corner........................53 G7
Willitoft 58 B3
Williton 16 B6
Willoughby, Warw 35 G4
Willoughby, Lincs 57 J6
Willoughby-on-the-Wolds 45 H5
Willoughby Waterleys 35 G1
Willoughton 56 D4
Wilmcote 34 C5
Wilmington, Devon......................8 D5
Wilmington, E. Susx 13 J6
Wilmington, Kent 21 K6
Wilmslow 53 K5
Wilnecote 44 D7
Wilpshire 61 K6
Wilsden 62 D6
Wilsford, Wilts 18 C5
Wilsford, Wilts 18 C7
Wilsford, Lincs 46 D3
Wilsill 62 E3
Wilson 44 F5
Wilstead 36 D6
Wilsthorpe 46 D6
Wilstone 20 D2
Wilton, Wilts 10 B1
Wilton, Wilts 18 D4
Wilton, N. Yks 64 F4
Wilton, Cleve 69 H5
Wilton Dean 73 K2
Wimbish 38 A7
Wimbish Green 38 B7
Wimbledon 21 G6
Wimblington 37 H1
Wimborne Minster 10 B4
Wimbotsham 48 B7
Wimpstone 34 D6
Wincanton 9 J2
Wincham 53 H6
Winchburgh 86 D7
Winchcombe 30 E5
Winchelsea 14 F7
Winchelsea Beach 14 F7
Winchester 11 F2
Winchfield 19 J5
Winchmore Hill, Bucks 20 D4
Winchmore Hill, G. Lon 21 H4
Wincle 54 C7
Windermere 67 G7
Winderton 34 E6
Windlesham 20 D7
Windley 44 E3
Windmill Hill, Somer 8 E3
Windmill Hill, E. Susx 13 K5
Windrush 31 F6
Windsor 20 D6
Windygates 87 G4
Wineham 12 F4
Winestead 59 H4
Winfarthing 39 G2
Winford 17 G4
Winforton 29 G3
Winfrith Newburgh 9 K6
Wing, Leic 46 B7
Wing, Bucks 20 C1
Wingate 69 G3
Wingates, Northum 75 G4
Wingates, G. Man 53 H3
Wingerworth 55 G7
Wingfield, Beds 36 D8
Wingfield, Suff 39 H3
Wingfield, Wilts 17 K5
Wingham 15 J3
Wingrave 20 C2
Winkburn 56 B8
Winkfield 20 D6
Winkfield Row 20 C6
Winkhill 44 B2
Winkleigh 7 G5
Winksley 63 F2
Winless 115 J4
Winmarleigh 61 H5
Winnersh 20 B6
Winscales 66 C4
Winscombe 17 F5
Winsford, Ches 53 H7
Winsford, Somer 7 K2
Winsham 8 E4
Winshill 44 D5
Winskill 67 H3
Winslade 19 H6
Winsley 17 K4
Winslow 35 J8
Winson 30 E7
Winster, Derby 55 F7
Winster, Cumbr 67 G7
Winston, Durham 68 D5
Winston, Suff 39 G4
Winstone 30 D7
Winswell 6 E4
Winterborne Clenston 9 K4
Winterborne Herringston 9 H6
Winterborne Houghton 9 K4
Winterborne Kingston 9 K5
Winterborne Monkton 9 H6
Winterborne Stickland 9 K4
Winterborne Whitechurch 9 K4

Winterborne Zelston 9 K5
Winterbourne, Berks 19 F3
Winterbourne, Avon 17 H2
Winterbourne Abbas 9 H5
Winterbourne Bassett 18 C3
Winterbourne Dauntsey 10 C1
Winterbourne Earls 10 C1
Winterbourne Gunner 10 C1
Winterbourne Monkton 18 C3
Winterbourne Steepleton 9 H6
Winterbourne Stoke 18 B6
Winterburn 62 C4
Winteringham 58 D4
Winterley 53 J8
Wintersett 55 G2
Wintershill 11 G3
Winterton 58 D5
Winterton-on-Sea 49 K6
Winthorpe, Notts 46 B2
Winthorpe, Lincs 57 K7
Winton, Dorset 10 B5
Winton, Cumbr 67 K5
Wintringham 65 F5
Winwick, Cambs 36 E2
Winwick, Northnts 35 H3
Winyates 34 B4
Wirksworth 44 D2
Wirswall 43 G3
Wisbech 47 H7
Wisbech St Mary 47 H7
Wiseton 56 B5
Wishaw, Warw 44 C8
Wishaw, Strath 78 E4
Wispington 57 G6
Wissett 39 J3
Wistanstow 32 D2
Wistanswick 43 H5
Wistaston 43 H2
Wiston, W. Susx 12 E5
Wiston, Dyfed 26 E6
Wiston, Strath 79 G6
Wistow, Cambs 37 F2
Wistow, N. Yks 63 J6
Wiswell 61 L6
Witcham 37 H3
Witchampton 10 A4
Witchford 37 J3
Witham 22 E2
Witham Friary 17 J6
Witham on the Hill 46 D6
Witherenden Hill 13 K4
Witheridge 7 J4
Witherley 44 E8
Withern 57 J5
Withernsea 59 H4
Withernwick 59 F2
Withersdale Street 39 H2
Withersfield 38 B6
Witherslack 61 H1
Withiel 3 H3
Withiel Florey 7 K2
Withington, Glos 30 E6
Withington, Shrops 43 G6
Withington, H. & W. 29 K3
Withington, G. Man 53 K4
Withington, Ches 53 K7
Withington Green 53 K6
Withleigh 7 K4
Withnell 61 K7
Withybrook 34 F2
Withycombe 16 B6
Withyham 13 H3
Withypool 7 J2
Witley 12 C2
Witnesham 39 G5
Witney 31 H7
Wittersham 14 E6
Witton Bridge 49 J4
Witton Gilbert 68 E2
Witton-le-Wear 68 D3
Witton Park 68 D3
Wiveliscombe 8 B2
Wivelsfield 13 G4
Wivelsfield Green 13 G5
Wivenhoe 23 G1
Wiveton 48 F3
Wix 39 G8
Wixford 34 B5
Wixoe 38 C6
Woburn 36 C7
Woburn Sands 36 C7
Wokefield Park 20 A7
Woking 20 E8
Wokingham 20 C7
Woldingham 13 G1
Wold Newton, Humbs 59 G7
Wold Newton, Humbs 65 H5
Wolferlow 33 F4
Wolferton 48 B5
Wolfhill 86 E1
Wolf's Castle 26 D5
Wolfsdale 26 D5
Woll 80 C7
Wollaston, Northnts 36 C4
Wollaston, Shrops 42 E6
Wollerton 43 H4

Wolsingham 68 C3
Wolston 34 F3
Wolvercote 31 J7
Wolverhampton 43 L8
Wolverley, Shrops 43 F4
Wolverley, H. & W. 33 H3
Wolverton, Bucks 36 B6
Wolverton, Warw 34 D4
Wolveshewton 29 J8
Wolvetton 19 G5
Wolvey 34 F2
Wolviston 69 G4
Wombleton 63 K1
Wombourne 43 K8
Wombwell 55 G3
Womenswold 15 J3
Wonastow 29 J6
Wonersh 12 D2
Wonson 5 G3
Wonston, Hants 19 F7
Wonston, Dorset 9 J4
Wooburn 20 D5
Wooburn Green 20 D5
Woodale 62 D2
Woodbastwick 49 J6
Woodbeck 56 B6
Woodborough, Wilts 18 C5
Woodborough, Notts 45 H3
Woodbridge 39 H6
Woodbury 8 B6
Woodbury Salterton 8 B6
Woodchester 30 C7
Woodchurch 14 F5
Woodcote 20 A5
Woodcroft 29 K8
Wood Dalling 49 F5
Woodeaton 31 K6
Woodend, Cumbr 66 D7
Wood End, Warw 44 D8
Wood End, Herts 37 G8
Woodend, Northnts 35 H6
Wood Enderby 57 G7
Woodfalls 10 C2
Woodford, Northnts 36 C3
Woodford, Corn 6 C4
Woodford, Devon 5 H6
Woodford, G. Lon 21 J4
Woodford, G. Man 53 K5
Woodford Bridge 21 J4
Woodford Green 21 J4
Woodford Halse 35 G5
Woodgate, W. Mids 34 A2
Woodgate, H. & W. 34 A4
Woodgate, W. Susx 12 C6
Woodgate, Norf 48 F6
Woodgreen, Hants 10 C3
Wood Green, G. Lon 21 H4
Woodhall 68 B7
Woodhall Spa 57 F7
Woodham 20 E7
Woodham Ferrers 22 D4
Woodham Mortimer 22 E3
Woodham Walter 22 E3
Woodhaven 87 H2
Woodhead 101 G5
Woodhill 33 G2
Woodhorn 75 J5
Woodhouse, Leic 45 G6
Woodhouse, S. Yks 55 H5
Woodhouse Eaves 45 G6
Woodhouselee 79 K3
Woodhurst 37 G3
Woodingdean 13 G6
Wooditton 38 B5
Woodland, Durham 68 C4
Woodland, Devon 5 H5
Woodlands, Dorset 10 B4
Woodlands, Hants 10 E3
Woodlands, Grampn 93 J2
Woodlands Park 20 C6
Woodlands St Mary 18 E3
Wood Lanes 53 L5
Woodleigh 5 H7
Woodlesford 63 G7
Woodley 20 B6
Woodmancote, Glos 30 D5
Woodmancote, Glos 30 E7
Woodmancote, W. Susx 12 F5
Woodmancote, W. Susx 11 J4
Woodmancott 19 G6
Woodmansey 58 E3
Woodmansterne 21 G7
Woodminton 10 B2
Woodnesborough 15 K3
Woodnewton 46 D8
Wood Norton 48 F5
Woodplumpton 61 J6
Woodrising 48 E7
Woodseaves, Shrops 43 H4
Woodseaves, Staffs 43 K5
Woodsend 18 D3
Woodsetts 55 J5
Woodsford 9 J5
Woodside, Berks 20 D6
Woodside, Tays 92 D8
Woodside, Herts 21 G3
Woodstock 31 J6

Wood Street 12 C1
Woodthorpe, Leic 45 G6
Woodthorpe, Derby 55 H6
Woodton 49 H8
Woodtown 6 E3
Woodville 44 E6
Woodwalton 36 F2
Woodyates 10 B3
Woofferton 32 E4
Wookey 17 G6
Wookey Hole 17 G6
Wool 9 K6
Woolacombe 6 E1
Woolage Green 15 J4
Woolaston 29 K8
Woolavington 16 E6
Woolbeding 11 K2
Wooler 81 H7
Woolfardisworthy, Devon 6 D3
Woolfardisworthy, Devon 7 J5
Woolfords Cottages 79 H4
Woolhampton 19 G4
Woolhope 29 L4
Woolland 9 J4
Woolley, Cambs 36 E3
Woolley, W. Yks 55 G2
Woolmer Green 21 G2
Woolpit 38 E4
Woolscott 35 F4
Woolstaston 42 F8
Woolsthorpe 46 B4
Woolston, Shrops 32 D2
Woolston, Shrops 42 E5
Woolston, Hants 10 F3
Woolston, Ches 53 H5
Woolston, Devon 5 H7
Woolstone, Bucks 36 B7
Woolstone, Oxon 18 D2
Woolston Green 5 H5
Woolton 52 F5
Woolton Hill 18 F4
Woolverstone 39 G7
Woolverton 17 J5
Woolwich 21 J6
Woore 43 J3
Wooton 31 J6
Wooton, Staffs 44 C3
Wooton, Oxon 31 J7
Wootton, Hants 10 D5
Wootton, Beds 36 D6
Wootton, Humbs 59 E5
Wootton, Kent 15 J4
Wootton, Northnts 35 J5
Wootton, Oxon 31 J7
Wootton, Staffs 43 K5
Wootton Bassett 18 B2
Wootton Bridge 11 G5
Wootton Common 11 G5
Wootton Courtenay 7 K1
Wootton Fitzpaine 8 E5
Wootton Rivers 18 C4
Wootton St Lawrence 19 G5
Wootton Wawen 34 C4
Worcester 33 H1
Worcester Park 21 G7
Wordsley 33 H2
Worfield 43 J8
Workington 66 B4
Worksop 55 J6
Worlaby 58 E5
World's End 19 F3
Worle 16 E4
Worleston 43 H2
Worlingham 39 K2
Worlington, Cambs 38 B3
Worlington, Devon 7 H4
Worlingworth 39 H4
Wormbridge 29 J4
Wormegay 48 B6
Wormelow Tump 29 J4
Wormersley 55 J2
Wormhill 54 E6
Wormiehills 93 H8
Wormingford 38 E7
Worminghall 20 A3
Wormington 34 B7
Worminster 17 G6
Wormit 87 G2
Wormleighton 35 F5
Wormley 21 H3
Wormley West End 21 H3
Wormshill 14 E3
Wormsley 29 J3
Worplesdon 12 C1
Worrall 55 G4
Worsbrough 55 G3
Worsley 53 J3
Worsthorne 62 B6
Worston 62 A5
Worth, W. Susx 13 F3
Worth, Kent 15 K3
Wortham 39 F3
Worthen 42 E7
Worthenbury 42 F3
Worthing, Norf 48 E6
Worthing, W. Susx 12 E6

Worthington 44 F5
Worth Matravers 10 A7
Wortley 55 G4
Worton 18 A5
Wortwell 39 H2
Wotherton 42 D7
Wotter 5 F5
Wotton 12 E2
Wotton-under-Edge 30 B8
Wotton Underwood 20 A2
Woughton on the Green 36 B7
Wouldham 14 D2
Wraness 39 G7
Wrafton 6 E2
Wragby 57 F6
Wramplingham 49 G7
Wrangham 100 F5
Wrangle 47 H2
Wrangway 8 C3
Wrantage 8 C2
Wrawby 58 E6
Wraxall, Avon 17 F3
Wraxall, Somer 9 H1
Wraxall, Wilts 17 K4
Wray 61 K3
Wraysbury 20 E6
Wrea Green 61 G6
Wreay, Cumbr 67 G2
Wreay, Cumbr 67 G4
Wrekenton 75 J8
Wrelton 64 E4
Wreningham 49 G8
Wrentham 39 K2
Wressle 58 B3
Wrestlingworth 36 D4
Wretham 38 E1
Wretton 48 B8
Wrexham 42 E2
Wribbenhall 33 G3
Wrightington Bar 53 G2
Wrinehill 43 J3
Wrington 17 F4
Writtle 22 C3
Wrockwardine 43 H6
Wroot 58 B6
Wrotham 14 C3
Wrotham Heath 14 C3
Wroughton 18 C2
Wroxall, Warw 34 D3
Wroxall, I. of W. 11 G7
Wroxeter 43 G7
Wroxham 49 J6
Wroxton 34 F6
Wyaston 44 C3
Wyberton 47 G3
Wyboston 36 E5
Wybunbury 43 H3
Wychbold 33 J4
Wych Cross 13 H3
Wyche 33 G6
Wyck 19 J7
Wyck Rissington 31 F5
Wycombe Marsh 20 C4
Wyddial 37 G7
Wye 15 G4
Wyke, W. Yks 62 E7
Wyke, Shrops 43 H7
Wyke, Dorset 9 J2
Wykeham, N. Yks 64 F5
Wykeham, N. Yks 65 G4
Wyke Regis 9 H7
Wyke, The 43 J7
Wykey 42 E5
Wylam 75 H7
Wylde Green 44 C8
Wylye 10 B1
Wymering 11 H4
Wymeswold 45 H5
Wymington 36 C4
Wymondham, Leic 46 B6
Wymondham, Norf 49 G7
Wymondham 25 H5
Wynford Eagle 9 G5
Wyre Piddle 34 A6
Wysall 45 H5
Wythall 34 B3
Wytham 31 J7
Wythenshawe 53 K5
Wyverstone 38 F4
Wyverstone Street 38 F4

Y

Yaddlethorpe 58 C6
Yafford 11 F6
Yafforth 69 F7
Yalding 13 L1
Yanworth 30 E6
Yapham 64 E7
Yapton 12 C6
Yarburgh 57 H4
Yarcombe 8 C3
Yardley 34 C2
Yardley Gobion 35 J6
Yardley Hastings 36 B5

Yardro 29 G2
Yarkhill 29 L3
Yarlet 43 L5
Yarlington 9 H2
Yarm 69 G5
Yarmouth 10 E6
Yarnfield 43 K4
Yarnscombe 7 F3
Yarnton 31 J6
Yarpole 32 D4
Yarrow 80 B7
Yarrow Feus 80 B7
Yarsop 29 J3
Yarwell 46 D8
Yate 17 J2
Yateley 20 C7
Yatesbury 18 B3
Yattendon 19 G3
Yatton, H. & W. 32 D4
Yatton, Avon 17 F4
Yatton Keynell 17 K3
Yaverland 11 H6
Yaxham 48 F6
Yaxley, Cambs 36 E1
Yaxley, Suff 39 G3
Yazor 29 J3
Yeading 21 F5
Yeadon 62 F5
Yealand Conyers 61 J2
Yealand Redmayne 61 J2
Yealmpton 5 F6
Yearsley 63 J2
Yeaton 42 F6
Yeaveley 44 C3
Yedingham 65 F5
Yelden 36 D4
Yelford 31 H7
Yelland 6 E2
Yelling 37 F4
Yelvertoft 35 G3
Yelverton, Devon 5 F5
Yelverton, Norf 49 H7
Yenston 9 J2
Yeoford 5 H2
Yeolmbridge 4 D3
Yeo Mill 7 J3
Yeovil 9 G3
Yeovil Marsh 9 G3
Yeovilton 9 G2
Yerbeston 26 E7
Yesnaby 116 B5
Yetlington 75 G3
Yetminster 9 G3
Yettington 8 B6
Yetts o' Muckhart 86 D4
Y Fan 41 J5
Y Felinheli 50 E4
Y Ffor 50 C7
Yieldshields 79 F4
Yiewsley 20 E5
Ynysboeth 25 J5
Ynysddu 25 K5
Ynyshir 25 J5
Ynyslas 40 F4
Ynysybwl 25 J5
Yockenthwaite 62 C2
Yockleton 42 F6
Yokefleet 58 C4
Yoker 85 J8
Yonder Bognie 100 F4
York 63 K4
Yorkletts 15 G3
Yorkley 29 L7
Yorton 43 G5
Youlgreave 54 F7
Youlstone 6 C4
Youlthorpe 64 E7
Youlton 63 H3
Young's End 22 D2
Yoxall 44 C6
Yoxford 39 J4
Ysbyty Ifan 51 H6
Ysbyty Ystwyth 41 G6
Ysceifiog 52 C6
Ysgubor-y-coed 41 F4
Ystalyfera 25 F4
Ystrad 25 H5
Ystrad Aeron 27 K2
Ystradfellte 25 H3
Ystradffin 28 B3
Ystradgynlais 25 F4
Ystradmeurig 41 G7
Ystrad Mynach 25 K5
Ystradowen, Dyfed 25 F3
Ystradowen, S. Glam 25 J7
Ythanbank 101 J5
Ythanwells 100 F5
Ythsie 101 H5

Z

Zeal Monachorum........................7 H5
Zeals 9 J1
Zelah 3 G4
Zennor, Corn 2 C6

Key to 1:250 000 Maps, atlas pages 2-121

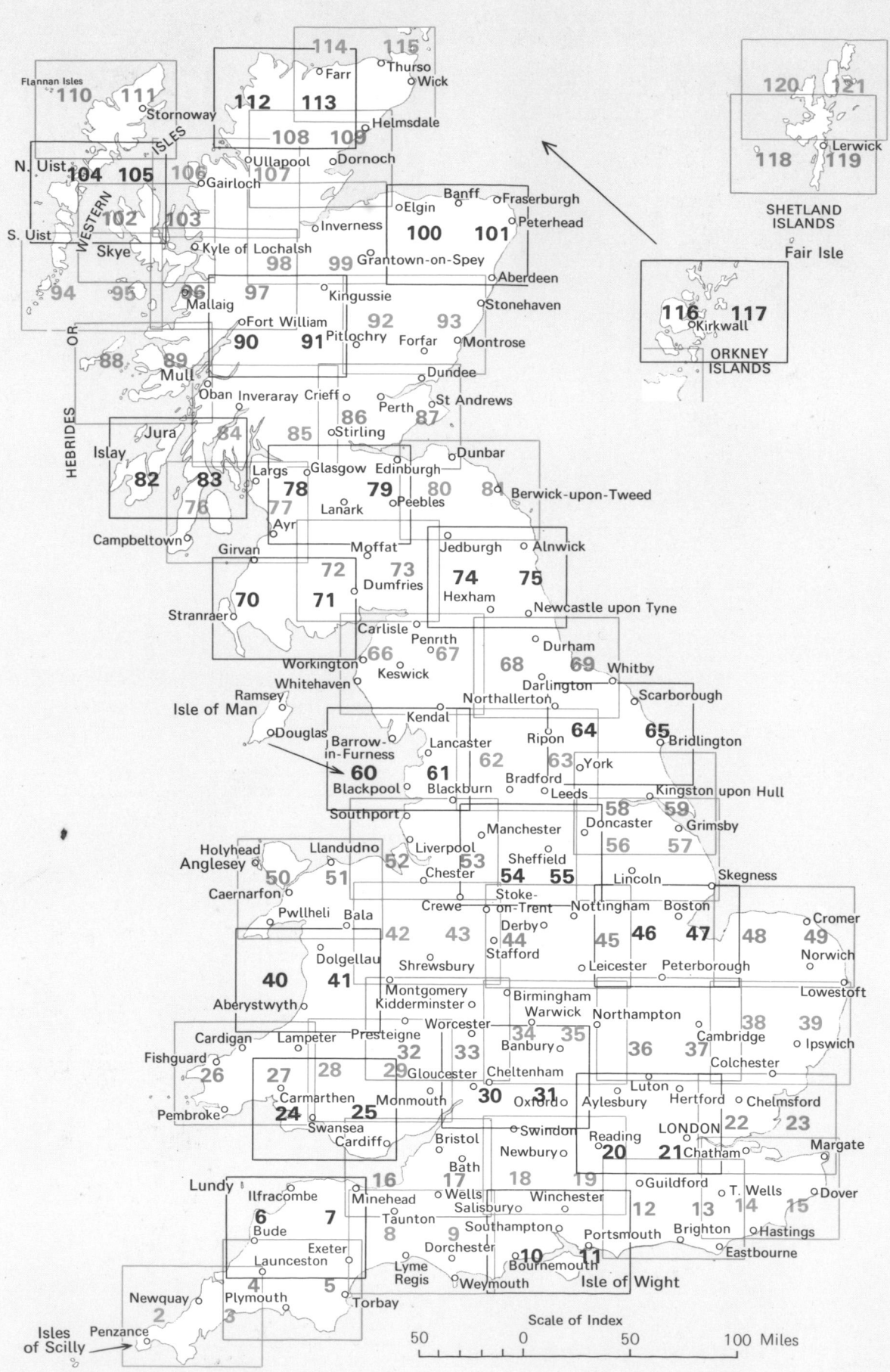

Flannan Isles
110 111
Stornoway
ISLES
N. Uist 104 105 106
102 103
S. Uist
WESTERN
Skye
94 95 96
88 89 Mull
Oban
Jura 84
Islay
HEBRIDES
82 83
76
Campbeltown
70 71
Stranraer
112 114 115
Farr Thurso
Wick
113
108 109 Helmsdale
Ullapool Dornoch
Gairloch
106
Kyle of Lochalsh 99 Grantown-on-Spey
98 Inverness 100 101 Peterhead
Banff Fraserburgh
Elgin
97 Kingussie Aberdeen
Mallaig 92 93 Stonehaven
Fort William 90 91 Pitlochry Forfar Montrose
Inveraray Crieff Dundee
Perth St Andrews
86 87
85 Stirling
Dunbar
78 79 80 8 Berwick-upon-Tweed
Largs Glasgow Edinburgh
77 Lanark Peebles
Ayr
Moffat Jedburgh Alnwick
Girvan 72 73 74 75
Dumfries Hexham
Newcastle upon Tyne
Carlisle
66 67 Penrith Durham
Workington 68 69 Whitby
Whitehaven Keswick Darlington Scarborough
Ramsey Northallerton
Isle of Man Kendal 64 65 Bridlington
Douglas Lancaster Ripon
Barrow- 62 63 York
in-Furness Bradford Kingston upon Hull
60 61 Leeds
Blackpool Blackburn 58 59
Southport Manchester Doncaster Grimsby
56 57
Holyhead Llandudno Liverpool Sheffield
Anglesey 52 53 Lincoln Skegness
50 51 Chester 54 55
Caernarfon Stoke- Nottingham Boston
Crewe on-Trent 46 47 48 Cromer
Pwllheli Bala Derby 49
42 43 44 45 Norwich
40 41 Dolgellau Stafford Leicester Peterborough
Shrewsbury 38 39
Aberystwyth Montgomery Birmingham Northampton Cambridge Ipswich
Kidderminster Warwick 36 37 Lowestoft
Cardigan Lampeter Presteigne Worcester 34 35 Colchester
Fishguard 32 33 Banbury
26 27 28 29 Gloucester Cheltenham Luton 22 23
Carmarthen Monmouth 30 31 Oxford Hertford Chelmsford
Pembroke 24 25 Aylesbury LONDON Margate
Swansea Swindon Reading
Cardiff Bristol 20 21 Chatham
Newbury
Bath
Lundy 16 17 18 19 Guildford T. Wells Dover
Ilfracombe Minehead Wells Winchester 14 15
6 7 Salisbury 12 13 Hastings
Bude Taunton Southampton Brighton
8 9 Portsmouth Eastbourne
Exeter Dorchester 10 11
Launceston Lyme Bournemouth Isle of Wight
4 5 Regis Weymouth
Newquay Plymouth Torbay
2 3
Isles Penzance
of Scilly

SHETLAND
ISLANDS
120 121
118 119
Lerwick

Fair Isle

116 117
Kirkwall
ORKNEY
ISLANDS

Scale of Index
50   0   50   100 Miles